INTRODUCTION
TO CRIMINOLOGY

INTRODUCTION TO CRIMINOLOGY

9th Edition

David Kauzlarich
and
Hugh Barlow

ROWMAN & LITTLEFIELD PUBLISHERS, INC.
Lanham • Boulder • New York • Toronto • Plymouth, UK

ROWMAN & LITTLEFIELD PUBLISHERS, INC.

Published in the United States of America
by Rowman & Littlefield Publishers, Inc.
A wholly owned subsidary of The Rowman & Littlefield Publishing Group, Inc.
4501 Forbes Boulevard, Suite 200, Lanham, Maryland 20706
www.rowmanlittlefield.com

Estover Road
Plymouth PL6 7PY
United Kingdom

Copyright © 2009 by Rowman & Littlefield Publishers, Inc.

British Library Cataloguing in Publication Information Available

Library of Congress Cataloging-in-Publication Data

Kauzlarich, David.
  Introduction to criminology / David Kauzlarich and Hugh Barlow. — 9th ed.
    p. cm.
  Includes index.
  Rev. ed. of: Introduction to criminology / Hugh D. Barlow and David Kauzlarich. 8th ed.
  ISBN-13: 978-0-7425-6186-1 (pbk. : alk. paper)
  ISBN-10: 0-7425-6186-0 (pbk. : alk. paper)
  eISBN-13: 978-0-7425-6577-7
  eISBN-10: 0-7425-6577-7
  1. Criminology. 2. Criminal justice, Administration of. I. Barlow, Hugh D. II. Barlow, Hugh D. Introduction to criminology. III. Title.
  HV6025.B29 2008
  364—dc22   2008010180

TABLE OF CONTENTS

PREFACE

We are delighted to offer this ninth edition of *Introduction to Criminology*. As with previous editions, we have continued our effort to provide students with an understanding of crime that is both methodologically and theoretically diverse and which pays close attention to the historical development of crime, law, and criminal justice. Throughout the book, we also devote considerable attention to social inequality as it relates to crime along with the implications of viewing crime as both a social construction and an objective phenomenon.

In addition to the updating of statistics, studies, and theories in criminology, we have also rearranged and added some chapters. We collapsed our discussion of drugs, prostitution, and organized crime into one chapter while creating new chapters on critical theories and biological, psychological, and evolutionary explanations of crime. These bodies of work have become so diverse that it is impossible to sufficiently review their substance in any other way.

Perhaps the largest change from previous editions is that we have taken a special effort to include more illustrations and examples of crime from popular culture. Throughout the text students will find references to films and music that we believe will help them make stronger intellectual connections to the material. Finally, we have added an epilogue that we hope students will find valuable in thinking through common criminological issues and questions they are likely to encounter in everyday conversation. The purpose of this epilogue is simple: We want students to be able to say something meaningful and concise about the causes of crime after taking an introductory criminology course.

We are indebted to many people who have shaped our thinking about crime over our careers. Chief among these colleagues are Bill Chambliss, Ronald V. Clarke, Steven Egger, Gil Geis, Jack Gibbs, John Farley, Paul C. Friday, David Friedrichs, Ron Kramer, Rick Matthews, Ray Michalowski, Chris Mullins, Richard Quinney, and Dawn Rothe. We also wish to thank the reviewers of this edition of the book as well as our editor, Alan McClare. Alan has been a pleasure to work with and we have appreciated his enthusiasm about this project. We also thank Karen Ackermann for the excellent production work on the manuscript as well as several graduate students who have helped us develop this book, especially Josh Lucker, Eva-Sophia Clark, and Tracey Hayes.

This book is dedicated to our beautiful children: Alison, Melissa, Eric, Colin, Chelsea, Kelsey, Elaina, and Jake.

1

CRIME AND CRIMINALITY

AP5CE6 Alamy

If the media were the sole source of information about crime and criminals, the picture would be highly distorted. For example, violent crimes are much more often publicized than property crimes, but the real frequency of these phenomena is the reverse: The vast majority of crimes are property offenses. Editors weigh the information they receive according to its newsworthiness, and then report it selectively. Furthermore, conjecture and opinion are presented and "experts" are used whose views fit the particular version of the story being told (Jewkes, 2004; Kappeler, Blumberg, and Potter, 2000). The resulting "reality" is generally far from the truth, or at least the whole story. The reality of crime reported by the press is one of exceptionally violent, exceptionally greedy, or exceptionally corrupt people picking on exceptionally vulnerable victims. In addition, the coverage is often racially biased, especially against African American males (Barlow, Barlow, and Chiricos, 1995a; Young, 2007). The image portrayed on TV and movie screens is even more distorted. Consider shows such as *Law & Order*, *NYPD Blue*, and *CSI: Crime Scene Investigation*, which have also been shown to play on racial and gender stereotypes (Eschholz, Mallard, and Flynn, 2004). Often these types of television programs portray criminal justice practitioners saving the world from serial murderers and child molesters.

Uncovering the "True" Story of Crime

Criminologists try to uncover the "true" story of crime. But the truth is socially constructed. What we know about the world of crime is a product of how people—particularly those in power—define, interpret, and react to crime. What "officially" counts as crime depends on, among other things: what behaviors legislators declare as punishable; whether or not a victim decides to report an incident to the police; how the police exercise discretion in making a stop, search, or arrest; what specific charges the

M ost Americans are touched by crime at some point in their lives. If they are not directly victimized, they see or hear of others being victimized. Despite the fact that crime surrounds us, it is often misunderstood. In large measure this has to with how the media portrays the crime "problem." Open almost any newspaper or news Web site and you will find at least one item about crime. However, these sources do not bother to report petty thefts and vandalism, or even most robberies, assaults, and burglaries, although small-town media sources often make them headline news. Big-city newspapers and major news Web sites seldom give coverage even to rape or murder unless there is a sensational angle to it.

prosecutor's office decides on and whether they drop the case or continue with it; and what the courts declare as fair and reasonable evidence. So when people speak of the nature, extent, and distribution of crime, it is important to consider the sources upon which those claims are based.

In sum, when we speak of "crime" or "criminals," our images and ideas are influenced by the people and institutions that regulate human behavior, and by those who sell the images to us. Even self-report and victimization surveys of crime (discussed in chapter 2) are based on socially constructed images. One person's experience and understanding of crime may not be the same as another's, even though the objective facts are the same. Simply put: "There is no such thing as a pure fact innocent of interpretation" (Zinn, 1999: 658).

Criminology is, nevertheless, interested in seeking out the facts about crime. Exposure to these facts is sometimes painful and often surprising. As you read through the sixteen chapters of this text, you will learn that the most likely victims of crime are the poor; you will learn that crime is like a huge iceberg, and only the tip is reported to and by the police; you will learn that most criminals are not punished for their crimes. You will also learn that the most common place where women and children are assaulted is the home, and the numbers are staggering—as many as 4 million women and 3 million children are abused by family members in the United States each year. You will learn that gang violence and drug use are widespread—but also that many youth gangs spend most of their time doing other things. You will learn that American jails and prisons are full of young

Box 1.1. Some Facts about "Street" Crime

The text mentions various facts about crime that challenge conventional wisdom and illuminate the limitations of media portrayals of crime and justice in America. Here are some other facts about street crime that are true in America as well as in many other countries.

- Crime is committed disproportionately by males.
- Crime is committed disproportionately by fifteen- to twenty-five-year-olds.
- Crime is committed disproportionately by people living in large cities.
- Crime is committed disproportionately by those who live in areas of high residential mobility.
- Young people who are strongly attached to their school are less likely to engage in crime.
- Young people who have high educational and occupational aspirations are less likely to engage in crime.
- Young people who do poorly in school are more likely to engage in crime.
- Young people who are strongly attached to their parents are less likely to engage in crime.
- Young people who have friendships with criminals are more likely to engage in crime themselves.
- "Street" crime is a term that identifies common crimes such as burglary, assault, drug possession and sales, robbery, rape, and many less serious offenses involving theft or destruction of property. It excludes corporate crime, state crime, tax evasion, embezzlement, and a variety of other offenses committed in connection to work.

Source: Braithwaite (1989a): 44–46.

males, half of them African American, and most of them from city neighborhoods in which joblessness, overcrowding, and physical deterioration are commonplace. You will learn that even though the costs of corporate and governmental crime far exceed those of traditional street crimes such as robbery, burglary, and auto theft combined, white-collar criminals are less likely than others to be arrested and prosecuted—and, if convicted, less likely to go to jail or prison. Box 1.1 provides some other well-known facts about crime.

One of the goals of criminology is to separate fact from myth. Sometimes the reality contradicts not only media representations, but our own personal beliefs as well. For example, many students we talk to believe that the crime rate has risen to all-time highs in recent years. However, the reality is that all available measures show an overall *decrease* in nearly all forms of traditional street crime and victimization over the last thirty years. Figures 1.1 and 1.2 show this trend based on victimization rates: in this case, the number of households per thousand experiencing a crime against one or more members from 1976 to 2006. Public opinion surveys, however, reveal that more than half of the American public believes that crime has increased every year over the last two decades (Maguire and Pastore, 2007).

While every science tries to distinguish between myth and reality, the task is especially difficult in criminology, because stu-dents often come to the study of crime with preexisting assumptions and conclusions. Some students have strong opinions about the causes of crime and what to do with people convicted of crimes; rarely does someone walk into an introductory biology class with a strong moral or political opinion on zygotes or photosynthesis. The challenge of understanding crime demands the ability to suspend final judgment until we can base our conclusions on valid and reliable information. Most people, however, simply have not had the opportunity to study crime in detail. This text is designed to provide readers with this opportunity.

WHAT IS CRIMINOLOGY?

Criminology can be defined in any number of ways, but Sutherland and Cressey (1974) provide the clearest definition: **Criminology** is the study of lawmaking, lawbreaking, and the reactions to crime. There are many specialties in criminology, and box 1.2 provides a list of some of the major ones.

Lawmaking

The first part of the definition of criminology includes the study of *lawmaking*. This area of inquiry generally focuses on the various political, economic, and cultural factors that help shape laws and criminal justice policies. For example: Why and how

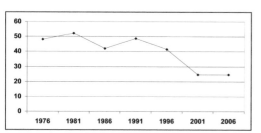

▲ **Figure 1.1.**
Violent Crime Victimization Rates per 1,000 Households, 1976–2006
Source: Bureau of Justice Statistics (2007).

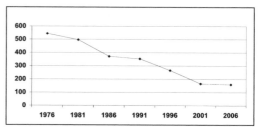

▲ **Figure 1.2.**
Property Crime Victimization Rates per 1,000 Households, 1976–2006
Source: Bureau of Justice Statistics (2007).

BOX 1.2. SOME MAJOR SUBJECT AREAS IN CRIMINOLOGY

Age and Crime
Alcohol, Drugs, and Crime
Biology and Crime
Comparative Criminology
Crime and Public Policy
Crime and the Media
Criminological Theory
Economic Class and Crime
Environmental Criminology
Fear of Crime
Gender and Crime
Guns and Crime
Hate Crime
Juvenile Delinquency
Race, Ethnicity, and Crime
Research Methods
Social Control Institutions (Police, Courts, and Corrections)
Victimology
Violence against Women
White-Collar Crime (including State and Corporate Crime)

are certain behaviors crimes? Why has there been a historic lack of effective laws protecting women and children from abuse in the home? Why and how were early laws prohibiting theft developed? Why and how were "three strikes" policies created (and why are they strongly supported)? The criminological study of lawmaking, sometimes called the sociology of law, has shown that law and policy reflect the interests of those in power. For example, the history of rape laws has largely been the history of males exercising power over females. This is discussed in more detail in chapter 4.

Lawbreaking

The second major part of the definition of criminology is the study of *lawbreaking*. Here criminologists are interested in how and why people commit crime. Criminologists might study the causes and correlates of juvenile delinquency, drug and alcohol use, violent

crime, property crime, hate crime, violence against women, or literally dozens of other types of crime. They might also focus on what specific things draw people toward or away from crime, such as family relationships, peers, neighborhood, social class, gender, race, and employment status.

One example of how some criminologists have addressed the question of lawbreaking can be seen in the area of race and crime. Although the risk of being a victim of most street crimes has remained relatively stable or even declined during the past fifteen years, the risks are not borne equally: African Americans have higher rates of victimization than whites for many offenses, including violent crimes (see figure 1.3). Most of this crime involves young black males victimizing other blacks. When explaining this fact, it has become fashionable in some circles to downplay the dehumanizing and disruptive setting in which many urban blacks spend their lives, as if their behavior is somehow

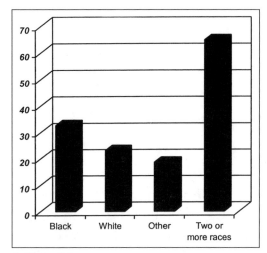

▲ **Figure 1.3.**
Violent Crime Victimization by Race
(per 1,000 persons), 1976–2006
Source: Bureau of Justice Statistics (2007).

unaffected by the environment and they are personally responsible for (or deserve) the ills that confront them.

A good place to begin studying the plight of America's underclass from a sociological perspective is by reading William Julius Wilson (1987) and Elijah Anderson (1990; 1994; 1999). These scholars have documented the life experiences of young black males in the inner city, and the picture is grim. On the issue of violence, for example, Anderson has this to say:

> The inclination to violence stems from circumstances of life among ghetto poor—the lack of jobs that pay a living wage, the stigma of race, the fallout from rampant drug use and drug trafficking, and the resulting alienation and lack of hope for the future. (1994: 81)

While this is only one view on the complicated topic of race and crime, much criminological theory and research supports this interpretation, as will become evident in later chapters.

Reactions to Crime

The third major area of inquiry within criminology is the study of the *reactions to crime*.

This includes the study of the state's reaction—the police, courts, and correctional institutions—as well as the analysis of various other criminal justice policies and practices, for example, capital punishment. Criminologists also study the public's reaction to crime. One well-researched topic in this area is the fear of crime.

Fear of Crime

Many Americans fear crime. Public opinion surveys show that nearly 40 percent of those polled are afraid to walk alone at night in their own neighborhoods (Maguire and Pastore, 2007). Fear of crime is greater for some groups of people than for others. For example, women are almost three times more likely than men to feel unsafe in their own neighborhoods at night. Some other findings are that African Americans are more fearful than whites, and that fear tends to go up as income goes down. Over the years since 1971, these findings have not changed in any meaningful way.

Conventional wisdom holds that the people most afraid of crime are the ones who have been personally victimized by it. While this is true to some extent, the relationship between experiencing crime and fearing crime is not simple. Elderly women, for example, are most afraid yet least often victimized, and young men are least afraid yet most often victimized (Maguire and Pastore, 2007). Those who have experienced crime themselves are no more likely to be afraid than people who have merely heard about other people's victimization. In fact, one researcher discovered that actual criminal victimization is less important as a cause of fear than the physical and social environments in which people live (Skogan, 1986). So-called social and physical incivilities in a neighborhood—such as unkempt lots, graffiti, homeless people, drunks, and trash—may raise levels of fear among both residents and visitors by affecting people's *perceptions* of the risk of being victimized (La-Grange, Ferraro, and Supancic, 1992; Weitzer

BOX 1.3. THREE CHALLENGES TO THE LEGALISTIC DEFINITION OF CRIME

The legalistic definition of crime is popular for its simplicity, but has been challenged for various reasons, as discussed in the text. The following quotes illustrate three different positions on the definition of crime.

[The] argument for limiting criminological inquiry to the specifications of the law overlooks the fact that the law itself reflects a set of subjectively held values, and limiting investigation within its boundaries reflects a no more inherently "scientific" choice than expanding inquiry beyond the law. . . . Right and wrong are moral concepts. The criminal law is essentially a politically enforced definition of right and wrong. Therefore, neither those who support a criminology that goes beyond the law's definition of right and wrong nor those who wish to keep it within these limits are making morally neutral choices. Any moral choice, even those about "scientific" data, will reflect the individual's values. (Michalowski, 1985: 317)

Criminologists often complain that they do not control their own dependent variable, that the definition of crime is decided by political-legal acts rather than by scientific procedures. The state, not the scientist, determines the nature or definition of crime. This book breaks with this tradition of passive compliance and attempts to construct a definition of crime consistent with the phenomenon itself and with the best available theory of criminal behavior. . . . [C]rimes [are] acts of force or fraud undertaken in pursuit of self-interest." (Gottfredson and Hirschi, 1990: 3, 15)

Only those are criminals who have been adjudicated as such by the courts. Crime is an intentional act in violation of the criminal law. . . . Criminology . . . cannot tolerate a nomenclature of such loose and variable usage [by anti-legalists]. (Tappan, 1947: 100)

It should be remembered that all legal systems are contextual in that they reflect the particular cultural and political characteristics of the times and places in which they were created or modified. This means that the legalistic elements of a crime may not be the same over time or in different jurisdictions.

and Kubrin, 2004). Finally, there is evidence that television news broadcasts have a strong impact on people's fear of crime, perhaps regardless of their victimization experiences or local crime rates (Chiricos, Padgett, and Gertz, 2000; Weitzer and Kubrin, 2004).

The remaining sections of this chapter discuss some of the important concepts and ideas that define the subject matter of criminology: What is crime? Who is the criminal? Where does law come in? What is the connection between crime and public policy?

WHAT IS CRIME?

The legal—or *legalistic*—definition of crime is a departure point for considering the subject matter of criminology. The definition simply states: Crime is a human act that violates the criminal law.

This definition has two important components. First, crime involves behavior: Someone has to perform some act. Second, this behavior is identified in terms of a body of substantive law. According to that law, a number of specific criteria must normally be met for an act to be considered a crime and the perpetrator a criminal. First, there must be conduct, or *actus reus* (mere thoughts, no matter how terrible, are not crimes). Second, the conduct must constitute a social harm: that is, the conduct must be injurious to the state (or "the people"). Third, the conduct must be prohibited by law. Fourth, the conduct must be performed voluntarily. Fifth, the conduct usually must be performed intentionally (the issue here is criminal intent, expressed in the concept of *mens rea*, meaning guilty mind); however, unintentional acts of negligence or omission may qualify as crimes in some cases. Sixth, the harm must be causally related to the conduct: that is, the act must produce the harm. Finally, the conduct must be punishable by law (in fact, the punishment must be specified in advance of the conduct).

The legalistic definition of crime is popular among both criminologists and the general public; however, it has not gone without challenge. (See box 1.3 for example quotes.) Many years ago Thorsten Sellin (1938) argued for a more universally applicable definition that would encompass any violation of what he called *conduct norms*. Sellin believed that the legal criteria used in legal definitions of crime are at best artificial and arbitrary, and at worst ignore other actions that conflict with the "general social interest." In Sellin's view, criminologists should study all conduct that violates group norms.

Around the same time, Edwin H. Sutherland (1945) argued that crime should be defined not only in terms of traditional criminal law, but also in terms of regulatory law, for example, restraint of trade, antitrust, and unfair labor practices, rules, and regulations. Sutherland, who coined the term *white-collar crime*, argued that criminologists who study only robbery, burglary, and theft are biased because they neglect the crimes of the more powerful members of society. Sutherland's viewpoint was very influential, giving rise to the study of white-collar crime, an important subfield of criminology that is the subject matter of chapter 6.

Other critics of the legalistic approach to the definition of crime include Jeffrey Reiman and Herman and Julia Schwendinger. Reiman (2007) lists a variety of acts and conditions that are similar to crime in terms of their consequences: for example, loss of life, physical injury, or property loss. He argues that when we are in the workplace, under medical care, and even simply breathing outside air, we are

at risk of unnecessary harm that dwarfs that which is caused by traditional street crimes. Reiman believes that the legal definition of crime does not encompass all—or even the most—socially injurious acts.

Some time ago the Schwendingers argued that the definition of crime does not have to be associated with law. They propose that criminologists can and should study things such as imperialism, racism, sexism, and other violations of human rights:

> Our disagreement with such social scientists as Thorsten Sellin and Edwin Sutherland ... is not over the independent character of criminal behavior. Instead, the issue at hand is whether social scientists have been fully justified in regarding the legalistic definitions of the behavior under study as the only justifiable definitions of what can be treated as crime (1970: 73).

Other criminologists argue that crimes include violations of international law, such as the Declaration of Human Rights, the Nuremberg Principles, and the Geneva Conventions (Kauzlarich and Kramer, 1998; Mullins and Rothe, 2008).

Michael Gottfredson and Travis Hirschi (1990) take a quite different approach, although they too believe that the subject matter of criminology should not be restricted to strictly legal categories of crime. They believe that many acts are similar to common crimes, from smoking cigarettes and eating between meals to gambling and speeding. Just like robbery, murder, rape, employee theft, and drug use, these acts are easy to commit, require little or no planning or skill, and are exciting, risky, or thrilling.

Finally, the so-called **labeling perspective** argues that crimes are distinguished from other acts precisely because they have been defined as crimes by people whose reactions matter. In other words, the social significance of a given act is in the reactions it calls forth. As Howard Becker has observed:

> [D]eviance is not a quality of the act the person commits, but rather a consequence of

the application by others of rules and sanctions to an "offender." The deviant is one to whom the label has been successfully applied; deviant behavior is behavior that people so label. (1963: 9)

Pursuing this reasoning, what makes behavior distinctive is the kinds of reactions it calls forth. The distinctive aspect of criminal behavior is that the behavior in question has been labeled crime (Hartjen, 1974: 5–8). When labeled as crime, behavior is transformed into criminal behavior, and the actor may be transformed into a criminal. This transformation is called **criminalization.** The opposite process—when the label criminal is removed from an action, event, or person—is called **decriminalization**. The labeling perspective views crime as status rather than as behavior. Bearing these points in mind, an alternative definition of crime might be stated as follows: Crime is a label that is attached to behavior and events by those who create and administer the criminal law.

While sensitive to the complex issues surrounding definitions of crime, in the end many criminologists use the legalistic definition. Even though most of the activities and events called *crime* in this text fall under the legalistic definition, we prefer a definition that treats crimes as both a behavior and a status. In this text, therefore, we define **crime** as "actions and/or labels that represent violation of criminal laws and other regulations designed to protect individuals and groups from victimization." Consistent with this definition, a **criminal** is "a person whose actions violate the criminal law, and/or have been called crimes."

VICTIMS OF CRIME

Victims are arguably the forgotten people in the crime scene. The primary reason is historical: The development of modern criminal law and the corresponding decline of primitive law (discussed in the next section) left victims no formal role in the criminal process. Historically, the word *victim* did not even appear in many statute books, nor were individuals thought of as victims—"the state" or "the people" were the victimized by any crime. This is why criminal cases are usually titled "The People" or "The State of X" versus a defendant.

A secondary reason relates to the orientation of science and public policy in criminal matters, which has traditionally focused on how to explain and deal with the behavior of criminals. Little attention has been paid to victims, and when they are brought in it is either as contributing causes of crime (especially common in discussions of assault, rape, and murder), in debates over whether some crimes are victimless (consensual sex offenses and drug use, for example), or as people who can help convict the offender.

But this picture has been changing dramatically in recent years. An international effort is under way to study the victimizing effects of crime (and other social ills) and to bring the real victim back into the picture. Much of this effort has been directed at changing criminal justice policy and practice to accommodate a more active role for victims.

For years, victims have been "twice victimized"—first by the criminal, and then by the very system to which they have turned for help. Women who have been raped are particularly at risk for this type of multiple victimization. Treated as nonentities, victims have been shuffled around, kept in the dark, had their property taken and not returned, and, worse still, they have been subjected to abuse and ridicule in court.

A variety of constructive responses are now being directed at the needs of crime victims. Some of these responses seek to reduce the probability of victimization, and, in that sense, are part of crime prevention efforts. Neighborhood crime watch programs and Operation Identification are examples. Other responses seek to improve the treatment of victims by the judicial process, and still others seek to redress the grievance occasioned by crime. The latter are generally divided into two kinds of support: *restitution*, where victims are compensated for their loss by the offender, either through fines or work; and *compensation*, where the state provides resources to help victims deal with the monetary loss resulting from crime. Today, all fifty states and the District of Columbia have compensation programs, and judges in most states are permitted to include some form of restitution in their sentencing options Many jurisdictions have also established formal organizations, such as victims' advocate offices, to specifically help victims of a variety of crimes. As of April 2008, more than three dozen states had constitutional amendments listing victims' rights (National Center for Victims of Crime, 2007). A federal constitutional amendment similar to those enacted in many states has been stalled in Congress for some time, but may by now have been reintroduced. The majority of these amendments require that victims be treated with "fairness, dignity, and respect." They are also entitled to the right to be informed, present, and heard at significant criminal justice proceedings. Approximately one-half of the states give victims the right to notice of the release of the offender, while about one-third of the states require a speedy resolution of the case and reasonable protection from the accused (National Center for Victims of Crime, 2007).

The impact of crime on victims can be devastating. Horror stories abound about victims who were horribly mutilated, killed, driven insane, or made penniless by crime. Every time gruesome murders come to light—the Virginia Tech atrocity, the bombing of the Murrah Federal Building in Oklahoma City, the Columbine school shooting, the "Manson family" murders—our sympathies go out to the families and friends of the victims. But, on a much more mundane level, millions of crime victims—many not even realizing they are victims—suffer unsensationally and find that few seem to care about their plight. Criminologists agree that the people most likely to be victim-

ized by crime are the very same people who are least equipped to deal with it and least able to change their social situation: the poor, African Americans, people living in public housing, the divorced, and single-parent families.

There are some critics who fear that the victim movement has been co-opted and manipulated by politicians and criminal justice officials whose real agenda is to secure more resources and public support for cracking down on criminals rather than reducing the pain of victims (Elias, 1993). The true picture is probably somewhere in between: Victims *are* more significant players than they used to be, and they *are* receiving more services and support than they used to; however, the reforms have been piecemeal, and the social injustices that underlie much victimization—and which victimization makes worse—have not really been addressed.

SOCIAL CONTROL AND LAW

Crime and law are intertwined. As a type of law, criminal law is generally regarded as a relatively recent development. Although no specific date of origin can be identified, criminal law in the Western world developed two thousand years ago from already existing systems of law and began to take shape in the later years of the Roman Empire. In considering the development of criminal law, an examination of the nature of law in general is desirable.

In any social group, efforts are made to ensure that members behave predictably and in accordance with the expectations of others. These efforts are at the heart of social control, and their success is thought to be indispensable to orderly group life. It is difficult to imagine how group life could endure if members simply acted impulsively or in continued violation of the expectations of others.

Social control may be informal or formal: It may appear in facial expressions, gestures, gossip, or ostracism. It may consist largely of unwritten rules passed on by word of mouth or by example, or it may take the form of written rules backed by force. Conformity is promoted sometimes through the use of rewards (positive sanctions) and sometimes through the use of penalties (negative sanctions). The effect of all these measures may be to create a sense of guilt and shame, which becomes an internal control.

Law is a type of formal social control, which "is characterized by (1) explicit rules of conduct, (2) planned use of sanctions to support the rules, and (3) designated officials to interpret and enforce the rules, and often to make them" (Davis, 1962: 43).

Origins and Development of Criminal Law

Much of what is known about the origins and development of criminal law has come through the efforts of legal historians and cultural anthropologists. Classic historical works such as *Ancient Law* by Sir Henry Sumner Maine (1905) and *The Growth of Criminal Law in Ancient Greece* by George Calhoun (1927) provide important interpretative accounts of early law. Twentieth-century anthropologists have added to the store of knowledge through their studies of primitive societies. Works by A. R. Radcliffe-Brown (1948), Bronislaw Malinowski (1926), E. Adamson Hoebel (1941), and E. E. Evans-Pritchard (1940) are among the best-known studies.

The Decline of Primitive Law

It is generally agreed that *primitive law*—the system of rules and obligations in preliterate and semiliterate societies—represents the foundation on which modern legal systems were built. Primitive law contains three important features:

1. Acts that injured or wronged others were considered "private wrongs": that is, injuries to particular individuals rather than the group or tribe as a whole. (Exceptions to this were acts deemed harmful to the entire community: for example, aiding an enemy or witchcraft.)
2. The injured party or family typically took personal action against the wrongdoer, a kind of self-help justice.
3. This self-help justice usually amounted to retaliation in kind. Blood feuds were not uncommon under this system of primitive justice.

Strongly held customs and traditions, the relative independence of the family, the similarities among people and their activities, and other features of primitive life changed as technological progress and a growing division of labor moved society toward the modern era. Growing differences in wealth, prestige, and power were associated with new patterns of authority and decision making. The rise of chieftains and kings and the centralization of political authority set the stage for the emergence the civil state. The handling of disputes slowly moved out of the hands of the family and into the hands of sovereign and state. Eventually, the creation of legal rules became the responsibility of heads of state, acting "in the name of the people."

These changes did not happen overnight. Today's criminal law is a product of centuries of change. The earliest known code of written law dates back to the twenty-first-century BC. This is the code of Ur-Nammu, the Sumerian king who founded the Third Dynasty of Ur. The famous Code of Hammurabi was discovered in 1901 in Susa, near the Persian Gulf. This code dates from around 1750 BC. Other ancient codes of law include the Twelve Tables of Rome, the Mosaic code, the laws of ancient Greece, and the laws of Tacitus. All these codes show strong ties with the self-help justice typical of more primitive eras. As Maine (1905: 341–42) notes, early penal law was primarily the law of torts (or private wrongs). The Twelve Tables treated theft, assault, and violent robbery as *delicta* (private wrongs), along with trespass, libel, and slander. The person, not the state or the public, was the injured party.

The maturing legal systems of ancient Greece and Rome moved steadily toward the formulation of offenses against the state (public wrongs, or *crimena*) and the establishment of machinery for administration and enforcement. According to Maine, the legislative establishment of permanent criminal tribunals around the first century BC represented a crucial step in the emergence of true criminal law.

One of the most interesting features of these early codes is the number of activities they cover. The Code of Hammurabi is particularly wide ranging. The laws covered such diverse areas as kidnapping, unsolved crimes, price fixing, rights of military personnel, sale of liquor, marriage and the family, inheritance, and slavery (Gordon, 1957). The contents of these early codes suggest three observations: (1) some laws articulate long-established customs and traditions and can be thought of as formal restatements of existing mores; (2) some laws reflect efforts to regulate and coordinate increasingly complex social relations and activities; and (3) some laws articulate prevailing moral standards and show close ties to religion.

Mala Prohibita *and* Mala in Se

In the minds of some people, law is based on moral beliefs and criminal codes are a sort of catalog of sins. But others have argued that there is much in criminal codes that bears no obvious connection with ethics or morality. In what sense, for example, are laws prohibiting certain forms of drug use or certain kinds of business activities matters of sin?

Laws were once indistinguishable from the general code governing social conduct. As primitive societies became more complex, law and justice were identified as concepts that regulated the moral aspects of social conduct. Even the extensive legal codes of Greece and Rome fused morality with law. In some languages (Hungarian, for example)

the word for "crime" means not only an act that is illegal but also one that is evil or sinful (Schafer, 1969). In time, criminal codes expanded and laws were passed to regulate activities in business, politics, the family, social services, and even people's intimate private lives. The connection between law and morality became less clear, and people categorized crimes as **mala prohibita**, meaning bad or evil because they are forbidden, or **mala in se**, meaning bad or evil in themselves. *Mala prohibita* crimes include drug offenses, traffic violations, and embezzlement; examples of *mala in se* crimes include incest, murder, arson, and robbery.

Interests and the Development of Law

Studies of the history of criminal law have documented the role that interests play in the creation, content, and enforcement of legal rules. Interests are simply the things people value, and different people sometimes value different things.

One of the first systematic discussions of interests in the formulation of law was by Roscoe Pound. According to Pound, law helps to adjust and harmonize conflicting individual and group interests:

> Looked at functionally, the law is an attempt to satisfy, to reconcile, to harmonize, to adjust these overlapping and often conflicting claims and demands, either through securing them directly and immediately, or through securing certain individual interests, or through delimitations or compromises of individual interests, so as to give effect to the greatest total of interests, or to the interests that weigh the most in our civilization, with the least sacrifice of the scheme of interests as a whole. (1943: 39)

The **functionalist theory** of sociological jurisprudence offered by Pound has been attacked for its emphasis on compromise and harmony and for its suggestion that there will be consensus where important social interests are concerned. Some scholars believe a **conflict perspective** better reflects the real workings of societal institutions. According to Richard Quinney,

> [S]ociety is characterized by diversity, conflict, coercion, and change, rather than by consensus and stability. Second, law is a result of the operation of interests, rather than an instrument that functions outside of particular interests. Though law may control interests, it is in the first place created by interests. Third, law incorporates the interests of specific persons and groups; it is seldom the product of the whole society. Law is made by men, representing special interests, who have the power to translate their interests into public policy. Unlike the pluralistic conception of politics, law does not represent a compromise of the diverse interests in society, but supports some interests at the expense of others (1970: 35).

Historically, those low in status or power have been labeled criminals most often and punished most severely for their crimes (Chambliss, 1973). Early legal codes specified different reactions according to distinctions of status: The most powerful were the most privileged. Conflict and power help explain why some activities are not crimes. This is especially evident in matters relating to business and government, but also applies to laws regarding sexual assault. Today, women and poor people still find it hard to protect their interests through law. In part this is because the state must support not only certain economic relationships, but other social relationships and institutions that can and often do reflect social inequality (Chambliss, 1988). The relationship between law and *patriarchy*, a social condition in which men have disproportionate power and privilege over women in a society, is one such example. Gender bias exists not only in law, but also in official data-gathering processes by the state and in formal social control institutions, such as the police and courts. For example, until very recently, few states considered it criminal for a man to rape his wife (Caulfield

and Wonders, 1993). Laws, criminal justice institutions, and actors within those institutions have gradually become more sensitive to issues such as violence against women. As long as a society is structurally and culturally organized around patriarchy, however, there will continue to be relationships and institutions within criminal justice that reflect—and sometimes promote—gender inequality.

Another example of how law does not necessarily reflect the interests of the majority can be illustrated by a relationship between a multinational corporation and third world mothers. Some years ago Nestlé launched an international campaign to promote its infant formula. Ads proclaiming "Give your baby love and Lactogen" were used to promote the product in less developed countries, where families are typically large. However, the promotion discouraged mothers from breastfeeding and encouraged practices that were more expensive, irreversible, and, because of contaminated water supplies, potentially harmful. Many babies became ill, and some died. But Nestlé had committed no crime, legally speaking, nor were any sanctions imposed on the company. In effect, the law both here and abroad protected the company, and had it not been for publicity surrounding the efforts of social activists in England and America, the company doubtless would have continued its legal but ultimately victimizing practices (Post and Baer, 1978). Corporations from developed countries often operate internationally because they can engage in practices that would be illegal in the United States but are not illegal in the host country (Kramer and Michalowski, 1987; 1999).

The advantages enjoyed by corporations in matters of crime also extend to situations in which corporations are the victims of crime: "The form and content of criminal justice in modern capitalistic societies supports and legitimates the use of criminal law for the protection of corporate property against individuals. That is . . . the modern criminal justice system better serves corporate than individual interests" (Hagan, 1982: 1019). These issues are examined in detail in chapter 6, but they are discussed from time to time throughout the text.

Anglo-American Criminal Law

Criminal law in the United States draws mainly from Greek, Mosaic, and Roman law via English law. The common law of England can be traced to the reign of Henry II (1154–1189). For centuries English law had been a system of tribal justice, the primitive law of private wrongs and self-help retaliation. As feudalism took hold in the eighth and ninth centuries, Anglo-Saxon society underwent important changes. The family lost its autonomy, kings and kingdoms emerged, and the blood feud was replaced by a system of material compensation (usually money) directed by individuals with special status—king, lord, or bishop. Equally important, political unification was underway, as territorial acquisitions by the new kings transformed a patchwork of small kin-dominated domains into a smaller number of larger kingdoms. With the Norman conquest of 1066, complete political unification was but a short step away.

The Normans centralized their administrative machinery, including that of law. During the reign of Henry II, new legal procedures emerged, including a court of common law. Those with complaints against others could take them to traveling courts, and justice dispensed there became a body of precedent to guide future judgments. During this period certain acts were identified as offenses against king and country ("Breaches of the King's Peace"), and these are the bones of modern criminal law. The Puritans took English criminal law to the New World. Over the next four hundred years, English common law was slowly Americanized.

The rules embodied in American criminal law come from four sources: (1) federal and state constitutions; (2) decisions by courts (common law or case law), including deci-

sions of precedent and Supreme Court rulings; (3) administrative regulations—those policy decisions employed by agencies on the federal, state, and local levels as they carry out their legal duties; and (4) statutory enactments by legislatures.

A distinction is made between **procedural rules** and **substantive law.** This distinction draws attention to two basic issues: (1) the question of procedure (how the authorities handle lawbreaking and lawbreakers), and (2) the question of substance (the content of the specific rules making up the body of criminal law). Thus substantive criminal law spells out the nature of criminal acts and the punishments associated with them.

Procedural rules govern the way lawbreaking and lawbreakers are handled by the criminal justice system. They are applicable at all stages of the legal process. Procedural rules shape the administration of criminal justice and help determine whether given acts and individuals will be officially identified as criminal, how offenders will be "processed," and what will happen to them if they are found guilty of a crime. Procedural aspects of criminal law set the tone for the process of criminalization and provide insights into criminal law in action. Together with the substance of criminal prohibitions, procedural rules reflect and reinforce public policy and the ideology that underlies it. The following section deals with the important topic of public policy.

CRIME AND PUBLIC POLICY

Public policy impinges on all aspects of the crime scene. Its impact begins with official decisions about what and whom to identify as criminal, and continues through all phases of the criminal process. Policy influences arrest, prosecution, trial, and sentencing. It also influences penalties and how punishment is carried out.

Many things shape public policy, whether on crime or anything else. The attitudes, beliefs, ideas, and assumptions about crime held by people in power help comprise the ideological underpinnings of policy and shape the positions taken on specific issues. These positions are often uncritically adopted by the public. This is called the *hegemonic effect* of ideology. The particular ideology underlying public policy is not always obvious, but it is there nonetheless, and actual policy decisions cannot be divorced from it. As noted thirty years ago, "ideology is the permanent hidden agenda of criminal justice" (Miller, 1973: 142)

The same ideology is not, of course, shared by everyone, or even by all those who work in the criminal justice system. For example, a study of attitudes among criminal justice practitioners found that prosecutors and judges were less likely than probation officers and defense attorneys (1) to agree among themselves and (2) to advocate alternatives to prison as punishment for crime (Lein, Richard, and Fabelo, 1992).

Nor does a particular ideology necessarily retain its influence over time. Policies change as time passes. Different assumptions and beliefs about criminal matters have achieved prominence at different times. The underlying ideology sometimes stimulates policy changes and sometimes reinforces existing policies. The influence of a particular ideology on policy depends on many things, and most important are the power and influence of those subscribing to it.

Samuel Walker (2005) claims that both liberals and conservatives are guilty of "peddling nonsense" about crime. Most people, Walker notes, base their ideas about crime and justice on "faith" rather than facts. This faith serves to undermine the sensible and successful implementation of crime and criminal justice policy. This echoes the theme we began this chapter with—that perceptions about crime are often biased.

Despite the obvious importance of ideology, there have been few attempts to identify and classify beliefs and assumptions about crime. Nearly forty years ago, Walter Miller

(1973) developed one of the most detailed statements on major ideological positions; it is still relevant today. Miller analyzed public statements on criminal matters made by a variety of Americans, including novelists, sociologists, journalists, government officials, lawyers, police, clergy, historians, and labor leaders. Though one does not hear so much these days from the radical left, the distinctions that Miller presents provide a useful starting point in thinking about ideology and public policy on crime.

Miller placed the different ideological positions he was able to identify on a one-dimensional scale:

Leftist					Centrist					Rightist
5	4	3	2	1	0	1	2	3	4	5
radical										conservative

The most extreme ideological positions were given the value 5. More moderate ones ranged between the extreme left and extreme right positions. The ideological position left 3 is more leftist than position left 1 but less leftist than position left 5. Each ideological position Miller identified concerns a specific crime issue and is made up of assumptions and beliefs about that issue.

For example, left 5 opinions on the causes of crime include assertions that the behavior called crime by the ruling elite "is an inevitable product of a fundamentally corrupt and unjust society. True crime is the behavior of those who perpetuate, control, and profit from an exploitative and brutalizing system" (Miller, 1973: 155). This, of course, is a radical conflict perspective.

In contrast, right 5 views on the causes of crime include assertions that "crime and violence are a direct product of a massive conspiracy by highly organized and well-financed radical forces deliberately seeking to overthrow the society . . . [through an] . . . unrelenting attack on the fundamental moral values of the society" (Miller, 1973: 156).

More moderate views are reflected in left 3 and right 3 positions. Left 3 views place the re-

sponsibility for crime on the shoulders of public officials who allocate "pitifully inadequate
resources to criminal justice agencies" and on
the shoulders of "damaging social conditions":
poverty, urban collapse, lack of jobs and educational opportunities, and race/ethnic segregation (Miller, 1973: 156–57). This may be
called the classic liberal position on crime (see
Walker, 1998). Right 3 views include this sort of
statement: "The root cause of crime is a massive erosion of the fundamental values which
traditionally have served to deter criminality,
and a concomitant flouting of the established
authority which has traditionally served to
constrain it. The most extreme manifestations
of this phenomenon are found among . . . the
young, minorities, and the poor" (Miller, 1973:
157). This view underlies the classic conservative policy position summarized by Messner
and Rosenfeld as follows:

The police will act swiftly to remove criminals from the streets; prosecutors will vigorously bring their cases to court without plea-
bargaining them to charges carrying lesser
penalties; judges and juries will have less
discretion in determining the penalties imposed; and more criminals will serve longer
sentences for their crimes. (1994: 94)

People's views about the proper ways to
deal with criminals and the proper operating
policies of criminal justice agencies are consistent with their views about the causes of
crime. In Miller's study, more radical opinions
stressed the brutalizing and militaristic strategies of government crime control, while more
conservative views stressed the dangerousness
of offenders and the need for swift, certain,
and severe punishment.

Left 1 and right 1 opinions show that the
moderate left and right converge on policy
matters. Moderate liberals stress a holistic
approach to crime in which the criminal
justice apparatus is coordinated with other
agencies that serve the general welfare of the
community and where the role of the federal
government is to finance and oversee reform

of the criminal justice system. Moderate conservatives also stress system reform, but put
more emphasis on increasing criminal justice
efficiency through modern management and
information-processing techniques.

Miller believes that both left and right can
be reduced to basic governing principles or
values and that few Americans would quarrel
with them, since they are "intrinsic aspects of
our national ideals":

For the right, the paramount value is order—
an ordered society based on a pervasive and
binding morality—and the paramount danger is disorder—social, moral and political.
For the left, the paramount value is justice—a
just society based on a fair and equitable
distribution of power, wealth, prestige, and
privilege—and the paramount evil is injustice—the concentration of valued social
resources in the hands of a privileged minority. . . . Stripped of the passion of ideological conflict, the issue between the two sides
could be viewed as a disagreement over the
relative priority of two valuable conditions:
whether order with justice, or justice with
order should be the guiding principle of the
criminal justice enterprise. (1973: 148).

While Miller's research is valuable, liberals and conservatives probably have more
in common when it comes to crime control
policy than anything else. Former U.S. president Bill Clinton, for example, who was considered fairly liberal, often supported very
conservative crime control measures, such
as limiting death penalty appeals, adding
more police officers, and advocating longer
prison terms (Kramer and Michalowski,
1995). While some of the policies Clinton
supported are closer to classic liberal thinking, such as his support of community policing and certain rehabilitation programs, the
traditional conservative ideology appears to
have influenced liberals more than liberal
ideology has influenced conservatives. Indeed, President George W. Bush's policies
do not appear to be significantly different
from those of his "liberal" predecessors, as

indicated by widespread bipartisan support of key elements of the Patriot Act, which are clearly within the crime control perspective.

The expectation that ideology influences public policy is based on the assumption that views or theories about an issue largely determine how people deal with it. In the last hundred years or so, public policy on criminal matters has indeed incorporated competing crime strategies. Two "ideal type" models of organized reactions to crime and criminals have been identified. One rests heavily on *order* with justice, the other on *justice* with order. Although neither model exactly reproduces the real world, both are drawn from criminal justice in action and emphasize what are thought to be fundamental divergences in assumptions and beliefs about the correct way to deal with criminals. The models were first suggested by Herbert L. Packer (1964, 1968), who calls them the crime control model and the due process model.

Order with Justice: The Crime Control Model

According to Packer, the ideology underlying the **crime control model** emphasizes repression of criminal behavior as the most important function of the criminal process:

> The failure of law enforcement to bring criminal conduct under tight control is viewed as leading to the breakdown of public order and thence to the disappearance of an important condition of human freedom. If the laws go unenforced—which is to say, if it is perceived that there is a high percentage of failure to apprehend and convict in the criminal process—a general disregard for legal controls tends to develop. The law-abiding citizen then becomes the victim of all sorts of unjustifiable invasions of his interests. His security of person and property is sharply diminished, and, therefore, so is his liberty to function as a member of society. The claim ultimately is that the criminal process is a positive guarantor of social freedom. (1968: 158)

To support this ideology, the crime control model pays the most attention to the capacity of the criminal justice system to catch, prosecute, convict, and dispose of a high proportion of criminal offenders. With its emphasis on a high rate of apprehension and conviction, and given limited resources, the crime control model places a premium on speed and finality. Speed is enhanced when cases can be processed informally and when procedure is uniform or standardized; finality is secured when the occasions for challenge are minimized. To ensure that challenges are kept to a minimum, those who work in criminal justice presume that the apprehended are in fact guilty. This places heavy emphasis on the quality of administrative fact-finding and the coordination of agency tasks and role responsibilities. Success is gauged by how expeditiously nonoffenders are screened out of the process and whether offenders are passed through to final disposition. Packer likens the crime control model to a conveyer belt, down which flows an endless stream of cases processed by workers who perform routine tasks.

Justice with Order: The Due Process Model

Whereas the crime control model resembles an assembly line, Packer visualizes the **due process model** as an obstacle course: "Each of its successive stages is designed to present formidable obstacles to carrying the accused any further along in the process" (1968: 163).

The due process model sees the crime control function as subordinate to ideals of justice. This model emphasizes ensuring that the facts about the accused are subjected to formal scrutiny; that the accused is afforded an impartial hearing under adversary procedures; that coercive and stigmatizing powers are not abused by those in an official position to exercise them; that the presumption of innocence is maintained until guilt is legally proven; that all defendants are given equal protection under the law, including the chance to defend themselves adequately; and that suspects and convicted offenders are accorded the kind of treatment that supports their dignity and autonomy as human beings. The emphasis, then, is on justice first.

U.S. Crime Policy: Due Process or Crime Control?

American public policy on crime appears to be dominated by the ideology and practices of the crime control model. Through the years there has been a proliferation of public and private police forces whose primary goal is the detection and apprehension of criminals and the defense of order. There have been continued efforts to create and enforce laws dealing with moral questions and essentially private behavior. There have been increasing efforts to unite and coordinate crime control at the federal, state, and local levels. There has been a growing emphasis on informality in the criminal process, best exemplified in the extensive use of plea bargaining. There have been continued efforts to promote efficiency, productivity, and professionalism in the activ-

ities and personnel of law enforcement agencies. There have been, conversely, a paucity of judicial decisions supporting due process values and few serious efforts to organize and fund programs that ensure equal protection under the law and guarantee the dignity and autonomy of either victims or offenders.

Important congressional support for the crime control model came in 1968 when Congress passed the Omnibus Crime Control and Safe Streets Act. Under Title 1 of the act, Congress established the Law Enforcement Assistance Administration (LEAA) under the Department of Justice. Through this move, Congress extended federal involvement in the enforcement activities of state and local governments and helped establish what were to become the primary crime strategies throughout the nation. Although the Constitution specifically places the major responsibility for criminal matters in the hands of the states, the federal government was able to assume considerable power and influence in such matters. To help the LEAA carry out its mandate, Congress allocated just over $60 million for operation in 1969. Over the next few years, the LEAA was one of the fastest-growing

7698477 Getty

Police detection and apprehension of suspected criminals is heavily emphasized by the crime control model of criminal justice

federal agencies; in 1971 its annual budget reached half a billion dollars, then it climbed to over $800 million, and by 1976 it stood at $1.015 billion (U.S. Department of Justice, 1976: 42). As a result of numerous criticisms of agency practices during the 1970s, however, Congress voted the LEAA only $486 million in 1980 before scrapping the agency altogether. The Justice System Improvement Act of 1979 established as its successor agency the Office of Justice Assistance, Research and Statistics (OJARS). Its budget for fiscal 1981 was $144,397,000, and, after a couple of leaner years, grew to $197.3 million in 1984 (McGarrell and Flanagan, 1985: 25). In 1984 Congress created the Office of Justice Programs (OJP) as successor to OJARS, and the OJP budget over the last few years has been between $4 and $5 billion (U.S. Department of Justice, 2006). More generally, current funding approved for federal criminal justice activities is estimated to be much higher, around $47 billion (Maguire and Pastore, 2007: 15).

Most of the federal money goes to police agencies. In 2007, for example, just under half of all federal expenditures on criminal justice went to police protection (Maguire and Pastore, 2007). Funds are used to purchase new, sophisticated police equipment (from weapons and ammunition to vehicles, computers, and bulletproof clothing), to train officers and to reorganize police departments, to finance management training programs and operations research, to fund scientific and technological research, and to plan future policy throughout the various levels of the legal process. Furthermore, the police, even those in relatively small towns, are becoming more militarized. A study of local police agencies serving populations of twenty-five to fifty thousand people found that more than 80 percent of them had "MP5 submachine guns, tactical semiautomatic shotguns, night vision equipment, sniper rifles, flash-bag grenades, tactical shields, battle dress uniforms, and specialized dynamic entry tools." Fifty percent of these small-town policing agencies had "electronic surveillance equipment, tactical helmets, tactical communication headsets, and a . . . SWAT van" (Kraska and Cubellis, 1997: 612). Prisons, jails, and various correctional programs have also experienced a boom in funding. From 1980 to 2003, state expenditures rose nine times over (Maguire and Pastore, 2007).

The crime control approach is also reflected in "three strikes" policies and the passage of multiple forms of federal legislation over the past decade. Besides authorizing the use of capital punishment for some sixty offenses, specific 1996 Crime Act provisions included $10.7 billion for state and local law enforcement agencies, including $8.8 billion to put one hundred thousand police officers on the streets in community-policing programs and $1 billion for drug enforcement; $8.3 billion to states for construction of new prisons and development of prison alternatives; $2.6 billion for federal enforcement agencies, including $1 billion for the Immigration and Naturalization Service and the U.S. Border Patrol; $1.8 billion in direct funding for local anticrime efforts such as drug treatment, education, and jobs; $1.3 billion for "drug court" programs providing at least six hundred thousand nonviolent offenders with substance abuse services over six years. In sum, more than two-thirds of its $30-billion budget was earmarked for law enforcement.

Recent state expenditures mirror the federal outlays on crime control. Nearly every state spends more than half of its criminal justice funds on policing (Maguire and Pastore, 2007). This funding policy gives rise to a "structural imbalance" in the criminal justice system, reducing the capacity of nonpolice agencies to handle violators and thereby undermining the crime control capacity of the system as a whole.

PUBLIC POLICY AND CRIMINAL STEREOTYPES

Every president since Lyndon Johnson has called for some form of "war on crime." The passing of the Omnibus Crime Control and Safe Streets Act in the late 1960s drew attention only to certain crimes and certain criminals. Despite using such broad expressions as "lawlessness in America," political officials considered the real crime problem to be the overt threats to public order and prevailing institutions represented in street crimes—muggings, forcible rapes, burglaries, assaults, and armed robberies—and the activities of junkies and dope pushers, militant activists, and other so-called radicals. Except for the last two groups, the bulk of those identified as the real threat to law and order are minorities and lower-class individuals living mostly in the poverty areas of the nation's cities (Chambliss, 1999). Nineteenth-century officials dubbed such persons "the dangerous classes."

Because current crime policies show little evidence of changing focus, people have no incentive to alter their long-held stereotypes of the criminal. On the contrary, current policies merely reinforce these stereotypes. Americans are encouraged to view the streets as the unsafe turf of the criminal class. They are encouraged to distrust less well-off neighbors and to demand speedy and harsh disposition of criminal offenses. Criminal stereotyping at work is found in the practice of **racial profiling.** This term describes a practice in which a person's race or ethnicity strongly influences police decisions to stop, search, or make an arrest. It came to national attention in the mid-1990s following a highly publicized case in New Jersey. Over a short period of time, twenty-five African Americans had been pulled over by the New Jersey State Police in one particular area of the the New Jersey Turnpike. The defendants' cars were stopped and subsequently searched, and drugs were found. Defense attorneys suspected that their clients were pulled over only because they were African American. A study was commissioned to see if a higher proportion of African Americans were using that part of the highway or if African Americans were simply being pulled over more frequently (Lamberth, 1998). The study found that blacks did not use the road more frequently, nor did they violate traffic laws more frequently than other racial groups. It appeared that race was the key to the traffic stops. Armed with corroborating testimony from state troopers, a New Jersey state court found Lamberth's study compelling and ruled that the police had been engaging in racial stereotyping. "Driving While Black" (DWB) is the expression commonly used to refer to this type of racial profiling. Multiple studies over the last decade have confirmed the ubiquity of racial profiling (Birzer and Birzer, 2006).

Stereotyping can also result in the view that criminals are categorically "bad" people and victims of crime are categorically "good" people. This has been called *moral polarization*—the "tendency to locate participants in criminal events on opposite and extreme sides of a moral continuum" (Claster, 1992: 196). In reality, as we have seen, criminality and victimization are interwoven, and cannot be easily distinguished from each other.

The targets of crime policy (and also many victims of crime) feel oppressed by the authorities (Allen, 1974; Maguire and Pastore, 2007). Crime control policy further alienates and aggravates the disadvantaged segments of society when they realize that middle-class criminality escapes the serious attention of the state. With all the money spent on projects and programs dealing with drugs, burglary, robbery, and street crimes generally, the government has little left over to spend on policing the middle class even if it wanted to.

This does not mean that street crimes should receive no attention, or even that they should receive less attention than they do. The issue is how much and what kind of attention they receive relative to other forms of criminality. The relative lack of attention authorities give to white-collar, state, and corporate crime is hard to justify because its negative impact on society is arguably greater than that resulting from street crimes. Chapter 6 looks at this issue in detail.

Jeffrey Reiman (2007) provides an interesting interpretation of this problem. He believes that the criminal justice system has failed to reduce crime and to protect society precisely because that failure benefits those who are wealthy and powerful. How can that be? Reiman asserts that this failure performs an ideological service by funneling discontent toward those depicted as responsible for crime—the poor, minorities, the lower classes—and away from the rich and powerful. At the same time, the system focuses on individual wrongdoing rather than on the organizations and institutions that make up social order, which ultimately eliminates the interest in examining the root economic, political, and social causes of crime. If social conditions are not responsible for crime, then cries for fundamental change in the social order are without substance; the "radical" threat can be resisted by a united middle class urging continuation of prevailing policies. As William Chambliss (1999) maintains, criminal stereotyping gives us an inaccurate picture of both victimization and victimizers.

CHAPTER SUMMARY

This chapter began with the observation that the media image of the crime scene is highly distorted. The emphasis on crimes that are especially violent or sensational helps fuel widespread fear of crime, which leads many people to retreat behind locked doors, making the streets even more dangerous for those who venture out.

Criminologists try to uncover the "truth" about crime and criminals. The chapter discussed various concepts, definitions, and perspectives that criminologists have developed. The legalistic definition of crime is behavior that violates the criminal law; criminals are people who engage in that behavior. Others have argued that the definition of crime need not be based on law. Another definition proposed is that crime and criminal are labels attached to behavior, events, and individuals by people in positions of authority or power. This text favors a definition that sees crime as both a behavior and a status.

Criminal law formally creates crime by defining it into existence. It is the application of law, however, that criminalizes actual behavior, people, and events. This process is influenced by interests: the things that people value. When interests are in conflict, as they often are, law usually reflects the interests of the more powerful groups in society. As later chapters will show, even laws supported by broad public consensus—rape statutes, for example—may actually serve the interests of the more powerful (males) at the expense of the less powerful (females).

Public policy on crime is shaped by historical forces as well as by the attitudes and beliefs of people in power. The crime control model emphasizes order with justice and pays most attention to the capacity of society to catch, prosecute, and dispose of a high proportion of guilty defendants. The due process model emphasizes justice with order and sees the crime control function as secondary to the protection of individual liberties and the right to equal treatment under the law.

American public policy on criminal matters is dominated by the crime control model. Government spending is used largely to improve apprehension and conviction rates of criminals rather than to prevent crime in the first place or to ensure that the rights of offenders and victims are protected. Criminal stereotypes abound, and this clouds our understanding of other threats to life and property such as white-collar and corporate crime.

KEY TERMS

conflict perspective
crime
crime control model
criminal

criminalization
criminology
decriminalization
due process model
functionalist theory
labeling perspective
mala in se
mala prohibita
procedural rules
racial profiling
social control
substantive law

RECOMMENDED READINGS

Barak, Gregg. (1994). *Media, Process, and the Social Construction of Crime: Studies in Newsmaking Criminology.* New York: Garland.

Best, Joel. (1999). *Random Violence: How We Talk about New Crimes and New Victims.* Berkeley and Los Angeles: University of California Press.

Chambliss, William J. (1999). *Power, Politics, and Crime.* Boulder, CO: Westview

Criminal Justice Collective of Northern Arizona University. (2000). *Investigating Difference: Human and Cultural Relations in Criminal Justice.* Boston: Allyn and Bacon.

Jewkes, Yvonne. (2004). *Media and Crime.* London: Sage.

Surette, Ray. (2006). *Media, Crime, and Criminal Justice: Images, Realities and Policies.* Belmont, CA: Wadsworth.

RECOMMENDED WEB SITES

American Society of Criminology (http://www.asc41.com). A professional association for criminologists and all other students of crime.

Sourcebook of Criminal Justice Statistics (http://www.albany.edu/sourcebook/index.html). Copious information on crime and victimization in the United States.

CHAPTER

2

CRIME DATA AND THE METHODS OF CRIMINOLOGY

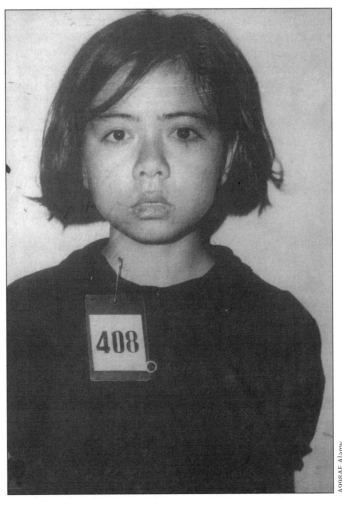

A998AE Alamy

The newspaper headlines read: "Crime Is Down," "Murder on the Decline," and "Hate Crime on the Rise." What do these statements really mean, and on what information are they based? Indeed, how do we even know how much crime there is in the United States? Fortunately, both the government and criminologists have devised various ways to measure the volume of crime. In addition, researchers have developed ways of identifying where crimes occur, the relationship between offenders and victims, and the age, gender, and race of those involved in crime. In the first section of this chapter, we will describe how crime data are constructed and gathered; the second part of the chapter provides a review of the basic research methods used by criminologists to study crime. It is important to remember throughout the following discussion that science requires that valid and reliable data be used to build knowledge. If a data source or research strategy is poor or inappropriate for studying the problem at hand, then the results are questionable. Just as it is important to consider the source when hearing a story, it is also important to consider the source when reading information on crime and criminality.

TYPES OF CRIME MEASUREMENT

There are three major sources of crime data in the United States: (1) information on crimes submitted by police agencies to the Federal Bureau of Investigation (FBI); (2) information on crime victimization gathered through interviews with citizens; and (3) information on crime and delinquency supplied through interviews with citizens who admit their own criminality. Each of these sources is discussed in turn.

Uniform Crime Reports (UCR)

The most widely used national data source on official crimes and criminals is the FBI's **Uniform Crime Reports (UCR)**. These reports were the brainchild of J. Edgar Hoover, the first director of the FBI. More than sixty years ago, Hoover recognized the need to compile nationwide data on crime as an aid to law enforcement and research on crime and criminals.

When you read or hear about crimes rates, UCR statistics are often the primary source of the information. The UCR is compiled by the FBI based on police department reports of crime. Crimes generally come to the attention of the police when a victim or observer reports a possible crime or if the police happen to discover one through routine patrol, detective work, or informants. Police departments report their crime statistics to the FBI on a monthly basis. The specific offenses reported under the UCR are divided into two categories: Part I and Part II. Part I offenses—also called **index offenses**—are thought to be the crimes most likely to be reported to the police and occur with some regularity in all jurisdictions (Federal Bureau of Investigation, 2008). The following are index offenses, with brief definitions:

- *CriminalHomicide*: The willful killing of one human being by another
- *ForcibleRape*: The carnal knowledge of a female forcibly and against her will
- *Robbery*: The taking or attempting to take anything of value from the care, custody, and control of a person by force or the threat of force
- *AggravatedAssault*: An attack by one person upon another for the purpose of inflicting severe or aggravated bodily harm
- *Burglary*: The unlawful entry of a structure to commit a felony or a theft
- *Larceny-Theft*: The unlawful taking away of property from another
- *Motor Vehicle Theft*: The theft or attempted theft of a motor vehicle
- *Arson*: Willful or malicious burning down or attempt to burn a dwelling house, public building, motor vehicle or aircraft, or the personal property of another

Notice that four of these eight crimes involve violence or the threat of violence against a person, while four are crimes against property. Also notice in these definitions that male victims of rape are excluded, attempted murder is not formally considered criminal homicide, and robbery involves elements of both theft and the use or threat to use violence.

Part II offenses contain a range of crimes that vary significantly in their frequency and seriousness. Twenty-one crimes are defined as Part II offenses, ranging from simple assault, forgery, and vandalism to gambling, prostitution, vagrancy, drunk driving, and drug abuse.

The FBI's UCR report, titled *Crime in the United States*, contains a wealth of data, including:

- Aggregate statistics on the overall crime rate, and trends over the last few years
- The relative frequency of index offenses (see figure 2.1), trends over the last few years, and, for some, the relationship between the offender and victim
- Statistics on the race, gender, and age of victims and offenders
- Data on the amount and type of crime in various cities, counties, and states
- Data on the police **clearance rate**: the percentage of reported crimes that result in an arrest
- Data on law enforcement personnel, including those on college campuses

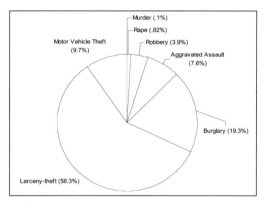

▲**Figure 2.1.**
Distribution of Part I Offenses (Excluding Arson)
Source: Federal Bureau of Investigation (2008).

UCR Crime Rates

The FBI presents much of its data in the form of rates. A **crime rate** is a very important concept, as we shall see. It is conventionally computed by dividing the number of crimes known to police in a jurisdiction by the population of the jurisdiction. The result is multiplied by 100,000 to avoid fractions. To illustrate, suppose we look at data from the states of California and Delaware.

State	Population	Violent Crimes	Rate
	(1)	(2)	(3)
California	36,132,147	190,178	526.3
Delaware	843,524	5,332	632.11

The Index crime rate for Delaware shown in column 3, was computed as follows:

$$\frac{5,332}{843,524} \times 100,000 = 632$$

Rates are more useful for comparative purposes than absolute numbers. This can be illustrated by using the above information. If you heard that California had around thirty-five times as many violent crimes as Delaware, you might think California a less safe place to live than Delaware. But the overall chances of being victimized by crime were actually *higher* in Delaware.

Modification to the UCR: The National Incident-Based Reporting System

In 1991, the FBI initiated a more comprehensive and detailed reporting system known as the **National Incident-Based Reporting System** (**NIBRS**). The plan is to replace the UCR with this incident-based system (Bureau of Justice Statistics, 2007).

The difference between the traditional UCR and NIBRS is basically this: Under NIBRS, individual police records on each official criminal incident and related arrest—rather than monthly summaries—will make up a database that can be used by criminal justice practitioners, policy makers and researchers to answer a wide variety of questions. Information on crime incidents will be taken directly off the reports officers make at the scene, as well as from reports maintained by prosecutors and the courts. An immediate advantage of NIBRS is that all offenses within a given crime incident can now be recorded, as opposed to only the most serious offense, as is the case with the UCR. Another advan-

tage concerns the breadth of information that will be available. Under NIBRS, information will be available on a wide range of details, from demographic information, time of day, weapon use, victim resistance, location of offense, and residence of victims and suspects to police response times, whether or not the crime was completed, and what eventually happened to the suspect, if there was one. In addition, NIBRS will contain incident-based data on the entire list of Part I and Part II offenses.

The promise of NIBRS is substantial but as yet unfulfilled. The U.S. Department of Justice has reported that NIBRS was not moving along as quickly as hoped. Implementing the NIBRS has proven to be difficult, but even when fully operational, NIBRS will still capture only official police-generated data. Nevertheless, the FBI reports that as of August 2007, thirty states have been NIBRS certified, while others are in the process of conversion (Federal Bureau of Investigation, 2008).

Drawbacks of the UCR

There are many limitations of the UCR. For example, most white-collar, corporate, and state crimes are excluded, as are federal crimes. In multiple-offense situations, as when a robbery also involves an assault or a weapons offense, only the most serious offense is recorded. In addition to these limitations, there are three other problem areas: (1) many crimes are not reported to the police, (2) there is routine underreporting of crime by the police, and (3) some areas and populations are overpoliced. These will be discussed in turn.

Underreporting of Crimes to the Police

Perhaps the most significant problem with the UCR is that it provides information on only those crimes that come to the attention of the police. Indeed, we know that there is a massive amount of crime that never becomes known to the authorities. Those crimes that do not show up in the official UCR statistics are referred to as the "**dark figure of crime**."

National surveys indicate that fewer than half of all serious crimes are reported to the police, and the situation is not much different in other countries such as Canada, Australia, and Britain (Bureau of Justice Statistics, 2007; Mirrlees-Black, Mayhew, and Percy, 1996). Although it is true that more serious crimes tend to be reported more often than less serious crimes, differences among serious crimes make some more likely to be reported than others. For example, crimes resulting in high losses or injuries that require medical attention tend to be reported more often than other crimes. Murders are reported most often—it is hard to ignore a dead body. Among other serious offenses, motor vehicle theft heads the list at around 83 percent being reported, followed by aggravated assault (62 percent), and burglary (56 percent) (U.S. Department of Justice, 2006).

The reporting situation with violent crimes is complicated. On the whole, violent crimes are more likely to be reported if they involve female victims or weapons, or result in injuries (Gottfredson and Gottfredson, 1988; Bureau of Justice Statistics, 1994). Surprisingly, assaults involving strangers are no more likely to be reported than incidents involving people who know each other. This is a recent change and may be due to the fact that domestic violence has received a lot of negative publicity over the past few years. The major exception to this pattern is sexual assault: Assaults by strangers are more likely to be reported than assaults by acquaintances or family members.

Why do many violent crimes go unreported to the police? The most frequent reason given by victims is that the incident is "personal" or "private" (Hart and Rennison, 2003). This reason is less likely to be given when the victim is attacked by a stranger (Harlow, 1991: 3); in these cases victims who don't report the crime usually say they felt nothing could be done. In fact, this is the most common reason for not reporting any type of serious crime. The second most common reason is that the victim felt the police would not want to be bothered. These responses may reflect unpleasant prior experiences with the police or belief that the police are uncaring or incompetent.

Sometimes, a decision not to call the police is stimulated by fear of reprisal by the offender. This is most likely to arise with domestic violence or incidents involving friends. Victims feel that reporting the offender to police will result in more violence against them: if not immediately, then later on. Yet studies have shown that calling the police may actually prevent future domestic violence, especially when offenders are subject to treatment after arrest (Sartin, Hansen, and Huss, 2006).

Underreporting by the Police

Although the public has a very important role in producing official data on crime, the police have the last word. This is true of both data on crime and data on criminals. A complainant may call the police to report a crime, but the police decide whether or not the incident will be treated as a crime. This is called the **founding decision**. Since the police have considerable discretion in deciding whether or not to treat a complaint as a crime, the amount of crime officially recorded is directly shaped by how that discretion is exercised. This means that a rise (or decrease) in published crime rates may reflect changes in police founding decisions rather than changes in the amount of crime itself. One study of this issue has shown that a twenty-year upward trend in violent crime rates from 1973 to 1992 was largely due to greater police productivity in recording and reporting crime (O'Brien, 1996).

The founding decision is sometimes inaccurate and may even be intentionally falsified. Internal audits of police founding practices in Chicago and in Portland, Oregon, found that 50 to 70 percent of "unfounded" felony crimes had been incorrectly labeled (Schneider, 1977). Accusations of deliberate falsification are difficult to document, but not hard to imagine. In one study of founding behavior by English police, the authors discovered several reasons why the police would not record an incident as founded even though it was in fact a crime:

- The police considered it too trivial.
- The victim was unlikely to prosecute the offender.
- The incident was "not police business."
- The crime was too difficult to investigate or prosecute.
- The incident was not "real" crime. (Kinsey, Lea, and Young, 1986)

Underrecording of crime by police is related to the type of crime involved and the people victimized by it (Kinsey, Lea, and Young, 1986; Elias, 1993). Fights among lower-class or minority individuals and domestic assaults involving female victims are examples of underrecorded crimes. In Canada some police officers in one large city made a distinction between the public—whom they served—and the "dregs" or "scum" (Shearing, 1979). The scum, drawn mainly from lower-class minority groups, were often not taken seriously when they complained of crime.

Overpolicing

Since poor and minority neighborhoods tend to experience an underrecording of crime, it may come as a surprise to learn that police also tend to concentrate law enforcement efforts in the same neighborhoods. These areas become overpoliced relative to other parts of the city (Hagan, Gillis, and Chan, 1978; Smith, 1986). To some extent this reflects the distribution of crime itself: Violent crimes such as robbery, aggravated assault, and murder tend to be concentrated in the inner city. But it also reflects stereotypes held by both police and public about the origins, characteristics, and dangers of "real" crimes and "real" criminals. Police go where they expect to find real criminals committing real crime. Using computerized geographic information systems (GIS) to map crime locations, many

large urban police forces today keep track of crime "hot spots" and concentrate their personnel in those areas, although software limitations raise serious questions about reliability (Bichler and Balchak, 2007). A hot spot may be a city block, a bar, an intersection, or even a residence.

Since overpolicing and underrecording of crime tend to occur in the same parts of the city, the impact on police clearance rates is substantial. Overpolicing inflates the numerator of the clearance rate (the numbers of arrests), while underrecording of crime lowers the denominator (the number of crimes known to the police). The resulting clearance rate is thus artificially inflated, suggesting that there is greater police efficiency in a community than is really the case. It distorts the true picture of a community's experiences with crime: Underrecording downplays the suffering that occurs in inner-city areas and poorer neighborhoods, while overpolicing subjects residents to increased surveillance and risk of arrest. The result can be a sense of neglect on one hand and a sense of abuse on the other (Bourgois, 2004; Kinsey, Lea, and Young, 1986). In any case, the true clearance rate is typically lower than the published statistics indicate.

The National Crime Victimization Survey (NCVS)

Every year since 1973 the U.S. Department of Justice has sponsored a nationwide survey to find out more about crime in America. Called the National Crime Survey until 1991, and now called the **National Crime Victimization Survey (NCVS)**, the program has become an international model. The Bureau of Justice Statistics (BJS), which runs the survey, interviews more than 130,000 individuals ages twelve and above from about 75,000 different households in the United States.

The NCVS begins with a series of screening questions conducted over the telephone or in face-to-face interviews with respondents. These questions identify whether the respondent recalls being personally involved in a crime during the previous year. For example, here is Question 42 from the NCVS Basic Screen Questionnaire used in the 2005 survey:

42a. People often don't think of incidents committed by someone they know. Other than incidents already mentioned, did you have something stolen from you or were you attacked or threatened by:
(a) Someone at work or school?
(b) A neighbor or friend?
(c) A relative or family member?
(d) Any other person you've met or known?
42b. Did any incidents of this type happen to you?
42c. How many times?

These questions help jog the respondent's memory and the answers tell interviewers where to go next. When probing about some incidents, interviewers are able to identify elements that indicate the event involved other crimes as well. For example, here is the way interviewers can establish whether a crime might have been motivated by hate:

46g. An offender(s) can target people for a variety of reasons, but we are only going to ask you about a few today. Do you suspect the offenders(s) targeted you because of:
a. Your race?
b. Your religion?
c. Your ethnic background or national origin?
d. Any disability?
e. Your gender?
f. Your sexual orientation?

Sometimes an incident is revealed not to be a crime; other times it turns out to be a different crime than initially believed. For example, a broken window may at first suggest a case of attempted burglary, but further questioning could reveal that it was more likely vandalism. In addition, detailed questioning provides information about such things as the actions of offenders and victims, the extent of injury or loss, the type of weapons used, and the reasons for reporting or not reporting incidents to police.

Limitations of Victimization Surveys

Victimization surveys have their limitations. First, findings are based only on recall, and people's memories are often flawed. Second, respondents may intentionally deceive interviewers, though this is a risk that carefully constructed questionnaires and well-trained interviewers can reduce. Deception is more likely to be a problem for some crimes and some victims than for others. For example, it is likely that victimization of women and children is underreported by victimization surveys because of embarrassment or fear. In fact, the offender may even be in the same room with the research subject!

Another problem with victimization surveys is the possibility that they overestimate the proportion of crimes involving black suspects. This is less likely to result from victims intentionally lying about a suspect's race than from the fact that some victims hold stereotypical images of criminals. In one interesting study of this issue, white and black subjects were asked to describe a picture they had been shown of a white man holding a razor during an argument with a black man; a majority of the white subjects recalled that the black man had been holding the razor! Black subjects were more likely to recall the picture accurately (McNeely and Pope, 1981). It is possible, too, that errors in racial identification could be made if some white offenders conceal their race by wearing masks and gloves or by blackening their hands and face when committing crimes at night.

Victimization surveys nevertheless provide useful information on a broad range of issues. For example, researchers can learn about the protective measures victims take when they are assaulted, robbed, or raped; about relationships between victims and offenders; about the distribution of crimes in time and space; and about the nature and timeliness of the police response. NCVS data have also shown us that the risks and burdens of crime victimization are not borne equally. This is particularly true of violent crime, as table 2.1 illustrates. Except for sexual assaults, those most likely to be victimized by violent crime are males, the young, African Americans and Hispanics, and people from low-income households.

Comparing the UCR and NCVS

The NCVS was designed to complement the UCR. The two programs are not directly comparable, for, as we have seen, they use different methods, calculate crime rates differently, and provide different kinds of information. However, sometimes it is possible to manipulate the data from both programs to overcome some of the differences between them. Even though the NCVS still records more crimes, long-term trends in some offenses look remarkably similar

Table 2.1. Who Is Victimized Most by Violent Crime?

The burden of crime victimization is not borne equally. This is particularly true of violent crime. NCVS reports show which Americans are more and which are less likely to be victimized by violent crimes. The following shows some of these differences based on a rate per 1,000 people age 12 or older.

Sex

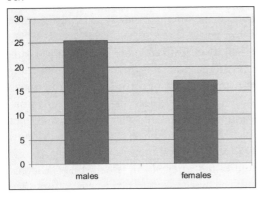

Race/Ethnicity

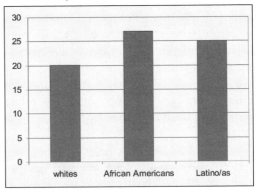

Age

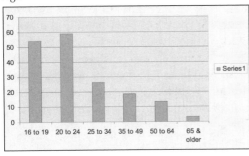

Household Income

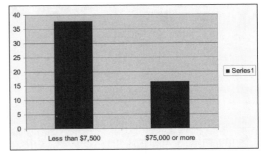

Violent crimes are rape, sexual assault, robbery with or without injury, aggravated assault with injury, and simple assault with minor injury. The data include attempts to commit robbery or rape, and threats of assault involving weapons.

Source: Bureau of Justice Statistics (2008).

in both UCR and NCVS data sets. For example, if robberies of commercial establishments such as gas stations, convenience stores, and banks are excluded from the UCR, the long-term rates closely correspond with those of the NCVS, which measure noncommercial robbery.

Not surprisingly, the National Crime Victimization Survey provides virtually no information on crimes that victimize society rather than individuals—for example, drug offenses, treason and espionage, or environmental crimes. Nor does it collect information on crimes committed in connection with a person's job such as embezzlement, price-fixing, or bribery.

The UCR hardly does any better in this regard, reporting only on fraud and embezzlement. In fact, it would not be easy to collect information on white-collar crimes under either format. There is little systematic policing of the workplace, and agencies that investigate such crimes do not generally report them to the FBI's UCR program—even if there were a category to put them in. In addition, people who are victimized by such crimes often have no idea what to call them or where to report them. Being the target of consumer fraud at an appliance store is different from having one's purse snatched or coming home to a ransacked house.

The absence of a regular national data collection effort designed to measure white-collar crime is unfortunate, because the costs to individuals and society are far above those associated with street crimes and personal offenses against individuals. While we discuss the costs of white-collar crime in a later chapter, it is clear that the dark figure of crime will remain hidden as long as there is no systematic national effort to collect victimization data on white-collar crime.

Self-Report Surveys

A well-known nationwide survey illustrates the **self-report** technique. In the mid-1970s, criminologists at the Behavioral Research Institute of the University of Colorado interviewed a representative sample of American youth born from 1959 through 1965 to find out about their delinquent activity (National Youth Survey, 2007). In 1977, 1,725 adolescents were surveyed, making up the first "wave" or "panel" of the study, called the **National Youth Survey (NYS)**. Now known as the National Youth Survey–Family Study, the subjects have been interviewed periodically over the last several decades. As you would expect, some of the original sample dropped out of the study because researchers could not find them or they refused to participate further. Only three-quarters of the original sample remain. This respondent loss is referred to as *attrition*, and it is a problem faced in all studies that follow the same group of people over time.

The subjects of the National Youth Survey were asked whether they had committed any of an extensive list of delinquent and criminal activities during the year preceding the survey. Box 2.1 lists the items, and, where appropriate, the year they were added to the original 1977 survey. The list shows a mixture of serious and less serious offenses, from joy-riding and minor theft to assault, strong-arm robbery, and weapons offenses. The original survey also included some *status offenses*—for example, cheating on school tests, skipping classes, and running away from home.

The NYS has produced a wealth of information about delinquency and crime, and criminologists are still learning new things from it. Because the study collected information on both the prevalence and incidence of delinquency and crime over a number of years, it is possible to identify the frequency of an offense as well as its seriousness and duration. The NYS confirmed, for example, that although most delinquency is sporadic and minor in nature, a small group of "chronic delinquents" is responsible for a disproportionate amount of all types of self-reported delinquency (Dunford and Elliot, 1984). Although some authors have criticized general youth surveys because they underrepresent truly serious chronic offenders who are incarcerated during the interview periods

BOX 2.1. SELF-REPORTED DELINQUENCY ITEMS FROM THE NATIONAL YOUTH SURVEY.

The following items make up the self-report delinquency measure used in the 1976–1993 National Youth Survey. This list omits status offenses but includes some items added to the original 1977 questionnaire, with dates shown in parentheses.

Question: "How many times in the last year have you:

1. Purposely damaged or destroyed property belonging to your parents or other family members
2. Purposely damaged or destroyed property belonging to a school
3. Purposely damaged or destroyed other property that did not belong to you
4. Stolen (or tried to steal) a motor vehicle, such as a car or motorcycle
5. Stolen (or tried to steal) something worth more than $50
6. Knowingly bought, sold, or held stolen goods (or tried to do any of these things)
7. Carried a hidden weapon other than a plain pocket knife
8. Stolen (or tried to steal) an item worth $5 or less
9. Attacked someone with the idea of seriously hurting or killing them
10. Been involved in gang fights
11. Sold marijuana or hashish (grass, pot, hash)
12. Stolen money or other things from your parents or from other members of your family
13. Hit (or threatened to hit) a teacher or adult at school
14. Hit (or threatened to hit) one of your parents
15. Hit (or threatened to hit) other students
16. Sold hard drugs such as heroin, cocaine, and LSD
17. Taken a vehicle for a ride (drive) without the owner's permission
18. Had (or tried to have) sexual relations with someone against their will
19. Used force (strong-arm methods) to get money or things from other students
20. Used force (strong-arm methods) to get money or things from a teacher or other adult at school
21. Used force (strong-arm methods) to get money or things from other people (not students or teachers)
22. Stolen (or tried to steal) things worth $5 to $50
23. Stolen (or tried to steal) something at school, such as someone's coat from a classroom, locker, or cafeteria, or a book from the library
24. Broken into a building or vehicle (or tried to break in) to steal something or just to look around
25. Used or tried to use credit cards without the owner's permission (1978)
26. Used checks illegally or used phony money to pay for something (includes intentional overdrafts) (1979)
27. Tried to cheat someone by selling them something that was worthless or not what you said it was (1979)
28. Purposely set fire to a building, car, or other property, or tried to do so (1980)
29. Hit or threatened to hit your supervisor or other employee (1986)
30. Forged or copied someone else's signature on a check or legal document without their permission (1993)

31.   Made fraudulent insurance claims, that is, falsified or inflated medical bills or property or automobile repairs or replacement costs (1993)

32.   Beaten up on someone so badly they probably needed a doctor (1993)

Source: Maguire and Pastore (1996), appendix 11.

(Cernkovich, Giordano, and Pugh, 1985), the NYS is generally recognized as one of the best self-report surveys.

Shortcomings of Self-report Surveys

In the early days of self-report studies, especially those using adolescents, the surveys were full of questions about status offenses, with only one or two tapping participation in serious crimes. Not surprisingly, the prevalence of self-reported delinquency turned out to be similar across class, race, and gender lines (Hindelang, Hirschi, and Weis, 1979). Critics argued that the surveys trivialized juvenile crime by underemphasizing serious offenses. More recent surveys have tried to correct this imbalance by including more questions addressing major crimes such as robbery and assaults involving injuries or weapons. Although overall rates of self-reported delinquency still do not vary much by class, race, or gender, serious offenses involving violence are more commonly reported by males, lower-class individuals, and African American youth (Barlow and Ferdinand, 1992: 60–69).

Although self-report studies now tap more serious crimes, they have largely neglected white-collar crimes, especially corporate crimes. There are two major reasons for this. First, it is difficult to gain information from corporations about their potentially illegal activities. Second, even if corporate executives were willing to consider being questioned about illegal activity, the researcher has little to offer in the way of inducement. Adolescents in school no doubt enjoy the momentary distraction from regular studies, but the situation is surely different for executives, who may also feel that they are taking unnecessary risks by opening up to strangers. The few in-depth studies of corporate crime that have involved personal interviews were completed only after elaborate steps were taken to ensure confidentiality and to gain the trust of respondents (Jackall, 1988; Clinard, 1989).

Trust is important in all interview situations, but especially with crime, a topic that is often embarrassing or humiliating, or involves behavior that would ordinarily get a person into serious trouble. An interview subject may well wonder whether cooperation is worth it, so interviewers must be adequately trained to overcome such negative reactions. Even then, problems may remain. For example, those people who agree to be interviewed may have had different experiences with crime from those who refuse; clearly, this would bias the results. Some respondents may conceal past criminal activities and others may exaggerate them. Some youths think it "cool" to report doing things that in fact they have never done. Although all these problems create potential pitfalls in the use and interpretation of self-report studies, the knowledge gained still adds new pieces to the puzzle of crime in America and helps uncover the dark figure of crime.

METHODS OF CRIMINOLOGICAL RESEARCH

There are a variety of ways criminologists carry out their research. The method and design of a study depends on what the researcher wishes to study, whether a theory is to be tested or created, and the previous research on the subject under study. Selecting one method over another can also be based on the time and cost involved, as well as the researcher's particular skills. The major forms of criminological research include: (a) surveys, (b) field research, (c) case studies, (d) comparative and historical research, (e) experiments, and (f) content analyses. Before discussing each method, it is important to keep in mind some basic issues about social research.

Some Basic Issues in Research
Dependent and Independent Variables

An important issue in most research is the specification of independent and dependant variables in a study. A variable is anything that can vary in quality or quantity; for example, age, gender, crime rates, or attitudes toward punishment. Much scientific research attempts to show that change in one variable is influenced or caused by change in another variable (or variables). The first variable—the one being influenced—is called the **dependent variable**; the second variable—the one doing the influencing—is called the **independent variable**. For example, suppose a criminologist has hypothesized that concentrated poverty within a population is the cause of higher rates of violent crime and sets out to study this relationship by collecting relevant data from U.S. cities (Lee, 2000). The primary independent variable in this analysis would therefore be concentration of poverty; the dependent variable might be the homicide rate. The selection of independent and dependent variables for any study is influenced by many things, including the previous research conducted on the subject, the insights of theory, and, of course, the individual intellectual interests of the criminologist.

Validity and Reliability

Researchers try to ensure that their measurements of variables are valid and reliable. Texts on research methods cover this topic in detail. Briefly, **validity** refers to the extent to which the method captures what it is designed to measure. Since the nature of social reality is very complex, attempts to measure key concepts and ideas may not work well. Measuring instruments tend to be "vulnerable to contamination from various sources outside (exter-

nal) or inside (internal) the instrument itself" (Champion, 2000: 377). So researchers struggle to find ways to reduce the contamination, a task made more difficult in many studies by the absence of standard measures in the social and behavioral sciences. Even if standard measures do exist—such as crime rates based on the Uniform Crime Reports—they may be a weak or misleading measure of this dependent variable, as, in this example, the Uniform Crime Reports may provide a better measure of police productivity than of crime rates.

Researchers also aim for **reliability** in their studies. Reliability refers to the extent to which particular methods or instruments yield consistent results when used repeatedly. For example, suppose a criminologist is interested in studying the attitudes of property offenders through the use of questionnaires. If the subjects are interviewed in October, and then reinterviewed in November, the answers should be the same or similar if the instrument is reliable. If significant differences emerge between the two survey dates, then either the instrument is not reliable or something significant has happened to change responses. And this points to an enduring problem: Reliability—or lack of reliability—can be established conclusively only when other influences can be ruled out.

Research Ethics

Research should always be conducted ethically. Research ethics refers to basic principles that prescribe the appropriate ways to conduct research. One of the underlying concerns in most social research is protecting the rights of the people whose attitudes and behaviors are being studied. Generally, ethical research allows participants to drop out of the study at any time; protects the anonymity and/or confidentiality of participants; and secures the voluntary, informed consent of participants. This is particularly important when a study might result in physical or mental injury or might damage a person's reputation or relationships with others. Ethical researchers always alert participants to possible dangers associated with their work.

The American Society of Criminology has proposed a Code of Ethics for its members. Here are a few items from that document:

- Criminologists should not misuse their positions as professionals for fraudulent purposes or as a pretext for gathering intelligence for any organization or government.
- Criminologists should not mislead respondents involved in a research project as to the purpose for which that research is being conducted.
- Subjects of research are entitled to rights of personal anonymity unless they are waived.
- The process of conducting criminological research must not expose respondents to substantial risk of personal harm. Investigators must make every effort to ensure the safety and security of respondents and project staff. Informed consent must be obtained when the risks of research are greater than the risks of everyday life. All research must meet the human subjects requirements imposed by educational institutions and funding sources.

Colleges and universities have created institutional review boards (IRBs) to help guard against unethical research being carried out under their auspices. All university research involving human subjects must be reviewed by an IRB, although class-related projects may be exempt. It is always a good thing to check with your instructor before engaging in any research activity that involves human subjects.

Survey Research

The use of surveys is perhaps the most popular method of conducting criminological research. **Survey research** generally involves administering a questionnaire to a group of people in order to understand their attitudes, experiences, and behaviors. The best surveys use *representative random samples* of relevant populations, meaning that everyone in the population has an equal chance of being picked. Randomness reduces bias and allows for generalizations beyond the individuals actually included in the study.

The quality of survey designs differs dramatically, sometimes because of simple things such as cost and time. At one extreme, students often carry out "research" as a class project. But students generally have neither the time nor the money to engage in serious survey research, so they will "sample" a few

The use of surveys, a popular method of conducting criminological research, usually involves administering a questionnaire to a large group of people in order to understand their attitudes, experiences and/or behavior

people on campus or some of their family and friends. These "convenience" samples may leave the student with impressions and suggest hypotheses for future study, but the results are of little scientific value. At the other extreme, the National Crime Victimization Survey collects data on a representative random sample of more than 100,000 households in any given year and is able to generalize to the entire U.S. population over age twelve, which is more than 300 million people.

While some criminologists do conduct national surveys with random samples, this is unusual. Indeed, the NCVS and NYS are exceptions to the custom. Most of the time, criminologists will try to randomly sample a university, city neighborhood, school district, or some other regional population.

Surveys are generally designed for *quantitative* analysis, a process that reduces information to numbers that can be manipulated mathematically. After the responses are collected, researchers generally store the data on computer disks and then use statistical software packages such as Statistical Package for the Social Sciences (SPSS) to identify relationships among the study's variables.

In contrast, *qualitative* survey research analyzes the complete statements or verbal interactions of survey subjects in an attempt to identify meanings and common patterns. A criminological study might incorporate both quantitative and qualitative survey research, although this is rare because of the cost and time involved. One example of a survey design that is both qualitative and quantitative is found in Ken Tunnell's (1990) interviews with imprisoned property offenders.

Field Research

One way of tapping meanings and common patterns in attitudes and behavior is through **field research.** In criminology, this form of research generally involves far-ranging interviews and discussions—sometimes over many hours or days—during which subjects give detailed accounts of their criminal activities and associated lifestyles. Researchers often spend considerable time in the natural environments of their subjects, either as *participant observers*—doing many of the same things group members do, though not necessarily committing crimes—or as *unobtrusive observers*—watching but not participating in the group. Criminologist Paul Cromwell has assembled a remarkable volume of studies titled *In Their Own Words: Criminals on Crime* (2006). It covers thieves of all sorts: gang members, rapists, murderers, drug dealers, and doctors who defraud the Medicaid system. Jeff Ferrell and Mark Hamm's book *Ethnography at the Edge* (1998) includes a collection of very interesting and sometimes shocking accounts of the experiences of criminological ethnographers.

Another example of field research is a study of the street life of residential burglars in St. Louis (Wright and Decker, 1994). Some of the problems mentioned earlier were also experienced in this study: convincing subjects to participate, gaining trust, assessing the truthfulness of what subjects said, and protecting the researchers' own safety. Safety is often a problem in field research dealing with crime, all the more so if researchers spend hours and hours with subjects on their own turf. A social researcher who was studying Chicago area gangs in the 1950s told how boys would constantly test him by frightening, "baiting" or "ranking" him, and subjecting him to minor acts of violence (Spergel, 1964). More recently, Phillipe Bourgois' (2004) masterful study of crack dealers in New York City illustrates the sometimes scary situations field researchers encounter.

Locating the interview subjects in the first place was a problem for the St. Louis researchers. The authors solved this by using the *snowball technique*: A former student of theirs was a retired criminal with hundreds of offenses, but very few arrests. The authors hired him to put the word on the street that active burglars were being sought for interviews. One person told another, and through these informal referrals the authors eventually built up a sample of 105 active burglars (Wright and Decker, 1994). These burglars described their lives and crimes, and 70 of them agreed to visit sites of successful burglaries they had committed to reconstruct the crimes. The researchers were able to place targets in their neighborhood context and also develop a clear picture of how these offenders typically went about their business of residential burglary.

Other outstanding examples of field research include Martin Sanchez Jankowski's (1991) study of several street gangs and Jeff Ferrell's (1993) field research on an urban graffiti subculture. Both of these works helped separate myth from fact in understanding gangs and people who engage in graffiti writing. Jankowski's methodology is quite interesting, and the following excerpt from his book *Islands in the Street* helps us better understand ethnography:

> I participated in nearly all the things they [gang members] did. I ate where they ate, I slept where they slept, I stayed with their families, I traveled where they went, and in certain situations where I could not remain neutral, I fought with them. The only things that I did not participate in were those activities that were illegal. (1991: 13)

The main advantage of field research is that it allows a researcher to gain in-depth information about experiences, beliefs, and behaviors that might otherwise go unnoticed through other research methods (Bourgois, 2004; Muzzatti, 2000). As a general rule, surveys give the researcher more breadth, while ethnography gives more depth.

One type of ethnography is called the *life history*, often referred to as **biographical research**. This way of gaining knowledge about crime has been used throughout the twentieth century by some very famous criminologists, among them Clifford Shaw. Shaw wrote *The Jack-Roller: A Delinquent Boy's Own Story*

(1930) based on interviews and interaction with a boy named "Stanley." Only twelve when Shaw met him, Stanley had already run up an extensive arrest history and had spent almost half his life in institutions. By the time he was seventeen, Stanley had thirty-eight arrests, mostly for petty offenses but also for assault and "jackrolling." Jackrolling involved robbing drunks or homosexuals. In Stanley's own words: "We sometimes stunned drunks by 'giving them the club' in a dark place near a lonely alley. It was bloody work, but necessity demanded it—we had to live" (85).

Through Stanley's story and those of other delinquent youths, Shaw shows how delinquent attitudes and practices develop and are transmitted from boy to boy, and also how individual delinquent careers develop. Friendships, neighborhood traditions, and relationships with parents played important roles in the development of delinquent careers, Shaw found. In addition, the work of Shaw and his colleagues helped in the construction of delinquency prevention programs, such as the Chicago Area Project. This program, which lasted many years, focused on changing a delinquent child's social environment through neighborhood reconstruction organized via community self-help projects. Since Shaw's day, biographical research has contributed a great deal to our understanding of criminality (e.g., Sutherland, 1937a; Chambliss, 1972; Klockars, 1974; Steffensmeier, 1986).

Case Studies

Case studies, while not as popular as surveys and ethnography, have been a mainstay of criminological research for some time. Case studies involve the detailed reconstruction of an event or process in order to develop or test theories or ways of understanding crime. This method is generally qualitative in design, but quantitative analyses can also be conducted.

Studies of state-corporate crime, a phenomenon reviewed in chapter 6, provide excellent illustrations of the case study method.

State-corporate crimes are violations of law that result from the cooperation or shared activities of both a governmental agency and a private corporation. Case studies have been conducted on the 1986 space shuttle *Challenger* explosion (Michalowski and Kramer, 2006); on the deaths of two dozen workers in a fire at a chicken food processing plant in North Carolina (Aulette and Michalowski, 1993); on the environmental crimes committed through the production of nuclear weapons (Kauzlarich and Kramer, 1993); and on the 1996 crash of ValuJet flight 592 in the Florida Everglades (Matthews and Kauzlarich, 2000). In all of these examples, the researchers collected as much information about the cases as possible, using both primary sources, such as interviews, and secondary sources, such as governmental reports, investigations, and internal organizational memos. Using multiple sources of data in case studies increases the validity and reliability of a study (Yin, 2002).

Good case study research produces a precise and multidimensional analysis of how and why a crime or event happened. Case studies also aim to create or test new conceptual or theoretical ideas that shed light on why the crime occurred and perhaps how similar crimes might be explained. Diane Vaughan's (1996) monumental case study of the space shuttle *Challenger* explosion is one example of the rich insights that can be derived from the case study method.

Comparative and Historical Research

Long ago, French sociologist Émile Durkheim observed that there is no known society without crime: "Its form changes, but everywhere and always, there have been men [*sic*] who have behaved in such a way as to draw upon themselves penal repression" (1964b: 65). In order to find out whether and how crime varies from place to place, or from time to time, criminologists use **comparative and historical research** methods. Ideally, comparative research compares different societies at the same point in time; historical research examines the same society at different periods in its history. The methodologies can be combined, though this strategy also combines their difficulties and limitations.

These difficulties and limitations include the costs and time involved, language barriers, political obstacles, lack or poor quality of data, noncomparable definitions of crime and delinquency, and the ethnocentric tendency of researchers living in one society or time period to see their own as the "standard" against which to measure others. *Ethnocentrism* can be illustrated by the assumption held by some prominent criminologists that American views of crime and delinquency can be applied everywhere. At the very least, researchers must be sensitive to the fact that in other societies and time periods, the actions and meanings associated with crime are likely to differ from their own (Beirne, 1983).

If these difficulties can be overcome, the benefits of comparative and historical research are considerable. One clear benefit of this method is in its ability to test criminological theories. Do theories developed in the Western world have any applicability to crime in Zimbabwe or Iraq? If criminology as a social science is truly interested in finding universal laws, we must test our theories in many areas around the globe (Barak, 2000; Heiner, 1996). Comparative and historical criminologies also have the benefit of allowing us to understand our own culture by examining its history or its similarities and differences to other cultures. For example, in the United States, laws prohibiting child labor, domestic assault, and many drugs were not invented until the twentieth century. Likewise, there are a number of countries, particularly postindustrialized Western countries, who placed those laws on the books at roughly the same time. However, there is a significant difference in, for example, the nature of drug laws globally—in some countries like India and the Netherlands, marijuana possession and consumption is not criminally prohibited.

Louise Shelley's classic book *Crime and Modernization* (1981) is an excellent example of the benefits of historical and comparative research. Shelley analyzed crime data going back about two hundred years in several countries. Her main finding is that the process of modernization affects crime in a very significant way. First, modernization brings about gradual social change in the norms of a culture, so that the small, homogenous community no longer has the ability to practice successful social control. The traditional norms of a community, Shelley continues, become less powerful in times of great change. Shelley also found that as societies advance, violent crime decreases and property crime increases, and that those countries with lower overall crime rates in the modern period (such as Sweden and Japan) have successfully defeated the cultural and normative change that often accompanies modernization.

Experiments

When researchers wish to establish whether one variable causes another, they will think first of conducting an experiment. The **experimental method** is generally considered the ideal way to measure causation because the experimenter can control the research process. A "true" or "classic" experiment requires one to show that independent variable X causes dependent variable Y. An experiment tries not just to show that variables are related, or "correlated," but that they operate in a linear and temporal (time-related) way. To satisfy the three criteria of causation (association, temporal order, and the exclusion of rival causes), the true experiment is usually conducted in a controlled laboratory setting, with the subjects randomly assigned to either experiential or control groups. Those subjects in the experimental group are exposed to manipulation of the independent variable, while those assigned to the control group are not. Then researchers examine whether the groups experience change. If there is a change in the experimental group and not in the control group, the case for causation is stronger. However, the experiment ought to be repeated with other subjects, for the sake of both reliability and validity.

In truth, criminologists rarely conduct the classic experiment. The ethical problems associated with experimenting on human social behavior are obvious, but it would also be very difficult to control the entire research process when studying crime and delinquency. The less a researcher has control over the research process, the less compelling and more questionable the findings will be. So, some criminologists who wish to use the experimental method will attempt to conduct a *field experiment*: conducting research in a natural setting in which social behavior occurs. A classic example of this method is the Provo, Utah, experiment designed to study the effectiveness of a community treatment program for youths who had committed serious offenses and/or were repeat offenders (Empey and Erickson, 1972). The 326 boys were randomly assigned to either probation or incarceration in one of four groups: probation experiment group, probation control group, incarceration experiment group, or incarceration control group. The boys assigned to the experimental probation group were placed in a special community treatment program, while their control counterparts were placed on regular probation. Those boys assigned to experimental incarceration were also placed into the social community treatment program, while their control counterparts were placed in a state training school. As you can see, this field experiment allowed the researchers to see whether one group of boys would reoffend less than the others. Ultimately, the results of the study were mixed (largely due to other methodological problems), but it did show that community-based group-centered treatment was more beneficial as an alternative to incarceration than as an alternative to regular supervised probation.

Content Analysis

In chapter 1 we discussed the images of crime portrayed by the media. We argued that the images are highly distorted, leading one to believe that crime rates have increased of late, that violent crime is at least as wide spread as property crime, and that white-collar crimes are less injurious than traditional street crimes. One method criminologists have used to understand how newspapers, films, news shows, and other media create certain impressions of crime is through **content analysis**: A careful and scientific examination of the substance and spirit of representations of crime in print, audio, and/or video. Content analysis allows a researcher to understand how media agents "frame" the problem of crime. Three content analyses show how enlightening this method can be.

First, Kenneth Dowler (2004) was interested in knowing whether there were significant differences between Canadian and American local television coverage of crime. After examining, coding, and interpreting the television images, he concluded that that "sensational stories, live stories, and stories that report firearms are more likely to appear in U.S. markets" (573). However, he notes that both countries in general support dominant popular culture understandings of crime rather than those informed by academic research. Of course, as we discussed in chapter 1, this is not a surprising finding.

Second, Robert Jerin and Charles Fields (1994) were interested in the type of subjects covered in the newspaper *USA Today*. Specifically, they were interested in the daily section of the newspaper called "News from Every State." The researchers analyzed and coded 26,301 news summaries for 1990 and found that while crime- and criminal justice–related new stories were not as common as other topics (such as government and politics), crime-related stories were more frequently about murder than about drug offenses or white-collar offenses. Then they compared the crime rates of each state with the type and quantity of crime stories in the newspaper and found that some states with low crime rates had a disproportionate number of crime-related stories. Jerin and Fields concluded that a major factor in a crime being reported by the media is "the circumstances surrounding the crime, the public nature of the offender or victims, or the humorous nature of the incident" (200).

Melissa Hickman Barlow, David Barlow, and Theodore Chiricos (1995a, 1995b) published two articles based on their content analysis of *Time* magazine. These criminologists examined not only what types of crime were given attention, but also the overt and subtle messages conveyed by the articles. They found that *Time* presented very superficial analyses of crime-related issues by, for example, ignoring the employment status of the offender, providing racially biased representations, and generally supporting the dominant political ideology.

CHAPTER SUMMARY

This review of data sources and research methods hardly does justice to a complicated topic. However, you should now have a much better understanding of the strengths, weaknesses, and utility of the information about crime and criminal justice presented in the chapters that follow. It is important to remember that no one research strategy or type of data stands above all the rest; each has its drawbacks and each has its benefits. In the last analysis, the appropriateness of a given method or body of data depends on the research questions being addressed.

Information on crime, criminals, and the justice system comes from a variety of sources: local police departments, who report to regional clearing houses and ultimately to the FBI; the National Crime Victimization Survey; and thousands of studies conducted by university researchers, governmental offices, and private corporations. The data collected are used to help test or form theories of crime, instruct social policy, and provide resources to criminal justice and social service agencies. It is crucial when using this data to understand that the "official" crime rate is an estimate of the real amount of crime based on reports to police or reports by victims or offenders. As such, the data must be carefully interpreted to avoid confusion and distortion.

Criminologists employ a variety of research methods. There are some near-universal issues a scholar must attend to, including research ethics, validity, and reliability, among others. The major methods of criminological research are survey, ethnography, case study, comparative and historical research, experiments, and content analysis. Some of these methods are quantitative and others are qualitative, but all of them are used to gain a clearer and less subjective understanding of the nature of crime. Most criminologists aspire to be objective and value free in their research, although that goal is more difficult to reach than might be expected.

KEY TERMS

biographical research
case studies
clearance rates
comparative and historical research
content analysis
crime rate
dark figure of crime
dependent variable
experimental method
field research
founding decision
independent variable
index offenses
National Crime Victimization Survey (NCVS)
National Youth Survey (NYS)
National Incident-Based Reporting System (NIBRS)

reliability
self-report
survey research
Uniform Crime Reports (UCR)
validity

RECOMMENDED READINGS

Bourgois, P. (2004). *In Search of Respect: Selling Crack in El Barrio.* 2nd ed. New York: Cambridge University Press.

Ferrell, Jeff, and Mark S. Hamm, (1998). *Ethnography at the Edge.* Boston: Northeastern University Press.

Krippendorff, D. (2004). *Content Analysis: An Introduction to Its Methodology.* Thousand Oaks, CA: Sage.

Sanchez Jankowski, Martin (1991). *Islands in the Street: Gangs and American Urban Society.* Berkeley and Los Angeles: University of California Press.

Shelley, Louise I. (1981). *Crime and Modernization: The Impact of Industrialization and Urbanization on Crime.* Carbondale: Southern Illinois University Press.

Wright, Richard T., and Scott H. Decker (1994). *Burglars on the Job: Streetlife and Residential Break-ins.* Boston: Northeastern University Press.

RECOMMENDED WEB SITES

Bureau of Justice Statistics (http://www.ojp.usdoj.gov/bjs/). Access to victimization data and other criminological and criminal justice reports.

Federal Bureau of Investigation (http://www.fbi.gov). Reports and data on crime and criminal justice, including access to the UCR.

National Criminal Justice Reference Service (http://www.ncjrs.org). Access to all federal government criminal justice data and research, and links to other government publications.

CHAPTER

3

VIOLENT CRIME

ABHJP9 Alamy

On April 6, 2007, Seung-Hui Cho killed thirty-two people and seriously injured more than two dozen others on the Virginia Tech campus in Blacksburg, Virginia. Cho committed suicide at the end of his rampage. Videotapes he made prior to the murders and several papers he had written in college classes suggested that he was considering the killings for some period of time. The news media flocked to the scene, and reporters—and police—spent the next days and weeks digging up all sorts of information about Cho, his victims, the families involved, and the campus community. A lot was made of the killer's mental health history and his apparent feelings of rejection, alienation, and desire for revenge through violence. Yet despite extensive investigation and commentary from all sorts of experts, no adequate explanation of this terrible crime has been forthcoming.

Thankfully, mass murders such as that in Blacksburg and the more recent case at Northern Illinois University are rare. The violence discussed in most of this chapter may seem less interesting and less heinous, but there is much, much more of it. It includes homicide, aggravated assault, simple assault, and robbery. This chapter does not address violence committed by or on behalf of states or corporations; this topic is discussed in chapter 6.

VIOLENCE IN U.S. HISTORY

The Puritans came to America largely to escape repression. Perhaps because of this, violence by New Englanders was generally a rare occurrence. Violence in the name of justice, however, was not. Consider what happened during the celebrated Salem witch trials. In one year alone a score of executions were carried out in the name of justice—and more were to die before the witch scare died down (Erikson, 1966: 149).

Some people believe that violence is never right, that it is immoral and without justification no matter what the circumstances. Others think violence can be justified, though only under exceptional circumstances, such as for self-defense. Others contend that violence can be justified by its accomplishments: a greater good or the prevention of a greater evil (Runkle, 1976). Much of the violence that has marked America's history has been justified on the grounds that it brought about important, constructive changes in American society. The Revolutionary War, the Civil War, the Indian wars, frontier vigilante justice, and labor violence have been called examples of "positive" violence (Brown, 1969). The fact that thousands of people were killed, maimed, orphaned, and left homeless has been played down. The end apparently justified the means.

During the nineteenth century, riots plagued the major cities; feuds erupted in Kentucky, Virginia, West Virginia, and Texas; guerrilla bands roamed the Midwest in search of glory and fortune; outlaws plundered the frontier regions of the country, often chased by blood-thirsty posses; citizens formed groups of vigilantes; workers seeking the right to unionize took to the streets and were met by police and hired thugs; lynch mobs plagued the South and dealt their own brand of justice; and the mass destruction of Native Americans continued. Wherever it surfaced, conflict seemed destined to be violent.

The use of violence as a means of resolving disputes continued into the twentieth century. The labor movement was marked by violence as it confronted stubborn bosses and politicians. Especially violent were the clashes in the country's mining areas. In a mining strike against the Colorado Fuel and Iron Company from 1913 to 1914, more than thirty men, women, and children lost their lives (Brown, 1969: 55). The first half of the twentieth century also witnessed other forms of group violence: During and after Prohibition, gangland killings became routine events in some cities, Chicago in particular; the Ku Klux Klan became a national organization and brought its hatred and prejudice to bear on blacks, Catholics, Jews, and "radical" whites in brutal beatings and killings.

Throughout the 1960s and 1970s, overall levels of violent crime rose steeply in the United States. A national commission found about a 47 percent increase in the official rates for murder and nonnegligent manslaughter between 1958 and 1968. Rates for aggravated assault showed even higher increases, around 100 percent. FBI data confirm that aggravated assault rates continued to rise during the 1970s, although more slowly. From 1987 to 1991, serious assaults and homicides were on the rise after a leveling-off period during the mid-1980s (Federal Bureau of Investigation, 1991: 9, 24). However, National Crime Victimization Survey figures in the 1980s suggested that the police picture overstated the increase in assault rates. In fact, fewer assaults were reported in those surveys than at any time since the NCVS program began in 1973 (Bureau of Justice Statistics, 1988). From the 1990s to the present, both the violent crime rate (from 729.6 per 100,000 in 1990 to 473 in 2006) as well as the rate of property crime (from 5073.1 per 100,000 in 1990 to 3334.5 in 2006) have continued to drop (Federal Bureau of Investigation, 2007).

THE CURRENT PICTURE

Official rates of murder and nonnegligent manslaughter vary around the country. New England states typically have the lowest rates, while southern and western states lead the country. Rates also vary by size of city. The highest rates are found in cities with populations over 250,000, and the rates tend to decline along with city size. Homicide is primarily a large-city phenomenon. However, for many years, rural rates have been slightly higher than the rates for many small and medium-sized cities. One reason may be that the distance from and quality of medical services in rural areas make assaults more likely to turn into homicides (Barlow, 1985; Giacopassi, Sparger, and Stein, 1992; Long-Onnen and Cheatwood, 1992), although it has been found that hospital closures in urban areas also increase the severity of injury (Buchmueller, Jacobson, and Wold, 2005). Overall, it has been well established that the quality and availability of medical care can significantly affect whether an assault turns into a homicide (Thomas et al. , 2002).

More detailed information about official homicides is found in arrest data. Fortunately, official statistics on homicides are among the best available. This is because homicides rarely go unreported and suspects are usually apprehended and charged with the crime. Police departments generally take great pride in their ability to solve homicides, which is made possible by the existence of a corpse and the crime's typical circumstances. Although they have declined since 1970, probably due to increases in the proportion of stranger murders, clearance rates for homicide are markedly better than those for any other index crime. Figure 3.1 shows the clearance rates for seven offenses. Clearance rates refer to the percentage of crimes reported that result in arrest.

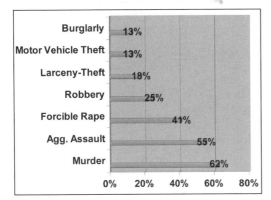

▲Figure 3.1.
Police Clearance Rates for Select Offenses
Source: Federal Bureau of Investigation (2008).

Note that clearance rates for property crimes are substantially lower than those for violent crimes. Since robbery involves elements of both, it is not surprising that it lies in between violent and property crimes.

As figure 3.2 indicates, after rising continuously during the 1960s and then remaining steady throughout the 1980s, homicide rates in the United States have declined in recent years. Whether this decrease is due to demographic changes, particularly the decrease in the proportion of people in the crime-prone age range of 15 to 24, the economy, other social and cultural changes, or criminal justice policies is a matter of great debate. However, the police in some cities have been claiming much of the credit, perhaps not without some justification, as explained in chapter 8.

Most homicides arrests occur in cities with populations over 250,000; of all those arrested in 2006, 89 percent were males and

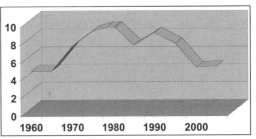

▲Figure 3.2.
U.S. Homicide Rate, 1960–2006, per 100,000 People
Source: Federal Bureau of Investigation (2008)

11 percent were under the age of eighteen. African Americans accounted for 50 percent of the arrests, while whites composed 48 percent of the arrests. Other facts about homicide include:

- Most murder victims are male.
- When the race of the murder victim was known, about half were white (49.8 percent), almost half were black (47.6 percent), and about 2.6 percent were of another race.
- When information on the victim-offender relationship was available, 77 percent of the offenders were known to the victim, while 23 percent were a stranger to the victim.
- Firearms were used in the majority of murders (70 percent).
- Homicide is generally intraracial, meaning that whites most often kill whites and African Americans most often kill African Americans.
- Arguments were the most often cited circumstance leading to murder (44 percent).
- Homicides occurred in connection with another felony in 23 percent of incidents. (Bureau of Justice Statistics, 2006; 2008)

Table 3.1 provides further information on the risks of victimization for different groups of people. Clearly, the risk is not shared equally, nor has it been for as long as national data have been collected.

Table 3.1. Murder Victims by Race and Sex, 2006

Race	Total	Male	Female	Unknown
			Sex	
Total	14,990	11,793	3,156	41
White	6,956	5,067	1,883	6
Black	7,421	6,294	1,126	1
Other race	406	301	105	0
Unknown race	207	131	42	34

Source: Federal Bureau of Investigation (2007), expanded homicide data, table 2.

Homicide in Large Cities

Although official statistics on homicide are valuable for assessing gross patterns and trends, those who desire a more complete picture will find a number of in-depth urban studies to which they can turn. The pioneering study of homicide was conducted by Marvin Wolfgang (1958) in the mid-1950s. Wolfgang looked at homicides that had come to the attention of Philadelphia police from 1948 to 1952. He investigated a host of variables, including race, sex, age, temporal patterns, spatial patterns, motives, and offender-victim relationships.

Since the publication of Wolfgang's study, there have been many other urban investigations of homicide (e.g., Lee and Ousey, 2005; Shihadeh and Shrum, 2004). These studies tend to confirm the following observations about homicide:

- Young black adult males are most likely to be identified as offenders and victims.
- Offenders and victims tend to be of low socioeconomic status and to reside in inner-city neighborhoods.
- Homicides usually occur during the late evening and early morning hours of the weekend.
- Around half of the known homicides occur in either the offender's or the victim's home.
- Homicides do not follow consistent seasonal patterns. They do not, as a prevalent myth has it, occur significantly more often during the hot months of the year.

- Offenders and victims are usually acquainted and often live in the same immediate neighborhood.
- Strangers are killed most often during the commission of another felony, such as robbery, rape, or burglary.

Recent homicide trends indicate that:

- The homicide offender is getting younger—the proportion of offenses committed by persons under age 25 has been rising for many years.
- Interracial homicides seem to be on the rise, though the increases are small.
- The proportion of homicides involving strangers has been increasing over the past few years, though it still remains lower than the proportion involving people who know each other. (Federal Bureau of Investigation, 2007; Fox and Zawitz, 1999)

DISAGGREGATING HOMICIDE

Even though most killings occur in the context of an argument or dispute of some sort, homicide is not a unitary phenomenon:

> Homicide is not one type of event, but many. . . . Homicides that begin as different types of confrontation have different characteristics, occur in different areas of the city, affect different segments of the population, and have different strategies for prevention. (Block and Block, 1991: 6)

When homicide rates are compared across space or time, **disaggregation** uncovers important variations that would not otherwise be seen. Disaggregating is a technique that breaks down the total into its constituent parts. Various criteria have been used to identify the different parts—the weapon used, the relationship between offender and victim, the time and place of occurrence, and the context or circumstances of the killing.

Studies of Chicago homicide figures demonstrate the value of disaggregation in studying homicide trends (Block, 1995). The Blocks broke down the aggregate Chicago homicide figures for a twenty-five-year period into two underlying categories: *instrumental*, in which violence emerges out of a goal-oriented predatory attack (such as robbery) where the purpose is not primarily to kill or injure; and *expressive*, where violence erupts spontaneously as part of a confrontation and as an end in itself. These two categories are considered opposite ends of a continuum, and they "seldom occur in their pure form. Thus, the acquisition of money or property may occur as an afterthought in expressive violence, or it may be an additional way of hurting the victim" (see also Katz, 1988).

The Chicago researchers found five contexts (called *syndromes*) in which violent crimes like homicide and aggravated assault occur:

1. *Interpersonal disputes*: disagreements between people regardless of their relationship
2. *Instrumental felony offenses*: violent crimes committed during the commission of another felony
3. *Group-based violence*: examples include gang-related violence
4. *Chronic offenders*: individuals with a very long history of violent offenses
5. *Politically motivated violence*: violence intended to further a political or ideological cause (Block, 1995)

Other researchers have broken down homicide by the relationship between the victim and the offender and have shed new light on topics that have interested criminologists for years. The relationship between income inequality, unemployment, poverty, and homicide is one such topic. A study of 190 U.S. cities found that while socioeconomic variables are linked to homicide regardless of victim-offender relationship, "poverty and unemployment are more important factors in

acquaintance homicide than in other categories" (Kovandzic, Vieraitis, and Yeisley, 1998: 592). Since this study also found that the racial composition of cities was a crucial factor relating to variations in homicide rates, the authors recommend further research involving disaggregation by race.

Race and Homicide

It is generally recognized that the complexities of homicide in America will not be unraveled until homicide data are disaggregated by race. It is well known that African Americans are disproportionately victimized and arrested for homicide, yet a more complicated picture emerges when one examines this relationship by county, state, and region (Hawkins, 1999). It turns out that urban, rural, and suburban areas have different homicide rates by race. One study found that rates of both black and white homicide are related to changes in the local economy: The decrease in the availability of entry-level jobs results in greater economic deprivation, which in turn raises levels of violence (Shihadeh and Ousey, 1998). A similar finding was made by Lee and Ousey (2005), who found that African Americans' access to churches and other social/civic institutions in cities is negatively associated with homicides rates in those areas. Here is another fact to consider: African Americans in the North are predominantly living in cities, while in the South there are sizable proportions of African Americans who live in suburbs and rural areas. Black-white homicide arrest and imprisonment ratios are closer in the South, which suggests that the place of residence might be a significant variable in understanding racial differences in homicide (Hawkins, 1999; Stark, 1987).

There is good ethnographic research that bolsters the argument that homicide is not a unitary phenomenon, and therefore that disaggregation is important, particularly by race. Consider Elijah Anderson's study of violence in poor inner-city black neighborhoods in Philadelphia. Here's how Anderson accounts for the higher rates of violent crime in these neighborhoods:

> the lack of jobs that pay a living wage, limited basic public services (police response in emergencies, building maintenance, trash pickup, lighting, and other services middle class neighborhoods take for granted), the stigma of race, the fallout from rampant drug use and drug trafficking, and the resulting alienation and absence of hope for the future. (1999: 32).

Anderson (1999: 28) also found that these conditions foster a "**code of the streets**" within the inner city. This code, which entails a need for respect, not being "dissed," and being treated "right," is "normative for only a segment of the community" (1999: 2), but other blacks are drawn under its influence. Thus, black families that are regarded as "decent" (the subjects' own words) and not into the "street" culture often feel compelled to act in accordance with the code for their social, and even their physical, survival. For many inner-city youth, violence is everyday fare. In one review of the literature, it was found that 20 to 40 percent of schoolchildren in inner-city neighborhoods have seen someone shot, stabbed, or killed in street violence (Green, 1993; see also Berton and Stabb, 1996; and Schwab-Stone et al., 1999; and a comprehensive review of the matter by Stein et al., 2003).

Gender and Homicide

The people most often victimized by and arrested for homicide are male, but what about female victims and offenders? Most studies suggest that the reasons why women kill and the circumstances surrounding female violence are different from those attributed to males. Female homicides are often precipitated by the violence of the men they kill (Browne, Williams, and Dutton, 1999; Campbell et al., 2007).

Most spousal homicides follow this pattern, and the wives who eventually become murderers have often been physically abused by their husbands over a long period of time. Ironically, the men are usually killed by their own weapons (Browne, 1987).

Comparing intimate relationships that end in homicide and those that involve lesser violence, it has been found that women who kill

- were assaulted more frequently
- sustained more serious injuries
- were more frequently raped and sexually assaulted
- were in relationships where the male had higher levels of alcohol and drug use
- experienced more death threats from their intimate

Unlike their male counterparts, women who kill generally have less extensive criminal histories, and they are rarely the first to use potentially lethal violence in an altercation. Also unlike males, women are most likely to kill their domestic partners than others. However, women are two to five times more likely to be killed than male partners (Browne, Williams, and Dutton, 1999: 150; Campbell et al., 2007). We discuss some of the reasons for this in chapter 4.

Coramae Mann (1996) studied a sample of all the women arrested for homicide in six major U.S. cities in the years 1979 and 1983. She found that women who kill do so in the home they share with the victim. Indeed, 70 percent of the murders were domestic. One respect in which female homicides mirror male homicides concerns the presence of alcohol: Mann found that more than 33 percent of the women and 50 percent of their victims had been drinking at the time of the murder. We will return to this issue later in the chapter.

Aggravated Assault

Aggravated assault is not as thoroughly researched as homicide. What is known about it, however, suggests a striking resemblance to homicide. This should not surprise any-one, because the essential difference between the two is the existence of a corpse. Indeed, one study of twelve hundred homicides and thirty-two thousand serious assaults in Dallas over a period of five years found that

> [e]xcept for their fatality, homicides share socio-economic, temporal, racial, age, and gender characteristics of assaults. . . .
>
> Differences between homicides are due primarily to (1) variations in the lethality of weapons, and (2) the analytical mixing of primary [i.e., personal injury is the immediate objective of the assailant] and secondary [i.e., injury is incidental to some other immediate objective, for example, rape or robbery] homicides. (Harries, 1989: 37; see also Miethe and McCorkle, 1998)

Those arrested for aggravated assault are disproportionately young black males who come from low socioeconomic backgrounds and reside in large cities. The victims also fit this characterization; however, Native

Americans experience the highest rates of aggravated assault victimization of all racial and ethnic groups (see box 3.1). Most studies have focused on who is victimized by whom, and they show that whites and blacks are generally victimized by members of their own races. But in one study, the author turned the question around and asked, "Who do members of each race choose as victims?" (Wilbanks, 1985). This analysis of nationwide victimization data showed that whereas 81.9 percent of black victims were assaulted by black offenders (the usual way of looking at things), 55 percent of black offenders had assaulted *white* victims. This is probably a result of opportunity rather than any sort of race-related motivation on the part of offenders. Whether this pattern holds for different regions and cities, different time periods, or other racial and ethnic groups was not explored.

As with homicides, aggravated assaults often occur inside the home or around bars and street corners. Not surprisingly, knives, blunt

BOX 3.1. NATIVE AMERICANS AND VIOLENT CRIME VICTIMIZATION

There are more than 2.5 million Native Americans living in the United States (about 0.9 percent of the total U.S. population). Victimization data shows that this group is more likely to be violently victimized than whites, Asians, *and* African Americans. Indeed, over a ten-year period of time (1992–2002), the rates of victimization per 1,000 persons are as follows:

	Native Americans	Whites	African Americans	Asians
Aggravated Assault	25	8	13	5
Rape/Sexual Assault	5	2	2	1
Simple Assault	61	27	26	12

Interestingly, arrest data shows that Native Americans do not commit a seriously disproportionate amount of these offenses. For example, they accounted for only 1 percent of all arrests for aggravated assault, 1 percent for sexual assault, and 1 percent for other assaults (Federal Bureau of Investigation, 2007). There is evidence to suggest, however, that Native Americans may be sentenced more harshly and serve a greater proportion of their sentences than other groups (Alvarez and Bachman, 2005; Nielsen, 2000: 51–52; also see Nielsen and Silverman, 1996).

Sources: U.S. Department of Justice (1999); Federal Bureau of Investigation (1998; 2007); Alvarez and Bachman (2005); and Perry (2004).

objects, and fists are the weapons most often used (were guns more often used, assaults would more often be homicides). As with homicide, victim actions often contribute to the initiation of violence. Verbal confrontations between males are especially prone to result in physical attacks, not just in American cities but universally (Polk, 1991).

Serial Murder

Serial murder is an extremely rare but much-publicized phenomenon. The best estimates of the numbers of serial killers and their victims indicate that serial murder represents "an extreme fringe of the American homicide problem" (Jenkins, 1994: 29; Egger, 2002; Fox and Levin, 2005), certainly no more than 1 percent of all homicide victims each year, and probably a lot less. The myth that serial murder has reached an epidemic has perhaps subsided a bit, but several other myths continue to survive. Box 3.2 identifies other myths about serial murder.

As one type of multiple murder, **serial murder** generally refers to killings that take place over weeks, months, or years, often with an inactive period in between. In contrast, **mass murder** is a multiple murder that occurs within minutes or hours, generally in one place, while **spree killings** are multiple murders that occur over a day or two (Fox and Levin, 2005). A stereotypical image of the serial killer emerged during the 1980s, that of a lone white male in his thirties or forties whose killings are motivated by sex or thrill seeking. Jeffrey Dahmer, Ted Bundy, and John Wayne Gacy all fit this image. However, this stereotype has been challenged by some who note that serial killers do not always act alone, nor do they always act from sexual motives (Egger, 1998; Fox and Levin, 2005; Jenkins, 1994). Further, while most American serial killers have been male and white, there have been serial killings by women and nonwhites as well, and some authors suggest that serial killing by women is increasing (Hickey, 1991; Holmes and Holmes, 1994).

BOX 3.2. MYTHS ABOUT SERIAL MURDER

Myth 1: *Serial murder has reached epidemic proportions.*
   In fact, it is extremely difficult to obtain data on this crime. No scientific evidence has shown that serial murder is on the rise (Fox and Levin, 1999).
   Myth 2: *Serial killers are unusual in appearance and lifestyle.*
   Many serial killers, on the contrary, look "normal" and oftentimes are not obviously alienated from the workforce or community (Egger, 1998, 2002; Fox and Levin, 1999).
   Myth 3: *Serial killers are insane, sex-starved, and/or totally sociopathic.*
   Some serial killers divide the world into "good" and "bad" people. Many also would not consider killing their parents or children, the "good" people (Fox and Levin, 1999).
   Myth 4: *Serial killers had terrible childhoods, were beaten, and sexually abused. They are also likely to have been adopted.*
   The evidence simply does not support these claims. While some serial murderers have come from abusive families, more have not (Egger, 1998; 2002; Fox and Levin, 1999).
   Myth 5: *Serial killers prey on anyone who crosses their path.*
   Most of the time, serial killers are looking to victimize someone who fits their definition of "expendable," "bad," or "scum." A disproportionate amount of prostitutes, skid-row alcoholics, and drug addicts are victimized by serial killers (Egger, 1998).

   Further reading: James Alan Fox and Jack Levin. (2005). *Extreme Killing: Understanding Serial and Mass Murder*. Thousand Oaks, CA: Sage.

Still, the paucity of women and blacks among officially documented serial killers begs the question "Why?" Regarding black offenders, Philip Jenkins (1993) has suggested that the low level of black involvement might result from the way in which law enforcement agencies identify and investigate murder: When victims are black, he suggests, police may be "less likely to seek or find evidence of serial murder activity" (47). Using the case of Calvin Jackson, an African American serial killer who murdered a number of poor, isolated, and elderly residents of a New York apartment building, Jenkins shows that the police did not establish any link among the killings until Jackson confessed. The oversight is explained as follows:

> [T]he police approach a suspicious death with certain pre-conceptions that depend on both the nature of the victim and the social environment in which the incident occurs. In some contexts, a sudden death can be explained in many ways without the need to assume the existence of a random or repeat killer; serial killer activity is thus less likely to be noted. This is particularly true of urban environments characterized by poverty, isolation, transience and frequent violence. (470)

Jenkins's argument might explain some of the disparity in black/white involvement in serial murder, but how much is unclear and in any case it remains an untested proposition. It is important to remember that among the population as a whole, African Americans make up only around 13 percent. This means that for every one hundred white serial killers, we should expect to find thirteen black serial killers. Consider how few serial killers are identified in any given year. Eric Hickey (1997) estimates that there have been between 2,526 and 3,860 victims and 399 serial killers in the entire period from 1800 to 1995. We would need to find very few black serial killers to bring their proportion in line with the black/white ratio in the U.S. population as a

whole. On the other hand, we would need a lot more to bring the black/white ratio in line with that of homicide arrests generally.

The issue for women is clearly different, since they constitute 51 percent of the population but only 17 percent of Hickey's count of serial killers. Quite a few women serial killers would have to be discovered to bring male/female proportions in line. On the other hand, what we know about homicide in general would not lead us to expect more female involvement. In fact, the ratio of known female to male serial killers is actually *higher* than that expected based on the proportion of all arrested homicide offenders who are female (around 10 percent). Simply put, in the absence of further research specifically addressing the issue of minority and female involvement in serial murder, the disparities by race and gender will remain something of a mystery.

Perhaps the most interesting aspect of serial murder from a sociological point of view is the way in which the phenomenon has been elevated in social consciousness from a rare, aberrant occurrence into a pressing social problem. Jenkins (1994) believes that the American public "discovered" serial murder during the 1970s, thanks largely to aggressive media coverage of a few sensational cases—Juan Corona, "Son of Sam" killer David Berkowitz, Kenneth Bianchi and Angelo Buono (the "Hillside Stranglers"), John Wayne Gacy, Ted Bundy, Wayne Williams (the Atlanta Child Murders), and the California Freeway Killers (actually two serial killers operating independently). The considerable attention given to this infrequent form of killing, Jenkins argues, helped support conservative crime control policies and agendas during the 1980s and early 1990s. A recent study also found that fear of crime increases in communities where serial murder is reported to have taken place, although the fear rises moderately, not extremely, and that this fear goes away once a serial killer is apprehended (Lee and DeHart, 2007).

School Violence

It is impossible to discuss criminal violence these days without saying something about the problem of violence in the schools. Fifty years ago, schoolteachers worried about students talking out of turn, chewing gum, violating the dress code, cutting in line, and littering. By 1980 a survey found that they worried about far more serious concerns: drug abuse, pregnancy, suicide, rape, robbery, and assault (Glazer, 1992: 797). From 1986 to 1990, an estimated 48 people died and 156 were wounded from gunshots in public and private schools in just ten states. From 1992 to 1999, 211 children died as a result of violence in school (Hinkle and Henry, 2000). Not surprisingly, high schools represent the greatest portion of gun-related incidents on school property (about 60 percent), but this still leaves 40 percent occurring in junior high and elementary schools.

Several high-profile murders were committed by high school students in the 1990s, leading many Americans to believe that school violence was on the rise and out of control. Understandably, the 1999 Columbine High School massacre drew most attention because it was the worst instance of school killings in United States history. Yet available data show that school violence has either declined or held constant over the last several years (Hinkle and Henry, 2000; U.S. Department of Education, 2000). Other facts about school violence include:

- Less than 1 percent of the total number of murders of children and youth in the United States occur in schools.
- Almost half of the offenders gave some type of signs (e.g., a threat, a note) prior to the event.
- 20 percent of perpetrators were victims of bullying and 12 percent had expressed suicidal thoughts or engage in suicidal behavior. (Centers for Disease Control and Prevention, 2007)

During the 1990s the problem of school crime and violence gained enough attention for the U.S. Congress to pass the Safe and Drug-Free Schools and Communities Act of 1994. This legislation required the National Center for Education Statistics (NCES) to collect data on the amount and seriousness of crime and violence in elementary and secondary schools. Findings from this nationally representative random study include:

- Serious violent incidents occur at a rate of less than 2 per 1,000 students at most grade levels.
- Schools in urban areas and those with higher numbers of people of color report higher incidences of violent crime.
- Similar to offending patterns in general, thefts are reported at higher levels than serious violent crimes (4.3 to 1.2, respectively).
- Hate crimes are rare in all levels of school, with an overall rate of 0.1 per 1,000 students. (National Center for Education Statistics, 2006)

The problem of school violence is understood by most criminologists as a reflection of trends in the larger society (Elliott, Hamburg, and Williams, 1998; Kramer, 2000). If, for example, youths become more alienated from conventional norms and values, one is likely to see a rise in violence both in and outside of the schools (Yogan, 2000). In this sense school is "a microcosm of society" (Lawrence, 1997: 4).

Children are three times more likely to be victimized outside of school than in school (Fogarty, 2006; U.S. Department of Education, 1999). School crime is a community problem that requires a "team" approach for solution. This means that parents, the police, organizations, and educational programs should be synchronized so that youths receive consistent definitions unfavorable to violence from as many agents of socialization as possible. It also means that schools should consider offering violence prevention programs, counseling, and, more generally, a proactive approach to identifying and helping children who might be prone to violence (Elliott, Hamburg, and Williams, 1998). This latter approach has gained increased popularity in the wake of the Columbine murders (National Center for Education Statistics, 2006).

Mass Murder

Some recent high school and university killings are properly characterized as mass murders. Aside from the Columbine killings, which involved thirteen victims, several other school killings involved multiple victims murdered over a short period of time: In 2007, as previously discussed, Seung-Hui Cho killed thirty-two people and injured over two dozen others on the Virginia Tech campus; in 1998 Michael Johnson and Andrew Golden killed four students and a teacher in Jonesboro, Arkansas; in 1996, mass murders occurred on school grounds in Pearl, Mississippi, and West Paducah, Kentucky. Sometimes, mass murders on school property have involved outsiders and adults, as was the case in 1989 in Stockton, California, when Patrick Purdy shot and killed five Southeast Asian children while they played during recess.

Of course, mass murders can take place almost anywhere. During the last sixty years, they have occurred in fast-food restaurants, in post offices, in an online brokerage firm, on a commuter train, outside the CIA, in an insurance company office, in a university lecture hall, and, most famously, from a university tower. A determined killer needs only the opportunity to become a mass murderer.

What do we know of mass murder and mass murderers? Two of the best-known criminologists who have studied mass murder are James Alan Fox and Jack Levin (2001; 2005), who describe the typical mass murderer as follows:

Most mass killers do not just snap and start shooting anything that moves. Typically, these murderers generally act with calm deliberation, often planning their assault days, if not months, in advance. . . . [M]ass murderers tend to be quite selective in targeting their victims. They aim to kill those individuals they are convinced are responsible for their miseries, frequently ignoring anyone not implicated in the plot against them (2001: 117).

The offenders are most often middle-aged males, but the sex and age of the victims of mass murderers vary considerably. Furthermore, victims come from all social strata. However, it appears that victims are more often white—which is also the race of the most common offender. Victims of the mass killer may be classmates, coworkers, relatives and family members (including young children), or complete strangers. Most often, the underlying motivation for mass murder is the resolution of intense anger brought about by frustration and feelings of injustice. Interestingly, most mass murderers think of themselves as law-abiding citizens, not criminals (Fox and Levin, 2001: 125). In this respect, mass murderers are similar to terrorists and hate mongers; they all see their actions as justifiable and rational responses to circumstances they find distasteful, offensive, or threatening.

Robbery ↓ hate

Robbery, unlike the typical murder and aggravated assault, is almost always an instrumental crime designed to gain property or money. It is considered a violent crime because it involves the threat or use of force.

According to the FBI statistics, there were almost a half milllion reports of robberies in the United States in 2006. Each year robberies account for about 4 percent of all Index Offenses, and on average $1,268 is netted by the offenders per incident (Federal Bureau of Investigation, 2007). The National Crime

Victimization Survey, however, has consistently found evidence that there are perhaps twice as many robberies than reported in the FBI's Uniform Crime Reports. Recall from chapter 2 that the NCVS interviews victims of crime, so it generally finds more crime than that reported to police. Like most crimes, the robbery rate has decreased considerably in the last decade. In fact, since 1997 it has decreased over 10 percent (Federal Bureau of Investigation, 2007: 10).

Official data and studies by criminologists (e.g., Conklin, 1972; Gabor et al., 1988) have consistently shown that:

- Robbery occurs most frequently in the more highly populated cites of the country. Larger cities experience higher rates than smaller cities, and the lowest rates are found in rural areas (see also Bureau of Justice Statistics, 2006, 2007).
- Robbery usually involves offenders and victims who are strangers. Although the percentages vary from study to study, estimates of the proportion of incidents involving strangers reach as high as 80 percent, though the more probable figure for the United States as a whole is around 60 to 70 percent (Bureau of Justice Statistics, 2006).
- Offenders tend to be younger males. Males between the ages of fifteen and thirty predominate in arrest statistics for robbery. Black males are more likely than white males to be identified as the offenders in robbery incidents.
- Victims are usually white males over age twenty-one. Males are much more likely than females to be the victims of robbery. Whereas offenders are more likely to be black, the most likely victims are white males. Robbery is also more likely to be an interracial offense than any other violent crime (Bureau of Justice Statistics, 2006).
- Robbery tends to take place "on the street." Although the percentages vary from city

to city and from one part of a city to another, nationally, at least half of recorded robbery incidents occur in the open—in alleys, outside bars, in streets, in parking lots, or in playgrounds (Federal Bureau of Investigation, 2007).

- Offenders usually have a weapon of some sort. The most typical robbery is an armed robbery, with knives and handguns the preferred weapons. Robbery by a stranger is more likely to involve a firearm than robbery by an acquaintance. Not surprisingly, therefore, guns are used most frequently in commercial robberies. Black victims are more likely than white victims to face an armed robber, especially one armed with a gun. However, weapons are rarely used to inflict injury.
- Victims tend not to be injured or to be only slightly injured during the commission of a robbery. Victimization data show that seven out of ten victims are not injured. One in twelve robbery victims, however, is seriously injured, from broken bones to gunshot wounds or rape. The most likely situation in which a robbery victim is physically attacked is when the incident involves two or more armed offenders who rob a female late at night. However, white robbery victims are more likely than black victims to be physically attacked. No matter who the victim is, resistance significantly increases the chance that the victim will be injured, but it also increases the likelihood that the robbery will be unsuccessful.

This last point deserves further explanation. In a study of armed robbers in St. Louis, Missouri, it was found that most armed robbers attempt to create an "illusion of impending death" when they confront a victim (Wright and Decker, 1997). The robber threatens the victim with death to increase the probability of victim compliance. The robber implies that if the victim does comply, only property will be taken, not life. Two statements from Richard Wright and Scott Decker's interviews with active armed robbers illustrate this point.

One offender stated:

> Robbery itself is an illusion. That's what it's about. . . . Here is a person that you stick a gun in his face, they've never died, they don't know how it feels, but the illusion of death causes them to do what you want them to do.

Several offenders use language like this in confronting their victims:

> This is a robbery. Don't make it a murder! (132)

Injury is more likely to occur in cases in which the offenders are unarmed than when they are armed. Robbery infrequently involves shooting or stabbing. It is far more likely to involve kicking, shoving, beating, or knocking down. On the other hand, fatal injury is far more likely to occur in armed robbery than when robbers are unarmed (Cook, 1987: 366). The greater likelihood of violence erupting in unarmed robbery incidents is not hard to explain. First, the absence of a gun, knife, or club means that offenders have no obviously deadly weapon with which to intimidate the victim. "Lacking a credible threat," Marc Riedel writes, "the offenders will be unable to convince the victims to surrender the goods" (1993:155). This is consistent with Wright and Decker's St. Louis research. With a gun or knife present, actual violence may be unnecessary—the victim is sufficiently intimidated and offers no resistance. Second, much unarmed robbery involves a sudden attack. A successful sudden-attack robbery depends as much on the element of surprise and the speedy commission of the theft as it does on intimidation. The robber, bent on taking as much as possible as quickly as possible, uses violence in an instrumental way: It helps ensure that the victim is in no position to resist even if he or she wanted to do so, and it makes escape more likely. It may also lessen the chances that the victim will be clearheaded enough to identify the robber for the police.

For obvious reasons, robberies of street drug dealers are seldom reported to the police. In this case, the offender usually takes precautions against being fingered, assaulted, and possibly killed on the street by the victim or the victim's associates. Such precautions are the use of extreme intimidation, using a disguise, selecting a stranger to rob, and becoming hypervigilant on the street after the offense (Jacobs, Topalli, and Wright, 2000).

"Doing Stickup"

Jack Katz argues that the violence in "doing stickup" is more than simply a means of securing compliance from the victim: "The more closely we examine violent interactions in robbery, the more we will appreciate that situational rationality will not do for the final analysis" (1988: 181). Katz believes that violence, especially killing, in robberies reflects "a commitment to be a hardman—a person whose will, once manifested, must prevail, regardless of practical calculations of physical self-interest" (187). The use of violence among "career" or "heavy" stickup men, Katz argues, is a way of demonstrating to victims and to themselves that they really mean it. However, "[t]he ultimate challenge for the would-be stickup man is to convince himself not to give up" (194).

The stickup man anticipates violence at any time, anywhere. This is part of the "chaos" that career criminals live with, according to Katz. It is bound up with the constant threat posed by police, victims, other hardmen, and even the "action" lifestyle typical of hardmen: heavy drinking and partying, sexual exploits, drugs, gambling, being "on the run," fast and heavy spending, and (consequently) persistent episodes of criminal activity week after week.

Katz constructs his picture of stickup men from the vantage point of offenders themselves, asking: "What are they trying to do?" His analysis is based on detailed police reports of Chicago robberies, ethnographies of street criminals, and autobiographical life stories such as that by John Allen (1977), whose criminal life began in his early teens and extended well into adulthood. The use of violence in these men's lives originates in the adolescent claims of the "badass" and becomes increasingly a persistent aspect of an existence framed by chaos and the never-ending challenge of demonstrating control.

Viewed in this light, the apparently "senseless"—that is, unprovoked, unnecessary, and irrational—violence described in accounts of some robberies takes on new meaning. In his Boston study, John Conklin (1972) found that one in six robbers with guns and one in three with knives used force even though victims offered no resistance. A bank robber interviewed by Peter Letkemann tells of seemingly gratuitous violence during a bank robbery:

> So they froze there—their reaction is one of extreme fear and they drop to the floor and sometimes we select the strongest person—the manager especially or another teller which is very big—a six-footer, or something like that, you know. And we won't say a word, we just walk up to him and smack him right across the face, you know, and we get him down. (1973: 110)

Katz argues that for "both the offender and the victim, the perception of whether the victim is resisting or not, is not as clear-cut as researchers often assume" (1988: 189). Katz illustrates with the following example:

> A 33-year-old male is sitting in his car when he is approached by a male of about 25, who opens the car door, displays a handgun, and demands money. The victim gives all his money. The offender then begins hitting the victim, requesting more money. The victim gives his wallet to the offender, who then runs off. (189)

Violence is a way to manage the uncertainties and suspense inherent in the robbery confrontation; however, the robber's understanding that he is able and willing to use violence—and that he is comfortable with it—transcends the specific event and is part of the "spiritual commitment" that transforms occasional and adolescent muggers into persistent offenders. The barrier to going on with robbery is the robber's inability to manage fear and uncertainty.

Professional and Amateur Robbers

According to Conklin (1972), two main types of professional criminals are involved in robbery: those who do it almost exclusively and those who have other "lines" (such as burglary) but may occasionally commit a robbery. The professional robber is one who engages in robbery almost exclusively and for whom it is the main source of income. Relatively few robbers are properly called professionals; nevertheless, they are responsible for a disproportionate number of armed robberies and for most of the big jobs.

Professionalism means more than quasi membership in a criminal subculture. It means developing skills, talents, know-how, competence, viewpoints—a way of life. It means weighing risks, choosing among alternatives, planning, using caution, and subscribing to a code of conduct. Professionalism in robbery means that robbery is a part of one's way of life. Werner Einstadter (1969) found that many professional robberies had been fully planned and calculated and were not incidental to some other form of crime. His subjects also considered themselves robbers and had spent considerable time in that line of work. When professional robbers work together, proceeds are shared equally; if arrested, team members are on their own—they are under no obligation to keep quiet, nor are their colleagues under any obligation to help them. If they do "rat," however, they will lose their share. The group has little cohesion. Members come in and leave the team as occasion necessitates, and leadership roles are filled more or less at will. Members of the team and other professional robbers are expected to deal honestly with one another, at least as it bears on the work itself. Members have a fatalistic attitude toward events that might transpire during a robbery. Other aspects of the professional robber's code and social organization concern cooperation, partnership consensus, planning the "hit," assigning roles (usually done on the basis of skill and knowledge), and decision making.

Today, many of the forms of robbery that in the past were the primary activity of professionals are now committed as often, if not more often, by amateurs—those who are unfamiliar with the skills, techniques, and other professional aspects of career robbery. Bank robbery is an example. The amateur status of many contemporary bank robbers is confirmed by newspaper accounts of robbers who hold up tellers while cameras take clear pictures of their undisguised faces. Other accounts describe robbers who try to rob drive-up facilities in which tellers are protected by bulletproof glass and are sufficiently hidden from view so that they can summon the police via silent alarm systems.

Indications of amateurism in bank robbery are also found in estimates of the amounts of money lost in such robberies and in the arrest rates of the last few years. Not only are arrest rates higher now for bank robbery than for any other felony property crime, but the average amount lost has decreased or remained stable during the last few decades. In 1932 the average loss was $5583, compared with $3177 in 1991 and just over $4,300 in 2006 (Federal Bureau of Investigation, 2006a). Of course, one reason for this is changes in banking procedures in the handling of cash. A professional will know this, however, and will not waste time on petty "scores" unless hard pressed. Considering the impact of inflation, bank robbery is certainly less lucrative than it used to be.

Research on amateur robbers suggests that quite a few take a "highly casual approach to their crimes" (Feeney, 1999: 122). Unlike professional robbers, more than half of Feeney's sample had done no planning at all and a third did only minor planning. The motivations for the robberies were found to be tremendously variable: Some needed money for drugs, housing, food, and clothes, while others, interestingly enough, were simply bored or angry at "the world."

Hate Crime

Hate crime, also called *bias crime*, does not necessarily involve violence, but physical assaults, even murders, are its hallmark. In 1990, under the Hate Crime Statistics Act, the FBI began a program of systematic data collection on hate crime. The FBI's definition of hate crime was then revised in 1994 to include acts targeting people with disabilities. Officially, then, hate crime, is defined as

> a criminal offense committed against a person, property, or society which is motivated, in whole or in part, by the offender's bias against a race, religion, disability, sexual orientation, or ethnicity/national origin. (Federal Bureau of Investigation, 2007)

The official FBI record on hate crime in the United States in 2006 (the most recent data available at the time of this writing) is represented in box 3.3. It is important to note that groups such as the Southern Poverty Law Center and the Anti-Defamation League consistently find that FBI figures undercount the amount of hate or bias crime in the United States.

Most hate crimes involve simple assault, intimidation, or damage to property. Contrary to the overall crime distribution, however, the majority of hate crimes are crimes against the person, not property offenses. While very few people are murdered because of hate or bias, several incidents in the last decade have drawn attention to the gravity of hated-inspired violence.

In the mid 1990s, at least a dozen southern black churches were set on fire, vandalized, or damaged. It is suspected than the offenders were racist white youths venting their rage and hatred at an extremely vulnerable target—small Christian churches composed of largely impoverished African Americans. Another case that drew worldwide attention

BOX 3.3. INCIDENTS, OFFENSES, VICTIMS, AND KNOWN OFFENDERS BY BIAS MOTIVATION, 2006

Bias Motivation	Incidents	Offenses	Victims	Known Offenders
Total	7,722	9,080	9,652	7,330
Single-Bias Incidents	7,720	9,076	9,642	7,324
Race	*4,000*	*4,737*	*5,020*	*3,957*
Anti-White	890	1,008	1,054	1,074
Anti-Black	2,640	3,136	3,332	2,437
Anti-American Indian/Alaskan Native	60	72	75	72
Anti-Asian/Pacific Islander	181	230	239	181
Anti–Multiple Races, Group	229	291	320	193
Religion	*1,462*	*1,597*	*1,750*	*705*
Anti-Jewish	967	1,027	1,144	362
Anti-Catholic	76	81	86	44
Anti-Protestant	59	62	65	35
Anti-Islamic	156	191	208	147
Anti–Other Religion	124	140	147	63
Anti–Multiple Religions/ Group	73	88	92	49
Anti-Atheism/Agnosticism/ etc.	7	8	8	5
Sexual Orientation	*1,195*	*1,415*	*1,472*	*1,380*
Anti–Male Homosexual	747	881	913	914
Anti–Female Homosexual	163	192	202	154
Anti-Homosexual	238	293	307	268
Anti-Heterosexual	26	28	29	26
Anti-Bisexual	21	21	21	18
Ethnicity/National Origin	*984*	*1,233*	*1,305*	*1,209*
Anti-Hispanic	576	770	819	802
Anti–Other Ethnicity/ National Origin	408	463	486	407
Disability	*79*	*94*	*95*	*73*
Anti-Physical	17	20	21	17
Anti-Mental	62	74	74	56
Multiple-Bias Incidents	2	4	10	6

Source: Federal Bureau of Investigation (2007).

because of its brutality was the 1998 murder of a young black man named James Byrd Jr. in Jasper, Texas. Byrd was chained to a pickup truck by three young white males who then drove off, dragging Byrd behind. His body was found in pieces when the police arrived at the scene (State of Texas, 1998).

Hundreds of Jewish synagogues and community centers were destroyed, damaged, or defaced by fire and graffiti during the 1990s. Jews have encountered significant violence, discrimination, and prejudice for centuries, not only in the United States and Germany, but in many areas of eastern and western Europe. Jews have been one of the most victimized groups in history. The Nazi Holocaust alone resulted in the loss of 6 million Jews. Unfortunately, anti-Semitism is still strong today in the United States, in part because of deeply imbedded stereotypes, myths, and conspiracy theories about Jews.

Finally, the age-old hate crime of violence against homosexuals has received more attention in the wake of the 1998 murder of University of Wyoming freshman Matthew Shepard, who was lured from a bar into a truck, robbed, beaten severely, and tied to a fence outside of town, where he was left to die. His attackers,

two young white males, were characterized as extremely homophobic (State of Wyoming, 1998). They were convicted, but escaped the death penalty largely because Shepard's father agreed to a sentencing bargain before that phase of the trial took place. Here is part of a statement Mr. Shepard made to the court following the sentencing agreement:

> It has been stated that Matt was against the death penalty. [This statement is] wrong. We have held family discussions and talked about the death penalty. Matt believed that there were incidents and crimes that justified the death penalty. For example, he and I discussed the horrible death of James Byrd Jr. in Jasper, Texas. It was his opinion that the death penalty should be sought and that no expense should be spared to bring those responsible for this murder to justice. Little did we know that the same response would come about involving Matt. I, too, believe in the death penalty. I would like nothing better than to see you die, Mr. McKinney. However, this is the time to begin the healing process. To show mercy to someone who refused to show any mercy. To use this as the first step in my own closure about losing Matt. Mr. McKinney, I am going to grant you life, as hard as that is for me to do, because of Matthew. Every time you cel-

Hate crime has existed for centuries but only in the last few decades has the problem been seriously recognized by the media, government, and general public. Demonstrations such as the one pictured here have become far more prevalent in recent years

ebrate Christmas, a birthday, or the Fourth of July, remember that Matt isn't. Every time that you wake up in that prison cell, remember that you had the opportunity and the ability to stop your actions that night. Every time that you see your cell mate, remember that you had a choice, and now you are living that choice. You robbed me of something very precious, and I will never forgive you for that. Mr. McKinney, I give you life in the memory of one who no longer lives. May you have a long life, and may you thank Matthew every day for it. (Wired Strategies, 2006, available at http://www.wiredstrategies.com/shepardx.html)

The national ledger on hate crime is murky, but few experts doubt its extensiveness. One of the biggest problems in gathering data is that many victims of hate crimes do not report the attacks, often out of fear or simply because they consider it a private matter—as many victims of violence do anyway. Another problem is that law enforcement officers and prosecutors may have differing interpretations of the definitions of crimes motivated by hate or bias. Nevertheless, some believe that hate groups and hate crime in general is increasing in the United States, particularly crimes against gays, lesbians, and Muslims (see Levin and McDevitt, 1993; Southern Poverty Law Center, 2007).

Some perpetrators of hate and bias crime have links to white supremacist groups such as the skinheads, the White Brotherhood, the Invisible Empire (part of the Ku Klux Klan), the Christian Patriot Defense League, or the confederacy known as the Aryan Nations. But whites certainly have no monopoly on hate crime. Homophobia and racism are only two of the many underlying motivations for hate. Besides, hate does not have to be organized to result in violence.

Nor is hate crime a distinctly American problem. The Australian National Committee on Violence published a report on racist violence, suggesting that racist attacks were on the increase in that country, and that much of it was organized (National Committee on Violence, 1989). The skinheads originated in England, where for many years they operated as a loosely knit national group of young racist thugs. Skinheads are now found in the United States, as well as in Germany, Canada, the Netherlands, and other parts of Europe (see Hamm, 1993; 1994). They tend to be associated with the conservative far-right, although their beginnings in England grew out of an attempt among working-class youths to set themselves apart from society by showing pride in their blue-collar roots and sharing a common interest in Reggae music (Aronowitz, 1994).

Hamm's (1993; 1994) studies of American skinheads appear to be consistent with research done on this group in other areas of the globe. For the most part, skinheads are likely to be white youths in the working class who became radicalized through music, the Internet, and hard-to-find racist books, films, and journals. Interestingly, many of those in his sample were from nonabusive families, procured high school diplomas, and some were enrolled in colleges and universities.

Gang Violence

What is a gang? While there are many definitions of gang currently in use, Moore (1998) offers a useful perspective based on criminological research. **Gangs** (as opposed to youth groups), can be distinguished in the following ways:

1. The group in question must define itself as a gang. An indicator of this is that the group has adopted a name, such as "Crips" or "Bloods."
2. There exists significant socialization and the transmission of norms and values among the group members. This means that the primary agents of socialization are found in the "street," not in the family, school, or other conventional groups and institutions.
3. A group is more likely to be a gang if it recruits members and becomes institutionalized in the community.

4. A group is more likely to be a gang if it has been involved in a sufficient number of illegal incidents that have prompted negative responses from formal social control agencies and the larger community.

The juvenile gang provides the setting in which many young inner-city males explore violence. The ideals of masculinity, toughness, excitement, and reputation are stressed in gang activities (see Sanchez-Jankowski, 1991; Moore, 1998) Members must show that they can take care of themselves when threatened or provoked, and much emphasis is placed on the conquest and dominance of women (an issue of great relevance to discussions of sexual violence).

Gang members often carry weapons and are more likely to use violence or the threat of violence to solve problems and gain respect. When approved by the group, violence can be used as a means to achieve prestige, honor, and recognition. Some criminologists believe that the meanings associated with violence for some groups of Americans reflect the existence of a **subculture of violence** (e.g., Wolfgang, 1958; Wolfgang and Ferracuti, 1967). Within this subculture, aggression is expected and legitimized in situations where it is not supported by the dominant culture: "Quick resort to physical combat as a measure of daring, courage, or defense of status appears to be a cultural expectation" (Wolfgang, 1958: 189).

Viewed in this way, violence has positive consequences for male gang members: It deters rivals and improves a youth's competitive edge, while at the same time it enhances a member's reputation and social status (see also Horowitz, 1987; Daly and Wilson, 1988a: 129). Not only does violence help gang members gain a tough reputation for themselves and their gang, but it helps protect that reputation. Ruth Horowitz reports how members of a gang "gathered in an alley to discuss how they could regain the reputation they had lost when [two of their] members were

beaten" (44). All favored some sort of violent response. William Sanders (1994), in the best ethnographic study of juvenile gang violence to date, shows how drive-by shootings are understood and justified by gang members in terms of rivalry, honor, protection, rationality, and defense.

Two additional points about youth gangs need emphasis. First, drug trafficking and other criminal enterprises are commonplace activities of many big-city gangs. As a result, a certain amount of instrumental violence surfaces as gangs compete with rivals and try to protect themselves from police. But again, the well-publicized gang-drugs-violence connection may be overstated: A three-year study of four of the largest street gangs in Chicago (Black Gangster Disciples Nation, Latin Disciples, Latin Kings, and Vice Lords) found that of 288 gang-motivated homicides, only 8 were related to drugs. The most prevalent context in which murder and assault occurred among the gangs was turf related (Block and Block, 1993). Of course, the findings of this study may not generalize to other locations (see Goldstein, 1993, for a study of East Harlem in New York City).

Second, there is little evidence to suggest that youth gangs in general have adopted murder and mayhem as a way of life, or even that they are predisposed to violence. Youth gangs provide comradeship and a way to have a good time. While the adventures of adolescence often bring gang members into conflict with middle-class ideals and the law, most youths mature out of crime and go straight.

Based on interviews with members of nineteen African American gangs in Milwaukee, John Hagedorn (1991) concludes that black gangs are part of an urban minority underclass—members tend to stay involved in gangs into adulthood, and the persistence of neighborhood gangs is supported not only because there is a lack of work but because neighborhoods in poverty lack effective social institutions. There are no chain grocery stores, no banks or check-cashing facilities, no alcohol or drug treatment facilities, and no community agencies. Neighborhood segmentation, drug dealing, and periodic shootouts contribute to tensions and reinforce gang violence.

The plight of African Americans living in the inner city is summed up in this quote from Elijah Anderson, which also contains a warning:

> A vicious cycle has thus been formed. The hopelessness and alienation many young inner-city black men and women feel, largely as a result of endemic joblessness and persistent racism, fuels the violence they engage in. This violence serves to confirm the negative feelings many whites and some middle-class blacks harbor toward the ghetto poor, further legitimating the oppositional culture and the code of the streets in the eyes of many poor young blacks. Unless this cycle is broken, attitudes on both sides will become increasingly entrenched, and the violence, which claims victims black and white, poor and affluent, will only escalate. (1994: 94)

SITUATIONAL FACTORS AND VIOLENCE

It is important to recognize that whether or not people are predisposed to violence when they enter a situation, the likelihood of violence can be influenced by factors that are present in, or develop out of, the situation itself. Examples of situational elements that promote violent outcomes are guns, alcohol, victim precipitation, and the encouragement of witnesses. While such situational factors raise the risk of homicide and serious injury in any encounter, they are most likely to be implicated in expressive homicides, where violence is an end in itself (Block, 1993: 302).

Guns and Violence

Guns are used in large numbers of violent crimes, but mostly by men. The Bureau of Justice Statistics (2007) indicates that guns were used in over 25 percent of all violent crimes,

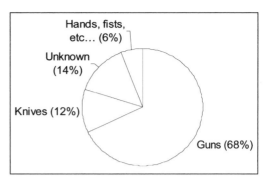

▲Figure 3.3.
Distribution of Murder Weapons, 2007.
Source: Federal Bureau of Investigation (2008).

including a quarter of robberies, and 6 percent of assaults. As figure 3.3 shows, the most common murder weapon in the United States is a firearm. Among firearms, handguns were used in the majority of cases. A classic study of 9,054 handgun murder victims in 1986 found that half were blacks, a victimization rate nearly eight times that for whites (Rand, 1990). Blacks aged twenty to thirty-four were victimized at a rate nine times greater than the population as a whole, regardless of age. In contrast, white rates of victimization were only slightly higher than average. Male rates of handgun murder victimization were five times those for women. A majority of all victims were shot and killed during arguments, but nearly 30 percent were killed during a robbery or other crime. Research shows that 90 percent of gang-related killings involved guns (of all types), compared with around 60 percent of argument-related homicides and 70 percent of homicides occurring during the commission of another crime (Fox and Zawitz, 1999).

Estimates of the number of firearms in private hands in the United States vary, and it is important to recognize their source. One should be wary of estimates made by people with financial or political interests in guns. Probably no one claims to know the exact number, and so any figure must be treated as a more or less educated guess. Having said this, academic estimates from the late 1970s placed the figure at 120 million, plus or minus 20 million, with handguns making up about 30 percent of the total (Wright and Rossi, 1981). In 1985 it was estimated that the number of handguns in private hands was 65 million, roughly two per household. More recent estimates suggest that perhaps as many as 300 million firearms (including rifles and shotguns) are privately owned in the United States (Hepburn et al., 2007).

National surveys show that almost half of those interviewed report having at least one gun in their homes (Bureau of Justice Statistics, 1998; Hepburn et al., 2007). About 25 percent of private guns are kept for protection and self-defense, also the primary reasons voiced by children who carry guns (Hepburn et al., 2007; Wright and Rossi, 1981; Wright, Sheley, and Smith, 1992: 70). Clearly, many Americans are fearful for their lives or property. By comparison, relatively few people actually die from firearm injuries—around thirty thousand annually.

In response to growing concern about the problem of assault-style weapons, on May 5, 1994, Congress voted to ban nineteen assault weapons despite vigorous opposition from the gun lobby. President Bill Clinton quickly signed the bill, and gun shops were immediately inundated with orders for the guns from thousands of potential customers (and, needless to say, prices skyrocketed). This step certainly has considerable symbolic value for the peace and antigun lobbies, but its impact on the practices of criminals may actually be small: A survey of state prison inmates estimated that fewer than 1 percent of all inmates used assault weapons in committing their crimes (Bureau of Justice Statistics, 1993: 18). Furthermore, the federal Bureau of Alcohol, Tobacco, and Firearms traced 56,509 firearms for law enforcement agencies during the 1990–1991 period, finding that two of the top three most frequently traced guns were cheap semiautomatic handguns: the Raven Arms MP-25 (about $60), and the Davis Industries P-32 ($85–$100).

In 1993 the Brady Law, which requires a five-day waiting period before the sale of a handgun, was passed by Congress. During the waiting period, local authorities are required to make a "reasonable effort" to find out if the buyer has a felony record, a history of mental illness or drug use, or some other problem that would make the sale illegal. Solid studies on the effects of the Brady Law are hard to find, but the public generally supports waiting periods for handgun purchases.

Some claim that if people could not readily acquire guns, there would be less killing. Others argue that the availability of guns has no bearing on homicide rates—that people kill, not guns. The debate on the issue is fierce and seems unlikely to be resolved in the near future. Since guns are a fact of life in the United States and have been widely owned for at least two centuries, talk of civilian disarmament generally falls on deaf ears. Powerful interest groups such as the National Rifle Association (NRA) and the highly profitable gun industry, which earns more than $2 billion a year, strenuously resist any stringent controls. Actor Charlton Heston became president of the NRA in 1998 and was reappointed for an unprecedented third term in 2000. The pro-gun lobby claims widespread support, and, indeed, opinion surveys consistently report that most Americans believe they have a right to own a firearm, though opinions are divided on whether handguns should be banned in the respondents' own communities (Bureau of Justice Statistics, 1998). In view of the demographics of homicide discussed earlier, it is perhaps no surprise that blacks are much more likely to favor stricter gun control laws than are whites. Thus, in 2007 a Gallup Poll found that 58 percent of black respondents favored stricter gun laws, versus 47 percent of whites (Maguire and Pastore, 2008).

The presence of a gun does not mean a murder will occur. Millions of Americans have access to guns, but relatively few kill or are killed by them. Nor does the widespread availability of firearms in the United States account for all the disparity between U.S. homicide rates and those of other countries. As Steven Messner and Richard Rosenfeld put it, "even if none of these weapons were ever used in another killing, the United States would still have the highest homicide rate of any advanced industrial nation" (1994: 25). Yet the presence of a gun increases the probability that someone will die if a dispute erupts and neither party can successfully defuse the situation. The gun is a situational factor providing an easily accessible opportunity for murder.

The situational importance of guns to homicide is revealed in studies in Chicago (Zimring, 1972) and St. Louis (Barlow, 1983; Barlow and Schmidt Barlow, 1988). Both studies found not only that guns were more lethal than knives but also that some guns were more lethal than others. In Chicago .38 caliber handguns were twice as deadly as .22s; .32 caliber handguns were more lethal than .25s; and .25s were more lethal than .22s. The St. Louis study found that 47.7 percent of those victims shot by "large-caliber" weapons (i.e., .38, .357, .44, or .45) died, compared to 33.3 percent of those shot with .32 or smaller caliber handguns. In further contrast, only 18.5 percent of stabbing victims died.

It should be pointed out that the relative lethality of different firearms is affected by the location of the wound. In general, wounds to the head are more likely to be fatal than wounds to other parts of the body. However, Barlow's study also found that the difference in lethality between large-caliber and small-caliber handguns virtually disappeared in head wound cases. Shoot someone in the head and it matters little whether the gun is a .357 magnum or a .25 caliber derringer (Barlow and Schmidt Barlow, 1988).

According to interviews with prison inmates, when used in the commission of crime, guns (and knives) are carried primarily for purposes of scaring the victim or for self-protection (Bureau of Justice Statistics, 1993: 18).

Typically, when killings occur in which guns are used, there has been a predictable chain of events: One person acquires a firearm, two or more people come within reach of the firearm, a dispute escalates into an attack, the weapon is fired, it causes an injury, and the injury is serious enough to cause death (Roth, 1994: 2).

Roth (1994) suggests that when viewed as a chain of events, the problem of guns and violence can be analyzed as a series of measurable risks. For example, greater gun availability increases the overall risks of firearm deaths as well as the likelihood that a gun will be selected as weapon of choice in the first place; greater availability increases the ease and lowers the cost of acquiring a gun; and the selection of a gun as a weapon of choice actually reduces the risk of death in some crimes (in robberies and rapes, for example, guns generally intimidate victims into surrendering) but significantly raises it in others (assaults, for example, where the intent is to injure, though not necessarily to kill).

Alcohol and Violence

Just as guns turn up as the weapon used in most homicides, so alcohol emerges as a situational element in many homicides and assaults. Wolfgang found that alcohol was present in 63.6 percent of 588 homicide cases in Philadelphia. Other studies have found alcohol to be present in similar or greater proportions (Wolfgang, 1958: 136; Bureau of Justice Statistics, 1998). More often than not, both offender and victim had been drinking immediately before or during a homicide or assault.

Does this mean that alcohol in some way caused the violence? Most authors acknowledge the statistical association between alcohol and homicide but do not speak of the relationship in causal terms. True, alcohol is a psychoactive drug, meaning that it produces mental changes in people who consume it. Some scholars believe that alcohol directly increases aggressive tendencies through its pharmocological effects (see Roth, 1994). The kind of changes that occur and how extensive they are depend on numerous factors, including the quantity consumed, the consumer's physiological state, the consumer's tolerance for the drug, and whether or not the individual has just eaten. There are also social factors to keep in mind: Alcohol is often consumed in settings where expectations of violence may exist, for example, at some sporting events, in notorious bars, and during binge-drinking sessions among males.

In short, alcohol is best viewed as a precipitating factor in violence. To the extent that alcohol lowers social inhibitions and reduces anxiety and guilt, people who have been drinking may act more aggressively than otherwise would have been the case. The underlying dispute may have erupted anyway, and the individuals concerned may have been predisposed to seek a violent solution. With the situational influence of alcohol missing, however, fear, anxiety, guilt, and social inhibitions are there to serve as constraints. On the other hand, being drunk may be a factor in violence for an entirely different reason. People who anticipate getting into a dispute may prepare themselves by getting drunk. Being intoxicated may provide a convenient rationalization—and the courage—for violence (Kantor and Straus, 1987).

Victim Precipitation

It is often argued that many homicide victims precipitate their own deaths. Many years ago Hans von Hentig (1948) said that killers are often driven to murder as much by their victims' actions as by their own inclinations. This is most likely to occur when those involved know each other well. Tensions and mutual aggravations reach the point where people see reconciliation only through violence. This can occur suddenly or develop over a long period of time. The violence is an outcome of interaction and not merely the result of a killer's actions.

A standard definition of **victim precipitation** is given by Wolfgang:

> The term victim-precipitated is applied to those criminal homicides in which the victim is a direct, positive precipitator in the crime. The role of the victim is characterized by his having been the first in the homicide drama to use physical force directed against his subsequent slayer. The victim-precipitated cases are those in which the victim was the first to show and use a deadly weapon, to strike a blow in an altercation—in short, the first to commence the interplay of resort to physical violence. (1958: 252)

Examples given by Wolfgang, taken from Philadelphia police files, illustrate typical situations of victim-precipitated homicide:

> During a lover's quarrel, the male [victim] hit his mistress and threw a can of kerosene at her. She retaliated by throwing the liquid on him, and then tossed a lighted match in his direction. He died from the burns.

> A victim became incensed when his eventual slayer asked for money which the victim owed him. The victim grabbed a hatchet and started in the direction of his creditor, who pulled out a knife and stabbed him. (1958: 253)

Identifying the number of victim-precipitated homicides is virtually impossible because doing so requires knowledge of the interaction between victim and offender. Because one party is dead, re-creation of the incident must rely on accounts by the killer or witnesses. Estimates have nevertheless been made, and these range from around 25 percent of homicides to upward of 50 percent. The picture for nonlethal assaults is even more uncertain, especially since so many incidents are hidden. In all probability, a high proportion of assaults are precipitated by the victim's actions, but even pinpointing who the victim is may be moot, since both parties may be injured and each is likely to blame the other for "starting it."

Violence as a Situated Transaction

All social situations possess unique characteristics, yet so many violent incidents look alike that the similarities lead one to ask whether there is some typical dynamic characterizing the events. David Luckenbill (1977) looked at homicide incidents with just this question in mind. He found evidence of six stages in the interaction between actors in the typical homicide drama. We may call this phenomenon a **situated transaction.**

In the first stage one person insults or offends another. To onlookers the action may not seem particularly offensive, but the person to whom it is directed is angered by it. In stage two the offended individual sees that the insult is directed at him or her personally. Sometimes this clarification results from meanings assigned by onlookers or friends; sometimes it derives from the history of interactions between the parties involved, as when, for example, a husband has previously fought with his wife and now interprets the present situation as similar.

Stage three involves decisions about reactions to the insult or affront. The offended individual may excuse the other's behavior, rationalizing that the person is just drunk, joking, or acting "crazy." If such face-saving techniques do not work or are inappropriate, the individual must retaliate or back down. Retaliation is usually the route taken in homicide situations and those in which someone is severely injured.

In a search for the situational, proximate, or close-in causes of murder, Katz asks, "What is the killer trying to do in a typical homicide?" (1988: 13). He believes that many murders represent an impassioned attack, or "righteous slaughter," in which the killer makes a last-ditch effort to defend his basic worth. Insults about sexual prowess (for men) or

continued sexual violation (of women) are felt to be deeply humiliating. When humiliation turns to rage, the would-be killer tries to settle things once and for all. In rage, the killer "confirms his humiliation through transcending it. In rage, he acknowledges that his subjectivity has been overcome by implicitly acknowledging that he could not take it anymore. But now the acknowledgment is triumphal because it comes just as rage promises to take him to dominance over the situation" (26).

Sometimes death or injury occurs in stage three. If not, a fourth stage may be entered, in which counterretaliation takes place. In stage four the original offender continues or escalates the insulting behavior, perhaps using violence. In this stage, onlookers may take sides in the dispute, escalating and even directing the conflict.

In stage five both parties are unable to back down without losing face, and weapons will be produced if they have not already appeared. In Luckenbill's study, many disputants already carried guns or knives with them. Others used bottles, pool cues, and other handy implements, or temporarily left the situation to get a gun or knife. With weapons at hand, either one party kills the other quickly or a battle ensues.

Throughout these five stages, no one has given much thought to the police. In stage six the police enter the picture. Some killers flee, some are restrained by onlookers, some are aided by friends, and some call the police themselves. The interactions themselves have thus created a new situation in which outsiders are involved and must be reckoned with.

This view of violent situations is not intended to describe all murderous encounters. However, as a depiction of the most "normal" homicide and serious assault, it describes the dynamics well. Conflict, victim precipitation, face saving, retaliation and escalation, and the presence of weapons conspire to produce deadly violence. That many situations also involve alcohol, drugs, or partying makes defusing the process a difficult, if not impossible, task. One often hears about people who have tried to break up a fight, only to be injured or killed themselves.

Looking at violence as an event draws attention from background factors and toward the situation elements that are intrinsic to violent encounters—victim precipitation, weapon availability and selection, witness behavior, offender-victim interaction, number and location of wounds, action and reaction, and the impact of opportunity and ability. There is also the medical factor. When victims do not immediately die, there is a chance that emergency medical care can be delivered in a timely fashion and their lives can be saved. Figure 3.4 illustrates how the intrinsic factors in violent events are linked with one another, and also with extrinsic factors that are in the background (e.g., culture, social structure, experience, and knowledge) or introduced into a situation after an attack occurs (e.g., victim assistance and the medical factor).

CHAPTER SUMMARY

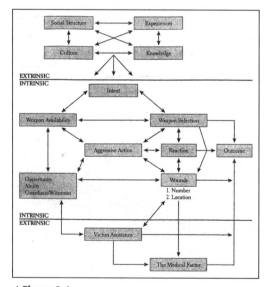

▲Figure 3.4.
The Violent Event: Elements and Linkages

This chapter has explored the character and extent of murder, assault, robbery, and other violent crimes. The United States ranks first in homicide among industrialized countries, and has for many years. Homicide offenders and victims are most likely to be young males of relatively low socioeconomic status who know each other. The same is true of nonlethal assaults, which are like homicides in most respects. The essential difference between a homicide and an assault is the existence of a corpse.

Robbery is a crime that involves an attempt to gain possession of material belongings through the use of—or threat to use—force. Robbers may be professionals or amateurs, but often times they attempt to create "the illusion of impending death" when confronting a victim during a street robbery. This raises the likelihood that the offender and the victim will leave the transaction without physical harm.

Serial murder is an infrequent but strangely attractive area of concern for people around the globe. A far more frequent type of violence is hate crime, which stems from racial, homophobic, religious, antidisability, and ethnic biases. Schools are in some ways a microcosm of the broader society, and violence in grade schools and high schools is still infrequent, but an emerging concern for criminologists and the general public. Gang violence, studied by criminologists since the 1950s, has also received much attention. An understanding of gang behavior requires attention to the social and structural pushes and pulls youths become subject to as they pass through adolescence and the teenage years.

Certain situations are prone to turning violent: The presence of a weapon, the consumption of alcohol, and victim precipitation are examples of situational elements that contribute to violent outcomes. Many violent events follow similar stages in which someone is offended by an insult and the offended person retaliates in a face-saving ritual that in turn provokes a counterreaction.

KEY TERMS

code of the streets
disaggregation
gangs
hate crime
mass murder
serial murder
situated transaction
spree killings
subculture of violence
victim precipitation

RECOMMENDED READINGS

Anderson, Elijah. (1999). *Code of the Street.* New York: Norton.

Egger, Steven A. (1998). *The Killers among Us: An Examination of Serial Murder and Its Investigation.* Upper Saddle River, NJ: Prentice-Hall.

Jenkins, Philip. (1994). *Using Murder: The Social Construction of Serial Homicide.* New York: Aldine De Gruyter.

Katz, Jack. (1988). *Seductions of Crime: Moral and Sensual Attractions in Doing Evil.* New York: Basic Books.

Mullins, Christopher W. (2006). *Holding Your Square: Masculinities, Streetlife and Violence.* Portland, OR: Willan.

Sanchez Jankowski, Martin. (1991). *Islands in the Street: Gangs and American Urban Society.* Berkeley and Los Angeles: University of California Press.

Wright, Richard, and Scott Decker (1997). *Armed Robbers in Action.* Boston: Northeastern University Press.

RECOMMENDED WEB SITES

Anti-Defamation League (http://www.adl.org). A great source for information on anti-Semitism.

Southern Poverty Law Center (http://www.splcenter.org). Copious amounts of information on all varieties of hate crime.

Safe and Drug-Free Schools Program (http://www.ed.gov/offices/OESE/SDFS/). Information and reports on school safety.

═CHAPTER═

4

VIOLENCE AGAINST
WOMEN AND CHILDREN

ABFEE9 Alamy

Only a few decades ago, domestic violence, rape, and other sexual assaults were only mentioned in sensational news stories and discussed in secretive whispers. Even the scientific community kept the subject at arm's length. The sensitive nature of the subject may account for some of this, but the historical failure to address these acts seriously may have a deeper meaning: It is women, not men, who are the usual victims of sexual assault and domestic violence, and female problems are not viewed with urgency in patriarchal societies. In addition, it was long believed that sexual assault was a rare thing that cropped up from time to time, but not often enough to merit real concern, even among women.

In recent years, sexual assault and domestic violence have become a major focus of writing and research. This development is largely due to the efforts of women who have sought to dispel the myths and mystique surrounding rape and the sexual abuse of children, and who have fought to help the victims.

DOMESTIC VIOLENCE

Much violence, including homicide and serious assaults, occurs in the home. **Domestic violence** can be defined as crimes committed by and against one or more family members, cohabitants, or intimates.

If there are doubts that violence is widespread and gendered in the American family and in intimate relationships, consider the following facts:

- Women are four times more likely to be killed by their husbands than husbands by their wives. The same ratio hold true for boyfriends and girlfriends. (Federal Bureau of Investigation, 2006a)
- Twenty-eight percent of women who are sexually assaulted were victimized by a close intimate (usually a husband, ex-husband, boyfriend or ex-boyfriend). (National Crime Victimization Survey, 2006)
- Almost a million children in the United States suffer from abuse or neglect. Children three years of age and under experience the highest rate of victimization. (U.S. Department of Health and Human Services, 2007)
- Ninety percent of the children of physically and sexually assaulted mothers witnessed the crime when it occurred. (McFarlane and Malecha, 2005)

Characteristics of Domestic Violence

Women are much more likely than men to be victims of domestic violence; therefore, much of what is called "family violence" and "domestic violence" is in fact *crime against women* (Renzetti, Edleson, and Bergen, 2001). The typical assailant is a husband; the next most common, an ex-husband.

Yet there is much evidence that the problem of intimate violence is not limited to heterosexual relationships. Although estimates vary, partner violence in lesbian relationships has been found to be frequent and serious enough to warrant the concern of social scientists, public officials, and domestic violence workers (McClennen, 2005; Renzetti, 1998). However, studies of lesbian battering have been conducted with very small samples and are therefore not very good measures of prevalence. The same is true of studies of intimate violence among men in homosexual relationships (Merrill, 1998). One cannot say with confidence that there is more or less violence in gay and lesbian relationships than in heterosexual relationships.

Uncovering family violence directed at women and children is not easy, partly because there is uncertainty and disagreement about what constitutes criminal violence in family settings (Mihalic and Elliott, 1997). When does the spanking of a child or other disciplinary action become abuse or crime? Consequently, even the most nonthreatening interviews often fail to uncover cases of family violence that respondents have not defined as such. This may explain why parental abuse of children is less often reported than spousal violence in victimization surveys.

In addition, many people believe that what happens within the family is a private matter, and this view is shared by men and women. NCVS surveys have consistently shown that around 60 percent of women who did not report being attacked said they considered the matter a private or personal one or they felt the offense was minor. When victims do make a decision to call officials for help, however, some find that they are physically restrained from making the call to police, or are threatened with more violence (Fleury et al., 1998;

Gracia, 2004). In the end, the most common reaction among victims who seek assistance is to approach relatives, friends, or neighbors; however, it often takes more than one episode of abuse before a battered woman seeks any assistance.

There is no typical female victim of spousal abuse, nor is it easy to predict when an assault will occur or its level of violence, although the majority of known incidents do not result in serious physical injury (Crowell and Burgess, 1996; Felson and Cares, 2005; Bergen, 1998). Where there is spousal abuse there are also likely to be abusive relationships among other family members, including abuse of children (Bergen, 1998). This provides an intergenerational link for domestic violence among family members and helps explain why violent adults often recount experiencing abuse as children (Heis, 1998). In one study investigating this "cycle of violence," being physically abused as a child *or* as an adolescent significantly increased the odds of future delinquency and adult criminality, and such children had the highest probability of future arrests for violent crime (Brezina, 1998; Office of Justice Programs, 1996; Widom, 1992). Indeed, a man who commits domestic assault is much more likely to come from a violent home in which his parents hit him as well as each other (Hanson et al., 1997; Pollack, 2004).

Although most incidents of family violence do not result in severe physical injury, there is a tendency for incidents within a family to escalate in frequency and severity with the passage of time (Crowell and Burgess, 1996). People often wonder why most battered women do not end their abusive relationships by leaving their husbands or boyfriends. The answer is complex, but revolves around vulnerability and values. Battered women who leave are often subject to criticism from family and society because they leave; if they stay they may be labeled emotionally dependent, unmotivated or dysfunctional. It is not unusual for battered women to feel some responsibility for the battering behavior of the offender: The violence reflects their failings or shortcomings as a wife or mother. Financial vulnerability may also play a role in the decision to stay, especially if there are children (Crowell and Burgess, 1996; Waldrop and Resick, 2004). A low-income or unemployed mother often faces a frightening "Catch-22": If she leaves with her children, her weak financial situation may threaten her children's welfare (they might even become homeless); if she stays, their physical safety may be in jeopardy and she may be prevented from seeing them. Women in rural areas are more likely to face major obstacles in seeking help or leaving a violent intimate relationship:

> Isolation, inadequate transportation and communication, the prevalence of guns in the home, social norms and values in rural communities, the nature of policing in rural areas, the lack of social and health care services, and inadequate housing all make it more difficult for rural battered women to deal effectively with the abuse. (Orchowsky, 1998: 1)

Some women stay in the hope that if they change their own behavior, the battering will end. It rarely, if ever, does.

When young children are victims of family violence, the potential for serious injury is always present, even though fatality rates are relatively low. Typical child injuries from severe beatings include brain damage, skull and extremity fractures, internal bleeding, and other traumas. While this type of violence can be found in all social classes, evidence indicates that it is more commonly found in poor families. In this respect, family violence reproduces the uneven class representation found for homicide and aggravated assault in general.

Significant social and psychological harms are caused by acts of violence in the family. However, abuse of women also takes place in dating relationships. One study has challenged the idea that violence is mainly found in marital relationships by conducting research on abuse of women on both U.S. and Canadian college campuses (DeKeseredy and Schwartz, 1998: 65). Surveys of college men and women show that around 75 percent of men admit having been psychologically abusive and nearly 15 percent admit physical abuse. Sexist and patriarchal beliefs on college campuses not only encourage abuse of women, they legitimize it as well. The same study found that men who abuse their partners or girlfriends in college share a number of characteristics: They tend to have patriarchal views on the family, friends who perpetrate and legitimize abuse of women, experience with pornography, and they drink and/or use drugs often, frequently with their dating partners (DeKeseredy and Schwartz, 1998: 123). We shall return to these features and their relationship to crime later in this chapter.

RAPE

Around the early 1970s, this argument surfaced in the emergent feminist literature (Brownmiller, 1975; Russell, 1983): There is a popular image of rape that has been fostered by males and that sustains certain myths about rape and the rapist. This image emphasizes the violence of male attackers who appear from nowhere to vent their repressed sexual desires by raping unsuspecting females who do everything possible to prevent the rapist from succeeding. This popular view reflects and perpetuates the following ideas:

- Males dominate females.
- A woman's body, especially her vagina, is a man's property, and, like any other property, can be stolen by those to whom it does not belong. (Historically, when married women took the name of their husband, this signified a property relationship.)
- "Good" women will defend that property at almost any cost.

- Normal males will not need to resort to force in order to acquire the sexual property represented by a woman—they learn to do it in other ways.

Armed with these images, society is encouraged to view true rape as infrequent, extreme behavior, whereas "normal" male sexual—and political, economic, legal, and cultural—domination of women is considered appropriate and acceptable.

Rape and the Criminal Law

Not surprisingly, then, the popular image of rape has been mirrored in legal definitions of the offense. Common-law tradition long emphasized lack of victim consent, physical resistance, the use of force, actual penetration of the vagina, and no prior offender-victim sexual intimacy. Physical injuries, torn clothing, and disarray at the scene of the alleged rape were just some of the things courts looked for in establishing that force occurred and was met by active resistance. Under common law, the victim was expected to resist vigorously and repeatedly. Modern courts, though recognizing that resistance is not a clear-cut issue, are inclined nevertheless to treat active physical resistance as an important factor in establishing that rape actually occurred. Historically, prosecutors screened out cases where evidence of force and active resistance was weak, and the practice still continues.

Offender-victim relationships are also important. Historically, and to some extent today, rape accusations are looked upon with suspicion in cases where there is anything more than passing acquaintance. For example, jurisdictions now acknowledge that it is possible for a husband to rape his wife, although there are often legal loopholes. Traditionally, a rape defendant who could show that he has had prior sexual intimacies with his accuser has a strong point in his favor if the case reached court.

With the advent of so-called **rape shield laws,** states can bar evidence of previous consensual sex between victim and suspect. Retired U.S. Supreme Court judge Sandra Day O'Connor once said: "Rape victims deserve heightened protection against surprise, harassment and unnecessary invasions of privacy" (quoted in Gibbs 1991: 4). By the mid-1980s most states as well as the federal government had introduced some version of rape shield laws. Now every state has them in place. However, testimony about the prior sexual activity of the victim may be permissible in certain cases, such as when a judge feels it is necessary in order to protect the rights of the accused.

From the time of the earliest legal codes, the true rape victim has been pictured as a sexually naive woman, usually a virgin. Indeed, the Code of Hammurabi and the ancient Jewish laws specifically distinguished between virgins and nonvirgins in their treatment of rape. According to these early codes, a married woman could not be raped, but if she were sexually assaulted by someone other than her husband, both parties could be charged with adultery, a capital offense. Furthermore, ancient Jewish laws did not rely solely on the distinction between virgins and nonvirgins, for they ignored the virginity of those women raped within the city walls. In such cases, complicity was assumed, "for the elders reasoned that if the girl had screamed she would have been rescued" (Brownmiller, 1975: 20).

The traditional view of rape has focused on penile-vaginal intercourse, but feminists have been successful in getting some states to change rape laws to include oral and anal sex and the use of any object to effect even the slightest degree of penetration. Diana Russell comments on the traditional definition, saying,

> The focus on [penile] penetration of the vagina has often been seen as a vestige of an outdated patriarchal notion that female purity and virtue requires a vagina that has not been penetrated. According to this perspective, a female who has experienced all manner of "foreplay," including oral or anal sex, whether voluntary or involuntary, may still be regarded as a virgin. (1983: 43)

The Official Record on Rape

According to the FBI, nearly 100,000 rapes are reported to the police each year in the United States. The FBI considers not only completed rapes under its definition, but also assaults and attempts to commit rape as well. As you might expect, however, the true rate of victimization is far, far greater. Some estimates put the figure at ten times the official rate, but many of these are based on definitions of rape that include almost any unwelcome sexual contact. The National Crime Victimization Survey, which has recently revised its questions on rape and sexual assault, indicates that there were approximately 272,000 rapes in 2006 (Bureau of Justice Statistics, 2007).

There is one point of agreement between these two official counts of rape: Both the UCR and the NCVS report that the rate of *completed* rapes has declined over the last several decades, although recently the rate has increased (see figure 4.1).

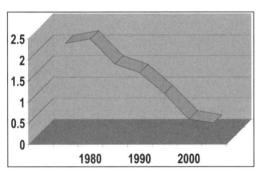

▲ **Figure 4.1.**
Rape/Sexual Assault Victimization per 1,000 Persons Aged Twelve and Over, 1975–2006.
While the rape and sexual assault victimization rate declined from 1980 to 2000, the rates have increased in the last few years.
Source: Bureau of Justice Statistics (2007).

As far as *intra*gender rape is concerned—men assaulting other men and women assaulting other women—the picture is even more murky. Estimates of the extent of intragender sexual assault vary considerably, but there seems to be no question that the true rate is far greater than official records indicate

(Preble, Groth, and Sgroi, 2002). According to NCVS data for the years 1987 through 1991 and 1998, the rape victimization rate for males was twenty per one hundred thousand males. More recent NCVS data indicate that about 7 percent of the victims of rape are men, presumably victimized by other men (Bureau of Justice Statistics, 2006).

Reporting and Nonreporting of Sexual Assault

The difference between police and other rates can be explained in large part by two things: victim reluctance to report offenses and police labeling practices. For example, NCVS data has shown for many years that fewer than half of all rapes are reported to the police. The most recent NCSV statistics suggest that the reporting of rape is even less, at 41 percent (Bureau of Justice Statistics, 2007). The likelihood that a victim will not report the offense increases if she knows her attacker, if no weapon is used, and if she is not physically injured.

The most common reasons given for not reporting a sexual assault are:

- It was considered private or personal, or the victim would take care of it herself.
- The victim feared reprisal.
- Police would be inefficient, ineffective, or insensitive.
- The victim had little or no proof, or no way to find the attacker.
- The victim reported it to someone else.

When victims do report the rape to police, the most common reasons are:

- The victim wished to keep the incident from happening again.
- The victim wished to punish the offender.
- The victim wished to fulfill what he or she saw as a duty.
- The victim wished to get help. (Office of Justice Programs, 2003; also Bachman, 1994: 12)

The reasons for reporting or not reporting vary according to whether the victim was attacked by a stranger or an acquaintance. Victims of rapes by strangers are much less likely to consider the matter private or personal and are less likely to fear reprisal. Victims who did report rapes were more likely to cite punishing the offender or fulfilling one's duty when the rapist was a stranger (Harlow, 1991: 13). Other studies generally confirm these findings (e.g., McDermott, 1979).

Using victimization data, Alan Lizotte (1985) concluded that factors likely to make the legal case strong—the offender is a stranger, he did not belong where the rape occurred, and the victim sustained injury—weigh more heavily in the victim's reporting decision in rape incidents than in other assaults. However, Lizotte also found that white women raped by black men were less likely to report the assault to police. He speculates this may be due to humiliation and embarrassment or the failure to appreciate that the chances of prosecution and conviction are increased in this situation.

Victimization surveys unlock the door to the dark figure of crime, but how wide the door is opened is a matter of debate, especially with regard to crimes such as rape and sexual molestation. Elizabeth Stanko found that much violence against women is hidden in that incidents are not easily called to mind even by victims who want to do so:

> One woman, a 63-year-old widow, assured me that she would not have very much to contribute to my study. When the interview was complete, she recalled being fondled by a shop owner when she was 8, feeling physically threatened by her brother as an adult, being attacked as a nurse while working at night in a hospital, and being hassled by men for sexual favors after the death of her husband. (1990: 11)

As women began to talk more freely about rape, the manner in which rape complaints were received by police officials surfaced time and again as a factor in nonreporting. Rape victims are often subjected to intense and sometimes hostile questioning quite unlike that experienced by victims of burglaries, robberies, and other crimes. One victim gave this account of her experience:

> They rushed me down to the housing cops who asked me questions like "Was he your boy-friend?" "Did you know him?" Here I am, hysterical, I'm 12 years old, and I don't know these things even happen to people. Anyway, they took me to the precinct after that, and there, about four detectives got me in the room and asked how long was his penis—like I was supposed to measure it. Actually, they said, "How long was the instrument?" I thought they were referring to the knife—how was I supposed to know? That I could have told them 'cause I was sure enough lookin' at the knife. (Brownmiller, 1975: 365)

In court, rape victims are subject to the rigors of a cross-examination in which they are required to recall, in explicit detail, the humiliating and frightening encounter with the alleged rapist. Of course, rape is a serious offense in all jurisdictions, and defense attorneys quite naturally seek to discredit the testimony of victims and demonstrate that a real rape did not occur. From the standpoint of the victim who wonders whether to report her rape to the authorities, however, the problem is a very real one and may be resolved only by a decision to keep silent.

People and Circumstances

Studies of rape during the 1960s and early 1970s suggested that the popular image of rape accurately depicts only a small portion of all rape incidents (see Amir, 1971; Brown, 1974). The publication of more recent research has left some of the earlier findings in doubt (e.g., Bachman, 1994). Before turning to the conflicting evidence, however, points of agreement will be reviewed.

First, both rape offenders and victims tend to be young, usually under twenty-five. In absolute terms, more white women are raped than black women, and more white men rape than black men. However, the probabilities of being a victim or an offender are significantly higher for African Americans than for whites. The most likely victims and offenders in rape incidents, regardless of race, come from relatively low socioeconomic neighborhoods in the nation's larger cities, again mirroring other interpersonal violence (Office of Justice Programs, 2006).

Second, rape is mainly an intraracial offense when seen from the victim's viewpoint—black women are most often raped by black men, and white women by white men. However, when viewed from the offender's standpoint, around half the black assailants in victimization surveys raped white women, while white assailants almost never raped black women. The percentage of rapes that are interracial—black on white or white on black—increases considerably when there is more than one assailant.

Various reasons may be suggested to account for the white/black disparities in rape victimization. Opportunity may be a factor in that the greater mobility of white women relative to black women makes them more vulnerable to sudden-attack predatory crimes by strangers. However, it could also be that cultural and historical images of race and gender, reinforced by structured inequities, make sexual assault of white women appealing to some black males as a means of demonstrating power and control while demeaning whites in the process. On the other hand, for many black offenders this sort of politicization of rape may be far from their minds; they may choose white women as targets because mainstream white society bombards them with cultural stereotypes of the desirability and attractiveness of white women. The impact of such cultural stereotypes is surely heightened by the aura of forbidden fruit: Sexual intimacy between black men and white women is still frowned on in many quarters.

A third point of agreement in the research on rape is that most rapes are likely to occur in private or semiprivate locations such as homes, apartments, automobiles, or parking garages. This is especially true when the rapist is known by the victim. When strangers are involved, initial contact between the rapist and victim often occurs outdoors or in public places such as bars and theaters, but the single most common location for the actual assault is inside a home, usually the victim's. Women living alone are most vulnerable to rape.

Fourth, rapists are usually unarmed. NCVS data from 2005 shows that 85 percent of rapes are committed without a weapon, 3 percent with a gun, and 3 percent with a knife (Bureau of Justice Statistics, 2006). When they are armed, rapists who know their victim tend to carry knives, while strangers are as likely to carry guns as they are knives (Bachman, 1994: 12). Even though it is rare, the presence of a weapon significantly increases the probability that the rape attack will be completed.

Finally, the vast majority of women who are raped (73 percent in 2005) are victimized by someone they know; most of the offenders are identified as friends or acquaintances (Bureau of Justice Statistics, 2006). This is explained partly by convenience and opportunity, and partly by the fact that potential offenders more easily rationalize and justify sexual attacks against women they already have a relationship with or know well.

One point of debate is the extent of injury associated with rape. There is no question that the psychological trauma associated with rape victimization is severe and potentially devastating—*Rape Trauma Syndrome* is the medically accepted term for it—but what about physical injuries? An early national victimization survey looked in detail at the injury question, and M. Joan McDermott concludes:

> Briefly, most rape and most attempted rape victims who were attacked were injured. Injuries included rape and attempted rape injuries, as well as additional injuries....

[M]ost often the additional injury was in the form of bruises, cuts, scratches, and black eyes. These survey data on injury suggest that the element of violence in rape is the physical force used to attempt and/or achieve sexual intercourse with a woman against her will. Generally, it does not appear to be violence in the form of additional, capricious beatings, stabbings, and so forth.

This conclusion receives confirmation from more recent studies (Crane, 2006; National Research Council, 1996). (1979: 36–38)

Both popular and legal images of rape place considerable emphasis on the violence of rape and the physical resistance of the victim. The impression gained from Amir's Philadelphia study is that rape victims put up token verbal resistance. The national victimization surveys, using a different categorization of resistance, established a rather different picture. Most victims took measures to protect themselves by screaming, by trying to use some form of physical force against the attacker, or by attempting to flee. A study of rapes in London also found that most victims took protective measures (Smith, 1989).

When potential victims resist a rape attack they increase the chances that the rape will not be completed, but at the same time they may increase the risk of more serious injury. A review of the available research "suggests that resistance does not result in an increase in *severe* injury . . . and that it is the attacker's level of aggression and not the victim's level of resistance which is more directly correlated with injury" (Grace, 1993: 23). While most of the research focuses on the victim, it is the offender's *perception* of the effectiveness of resistance that is surely an important element in his behavior.

One study using NCVS data found that when victims resist *with a weapon*, the chances of further injury are significantly reduced. The authors conclude that since victims cannot predict what an attacker will do, "the best course of action for most rape victims is to resist, preferably with a weapon" (Kleck and Sayles, 1990: 161). The authors also list attracting attention, running away, and hiding as appropriate types of resistance if a victim does not have a weapon at hand. However, any blanket recommendation about resistance as a strategy for women (or men) should acknowledge research showing that resistance is least likely to be successful when the attack occurs indoors and when the offender is someone the victim knows (see Grace, 1993: 21).

Marital Rape

Legal developments in recent years have led to a significant change in the scope of rape laws: A husband may be held liable for rape if he forces sexual intercourse on his resisting wife. This possibility has existed for many years in Norway, Sweden, and Denmark and in many communist countries, but only since the late 1970s has Anglo-American law encompassed the idea. By the early 1990s a number of Australian states, Canada, New Zealand, and Great Britain had abolished the marital rape exemption. Earlier, in 1980, the Israeli Supreme Court had dismissed a husband's appeal of his conviction for marital rape, arguing that the Talmud prohibits forced sexual intercourse between a man and his wife (Russell, 1983: 336).

In America today the possibility of rape in marriage is recognized in all states and by the federal criminal code (Bergen, 1996; 2006). One landmark decision that helped pave the way for the burgeoning of laws against marital rape was a 1985 Georgia Supreme Court ruling that upheld the conviction of a man who raped and sodomized his wife. The court argued that the marriage vow does not mean that a wife must always submit to a husband's sexual demands (Reid, 1989: 152).

This represents a significant departure from legal tradition going back hundreds—even thousands—of years. These traditions were born of patriarchy, with the wife always the loser. Matthew Hale, the seventeenth-century English jurist whose caution on rape (that it is easy to charge and difficult to defend) has long guided judges and legislators, was unquestionably a misogynist (Geis, 1978b; Bergen, 1996). Recent changes in marital rape laws also reflect the influence of the feminist movement, showing yet again how important the pressure of organized interest groups is in the realm of law.

A recent study found that between 10 and 14 percent of all married women are sexually assaulted in their marriage (Martin, Tafta, and Resick, 2007). This estimate is consistent with other studies of marital rape. One of the earliest and most well-known studies was conducted by Diana Russell. She conducted interviews with 930 women aged eighteen and over living in San Francisco, and of these women, 644 were or had been married and were the major focus of her study. Russell defined rape as forced sexual activity that involves intercourse, oral sex, anal sex, or forced digital penetration. One in seven of these women had been the victims of at least one completed or attempted rape by a husband or ex-husband, 10 percent had been the victims of both rape and other forms of physical abuse, and 15 percent had been victims of either rape or other abuse, but not both. Most of the completed incidents involved penile penetration: 9 percent involved anal or oral sex. Thirty-one percent were isolated cases, but another 31 percent involved more than twenty different attacks, sometimes over a period of weeks or even over a period of more than five years. Alcohol was frequently present before or during the incidents, though Russell points out that no simple connection could be identified: Sometimes it appeared to be a factor and sometimes it did not (1983: 156–66).

The demographics of Russell's marital rape cases are particularly striking in light of other research on rape. White rapists were slightly overrepresented, and husbands were equally likely to hold lower-class, middle-class, or upper-middle-class jobs. Most of the husbands had at least some college education, and fewer than 20 percent were living at or

below the poverty line at the time of the first incident. The majority of rapists were between the ages of twenty-one and thirty-five. These findings depart from those commonly reported for rape in general. Russell warns against generalizations, however, as her study was plagued by refusals from many of the subjects initially contacted for interviews. On the other hand, it is probable that if cases such as those described by Russell were fully represented in victimization surveys, the demographics of sexual assault would look less young, less black, and less lower class.

Angela Browne's interviews with battered wives disclosed that many had also been raped. But the interviews also disclosed that women who eventually killed their husbands were more likely to report they had been raped often and violently. Many of these women felt that the only way out of their fearful and humiliating marital life was by the death of their tormentors, yet most were also sorry that their husbands had died (1987: 140–41).

David Finkelhor and Kersti Yllo (1985) conducted in-depth interviews with fifty women who had been sexually abused by their spouses. They constructed a typology of rapes based on their findings:

- *Battering rapes*: The sexual violence is part of a generally abusive relationship.
- *Nonbattering rapes*: The sexual violence grows out of other sexual conflicts, for example, a long-standing disagreement over the timing or setting of sex, or even the act itself.
- *Obsessive rapes*: These reflect bizarre sexual obsessions on the part of the male, perhaps related to pornography, sometimes a result of the need for force or ritual in order to get aroused.

Battering rapes were the most common; obsessive rapes, the least.

Another study of marital rape was authored by Raquel Kennedy Bergen. She interviewed forty survivors of wife rape and found that they had very different experiences. Some were physically forced into the act, others were physically battered as a means to rape, and still others were sadistically raped. Many of the women had difficulty defining their rape as indeed "rape":

> They may see sex in marriage as their obligation, or laws and stereotypes about "real rape" in this society may hinder their ability to name their experience wife rape.... [H]aving redefined their experiences as rape, many women decide to end the violence. (Bergen, 1996: 94)

Ultimately, many of the victims traced the source of their rape to the husbands' desire for control or to punish their spouse, or to their view that sexual assault of a wife was a matter of "entitlement."

Date Rape

Historically, dating has been an important social institution for both males and females. For the female it marked the conventional road to courtship and marriage and provided the opportunity to practice her "proper" role as the deferential, acquiescent, admiring, and passive partner. For the male dating provided the conventional road to marriage, but it also gave him the chance to demonstrate independence, masculinity, and action. As the expected initiator of sexual play, the male has been encouraged to view his female companion as a sexual object to be won. His success is measured by how far he gets.

The goal of success in this particular demonstration of masculinity may not be shared by the man's female friend. When this happens, the interaction may become a physical confrontation. Influenced perhaps by the effects of a few drinks or by what he has wrongly interpreted as sexual acquiescence by his female companion, the rejected male refuses to back off. He reaches a point at which, in his own mind (and, he presumes, in the minds of other males), his masculinity is being put to

the test (see Schwartz and DeKeseredy, 1997; Weis and Borges, 1973). Indeed, "[f]or many young women, negotiating adolescent heterosexuality is also negotiating sexual safety. How to say no or yes, without losing companionship, intimacy and the status involved in coupledom, is learnt from experience. Young women juggle sexuality and safety and, at the same time, keep their eye on their social respectability" (Stanko, 1990: 94).

Certainly, not all males subscribe to the masculine ideal of sexual conquest, nor do most dates end in physical confrontations and sexual assault. However, studies indicate that rape and attempted rape during a date are by no means rare, and when they occur, offenders come from all walks of life. Studies on college campuses show that both male and female students—in some cases as many as 27 percent of those interviewed—could recall instances in which they had committed or been the victims of sexual assault during a date, and as many as 60 percent recall being petted, fondled, or kissed against their will (Schwartz and DeKeseredy, 1997; Murphy, 1984; Warshaw, 1989; Feltey, 1991; Allison and Wrightsman: 1993: 6).

Many, perhaps most, date rapes go unreported, but one thing is clear: It is unlikely that date rape will fade from the cultural landscape anytime soon. And this is partly because of enduring myths and misconceptions about rape.

Myths and Misconceptions about Rape

Some—perhaps many—males are quick to point out that rape can be justified. Such a view is characteristic of a patriarchal society in which social interaction is gender based and males are structurally and culturally dominant:

> Rape and sexual violence against women are reproduced and legitimated through culturally mediated interpretative devices which justify, excuse, and glorify male violence against females. Rape myths, techniques of neutralization, or, more generally, patriarchal ideologies provide the linguistic rationaliza-

tions and interpretive frameworks for assessing the rape incident: for making sense of what happened, and for legitimating the sexual scripts governing male-female interactions. (Matoesian, 1993: 13)

A number of myths and falsehoods mark the female as a legitimate target of male sexual aggression (see box 4.1). Some women, it is said, need to be raped: They have stepped out of line; they are not passive or submissive and thus must be reminded of their place. Some women, it is said, deserve to be raped: They have been too submissive, and thus any man can have them, or they have (heaven forbid) rejected the male as a sex partner altogether. Then again, some men say, "When a woman says no, she really means yes," or "In their hearts all women want to be raped."

A survey of Minnesota men provides evidence of the prevalence of such views. Seventy-one percent of the respondents believed that women have an unconscious desire to be raped, and 48 percent felt that going bra-less and wearing short skirts was an invitation to rape (Hotchkiss, 1978).

If you think rape myths are a thing of the past, recent research has shown that they still exist (Johnson, Kuck, and Schander, 1997; Schwartz and DeKeseredy, 1997). One study found that of the 143 college students surveyed, about 33 percent of the respondents said that men "have sexual urges they cannot control" and 43.9 percent thought that "all men are capable of rape, given the right situation" (Johnson, Kuck, and Schander, 1997: 696). This study also found that "males and those upholding traditional gender role beliefs were more likely to accept certain myths that blame the woman, excuse the male, and justify acquaintance rape compared to females and those who supported less traditional gender role beliefs" (697). A more recent study found that men who are members of fraternities, and particularly those males who place "pinup" posters on their walls, are more likely to accept rape myths (Bleecker and Murnen, 2005).

One of the best ways to look at the absurdity of rape myths and justifications is by applying them to bank robbery. Among possible justifications would be:

1. The bank says "yes" to a loan and then changes its mind.
2. The bank has led the applicant to believe he/she will receive a loan.
3. Through advertisement, the bank has got the loan applicant "excited."

BOX 4.1. SOME MYTHS ABOUT SEXUAL ASSAULT

Despite dramatic cultural changes over the last few decades in the United States, myths about rape and sexual endure.

- Women are sexually assaulted because they "ask for it" in some way.
- Sexual assault cannot happen to a respectable woman.
- Only the young or beautiful are sexually assaulted.
- Most women fantasize about rape and actually enjoy it.
- Sexual assaults are usually a spontaneous result of an urgent need for sex.
- Most sexual assaults are interracial.
- Most sexual assault victims react hysterically.
- Men cannot be sexually assaulted.
- Sexual assault only occurs in dark alleys and isolated areas.
- Most victims are assaulted by strangers.
- Rape is no big deal; it's only sex, and most women aren't really hurt anyway.

4. The bank has given the person a loan before.
5. The applicant "really needs" the money.
6. The bank has loaned other people money.
7. The loan officer goes to a party with the applicant where he knows drinking and drug use will be going on. (Sanders, 1983: 266)

It is small wonder that progressive people, feminist groups, and some politicians are calling for urgent and continued efforts to educate people of all ages and backgrounds in the realities of sexual violence. This is one step toward removing the myths and confusion surrounding rape and other sexual abuse. In spite of this, many people—women included—persist in blaming the victim.

Blaming the Victim

It is not unusual for victims to be blamed for their suffering, and this practice diverts attention from the real causes of victimizing behavior. Implied **victim blaming** phrases might include: "Don't hitchhike"; "Don't accept when a new acquaintance invites you to his apartment for drinks"; "Don't go out at night on your own"; "Don't wear sexy clothes"; "Don't initiate sexual play"; and, above all, "Don't promise what you won't deliver!" If you are a woman, be what you are supposed to be: vulnerable, demure, passive, dependent, and proper.

Although victim blaming seems to be a generalized response to rape in our culture, it is most likely to surface in the following situations:

- when there has been a prior association between the assailant and victim;
- when the victim has behaved in a nontraditional way;
- when the rape occurred close to the victim's home;

- when the community as a whole espouses patriarchal values and has rigid sex-role traditions; and
- when observers see themselves as vulnerable to rape but have followed "rules" to avoid it.

A study of events following the infamous "pool table" gang rape of a woman who stopped into a bar for a drink in New Bedford, Massachusetts, shows also that victim blaming may be linked to a community's efforts to defend itself in the glare of publicity (Chancer, 1987).

Some victim blaming is really a denial that women are rapable. Consider this comment from a male juror:

I don't think a woman can be raped. . . . I ask why are they out at that time of the night? What did they do to provoke it? . . . A judge over in Ohio told me that a woman can run faster with her pants down than a man, and I believe that. . . . If you want to say rape, then she must be unconscious. She can scream and kick if she's awake and doesn't want it. (LaFree, 1989: 225)

Myths about rape impede the search for understanding and reinforce stereotypes and bigotry that often surround them. This is no less true in the case of intragender rape:

Myths about the nature of rape impede awareness and recognition; many people assume that male-to-male rape occurs only among homosexual or heterosexual men who are incarcerated and have no other sexual outlet. In actuality, like female victims, most male victims are assaulted by an acquaintance. Furthermore, neither the perpetrator nor the victim is necessarily homosexual. (Allison and Wrightsman, 1993: 48–49)

Pornography and Rape

Pornography mostly involves the objectification of women so that their body parts are defined as sex instruments. Furthermore, in some pornography, rape is represented as a part of sexual relations, and the victim is usually depicted as being aroused by the experience, if not actively enjoying it (Ashley and Ashley, 1984). Several studies of convicted rapists have discovered that many of the victimizers justified their violent infliction of pain on the grounds that the victim had experienced an orgasm (Scully and Marolla, 1985: 253).

If there is a causal relationship between pornography and sexual violence, it remains unclear, despite—or perhaps because of—the 1986 report of the Commission on Pornography headed by former attorney general Edwin Meese. This commission did no research of its own, nor did it even conduct a comprehensive literature review, relying instead on testimony at six public hearings around the country. Much of the testimony was composed of horror stories from people claiming to have been victimized by pornography and from representatives of antipornography groups (see also Baron and Straus, 1990: 189). Testimony from social scientists was inconsistent and often cautionary, but a majority of the commission's members chose to ignore this fact.

There seems to be growing consensus that the portrayal of women in pornography, especially pornography depicting force or violence, provides cultural approval of the sexual objectification of women and their subordination to the desires and commands of men. To that extent, pornography provides part of the culturally acquired vocabulary that can be used to justify and excuse male sexual violence directed against women. In their study of state variations in rape rates, Larry Baron and Murray Straus (1990) found a positive correlation between the circulation of sex magazines and rape rates among states, and their interpretation of the finding is consistent with this argument.

However, these authors also caution against censorship of pornography on the following grounds:

1. It "paves the way for prohibition of controversial or unpopular political ideas, including feminist ideas, and helps to establish a social climate in which censorship is morally acceptable."
2. "[T]here is no scientific evidence that pornography without violent content increases aggression toward women."
3. "[V]iolence not sex is the real problem."
4. "[P]ornography is less violent than other media."
5. "[P]ornography is no more sexist than other media."
6. There are more important ways that society can combat violence and sexism. (Baron and Straus, 1990: 190–91)

Many rapists see women "as sexual commodities to be used or conquered rather than as human beings with rights and feelings. Rape "is not an idiosyncratic act committed by a few 'sick' men. Rather, rape can be viewed as the end point on a continuum of sexually aggressive behaviors that reward men and victimize women" (Scully and Marolla, 1985: 261–62). According to a study of 132 rapists, these rewards are numerous, including revenge and the ability to exact punishment, to express anger, and to exercise power and control (Hale, 1997). Some women were raped because they had had an affair, some because they filed for divorce, and others merely because the offender was having a "bad day."

SEXUAL ABUSE OF CHILDREN

Although the most likely victims of rape are older teenagers and young adults, children, including the very young, are sometimes the victims of sexual assaults. In addition to sexual assault, the wider problem of **child maltreatment** includes instances of physical abuse, neglect, and emotional abuse. We will focus on the former, which is defined as the exploitation of a child for the sexual gratification of an adult, as in rape, incest, fondling of the genitals, exhibitionism, or pornography. Studies have generally found that about 16.8 percent of adult women and 7.9 percent of men were sexually abused in some way when they were children (Putnam, 2003). As figure 4.2 shows, young females suffer from the highest rate of rape.

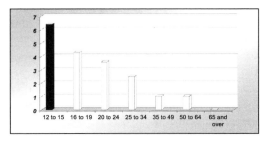

▲ Figure 4.2.
Distribution of Sexual Assault by Age Groups
Victimization surveys show that younger women are more likely to be raped than older women. Of those over twelve years of age, those between the ages of sixteen and nineteen have the highest rate of victimization (3.2 per 1,000 persons.)
Source: Office of Justice Programs (2006).

As with the rapist, there is a popular image of the child molester. He is the stranger who lurks around playgrounds, parks, and other places where children wander and who lures or drags his victims into his car or home, where he then sexually assaults them. This image is no more accurate than the one of rape and the rapist. For example, the child molester is not usually a stranger. Several studies show that this type of context is rare, accounting for only 3 to 4 percent of all sexual assaults on children. In studies both in the United States and abroad, researchers are finding that in most cases of child molestation the offender and victim are acquainted with each other. More than 70 percent of the perpetrators of sexual abuse against children are males, while most charged with neglect are female (U.S. Department of Health and Human Services, 2007).

It is estimated that one in five sexually abused boys goes on to molest children sexually (Watkins and Bentovim, 1992). Female incest victims are more likely than non-sexually abused females to die at a young age, commit suicide, become addicted to hard drugs and alcohol, prostitute themselves, and suffer a host of psychological and developmental problems (Fraad, 1997). One study found that 38 percent of women and girls who were incestuously victimized by their fathers attempted suicide (Fraad, 1997).

There are many forms of child maltreatment. Emotional and physical threats carried out by parents and caretakers are particularly likely to escape official criminal justice system scrutiny

Most experts believe that molesters rarely resort to physical violence, and when a child does offer resistance it is most likely overcome by threats of deprivation (loss of love, affection, or privileges) or by rewards (candy or money) (Schneider, 1997). Victim resistance and use of physical coercion by offenders most often occur in sexual incidents involving strangers, which is what one would expect. Victim compliance is problematic when love and affection or familial ties are absent.

Some important points of agreement among researchers are that child molesters come from all walks of life, are of varied ages, engage in different sorts of sexual acts, and choose different types of child victims. About the only common characteristic is that they are most often males who target young females—the most likely victim is eleven to fourteen years old (Vander-May and Neff, 1984; Schultz, 2005).

There are four basic types of child sexual abusers:

1. the regressive offender, who turns to children after rejection by those in his own age group;
2. the fixed offender, who is fixated on and fanatically obsessed with children as sexual objects;
3. the exploiting offender, who generally desires power over children and obtains this power through sexual means; and
4. the sadistic offender, who gains sexual pleasure by inflicting physical pain or killing children. (Bartol, 1995)

Sadistic offenders are the least common and exploiting offenders are probably the most common. According to a recent study of 140 child molesters, Dawn Fisher, Anthony Beech, and Kevin Browne (1999) found that child molesters have lower levels of self-esteem, higher levels of loneliness and personal distress, and little empathy for victims. This may underscore the motivations for the regressive offender and the exploiting offender.

As we indicated above, most sexually abused children are victimized by someone they know. The most frequent group of offenders are family members, including fathers, grandfathers, uncles, and males in stepfamilies. The next most frequent group of offenders are nonfamilial acquaintances such as neighbors, babysitters, teachers, and members of the clergy (Schneider, 1997). In cases in which family members or relatives of the molester are victimized, the offense has usually been committed over a period of weeks, months, or years. Given the ongoing intimate but nonsexual interaction between relatives and family members, this is not surprising. In addition, the sexual encounters themselves may have developed in an atmosphere that encouraged physical demonstrations of affection and love. Incestuous desire on the part of both adult and child may be a natural—though not condoned—consequence of close, personal, and satisfying relations between family members. Thus, what begins as a loving nonsexual relationship between an adult and a child may, with the passage of time, expand to include repetitive sexual interactions (White, 1972: 160–71).

As noted, most societies do not condone incest or other sex acts between family members or between adults and children in general. It is hard to imagine that molesters are, as a group, unaware that they have moved beyond acceptable boundaries of sexual conduct. Like other sex offenders, a few may be mentally deficient or suffering from severe psychiatric disorders, but most are clearly aware of their transgressions, and, like many other criminals, they disavow their actions or try to justify them (Schneider, 1997).

When asked to account for their actions, child molesters explain away their conduct in various ways: by blaming it on a temporary loss of sense or rationality ("I was drunk"; "I didn't know what I was doing"; "Everything went blank"), by blaming it on the behavior of the victim ("She wanted me to do it"; "He started it"), or by blaming it on conditions of family life or on other personal troubles. A classic study found that the most common single response to the question "Why?" was to blame the offense on a temporary loss of rationality (McCaghy, 1967; also see Schneider and Wright, 2004). The offenders most likely to deny their deviance in this way were those who had used force to obtain compliance and those who had molested female children.

Finding Out about Sexual Molestation

Learning the details surrounding cases of child molestation is not easy, especially when very young children are victimized. Except when brutal physical abuses are involved (a small minority of known cases), even the nature of the sexual encounter itself may be difficult to determine. From the standpoint of criminal law, the nature and gravity of the offense hinge on the details of the encounter. Especially important when the victim is an older child, fourteen or fifteen years old, are the issues of resistance and consent. Did the child resist? Did the child consent to the sexual act or even encourage it? Was compliance secured by the use or threat of physical force? In dealing with those questions, investigators are often confronted with conflicting pictures of an incident. However, even young children remember details and testify more accurately than is generally believed. This has been supported by recent research, which, for example estimates that less than 10 percent of children's portrayal of the events could be reasonably judged as false (Schneider, 1997). However, one potential problem for a prosecutor in sexual abuse cases is that child victims remember much more about the actions that took place than about when and where they took place or the identity of the offender. The view that there is a pressing need for better methods of interviewing children is widely shared, and government-funded research is now addressing the problem.

Not surprisingly, many children who are sexually abused find it difficult to report their experience to the authorities, especially so if they were victimized by a family member or acquaintance. Even when reported, children face other problems. As one study found:

> Participants (sexually abused children) reported little support from parents when disclosing sexual abuse. Participants who disclosed sexual abuse described being discouraged from initiating protective action against a boyfriend, father, friend, or relative. A female participant who had been sexually abused by a stranger stated that after disclosure, her father threatened to file charges against the abuser, yet called the participant who was raped a "whore." (Champion, 1999: 712)

Significant numbers of legitimate complaints of child sexual abuse are designated as "unfounded" by authorities. One study looked at 576 reports of sexual abuse received by the Denver Department of Social Services and found that 47 percent had been designated as unfounded. However, after review, the authors concluded that only 8 percent of these cases were probably fictitious reports. The remainder had been classified as unfounded primarily because of insufficient information or because appropriate suspicion could not be substantiated through investigation (Jones and McGraw, 1987).

Various strategies have been advanced to reveal the facts behind reports of child sexual abuse. These range from the use of anatomically correct dolls to videotaping testimony and the use of closed-circuit television to allow victims to testify in court from another room (see Freeman and Estrada-Mullaney, 1988; Whitcomb, 1985). However, the U.S. Supreme Court ruled in *Maryland v. Craig* (1990) that alternatives to courtroom confrontation of the witness may be made available only to children expected to suffer severe emotional trauma if made to testify in the traditional manner. In addition, innovative methods may not be necessary in most cases of abuse.

The primary reason for concern over courtroom testimony of child victims is the trauma associated with it. Available research indicates that most children deal with the experience reasonably well, but long-term effects are less predictable. Three studies of the problem found that while children score high on anxiety and stress prior to their involvement in the court process, most improved with the passage of time regardless of their experience in court. Further, the improvements in these children's mental health were directly associated with the strong support of their mothers (Whitcomb et al., 1994). However, an important difference in findings also emerged: In one study children who testified showed more improvement in their mental health than those who did not, while in the other two studies the reverse was found. The report concludes: "Based on these studies it cannot be stated conclusively that testifying is either harmful or beneficial to sexually abused children" (Whitcomb et al., 1994, 5).

Any complete and accurate picture of child molesting and the child molester is far away. Much research is still needed, and the greater willingness of people to talk about sensitive sexual issues will aid in that endeavor. Even so, most incidents of child molestation will remain hidden, particularly those offenses in which physical force and abuse are not employed and that involve offenders and victims who are familiar with each other and are associated in continuing relationships of a nonsexual kind. Many states now have child abuse hotlines and mandatory reporting laws. These will undoubtedly result in many more cases coming to light, but there is a downside: Some parents will not take their child to a counselor or seek other help precisely because they do not want the incident reported.

REACTIONS TO DOMESTIC VIOLENCE, RAPE, AND THE SEXUAL ABUSE OF CHILDREN

Although it has been a problem for centuries, domestic violence has only recently become the subject of a formalized criminal justice response. Rape and sexual acts with minors, on the other hand, have long been regarded as heinous crimes. Even when legal codes were in their formative stages, little sympathy was extended to rapists, child molesters, and those committing incest with children. The usual penalties were death, banishment, and, in recent years, long prison sentences. Notwithstanding this tradition, public and official reactions to offenders have not been clear-cut. Though generally punitive, reactions have depended on who the offender is, who the victim is, and what kind of interactions the two had.

Reactions to Domestic Violence

The conventional response to domestic violence has been a restrained one at best, and more typically one of disinterest. This reflects a reluctance to get involved in family disputes: When men were asked by researchers what they would do if a friend was hitting his partner in front of them, this reply was typical: "Nothing . . . it's none of my business is it? . . . it's between those two. I'd tell him he was out of order afterwards and that he should go back and make sure she's alright and that but I wouldn't interfere" (Bush and Hood-Williams, 1995: 13). Even many victims feel that domestic violence is a private matter.

Some police officers believe that responding to domestic disturbances is not real police work. It is often seen as "uninteresting and unexciting, ranking alongside lost dogs, rowdy youth and bothersome drunks" (Grace, 1995: 1). Even when serious violence is involved, a recent study of police actions in Chester, Pennsylvania, found support for a leniency hypothesis: Police there treated men who beat their wives more leniently than men who committed similar violence in other contexts (Fyfe, Klinger, and Flavin, 1997). A study of the police response in London during the 1980s found that it was often slow, and that when police did arrive it was not uncommon for them to side with the assailant, who was rarely arrested (Edwards, 1986). This picture also fits the situation in Australia, Canada, and the United States.

Besides being reluctant, the conventional police response to domestic violence is a *reactive* one (Sherman, 1992: 208). This is largely because domestic disturbances are considered unpredictable events—and this includes the type and degree of violence involved. This unpredictability discourages the development of proactive policing strategies. Furthermore, although few people would question police who invaded a home because they thought someone was about to be stabbed, raped, or murdered, they would probably be alarmed if police routinely monitored and inspected homes or planted informants so as to prevent domestic disputes from occurring. (More details about the traditional police response to "domestics" are found in Barlow, 2000: 300–3).

Changing Responses to Domestic Violence

The women's movement can claim much of the credit for bringing domestic violence into the open. By the 1980s police departments around the country found themselves being sued for denying female victims of domestic violence equal protection of the law. A now-famous experiment conducted in Minneapolis in the early 1980s—but not confirmed by subsequent replications in other cities—also gave impetus to change by showing that domestic assailants who were arrested were less likely to commit repeat offenses during a six-month period following the experiment (Sherman and Berk, 1984). From 1984 to 1986, the proportion of urban police departments encouraging officers to make arrests grew fourfold and several states made arrests mandatory (Sherman, 1992: 203). Special prosecution units were also established in some states to ensure vigorous prosecution (Fagan, 1996).

Would more aggressive "proactive" criminal justice strategies reduce the incidence of domestic violence, and perhaps also the homicides that sometimes result from it? For example, by keeping track of calls to specific addresses, police can identify "hot spots" of domestic violence. In Milwaukee, for example, the police found that most couples with seven or more prior reports over a three-year period will have another one during that time period. If police acted on that prediction, they would be wrong in only one out of four cases. In addition, there are various other ways proactive policing might be conducted. For example, high-risk couples or families with repetitive police visits might be sent letters via mail, or beat officers might threaten more severe penalties the next time an incident occurs. This sort of approach could be tested experimentally. Another idea is repeat random visits by patrolling police to households with a specified number of prior domestic violence calls (Goldstein, 1990: 104–14). Families would be notified that police would be calling periodically to see how things were going.

Even if successful policing strategies could be developed for dealing with domestic violence, there will probably be little change in the demographic most likely to be targeted by the criminal justice system. The policing of domestic conflicts will continue to focus on the lower classes. Not only are lower-class people stereotypically linked with violence, as we have seen, but their lack of resources and their self-help traditions mean that personal problems are rarely addressed through counseling, mediation, education, or restitution—forms of social control that are available to the middle and upper classes (Manning, 1994: 89). In other words, the policing of domestic violence will likely remain concentrated in neighborhoods where there is already a disproportionate police presence.

Reactions to Rape

Most state codes have, at one time or another, identified rape as a capital crime, and those offenders most likely to receive the death penalty have been blacks. Since 1930 there have been 455 executions for rape; of those executed, nearly 90 percent were black. To these legal executions one must add the hundreds of blacks who were lynched for alleged sexual offenses against white women. The feeling among some whites, particularly in the South, seems to have been that only the most severe penalty matches the outrage committed when a black man violates the social taboos surrounding white-black relations and has sex with a white woman. Whether rape was actually committed—and in numerous cases this certainly was not established—seems to have been largely beside the point. A black simply did not become "intimate" with a white, especially a white woman. The charge of rape justified the imposition of death, which matched the legal punishment for rape. Also important to note is that it exonerated the white female, who, whites could argue, would never have consented to sexual intimacies with a black. The charge and the punishment thus reinforced racist practices.

The general sense of what "true" rape and molestation are affects trial and sentencing. Important to this image are the characteristics of the victim and how she behaved before and during the rape. If she is a virgin, a minor, or very old, and if there is circumstantial evidence that she put up resistance and was overcome by force, the offender is likely to be convicted and receive a severe sentence.

The moral categorization of women as "rapable/virtuous" and "nonrapable/unvirtuous" (MacKinnon, 1989: 175) is a manifestation of patriarchy that is reproduced in courtroom behavior. In rape trials, patriarchy, law, and the dynamics of courtroom behavior blend together and reproduce the relations of domination that structure interaction between men and women in everyday life (Matoesian, 1993). Acquittals are often a matter of transforming a woman's rape into an act of consensual sex (Sanday, 1996). Years ago, judges in a Philadelphia court, for example, admitted placing considerable weight on the victim and her behavior. They acquitted defendants when they perceived that the sex had been consensual (described by some judges as "friendly rape," "felonious gallantry," "assault with failure to please," and "breach of contract"), or the result of "female vindictiveness" (Bohm, 1974).

But how did they arrive at this judgment? How do defense attorneys transform a woman's rape into a consensual act? Gregory Matoesian (1993) explored these very questions through an analysis of trial talk—the verbal exchanges between prosecution, defense attorney, defendant, victim, witnesses, and judge. Talk is "socially structured" in that "[w]ho gets to say what, when they get to say it, and how much they get to say is contingent upon the social organization of the courtroom system, the distribution of power among its participants, and the larger system of patriarchy within which these actions are embedded" (32). Matoesian demonstrates that the moral categorization of the victim is not determined by virtue of her standards, but "according to male definitions through which rape is organized, interpreted, and legitimated" (30). Through analyzing trial talk as it occurred, he shows how defense attorneys succeed and fail in convincing the court that the victim was no victim at all. The strategy is to impugn the victim's sexual/moral character, even though rape shield laws ostensibly forbid this. One illustration: Although in pretrial motions in one case, the judge ruled that the marital status of an unmarried pregnant victim could not be introduced, the defense attorney "consistently referred to her as 'Miss' during the trial" (31).

Posttrial interviews with jurors show how blame can be attributed to some victims of rape (LaFree, Reskin, and Visher, 1991). Defendants were more likely to be acquitted when there was evidence of the victim's drinking, drug use, or extramarital sex. However, these characterizations were cited most often in cases where the defense attorney had argued for consensuality or diminished responsibility. If the defense attorney does not impugn the victim's character as the story is reconstructed in court, it appears jurors accept the implication that she is rapable (see also Lafree, 1989: 200–33). Furthermore, as Peggy Reeves Sanday (1996) and others have noted, jurors were actually told by judges in the United States that accusing someone of rape is easy, but the accusation is much harder to be defended, even if one is innocent.

Reactions to Child Sexual Assault

Sexual assault of children commonly provokes severe reactions. Just the attempt to sexually molest a minor is generally near the top of public polls on the seriousness of crimes. Judicial attitudes toward sexual assault of young children are generally severe. When pubescent children are involved, marked variations in official reactions have been observed. Again, much is made of the victims themselves and their apparent role in triggering the offense. Two examples from England serve to illustrate. In one case, a young man had numerous episodes of sexual intercourse with a fourteen-year-old girl he had met at a dancing school; "[i]t was accepted that the girl was a very willing participant" (Thomas, 1967: 515). In another case, a married father of four children had repeated acts of sexual intercourse with his fifteen-year-old sister-in-law. Circumstantial evidence was entered to support the view that the girl "had been the real instigator" (515). In both of these cases, an appeals court reduced the sentences imposed by the trial judge on the grounds that the victims wanted sex and willingly participated in the act.

A retrospective study of 350 cases of child sexual abuse occurring in a Texas county from 1975 to 1987 found that prosecution and conviction was more likely when (1) there was medical evidence to substantiate the charge, (2) the suspect made a statement of implication, (3) the time between the incident and the reporting of it was relatively short, and (4) the seriousness of the offense was greater (Bradshaw and Marks, 1990). Another Texas study found that a victim/witness program designed to help children in the difficult process of prosecution affected cases in a variety of ways: It (1) increased the percentage of convictions at trial from 38 to 72 percent, (2) resulted in fewer plea bargains, (3) increased the percentage of offenders receiving prison terms from 25 to 48 percent, and (4) increased the average length of sentence for all child sex abuse cases, whether pled or not (Dible and Teske, 1993).

If there is some ambivalence in the societal response to sexual victimization of older children, even the sentences handed down to molesters of young children are sometimes light—for example, probation with counseling. This usually occurs as a result of plea bargains in which defendants plead guilty to misdemeanor sex offenses. When convicted of felony sexual assault, mandatory sentencing laws in many states make imprisonment inevitable, and most states now force the offenders to register with authorities after they have served time and (where appropriate) completed parole. This information is then made public under the so-called Megan's Law.

In 1995 New Jersey passed Megan's Law, named after seven-year-old Megan Kanka, who was raped and murdered by a known child molester who had moved in across the street. Megan's Law requires authorities to notify communities of convicted sex offenders in their neighborhoods. As of this writing, all states have some form of sex offender registries, and many are posted on the Internet with complete search capabilities. Megan's Law has been upheld by the U.S. Supreme Court, despite objections that it violates the constitutional rights of people who have already been punished for their crimes. Some states have also passed new laws allowing certain repeat sex offenders to be committed to secure mental facilities indefinitely after they have completed their prison sentences. A civil proceeding is held, and the burden of proving why commitment should not occur rests with the defendant.

There is no better way to sum up the tragedy of rape and sexual assault generally than from a woman's perspective. Elizabeth Stanko writes:

> Wherever women are, their peripheral vision monitors the landscape and those around them for potential danger. . . . For the most part, women find they must constantly negotiate their safety with men—those with whom they live, work and socialize, as well as those they have never met. Because women are likely to be physically smaller than men, as well as emotionally and economically dependent on them, they must bargain safety from a disadvantaged position. . . . The very people women turn to for protection are the ones who pose the greatest danger. (1990: 85–86)

If the criminal justice "management" of sexual assault of women is to do more than merely mirror the sexism of a patriarchal society, it must be recognized "that all women are entitled to be protected from rape and whatever a woman's behavior, there is no justification for rape" (Box-Grainger, 1986: 32). An excerpt from Marge Piercy's famous poem about rape is stark in its portrayal of victim blaming:

> There is no difference between being raped and being run over by a truck except that afterwards men ask if you enjoyed it. . . .
>
> There is no difference between being raped and being bit on the ankle by a rattlesnake except that people ask if your skirt was short and why you were out alone anyhow.
> (Quoted in Odem and Clay-Warner, 1998: 3)

CHAPTER SUMMARY

This chapter has discussed domestic violence and sexual assault of women and children. Both legal and scientific perspectives have been shaped by historical conflicts of interest between men and women, and by the societal dominance of males and adults.

Domestic violence is kept largely under wraps, but it affects a large number of women and children. Victims often remain silent, and offenders often don't see themselves as criminals. Violence among intimates is regarded as a private affair. There has even been a tendency among police officers, both in the United States and abroad, to treat domestic violence as not worthy of serious police activity. Considering that women and children are the most common victims of domestic violence, this sends a strong message that it's okay for adults, men in particular, to use physical force against other family members. Men who persist in using violence generally escalate the seriousness of the attacks, sometimes to the level of homicide; at the same time, some victims turn the tables and murder their assailants.

In recent years feminists have led the way to more open and enlightened exploration of domestic violence and sexual assault. Research findings show that sexual assault is widespread, that it often involves people who know each other or are related, that victims are often humiliated and frustrated in their search for justice, and that reactions to rape are influenced by myths, stereotypes, and prejudices that generally serve the interests of men.

Current explanations of sexual assault focus on domination rather than on sex. The sex act itself is less important than what it represents—the humiliation of another person through intimate violation of that person's body and mind. Some people argue that high rates of sexual assault reflect the existence of subcultures of violence, while others suggest that aggressive male dominance of females is also valued in middle-class culture and encouraged through the institution of dating, through pornographic imagery, and by prevailing stereotypes of "proper" womanhood as weak, passive, and submissive to man.

Sexual assault of children is also widespread, and most of it remains hidden from authorities. Child molesters come from all walks of life, but the offenders are most often male and the victims are more often girls than boys. When questioned by authorities or researchers, many heterosexual child molesters either disavow their actions or blame them on the victim or on forces beyond their control.

KEY TERMS

child maltreatment
domestic violence
rape shield laws
victim blaming

RECOMMENDED READINGS

Bergen, Raquel Kennedy. (1998). *Issues in Intimate Violence*. Thousand Oaks, CA: Sage.

Brownmiller, Susan. (1975). *Against Our Will*. New York: Simon and Schuster.

Odem, Mary E., and Jody Clay-Warner. (1998). *Confronting Rape and Sexual Assault*. Wilmington, DE: SR Books.

Renzetti, Claire M. (1992). *Violent Betrayal: Partner Abuse in Lesbian Relationships*. Thousand Oaks, CA: Sage.

Renzetti, Claire M., and Lynne Goodstein. (2001). *Women, Crime and Criminal Justice: Original Feminist Readings*. Los Angeles: Roxbury.

Sanday, Peggy Reeves. (1996). *A Woman Scorned: Acquaintance Rape on Trial*. New York: Doubleday.

Searles, Patricia, and Ronald J. Berger. (1995). *Rape and Society: Readings in the Problem of Sexual Assault*. Boulder, CO: Westview.

RECOMMENDED WEB SITES

Violence Against Women Program, U.S. Department of Justice (http://www.ojp.usdoj.gov/vawo). Information, links, and reports on crimes against women.

National Organization for Women (http://www.now.org). A wide range of studies, positions, and data relating to crimes against women.

National Clearinghouse on Child Abuse and Neglect (http://www.calib.com/nccanch/). Volumes of information on all forms of child maltreatment.

5

NONVIOLENT THEFT

ACBAR5 Alamy

Consider how many opportunities there are for theft around your college or university. There are books and bookbags left lying around, cars to be broken into, and office, computer, and classroom equipment in plain view of thousands of people each day. All American universities are now required to publish crime statistics under a 1990 federal law known as the Jeanne Clery Act, in honor of a woman who was murdered on a college campus. These statistics suggest that while most college and university campuses have lower than average overall crime rates, they are certainly not immune to crime, including theft.

Theft is the most common class of crime in most societies. It is also the crime least likely to result in arrest when reported. If people do not steal themselves, then they are victims or they hear about thefts involving others. Many people may be the victims of theft without even knowing it. Only three conditions are necessary to make theft possible: (1) goods or services capable of being stolen, (2) someone from whom they can be stolen, and (3) someone to do the stealing.

As one might expect, the legal notion of theft is not uniform across different societies. If property or material possessions do not exist, people are unlikely to have any notion of stealing. The types of possessions that can be stolen, the methods used, and the kinds of people who are victims are all influenced by culture, by the way people live, and by their attitudes and values.

In a society that places a premium on the acquisition of personal property, theft is likely to be a serious offense. However, those same values may also encourage the very behavior that is condemned. If possession of material wealth is highly valued, then people may stop at nothing to accumulate it. If people could acquire whatever they wanted through culturally acceptable channels, then theft might not exist. But when some people are systematically excluded from access to acceptable channels of acquisition or cannot acquire what they want even with such access, then stealing may be an alternative way to achieve material wealth. Though it is popular to think that thieves are primarily the poor and disadvantaged, people from all walks of life—even those with all kinds of advantages—steal from others. This will be the main topic of chapter 6. This chapter concentrates primarily on forms of common theft committed outside the context of legitimate work.

THEFT IN HISTORY

Theft has a long and interesting history. In early legal codes theft was a rather vague term, though most known codes maintained laws identifying theft as punishable behavior. More interesting, perhaps, is that many of these early codes tried to distinguish among different methods of stealing and different classes of victims. For example, the Roman law of the Twelve Tables designated theft by night as a more serious offense than daylight theft. The Code of Hammurabi placed the interests of church and state above those of the citizenry as a whole: Those who stole from temples or royal palaces were punished by death, whereas those who stole from private citizens merely had to pay compensation.

It is mainly in English law that the roots of modern criminal law conceptions of theft are found. Even before the Norman conquest of 1066, theft was an offense. Many people are familiar with the adage "Possession is nine points of the law," but in early English law possession was everything. It was in terms of possession that theft was identified and the thief so labeled. Ownership was a notion quite alien to early English society. One did not own something; it was in one's possession. To identify theft it was necessary to show, first, that the thief did not have lawful possession of the object in question and, second, that the person who claimed lawful possession could rightly do so. In practical terms this meant that to establish theft it was important to produce the thief, and the best way to do this was to catch the person red-handed.

Similar to the American "posse," the English chase was thus an integral part of the theft scene. If the suspect was caught while transporting stolen goods from the crime scene, then the theft was "manifest" and justice could be meted out swiftly and severely—and often was. If the chase was unsuccessful or the lawful possessor failed to pursue the thief, then the theft was "secret" and justice was often slow and tortuous. All things considered, it was certainly in the interest of the victim to catch the thief in the act of fleeing with the loot.

Another important aspect of common law conceptions of theft was a civil law violation: trespass. The common legal term for theft was—and still is—larceny. Larceny was an extension of trespass. Under Roman law, larceny (*latrocinium*) was defined as almost any type of deceit and trickery, but this was not the case in England. Larceny meant laying hands on another's possessions without permission: "Simply to lay a hand on a man's thing without his permission would be trespass; therefore it was argued that there could be no larceny without trespass" (Turner, 1966: 267). Larceny went beyond trespass in the notion of *animus furandi* (intent to steal); trespass turned into larceny when the trespasser intended to steal from the victim. The notion of trespass is still retained in many state laws dealing with theft.

Regarding what could be stolen, the idea of "movable" possessions remained central in emerging criminal law. The old charge that the thief "stole, took, and carried away" emphasizes this idea. In medieval times the most prized movables were agricultural chattels—farm animals such as oxen, cows, horses, and pigs, which often also served as money. Not surprisingly, these were the movable possessions to which early theft laws most often applied. But the creators of law have never been bound by tradition. One Anglo-Saxon king declared: "Men shall respect everything the king wishes to be respected, and refrain from theft on pain of death and loss of all they possess" (Attenborough, 1963: 137). Though the king put the matter bluntly, the point is obvious: Those who shape legal conceptions of what can be stolen are in a position to impose their own ideas about what is valuable and to determine what will and will not be deemed stealable (Hall, 1952).

The actual value of goods has traditionally been irrelevant to the identification of theft. It matters little whether you steal a coat worth five thousand dollars or one worth only five cents—a theft has still been committed. But value clearly does matter in what happens to the thief. From at least Anglo-Saxon times, distinctions in theft have been based on the value of the property taken. Just as today many states treat theft under three hundred dollars (or some other figure) as petty theft and anything more than that as grand theft, similar distinctions have been made throughout the history of theft laws. The penalties for grand theft, a felony, are more severe. If value is an indication of seriousness, which such rules imply, then such distinctions may be justified on the grounds that they provide a workable solution to the problem of "making the punishment fit the crime." Some authors have argued, however, that distinctions of value merely reflect the operation of class interests and ignore that what may be a great loss to one person may be trivial to another. More wealthy theft victims realize more in the way of "justice" than do poorer ones, whose losses may actually be more significant (Mannheim, 1946).

Interests and Theft Laws

Criminal law is constantly changing. For one thing, legal formulations prove inadequate when confronted by changing social conditions and interests. Theft laws have continually been revised and extended, and one result is that new forms of theft keep emerging. One particularly significant development in criminal theft occurred during the late 1400s, and it shows the impact on criminal law of emergent social conditions and interests (see Hall, 1952).

The "Carrier's Case" involved a man who was hired to carry some bales of merchandise to Southampton, an English port city. Instead of doing this, he broke open the bales and took their contents. He was subsequently caught and charged with felony theft. As the larceny law then stood, however, his actions did not legally constitute theft: He had entered an agreement in good faith, and he thus had lawful possession of the bales. Under the possession rules he could not steal from himself or from the merchant who hired him. After much debate, a majority of the judges in the case finally found him guilty of felony theft and in doing so extended the law of

larceny to cover cases of "breaking bulk," as it was called.

Most people would probably argue that this verdict and the legal precedent it established are reasonable enough. After all, if you hire a truck driver to deliver goods, you would surely be angry if the driver stole them. But if no laws could be applied in your particular case, then what satisfaction could you hope to receive? To judge from the Carrier's Case, successful resolution of the problem would depend on how much pressure you could bring to bear on authorities to protect your interests. It so happens that at the time of the Carrier's Case, the judges were faced with a number of outside pressures:

> The most powerful forces at the time were interrelated very intimately and at many points: the New Monarchy and the nouveau riche—the mercantile class; the business interests of both and the consequent need for a secure carrying trade; the wool and textile industry, the most valuable by far in all the realm; wool and cloth, the most important exports; these exports and foreign trade; this trade and Southampton, chief trading city with the Latin countries for centuries; the numerous and very influential Italian merchants who brought English wool and cloth inland and shipped them from Southampton. The great forces of an emerging modern world, represented in the above phenomenon, necessitated the elimination of a formula which had outgrown its usefulness. A new set of major institutions required a new rule. (Hall, 1952: 33)

So, as William Chambliss states: "The judges deciding the Carrier Case had, then, to choose between creating a new law to protect merchants who entrusted their goods to a carrier or permitting the lack of such legal protection to undermine trade and the merchant class economic interests. The court decided to act in the interests of the merchants despite the lack of a law" (1975a: 7).

The revision and expansion of theft laws continued to the present day. Many of the changes were designed to plug gaps and crevices in prevailing common law. Embezzlement, for example, emerged in its modern form in 1799, when Parliament passed a statute to cover cases of servants misappropriating goods placed in their possession in the course of employment. It was later extended to cover brokers, bankers, attorneys, and others in positions of trust as agents for third parties.

Embezzlement statutes covered only the illegal transfer of possession. For cases of ownership fraudulently acquired—as when one signs over property to another after being tricked into doing so—the law remained inadequate until a statutory decree in 1861 created the offense of obtaining goods by false pretenses. This new offense was basically an extension of the earlier common-law crime *larceny by trick and device.*

THEFT: THE CURRENT PICTURE

Much theft, like all crime, remains beyond the reach of bureaucratic data collection. Accordingly, national data on theft are extremely difficult to assess and interpret. When one considers the fact that only a relatively minute number of thefts are ever solved, the difficulties become obvious.

Published national data provide an idea of the dimensions of the theft problem from the standpoint of the criminal justice system. In 2007, burglary, larceny theft, arson, and motor vehicle theft accounted for approximately 10 million of the index offenses, accounting for $17.6 billion in losses reported by the FBI (2008). This represents about 90 percent of all index offenses. Incidences of all three offenses steadily increased during the 1960s, with burglary and larceny continuing to climb, though more slowly, during the 1970s. During the 1980s all three offenses increased again, according to police figures. As figure 5.1 shows, property crime rates, like the rates for most crimes, have consistently declined in the last several years.

The published national data indicate other characteristics of these three index offenses:

- Rural rates are substantially below those found in both cities and suburbs.
- The young tend to be most victimized.
- The higher one's income, the *higher* the rate of victimization for *personal theft.* The higher one's income, the *lower* the rate for *burglary* victimization.
- African Americans are more likely to be victimized than whites and Hispanics.
- Most thefts are not reported to the police. If reported, fewer than 20 percent are cleared by arrest.
- The most common form of larceny theft involves thefts related to motor vehicle parts, accessories, and other contents. (Federal Bureau of Investigation, 2006b)

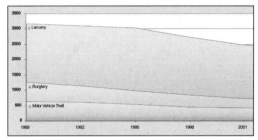

▲ **Figure 5.1.**
Property Crime Rates, 1990–2007.
Source: Federal Bureau of Investigation (2008).

Specialization and Varieties of Theft

Thieves rarely spend all or even most of their time in one particular line of theft (Cromwell, 1999). Explaining why most thieves diversify, one professional thief had this to say:

> Stealing for a living isn't just being a burglar or stick-up man. You've got to be able to look around and recognize opportunities and be able to take advantage of them regardless of what the conditions are. A lot of people think once a stick-up man, always a stick-up man. Well, you can't run around stickin' up people every day of the week like a workin' man. Maybe something worth-while sticking up only shows up every two or three months. In the meantime you're doing this and that, changing around, doing practically anything to make a dollar. (Martin, 1952: 117)

Some thieves develop interests and talents so that they can concentrate on specific crimes. They "have a line." Some express interests in the theft of only certain types of merchandise—for example, credit cards, jewelry, or furs—and others see their talents put to the most productive (and secure) use in one line of work—picking pockets, sneak theft, forgery, or con games. On the whole, however, thieves are generalists rather than specialists. Some may even be adamantly opposed to specialization: It reduces the chances of remaining anonymous and increases the risks of being "fingered" for a caper known to be their style. Professionals give recognition to those who can say they "have a line," but this denotes their preference and skill rather than day-to-day activity.

Varieties of theft involving high levels of skill, organization, and planning and those requiring substantial resources (some big cons) are usually outside the reach of the typical amateur. Many types of theft attract both professionals and amateurs, however. Within these types, some of the major characteristics distinguishing amateurs from professionals are arrest and conviction history, size of the heist, level of technical skill involved, and type of fencing arrangement employed. Amateurs tend to be arrested and convicted more often, to leave with smaller (or no) payoffs, to employ little in the way of manipulative and technical skills, and to steal for themselves or for their friends. Both professionals and amateurs are involved in burglary, sneak theft, forgery, and auto theft. Amateurs rarely perform confidence swindling, counterfeiting, or extortion.

SHOPLIFTING: THE FIVE FINGER DISCOUNT

When people steal from under the nose of their victims, it is commonly called sneak theft. Examples include shoplifting, pocket picking, and "till tapping" (stealing from cash registers).

Of the many varieties of sneak theft *not* committed by employees, shoplifting has no equal. The number of shoplifting incidents and the total dollars lost from this crime are unknown and impossible to determine, but the estimates are staggering. While almost a million shoplifting incidents were reported to the police in 2005, estimates as early as 1984 put the real figure closer to 200 million incidents per year (Federal Bureau of Investigation, 2006b; Baumer and Rosenbaum, 1984). What about the cost of it all? The authors of the respected *National Retail Security Survey* estimate that the U.S. retail industry alone loses about $35 billion each year from theft, $11.5 billion of which is from shoplifting (Hollinger, 2005). The remaining amount is lost by, in order of frequency, employee theft, administrative errors, and vendor fraud. The average shoplift results in a loss of about two hundred dollars (Federal Bureau of Investigation, 2006b; National Retail Security Survey, 2006). The dollar amount of the theft is important because, in many jurisdictions, a theft over three hundred dollars is considered a felony and therefore could result in more serious punishment.

Shoplifting is not new, nor have the methods changed much in a hundred years. To be sure, there have been changes in the architecture of stores and in the overall character of the shopping experience, but shoplifters still employ time-honored methods: concealing items under their clothes, hiding them in false-bottomed cases, "bad bagging" them (putting them in well-worn shopping bags), and using "booster boxes" (cartons and packages that appear sealed but in fact have an opening through which to put lifted items (see Edwards, 1958: 4–15; Klemke, 1992).

Shoplifting is dominated by amateurs and opportunists, and it cuts across age, sex, race, economic status, and educational distinctions. It used to be thought that females stole from stores more frequently than males did—a reasonable belief, perhaps, in light of traditional sex roles and what official data tell us about gender and crime. However, more recent evidence suggests that males steal just as often as females—and tend to steal more items per visit (Buckle and Farrington, 1984, also see Clarke, 2003; Klemke, 1992). Few shoplifters are kleptomaniacs, and most say they steal simply because they didn't *want* to pay for the item, not because they *couldn't* possibly pay for the item (Cromwell, Parker, and Mobley, 1999). One shoplifter explained it this way: "I did it because I didn't want to pay for anything. I've got better things to do with my money"(62). Box 5.1 provides similar insights about college students who shoplift.

Reactions to Shoplifting

Reactions to shoplifting and shoplifters reveal an intriguing facet of this crime. Time and again studies indicate that although most shoplifters are never apprehended, those who are sometimes face little more than a scolding and are sent on their way after returning or paying for the merchandise. The shoplifter's chances of a lenient reaction depend on age, sex, ability to pay, attitude, apparent social class, and whether or not he or she is a known or suspected professional. Overall, it appears that the value of the stolen items is the best predictor of whether the shoplifter will get by with verbal scolding or whether police will be notified and prosecution pursued (Hindelang, 1974, see also Cromwell, 1999).

Because detection and arrest of shoplifters are commonly the responsibility of store personnel, arrest and prosecution are largely influenced by the policies of store management. The typical store policy is usually one of caution and leniency. The primary objective is to deter shoplifting while avoiding anything that might hurt store business. Store management usu-

Box 5.1. THE THRILL OF SHOPLIFTING

Jack Katz has argued that shoplifting, like vandalism and joyriding, is a sneaky crime that often provides the offenders with a "thrill." This thrill and risk-taking seductions of crime is more powerful than criminologists have realized in the past. The "sneaky thrill" of shoplifting is evident, according to Katz (1988: 52), because of the seduction of the objects in time and place, the possibility of getting caught, and the sense of euphoria one experiences when doing and recounting the act. Here are some quotes from Katz's criminology students who recounted their thoughts on shoplifting.

On the attraction:
"I felt an overwhelming urge" (55).
"I'm not quite sure why I must have it, but I must." (55).
Keeping up normal appearances:
"I proceeded to make myself look busy as I tried on several pairs of earrings. My philosophy was that the more busy you look the less conspicuous." (60).
"The whole time as we approached the exit I remember looking at it as a dark tunnel and just wanting to run down and disappear"(62).
After the exit:
"Once outside the door I thought Wow! I pulled it off, I faced danger and I pulled it off. I was smiling so much and I felt at that moment like there was nothing I couldn't do." (64).
"[T]he thrill of getting something for nothing, knowing I got away with something I never thought I could, was wonderful" (64).
These quotes suggest that there is a lot more going on in the decision to shoplift than the interest in having "more things" or "saving a few bucks," at least according to Katz's sample.

ally wants to avoid embarrassing situations on the shop floor that might adversely affect the attitudes and behavior of customers. Equally important, it wants to minimize the time and expense involved in carrying through official prosecution of suspects. Finally, it wants to avoid unnecessary publicity that might mark the store as unfriendly or harsh, or as a place frequented by shoplifters (Cromwell, Parker, and Mobley, 1999; Klemke, 1992; Waltz, 1953). If the store can recover the items or obtain payment through informal and discreet means, then its interests are partially met.

Other aspects of the informal approach should be kept in mind. Store management knows that most pilferers are amateurs and that when confronted with their attempted theft, most are shaken up so badly that they will do almost anything to avoid official attention. Further, they will probably refrain from stealing in that store, at least for a time. Studies have shown that typical pilferers are what the criminal subculture labels as *square johns*—those who neither systematically involve themselves in criminal pursuits nor identify themselves as criminals. They are typically people who adhere to the dominant cultural values and spend most of their time in legitimate pursuits. When caught, amateurs (particularly adults) display their commitment to dominant values and strenuously deny that they have done anything wrong or that they are criminals. Here is a typical verbal response from the amateur on being apprehended:

> I didn't intend to take the dress. I just wanted to see it in the daylight. Oh! what will my husband do! I did intend to pay for it. It's all a mistake. Oh! my God! what will mother say! I'll be glad to pay for it. See, I've got the money with me. Oh! my children! They can't find out I've been arrested! I'd never be able to face them again. (Cameron, 1964: 164)

To arrest a misdemeanor suspect (the usual case in shoplifting incidents) is to do so at peril, because lawsuits charging false imprisonment or false arrest may result (Cromwell,

Parker, and Mobley, 1999). Not surprisingly, retailers in recent years have pressured legislatures to amend regulations dealing with the apprehension of suspected shoplifters. Most states now permit store personnel to detain suspects under certain broad conditions and without fear of civil suits charging false arrest or imprisonment. This may mean an increase in police arrests (and thus an increase in official rates of shoplifting), though the considerations reviewed in this section will continue to play an important part in management decisions. In addition, since shoplifting is usually a misdemeanor committed by amateurs, authorities may decline to arrest or prosecute whenever jail space is tight.

The informal handling of shoplifters may have important ramifications for the way shoplifting is viewed by those arrested as well as by the general public. The fact that many shoplifters are generally law abiding suggests that in order to engage in shoplifting in the first place—which they recognize is wrong and illegal—they may have convinced themselves that in their case it is not really theft, certainly not crime. As already seen, many apprehended amateurs think of their actions this way. How do they arrive at this conception? How is it that what they do is not crime, but what someone else does—for example, robbery and burglary—is crime?

What society views as crime is influenced partly by prevailing cultural conceptions of crime and partly by the consequences of criminal behavior. If people do things they expect will result in being labeled a criminal, then being so labeled comes as no surprise and reinforces the belief that the act is criminal. But if people are not sure that the actions are criminal or if they have adopted the view that they are not, there will be no reason to alter their view when reactions do not match what they think happens to "real" criminals committing "real" crimes. So upright citizens who occasionally shoplift and who are treated informally and discreetly by store personnel are under little pressure to alter their conception of themselves or their behavior: They believe that what they do is not criminal and that the criminal is quite another sort of person.

Interestingly enough, American business practices may encourage amateur shoplifting in other ways. Businesses spend billions of dollars every year on campaigns designed to convince Americans that they need and want items offered for sale. Already attuned to the values of an acquisitive society, Americans are reminded constantly to spend as much money as they can. They are continually exhorted to buy now, buy more, buy better, and pay later. During the Christmas shopping season, when shoplifting is at its yearly peak, the glitter and the temptation are at their height. Even if people cannot afford an item, they are discouraged from forgetting about it and instead are exhorted to find a way to buy it. When continually pushed to conceive of the meaning of life in material terms, people are measured by what they possess, what they can afford, and what they consume, rather than by who and what they are (Berlin, 1996).

BURGLARY

Burglary is the illegal entry of a structure (usually a house or store) with the intent to commit theft. According to victimization surveys, burglary is the most common and, to many Americans, one of the most frightening felony crime. Victims often report that they felt as if their very person had been violated. People cherish the privacy and security of their homes and feel anger and resentment when these are breached. Women have a very special and justified fear: that an intruder will rape as well as steal. There is some research to support this concern, as violence is likely to erupt in about 30 percent of incidents in which someone is at home during a break-in.

Researchers have compiled a list of the most significant risk factors associated with household burglary (Mayhew, Maung and Mirrlees-Black, 1993; Tseloni et al., 2004).

Among those risk factors were:

- inner-city location;
- no security devices;
- only one adult living in a household (this risk was heightened for people living alone in an apartment); and
- being away from the residence during the evening.

However, when researchers checked to see whether the different variables might "interact"—that is, influence each other—it was discovered that houses without security devices are more vulnerable to burglary regardless of whether they are left unoccupied in the evenings. By the same token, security devices were more important for people living alone than for households with two or more adults.

During the last few years, the fears of middle-class homeowners have heightened as suburban burglary rates have increased faster than central city rates. Communities have organized "crime watch" groups to patrol their neighborhoods in an attempt to protect themselves from the burglar and other criminals.

Whether committed in the suburbs, in rural areas, or in cities, most burglaries are the work of relatively unskilled individuals who commit occasional burglaries among a variety of other offenses and who live in or near the places they burglarize (Shover, 1991). They look for cash and for items that can be readily disposed of via fences and pawnshops. Their methods are scorned by professionals, often known as "good burglars." Professionals take pride in their ability to gain entrance without force and noise and to pull a job speedily and profitably. The unskilled, often youthful burglars are called "door shakers," "kick-it-in men," "loidmen," and "creepers," names that reflect their amateur techniques (Pileggi, 1968).

Good burglars choose targets they have selected in advance, sometimes after carefully casing them (Wright and Decker, 1994: 62–102); sometimes they work in well-oiled teams, with each member assigned a specific role based on experience and expertise, and they always work with quiet speed. In search of a lucrative target, the professional must deal effectively with security systems. The ability to disarm alarms separates the good burglar from both the amateur and the aspiring professional (Letkemann, 1973; Wright and Decker, 1994).

A number of research efforts during the past decade have aimed at identifying the major contours of burglary offenses and offenders. There is considerable agreement about the main characteristics. Losses are moderate, usually under nineteen hundred dollars (Federal Bureau of Investigation, 2007); most involve cash and cash-convertible items such as televisions, radios, and stereos; residential burglaries usually take place during the daytime, while those of commercial establishments take place at night, often on weekends; and most involve forced entry. It is perhaps significant that the clearance rate (proportion of incidents resulting in arrest) tends to be higher for burglaries in which there is no loss at all or only a small one. Presumably these are uncompleted burglaries, whose numbers are higher than might be expected—up to 33 percent of all incidents in some studies (e.g., Conklin and Bittner, 1973). They are often the work of amateurs who cannot find what they want or who are discovered or frightened away before they have started work.

Burglaries are more likely to occur in the daytime between 6:00 a.m. and 6:00 p.m. (Federal Bureau of Investigation, 2006b). In general burglars prefer not to enter houses that are occupied. In Wright and Decker's study of St. Louis burglars, nine out of ten burglars interviewed said they "*always* avoided breaking into a residence when they knew or suspected that someone was at home" (1994: 110).

Those arrested for burglary in the United States are disproportionately young and male. In 2005 more than 80 percent of those arrested were males, and 70 percent of all arrestees were white (Federal Bureau of Investigation, 2006b: 43). The gender gap for this crime is greater than for any index crime but rape. When women are involved, they are more likely than men to work in partnerships or in groups, although men also frequently work in teams at least some of the time (Wright and Decker, 1994). Most adult burglars have prior arrest records, often for burglary.

Once inside a building, burglars must find the cash or goods. If burglars are interested in cash, as many are, finding it is not always simple. Skilled burglars try to anticipate the behavior of their victims:

> In commercial establishments, [the burglar] may find it in the expected places, such as safes, cash registers, or in deliberately unexpected places, such as one shoe box among several hundred others. In residential dwellings, the burglar's task may be even more difficult, since the places where cash may be found are less predictable. A home does not have a cash register, nor, necessarily, a safe. Therefore, the burglar must make quick interpretations as to the most probable location of cash. The mental activity here is really a game of wits—or operating on the basis of reciprocal expectations. He proceeds on the assumptions he has regarding routine family behavior, and he anticipates uniformities in architecture as well as in styles of placing valuables. (Letkemann, 1973: 55)

Among residential burglars in St. Louis, two main kinds of searches were identified: the *brief search* and the *leisurely search* (Wright and Decker, 1994). In the brief search speed is of the essence, and most burglars head straight for the master bedroom, where cash, jewelry, and guns are most likely to be found. Sometimes the kitchen is also searched, but only if time permits and doing so does not divert the burglar from his usual "script." The leisurely search is mentioned by a small number of burglars who like to make an exhaustive search of a residence if they feel reasonably certain they will not be interrupted.

In professional burglary, safecrackers are at the top of the status hierarchy, and their work makes some of the greatest demands on a thief's skill. Safecracking has been explored in detail by Letkemann (1973) and has been a pronounced theme in several movies, including *Ocean's Eleven* and *The Italian Job*. Among the basic tools and equipment are "grease" (nitroglycerine), made from a combination of sulphuric acid, nitric acid, and glycerine; soap, which must be pliable and is used for funneling grease into the door; and "knockers and string" (detonators and fuses). The most common technique of safecracking is the so-called jam shot, a procedure consisting of ten coordinated steps that, if done correctly, force the door of the safe to swing open on its hinges. When done incorrectly, the door is blown off the safe—or worse, the door *and* the safe buckle.

Professional safecrackers must remain knowledgeable about technological advances if they are to stay in business, and those who have been in the field long recognize the importance of information sharing. Safecrackers share information on jobs, techniques, new developments, and any related aspects of their line. Letkemann suggests that the already fairly strong social bonds linking safecrackers have been strengthened as a result of greatly restricted access to dynamite (a ready source of grease) and the resulting need to make their own nitroglycerine: "It enabled leaders to screen new 'recruits' and necessitated the development of a stronger subculture based on mutual aid and group loyalty" (1973: 88).

Sophisticated professional burglary has been swallowed up by the growing numbers of amateur burglaries committed by those in search of immediate economic rewards. It may be that decreased use of cash as a medium of exchange will help drive all but the most organized and skilled burglars into other "professions." On the other hand, the low risk of arrest coupled with initial successes may encourage many inexperienced burglars to continue in this line. They build their skills, their pride, and their fencing contacts. As

they develop friendships with other crooks and lose contact with "straight" friends, their commitment to burglary may increase and they will become new experts, replacing retiring or imprisoned professionals (Cornish and Clarke, 1986a: 13). This does not mean they drop other criminal activities; rather, they add burglary to a list of offenses they feel competent to commit successfully when the opportunity and incentive arise.

Why Burglary?

The question "Why?" can be asked of offenders in any crime, and the answers are bound to vary across offenses and offenders. But similar answers are also bound to appear, and if these cluster around a particular offense, criminologists can rightly claim to be a little closer to identifying the motivations behind particular crimes and to establishing differences in motivations among crimes. Unfortunately, the time, energy, and resources required for an in-depth comparative analysis of offender motivation across crimes would probably be prohibitive, and so research designed to uncover the whys and wherefores of crime tends to be more limited in focus. They are nevertheless crucial to building an understanding of specific crimes from the offender's perspective, and ultimately they help us with the larger jigsaw puzzle.

Such is a study of burglary by Wright and Decker. This groundbreaking work does not rely on information from imprisoned offenders (as many studies have) but is based on interviews with *currently active* burglars located by the researchers themselves through a "snowball" sampling strategy. This method involves recruiting an initial subject "who then is asked to refer further participants. This process continues until a suitable sample has been built" (see Wright and Decker, 1994: 16–25 for a complete account of their method and its pitfalls).

Wright and Decker's study sought answers to the whys and wherefores of burglary, and the authors wondered, like Katz (1988), what it feels like to do the crime. The immediate motivation for burglary appears no different than that for robbery: "a pressing need for cash" (Wright and Decker, 1994: 36). As one burglar put it:

> Well, it's like, the way it clicks into your head is like, you'll be thinking about something and, you know, it's a problem. Then it all relates. "Hey, I need some money! Then how am I going to get money? Well, how do you know how to get money quick and easy?" Then there it is. Next thing you know, you are watching [a house] or calling to see if [the occupants] are home. (Wright and Decker, 1994: 36)

The frequency of committing burglary is determined largely by how much money the offender has in his pocket at any one time. The money from burglary is then spent to maintain "high-living," or what Katz (1988) calls a life of "action." Much of this life involves getting and using drugs. It also includes wearing good clothes and gold jewelry and being able to flash money around, especially in the pursuit of women, whose conquest is the *sine qua non* of masculinity (see Messerschmidt, 1994).

But why burglary rather than legitimate work or some other crime? Many burglars speak of needing cash on the spur-of-the-moment and not being able to get it legitimately, whether through work or from friends and relatives (Wright and Decker, 1994; Tunnell, 2000). As for why burglary over some other crime, the answer is varied: Some burglars say this is their "main line," others have moral objections to alternatives such as robbery, and some have simply gone along with the suggestions of others. One subject reported: "I got a friend that do burglaries with me. He usually the one that sets them up. If he ain't got one set up, then I might go off into somethin' else" (Wright and Decker, 1994: 53). A few respondents mentioned the excitement of burglary, or its challenges. Excitement is also one of the things that drives auto thieves, as we will see in the next section.

Auto Theft

The movie *Gone in Sixty Seconds* glorified auto theft and emphasized the skills and risks involved. However, scholarly studies of auto theft are scarce, despite the fact that this crime is better reported and more costly per incident than any other street crime. Estimates of the direct losses to victims alone are put at over $7.9 billion. Auto theft is also a major contributor to the nation's felony crime figures, representing around 1.2 million offenses in 2006 (Federal Bureau of Investigation, 2007). The vast majority of car thefts take place in metropolitan areas, and, unlike most other major crimes, auto theft is almost always reported to the police—insurance claims are the primary reason for this.

NCVS data also show that the risk of being victimized by car thieves is not borne equally: Rates of victimization are higher in central cities and lowest in rural areas, higher for renters than for homeowners, and occur more frequently in the western part of the United States (Bureau of Justice Statistics, 2006).

Types of Auto Theft

There are four basic contexts for auto theft: (1) joyriding, when vehicles are stolen simply to be ridden around in for fun and recreation; (2) transportation, when a vehicle is stolen for personal use so that the thief can get from one place to another; (3) to commit other crimes, when a car is stolen to be used as transportation to and from a crime scene; and (4) profit, when a car is stolen so that it can be sold or dismantled for parts, which can be sold separately or combined ("chopped up") with other stolen parts to make "new" vehicles that are nearly impossible to trace (Fleming, 1999).

A significant amount of auto theft appears to be for profit, and while most are relatively simple operations, some thieves are involved in quite complex schemes. There are four complex insurance frauds involving auto theft:

- *Duplicate title frauds,* in which a person sells a car, obtains a duplicate title, then reports the car stolen and surrenders the duplicate title to the insurance company for payment.
- *Counterfeit title frauds*, where a heavily financed car is reported stolen and the insured provides a duplicate title listing himself as sole owner.
- *Paper vehicle frauds*, in which a fictitious vehicle is registered and insured, then "stolen" so the insurance can be claimed.
- *Salvage vehicle frauds*, similar to the preceding, except they involve actual vehicles sold as salvage, which are then registered, titled as operational, insured, then reported stolen. (Illinois Motor Vehicle Theft Prevention Council, 1993: 5–7)

Available research allows only inferences about the dynamic qualities of auto theft, including the perceptions, decisions, and reactions of car thieves themselves. A small sample of one hundred car thieves provided information on these issues in a British study (Light, Nee, and Ingham, 1993). Obviously, their views and experiences may not be typical even of British car thieves, let alone thieves operating in the United States or elsewhere. The main findings of the study, supported by the work of Fleming (1999), are summarized as follows:

- Most offenders began to steal cars in their early to mid-teens with the help of more experienced offenders.
- The influence of friends, the excitement of stealing cars, and boredom were the reasons given for first getting involved in car theft.
- Over time, the opportunity to make money from car theft seems to have be-

come more important, and more than a third progressed to "professional" car theft for financial gain.
- More than half described themselves as "specialists," stealing cars more or less to the exclusion of other crimes. Specialists were more likely to have had a youthful obsession with cars.
- Car alarms appeared to be of some deterrent value. A third said all alarms deterred them, while another quarter said some makes and models did.
- While accepting that car theft was morally wrong, most offenders did not consider it a serious crime.
- The excitement of car theft seemed to overcome any appreciation of the threat of punishment. Nine out of ten said they were not deterred by the prospect of being caught.
- Most of those who said they had stopped stealing cars put this down to increased responsibilities and maturity. The threat of penal sanctions seemed relatively unimportant in stopping offending.

Perhaps more than some other crimes, auto theft is complicated by its mixing of instrumental and expressive motives. When thieves steal cars to make money, the motive is clearly financial and the crime often has the hallmarks of the specialist; when a car is stolen for joyriding or as a gag, the crime is usually opportunistic and often ends with the vehicle being dumped somewhere in much worse condition. In both cases, however, the crime usually involves more than one person, which is also the case with confidence games, to which we now turn.

TRADITIONAL CONFIDENCE GAMES

Swindlers have been around for centuries. Swindlers and con artists rely on people wanting something for nothing, and they often say, "You can't cheat an honest man." There are no national data on **con games**, thefts committed through apparently legitimate but fraudulent means. Neither the FBI's Uniform Crime Reports nor the NCVS list them as an individual item. Partly because of this, most of the research has been impressionistic and anecdotal (Friedman, 1992: 21).

Variations on the con game are numerous. For at least two hundred years, two of the most common con games have been "ring dropping" and "purse dropping." Both involve simple techniques of manipulation, and both take advantage of the victim's gullibility and desire to make easy money. In ring dropping, a worthless piece of jewelry is dropped by one member of the con team (the "roper" or "steerer") near a stranger (the victim or "mark"). A second member of the team (the "inside man") rushes forward to pick up the jewelry and, after showing it to the mark, agrees to share the proceeds if the stranger will sell it. The mark is persuaded to leave something of value with the inside man as security—a token of good faith. The climax of the game is obvious—the inside man absconds with the security, leaving the mark to discover that the jewelry is worthless.

The game just described is one variety of swindles commonly referred to as "short con" or "bunco." The aim in short con is to fleece marks of whatever they have with them at the time or can obtain in a matter of minutes. In a short con, the amount of preparation needed and the size of the take are generally small. It can be put into motion at a moment's notice and the score is usually a matter of dollars and cents (Roebuck and Johnson, 1964). Another common version of the short con is the "pigeon drop," which operates along lines similar to ring dropping but requires more manipulative abilities by the bunco artist. In the typical pigeon drop, the victim is invited to share money that has supposedly been found by one member of the confidence team, but in order to qualify for a share the mark must first demonstrate good faith by putting up some of his or her own money. This money is then mixed with money supposedly put up by the con artist, but in fact the money is switched and the victim ends up with a bag full of worthless paper.

The successful con artist must accomplish at least three things: (1) make the mark trust the con operator; (2) make the mark believe that his or her part in the enterprise will be rewarding; and, most important, (3) convince the mark to part ("temporarily," of course) with some of his or her own money. Clearly, a good deal of smooth talking and friendly persuasion is usually necessary. This is where good con artists excel (Roebuck and Johnson, 1964: 236).

Big-con operators often adhere to a sequence of steps, each of which must be successfully accomplished if the con is to work. As each step is completed, it becomes more difficult for the mark to abandon the enterprise and more likely that the swindle will succeed. Seven major steps in the sequence have been identified:

- Step 1: Tying into the mark—finding a victim, gaining his confidence, getting him ready for step two.
- Step 2: Telling the mark the tale—showing the victim what is at stake for him, and how he can get hold of it.
- Step 3: Initial money gaff—letting the mark make some money to show how easy it is.
- Step 4: Putting the mark on the send—sending the victim for money.
- Step 5: Playing the mark against the store—fleecing him of his money.
- Step 6: Cooling out the mark—see explanation below.
- Step 7: Putting the mark in the door—getting rid of the victim. (Gasser, 1963: 48–51)

One of the most important steps in the sequence of events is "cooling out" the victim. Con artists recognize that victims will be angry when they discover they have been duped. Accordingly, they take a special step, the purpose of which is to reduce the chances that the mark will cause trouble. They hope the mark will be convinced to forget the whole incident.

Generally, con artists avoid using violence, even if it means losing the score (Roebuck and Johnson, 1964). How, then, do they cool out the mark? One method is to create a twist whereby victims become apparent accessories to a felony (sometimes murder) and hence think they have committed a crime. From being a victim, the mark is now a criminal, facing a prison sentence if caught. Of course, the whole situation is contrived; the con artists stage a fake murder. For example, the mark in the excellent film *The Sting*, assuming himself to be an accessory to murder, was only too glad to forget the whole incident.

Erving Goffman has discussed a second method of cooling out the mark. This method relies on "the art of consolation." Instead of generating fear in victims, the con artists help them redefine the situation and themselves so that they feel more comfortable with the outcome. By emphasizing that it was extremely hard to con the mark or that the mark presented a real challenge, the con operators help the victim regain a positive self-image. Although the stakes are higher, this method is rather like the situation in which a chess opponent who has just beaten you proceeds to commend you on your play and the challenge you offered. You have still lost the game, but you feel much better. Redefining the situation for the mark provides "a new set of apologies . . . [and] a new framework in which to see himself and judge himself" (1952: 456).

It is the nature of confidence games and swindles that the best targets are people with money but without the means to adequately protect themselves from the swindler's clever deceit. Elderly people are particularly vulnerable, and it should come as no surprise that they are more often targeted than any other group. A 1990 national survey of bunco investigators representing 331 police departments in thirty-nine states focused on the elderly

as victims in three types of swindles: the pigeon drop, the "bank examiner" swindle, and home improvement and repair frauds (Friedman, 1992). Since the first has already been described and the last is taken up in chapter 6, here we will discuss the bank examiner scheme. In this fraud, the mark is asked to help check out the honesty of a local bank teller suspected of stealing. The prospective victim is asked to help with this investigation by withdrawing a large sum of money from the bank in cash, often several thousand dollars, and making sure the withdrawal is handled by the suspected teller. When the victim returns home, he or she is met by a "bank examiner," who takes the withdrawn money for "laboratory analysis" after giving the victim an official-looking receipt (Friedman, 1992: 27–28).

Friedman's survey found that the victims of these three types of swindle were very similar: Most were white, unmarried women between sixty-five and seventy-nine years old, living alone and not working outside the home. When investigators were asked what characteristics would make an elderly person attractive to swindlers, the most common responses were being friendly to strangers and showing visible signs of financial assets such as expensive clothes and jewelry. Some differences among the three types of fraud emerged when investigators were asked to describe the typical characteristics of the bunco artists: Pigeon drop swindlers are most likely to work in teams of two, while home improvement swindlers work in teams of three or more; home repair swindlers are most likely to be white males, while pigeon drop teams are mixed race or black and mixed gender; on all dimensions, bank examiner swindlers tend to fall in between, according to police investigators.

FENCING STOLEN PROPERTY

Fencing overlaps the worlds of criminal enterprise and legitimate work. It binds theft to the larger social system. Without someone to dispose of stolen property (a **fence**), thieves would have to rely on their own connections, and the costs and risks of crime would increase substantially. For the rest of society, the fence provides an opportunity for people to buy something at less than market price.

The legal requirements for demonstrating that fencing has occurred are complex and help explain why police and prosecutors rely on highly specialized enforcement strategies in combating the crime. In America, as in England, there are four elements to the crime: (1) the property must have been stolen, (2) the property must have been received or concealed (though a fence may not have actually seen or touched it), (3) the receiver must have accepted it with the knowledge (in some states, merely the belief) that it was stolen, and (4) the property must have been received with criminal intent.

One must remember also that most fencing is carried on by "lay" or amateur fences, people who periodically deal in stolen property in networks involving family, friends, neighbors, and coworkers. Lay receivers may be essentially law abiding ("square johns") or may dabble in other forms of crime (Shover, 1973). The thieves they connect with are often young, usually amateurs, and many do not know professional fences. They have no alternative but to unload their booty on friends and acquaintances.

Ethnographic research on burglary shows that a majority of burglars sell directly to the public (Cromwell, Olson, and Avary, 1991; Wright and Decker, 1994). There are four main ways they do this: (1) selling directly to friends or neighbors; (2) selling at auctions, markets, trunk sales, or through classified ads; (3) selling to strangers in bars, clubs, amusement arcades, or Laundromats; and (4) selling to unsuspecting or unquestioning pawnbrokers and secondhand dealers (Sutton, 1993: 5).

Selling to strangers is probably more risky than the other methods, and this undoubtedly accounts in some measure for the fact that it is mentioned less often by active thieves. Even so, Wright and Decker found this method used by twelve of the ninety burglars who spoke to them about disposing of hot property (1994: 188–92). Some burglars express a carefree attitude:

> Man, just like if I see you on the street I walk up and say, "Hey, you want a brand new nineteen-inch color TV? . . . You say, "Yeah," and give me seventy-five dollars. I'll plug it in for you. (189)

Professional "businessman" fences and thieves are better organized and better connected than amateur thieves and lay fences. They buy from thieves with the intention of reselling, and they often keep a stock of goods on hand. The relationship between professional thieves and fences is one of mutual support. Though many professional fences remain on the periphery of professional theft, they are often a useful source of tips and information for thieves. By acting as a source of information, fences retain better control of their own business because they know what is "coming down" and which goods will be available. This works to the advantage of both fence and thief.

Networking

Connections are vital to the fence, whose business is essentially word of mouth. The importance of networking was first established by Marilyn Walsh (1977). She identified three types of networks: (1) kinship networks, dominated by family ties, often with young members stealing and older members selling; (2) workaday networks, often based on employer-employee relations, as when a fence with a legitimate business receives stolen merchandise from an employee; and (3) play networks, groups of "good" burglars and fences who meet socially and exchange information. Other research has documented the extensive contacts of successful fences (Klockars, 1974; Steffensmeier, 1986). They found that fencing requires resourcefulness, charisma, ingenuity, and a good grasp of market practices and the rules of economic competition. Pricing norms and prevailing market conditions are used to determine what is "fair," and a sense of justice is developed based on the risks borne by the thief. The motivation for being fair with thieves is rarely altruism; it stems from the need to maintain a good reputation and good relations with valued customers. In this respect, the fence is no different from anyone whose knowledge and power provide a temptation to exploit others that must be overcome if the goal is long-term prosperity.

To leave the topic of fencing with the impression that it is primarily an entrepreneurial activity carried out by astute businesspeople who make a good living at it ignores the extensive hidden trading among "ordinary people." A word, then, about Stuart Henry's (1978) important work: Henry studied amateur fencing, or "on-the-side" trading, as he calls it. He used information provided by friends, fellow workers, neighbors, relatives, university colleagues, and even the local hairdresser.

Most of the amateur trading took place within loose networks of collusion, and a participant's job usually provided the opportunity and incentive to get involved. But Henry points out that rarely was the incentive need or greed. He believes that on-the-side trading is largely inconsequential, if not actually unprofitable, from a material standpoint: Things are sold for no more, and often less, than they cost. A beer or a promise of favors returned is often sufficient payment. As one participant put it: "No one really makes any money. Not real money. . . . The bloke who sells it is not actually making anything either" (1978: 89). The real profits are of a social nature—forging and maintaining good relations with acquaintances, neighbors, and workmates, and the fostering of "community spirit." To be sure, these social benefits may have a material side, but Henry's informants rarely mentioned it.

All this may help explain why amateur trading is so extensive and why participants do not think of themselves as criminals. They see themselves as ordinary people who are not doing anything really dishonest. Since they do not "need" to steal, the stereotype of the "real" criminal doesn't apply: "People in ordinary, honest jobs know that they do not have to fiddle, pilfer, or deal in order to earn a living" (Henry, 1978: 76). Thievery is certainly more justifiable if its criminality can be defined away.

COMPUTER AND INTERNET CRIME

The increasing availability of personal computers has provided many new opportunities for criminal activity. While much theft and fraud by computer is committed by employees against their employers (discussed in chapter 6), our focus here is on nonoccupational computer crimes. We begin with hackers.

Hackers are people who break the security of an organization's computer network. Emmanuel Goldstein, editor of *2600: The Hacker's Quarterly*, once said: "While it's certainly possible to use hacking ability to commit a crime, once you do this you cease being a hacker and commence being a criminal. It's really not a hard distinction to make" (CNN, 2000).

Many hackers are simply motivated by the challenge of figuring out how to beat a security system. Both a science and an art, hacking involves a certain level of skill, knowledge, commitment, and creativity. It also takes higher than average intelligence to be a successful hack. The motivations for hacking vary. Sometimes hackers are simply interested in understanding how systems work and how they can be compromised. Other hackers have compared the challenge and high they receive with cracking a code. Some hackers vandalize, deface, or otherwise disrupt networks and Web sites, but do not actually steal information, commodities, or cash. They can nevertheless cause considerable harm. Major commercial Web sites, such as those maintained by CNN, Amazon.com, and E*TRADE, have been subject to *denial of service attacks*. This is when a "black-hat" hacker sends commands to other hackable "zombie" supercomputers, which then flood a targeted Web site with thousands of simultaneous requests. This disrupts the site's normal operation and may cause it to crash.

Similar attacks may come in the form of e-mail bugs, Trojan horses, and viruses that compromise (and sometimes destroy) e-mail networks and servers. Perhaps the most famous case involves the Melissa virus, which eventually caused $80 million in damages as a result of system damage to computer networks. Such attacks can disable Web sites and networks and companies can lose serious money in sales, repairs, and additional security and software expenses.

One of the most common forms of hacker computer crime is breaking into the network system of a credit card company or credit service bureau, stealing confidential information, and then using that information to obtain loans, cash advances, and, of course, merchandise. Even nonbanking Web sites—such as those run by colleges, universities, and employment exchange venues (such as monster.com)—are vulnerable to attack as criminal hackers seek to gain social security numbers, e-mail and housing addresses, and other personal information that could be used to steal someone's identity.

Anyone who regularly uses e-mail has probably received numerous messages from individuals pretending to represent a legitimate financial or state institution. Known as **phishing,** these communications are designed to trick people into providing the sender with personal information, which can be then used to commit other frauds or crimes such as identity theft. We receive several of these e-mail messages each day, many of which are masqueraded as communiqués from eBay, AOL, PayPal, Amazon.com, or any number of banks or foreign governmental agencies. Usually the messenger asks you to visit a Web site using a link embedded in the e-mail; the

link sends the user to a phony Web site that often looks quite legitimate. Once there, a user may have already given the phisher control of his or her computer or may be asked to enter personal information. If either happens, potentially serious financial harm could result through subsequent identity theft.

The range of crimes that can be committed via the computer is staggering: fraud, theft, extortion, piracy, intimidation, and even espionage. It is impossible to predict the future of computer crime, just as it was impossible for people fifteen years ago to understand how dramatically their lives would be transformed with the advent of e-mail and online commerce.

Entire subcultures have developed around computer hacking. So-called cyberpunk or phreak groups, like other subcultures, often times have unique norms and customs, such as specialized vocabularies and nicknames. The well-publicized release from prison of legendary hacker Kevin David Mitnick illustrates these subcultural elements. Mitnick was found guilty a few years ago for hacking into corporate Web sites and stealing software. Many fellow hackers protested the treatment of Mitnick and argued that while he did commit computer crimes, a five-year prison sentence was not justifiable. He is regarded as a martyr in the hacker community.

PROFESSIONAL THEFT

Professional theft has a history going back at least to Elizabethan times, when *conny catching* (a type of swindling) was a full-time profession. Through the years other varieties of theft became the focus of professionalization, with shoplifting and pocket picking two of the more common ones. Much of what is known about professional theft and the professional thief has come from firsthand accounts by thieves (both practicing and reformed), many of which are of the "as told to" variety. Among the best known are *The Professional Thief,* edited by Edwin Sutherland; Ernest Booth's *Stealing Through Life*; *My Life in Crime*, reported by John Bartlow Martin; and *Box Man: A Professional Thief's Journey*, as told to William Chambliss. To those must be added an assortment of books and articles focusing on professionalism in specific types of theft—for example, confidence games, burglary, forgery, and pocket picking.

By far the most influential work on professional theft has been Sutherland's *The Professional Thief* (1937b). Sutherland used the written accounts of one professional thief ("Chic Conwell") to illustrate the complex assortment of behavior characteristics, attitudes, organizational features, subcultural patterns, and worldviews that together make up a way of life shared by professional thieves.

In describing the world to which he belonged, Chic Conwell tells us that professional thieves (1) "make a regular business of stealing"; (2) acquire their skills and professional know-how through tutelage by and association with already established professionals; (3) develop highly skilled work techniques, the most important of which is the "ability to manipulate people"; (4) carefully plan everything they do in connection with their business; (5) look upon themselves as different from amateurs and superior to them, particularly those who indulge in sex crimes; (6) have a code of ethics that "is much more binding among thieves than that among legitimate commercial firms"; (7) are "sympathetic" and "congenial" with each other; (8) view successes and failures as "largely a matter of luck"; (9) have an established vocabulary of criminal slang, the main purpose of which is to enhance "we-feeling" and promote ease of intraprofession communication; (10) rarely engage in only one specialized form of theft (the notable exception being pickpockets, or "cannons"); and (11) usually operate in gangs, "mobs," or partnerships whose life span is generally short unless they are consistently successful (Sutherland, 1937b: 2–42).

Summarizing Conwell's account of professional theft, Sutherland offers this conception of the profession:

> The profession of theft is more than isolated acts of theft frequently and skillfully performed. It is a group way of life and a social institution. It has techniques, codes, status, traditions, consensus, and organization. It has an existence as real as that of the English language. It can be studied with relatively little attention to any particular thief. The profession can be understood by a description of the functions and relationships involved in this way of life. In fact, an understanding of this culture is a prerequisite to the understanding of the behavior of a particular professional thief. (1937b: ix–x)

A key feature of professionalism is the maintenance of a system that confers status and prestige. Status distinctions are based on a variety of things: type of theft engaged in, skill and technical competence, success, connections, and commitment. As in any other profession, participants confer prestige and recognition upon one another and distinguish the entire fraternity from outsiders—those who do not belong.

Within the ranks of professional thieves, certain specialties stand out. Confidence men and safecrackers have traditionally been considered at the top of the pecking order. Their work involves considerable skill and ability, and the payoffs can be substantial for those who succeed. At the other end of the status hierarchy are those whose jobs usually have a small payoff, involve more modest levels of skill and risk, and whose victims are typically individuals or small businesses. Cannons (pickpockets), "boosters" (professional shoplifters), and small-time burglars are examples of low-status thieves. Here is how two thieves view shoplifting:

> A booster is just about the lowest thief there is. Nobody has much to do with them. I mean, I seen one yesterday as a matter of fact. I saw this one, then talked to this other

guy who was a meter-robber; you know, a guy who robs parking meters. They make a lot of money. I was talking to this friend and he said he saw Charlie boosting the other day. I told him: "Gee, Charlie Jay? Man, I can remember when he was a real high-classed thief." "Oh," he said, "he's down at the bottom now." In our estimation he's down dragging bottom because he's boosting. And he used to be a real high-classed thief at one time. (King, 1972: 81)

It appears that "good" thieves also do not think much of women who venture into crime. In a rare investigation of the issue, Darrell Steffensmeier and Robert Terry (1986) interviewed forty-nine male thieves: most of them experienced, some of them probably ranking as professionals. These thieves identified various traits that they felt were particularly important to their trade, but which women were perceived to lack. In their view, successful thieves are physically strong, they have "heart" ("guts" or courage), they are aggressive when they need to be, they have endurance, they can be trusted when the chips are down, they are emotionally stable, they stay calm and cool under pressure, and they command respect. Most thieves claimed to have committed crimes with women at one time or another, but in no cases were the women full partners in the crimes, being relegated instead to peripheral sex/service roles for which they received a less-than-equal share of the "score." Even in crime, it seems, women are treated as second-class citizens.

In contrast to professional thieves, a considerable number of property offenders are not skilled in the finer techniques of theft. This other group of offenders has been called **persistent thieves,** those who continue their involvement in property offenses even after an arrest. These thieves often use the proceeds of their crimes to "party," that is, to consume heavy amounts of drugs and alcohol in a group setting (Shover and Henderson, 1995; Shover and Honaker, 1992; 1999). The phrase "life as party" refers to "the enjoyment of

'good times' with minimal concern for obligations and commitments that are external to the person's immediate social setting" (Shover, 1996: 93). This may include unconventional sleeping hours, just "hanging out" at home for days listening to music or watching television, and frequenting bars, taverns, lounges, and parks. Contrary to the professional thief, those stealing for party pursuits often do so spontaneously and unprofessionally. Several studies have shown that these offenders commit their crimes when they are high and drunk (e.g., Shover and Honaker, 1999)—hardly a very professional way to go about their thievery.

CHAPTER SUMMARY

This chapter has examined shoplifting, burglary, computer crimes, and confidence games, as well as fencing and the fix, which help support them. The social organization of professional theft was also examined, as well as the convergence of professional theft and occupational crime, the subject of chapter 6.

Stealing has a long history and is found in some form in many societies. Without private property, however, the concept of theft is moot. Theft laws have been shaped by conflicting interests and by the power of property owners to protect that property. A society that values the acquisition of material wealth but also has gross inequalities in the distribution of material resources finds itself encouraging theft, as appears to have happened in the United States. Many thefts are not reported to the police, but even those that are usually remain unsolved. In this respect, most forms of theft are low-risk crimes, a fact that also contributes to high offense rates.

Most thieves are opportunists who sporadically shoplift, forge checks, or burglarize businesses or residences with minimal planning or skill. Many do not think of themselves as criminals, either denying their crimes altogether or blaming their actions on situational pressures. Professional thieves, on the other hand, maintain a complicated system of roles and norms in terms of which participants gain status, prestige, and professional identity. In between the rank amateurs and the professionals are "ordinary property offenders," people who spend many years at crimes of all sorts, usually beginning at an early age, often spending considerable time in prison, and rarely making much money at crime. As they grow older they commit fewer crimes, and many eventually quit the largely unsuccessful criminal lifestyle to "go straight."

Fencing and the fix provide important links between legitimate society and the world of theft. Without them, neither theft nor thieves would prosper, and with them it is possible for ostensibly "straight" society to cash in on the criminality of others. In both fencing and the fix, information networks are vital for the success of the enterprise, and this draws knowledgeable, connected individuals to the center of power relations in the underworld.

KEY TERMS

burglary
Carrier's Case
con games
fence

hackers
persistent thieves
phishing

RECOMMENDED READINGS

Cromwell, Paul. (2006). *In Their Own Words: Criminals on Crime*. 4th ed. Los Angeles: Roxbury.

Katz, Jack. (1988). *Seductions of Crime: Moral and Sensual Attractions in Doing Evil*. New York: Basic Books.

Tunnell, Kenneth D. (1992). *Choosing Crime: The Criminal Calculus of Property Offenders*. Chicago: Nelson-Hall.

———. (2000). *Living Off Crime*. Chicago: Burnham.

Wright, Richard T., and Scott H. Decker. (1994). *Burglars on the Job*. Boston: Northeastern University Press.

RECOMMENDED WEB SITES

The International Association of Auto Theft Investigators (http://www.iaati.org/). Reports, statistics and links on all kinds of thefts.

Illinois State Police (http://www.state.il.us/isp/). Information on dozens of frauds and con games.

⬛CHAPTER

6 WHITE-COLLAR CRIME

A5T0B0 Alamy

So far the text has focused on what are "traditional" or "street" crimes. Robbery, rape, murder, assault, burglary, and other thefts are traditional crimes in a number of senses. First, they are among the activities that most readily come to mind when people think of crime. Second, they are the conventional targets of criminalization. Third, they have long been the prime focus of law-enforcement efforts. And fourth, it is primarily around these kinds of crime that criminologists have framed their theories.

Robbery, burglary, assault, and rape may be called traditional crimes, but this does not mean they are the most common forms of crime or that they create the most victims, the highest economic costs, or the greatest damage to social institutions. The crimes discussed in this chapter have far greater impact on society, and often on individual victims as well. A closer look at occupational and organizational crimes will show that "crimes in the suites" deserve far more attention than they commonly receive in the press—and in criminology.

Types of White-Collar Crime

The term **white-collar crime** was coined in 1939 by Edwin H. Sutherland. He defined it as crime committed by people of respectability and high social status in the course of their occupations. Sutherland also observed that criminologists had virtually ignored the illegal activities of those in business, politics, and the professions, concentrating instead on the world of lower-class criminality emphasized in crime statistics and in the criminal justice system. Lawbreaking, he argued, goes on in all social strata. Restraint of trade, misrepresentation in advertising, violations of labor laws, violations of copyright and patent laws, and financial manipulations were a part of what Sutherland called white-collar crime.

Over the years since Sutherland's groundbreaking work, other criminologists have refined the definition of white-collar crime. One of the earliest of these was Marshall Clinard and Richard Quinney's (1973) effort to define white-collar crime in more operational terms. They split the concept of white-collar crime into **corporate crime**—crimes organizationally based and directed towards reaching *corporate* goals—and **occupational crime**, acts committed by individuals in the course of their occupations for their own *personal* gain.

Another advance in white-collar crime research came when scholars argued that organizations are social actors in their own right and can be studied criminologically because they persist over time, develop and maintain procedures, and pursue goals (Hall, 1987). Furthermore, "[p]reoccupation with individuals can lead us to underestimate the pressures within society and organizational structure, which impel those individuals to commit illegal acts" (Schrager and Short, 1978: 410). Thus, "the principal rationale for distinguishing organizational crime is the assumption that organizational dynamics, conditions, and constraints . . . play a major part in their onset and course" (Shover and Wright, 2001: 3). **Organizational crime** can be defined as follows:

> Organizational crimes are illegal acts of omission or commission of an individual or group of individuals in a legitimate formal organization in accordance with the operative goals of the organization, which have a serious impact on employees, consumers, or the general public (Schrager and Short, 1978: 411).

Organizational crimes may be committed by a private or public organization. Thus, corporate crime is a type of organizational crime.

Another type of white-collar crime is **governmental crime** (sometimes called *political crime*), which may be committed by organizations or by individuals. There are several forms of governmental crime:

1. *State crime*: Illegal or socially injurious acts of omission or commission by an individual or group of individuals in an institution of legitimate governance that are executed for the consummation of the operative goals of that institution of governance. (Kauzlarich, 2007)

2. *State-corporate crime*: Illegal or socially injurious actions that result from mutually reinforcing interaction between institutions of political governance and institutions of economic production and distribution. (Michalowski and Kramer, 2006)

3. *Political white-collar crime*: Illegal activities carried out by political officials for direct personal benefit. (Friedrichs, 2004)

Clearly, there are many different offenses that fall within the realm of white-collar crime. Apart from the illegal activities already mentioned (restraint of trade, unfair labor practices, and so on), there are embezzlement, a variety of consumer frauds, thefts by computer, music and record pirating, prescription law violations, employee pilfering, food and drug law violations, bribery and other forms of corruption by public officials, kickbacks, illegal wars, and violations of human rights—the list could go on and on. As might be anticipated from this list, white-collar crime is by no means a new problem; it dates from the first time people regularly put time, energy, and ability into sustenance activities for which they received some form of reward.

As suggested by this discussion, white-collar crime varies by its organizational complexity and in its consequences for victims. One study looked at eight different offenses—antitrust violations, securities fraud, mail fraud, false claims, credit fraud, bribery, tax fraud, and bank embezzlement—in terms of these two dimensions. Securities and antitrust violations were at the high end of both dimensions, and tax fraud, credit fraud, and bank embezzlement at the other end (Weisburd, Waring, and Chavet, 1991). The other offenses fell in between.

When compared with "common crimes"—in this case, postal theft and forgery—the authors of the study found that their white-collar crimes differed noticeably from common crimes on these same two dimensions. Postal theft and forgery were less likely to victimize organizations, had mostly local impact, involved little potential gain, victimized far fewer people, were much less likely to involve five or more coconspirators, and seldom involved a pattern of offending. The largest difference pertained to duration of the crime: Very few common crimes lasted more than a year, while half the white-collar crimes did. We shall return to a comparison of occupational and street crimes later in this chapter.

WORK AND THE HISTORICAL DEVELOPMENT OF LEGAL CONTROLS

The regulation of economic behavior has a long history. Long before the modern era, there was widespread appreciation of the dangers and injustices of unregulated marketplace behavior. It requires little imagination to see how important orderly and fair economic relations must have been during a time when most people lived in small villages and knew each other.

However, the Industrial Revolution eventually pushed market exploitation "into the shadows, camouflaged by its remoteness, the diffuse nature of the harm it inflicted, and the obscurity of the source of the harm" (Geis, 1988: 15). As a result, the public sense of injustice and indignation waned. As a fledgling capitalist society applied itself to the practical problems of making capitalism work, industrial power and wealth reached heights never before imagined. During the late nineteenth century, there emerged a drive to check corporate power and the economic abuses spreading from it. First the railroads and later corporations in general became the targets of regulatory reforms. However, rather than a systematic response to problems, the

regulatory movement consisted of sporadic responses "to a series of disasters" (21), from coal mine explosions to deformed babies born to mothers who had taken thalidomide (Hills, 1971: 151).

The Role of Interests

The full flavor of laws relating to occupations is lost unless the role of special interests is considered. Besides the fact that many past laws were weighted in favor of elites—so the penalties for violation were less the higher one's social status—few laws formalized the obligations of masters and employers toward their servants, slaves, and employees. In addition, some laws were clearly designed to consolidate ruling-class control over economic and political activities and thus over the production and distribution of wealth and material advantages. Consider, for example, laws against criminal fraud.

Fraud

When people induce someone to part with money or valuables through the use of deceit, lies, or misrepresentation, they commit fraud, or what was called a "cheat" in earlier times. Under English common law, criminal liability extended only to situations in which (1) some false token or tangible device of trickery was involved and (2) the activity was such that reasonable prudence could not guard against it and any member of the general public was a potential victim (Turner, 1966). Under common law, personal fraud directed against a private individual was no crime, because it was customary to assume that individuals would exercise due caution in their financial dealings with others and because when an individual was deceived, civil remedies were available.

With the rise of capitalism, entrepreneurs throughout the business community urged Parliament to broaden the range of criminal liability associated with fraudulent practices. In

1757 a statute was passed establishing the crime of "obtaining property by false pretenses." Subsequently adopted in the American colonies, this law has remained one of the few specifically criminal statutes dealing with fraud.

Despite the extensive victimization associated with consumer fraud, the courts until recently had operated on the principle of *caveat emptor*—buyer beware. The idea was simply that in making purchases, consumers have only themselves to blame if they are "taken." Reasonable as this may sound, it actually encourages victimization in the modern marketplace, where the complex nature of many products, services, and organizations are such that even knowledgeable purchasers find it almost impossible to protect themselves against fraud. For example, because of modern supermarket packaging practices, shoppers can rarely inspect the products they want to buy in more than a superficial way, leading to the passage of laws protecting against consumer fraud in the food and drug industries.

Pure Food and Drug Laws

Interest in the regulation of the food and drug industries first gained prominence during the nineteenth century, as cities grew and consumers became increasingly removed from agricultural producers and the possibilities for adulteration, spoilage, exploitation, and fraud increased. Public awareness of the problem was stirred partly through the changing experience of buying itself, but mostly by newspaper editorials and by articles and books that stressed the dangers of existing business practices, sometimes in lurid and frightening detail.

The first major federal legislation aimed at regulating the food and drug industries was introduced in 1880 and soundly defeated, as were many subsequent bills: "It and other efforts like it were defeated by a durable alliance of quacks, ruthless crooks, pious frauds, scoundrels, high-priced lawyer-lobbyists, vested interests, liars, corrupt members of Congress, venal publishers, cowards in

high office, the stupid, the apathetic, and the duped" (Mintz, 1970: 78–79). When Congress finally passed the Federal Food and Drugs Act of 1906, it was only the first step in what has turned out to be a long and hard battle between public interests and the food and drug industries.

The 1906 law made it illegal to manufacture or introduce into the United States any adulterated or misbranded food or drug. Offenders could have their products seized, and those convicted of violating the law would be subject to criminal penalties. Thus a new area of occupational crime was born. But it has been argued that the new law contained inadequate regulation of advertising and provided no provisions applying to cosmetics or the use of health devices (Quinney, 1970). Indeed, "nearly 100 years after public interest was first mobilized, Americans could count on one hand the number of truly significant bills designed to regulate the powerful industries supplying their food, pharmaceutical products, and cosmetics" (79).

If it were not for the efforts of Ralph Nader, the American public might still be buying meat products largely unregulated by legal controls. In 1906 Upton Sinclair had described the disgusting conditions of meat slaughterhouses in his highly popular novel *The Jungle*. In 1967 Nader found that we were still "in the jungle." His investigation found meat that was contaminated with disease and spoiled carcasses—even manure and pus—and often sold in a deceptive and fraudulent manner. While cases of this magnitude are rare now, deliberate selling of unsafe food still happens. For example, in January 2000 a Grand Rapids, Michigan, food distribution firm pleaded guilty to selling adulterated and contaminated meat and poultry to a Detroit retail grocer (Food Safety and Inspection Service, 2000).

Like many problems related to consumer protection and safety, these appalling conditions in the meat and food industry are partly the result of the inadequacy of existing federal and state laws and partly the pitiful efforts to enforce them. Both problems are blamed on the cozy relationship among the United States Department of Agriculture (USDA), state agriculture agencies, and the meat production and processing interests. When Congress passed the Wholesale Meat Act of 1968—bringing intrastate meat processing under federal jurisdiction and establishing stricter controls—another small victory for public welfare was achieved and the range of legal penalties extended. However, the Reagan administration systematically undermined the law by cutting back on expenditures for enforcement, and states have generally done no better. The Clinton administration, however, increased efforts to control the quality of food with its support of the Food Quality Protection Act of 1996, but President George W. Bush has been less supportive of the measure.

THE COSTS OF WHITE-COLLAR CRIME

It is now appropriate to return to a matter raised in the opening paragraphs of this chapter: the costs of white-collar crime to individuals and society. A brief look at some of these costs should support a more balanced view of the impact of crime and serve as a reminder that societal reactions to a particular form of crime are not necessarily an accurate reflection of its impact on people's lives, their communities, and their institutions.

Financial Costs

The financial costs of white-collar crime far exceed those resulting from traditional crimes. This reflects the greater frequency with which white-collar crimes are committed and also the fact that a single offense can result in losses running into millions of dollars. Estimates place direct financial losses resulting from traditional street crimes such as burglary, murder, and robbery at $28 bil-

lion per year (Federal Bureau of Investigation, 2006a). By contrast, losses attributed to occupational fraud *alone* have been estimated at $652 billion per year (Association of Certified Fraud Examiners, 2006). Other white-collar crimes cost the public billions more: Financial fraud by the Enron Corporation cost investors and employees $25 to 50 billion (Greider, 2002); the savings and loan disaster of the late 1980s ended up costing more than $500 billion (Chambliss, 1999: 152); the extent of losses to employee theft is at least $15 billion a year (Hollinger, 2004); and price-fixing costs at least $60 billion a year (Simon, 2006). Although the overall financial costs of white-collar crime cannot be estimated with confidence—there are simply too many types and no systematic data collection for most of them—they are huge relative to street crimes. A recent conservative estimate puts the costs of street crime at only 6 percent of the costs of white-collar crime (Rosoff, Pontell, and Tillman, 2007).

Damage to Institutions and Moral Climate

Deception, fraud, price-fixing, bribery, kickbacks, and violations of trust undermine principles of honesty and fair play. They also foster a moral climate in which lawlessness provokes little indignation—especially when its victims are vague entities such as "the public," "the consumer," "the corporation," and "the government," and occurs largely free from any sense of guilt on the part of offenders. This results in the erosion of economic and political institutions. Looking out for number one, beating the system, getting something for nothing, or doing a favor for a price become accepted and expected practices for all social strata. When there is pervasive and unpunished thievery and corruption among leaders in business, the professions, and government, street criminals can easily rationalize their own illegal conduct as no different from that of their "betters" (Kauzlarich, Matthews, and Miller, 2001; Simon, 2006).

Personal Health and Safety

The greatest losses from white-collar crime involve personal health and safety. Occupational, organizational, and political crimes pose health and safety hazards in numerous ways:

- Companies violating safety standards for their products (cars, tires, electrical appliances, toys, nightclothes, Christmas tree lights, and many others) expose their customers to possible injury or death.
- Physicians who do unnecessary surgery expose their patients to the risk of surgical complications.
- Pharmaceutical companies conspiring to fix high prices threaten the well-being of those who need but cannot afford their products.
- Mine and factory bosses who violate health and safety regulations expose their workers to injury, disease, and death.
- Companies manufacturing or selling contaminated food products or mislabeled drugs expose their customers to unnecessary health hazards.

Now consider how state crime may produce physical injury and death:

- Illegal wars, invasions, and genocides have easily cost the lives of tens of millions of people in the twentieth and early twenty-first centuries. (Mullins and Rothe, 2008)
- U.S. governmental projects such as the manufacture and production of nuclear weapons have resulted in hundreds of thousands of deaths and perhaps millions of health problems.
- Illegal radiation experiments and nuclear weapons testing have claimed the lives of thousands of U.S. veterans and civilians. Thousands more have had their health compromised by such state actions. (Kauzlaric and Kramer, 1998)

- State regulatory agencies that ignore their mandate to protect workers, airplane passengers, and the environment have directly and indirectly led to death and injury. (Michalowski and Kramer, 2006)

There can be little doubt that when the health and safety of the population as a whole are considered, the threat posed by occupational, organizational, and political crime far exceeds that posed by traditional crimes. This is not to minimize the dangers associated with violence, rape, and robbery, but rather to place the two broad categories of crime in perspective. It is easy to overlook the dangers posed by white-collar crime because these are often less visible, less direct, and appear less concrete than those of street crimes. They are also commonly committed by people or groups in positions of considerable power. Yet these crimes are extensive. Take, for instance, the physical dangers associated with environmental pollution in the air, water, soil, workplace, and home. Millions of Americans are exposed every day to known carcinogens and other potentially lethal substances, often because corporations and businesses fail to meet environmental standards or find legal ways to circumvent them (Burns and Lynch, 2004; Clifford, 1998).

In Missouri the entire population of Times Beach was forced to evacuate because dioxin-tainted waste oil was sprayed on the roads to keep the dust down. Times Beach was a modern ghost town, with some former citizens suffering the delayed effects of dioxin (called *Agent Orange* during the Vietnam War). Many thousands of industrial workers will become ill or die because they work under conditions that needlessly expose them to carcinogens and severe respiratory ailments. Those in the rubber, steel, asbestos, coal, and chemical industries are especially vulnerable to such diseases. One of the most costly industrial disasters of all time has been tied to "unlawful, willful, malicious, and wanton" disregard for human safety—the December 1984 gas leak at the Union Carbide pesticide plant in Bhopal, India, which claimed 2,000 lives and injured 150,000 to 200,000 more. The Indian government eventually charged Union Carbide with moral responsibility and legal liability for the leak. For its part, the company accepted some responsibility but denied any criminal negligence.

As with most forms of crime, the risks and costs of being victimized by occupational crimes are not borne equally. The young, poor, and elderly are especially vulnerable to environmental crimes and to fraud of all sorts. As the population ages, we can expect to see more and more victimization of the elderly—not only by fast-talking salespeople, but also by corporate marketers who capitalize on their fear of change, their susceptibility to illness, their fear of having inadequate insurance, and their loneliness.

Occupational Crime: Violating the Law for Personal Gain

The motivations for occupational crime are varied and not simply economic. They include empire building, protection of top management from hostile takeovers, defense of activities that carry great prestige or confer respect, "glory, power, the exposure of traitors, a more just society, or simply easier ways of getting the job done" (Braithwaite, 1988: 628). This section explores crimes that are primarily committed by individuals for their own gain, in violation of loyalty to their employers or clients.

Embezzlement

There were about twenty thousand arrests for embezzlement in 2006 (Federal Bureau of Investigation, 2007). Embezzlement suspects are usually white, middle-class, middle-aged males, quite unlike the prevailing stereotype of the criminal (Poortinga, Lemmen, and Jibson, 2006). However, this police description of the typical offender may not be an accurate portrayal of the bulk of people embezzling

from their employers or clients. In terms of age and gender, Gottfredson and Hirschi (1990) believe that the typical embezzler is no different from the typical street criminal—that is, a young male—although their evidence for this claim is far from compelling (see chapter 15).

When the embezzler is a woman, she is usually a lower-level employee rather than an executive (Daly, 1988). Indications are that male and female rates of embezzlement are converging (Hirschi and Gottfredson, 1987: 961). It is not clear why this is so, but some believe it reflects increased employment of women in positions of financial trust, while others attribute it to the economic marginalization of many women, who find themselves in dire financial straits with families to support. It is probably a combination of both.

The embezzler has been called "the respectable criminal" (Cressey, 1965). Respectable or not, estimates of the frequency and costs of embezzlement are staggering. In 1967 the President's Commission on Law Enforcement and the Administration of Justice put the annual cost at more than $200 million; that figure is dwarfed by a 1974 estimate of $4 billion. The current figure is certainly much higher, perhaps in the hundreds of billions, although no reliable studies have been conducted on the exact cost (McMillan, 2006).

The respectability of embezzlers mentioned by many authors acknowledges not only the relatively high occupational status of many offenders but also the fact that they rarely have a delinquent or criminal record prior to their embezzling activities and rarely think of themselves as real criminals. According to a study of 1,001 embezzlers conducted some years ago, the typical male embezzler is the epitome of the moderately successful family man. He is "thirty-five, married, has one or two children. He lives in a respectable neighborhood and is probably buying his own home. He drives a low or medium priced car and his yearly income is in the top forty percent of the nation's personal income distribution" (Jaspan and Black, 1960: 24–25). The female embezzler also fits the picture of a respectable American, though her income was found to be in the bottom third of the nation's income distribution—a reflection of sex discrimination in jobs and salaries more than anything else.

In a classic study, Donald Cressey (1953) describes interviews with 133 embezzlers in penitentiaries in Illinois, Indiana, and California. His findings regarding the "etiology" of embezzlement—the factors leading up to it—show that embezzlers typically committed offenses after (1) coming up against a "non-shareable" financial problem, (2) recognizing that they could secretly resolve the problem by taking advantage of their positions of financial trust, and (3) engaging in rationalizations and justifications to protect their self-image as trustworthy employees or partners.

By a nonshareable problem, Cressey means almost any kind of financial difficulty the individual feels cannot be resolved by enlisting the help of another. It could be some unusual family expense or gambling debts, once thought to be the major cause of embezzlement. It could even be linked to attempts to keep up a particular standard of living. Rationalization occurs before or during the act of embezzling. Many of Cressey's subjects, and especially those who had been independent businesspeople, reasoned that they would be merely "borrowing" the money or that it really belonged to them anyway. The embezzlers-to-be often argued that they were merely adhering to a standard business practice: borrowing against future earnings. Looked at sequentially, then, a nonshareable problem leads to the search for a personal and secret solution, a position of financial trust provides the means to solve the problem, and rationalization provides the excuse.

One study could not substantiate Cressey's emphasis on the nonshareable financial problem as an impetus to embezzlement. Embezzlers were apparently driven to their crimes by temptation and avarice, and their jobs

provided the opportunity and the means (Nettler, 1974). A study of female embezzlers also challenges Cressey's explanation (Zeitz, 1981). In this research, subjects were more likely to justify their crimes in terms of family needs than in terms of a nonshareable problem.

Another point made by some criminologists is that embezzlement is more likely to be trivial and persistent than a carefully thought-out, last-ditch solution to a pressing financial problem (Gottfredson and Hirschi, 1990; Croall, 1989). This view receives some support from private security experts, who recommend that the best way to find embezzlers is to give employees a vacation that requires someone else to take over their duties: Embezzlers will resist the offer for fear their schemes will be uncovered in their absence (McMillan, 2006). A case came to light at our university precisely because the clerk involved had not taken a vacation for more than a year and thus drew the suspicions of her supervisor. She had been taking relatively small amounts of money over the course of three or four years, though in the aggregate her embezzlement reached hundreds of thousands of dollars. In any event, the explanation of embezzlement is not yet a matter of consensus.

FIDDLING AT WORK: PART OF THE HIDDEN ECONOMY

Operating within the legitimate world of work is a hidden economy in which goods and services are produced, stolen, or exchanged on the sly. There is no official record of this "fiddling," and the income obtained from it is rarely, if ever, taxed. Much of the activity is itself criminal, though rarely thought of as such by the participants or the general public. This quote illustrates the range of activities that make up the hidden economy:

A number of specific fiddles make up hidden property crime. These include ... taking company stock home to doing jobs "on the side." . . . Personal use of the firm's telephone, photocopying, or mailing service accounts for a certain amount of the kind of fiddling which may be claimed as perks, and overestimates of petrol [gasoline], food and travel allowances that appear as inflated expense accounts might also be seen in this light. In addition, there are a number of other . . . fiddles . . . such as short-changing, overloading, overestimating, under-the-counter selling, buying off-the-back-of-a-lorry [truck] goods, fiddling time, dodging fares, and smuggling duty-free goods. Nor should we neglect the numerous tax and social security fiddles involving undeclared income, falsely claimed allowances and misrepresented welfare benefits and rebate claims: nor corporate fiddles, such as computer fraud and industrial bribery. (Henry, 1978: 4–5)

Collectively, these fiddles cost billions of dollars (Friedrichs, 2004). In the United States, theft by retail employees is estimated by em-

ployers to account for almost half of their inventory shrinkage (National Retail Security Survey, 2005). Surveys of top management representing large and small firms across the United States show that no single generalization adequately describes the considerable differences in the nature and seriousness of employee crime across companies. However, executives are more likely to think that petty thefts, small frauds, and abuse of services are a more serious problem than large-scale thefts and frauds, violence, or sabotage (Baker and Westin, 1987).

This section focuses on pilferage on the job. There are many forms: Sometimes it is casual, sometimes systematic and repetitive; sometimes workers pilfer alone, at other times in more or less organized groups; and sometimes the pilferage victimizes the employer, sometimes the customer or client, and sometimes other workers. However, cash is rarely stolen directly, and the income obtained

Box 6.1. THEFT AND FRAUD BY CRIMINOLOGISTS

A nationally representative study of criminologists shows that fiddling and fraud exist among the ranks of those who study crime for a living. In "Criminologists: Are We What We Study?" Matthew Robinson and Barbara Zaitow (1999) present data based on a sample of 1,500 (N = 522) criminologists. Results of the study show that:

- 84 percent of the respondents reported that they had used departmental office supplies (pens, paper, copying, etc.) for personal rather than professional use. Eleven percent admitted to using grant money for personal use.
- 20 percent falsified travel receipts for reimbursement for things like conference attendance and participation.
- 18 percent admitted they had misrepresented their income to obtain a reduced membership fee in a professional organization. (Oftentimes membership fees are graduated).

Respondents were also asked to report on their nonoccupationally-related involvement in crime. A few of the findings: 22 percent admitted they had at least once engaged in burglary and 66 percent had at least once in their life driven a vehicle under the influence of alcohol.

Are criminologists, then, essentially "the pot calling the kettle black"? While the authors are cautious to conclude anything about prevalence of fraud and theft by criminologists compared to other groups, they did indeed establish that some criminologists do engage in the very behaviors they study.

through fiddling at work is generally considered secondary to that obtained legitimately (Friedrichs, 2004; Henry, 1978).

Certain jobs are associated with certain kinds of pilfering and pilferers. Gerald Mars (1983) identifies four types of work situations depending on the extent to which jobs constrain and insulate workers or foster reciprocity and competition among them, and the extent to which they give workers group support and control. Job pilferers are categorized as *hawks*, *donkeys*, *wolves*, or *vultures*.

Hawks

Hawks are found in jobs that stress individuality, competition, autonomy, and creativity. These jobs also have weak group support because workers largely control their own activities. Independent salespersons, successful journalists, small businesspeople, academics, and other professionals are likely to be hawks, but so too are waiters and owner-operator cabdrivers. Hawk fiddles usually involve the manipulation of time and work performance, and the scale of the fiddle increases with the status of the fiddler. Mars shows how accountants, lawyers, physicians, management consultants, and even university instructors are able to capitalize on their status and freedom from group control. Favorite fiddles of hawks are padding expense accounts and charging for work not actually performed. Professors have multiple opportunities to engage in hawkish fiddles, and, as box 6.1 shows, it appears as though quite a few criminologists do engage in minor forms of occupation fraud and fiddling.

Donkeys

Donkeys are in jobs characterized by isolation and relatively rigid constraints. Assembly line workers, supermarket cashiers, and retail salespeople are good examples. "The donkey type of fiddle is an appropriate response to this minimal autonomy. Since the job isolates the worker, the worker fiddles in isolation" (Mars, 1983: 71). New workers may learn of fiddling among their fellows, but there is no group support for it, nor is it practiced as a group activity. Bar stewards who give short-measured drinks, pocketing the difference between what each bottle would have brought in and actually does bring in, and cashiers who fiddle change or pocket money after ringing "no sale" on the till are examples of donkey fiddlers. Mars observes that donkey fiddles are often not motivated by material gain, but rather by the worker's greater sense of personal control. In addition, the absence of group controls may give rise to excessive fiddling, as when a short-order waiter skimmed $150 a day for a year before being found out (87).

Wolves

Wolf fiddlers operate in packs and are found in jobs in which the work is organized into crews: longshoremen, miners, prison guards, and garbage collectors are found in "wolf pack" jobs. The group comes to exercise a lot of control over the individual, and pilferage is organized and controlled by the group. Individualists are not welcome, and membership in the wolf pack is not automatic but through acceptance by other members. Members are held together by mutual dependence and trust, with much testing of the latter.

Dock pilferage by longshoremen in Newfoundland is typical of the wolf pack. Longshore work gangs are close knit, with controlled membership and a ranking system based on skill and trust that effectively controls any particular member's access to cargo by allocating work responsibilities. Only through access to cargo can a dockworker pilfer, and so jobs with such access are essential. On the other hand, the nature of dock work makes it important to have group support in order to pull off a fiddle. Since individual workers rarely have both access and support, dock pilferage remains group centered.

Vultures

Vultures hold jobs that offer autonomy and freedom but are subject to overarching bureaucratic control that encourages group influence. Vulture jobs are selling jobs, postal delivery, truck driving and other traveling jobs, taxi driving, and many service jobs. Fiddling tends to be exercised individually, but mutual self-interest keeps employees tied in a bond of sometimes uneasy cooperation. The relative instability of vulture occupations means that under the surface of cooperation there is competition, and when a particular fiddle threatens others' jobs, they close ranks against the offender.

One of us (Barlow) experienced a vulture fiddle. During a college vacation he was a delivery driver for Harrods department store in London. On the first day of work he learned from a codriver that two breakfasts, a two-hour lunch period, and an hour-long afternoon tea break on top of seven hours of delivering always produced a healthy overtime check. He also learned that his codriver expected him to conform to this schedule and that if he did not, it would not look good for the other drivers who were doing the same thing. The company supposedly knew about the time fiddle, and, so long as it did not become unreasonable, store management accepted it, he was told, in return for the drivers' staying nonunion. The other author of this text experienced vulture fiddles in a variety of jobs he took in college.

Obviously, employee theft is not a unitary phenomenon, occurring as it does in a great variety of contexts and involving different organizational characteristics, different levels of sophistication, and varying degrees of group support. On the other hand, some authors have argued that an underlying motive or drive behind much employee theft is worker perception of injustice in the workplace. Marginal, temporary, and socially isolated workers are at greatest risk of committing theft, since stealing provides a means of obtaining justice for their grievances (Tucker, 1989).

Tests of these hypotheses show inconsistent results. Interviews with retired garment workers found that employee theft was rarely selected because workers had grievances involving equity; rather, theft was explained in terms of work group influence and institutional supports promoted by the Garment Workers Union (Sieh, 1987). The idea that crime is driven by adversity (perceived or real) is an old one, and it has been the focus of considerable theory and research. Reasonable as the argument seems—most people would accept that angry and frustrated people often lash out at the perceived cause of their problems—as a general explanation this view has a difficult time accounting for the fact that employee theft seems to be a universal phenomenon found in all types of organizations, including those in which there is no evidence of low employee morale, job dissatisfaction, or perceived injustices (McMillan, 2006).

POLITICAL WHITE-COLLAR CRIME

Political white-collar crime is a violation of law by individuals in a position of governmental trust for their own personal gain. Political crimes committed for organizational gain are discussed later. Political white-collar crime manifests itself in two different, though often related, forms: (1) activities designed to bring about economic gain and (2) activities designed to perpetuate or increase political power (Friedrichs, 2004). Government officials who accept or demand kickbacks in return for a vote for legislation favorable to some individual or special group are engaged in corrupt activities that promise economic gains. Politicians who arrange to have cronies stuff ballot boxes with the names of nonexistent voters are engaged in corrupt practices designed to put keep themselves in office. Needless to say, those who gain economically from corrupt activities may also gain political power, and those who gain political power may also gain financially. Thus it is sometimes difficult to separate the economic and power dimensions of political corruption.

Finding out about political corruption is not easy, and this is as true for the criminologist as it is for the general public. One reason is the insider-outsider barrier that politicians erect in their dealings with others who are not part of the political establishment. Another is the cronyism characterizing relations among politicians and their friends in business and government. This encourages a "politics is politics" attitude among insiders, who would rather look the other way than make public trouble for a colleague. During the entire history of the United States Congress, only seven senators and nineteen representatives have been censured by their colleagues, although others have resigned before they could be censured.

A third reason it is difficult to learn about political corruption is that the agencies responsible for policing the politicians are themselves run by politicians. If an investigation of a particular official or agency is called for, it is usually pursued without fanfare and rarely results in the pressing of formal charges. Even when an investigation is reliably known to be underway, heads of the responsible agencies often deny it. Fourth, there are no official statistics on the kinds of occupational crime committed by those in politics and government. One looks in vain for "official misconduct," "high crimes and misdemeanors," "bribery," "influence peddling," and so forth in the annual Uniform Crime Reports. In fact, the only specifically occupational crime listed at all is embezzlement, which victimizes the establishment.

Political corruption is publicized primarily through the efforts of journalists and those who keep watch on government in the public interest: for example, Ralph Nader historically, and more contemporarily, a host of organizations with Web sites devoted to exposing political crime. Historically, Chicago has borne the brunt of media scrutiny for years, which has not blunted its reputation as the most politically corrupt city in America. From 1985 to 1988, federal grand juries indicted 265 public officials and government employees for corruption (*St. Louis Post-Dispatch*, October 16, 1988). Often, corruption comes to light because persons involved in it turn informer and approach the media or federal authorities. Someone who has been indicted may also "snitch" on others as part of a plea bargain.

Crimes for Money

Political crimes that come to light are usually notable because they have been committed by high officials, have involved substantial losses to the taxpayer, or have represented a systematic and extensive violation of public trust or civil rights. During the last few years, political corruption at the national and international levels has so dominated the headlines that local scandals seem mild by comparison. Actually, the victimization brought about by local corruption may have a more far-reaching and harmful effect on the lives of Americans. When—as happened recently in a midsized Illinois city—school board officials misappropriate thousands of dollars in school funds, it may take years to overcome the damage to local education, not to mention public trust.

In the course of their political careers, government officials sometimes find their pasts catching up with them after they have moved to national prominence. Such was the case with former vice president Spiro Agnew and former labor secretary Raymond Donovan. It was revealed in Agnew's case that when he was governor of Maryland, and earlier while a county official, he had received kickbacks from contractors doing business with the county and state governments. When this was publicly disclosed, Agnew resigned the vice presidency and subsequently pleaded no contest to an income tax violation charge ("no contest" is not a plea of guilty, but the defendant is still convicted). In Donovan's case, grand jury indictments charged him with fraud and grand larceny while he was in the construction business. Another case involved Judge Otto Kerner, formerly the governor of Illinois. Kerner was tied to an Illinois scandal involving offers of racetrack stock to politicians. He was subsequently convicted of numerous criminal offenses, including perjury, and became the first federal judge ever to spend time in prison. Former congressman from Illinois Dan Rostenkowski served prison time for illegally siphoning funds to support his personal lifestyle and political aspirations. Finally, the well-publicized political corruption trial and conviction of former Illinois governor George Ryan Sr. stands among the most famous examples of political white-collar crime (see box 6.2).

Political white-collar crime is encouraged by the tight links between politics and business. In addition to the fact that business provides financial support for political campaigns and governments disperse billions of dollars worth of contracts to industry, many government officials retain a financial interest in their business pursuits while in office. Members of Congress remain active in businesses ranging from real estate and insurance to construction, law, oil, and gas. Temptations to abuse their political connections abound, particularly when proposed laws or government contracts influence their personal finances and those of business colleagues.

ABSCAM

A major scandal involving several U.S. congressmen was uncovered in the 1980s. In the undercover FBI operation known as ABSCAM, one of its operatives posed as a wealthy Arab businessman seeking to obtain residency permits. Contacts were set up between the "Arab" and various congressmen, to whom large sums of money were offered in exchange for help. The FBI videotaped the meetings, and when the congressmen were eventually prosecuted the public saw film of elected representatives gleefully filling their pockets and briefcases with money.

Although all the offenders were initially convicted, some later filed successful appeals. These were heralded by many in Washington as the fitting end to an affair in which the FBI, not members of Congress, was the culprit. Accusations of entrapment and violation of privacy flowed from all sides, and if anyone emerged tarnished by the episode it was the FBI and the Department of Justice. Indignation like that directed at ABSCAM is noticeably lacking when similar police practices are directed at drug traffickers.

BOX 6.2. THE CONVICTION OF FORMER ILLINOIS GOVERNOR GEORGE RYAN SR.

In April 2006 former Illinois Governor George Ryan Sr. was convicted on eighteen counts of political corruption charges, including racketeering, mail fraud, obstruction of justice, and false tax filings. More specifically, the crimes committed by Ryan included:

- steering about $4.77 million in state contracts to his friends Arthur Swanson, Lawrence Warner, Donald Udstuen, and Harry Klein in exchange for gifts and vacations;
- leaking the selection of a new state prison, which resulted in improper profits for Swanson;
- diverting state resources and personnel to political campaigns; and
- lying to federal authorities in three interviews.

In September 2006 Ryan was sentenced to serve six and a half years in prison for his crimes.

Sources: O'Conner and Bush (2006a; 2006b).

Crimes for Power

Corruption for the purposes of acquiring, retaining, or increasing one's political power also occurs at all levels of government. Violations of fund-raising laws, ballot box stuffing, nepotism, and exchanging favors for votes are some examples.

The most famous example of political crimes for power at the national level is the 1972 Watergate scandal. Brought to light after a bungled burglary attempt at the Democratic National Committee headquarters in the Watergate hotel and apartment complex in Washington, D.C., the affair resulted in the first resignation of a U.S. president and touched people in all areas of national politics. Due in part to vigorous investigative journalism by *Washington Post* reporters Carl Bernstein and Bob Woodward, the American public was given a two-year, in-depth look at political corruption at its worst. Not only had the White House been deeply involved in the scandals, but also included were a former secretary of the treasury; the attorney general of the United States; officials of the FBI, CIA, and Internal Revenue Service; persons connected with organized crime; international terrorists; and even some street criminals.

The central theme around which the Watergate affair revolved was clearly one of political power. The involvement of the Committee to Re-Elect the President, the activities of White House staffers, and the routine subversive manipulation of government agencies by Richard Nixon and his allies bear this out. Here was an incident—or rather, a combination of incidents—in which maintaining and extending power stood as the central goal. Nixon's supporters and staffers committed various illegal actions:

- They used the U.S. Postal Service for fraudulent and libelous purposes, an aspect of the "dirty tricks" used to discredit Democratic opponents.
- They orchestrated the Watergate break-in for the purpose of "bugging" the Democratic National Committee headquarters and scrutinizing its files.
- They pressured the IRS to harass political opponents and Nixon's alleged enemies.
- They encouraged the FBI and CIA to obstruct justice so that these and other criminal activities would not come to light and, if they were revealed, would not be linked with the White House.
- They paid "hush money" to the Watergate burglars.
- They misused public funds and solicited campaign contributions in violation of federal laws.

In the summer of 1974 the House of Representatives Judiciary Committee voted to impeach Nixon. He was charged with obstruction of justice and failure to carry out his constitutional oath and duty to uphold the laws of the United States. He resigned on August 9, 1974. Much still remains unknown about political corruption in Richard Nixon's administration, and since Nixon's death, it is unlikely that the true nature of his offenses will ever come to light. One is certainly left wondering whether anything would have come to light had it not been for the ill-fated break-in at the Watergate and the tenacity of two young reporters in search of news.

ORGANIZATIONAL CRIME I: CORPORATE CRIMES

Organizational crimes arise in connection with business pursuits but are not the central purpose of the business. They are committed on behalf of business interests, sometimes by individuals, sometimes by groups; they surface among the self-employed and among executives of companies large and small. The discussion here will concentrate first on **corporate theft and fraud**, which are activities that violate laws governing commerce and trade. We will then address **corporate violence**, crimes that result in physical and social injury, pain, and sometimes death.

Corporate Theft and Fraud

This section explores a number of examples of corporate crimes involving theft or fraud. As noted earlier, this type of crime is arguably more extensive—and certainly more costly—than street crimes committed by individuals seeking personal gain.

Restraint of Trade

The first relevant federal statute relating to trade was the Sherman Antitrust Act of 1890. Designed to curb the threat to a competitive free-enterprise economy posed by the nineteenth-century spread of trusts and monopolies, this act made it a criminal misdemeanor for individuals or organizations to engage in restraint of trade by combining or forming monopolies to that end. In 1974 Congress made restraint of trade a felony, thus making it possible for convicted offenders to receive prison terms of a year or more. Antitrust violations contribute to the persistence of a "closed enterprise system," the very antithesis of what American business is supposed to be.

There are three principal methods of restraint of trade: (1) consolidation so as to obtain a monopoly position, (2) price-fixing to achieve price uniformity, and (3) price discrimination, in which higher prices are charged to some customers and lower ones to others. From the standpoint of those engaging in these practices, they make sense: The less the competition and the greater the control over prices, the larger the profits. But small and independent businesses will lose business, and the public at large will face higher prices and lose its discretionary buying power.

The most common violations of restraint-of-trade laws are price fixing and price discrimination. **Price-fixing** is an example of "horizontal" restraint of trade because it in-

volves people or organizations at the same level in the chain of distribution (i.e., manufacturing, wholesaling, or retailing). Examples of price-fixing include any agreement or understanding among competitors to raise, lower, or stabilize prices. **Price discrimination** represents "vertical" restraint in that it involves conspiracies across different levels—for example, between manufacturers and retailers. Sutherland (1949) describes a case involving Sears, Roebuck and Goodyear Tire Company: Goodyear charged Sears a lower price than its own independent Goodyear dealers for identical tires, allowing Sears to charge a lower retail price, to the disadvantage of the Goodyear independents.

In his investigation of seventy of the largest American corporations over a fifty-year period, Sutherland found that many of the suits charging restraint of trade through price-fixing or price discrimination were brought by private interests rather than by the Federal Trade Commission or the Department of Justice, the two agencies given primary responsibility for enforcing restraint-of-trade provisions. When corporate officers break the law on behalf of their organizations, criminal justice officials do not seem particularly aggressive in ferreting out violations and bringing charges. But this should hardly come as a surprise, given the close relationship between business and politics. Indeed, in Europe and the Far East, governments have historically encouraged cartels whose price-fixing activities are legendary.

Price-Fixing Conspiracies

In 1961, twenty-one corporations and forty-five high-ranking executives in the heavy electrical equipment industry were successfully prosecuted for criminal violations of the Sherman Antitrust Act. They had been involved in a price-fixing and bid-rigging scheme that, over nearly a decade, had bilked local, state, and federal governments (and taxpayers) out of millions of dollars on purchases averaging nearly $2 billion a year.

In carrying out their scheme—called by the trial judge the most serious breach of antitrust laws in history—executives of the conspiring companies met secretly under fictitious names in hotel rooms around the country. Referring to those in attendance as "the Christmas card list" and to the meetings as "choir practice," the conspirators arranged prices for equipment, allocated markets and territories, and agreed on which companies would supply the low bids on pending government contracts. The participants covered their tracks well and were discovered only because officials of the Tennessee Valley Authority received identical sealed bids on highly technical equipment. The companies involved in the conspiracy ranged from such giants in the electrical equipment business as General Electric, Westinghouse, and Allis-Chalmers, to smaller firms such as the Carrier Corporation, the I.T.E. Circuit Breaker Company, and Federal Pacific (for more on this famous price-fixing conspiracy, see Ermann and Lundman, 1982: 86–95).

This price-fixing conspiracy illustrates extensive collusion among corporations who have found a way to prosper without having to compete. Needless to say, cooperation is preferred when the benefits outweigh the risks of competition. Equally important, the cooperators usually gain over those who refuse to cooperate or simply cannot participate in the collusion. This advantage is precisely what restraint-of-trade laws are designed to curb, for its consequence is obvious: Fewer firms stay in business, and the prices of goods and services rise when the survivors exercise their monopoly power, keeping new competitors away and setting artificially high prices—in effect stealing from their customers. The cost of those higher prices can be staggering. In the heavy electrical equipment conspiracy, the cost approached $3 billion, "more money than was stolen in all the country's robberies, burglaries, and larcenies during the years in which the price fixing occurred" (Geis, 1978a: 281). There are countless illustrations of price-

fixing, although rarely will those accused of it admit the practice. Francis Cullen, William Maakestad, and Gary Cavender have argued that "conspiracy to set prices has become a way of life in some industries" (1987: 60).

The Savings and Loan Failures

When savings and loan companies began to fail around the country in the late 1980s, alarm bells sounded in homes and businesses around the country—and in Washington, D.C. Long thought to be among America's most stable and trustworthy institutions, savings and loans suddenly looked weak and vulnerable. Since the government insures savings up to $100,000 in individual accounts, small investors were not hurt; however, the private aggregate cost to taxpayers is estimated at over $500 billion. Mismanagement and mistakes in operating a business are not necessarily indications of criminal activity. Many believe that the S&L collapse was a product of systemic changes resulting from the deregulatory frenzy of the Reagan years (but see Ayres and Braithwaite, 1992) and the rise of the junk-bond market. Deregulators took the position that "the free enterprise system works best if left alone" (Calavita and Pontell, 1990: 312). The opportunities and incentives for S&Ls to embark on risky ventures were simply too compelling given the freeing of controls and the prospects of huge short-run profits. A sort of "casino" economy emerged in which speculation and deregulation created expanded opportunities for fraud and embezzlement. "Participants in this epidemic of fraud included both those who deliberately entered the thrift industry in order to loot it and legitimate thrift operators who found themselves on the 'slippery slope' of insolvency, unlawful risk taking, and cover-up" (240).

As details surrounding the collapse of Lincoln Savings and Loan—the largest thrift failure in U.S. history—emerged, it became clear that deceit, conspiracy, political corruption, and all manner of financial irregularities were involved. A sort of "collective embezzlement" occurred in which S&L executives siphoned off funds for personal gain, at the expense of the institution, "but with implicit or explicit sanction of its management" (Calavita and Pontell, 1990: 321). On December 4, 1991, a Los Angeles jury convicted S&L owner Charles H. Keating Jr. on seventeen counts of securities fraud. On April 10, 1992, he was sentenced to ten years in prison and fined $250,000—but how does one measure this punishment against the estimated $2.6 billion the collapse of Lincoln is estimated to have cost American taxpayers?

Fraud in Advertising, Sales, and Repairs

Consumers become the victims of fraud in many different ways, including misrepresentation in advertising and sales. Misrepresentation in advertising means that what prospective buyers are told about a product is untrue, deceptive, or misleading. Sometimes the misrepresentation concerns the quantity of a product or the actual contents of a package or container, sometimes it concerns the effectiveness of a product, and sometimes it involves lack of or insufficient information about a product or service such that buyers are misled. An illustrative case involved Chrysler Corporation. In 1987 the company admitted selling as "new" cars that had in fact been driven by executives. Another example is an ad campaign by Ralston Purina, the makers of Puppy Chow, in which the company seemed to be claiming that its product cured cancer (*St. Louis Post-Dispatch*, November 27, 1991: B1).

The fact that a fine line divides fraudulent from legitimate sales promotion becomes evident as one considers a problem faced by nearly all businesses: creating a need for their products and services. Many of the things considered necessities today—canned foods, refrigerators, automobiles, insurance policies—either did not exist a few decades ago or were thought of as luxuries, certainly not necessities. They have come to be thought of as necessities largely because the companies

selling them have convinced the public to see them that way. When things are necessities, people "need" to purchase them.

In their efforts to convince people of a need for goods and services, businesses use a variety of different ploys. *Fraudulent ploy* is the use of false claims as to the effectiveness of a product in doing what it is supposed to do. Those who believe the claims will see a need for the product. An example is the advertising plan followed some time ago by the makers of Listerine. In their campaign, the makers sought to create a need for Listerine as a mouthwash, a fairly new idea at the time; to establish that need, they presented fake claims about the germ-killing powers of the mixture.

It is only a short step from these strategies to those the common swindler uses. Consider the activities of the Holland Furnace Company. This company was in the business of selling home heating furnaces. With some five hundred offices and a sales force in the thousands, the company put its resources to work on a fraudulent sales promotion involving misrepresentation, destruction of property, and, in some cases, what amounted to extortion:

> Salesmen, misrepresenting themselves as "furnace engineers" and "safety inspectors," gained entry into their victims' homes, dismantled their furnaces, and condemned them as hazardous. They then refused to reassemble them, on the ground that they did not want to be "accessories to murder." Using scare tactics, claiming that the furnaces they "inspected" were emitting carbon monoxide and other dangerous gases, they created, in the homeowners' minds, a need for a new furnace—and proceeded to sell their own product at a handsome profit. They were so ruthless that they sold one elderly woman nine new furnaces in six years for a total of $18,000. The FTC finally forced the company to close in 1965, but in the meantime, it had done some $30 million worth of business per year for many years. (Leiser, 1973: 270)

Consumer fraud figures prominently in a list of the "Top 100 Corporate Criminals of

BOX 6.3. THE TOP CORPORATE CRIMINALS OF THE 1990S

R ussell Mokhiber (1999), editor of the journal *Corporate Crime Reporter*, has published a list of the top one hundred corporate criminals of the 1990s. Here are the top ten from that list.

1. F. Hoffmann-La Roche Ltd. was fined $500 million in an antitrust case for a conspiring to fix prices of several different types of vitamins. (*Corporate Crime Reporter*, May 24, 1999)
2. Daiwa Bank Ltd. was fined $340 million for fraud relating to the coverup of massive securities trading losses and defrauding bank regulators. (*Corporate Crime Reporter*, March 4, 1996)
3. BASF Aktiengesellschaft, a German Company, was fined $225 million in an antitrust case in which the bank conspired to raise and fix the prices of several types of vitamins. (*Corporate Crime Reporter*, May 24, 1999)
4. SGL Carbon Aktiengesellschaft was fined $135 million in an antitrust case stemming from attempts to fix the prices of graphite electrodes. (*Corporate Crime Reporter*, May 10, 1999)
5. Exxon Corporation and Exxon Shipping companies were fined $125 million for the violation of environmental laws that resulted from the grounding of the *Exxon Valdez*. (*Corporate Crime Reporter*, March 18, 1991)
6. UCAR International, Inc. was fined $110 million for antitrust activities associated with attempting to fix the prices of graphite electrodes.
7. Archer Daniels Midland was fined $100 million for antitrust conspiracies to fix prices in the lysine and citric acid markets. (*Corporate Crime Reporter*, October 21, 1996)
8. Banker's Trust was fined $60 million for financial crimes committed by falsely recording several millions of dollars as income and reserves that were in truth unclaimed customer funds. (*Corporate Crime Reporter*, March 15, 1999)
9. Sears Bankruptcy Recovery Management Services were fined $60 million for fraud relating to reaffirmation practices that led bankrupting Sears customers to believe they still owed the company money from previous credit card charges. (*Corporate Crime Reporter*, February 15, 1999)
10. Haarman & Reimer Corp. was fined $50 million for antitrust activities relating to the fixing of prices in the citric acid market. (*Corporate Crime Reporter*, February 3, 1997)

More information on these and other corporate crimes can be found in the above-cited editions of the *Corporate Crime Reporter* and on the Web site http://www.corporatepredators.org/top100.html#Briefs.

the 1990s" (see box 6.3). Twenty of the cases were instances of fraud in the electronics, medical, and financial service industries. The recent legal problems experienced by State Farm Insurance Company will serve as a final example of corporate theft and fraud.

A $238-million lawsuit accused State Farm of several fraudulent practices involving the sale of whole life and universal life policies from

January 1982 to December 1997. This lawsuit, which State Farm settled without admitting wrongdoing, claimed that policyholders were told to switch policies so they could receive greater benefits. In reality, these greater benefits were for the company, not the customer. Customers were also intentionally deceived about the rate of return on their policies and were given unreasonable predictions about the possible dividend (Gallagher, 1999). At about the same time, State Farm was found guilty of fraud in the use of generic replacement parts in auto body repairs. Auto body shops generally need the permission of insurance companies when installing replacement parts. State Farm mostly approved the use of generic replacements parts, not the more reliable original-equipment parts from car manufacturers. While State Farm acknowledged that it did recommended and approve the use of aftermarket parts rather than the "true" replacements, it claimed the practice was not illegal. The judge did not agree and slapped a $1.2-billion fine on the insurance company. This is believed to be the largest cash settlement against an insurance company. The case was reversed on appeal, but the plaintiffs are appealing this decision (Gallagher, 1999).

The BCCI Case

Established in 1972 by Pakistani financier Agha Hassan Abedi, the Bank of Credit and Commerce International (BCCI) became the first multinational bank originating out of the third world. Headquartered until recently in London, regulated (in a very loose way) by Luxembourg, and backed by Middle East oil revenues, BCCI had by 1990 more than $20 billion in assets in seventy-five countries, with more than four hundred branches and subsidiaries (*Newsweek*, July 22, 1991: 37; *Time*, July 29, 1991: 42). It gained a reputation for offering first-rate service to its large depositors—and for asking no questions. BCCI also knew exactly where to go in the political hierarchy of Western nations to get counsel and representa-

tion for its expansion—for example, to Clark Clifford, who "sat atop three branches of the capital's permanent government—law, money, and politics" (*Wall Street Journal*, June 14, 1991: 4). Clifford, a man of formerly unquestioned respect and integrity, became chairman of First American Bankshares following its purchase by Saudi investors in 1981 with money loaned by BCCI. The investors eventually defaulted, and BCCI (secretly, according to Clifford in congressional testimony) became the owner of First American.

In sixteen years of expansion, BCCI was not the legitimate banking operation it appeared to be. And there is evidence that officials in many countries—including the United States, England, Peru, and Argentina—knew it. They knew that BCCI was heavily involved in shady activities, and, far from doing anything about it, found their own illegal uses for the bank.

Drug trafficking was arguably BCCI's downfall. Indicted by a federal grand jury in 1988 for laundering millions of dollars in drug money, BCCI eventually pleaded guilty and was fined $14 billion in 1990 (*Time*, July 22, 1991: 46). Subsequent investigations produced an incredible array of charges: gunrunning, bribery and corruption, smuggling, terrorism, securities theft, property theft of all sorts, influence peddling, insurance fraud, covert operations for the CIA, bank fraud, espionage, extortion, kidnapping, and the violation of other domestic and international laws. The bank was closed down in July 1991, its assets frozen. In January 1992 BCCI pleaded guilty to racketeering; Clifford was indicted seven months later, along with his law partner, and many more indictments and convictions will surely follow.

Electronic technology has made international money transfers simple to commit and a nightmare to police:

> Bank-to-bank transfers of illegal funds can . . . be accomplished easily with the complicity of bank officials. The bank transfers by wire between its own (rather than a customer's) account and accounts in correspondent

banks, making the laundering of personal funds appear as legitimate bank business. Without other leads, bank-to-bank transfers of illegally obtained funds are almost impossible to distinguish from normal banking transactions. Furthermore, the sheer volume of all wire transfers made and the speed with which they are accomplished make it extremely difficult to trace these funds or document their illegal nature. (Webster and McCampbell, 1992: 5)

The Enron Case

Perhaps the most infamous case of corporate fraud in U.S. history took place in the late 1990s to 2001, when it was revealed that the energy giant Enron had seriously misrepresented its financial status for several years. At its core, the Enron case involved the company's fraudulent financial reports (concealment of debt and inflation of profits) and premeditated actions to cover up the company's declining value and forthcoming bankruptcy. It is also widely known that Enron company executives consistently provided messages to its employees and stock holders that the company was "doing great" and specifically encouraged others to buy more stock and invest more money into their pension plans because of the company's record "successes." Further, Enron executives Kenneth Lay and Jeffrey Skilling often took exorbitant bonuses and loans out for themselves through the company and its subsidiaries (some of which were shell companies), thereby diminishing the company's profitability and obligations to its line employees and stockholders. All told, it is estimated that the crimes of the Enron Corporation cost $2 billion in pension plans and $60 billion in lost markets shares/values (Friedrichs, 2004).

In 2006 both Lay and Skilling were convicted of multiple charges of securities and wire fraud, with Skilling receiving a prison sentence of twenty-four years. Lay died shortly after the guilty verdicts. More than a dozen other Enron executives have also been convicted or pleaded guilty to corporate fraud charges, such as investor relations manager Paula Rieker, who in September 2006 received two years' probation in exchange for her cooperation with authorities in other related cases. Another corporate giant, Arthur Andersen Accounting, was implicated in the Enron affair as well. Convicted on charges of obstruction of justice as a result of the shredding of Enron's financial documents, Arthur Andersen is also defunct.

Corporate Violence

While many corporate crimes result in economic harms, a sizeable number of corporate crimes are violent. It is clearly a myth that white-collar crimes can be correctly called "economic crimes." Here we review several instances of violent corporate crimes committed as a part of a company's pursuit of profit, a major cause of most forms of corporate crime.

Violence against Consumers

Most of us rely on corporations to provide us with the commodities we use in our daily lives. We assume these products will not expose us to unreasonable threats to our life and safety. Unfortunately, this assumption can be in serious error, as we shall see in the following illustrations.

Ford Motor Company's Pinto was designed in the late 1960s to compete in the "small car for a small price market," which at the time was controlled by Volkswagen. Ford president Lee Iacocca and other executives directed that the Pinto be produced quickly, weigh less than two thousand pounds, and cost less than $2,000. While the Pinto was being tested prior to its release into the marketplace, a major problem in the fuel system was discovered: When rear-ended, the Pinto's gas tank often ruptured. The problem could be fixed by placing a rubber bladder, or flak, within and/or around the tank or by locating the tank in a safer area. Ford executives rejected these avenues because the assembly line was already tooled for production, and it would cost the company several millions of dollars to redesign and produce a safer car. As a direct result of the deadly design of the Pinto, dozens of drivers and passengers of the vehicle were killed or seriously burned in rear-end collisions over the next several years (Cullen, Maakestad, and Cavender, 1987).

In the course of several successful civil suits against Ford and one unsuccessful criminal prosecution, it came to light that the company had made a conscious decision to risk the lives of consumers in order to make a profit. Ford calculated that a burn death would result in an average $200,000 loss and any injury less than death would cost them $67,000. Ford officials also calculated that the cost of fixing the problem with the Pinto's fuel tank placement would be a paltry $11 per vehicle. But with 11 million cars to fix, paying the estimated $49.5 million it would cost in lawsuits for deaths and injuries was a better business deal for the corporation. Ford was eventually forced to recall the Pinto after several successful product liability lawsuits (Mokhiber, 1988). No one was ever sentenced to prison for the deaths.

Two widely publicized cases of corporate violence against consumers are also crimes against women and children (Fox and Szockyj, 1996; Rynbrandt and Kramer, 1995). First, the Dalkon Shield, an intrauterine birth control device, was marketed and sold by the A. H. Robins Company in the 1960s. The device was popular in part because it supposedly did not have negative side effects, as the birth control pill did. It was also marketed as an extremely effective way of blocking pregnancy (Mokhiber, 1988). But because the shield was poorly designed (and poorly tested), it often caused severe pelvic infections, sterility, poor protection against pregnancy, and the spontaneous abortions of fetuses. Twelve women also died from using this device. The Robins Company, which knew of many of the problems with the Dalkon Shield but did nothing to protect consumers, escaped

criminal charges but has paid nearly $1 billion in damages (Mokhiber, 1988).

Another corporate crime against women and children involved the sale and distribution of the drug thalidomide. Many women were given prescriptions for thalidomide as a tranquilizer and to combat morning sickness while pregnant. The producer of the drug, the German company Chemie Grunenthal, had information that the drug could cause major health problems, including severe disturbances to the nervous system. This information was ignored and downplayed by Grunenthal for years, but the company was finally forced to come clean after overwhelming evidence of the drug's horrible side effects on fetuses. At least eight thousand children, the so-called thalidomide babies, were born with deformed genitals, eyes, and ears; brain damage; and shortened limbs. While Grunenthal escaped criminal fines, Distillers Ltd., a company that later distributed thalidomide under the name of Distaval in Britain, was forced to pay millions of dollars to British and German victims of this drug (Mokhiber, 1988).

Violence against Workers

According to the Occupational Safety and Health Administration (OSHA, 2007), there were 4.2 million work-related injuries and illnesses in 2006. OSHA also estimates that 5,703 workers died on the job that year. However, these statistics are conservative estimates of the risks involved in work. There is strong evidence to show that up to 100,000 workers in the United States lose their lives each year as a result of injuries and illnesses suffered at work (Friedrichs, 2004; Reiman, 2007). Many illnesses and injuries are simply not reported to the authorities, whether that authority is the company, OSHA, or the U.S. Department of Labor. Some workers also know that whistle blowing to agencies like OSHA could cost them their jobs.

A study of mining disasters in five countries concluded that most of them were related to violations of workplace safety laws (Braithwaite, 1985). Some of the violations were a cause of the disasters, while others made the disasters worse than they should have been. Workers are not the only ones at risk in the mining industry. In 1972 the entire community of Buffalo Creek, West Virginia, was virtually destroyed from a dam break (Erikson, 1976).

During the twentieth century, at least one hundred thousand U.S. miners were killed and 1.5 million injured (Mokhiber, 1988). Black lung disease, which took the life of the great-grandfather of one of this text's authors (Kauzlarich), is still a major problem today. It is now called *coal worker's pneumoconiosis*, and usually results from inhalation and exposure to assorted coal dusts and silica (U.S. Department of Labor, 2000). There is no doubt that many coal companies knew of the dangers of black lung but did nothing to prevent worker exposure to dangerous coal dust (Mokhiber, 1988). Even today a few companies do not adequately protect their workers from contracting the disease (OSHA, 2006).

Even if we use the conservative OSHA statistics, we get some sense of how routine violations of worker safety laws actually are in the United States. Federal and state OSHA agencies conducted one hundred thousand inspections in 2006, resulting in the uncovering of more than two hundred thousand violations of worker safety laws (OSHA, 2007). Here are two examples of these violations:

- Cintas Corporation was fined $2.78 million for forty-two willful violations of equipment safety regulations, which contributed to the death of an employee in 2007. The employee fell into an industrial dryer as he tried to clear washed laundry from a conveyor belt. (OSHA, 2007)
- Two Milwaukee companies were fined more than $50,000 for failing to ensure proper safety measures and inspections were taken pertaining to underground propane gas connections. Three employees of the companies lost their lives in an explosion and fire resulting from underground gas leaks. (OSHA, 2007)

Other examples of corporate violence against workers could be detailed here. For example, the owners and managers of the Imperial Food Products Company in Hamlet, North Carolina, routinely locked fire doors to prevent employees from stealing chicken. When a fire erupted in the plant on September 3, 1991, the workers were trapped—twenty-five were killed and another fifty-six were injured (Michalowski and Kramer, 2006). Another case centers around the Johns Manville Company's refusal to protect workers and others from exposure to asbestos. Even with the knowledge that the substance was harmful, Johns Manville allowed the product to be manufactured and distributed across the country. The company declared bankruptcy in the wake of a deluge of lawsuits (Friedrichs, 2004; Mokhiber, 1988).

Corporate Violence to the Natural Environment

The natural environment can also be a victim of corporate violence. Like most corporate crimes, corporate degradation of the natural and physical environment is largely an outcome of the pursuit of profit. The costs of compliance with federal and state regulations are often greater than the costs of paying fines. The median fine for environmental crimes by organizations, for example, is $50,000 (Cohen, 1998).

Perhaps the most devious environmental crime in United States history involves the actions of the Hooker Chemical and Plastics Corporation, who in the 1940s bought the Love Canal in Niagara Falls, New York, and buried dangerous toxic chemicals there. Hooker had sold the land for $1 to the local school board but did not notify the board or the community of the hazardous material buried there (two hundred or so dangerous chemicals were dumped there over several years), and it was eventually turned into a neighborhood playground and recreational

Harmful industrial pollution from factories like this constitutes a major form of corporate crime. Factories and other workplaces can pose another danger as well: In the United States, people are about five times more likely to die from avoidable diseases and workplace injuries on the job than from traditionally defined criminal homicide.

area for nearby residents. As time passed, residents complained of terrible odors emanating from the area, and high rates of emotional problems, miscarriages, and other illnesses were documented. It was also claimed that several died as a result of exposure to the chemicals. For years Hooker claimed it was not responsible for the problems, but eventually it was forced to pay millions of dollars to victims as well as to the federal government for the cleanup of the area (Mokhiber, 1988).

When the *Exxon Valdez* ran aground in 1989, about 12 million gallons of oil fouled the ocean near Prince William Sound in Alaska. About thirteen hundred miles of beach were affected by the spill. At least 250,000 seabirds, 2,800 sea otters, 300 harbor seals, 250 bald eagles, and 22 killer whales were killed. Billions of salmon and herring eggs were eliminated as well (Exxon Valdez Oil Spill Trustee Council, 2000). Thousands of people were directly affected by the spill: Millions of dollars were lost in tourism income and several commercial fishing enterprises folded.

Hearings eventually determined that Exxon was responsible for the disaster: The company had allowed an incompetent crew to run the ship under a captain known to have a drinking problem. It had also made cuts in necessary staffing. Exxon entered into a criminal plea agreement in U.S. District Court, which allowed them to pay only $25 million of a $150-million criminal fine. The company also paid $100 million in restitution and $900 million toward the cleanup (Exxon Valdez Oil Spill Trustee Council, 2000).

Small Business Crime

A variety of criminal activities are committed in the context of small business activity. Surprisingly, studies of small business as a setting and context of crime are few and far between. The following is a brief description of some of the factors that encourage criminal activity by companies, firms, and businesses that are owned by sole proprietors or business partners who directly supervise business activities and who personally authorize all transactions.

Mars's study of workplace fiddles, discussed earlier in this chapter, demonstrates that different occupational structures facilitate particular kinds of workplace crime, which are then supported and routinized by the attitudes and inclinations of those working within them. "Hawks," for example, are found in jobs that stress initiative, autonomy, competition and control, the typical small business environment. "All share certain attitudes: the most common are a resistance to external constraint and a high value placed on independence. Our small businessman is, therefore, typically and almost by definition a hawk (1982: 42–43).

Tax fiddles are the archetypal offense, a version of which is described by one of Mars's informants as follows:

> We fiddle part of our worker's wages. All the very small businesses that I know have to be in on this kind of fiddle. If you employ someone and he earns below the amount that allows him to get the maximum supplement as a low wage-earner—then you make sure he gets the supplement. You pay him just enough to qualify for the maximum and you make the rest of his wages up in cash. This is possible because we've got a lot coming through the till. (1982: 40).

Cash is the key here, as it is in other common tax fiddles, such as avoidance of sales tax. Cash transactions bypass bookkeeping and therefore are difficult to monitor and trace.

In conjunction with bypassing the checks and controls of the official economy, some small businesses become involved in networks of collusion. Besides supporting the shadow economy, these networks bridge the worlds of compliance and crime and provide opportunities and incentives for a wide range of illegal activities. Collusion supports small business crime in various ways: through group norms and values that say it's OK, by offering protection, by disseminating information, and by forging connections between participants. Indeed, crime networks are largely indistinguishable from networks of legitimate exchange, and each appears to feed off the other. As noted earlier in this chapter, noncriminal and criminal opportunities work together to stimulate crime.

The structure of the legitimate economy is characterized by differences in knowledge, control, power, and resources (Mars, 1982: 138). This gives rise to various "fiddle factors" that facilitate small business crime as well as many forms of state and corporate crime more generally.

For example, consider retail and service businesses in high-traffic areas that cater primarily to the tourist and convention trade. These contexts are fiddle prone because they involve "passing trade": The parties to a transaction typically meet only once. Because business customers are usually strangers in the community, possibly also of a different race, class, gender, or ethnicity than "regulars," the conventional morality governing free exchange (i.e., don't cheat) is suspended or modified, thus increasing the chances of consumer fraud.

As noted with respect to fraud in maintenance and repair (which is dominated by small businesses), there is widespread ignorance among customers regarding what they need and don't need, how to satisfy a need, and what to pay. This ignorance constitutes another fiddle factor, and a clear parallel can be drawn between fraud in this context and fraud among physicians, lawyers, and other professionals (see Jesilow, Pontell, and Geis, 1993).

ORGANIZATIONAL CRIMES II: CRIMES OF STATES AND GOVERNMENTS

State crime is a socially injurious and/or illegal act committed by states, state agencies, and state officials committed for the benefit of a state organization. These crimes cover a wide range of activities and consequently have a wide range of victims, including people targeted for genocide; individuals suffering from racism, sexism, and classism; involuntary research subjects in government-sponsored projects; countries and nations oppressed by more powerful states; suspects in criminal cases; and even passengers on airplanes (Kauzlarich, Matthews, and Miller, 2001).

Here we discuss five major examples of state crime, beginning with the Iran-Contra affair during the Reagan administration.

The Iran-Contra Affair

The Iran-Contra affair, arguably the worst scandal during the administration of Ronald Reagan, was an international conspiracy designed to secure the release of American hostages in Lebanon through the illegal sale of arms to Iran, and to shore up the Contra rebels in Nicaragua through illegal diversion of arms sales money to the rebels.

Investigations by congressional committees and by special prosecutors implicated members of the White House staff, the military, and the Central Intelligence Agency (CIA), and documented the involvement of businessmen and government officials from three continents. National Security Council aide Oliver North was at the center of the scandal, but other senior government officials were also implicated, though few have been charged and some convictions (including North's) were overturned on appeal.

It is interesting that the defense most often presented in state crimes is "I did what I thought was in the best interests of the country." This appeal to national security diverts attention from the core issue (willful violation of the law by those entrusted to uphold it), protects the public image of the wrongdoers as people of honor who go out on a limb to protect the national interest, and conveys the idea that the accused have been wronged and are therefore the real victims. It also helps legitimize covert crimes by government officials and cloaks the secretive underside of national politics with an aura of decency and honor: The people are doing their best to protect "good" against "evil." Appeals to higher loyalty are not confined to political criminals, it turns out, but are also invoked by common or garden-variety offenders and juvenile delinquents (see the discussion of techniques of neutralization in chapter 12 for more on this).

U.S. Nuclear Crimes

The U.S. Department of Energy and a host of other federal agencies have funded or otherwise managed thousands of human radiation experiments. Several of these experiments have been conducted in violation of the Nuremberg Code, which outlaws nonconsensual, reckless, deceptive, and coercive experiments. Two sets of studies have been found to be particularly unethical and illegal (Kauzlarich and Kramer, 1998).

From 1945 to 1947, a series of plutonium injection studies supported by the Manhattan Project and Atomic Energy Commission (AEC) were conducted on eighteen people. The subjects were expressly deceived into participating in the study: They were told that they were being *treated* for a life-threatening disease when in fact the studies were designed to help the state understand the effects of plutonium on the human body in the case of nuclear war. The victims of these experiments were poor and uneducated. The second series of experiments in violation of the Nuremberg Code were prison radiation experiments conducted from 1963 to 1973. One hundred thirty-one state prisoners in Oregon and Washington were subjects in a study to determine the effects of irradiation on the male reproductive system. Prisoners were given $25 per irradiation and informed of only some of the possible risks associated with the experiments. Prisoners are not in a position to exercise the type of free will envisioned by the Nuremberg Code. Clearly the victims of this state crime were poor, scientifically uneducated, and literally captive.

The production of atomic and nuclear weapons by the U.S. Department of Energy has resulted in massive environmental contamination. In violation of U.S. EPA laws, the Clean Water Act, and the Resource Conservation and Recovery Act, at least seventeen areas in the country have been substantially damaged and polluted. In Hanford, Washington, one hundred square miles of groundwater were contaminated with extremely high levels of tritium, iodine, and other toxic chemicals. Near the Savannah River Plant in the Carolinas, there have been massive releases of mercury into the air and tritium, strontium, and iodine into the soil (Kauzlarich and Kramer, 1998; 1993).

There is evidence to show that there are higher rates of miscarriages, leukemia, and other health-related problems in the areas where nuclear weapons have been produced, stored, or tested. The human effects of environmental degradation as a result of the hundreds of nuclear weapons tests in the western part of the United States are also examples of state crime. A recent study by the National Cancer Institute estimates that tens of thousands of people have developed thyroid cancer as a result of nuclear tests. The victims of these environmental crimes were not only the unknowing civilians who simply happened to be living near the test sites, but also military personnel who were forced to witness nuclear blasts and then tested for any negative side effects (Kauzlarich and Kramer, 1998). In these cases, the victims were unfortunately easily exploitable because they were either unknowing, powerless, or in subordinate organizational positions (Kauzlarich, Matthews, and Miller, 2001).

Finally, the development and use of weapons of mass destruction have been criminalized. On July 8, 1996, the International Court of Justice (ICJ) delivered an advisory opinion that the threat or use of nuclear weapons would generally be illegal. This historic ruling came in response to requests by the World Health Organization (WHO) and the United Nations General Assembly (UNGA) for advisory opinions on this important issue. In a complicated and controversial ruling, the ICJ stated that "the threat or use of nuclear weapons would generally be contrary to the rules of international law applicable in armed conflict, and in particular the principles and rules of humanitarian law" (International Court of Justice, 1996: paragraph 105 (2) E; Kauzlarich, 1997; Kramer and Kauzlarich, 1999). One of the relevant international laws the ICJ used to make their decision was the Nuremberg Principles (see box 6.4).

Violations of Human Rights and Economic Terrorism

One of the most widely recognized forms of state suppression of political rights was the FBI's COINTELPRO. Under this program, the

BOX 6.4. THE NUREMBERG CHARTER: AN INTERNATIONAL LAW GOVERNING STATE BEHAVIOR

(a) Crimes against Peace: namely, planning, preparation, initiation, or waging of a war of aggression, or a war in violation of international treaties, agreements, or assurances, or participation in a common plan or conspiracy for the accomplishment of any of the foregoing.

(b) War Crimes: namely, violations of the laws or customs of war. Such violations shall include, but not be limited to, murder, ill-treatment, or deportation to slave labor or for any other purpose of civilian population of or in occupied territory, murder, or ill-treatment of prisoners of war or persons on seas, killing of hostages, plunder of public or private property, wanton destruction of cities, towns or villages, or devastation not justified by military necessity.

(c) Crimes against Humanity: namely, murder, extermination, enslavement, deportation, and other inhumane acts committed against any civilian population, before or during war, or prosecutions on political, racial or religious grounds in execution of or in connection with any crime within the jurisdiction of the Tribunal, whether or not in violation of the domestic law of the country where perpetrated.

Source: Kauzlarich and Kramer (1998: 32).

political rights of dissident political groups like the Socialist Workers Party (SWP), the Southern Christian Leadership Conference (SCLC), the Black Panthers, American Indian Movement (AIM), and the Committee in Solidarity with the People of El Salvador (CIS-PES) were violated (Caulfield, 1991; Churchill and Vander Wall, 1990; Davis, 1992). Covert attempts by the FBI to "neutralize" political dissent included such illegal tactics as wire-taps, bugging, mail opening, and breaking and entering (Beirne and Messerschmidt, 2000). Other activities included group infiltration and death threats (Churchill and Vander Wall, 1990; Davis, 1992).

Economic terrorism involves coercion through economic means that is directed toward the civilian population of the target country to bring about a desired political or economic change, or to simply "punish" the target country (Dowty, 1994; Hass, 1998; Hufbauer, Schott, and Elliot, 1990). The effects of economic sanctions range from moderate discomfort to more serious consequences such as disease, malnutrition, and even death (Dowty, 1994; Hufbauer, Schott, and Elliot, 1990). Consider the case of Cuba. The passage of the Cuban Democracy Act (CDA) in 1992 and the Helms-Burton Act in 1996 were major steps in tightening the economic sanctions on Cuba. The tightening of the economic sanctions in 1992 created health problems for many Cuban citizens in the areas of malnutrition, water quality, and shortages of medicines and medical equipment (American Association for World Health, 1997).

The outright ban on the sale of American foodstuffs has contributed to serious nutritional deficits, especially among pregnant women. This has led to an increase in low-birth-weight babies. Food shortages have led to devastating outbreaks of neuropathy; the embargo has severely restricted access to water treatment chemicals and the parts needed to maintain Cuba's water supply system (American Association for World Health, 1997). This has led to rising incidences of morbidity and mortality rates from water-borne diseases. Finally,

> [o]f the 1,297 medications available in Cuba in 1991, physicians now have access to only 889 of these same medicines—and many of these are available only intermittently. Because most major new drugs are developed by U.S. pharmaceuticals, Cuban physicians have access to less than 50 percent of the new medicines available on the world market. Due to the direct or indirect effects of the embargo, the most routine medical supplies are in short supply or entirely absent from some Cuban clinics. (ii)

Historically, the use of economic sanctions has been viewed under both domestic law and international law as a "humanitarian" alternative to military force. Indeed, there have been instances where economic sanctions have been very successful in bringing about a desired change—the economic sanctions on Haiti and South Africa, for example. However, even when economic sanctions are "successful,"

> sanctions and humanitarianism often collide. Although in theory sanctions are motivated by an implicitly humane rationale, their implementation often wreaks great havoc and civilian suffering. Inherent in sanctions policy are uncomfortable and, for the moment, still imprecise calculations about inflicting civilian pain to achieve political gain. Where tolerable civilian discomfort begins and full-fledged humanitarian crisis begins is an elusive boundary, particularly because pre-sanction conditions in many countries are often so marginal. (Weiss, 1997: 30)

Each year since the passage of the CDA in 1992, the UN General Assembly has passed resolutions condemning the sanctions placed on Cuba. Cuba has maintained that the U.S. economic measures, which are intended to coerce changes in Cuba's political and economic institutions, violate principles of nonintervention and the sovereignty of states (Krinsky and Golove, 1993).

Genocide and Illegal War

Genocide is a collective and institutionally sanctioned effort to kill individuals because of their race, ethnicity, or cultural affiliation. Sadly, genocide is not just a ghost of the past, but continues to be a contemporary phenomenon as well. Many probably identify the term with the German Nazi Party's murder of more than 6 million Jews in the 1940s. However, genocidal activities continue to be investigated in several areas of the globe, including those occurring in Bosnia and Rwanda in the 1990s as well as the most recent violence in the Darfur region of Sudan (Mullins and Rothe, 2007; Rothe and Mullins, 2006). As noted at the beginning of this chapter, white-collar crimes are far more injurious to life and health than traditional street crimes, especially when one considers the immense suffering of victims of genocide.

Wars are illegal if they are not conducted out of strict self-defense or with the express approval of the United Nations Security Council. The technical illegality of the United States' latest war on Iraq has been thoroughly documented by criminologists (Kramer, Michalowski, and Rothe, 2005; Kramer and Michalowski, 2005). On the most basic level, any war not clearly in self-defense is prohibited by international law. The United Nations Charter, a principal source of the laws of war, specifies that "[a]ll members shall refrain from the threat or use of force against the territorial integrity or political independence of any state, or in any state in which the United Nations is taking preventive or enforcement action" (United Nations, 2006, article 2, chapter 1: 4). The only exception to Article 2(4) is found in Article 51 of the charter: "Nothing in the present Charter shall impair the inherent right of individual or collective self-defense if an armed attack occurs against a Member of the United Nations, until the Security Council has taken measures necessary to maintain international peace and security" (United Nations, 2006). The intention of this article is

to allow a state under direct attack to defend itself. Importantly, however, such a right is limited and executable only until the UN Security Council provides an international plan of action (Kauzlarich, 2007; Kauzlarich and Kramer, 1998).

In the history of the United Nations, the specific legal meaning of the Article 51 exception in relationship to Article 2(4) has been defined in only one case: *Nicaragua v. The United States* (1986). Here the ICJ ruled that Article 51 applies only when a state has been subject to an armed attack, and thus the decision reaffirms the fundamental precept of international law that war must be the very last measure taken in times of international dispute and conflict (Kramer and Kauzlarich, 1999). The Bush administration did half-heartedly attempt to gain the UN Security Council's permission to launch a war on Iraq in February 2003 when U.S. secretary of state Colin Powell presented what is now known to be mostly fictional information on Iraq's apparent possession of weapons of mass destruction and ties to Osama bin Laden, al-Qaeda, and the September 11, 2001, attacks on the United States. Finding the evidence unconvincing, the UN Security Council voted not to support a U.S. attack on Iraq, but this was ignored by the Bush administration and the war commenced shortly thereafter—in violation of the most basic principles of international law. While the war could be labeled criminal through a variety of nonlegal and humanistic definitions, there appears to be no clearer prohibition of the action than that found in the United Nations Charter (Kauzlarich, 2007).

State-Corporate Crime

While the study of state crime is still in its infancy, a promising and important development has recently been made by Ronald C. Kramer and Raymond J. Michalowski (1990) through the introduction of the concept of **state-corporate crime.** State-corporate crimes are

illegal or socially injurious actions that result from a mutually reenforcing interaction
between (1) policies and/or practices in pursuit of goals of one or more institutions of
political governance and (2) policies and/or
practices in pursuit of the goals of one or
more institutions of economic production
and distribution. (Kramer and Michalowski,
1991: 5; Michalowski and Kramer, 2006; also
see Aulette and Michalowski 1993: 175)

The concept of state-corporate crime has
been used to examine the space shuttle *Challenger* explosion (Kramer, 1992), the environmental devastation caused by U.S. nuclear
weapons production (Kauzlarich and Kramer
1993; 1998), and the previously mentioned
deadly fire at the Imperial Food Products
chicken-processing plant in Hamlet, North
Carolina (Aulette and Michalowski, 1993).
Other examples of state-corporate crime include the I. G. Farben Company's involvement with Nazi atrocities (Borkin, 1978); the
Wedtech case, involving defense contractor
fraud (Friedrichs, 1996); and the violent and
deadly crash of ValuJet flight 592 in May 1996
(Matthews and Kauzlarich, 2000; 2006).

Kramer and Michalowski (1990; 1991: 6)
identify two forms of state-corporate crime.
State-initiated crime occurs when corporations engage in organizational deviance at
the direction of, or with the tacit approval of,
the government. It includes cases such as the
space shuttle *Challenger* explosion and the
environmental and human injury caused by
nuclear weapons production. In both of these
instances, a government agency—NASA in
the *Challenger* case and the Department of
Energy in the nuclear weapons case—actively
pursued a shared goal with a private corporation—Morton Thiokol and Rockwell International, respectively. The day-to-day manufacture of various parts for the space shuttle
and nuclear weapons rests in the hands of
private corporations. Both the state and the
contracted corporation must produce a com-
modity in a timely and efficient way to achieve
mutually held organizational goals.

The illegal corporate practices (environmental contamination and the manufacture
of defective products) that resulted from
such contractual relationships were strongly
encouraged by the state agencies involved
(Kauzlarich and Kramer, 1993; 1998; Kramer,
1992; Matthews and Kauzlarich, 2000). In the
Challenger case, NASA pressured managers
at Morton Thiokol into granting permission
to launch the shuttle, even though scientists
at Morton Thiokol expressed great concern
that the O-rings would fail (Kramer, 1992;
Vaughan, 1996). Here, a state agency initiated
the socially injurious event. It was through
this interaction that a private corporation and
a public entity made a decision that ultimately
lead to the *Challenger* explosion.

The second form of state-corporate crime
is *state-facilitated crime*. This occurs when
"governmental regulatory institutions fail to
restrain deviant business activities, because of
direct collusion between business and government, or because they adhere to shared goals
whose attainment would be hampered by aggressive regulation" (Kramer and Michalowski
1991: 6). For example, the Imperial Food Products fire in North Carolina did not simply result
from the technical cause of injury (Imperial
Food Products' decision to lock fire doors), but
the twenty-five workers who died were the victims of "a series of social decisions made by a
broad array of institutions." These institutions
acted "like a noose . . . [that] . . . closed around
Hamlet which brought about the death of 25
workers" (Aulette and Michalowski, 1993: 203).
Likewise, if not for very specific omissions by a
number of institutional actors in both the private and public sectors within a lax regulatory
environment, ValuJet flight 592 would not have
crashed in the Florida Everglades (Matthews
and Kauzlarich, 2000; 2006).

CHAPTER SUMMARY

This chapter has explored the many dimensions of occupational and organizational

crime. Such crime occurs in connection with a person's job, with work providing the opportunity and/or motivation for criminal activity. The financial, medical, and social costs of white-collar crime far exceed those of such conventional street crimes as robbery, burglary, drug sales, murder, and assault.

Occupational crimes are committed for personal gain. These include embezzlement, political white-collar crime, and a host of other offenses ranging from simple fiddles to high-tech manipulations costing thousands of dollars. Other white-collar crimes are committed on behalf of an organization, as in the case of corporate crime and state crime.

As we will discuss in later chapters, no one theory adequately explains white-collar crimes, partly because the term covers diverse situations. It seems safe to argue, however, that many people and organizations who commit work-related crimes regard their behavior as normal rather than deviant or illegal—but not criminal. Situational incentives are reinforced by norms and values that define the behavior as appropriate, even expected. Under such circumstances it is the people who refrain from offenses who are regarded as deviant.

On the whole, however, official reactions to most white-collar crimes are more lenient than reactions to most street crimes, and rarely will a convicted occupational criminal go to jail (Benson and Cullen, 1998). Michael Blankenship wonders, "What conclusions can we draw about a society that is willing to impose the death penalty on the poor and the powerless but permits members of the upper class literally to get away with murder?" (1993: xxi).

American culture strongly supports the drive for profits and power, and in so doing provides rationalizations for executives who bend the rules, for politicians who deal in favors, and for officials who look the other way. It should come as no surprise, therefore, that the factory worker, office clerk, and salesperson have little trouble justifying their relatively petty crimes. They are taking advantage of the opportunities before them in the same enterprising spirit.

The irony, however, is that workers at all levels of responsibility and power actually have little choice in the matter: The structure and norms of work make occupational and organizational crime virtually inevitable.

KEY TERMS

corporate crime
corporate theft and fraud
corporate violence
governmental crime
occupational crime
organizational crime
political white-collar crime
price discrimination
price-fixing
state-corporate crime
state crime
white-collar crime

RECOMMENDED READINGS

Barak, Gregg. (1991). *Crimes by the Capitalist State*. Albany: State University of New York Press.

Kauzlarich, David, and Ronald C. Kramer. (1998). *Crimes of the American Nuclear State: At Home and Abroad*. Boston: Northeastern University Press.

Michalowski, Raymond J. and Ronald C. Kramer. (2006). *State-Corporate Crime: Wrongdoing at the Intersection of Government and Business*. New Brunswick, NJ: Rutgers University Press.

Simon, David R. (2006). *Elite Deviance*. 6th ed. Boston: Allyn and Bacon.

Tunnell, Kenneth D. (1993). *Political Crime in Contemporary America*. New York: Garland.

Rothe, Dawn, and Christopher W. Mullins. (2006). *Symbolic Gestures and the Generation of International Social Controls: The International Criminal Court*. Lanham, MD: Lexington Books.

RECOMMENDED WEB SITES

Amnesty International (http://www.amnesty.org). A plethora of information about state and corporate crimes, especially violations of human rights.

Association of Certified Fraud Examiners (http://www.cfenet.com/). Information and links on occupational and some organizational crimes, especially fraud and theft.

Occupational Safety and Health Administration (http://www.osha.gov). An enormous amount of information, data, and press releases on matters related to worker health and safety.

CHAPTER

7

Drugs, Prostitution, and Organized Crime

22850106 Jupiter

149

This chapter deals primarily with two major and often interrelated crimes: (1) the public order crimes of drug use and prostitution and (2) organized crime. Regarding the former, societies have grappled with the problem of what to do about activities that many regard as sinful and yet many others enjoy. As long as these behaviors are kept from public view, it is easy to deny that they really exist. Prostitution, pornography, drunkenness, and drug use and addiction are rarely hidden from the public eye, however, and for that reason they are often considered threats to public morality and order—and so are made illegal. In their criminal aspects, drugs and sex have some marked similarities:

- Participants in these crimes often do not view themselves as criminal, nor are they viewed as criminals by significant portions of the population.
- The criminal sides of sex and drugs have legal counterparts that are sometimes difficult to distinguish from them, except for their legality. For example, it is legal to buy and sell alcohol and caffeine but not heroin or marijuana. It is legal (in most places) to buy and sell *Hustler* and *Penthouse* magazines but not to dance nude in a bar.
- Illegal sex and drugs are sources of pleasure and tremendous profits. The profits, more than the pleasures, are a direct consequence of criminalization. The black market drives up prices, and entrepreneurs willing to take risks pay no taxes on their profits.
- Illegal sex and drugs are prime targets of organized crime, with all three feeding off one another. For example, many prostitutes are drug addicts, and vice versa. Organized crime controls large segments of drug trafficking and criminal sex, and, through the profits it makes, extends its control, protects itself from law enforcement, and increases the market for its products and services.
- The laws that apply to sex and drugs reflect both consensus and conflict, with special interests prominent in both their substance and enforcement.
- Enforcement of laws dealing with drugs and sex requires a special type of policing: the use of informants and un-

dercover police. It is also a major area of graft and corruption in the criminal justice system.

- Much of the behavior that is criminalized in both areas is said to be "victimless," in that participants consider themselves willingly involved rather than being offended against.
- Both areas of crime are prime targets of moral entrepreneurs, who see the behavior involved as evidence of declining morals and unreasonable permissiveness and who continually organize campaigns to broaden the laws and increase the penalties.

Historically, much organized crime has revolved around the so-called vice crimes, which are drug, prostitution, and gambling offenses. The second half of this chapter not only addresses the links between drugs, sex, and organized crime, but also considers other ways in which syndicated criminal networks operate more generally. Let us begin by taking a closer look at prostitution and drugs and what criminologists know about these phenomena.

PROSTITUTION

Some sex offenses are **victimless crimes**, meaning that they are conducted by consenting adults who voluntarily engage in an activity that happens to be illegal. Adultery, fornication, the sale and purchase of pornographic images and literature, and prostitution are possible examples. This section focuses on prostitution, which some consider a victimless crime but, as we shall see, can and does result in social and physical harms.

As many as 1 million male and female prostitutes are working at any given time in the United States (San Francisco Task Force on Prostitution, 2000). Yet prostitution is a violation of criminal codes in all states except Nevada, in which county governments decide on legality, and Rhode Island, where the law specifically criminalizes outdoor or public solicitations but contains a loophole that allows for private forms of prostitution behind closed doors. Prostitution has not always been illegal in the United States, and in some Western societies it is tolerated today. In Germany, Holland, and Denmark, for instance, female prostitutes are pretty much left alone as long as they ply their trade in designated areas and fulfill other requirements such as licensing and payment of taxes.

Selling Sex: The Prostitute at Work

Prostitutes work in various ways (Raphael and Shapiro, 2004; Weitzer, 2005). At one end of the spectrum and most numerous are the *streetwalkers*, or street hookers. These women may be readily encountered on the street, particularly where cheap hotels, bars, and mass transportation terminals are to be found.

The streetwalker is at the bottom of the pecking order among prostitutes. She works where the risks are greatest, she has little or no control over which clients she takes, she must put up with all kinds of weather, she must generally give a good portion of her earnings away for "protection," and she must usually work long hours to make enough from her "tricks" (paying customers, sometimes called *johns*) to meet her financial obligations.

There are three kinds of female streetwalkers in big cities:

(1) *Daytimers*, the "classiest" group, who usually work office buildings, comprised mostly of white, out-of-work models and actresses, and housewives supplementing their family income.

(2) *Early evening girls*, who finish by 11 p.m., are full-time, independent professionals working in and around hotels.

(3) *All the rest*, those who do not fit into the first two categories, including the old, the very young, the unattractive,

and the desperate, who work far into the night and turn as many tricks as they can (Sheehy, 1973: 30–32). The latter category includes women with drug addictions, who commonly render their "services" in cars, abandoned buildings, cheap hotels, or crack houses (French, 1994).

Even the "classiest" streetwalkers—those working office buildings or conventions—rarely gross more than $300 a day. The streetwalker does well to stay in business for more than a few years, and her earning capacity declines rapidly after she passes her twenty-second or twenty-third birthday.

Male prostitutes also work the streets; most are older teenagers and young adults. They rarely regard themselves as homosexuals, and prefer to be called *hustlers* (McCaghy and Capron, 1994: 442). Various roles are possible, and, as with female streetwalkers, young men and boys can be seen selling and negotiating on street corners, sometimes standing close together displaying their wares in what is known as the "meat rack."

Next up the social ladder are prostitutes who work in brothels (also called "bordellos," "cathouses," or "whorehouses"). Until World War II, brothels were the major outlet for prostitution in the United States. In major cities, brothels numbered in the hundreds, and they were usually located close together in areas that came to be known as *red-light districts*. Run by madams, who were often working prostitutes at one time, these brothels sometimes had a "stable" of twenty or thirty women working in shifts. Typically, half of each woman's earnings went to the madam to pay for room and board (see Wiltz, 1999).

Over the second half of the twentieth century, the number of brothels declined, mostly as a result of cleanup operations by city councils pressured by local citizen groups. Brothels still operate as the major context of prostitution in Nevada (the state frowns upon streetwalkers), and most large cities in the United States have brothels that maintain themselves solely through a system of informal referrals. Gone are the days, though, when a visitor could simply appear on the doorstep of a common brothel and buy himself sexual pleasure (Wiltz, 1999). The closing of brothels made the business of prostitution more unpleasant and dangerous for both clients and prostitutes (Daly, 1988: 199).

A study of male sex workers (MSWs) in Australia found that clients were primarily contacted through advertisement and escort services (Marino, Browne, and Jamieson, 1999). The study also found that half the surveyed MSWs considered themselves gay, 31 percent bisexual, and 5.5 percent straight. The MSWs reported that their clients were mostly middle aged and middle class.

Toward the top of the prostitution pecking order are call girls, who usually work through escort services. Though the operating methods differ, the established call girl usually secures her clients through individual referrals by customers, trusted friends, or through shady business entities (Bryan, 1965; Weitzer, 2005). She conducts the sexual transaction in her own apartment or in the office, home, or hotel room of her client. Many call girls work independently and exercise considerable discretion in their choice of clients. Most top-flight call girls are in their early twenties; they are generally from middle-class backgrounds, and some are college educated. The successful call girl is physically attractive, well groomed, and articulate, and she makes a pleasant date for those men who can afford the $500 to $1,000 it takes to purchase her company for an evening. By using the telephone rather than the street, call girls can be highly selective regarding customers.

Bars and Massage Parlors as Places of Prostitution

Public bars and nightclubs have long been frequented by prostitutes (Weinberg, Shaver, and Williams, 1999; Weitzer, 2006). These women often operate with the support of bar management. Prostitutes find bars good places for hustling. For one thing, they can work indoors; in addition, they have a constant flow of prospective clients, they can mingle with the crowd and thus not be too obvious, there are people around who can come to their rescue if trouble should arise, and they can choose their clients.

Massage parlors are also a lucrative setting for prostitution. Though some establishments provide only therapeutic massages by trained personnel, many of the thousands of parlors from coast to coast basically offer one service: sex. The range of sexual activities purchased extends from simple hand jobs—which are permissible in some jurisdictions—to blow jobs, straight sexual intercourse, and anything else the customer may desire and the "masseuse" is willing to do. The profits can be enormous for owners of these parlors.

Massage parlors are good fronts for prostitution because they provide a legal setting for customer contacts. "Employees" need not solicit business; it comes to them, as a typical customer is looking for more than just a massage. Furthermore, the masseuses are not dependent on the customers' purchase of sex because they receive a commission (usually 30 to 35 percent) on any legal massage they give—and these can cost $100 an hour for such frills as nude masseuses, champagne, and special baths. Other advantages to prostitution in this setting include a comfortable work environment, a potentially speedy turnover in customers, and some protection against arrest and criminal conviction for prostitution. Massage parlor prostitutes are protected from arrest and conviction partly by the semiprivate character of the parlor and partly because, by leaving it up to the customers to do the soliciting, they minimize the chances of a legal arrest. An undercover cop who first solicits sex and then arrests the masseuse may well be acting illegally under the rules of entrapment. These rules usually are interpreted as follows: Police may not entice a person into committing a crime and then use the offense and evidence of it to bring about a criminal conviction if the person would not normally have voluntarily committed the offense in question.

The Pimp

The **pimp** holds a key position in the world of prostitution (Miller, 1986; Romenesko and Miller, 1989; Weitzer, 2005). Though there is no way of knowing exactly what proportion of prostitutes work under the control of pimps, it is certainly the majority, and may be as high as 90 percent in some places (Farley et al., 1997; Weitzer, 2005). For a pimp, prostitution is the road to financial success; it is he, not his women, who reaps the real profits from the billion-dollar business. Despite this arrangement, many prostitutes would quickly fail in business without their pimp. Ironically, though, the fact that the pimp controls her earnings means that the typical female street hustler "cannot save or plan for the future *independently* of men" (Romenesko and Miller, 1989: 132).

The pimp's importance comes partly from the nature of prostitution itself and partly from his own business acumen and ability to manipulate people. Because prostitution is illegal, those involved are constantly threatened by arrest. Pimps can help protect prostitutes from legal troubles as well as provide financial and other assistance, such as posting bail. Pimps help defend their prostitutes against competition by establishing and maintaining control over particular territories. Independent prostitutes do not have that kind of security. Pimps also offer protection against physical or financial threat posed by drunks, toughs, and customers who want something for nothing. Most prostitutes have little control over men's access to them—indeed, they must make that access as free as possible—and when they are confronted by troublemakers, it is nice to have someone in the wings who can deal with the problem.

The dangers of prostitution open up a role for the pimp. Even so, his success also hinges on his adeptness in establishing and maintaining the prostitute's dependence on him and his control over her. Control and dependence are the central features of what is, at its heart, a relationship of exploitation. To establish that relationship, the pimp demonstrates that the practicing or would-be prostitute needs him for both material and emotional reasons. He shows his material importance by taking care of room and board, clothing, and medical expenses and by running the business profitably. On the emotional level, the pimp is there when the woman needs affection, advice, and love—but he also disciplines her when she falters.

Several studies have shown that prostitution is a significant source of income for women who use and/or are addicted to crack cocaine and powder cocaine (Gilchrist, Cameron, and Scoular, 2005; Ratner, 1994). While the levels of crack use have declined of late, many lower-class crack-addicted women sell sex for cash or exchange sex for crack. The women are often so desperate for money that they will perform sexual "tricks" for next to nothing, just to get a little closer to a hit on the crack pipe. Others give sexual favors to crack dealers or crack house operators in exchange for drugs. One crack-addicted woman put it this way:

> The rock is the pimp. . . . We go out there, we get all this money, first person we run to is to the dope man. The rock is the pimp. . . . So that's why they call us strawberries, 'cause we get the rocks and we will have oral sex, have you, have your brother too, all at the same time to get this cocaine. (Feucht, 1997: 135)

Another said: "I really didn't want to be with them, but I wanted to get high, so I just went ahead and had sex with them to get the money and go on and buy my [rock]" (136).

In any case, these women have very little control over their lives (Ratner, 1994). They also hold the lowest status on the street—the crack whore is disdained not only by the so-called professional street prostitutes, but also by her own clients (Boyle and Anglin, 1994).

DRUGS

Most Americans are consumers of drugs, but some do nothing illegal, whereas others do. The world of drugs, then, has two sides: the legal and criminal. Here the word *drug* will refer to any psychoactive substance. A **psychoactive substance** is one having the capacity to alter mental states. Identifying an altered mental state requires a subjective assessment by the drug user, which sometimes complicates the identification of a substance as a drug. However, there is widespread agreement on the following examples of currently abused drugs: alcohol, nicotine, caffeine, opiates, hallucinogens (LSD, DMT), cocaine, heroin ("boy"), barbiturates ("downers"), amphetamines ("speed"), ecstasy ("X"), marijuana, tranquilizers, and analgesics (painkillers).

Marijuana and the Drugging of America

Two trends that began nearly fifty years ago, taken together, explain much of the current drug problem, in particular its criminological aspects. First was the growing recreational use of drugs, especially among the young; second was the marked growth in the production and marketing of legal drugs. In the opinion of many experts, the first trend was helped along by the second.

In Search of Self: Marijuana

The preeminent illegal drug is marijuana. According to recent national surveys of use among high school students, 38 percent claimed to have used the drug once in their life (Maguire and Pastore, 2007). Almost half of all adults in the U.S. admit to using the drug at some point in their life. College students generally report a greater level of drug use than high school students. And while inner-city neighborhoods have received considerable publicity as being drug ridden, studies suggest that inner-city youth are no more at risk of becoming drug users than are other youths; however, they are more at risk of becoming *sellers* of drugs, including marijuana (Greenwood, 1992: 446).

There was a steep decline in the use of illicit drugs among Americans generally from the 1980s to early 1990s, although in recent years their use appears to be increasing (see figure 7.1). Marijuana is readily available: The majority of studies have found that around 85 percent of high school seniors surveyed think it would be easy to buy marijuana where they live (Maguire and Pastore, 2000). Further-

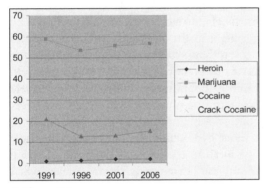

▲ **Figure 7.1.**
Percent of Young Adults Reporting Use of a Drug in Their Lifetime
Source: Monitoring the Future (2007). National Institute on Drug Abuse.

more, the availability of marijuana appears to have been increasing in recent years with expanded domestic cultivation.

Marijuana (cannabis) comes from the Indian hemp plant *Cannabis sativa* and has been used for centuries. The resin, called *charas* by Hindus and known as hashish today, was used for spiritual purposes by Native Americans and as a medicine by the ancient Chinese. When the top leaves of the hemp plant are cut and dried, they can be eaten or smoked. The mixture is less potent than hashish, and the Indians called it *bhang*; it is now called marijuana, grass, or pot, among other terms.

More than half of the marijuana supply in the United States comes from Mexico (U.S. Drug Enforcement Agency, 2007). Much of the remainder is locally grown.

How did marijuana emerge as America's most popular illicit drug? The answer lies partly with the growth of countercultures during the late 1950s and subsequent confrontations with "the Establishment" on college campuses during the 1960s. The Beat generation that emerged in New York and San Francisco in the 1950s emphasized an alternative lifestyle of autonomy, drugs (especially pot), music, free sexual expression, aversion to routine employment and politics, and disregard for the law (Polsky, 1967). Hippies succeeded the Beats and made famous the Haight-Ashbury district of San Francisco. They claimed a similar lifestyle, though jazz was replaced with acid rock or folk rock, and marijuana was joined by LSD. Hippies also enjoyed "putting on straights" and "blowing their minds" by rejecting all that was valued by the dominant middle-class culture. By the end of the 1960s the hippie culture—if not its ideology—had spread to all parts of the country, and rock music was one of its major vehicles. Another factor in marijuana's increasing popularity was the growing disenchantment among young people, especially college students, with the policies and practice of American government. Use of illegal drugs became a way of underscoring their opposition to the Establishment. In addition, marijuana and psychedelics were touted as a way to "expand the mind," to "trip," to "get your head right." They were perfect for the "now" generation: those who searched for meaning and heightened self-awareness (Carey, 1968).

In the past and present, those likely to use marijuana—and all illegal drugs—are precisely those who have grown up in a social environment in which legal drugs are commonly used (Abdelrahman et al., 1998). No matter whether it is cocaine, heroin, marijuana, or the psychedelics, studies consistently show generational continuity in drug use and in the progression from legal to illegal drugs (Vega and Gil, 1999). The important lesson is that illegal drug use is most likely to be found in a climate favorable to drug use in general. In fact, the most significant correlate of illegal drug use is the consumption of legal drugs.

Cocaine

Cocaine is extracted from the leaves of the plant *Erythroxylon coca*, which is found in South America. Coca leaves have been chewed for at least three thousand years by South American Indians. Cocaine use in America is not well documented but does not seem to have been particularly extensive until relatively recently. It was first used medicinally as an anesthetic in eye surgery in the early 1900s. It was also "used by many people in the form of tonic, wines, and teas" (Chaiken, 1993: 3). It was once a popular Yuppie drug, and its street use grew in the 1980s, especially in the form of crack.

The major site of coca cultivation continues to be Peru, but trafficking is dominated by Colombia, where the raw paste or cocaine base is converted into cocaine hydrochloride (HCl) for distribution to the United States. Generally, cocaine HCl is 90 percent pure when imported. The most common route of importation is through Mexico, followed by the Caribbean. Cocaine confiscations by the Drug Enforcement Administration (DEA) peaked in the early 1990s, from 399 pounds in 1977, to 81,823 pounds in 1987, 173,391 pounds in 1992, and, most recently, 153,600 pounds in 2006. DEA confiscations have tailed off in recent years, partially because of greater multiagency involvement in drug investigation. Additionally, methamphetamine distribution and consumption has drawn considerably more attention in recent years, as the DEA seized 1,711 kilograms of the substance in 2006, up from only 272 kilograms in 1990 (U.S. Drug Enforcement Agency, 2007). Cocaine use has been controlled since the Harrison Narcotics Act of 1914 restricted its manufacture, distribution, and sale. It is illegal in all states. Cocaine is not, in fact, a narcotic; it is a stimulant that acts directly on the "pleasure" or "reward" centers of the brain. It is so powerful that it undermines the brain's ability to regulate such functional necessities as sleeping, eating, and handling stress. Users describe the "high" as elation, warmth, vigor, friendliness, and arousal (Farrington, 2000; Grabowski, 1984). Because the subjective effects are so pleasant, cocaine is considered a prime target for abuse.

Crack

If anything accounts for the explosive growth in cocaine use in America during the 1980s and early 1990s, it was crack—a cheap, smokable form of cocaine. Crack, unlike other forms of cocaine, is inexpensive, and one can get high on the substance for a few minutes for less than $20. Like most commodities, the price does vary considerably from location to location. Crack is easy to make and extremely fast acting. It is produced by processing street cocaine with ammonia or baking soda to remove hydrochlorides. The resulting crystalline mixture gets its name from the crackling sound the baking soda residue makes when the mixture is smoked (National Institute of Drug Abuse, 2006).

Drug-dealing structures are not well studied, but some similarities appear to exist across drug types and may help explain the popularity of crack in the 1980s and early 1990s:

> First, the structure of distribution is better characterized as groups of dealers and individual entrepreneurs, rather than as a single, highly organized and centralized criminal operation; and second, entrance and acceptance into dealing groups are based on familiarity, friendship ties, situational factors ("the right place at the right time"), and available capital (Bourgois, 2004; Hunt, 1990: 181; Jacobs, 1999a; 1999b).

Crack can be manufactured in anyone's kitchen, and the "step from crack manufacturer to crack user is a short one" (Hunt, 1990: 179). Thus the entire crack business can be a local, neighborhood affair (Bourgois, 2004). Many crack dealers, however, try to be careful about their own use of crack because of its tendency to get in the way of good business decision making. Many do, however, smoke marijuana or consume other drugs (Bourgois, 2004; personal interview, March 2000; Jacobs, 1999b).

The presence of neighborhood gangs and cliques facilitates the production and distribution of illegal drugs. It is true that illicit drugs have been a feature of street-corner society for decades (see Merry, 1981; Schwendinger and Schwendinger, 1985), but the intensity of trafficking grew after crack appeared on the scene. Traditions of street drug use, black-market enterprise networks, protection of "turf," anonymity, and high rates of truancy and unemployment combine with ease of manufacture to promote trafficking in crack (Barr et al., 1993). Nevertheless, street gangs vary widely in the extent of their involvement in drug-related crime in general and with cocaine specifically, particularly crack cocaine. One former drug dealer explains the lure of trafficking from the standpoint of underclass black youths:

> See, where I come from, young people don't dream of becoming doctors, lawyers, teachers, or even professional athletes. They dream of becoming big-time drug dealers. Kingpins. I'll stand witness. . . . When I show people the pictures of my previous lifestyle and the material things I had, it's not to brag. It's just you can't tell them the whole truth without letting them see the traps—money, cars, fine women, bad rep and the feeling you're a big man. In some neighborhoods, if you aren't a drug dealer, you'll never get a girlfriend. Talk about pressure, especially for a teenager. (Alexander, 1994: 33)

The declining use of crack has placed considerable strain on dealers, who now compete in a high-risk/low-return environment. Bruce Jacobs (1999a; 1999b) has studied both heroin

and crack dealers in St. Louis and finds plenty of evidence to show that heroin has replaced crack as the drug of choice in the inner city. Many former crack dealers now prefer to sell heroin, while those who still sell crack often supplement their inventory with heroin. There are many interrelated reasons for this change in drug use and dealing: demand for crack is down, heroin is in some ways more powerful and more profitable than crack, some crack users have died or gone to prison and not been replaced, and there is increasing social stigma surrounding crack use—even among those on the "street." Many law enforcement agencies and researchers believe that heroin and methamphetamine has assumed the role crack once occupied (Jacobs, 1999a; 1999b; personal interview, 2007). One reason for this is the different pharmacological and psychological effects of the drugs. One user put it this way:

> You get a better high out of it (heroin). A crack high only last like maybe one, two, three, maybe five minutes man and then it's gone. . . . (With heroin) you spend (the same amount of money) . . . and get high all day, get high for two or three day. (1999a: 564)

While crack use and dealing is down across the country, the drug problem is far from over. The use of meth, which causes a high that can last for days, has grown substantially over the last decade. Easily produced in "meth labs" in homes or even vehicles, the drug has the effects of concentrated speed and is very addictive. Stepped-up law enforcement efforts in response to hundreds of deaths and thefts related to the drug have netted thousands of arrests of meth "cooks" and users, especially in areas of the Midwest. Additionally, cheap and potent forms of heroin, as we will see shortly, are becoming a major concern for communities and law enforcement agencies across the United States.

Heroin

The millions of Americans who routinely consume psychoactive substances with little thought that they are addicts, or even drug users, stand in stark contrast with the estimated 3.5 million people who have used heroin at least once in their lifetime or the estimated six to eight hundred thousand hardcore heroin addicts (Jacobs, 1999a; Office of National Drug Control Policy, 2007). Heroin has historically borne the brunt of public and legal intolerance (as crack does now), and the world of most heroin addicts is quite different from that of other, "respectable" drug users. It is a world in which getting the "shit" (or "horse," "smack," "skag," "junk," "tragic magic") and staying alive and out of jail consume much of every waking day.

The heroin addict craves has often traveled thousands of miles and passed across numerous links in a complex underground chain of importation and distribution. Over the past decades, the primary foreign sources of heroin have been the Middle East, Afghanistan, Pakistan, India, the Far East, Mexico, and Colombia. During the 1970s Mexico emerged as the major foreign source, a trend that continues today, although areas in South America comprise a close competitor (Drug Enforcement Administration, 2007).

The mechanics of importation vary according to the location and availability of raw opium—Mexico became an important source only after America withdrew from Vietnam and the Turkish government cracked down on opium production. Local dealers and vendors always remain the important final links in the chain and effectively control dealing at the street level. It is the pusher, the small-time vendor, who provides the addict and user with heroin. Pushers are usually addicts themselves; today, as they have for decades, pushers finance their own drug purchases through sales to others (Bourgois, 2004; Dunlap, Johnson, and Manwar, 1997; Preble and Casey, 1969).

Recall that heroin has replaced crack cocaine as the drug of choice in the inner city. According to Jacobs (1999a), heroin is usually dealt on the street in one of two forms: (1)

buttons, pills that contain black tar heroin and crushed sleeping pills, can be purchased for about $10 each; and (2) the more recent pure tar heroin, which is of better quality and sold for about $20 a tenth gram. Neither requires that the user "shoot up"—both can be snorted. This might make the drug more desirable to casual or recreational drug users, as illustrated in Plano, Texas, several years ago when nineteen young "middle-class white cheerleaders, football players, and preppies" died as a result of taking $10 heroin capsules (Gegax and Van Boven, 2000).

The Link between Drugs and Crime

Where there is illicit drug use, there is often other crime. Much of the associated crime relates to financing drug use, abuse, and addiction. This instrumental crime is most likely to be found among people who are poor, unemployed, or unemployable, and among those who are heavy users. Many inner-city crack and heroin addicts belong to both groups.

The relationship between the level of drug involvement and crime is confirmed by several studies (Allen, 2005; Anglin and Speckart, 1988; Bourgois, 2004). As the level of use increases, so does the amount of criminal activity, but also there seems to be a shift in the criminal activities of high-level users to more profitable types of crime (Anglin and Speckart, 1988). Wright and Decker (1994: 39) found that fifty-nine of sixty-eight burglary offenders who used proceeds for pleasure-seeking pursuits specifically mentioned how the money would be used to buy drugs: "For many of these respondents, the decision to break into a dwelling arose as a result of a heavy session of drug use. The objective was to get the money to keep the party going" (Shover 1996).

There is little argument that drug use and crime are related. What is a matter of dispute are the nature and direction of that relationship. In fact, drug use and crime may be connected in various ways: Drug use may give rise to crime, crime may give rise to drug use, or drug use and crime may be reciprocal—each giving rise to the other. All three views find support in criminological research, as does another: Commitment to a life of "action" produces both drug use and crime.

Most studies of chronic criminal offenders find heavy drug use and drug sales in their backgrounds, often beginning in their early teens (Allen, 2005; Harrison, 1992). What is not clear is how much of that crime is explained by drug use. The financial pinch that forces many drug users—especially the young and poor—into instrumental crime is clearly a factor; but it is nevertheless difficult to disentangle the offenses that are driven by drug abuse from those that are not and would have occurred anyway. As far as violence is concerned, it appears that drug (and alcohol) users who commit violent acts were likely to have been aggressive before they started using drugs (Fagan, 1990). So, too, one should recognize that there is a kind of systematic violence associated with the world of illicit drug use—violence that derives from the milieu rather than the drug-using behavior of individuals within it. Territorial fights, robberies of dealers and subsequent retaliation, the elimination of informers, and punishment for selling adulterated (or fake) drugs are examples (Allen, 2005; Hunt, 1990).

Although it is popular to think of drug use driving crime, criminal activity itself may lead to drug use among offenders. There are various ways this can happen:

(1) people who "earn" money like to spend some of it on pleasurable things; (2) a risky but successful venture should be celebrated; (3) a risky venture may need some special courage or other mental preparation; (4) the peer networks that facilitate delinquency and crime also facilitate drug use; and (5) drugs may substitute for cash or other profits. (Barlow and Ferdinand, 1992: 109)

Studies have shown that serious drug use is more likely to be an aspect of the lifestyles of chronic delinquents and criminals than chronic criminality is of the lifestyles of serious drug users. In part, this reflects the better economic backgrounds of chronic drug users compared to those of chronic delinquents. On the other hand, as illegal income increases, so does discretionary buying power, which means more money is available for drugs (Bourgois, 2004; Cromwell, 2006; Collins, Hubbard, and Rachel, 1985; also see Faupel, 1991; 1999).

Many people cling to the idea of a causal connection between drug use and antisocial behavior, even though association does not mean that one causes the other. There are various reasons for this belief. The idea helps one account for criminal behavior without imputing criminal intent; if a person were not "under the influence," a crime would not have happened. The drug becomes an excuse, a rationalization. Another reason pertains to enforcement: It is because people believe that illegal drugs cause terrible crimes that they accept and support severe penalties and secretive police tactics used against drug offenders, whereas ordinarily, people abhor "snitches" and distrust those who go about in disguise pretending to be what they are not.

Drug Arrests: A Major Police Activity

The police make many drug arrests, but mostly for possession. When combined with alcohol-related arrests in any given year, more arrests are made for drug-related offenses than for any other category of crime. In 2005, there were 1.85 million drug arrests and about 2.5 million arrests for drunk driving, liquor law violations, and drunkenness (Federal Bureau of Investigation, 2006a). Over the past twenty years, drug- and alcohol-related arrests have made up around 30 percent of all arrests.

Over the past few years, the rate of drug arrests of African Americans has been rising faster than those of whites. In 2005, for example, 34 percent of all those arrested for drug crimes were African American, despite the fact that this group comprises less than 13 percent of the U.S. population (Federal Bureau of Investigation, 2006a). The spread of crack in inner-city neighborhoods certainly accounts for some of the difference, but the complete story is not that simple. Many drug arrests are incidental to other police actions, and when police target minority neighborhoods with a reputation for crime and social disorder, many drug violations that might have escaped detection in other neighborhoods are likely to be uncovered (Beckett, Nyrop, Pfingst, 2006; Klofas, 1993). In fact, most drug arrests are made not by specialized narcotic units, but by police on routine patrol in nondrug stops and searches that reveal evidence of drug-related crimes.

ORGANIZED CRIME

Most Americans are familiar with the term *organized crime*, yet it is unlikely that many of them know much about it. They have probably heard of Al Capone, John Gotti, Joe Valachi, and Charlie "Lucky" Luciano. Most may also have heard of Eliot Ness, head of the Untouchables, the law enforcement team

assigned the task of breaking up Capone's bootlegging operations during Prohibition. It is common knowledge that Chicago and the New York–Philadelphia–New Jersey area are major centers of organized crime activities. What most people have learned about organized crime, however, has come from the mass media. Apart from periodic news items, which are usually colorful and designed to demonstrate some special kind of "inside" knowledge, the entertainment industry has been a major window on organized crime. The enduring popularity of films such as *Goodfellas* and *The Godfather* as well as the television show *The Sopranos* is evidence of the strong appeal of organized crime as entertainment. At best, the information available to the public via the mass media is fragmentary, superficial, and misleading; at worst, it is patently false and purely titillating. We also know that members and associates of the Italian organized syndicate **La Cosa Nostra** feel that there are widespread misperceptions about organized crime. Thomas Cupples and David Kauzlarich (1997) interviewed 150 such persons and found that only 20 percent of the respondents believed that the mob is accurately depicted in movies.

BOX 7.1. VARIOUS DEFINITIONS AND DESCRIPTIONS OF ORGANIZED CRIME

Organized crime means the unlawful activities of the members of a highly organized, disciplined association engaged in supplying illegal goods and services, including but not limited to gambling, prostitution, loan sharking, narcotics, labor racketeering, and other unlawful activities of members of such organizations.—The 1968 Omnibus Crime Control Act, Section 3701

Any enterprise or group of persons engaged in a continuing illegal activity which has as its primary purpose the generation of profits, irrespective of national boundaries.—1988 Interpol definition, in Bresler (1992)

Any group having a corporate structure whose primary objective is to obtain money through illegal activities, often surviving on fear and corruption.—Current Interpol definition, in Bresler (1992)

[A]ny group having some manner of a formalized structure and whose primary objective is to obtain money through illegal activities. Such groups maintain their position through the use of actual or threatened violence, corrupt public officials, graft, or extortion, and generally have a significant impact on the people in their locales, region, or the country as a whole.—Federal Bureau of Investigation (2007)

THE EXISTENCE OF ORGANIZED CRIME

Over the years a belief has grown that thriving within the United States is a national alliance or cartel of organized groups of criminals, dominated by Italian Americans, and involved in an extensive range of illicit, often violent activities. As we shall see, this view is now strongly challenged. There is also controversy surrounding the definition of organized crime. Box 7.1 includes various definitions of the phenomenon; note the vagueness of the wording.

The Case for a National Cartel of Crime Groups

In 1951 and then again in 1969, highly credible sources appeared to confirm that a national crime cartel does exist in the United States. First, the Kefauver Committee of the U.S. Senate reported that:

1. There is a nation-wide crime syndicate known as the Mafia, whose tentacles are found in many large cities. . . .
2. Its leaders are usually found in control of the most lucrative rackets in their cities.
3. There are indications of a centralized direction and control of these rackets, but leadership appears to be in a group rather than in a single individual.
4. The Mafia is the cement that helps bind the Costello-Adonis-Lansky syndicate of New York and the Accardo-Guzik-Fischetti syndicate of Chicago as well as smaller criminal gangs and individual criminals throughout the country. . . .
5. The domination of the Mafia is based fundamentally on "muscle" and "murder." The Mafia is a secret conspiracy against law and order which will ruthlessly eliminate anyone who stands in the way of its success in any criminal enterprise in which it is interested. It will destroy anyone who betrays its secrets. It will use any means available—political influence, bribery, intimidation, etc., to defeat any attempt on the part of law enforcement to touch its top figures or to interfere with its operations. (Tyler, 1962: 343–44)

The findings of the Kefauver Committee were based on information supplied mainly by police officials and informants. Using basically the same kinds of information, Donald Cressey summarized his investigation on behalf of the President's Commission on Law Enforcement and the Administration of Justice as follows:

1. A nationwide alliance of at least twenty-four tightly knit "families" of criminals exists in the United States (because the "families" are fictive, in the sense that the members are not all relatives, it is necessary to refer to them in quotation marks).
2. The members of these "families" are all Italians and Sicilians, or of Italian or Sicilian descent, and those on the Eastern seaboard, especially, call the entire system "Cosa Nostra." Each member thinks of himself as a "member" of a specific "family" and of Cosa Nostra (or some equivalent term).
3. The names, criminal records, and principal criminal activities of about five thousand of the participants have been assembled.
4. The persons occupying key positions in the skeletal structure of each "family"—consisting of positions for boss, underboss, lieutenants (also called "captains"), counselor, and for low-ranking members called "soldiers" or "button men"—are well known to law-enforcement officials having access to informants. Names of persons who permanently or temporarily occupy other positions, such as "buffer," "money mover," "enforcer," and "executioner," also are well known.
5. The "families" are linked to each other, and to non–Cosa Nostra syndicates, by understandings, agreements, and "treaties," and by mutual deference to a "Commission" made up of the leaders of the most powerful of the "families."
6. The boss of each "family" directs the activities, especially the illegal activities, of the members of his "family."
7. The members of this organization control all but a tiny part of the illegal gambling in the United States. They are the principal loan sharks. They are the principal importers and wholesalers of narcotics. They have

infiltrated certain labor unions, where they extort money from employers and, at the same time, cheat the members of the union. The members have a virtual monopoly on some legitimate enterprises. . . . Until recently, they owned a large proportion of Las Vegas. They own several state legislators and federal congressmen and other officials in the legislative, executive, and judicial branches of government at the local, state, and federal levels. Some government officials (including judges) are considered, and consider themselves, members.

8. The information about the Commissions, the "families," and the activities of members has come from detailed reports made by a wide variety of police observers, informants, wire taps, and electronic bugs. (1969: x–xi)

In Cressey's view, these crime families are organized along the lines of what sociologists call **formal organization**. In this structure, the labor is divided so that tasks and responsibilities are assigned primarily on the basis of special skills and abilities, there is a strict hierarchy of authority, rules and regulations govern the activities of members and the relationships among them and with the outside world, and recruitment and entrance are carefully regulated. In short, the crime families are, like other formal organizations, rationally designed for the purposes of achieving specified objectives.

Many other law enforcement officials still favor this description of La Cosa Nostra (LCN). In testimony in federal court, Rudolph Giuliani documented the existence of specific LCN families in New York, Philadelphia, Cleveland, Chicago, Milwaukee, Kansas City, and Los Angeles, and he described nationwide coordinated LCN control of the nation's largest union, the International Brotherhood of Teamsters (see Block, 1991).

Much-publicized recent successes by federal law enforcement officials in prosecuting reputed LCN members, primarily through the extensive use of wiretaps, lend credence to claims of LCN's existence and of considerable

interaction among Italian American crime families. However, Alan Block (1991: 13–14) believes they fall far short of proving the "big conspiracy," and he regards both the history of La Cosa Nostra and its sociology clouded in mystery.

An Alternative View

Not all authorities on organized crime agree entirely with Cressey's depiction of a national network of crime families. The **revisionist view** emphasizes more or less organized local criminal gangs, some of whose activities inevitably bring them into working contact with groups operating elsewhere. Advocates of this view see no real evidence of any centralized direction or domination of these localized syndicates. (Bell, 1965; Block, 1991: 8).

The notion of a formally organized, centrally directed national alliance of Mafia families has been rejected by Peter Reuter (1983) and to some extent by Donald Liddick (2004) and many others. Reuter and Liddick do not dispute the existence of Mafia families—most have continued in the same recognizable form for at least sixty years. Rather, Reuter, for example, believes that the relations among them are the result of occasional venture partnerships, occasional exchange of services, and attempts to reduce the uncertainty that arises when business takes a family into unfamiliar territory. Reuter also suggests that many of the connections among organized crime gangs resulted from Prohibition and from associations made while members served time in federal prisons (158).

Another point of contention concerns the degree and nature of organization. Some authors reject the idea that organized crime groups fit the formal organization model:

> Secret criminal organizations like the Italian-American or Sicilian Mafia families are not formal organizations like governments or business corporations. They are not rationally structured into statuses and functions in order to "maximize profits" and carry out

tasks efficiently. Rather, they are traditional social systems, organized by action and by cultural values which have nothing to do with modern bureaucratic virtues. Like all social systems, they have no structure apart from their functioning; nor . . . do they have structure independent of their current "personnel." . . . Describing the various positions in Italian-American syndicates as "like" those in bureaucracies gives the impression that they are, in fact, formal organizations. But they are not. (Ianni and Reuss-Ianni, 1973: 120–24)

A study of the South Philadelphia mob run by Angelo Bruno from 1959 until 1980, when he was assassinated, corroborates this view. Mark Haller (1991) analyzed all files of the Pennsylvania Crime Commission dealing with Bruno and his successor, Nicodemo Scarfo. He found that two organizational structures appeared to operate simultaneously: (1) a family structure comprising a network designed to help the individual enterprises of members and constituting a "shadow government" of rules and expectations that facilitate members' legal and illegal activities, and (2) an enterprise structure comprising the legal and illegal businesses run by individual members of the Bruno family. This enterprise structure involved cost, risk, and profit sharing (sometimes with non-family members), and most of the business was carried on informally, through "deals, negotiations, [and] whispered conversations," and through decentralized operations involving minimal oversight. According to Haller, this system not only fit the lifestyle of the men but also provided each participant wide discretion in doing "business."

Although some crime families or syndicates exhibit some of the elements found in highly rationalized bureaucratic structures, as Cressey showed, most do not. This distinction is important when one considers the growing organized crime involvement of blacks and Hispanics, and of street gangs, whom law enforcement officials have compared to the mobsters of Prohibition days. Some of these groups display only rudimentary organization, mostly operating in loosely connected networks, but others are highly organized.

Illegal Enterprise

Reuter's (1983) study of loan-sharking, gambling, and the numbers racket in New York City shows how illegality of products and services affects the organization of an economic market, keeping some enterprises localized and relatively small scale. The illegal market differs from its legal counterpart in various ways: (1) contracts cannot be enforced in a court of law, (2) assets associated with illegal operations may be seized at any time, and (3) participants risk arrest and imprisonment. These problems differ in significance from one illegal market to another, however: Heroin trafficking, for example, carries more risk than operating a numbers game.

These problems call for control over the flow of information about the operation. Those who participate are at different risk and pose different levels of threat to others. The entrepreneurs who control operations are at greatest risk from their agents or employees, who know the most about the business, but those risks are reduced by dividing up the tasks and responsibilities, by offering employees economic incentives, by ensuring that they are not employed elsewhere, through intimidation, and by recruiting based on family ties or the incorporation of employees into the family through rite or marriage. Risks to the employees come largely from other employees, thus encouraging entrepreneurs to keep operations small scale and/or dispersed in time and space (Reuter, 1983).

Another problem faced by illegal enterprise is financing. Reuter found that credit works differently in illegal markets: (1) There are no accurately audited books; (2) the lender is unable to control any assets placed as collateral against a loan because the borrower is likely to demand secrecy, and, in any case, lacks court protection (as a financer of criminal activities); and (3) the loan is to the individual entrepreneur and not to the enterprise, which has no legal existence apart from its owner (1983: 120). Therefore, the lender would have difficulty collecting from any successor.

These problems also constrain the growth of illegal enterprises, especially those in loan-sharking and gambling:

> Without smoothly working capital markets, the growth must be internally financed ... out of profits. In the heroin importing business, where each successful transaction may double the capital of the enterprise, this may be a minor restriction. For the numbers bank, with a relatively modest cash flow and a need for maintenance of a substantial cash reserve, this may be a very important constraint. (Reuter 1983: 121)

Haller (1990), arguably America's foremost authority on the history of organized crime, reminds us that illegal enterprise existed long before La Cosa Nostra. Indeed, it shaped the underworld of American cities for more than one hundred years before the rise of Italian American crime families. These enterprises included freelance prostitution, street-corner drug dealing, and neighborhood bookmaking. Entrepreneurs sometimes got together in cooperative ventures giving rise to networks of collusion.

The cooperative ventures of illegal enterprise rested on three important factors, according to Haller: (1) police or politician oversight that involved regular payoffs (kickbacks), limited competition, and encouraged avoidance of scandals and participation in "honest" crime; (2) flexible partnership arrangements allowing several entrepreneurs to share risks, to pool resources, and to combine their capital, influence, and managerial skills; and (3) internal economics—that is, the need to develop cooperative relations between buyers and sellers in order to protect both from the vagaries of doing business in the illegal marketplace.

Distinguishing Characteristics of Organized Crime

It is unlikely that criminologists will soon reach a consensus on the issues under discussion here. Even if detailed and dependable information were forthcoming, how complete a picture could be drawn from it? When dealing with people who place a premium on secrecy and engage in criminal activities, one is rarely able to learn everything one needs to know. Even those in a position to know more than most—a participant who turns informant, such as Joe Valachi, whose testimony before the McClellan Committee was influential (see Abadinsky, 1990: 473–75)—may know the facts about only some aspects of their own organization and thus cannot be considered authoritative sources of information on other aspects or other organizations (see Maas, 1968).

Al Capone, perhaps the most recognizable crime boss in the history of the United States, was never convicted of major racketeering or violent crime charges. He was, however, incarcerated at various points in his life on weapons, contempt of court, tax evasion, and prohibition charges.

As Steffensmeier notes: "No other area in the field is as difficult to define, describe . . . and conduct research on" (1995: 269). Even so, criminologists generally agree on some important features of organized crime that, when taken together, distinguish this type of criminal activity from others. First, organized crime is instrumental crime, the purpose of which is to make money. To accomplish this, participants organize in more or less complex networks. Second, most organized crime activities offer illegal goods and services. This does not mean, however, that those in organized crime have nothing to do with "traditional" crimes such as burglary or robbery.

A third important characteristic of organized crime is its connections with government and politics. Organized crime makes political and police corruption an integral part of its business. Indeed, political corruption is not merely a distinguishing feature of organized crime; it is critical to its survival

(Beare, 1998; Liddick, 2004; Simon, 2006). Take, for instance, what a kingpin revealed to Cupples and Kauzlarich about the need to protect illegal gambling activities:

[P]olice corruption was a thriving business . . . [B]ankers routinely paid protection money to . . . the police department. . . . [B]asically you can't operate a numbers business without taking care of the cops. (1997: 20)

The fourth feature of organized crime is its generational persistence. The syndicates or families involved in organized crime continue to operate despite the comings and goings of their members. Although the death or retirement of persons in leadership positions may result in significant changes, organized crime does not disappear and individual organizations usually do not cease to exist. The persistence of organized crime can be explained in part by a fifth important feature: sanctioned rules of conduct (sometimes called

Box 7.2. THE RICO STATUTE

The provisions of the Racketeer Influenced and Corrupt Organization Act (1970) include the following:

- It shall be unlawful for any person through a pattern of racketeering activity or through collection of an unlawful debt to acquire or maintain, directly or indirectly, any interest or control of any enterprise which is engaged in, or the activities of which affect, interstate commerce.
- It shall be unlawful for any persons employed by or associated with any enterprise engaged in, or the activities of which effect, interstate or foreign commerce, to conduct or participate, directly or indirectly, in the conduct of such enterprise's affairs through a pattern of racketeering activity or collection of unlawful debts.
- It shall be unlawful for any person to conspire to violate any of (these) provisions.

Pattern of racketeering means at least two acts of racketeering activity within ten years of each other (excluding any period of imprisonment).

Racketeering activity includes the following: (a) murder, kidnapping, gambling, arson, robbery, bribery, extortion, or dealing in narcotic or other dangerous drugs . . . and (b) any act indictable under (the Organized Crime Act), including those related to bribery, embezzlement from pension or welfare funds, mail fraud, wire fraud, obstruction of justice, interference with commerce, robbery or extortion, (and) racketeering.

Source: United States Code, Title 18, Part I, Chapter 96: Racketeer Influenced and Corrupt Organizations. Available online at http://www.law.cornell.edu/uscode/html/uscode18/usc_sup_01_18_10_I_20_96.html.

"the code"). The survival of any group or organization is problematic if the behavior of members is neither predictable nor conforming to the evaluations of at least some other members of the group. Rules of conduct help establish conformity and predictability; sanctions for violations of the rules help ensure that conformity and predictability persist over time. Sanctions are related to a final characteristic: ability and willingness to use force and violence to accomplish the organization's goals. Reuter (1983) points out that reputation may be more important than actual behavior: A gang that has a reputation for violence can accomplish the same results with fewer bad consequences (see also Block, 1991: 5).

When discussing what makes organized crime special, some authors emphasize its organizational features, while others note that organized criminals are able to commit a greater variety of crimes, on a larger scale, than are other offenders (Steffensmeier, 1995). Mark Moore believes that most recent research and policy has been guided by the first view rather than the second. For example, the Racketeer Influenced and Corrupt Organizations (RICO) Act of 1970 (see box 7.2) focuses on the specific organization of criminal groups and their capacity to continue operations despite government opposition. "The Policy goal . . . is to weaken and frustrate the enterprise rather than control their criminal offending" (Moore, 1986: 2). In addition, Moore argues, the organizational focus draws attention to the parallels between organized crime and legitimate enterprises. Indeed, these parallels are not lost on federal prosecutors, who routinely use RICO to crack down on corporate and other occupational crime, and who have recently used the statute to prosecute the recurring criminal activities of antiabortion groups—to which the U.S. Supreme Court gave unanimous approval in January 1993.

The Code

There is no conclusive evidence that one particular code, a set of sanctioned rules of conduct, is shared by the various criminal organizations. Investigators have found numerous obstacles to a definitive statement of what the code (or codes) might be, the most important being the veil of secrecy that surrounds organized crime and the difficulty of gaining access to its participants.

Cressey combined snippets of information from informants with clues deduced from an analysis of the social structure of La Cosa Nostra and suggested the following as the **code of organized crime:**

1. *Be loyal to members of the organization. Do not interfere with each other's interests. Do not be an informer.* This directive, with its correlated admonitions, is basic to the internal operations of the Cosa Nostra confederation. It is a call for unity, for peace, for maintenance of the status quo. . . .

2. *Be rational. Be a member of the team. Don't engage in battle if you can't win.* What is demanded here is a corporate rationality necessary to conducting illicit businesses in a quiet, safe, profitable manner. . . .

3. *Be a man of honor. Always do right. Respect womanhood and your elders. Don't rock the boat.* This emphasis on "honor" and "respect" helps determine who obeys whom, who attends what funerals and weddings, who opens the door for whom, . . . and functions to enable despots to exploit their underlings. . . .

4. *Be a stand-up guy. Keep your eyes and ears open and your mouth shut. Don't sell out.* A "family" member, like a prisoner, must be able to withstand frustrating and threatening situations without complaining or resorting to subservience. The "stand-up guy" shows courage and "heart." . . .

5. *Have class. Be independent. Know your way around the world.* . . . A man who is committed to regular work and submission to duly constituted authority is a sucker. . . . [Next], the world seen by organized criminals is a world of graft, fraud, and corruption, and they are concerned with their own honesty and manliness as compared with the hypocrisy of corrupt policemen and corrupt political figures. (1969: 175–78)

In discussing the code, Cressey points out that it is similar to the codes adopted by professional thieves, prisoners, and other groups whose activities bring them into confrontation with official authority and generate the need for "private" government as a means of controlling the membership's conduct (see also Salerno and Tompkins, 1969: 105–48).

Taking exception to Cressey's position, Francis Ianni (1973: 150–55; 1998) argues that the presumption of a shared code is based on the questionable belief that there is a single national organization, and that each individual organized crime group has achieved similar levels of organizational sophistication and has shared similar experiences.

From his two-year participant observation of one Italian American crime family operating in New York (the "Lupollo" family) and his later research on black and Hispanic groups in organized crime, Ianni found evidence of different codes for different groups. In the case of the Lupollo family, there were three basic rules for behavior:

(1) [P]rimary loyalty is vested in "family" rather than in individual lineages or nuclear families, (2) each member of the family must "act like a man" and do nothing which brings disgrace on the family, and (3) family business is privileged matter and must not be reported or discussed outside the group. (Ianni and Reuss-Ianni, 1973: 155; Ianni, 1998)

Ianni found that black and Hispanic organized crime codes differed from the Lupollo rules, as well as from each other. For example, whereas the black and Hispanic groups emphasized loyalty and secrecy (as did the Lupollo family), some of these organized crime networks also stressed the rules "Don't be a coward" and "Don't be a creep" (in other words, "fit in" with the group). Some stressed the rule "Be smart" (know when to obey but also when to beat the system), and some stressed "Don't tell the police," "Don't cheat your partner or other people in the network,"

and "Don't be incompetent" (Ianni, 1975: 301–305; 1998).

Which rules are stressed depends in large part on how the individual gang came together in the first place. Gangs with shared family roots place a premium on rules supporting kinship ties. On the other hand, gangs with origins in youthful street associations and partnerships tend to stress rules underscoring personal qualities ("Don't be a coward"). Those originating in strictly business or entrepreneurial associations tend to stress rules emphasizing more impersonal, activity-oriented obligations ("Don't be incompetent"). The code adopted by a criminal organization reflects far more than the mere fact that it is a secret association engaged in regular criminal activities. How and why the participants came together in the first place, how long the organization has been operating, the cultural heritage of its major participants, and the nature and range of its activities all influence the code of a particular crime group.

While there may be different codes for different groups, a 1989 undercover FBI recording of an LCN induction ceremony obtained by Cupples and Kauzlarich suggests that Cressey's work is still relevant. The following is an excerpt of that ceremony, recorded in a home in Boston, with Joseph Russo (*consigliere* or "counselor") and Biagio Di Giacomo (*capo* or "captain") swearing in Carmen Tortora:

Russo: In order to belong to us, to be a part of us, Carmen, you have to have truth and trust. Do you have that Carmen?

Tortora: Yes.

Russo: This is what you want. Do you have any brothers, Carmen?

Tortora: One.

Russo: If I told you your brother was wrong, he's a rat, he's gonna do one of us harm, you'd have to kill him. Would you do that for me?

Tortora: Yes.

Russo: Would you do that favor?

Tortora: Yes.

Russo: Anyone here asked for it?

Tortora: Yes.

Russo: You know that. So you know the severity of this thing of ours?

Tortora: Yes.

Russo: Do you want it badly and desperately? Your mother's dying in bed and you have to leave her because we called you. It's an emergency. You have to leave. Could you do that, Carmen?

Tortora: Yes.

Russo: Alright. This is what you want. We're the best people. I'm gonna make you part of this thing.

Di Giacomo: We gonna baptize you . . . Carmen. . . . You do not reveal any secrets of this organization . . . to the rest of the world this does not exist . . . they call it La Cosa Nostra, my organization. (1997: 18)

Finally, Cupples and Kauzlarich's research on 150 members of La Cosa Nostra in Philadelphia lends some support to the claims of *both* Cressey and Ianni:

- Eighty-eight percent of the respondents claimed they were "honest."
- Ninety-five percent said that loyalty to the group was important to them.
- Only 30 percent considered themselves religious.
- Half considered themselves "aggressive."
- Seventy-three percent were employed outside of mob duties.
- Most (62 percent) had graduated high school. (1997)

THE MONEY-MAKING ENTERPRISES OF ORGANIZED CRIME

During Prohibition, crime syndicates made the manufacture, distribution, and sale of alcoholic beverages their major business. Although extortion, blackmail, robbery, prostitution, gambling, and the sale of protection had been lucrative enterprises, bootlegging outweighed them all. Suddenly the law had made illegal something much in demand by all segments of the population. Fortunes could be made by those who cared to break the law and could organize to do it.

When Prohibition came to an end in 1933, the black market quickly fell apart. This did not mean that no money was to be made by dealing in booze, only much less. Actually, organized crime continues to dabble in the liquor business. Some jurisdictions are still "dry," and others permit only beer or only certain labels to be sold. Even where liquor of any sort is legal, however, money can still be made. With the right connections, profitable liquor licenses can be bought on behalf of the syndicate; through control of bottling, warehousing, and distributing, syndicate liquor finds its way into legitimate outlets (Dorman, 1972: 129).

Organized crime is not restricted to any one kind of activity, legal or otherwise, and, like any entrepreneur, it must keep up with changing times or go out of business. To fill the void created by the repeal of Prohibition, organized crime turned its attention to new avenues of profit and has continued to branch out ever since.

Criminal Enterprises

The major enterprises providing illicit profits are gambling, usury (loan-sharking), drug trafficking, theft, and **racketeering** (criminal network schemes). In all these areas the money to be made is enormous. Though one can only guess, it is generally held that profits from each one of these areas run into billions of dollars every year. Estimates of the annual gross from gambling enterprises go as high as $50 billion; drug trafficking is estimated to be a $75-billion business; and a conservative estimate of the gross from loan-sharking is $10 billion. Even the sale of sex, not one of the big money makers, is estimated to gross more than $2 billion a year. Recalling that organized crime avoids most, if not all, of the overhead and taxes legitimate businesses have to absorb, these gross figures indicate tremendous incomes for organized crime—a conservative estimate of the net profits would be 30 percent of the gross.

Gambling

Though some speculate that the money-making possibilities of illegal gambling may be on the decline following the spread of state lotteries, gambling remains one of the principal sources of income for organized crime (Pennsylvania Crime Commission, 1989). It is clearly a major enterprise of Italian-based organizations (Liddick, 2004). LCN capo Thomas Del Giorno once said that many people got their start in the mob through gambling and that it was steady, "relatively easy money" (Cupples and Kauzlarich, 1997: 20). George Anastasia has noted that mob related sports betting in Philadelphia is as pervasive as "soft pretzels and, in most cases, is considered as harmless as bingo" (1993: 49).

Most of the money from gambling is made from the policy, or numbers, racket. Legend has it that the term *policy* originated from the nineteenth-century practice among the poor of gambling with money set aside for insurance policy premiums; Cressey, however, suggests that the term came from the Italian word for lottery ticket, *polizza*. Whatever the truth, one fact is clear: Policy, or numbers, betting is predominantly a feature of urban slum life.

Numbers betting is a simple concept and easy to do. The gambler simply picks any three-digit number and bets that this number will correspond to the winning number, selected by some predetermined procedure. Over the years winning numbers have been computed from the number of shares traded on a stock exchange, the daily cash balance in the United States Treasury, and the payoffs at local pari-mutuel racetracks. At one time, the number was simply drawn from a revolving drum. The odds are 1000 to 1 against the bettor, whereas payoff never exceeds 600 to 1.

Though the specifics vary from place to place and from syndicate to syndicate, the numbers operation is organized along the following lines: The bets are picked up by "runners" from "numbers drops" in shops, factories, office buildings, and bars, or simply on the street. The runners pass the money and betting slips on to local "collectors," or "route men," in charge of their neighborhoods. The collectors pass the money and numbers tickets on to the "controller," who sends it on to the "district controller," who works for the "policy operator." The policy operator actually runs the enterprise and sometimes is known as the "banker" or "owner." He or she is usually one of a number of operators, all of whom pay a commission to the crime syndicate under whose overall supervision and control and in whose territory the racket operates. These policy operators may or may not be actual members of the crime family. At payoff time, the money simply follows the reverse route, usually starting at the "branch" or "district bank" run by the policy operator.

The numbers racket attracted organized crime not only because of the immense profits to be made from it but also because the game requires organization, money, and a good deal of corruption in the right places—things only organized crime had. Although small-scale games, involving small bets and a small betting clientele, have existed in the past, they were neither very profitable nor very secure for those who ran them. To work, the numbers racket needs organized crime. The boss of a New Jersey crime network explains why:

> Everybody needs the organization—the banker, the controllers, the runners, even the customers. Here's why. Only a big organization can pay up when the bank gets hit very hard. Suppose a lot of people play the same number one day. For example, when Willie Mays hit his 599th home run, a lot of black people played "600" the next day, figuring Willie was going to make it and so were they. If that number had come up, the banker would have been wiped out, and not only that, a lot of customers would have gone without their payoffs. The whole system would have collapsed. (Ianni, 1975: 59–60)

There is another reason the numbers racket needs the organization: Only the organization has the money and the muscle to keep the cops and politicians from breaking up the game and shaking down the players and operators. (Ianni, 1975: 59–60). Reuter (1983) found that New York City numbers games were not highly coordinated, though some apparently independent banks may have been branches of a single owner (see also Haller, 1991).

Loan-Sharking

Loan-sharking thrives because some people who need loans are unable or unwilling to secure them through legitimate lending institutions. Loan sharks will lend them the money, for a price. To make loans one needs money; organized crime has it. To ensure that the money is repaid, with interest, one needs organization and the ability to make collections; organized crime has it. Because usury is illegal, a lender must be able to collect without resorting to legal channels and without the interference of the law; organized crime accomplishes this through muscle and corruption.

Borrowers who come to a loan shark usually want quick loans with no questions asked. They may be gamblers in need of money to pay off debts or finance further play; they may be businesspeople faced with bankruptcy or wanting to invest in risky, perhaps illegal, ventures; they may simply be poor people in need of small loans but lacking the credit or collateral required by licensed lending institutions. The interest they pay depends on how much they borrow, the intended use of the loan, their repayment potential, and what they are worth to the mob if they cannot make their payments. Generally interest runs anywhere from 1 to 150 percent per week, with most smaller loans at 20 percent per week—the "six for five" loan, in which $6 must be paid back each week for every $5 borrowed. Usually a set time is established for payments, and if the required payment is not made on or before

that exact time, the borrower will owe another week's interest, computed from the principal plus the interest already accrued.

Various members of the South Philadelphia Bruno family operated loan-sharking businesses, and Haller (1991) uses two of them to illustrate contrasting operations within one crime family. On the one hand, there was Harry Riccobene, whose loans were mostly small (less than $1,000) and made to local hustlers and merchants: "Within their culture, borrowing informally from a loan shark was a normal and accepted business practice" (10). When customers fell behind in their payments, as most did, Harry used a combination of gentle chastisement and renegotiated (lower) payment schedules. Some of his agents did not approve of Harry's leniency, but Harry's revolving credit system prospered.

Also prospering was the loan-sharking operation of Frank Sindone, another Bruno family member. But Sindone's operation was different: He made much larger loans—up to $50,000 or higher—mostly to construction contractors and other legitimate businesses with credit and cash flow problems. He also took his operation further afield, to South Jersey and the Pennsylvania suburbs. His agents operated relatively independently, sharing in the profits, and together Sindone and his agents "had mastered the orchestrated use of vicious, vulgar, and convincing threats of violence to the borrower and the borrower's family" when dealing with delinquent loans (Haller, 1991: 12).

It is unusual for a borrower to be killed, for death means the money is lost forever. Though a killing may be committed occasionally to make the victim an example to others, the loan shark wants the money first and foremost, and if this cannot be obtained with threats, the loan shark will look for other ways to get it. Indeed, loans are sometimes made—at very high interest rates—not in the expectation that they will be repaid, but for other purposes. The mob may be looking to garner a controlling interest in a borrower's business, and when loan payments falter, this provides the leverage necessary to bring this about; the borrower simply turns over all or a part of the business in exchange for a temporary delay of the payments. The Bruno family's Sindone liked to operate this way (Haller, 1991: 12). This is one of the ways that organized crime secures a footing in legitimate business enterprises, though Reuter thinks it is rare among the small-time loan sharks, most of whom would not know how to carry out profitable fraud schemes involving legitimate businesses (1983: 101).

Drug Trafficking

Organized crime is involved in drug trafficking at all levels, but especially in importation and wholesale distribution. The need for organization, contacts, and large sums of money puts the business outside the reach of most individuals and small criminal groups (Liddick, 2004; Natarajan and Belanger, 1998). This emphasis on importing and wholesaling does not mean, however, that organized crime is not interested in what goes on at the neighborhood and street levels of the drug scene. Since its own profits depend on a healthy drug traffic, it observes the street closely and helps keep open the channels through which the drugs flow. The syndicate also supplies loans to dealers—at least the bigger, more successful ones—and, through loan-sharking and fencing on the street, endeavors to ensure that money circulates so that buys can be made. Today much of the local heroin trade is controlled by black and Hispanic criminal groups, and this has been one of the avenues giving these groups access to the world of organized crime.

In 1984 the so-called Pizza Connection was uncovered when Italian and American police arrested more than two hundred suspected Mafia members, including twenty-eight in America, after a high-ranking mafioso named Tommaso Buscetta turned informant. Buscetta had extensive operations in Italy and Brazil, and he detailed the existence of a Sicilian-based organized crime network operating outside the established American Mafia families. This network is reputed to have imported more than sixteen hundred pounds of heroin, with a street value of $1.65 billion, since 1979. Its American members were mostly pizza parlor operators—hence the name—located in rural parts of Wisconsin, Michigan, Oregon, and Illinois, and with connections in New York and Switzerland. In late 1988 another major drug ring was exposed, this one smuggling tons of marijuana into the United States from Colombia. Former race car driver Randy Lanier and two associates were charged with engaging in a "continuing criminal enterprise," a federal charge carrying a mandatory life sentence. The three conspirators were said to have smuggled 646,000 pounds of marijuana over a seven-year period, and to have accumulated assets worth more than $150 million (*St. Louis Post-Dispatch*, October 6, 1988).

Theft

Organized crime has been interested in theft since its earliest days. Today most organized crime efforts are directed at the kinds of thievery that promise high returns while avoiding high risk, such as truck hijacking, car theft, thefts from warehouses and docks, securities theft, and fencing. Once again, the organization, money, muscle, and contacts of organized crime are major factors in explaining syndicate activity in these areas.

Much has been made of syndicate involvement in securities theft and manipulation. Millions of dollars in securities disappear every year from the vaults of major brokerage houses; most of the lost bonds are stolen. Testimony before the Senate Committee on Banking, Housing, and Urban Affairs indicated that securities theft is a major problem these days and that organized crime syndicates lie behind much of the thievery (see also Abadinsky, 1990: 291–94). While estimates of the actual amounts stolen are difficult to make, the yearly totals are generally thought to exceed $2 billion, and may be much higher when thefts from the mails and manipulations during securities transfers are included (Conklin, 1973: 121–27; Metz, 1971).

To accomplish the theft and manipulation of stocks and bonds, organized crime needs insiders: persons employed by brokerage firms who have access to vaults or who routinely handle securities. Sometimes these important contacts are indebted to loan sharks and steal securities in exchange for a respite from their payments, sometimes extortion and intimidation are used to frighten employees into working with the underworld, and sometimes the mob manages to place one of its own in a position of trust within a brokerage firm. Once in syndicate hands, the stocks and bonds are often converted into cash. This can be accomplished by using the stolen securities as collateral for loans, as part of a company's portfolio of assets, or merely by reselling them through brokers here or abroad.

In the modern era, organized crime groups have capitalized on the digital age by creating pirated software programs, film, and music. Counterfeiting these commodities is big business. A few years ago a Windows counterfeiting operation run by Asian gangs in California produced millions of dollars in profits (Liddick, 2004).

Labor Racketeering

During the nineteenth century, organized criminal groups learned that money could be made in the fields of industrial organization and employee relations. Faced with the prospect of strikes and unionization, companies called on criminal gangs to help them combat these threats to their power and profits. The companies paid well for the gangs' muscle, and the gangs, in turn, were happy to oblige. Infiltration of the union movement by organized crime soon followed, and with it came money and power for leaders of the fledgling

unions. First the building trades and then the service industries fell under the influence and domination of corrupt officials backed by gangsters. Money was collected from both employers and employees, with organized crime playing off each side against the other (Hutchinson, 1969).

Racketeering is explained not merely by the corruption of union and company officials, nor by the fact that organized crime is in the business of making money any way it can. Rather, the spread of racketeering stems from a combination of conditions. Some are economic—for example, excessive entrepreneurial competition and an excess supply of labor. As Walter Lippmann observed many years ago:

> Given an oversupply of labor and an industry in which no considerable amount of capital or skill is required to enter it, the conditions exist under which racketeering can flourish. The effort to unionize in the face of a surplus of labor invites the use of violence and terror to maintain a monopoly of labor and thus to preserve the workers' standard of living. Labor unionism in such trades tends to fall into the control of dictators who are often corrupt and not often finical about enlisting gangsters to enforce the closed shop. The employers, on the other hand, faced with the constant threat of cutthroat competition, are subject to the easy temptation to pay gangsters for protection against competitors. The protection consists in driving the competition from the field. (1931: 61)

Additional conditions that support organized crime infiltration into unions includes (1) the traditions of frontier violence, (2) cultural values stressing individualism, (3) an entrenched philosophy of acquisition, (4) an admiration for sharp practices, (5) a tolerance of the fix, and (6) a legacy stressing politics as a source of personal profit (Hutchinson, 1969: 143). Companies and unions went along with the spread of racketeering because both saw benefits outweighing costs and because the conditions and temperament of the times presented no great obstacles. Actually, of course, both company officials and union leaders risk becoming pawns in the hands of organized crime syndicates—and this is precisely what has happened over the years, with the costs borne not only by the union membership but also by members of the general public who hold company stock or who are simply consumers of the companies' goods and services.

Nobody knows for sure how much organized crime syndicates make from labor racketeering. In 1958 the Senate Select Committee on Improper Activities in the Labor or Management Field found that $10 million in Teamsters Union funds had been siphoned off into the pockets of union officials and their gangster friends (Salerno and Tompkins, 1969: 295). The Teamsters Central States Pension Fund is widely acknowledged to have been under the control of syndicate figures. It is known that the mob helped pick Teamster presidents Jackie Presser and Roy Williams. Police informants have tied both men to organized crime groups in Chicago, New York, Kansas City, and Cleveland (*Los Angeles Times*, September 25, 1985). The pension fund is worth billions of dollars, and millions have apparently been spent without the knowledge of the rank-and-file membership whose money it really is (see also Block, 1991; Abadinsky, 1990).

Pseudolegitimate Enterprises

Apart from their patently illegal enterprises, organized crime groups have infiltrated the world of legitimate business. Though any complete list of the different businesses in which organized crime is involved would be impossible to compile, the following have been specifically identified: banking, hotels and motels, real estate, garbage collection, vending machines, construction, delivery and long-distance hauling, garment manufacture, insurance, stocks and bonds, vacation resorts, funeral parlors, bakeries, sausage manufacture and processing of other meat products, paving, tobacco, dairy products, demolition, warehousing, auto sales and leasing, meat packing, janitorial services, beauty and health salons, lumber, horse breeding, nightclubs, bars, restaurants, linen supply, laundries, and dry cleaning. There may well be no type of legitimate business enterprise in which organized crime does not have a financial interest (Liddick, 2004).

Organized crime has sought involvement in legitimate businesses for a number of reasons. First is the obvious economic incentive: Legitimate businesses are additional sources of income. Second, legitimate businesses can provide a front for illegal activities; owning a trucking firm, for example, gives a crime syndicate the means of transporting stolen property or a cover for bootlegging. Third, legitimate businesses can serve as important outlets for monies earned through criminal activities. Profits from the latter invested in businesses under syndicate control are made to appear "clean" (or "laundered"), as are the wages and salaries received by syndicate members from the companies. These salaries constitute the members' visible sources of income, and they declare this income on tax returns in a continuing effort to avoid federal prosecution. (Needless to say, those receiving such salaries often contribute little or nothing to the actual day-to-day operations of the companies concerned.) And fourth, legitimate business activity helps syndicate members avoid the costs and risks of continued exposure to law enforcement as a result of being able to "cover" their involvement in crime.

A final reason that organized crime has sought holdings in legitimate enterprises is respectability. Crime is not respectable work, and the profits from it are dirty money. A long-standing goal among higher-echelon mobsters, especially Italian Americans, with their traditions of family honor, has been the acquisition of respectability for their children and grandchildren, if not for themselves. Legitimate businesses provide a route to social acceptance. Instead of following in the footsteps of their elders, the younger generation is able to acquire the trappings of respectability by working in enterprises with no apparent connection to crime.

Organized crime moves into its pseudolegitimate enterprises in various ways. Some use intimidation and force, while others use more normal avenues of business acquisition. When interested in a particular business, it is common for the syndicate to use the carrot-and-stick approach—in Don Corleone's words, "I'll make him an offer he can't refuse." Such a case was reported in the New York State Court of Appeals in the late 1960s. An executive of several successful vending machine companies was simply told that he was to pass over to a certain family of interested persons a 25 percent share of his business interests. The request was backed up by assaults on his wife and various other forms of intimidation (Cressey, 1969: 103). Another way to infiltrate businesses is to arrange, through extortion or bribes, to have syndicate associates placed in executive positions, so that eventually the company is controlled by the syndicate. Yet another way is to purchase large blocks of company stock through legitimate trading channels, though under the cover of fictitious names and companies. Finally, loan sharks may turn delinquent loans into a means of acquiring a controlling interest in a business.

Current and Future Trends

Organized crime is undoubtedly here to stay, at least for the foreseeable future. But changes are afoot, just as changes occurred in the past. Ethnic succession has brought Chicanos, Puerto Ricans, Asians, and Cuban Americans into prominent positions in organized crime, especially in the highly populated Northeast and in Chicago and Miami (see Ianni, 1998). African Americans have also claimed a *more* prominent place in organized crime, moving beyond their traditional urban numbers rackets into drug trafficking and prostitution (see Venkatesh, 1998). There is also evidence

to suggest that Eastern European organized crime syndicates in the United States have grown considerably since the dissolution of the Soviet Union (Friedman, 2000; Liddick, 2004).

According to Ianni, the same ghetto conditions that spawned early organized crime helped produce the contemporary ethnic succession:

> It is important to note in this context of ethnic succession that none of these characteristics of or attitudes toward organized crime are culture bound: the structures of poverty and powerlessness, rather than the structures of the black and Puerto Rican cultures, seem most responsible. (1998: 127)

In addition, the Italian American crime syndicates themselves may have helped bring about change. Established organized crime groups inevitably came to employ ghetto residents as soldiers, lower-echelon pushers, and numbers runners in their own neighborhoods. Streetwise blacks, Chicanos, Puerto Ricans, and Cubans became vital links between the organization and street-level buyers of commodities and services. With involvement came knowledge, contacts, and—for some—wealth. With involvement also came efforts on the part of these groups to control the business in their own territory. An added incentive for Cuban involvement was the establishment of a cocaine and heroin connection from South America through Cuba and Miami.

Although mainly restricted to their own ethnic neighborhoods, the crime networks of blacks and Hispanics are emerging as the new forces in the organized delivery of drugs and sex and are gaining more control over the numbers racket and loan-sharking in the ghetto. In order to extend and expand, however, these newcomers will have to accomplish what the Italian Americans did before them: "(1) greater control over sectors of organized crime outside as well as inside the ghetto; (2) some organizing principle which will serve as kinship did among the Italians to bring the disparate networks together into larger criminally monopolistic organizations; and (3) better access to political power and the ability to corrupt it" (Ianni, 1974: 36; 1998). Although the first requirement may well be the easiest to meet because of their growing control over the drug traffic, much will depend on the willingness of established crime syndicates to allow a blossoming competition from these newcomers.

One can expect to continue hearing about organized crime. It should be apparent that organized crime is a consequence of numerous social, cultural, political, legal, and economic conditions, many of which seem destined to persist. The apparent international growth of organized crime, especially in Russia and areas in Southeast Asia, is interesting in this vein. Viewed from a rationality-opportunity perspective, as well as functionalist reasoning, organized crime will continue to flourish as long as illicit goods and services are demanded and capable people are willing to organize to supply them for a profit. As new opportunities for criminal enterprise appear, they will be grasped by criminally motivated individuals in a position to prosper from them.

One of the more interesting directions this line of reasoning takes us is reflected in the recent explosion of research on international organized crime (Frisby, 1998; Geis, 1997–98; Passas, 1999). The FBI has also extended its international investigations of organized crime to an unprecedented level. It now has Russian and Chinese organized crime "squads." The United Nations has also recently taken notice of the threat of global organized crime networks by establishing a special committee to promote an international convention against transnational organized crime. The committee is focusing on three areas not traditionally associated as main organized crime activities: the trafficking of women and children, migrants, and firearms. Clearly the range of activities available for organized crime groups can and will change as cultural and structural forces shape supply and demand.

CHAPTER SUMMARY

This chapter has examined prostitution and offenses involving drugs. There are many similarities in the criminological aspects of drugs and sex, including the fact that participants usually do not think of themselves as either criminals or victims. Prostitution thrives because there is widespread male demand for sexual encounters and a more or less organized network of suppliers prepared to meet that demand for a price. If there is a victim in prostitution, it is the prostitute herself. Among the various participants—prostitute, customer, and pimp or procurer—it is the prostitute who runs the greatest risk of arrest, jail time, assault, robbery, disease, and dependency.

Offenses involving heroin, cocaine, hallucinogens, and, to a lesser extent, marijuana, are the focus of extensive law enforcement efforts and can result in penalties that are more severe than those given to burglars, robbers, and rapists. Influenced by fears of a crumbling morality among youth and by the view that drug use causes other crime, the current furor over illicit drug use largely obscures the fact that much of the current drug problem in America is explained by three related historical processes: growth in recreational use of drugs, growth in the production and marketing of legal drugs, and the selective creation and enforcement of prohibitions dealing with essentially similar behaviors. This observation does not deny that the growing use of heroin is a serious problem that needs to be solved, but it serves as a reminder that crime is invariably shaped by social, political, and economic history rather than by the criminal motives of evil, or merely weak, individuals.

We have also explored the nature and role of organized crime in the United States. Criminals are considered part of organized crime if they combine into groups for the purpose of providing illegal goods and services or to engage routinely in illegal activities that profit the group. Political corruption is an integral part of organized crime, as is the ability and willingness of participants to use force in pursuit of the organization's goals and to ensure that members abide by its rules. Although there is disagreement on the extent to which organized crime is organized, it is generally agreed that even rudimentary organization means that participants are able to commit a wider variety of crimes on a larger scale than are other criminals.

Organized crime survives mainly because there is widespread demand for the illegal goods and services that it provides, because public officials are willing to be corrupted, and because moral entrepreneurs are successful in getting the authorities to criminalize activities that many people find pleasurable. In short, organized crime is functional. In addition, however, the existence of marked ethnic and racial inequality in an acquisitive society helps explain both the appeal and suitability of black-market enterprise for population groups isolated from the economic, social, and political mainstream.

KEY TERMS

code of organized crime
drug
formal organization
La Cosa Nostra
pimp
pornography
psychoactive substance
racketeering
revisionist view
victimless crimes

RECOMMENDED READINGS

Adler, Patricia A. (1993). *Wheeling and Dealing: An Ethnography of an Upper-Level Drug Dealing and Smuggling Community.* 2nd ed. New York: Columbia University Press.

Chambliss, William J. (1988). *On The Take: From Petty Crooks to Presidents.* 2nd ed. Bloomington: Indiana University Press.

Jacobs, Bruce A. (1999b). *Selling Crack: The Social World of Streetcorner Selling.* Boston: Northeastern University Press.

Liddick, Donald R. (2004). *The Global Underworld: Transnational Crime and the United States.* Westport, CT: Praeger.

Ratner, Mitchell S. (1994). *Crack Pipe as Pimp: An Ethnographic Investigation of Sex-for-Crack Exchanges.* New York: Lexington

RECOMMENDED WEB SITES

The Nathanson Centre for the Study of Organized Crime and Corruption (http://www.yorku.ca/nathanson/default.htm). Major reference service for academic and popular studies of organized crime.

National Institute on Drug Abuse (http://www.nida.nih.gov). Outstanding source of data for research on drug types and addictions.

U.S. Drug Enforcement Agency (http://www.usdoj.gov/dea/index.htm). Statistics, policies, programs, and interdiction effort information.

8

CRIMINOLOGY,
CRIMINAL JUSTICE, AND CRIME

34879680 photos.com

If we use the legalistic definition of *crime*—that the state creates crime—then it must also be, in some measure, the state's responsibility to deal with it. For this reason alone, crime and criminal justice are intertwined. This means that a comprehensive understanding of crime and criminality depends on knowledge of how the criminal justice system works. While most people correctly see criminal justice as the state's reaction to crime and criminals, others see it as a *cause* of crime as well. This is also correct, not only because the actions of authorities may encourage criminal activity, but also because some of those actions may be criminal in themselves. The study of the relationship between crime and criminal justice might be called a *criminology of criminal justice.*

Rather than provide a comprehensive description of the American criminal justice system—there are whole textbooks on this subject—this chapter looks instead at the criminology of criminal justice. After a brief introduction to the major actors and decision points in the system, the chapter discusses the nature and consequences of discretion, the crime-prevention function of the police, and the relationship between crime and punishment. The chapter also looks at crimes and other abuses committed by criminal justice authorities.

CRIMINAL JUSTICE: ACTORS AND DECISIONS

Criminal justice is a society's system of roles and activities for defining and dealing with crime. In the United States today, criminal justice involves the actions of

- state and federal legislatures, where rules governing crime and justice are enacted into law;
- administrative agencies such as the Internal Revenue Service and the Food and Drug Administration, which create rules that carry criminal penalties if violated;
- local, state, and federal law enforcement agencies;
- prosecution and defense, made up of attorneys who practice criminal law and handle criminal cases in the courts;
- municipal, state, and federal trial courts, where criminal cases are handled;
- state and federal appellate courts, which rule on the constitutionality of actions taken by lower courts and by police and correctional agencies;
- probation and parole agencies, which provide services to the courts and to correctional agencies;

- local, state, and federal correctional agencies, which carry out the punishment of convicted criminal offenders and oversee the operation of jails and prisons;
- justice professionals such as private detectives, medical examiners, expert witnesses, jury consultants, criminologists, and law professors;
- social service agencies, which provide treatment, counseling, and rehabilitation;
- private companies that provide goods or services to individuals and agencies involved in criminal justice or employ criminal justice personnel;
- special interest groups such as the National Rifle Association (NRA),

the American Civil Liberties Union (ACLU), the National Association for the Advancement of Colored People (NAACP), and the National Organization for the Repeal of Marijuana Laws (NORML);
- private citizens who are crime victims, witnesses, or complainants, or who have ties with offenders or criminal justice personnel; and, of course,
- criminal suspects, defendants, and offenders.

The relationship between these different actors is shown in figure 8.1, a "road map" of criminal justice in America (Barlow, 2000: 35). Decisions made at one point in the road

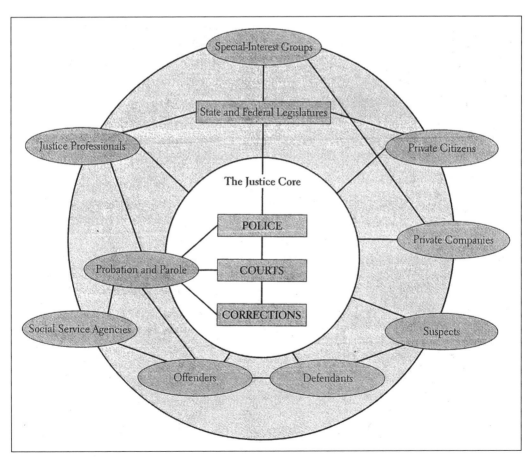

▲ **Figure 8.1.**
Criminal Justice System Relationships

flow along it and influence decisions made at other points. The core agencies, or pillars, of the criminal justice system are the police, courts, and corrections. However, actions taken outside the core influence what happens inside, and vice versa. For example, in 2000, former Illinois governor George Ryan Sr. placed a moratorium on the use of capital punishment in his state. Ryan and many others found that the state practice was incredibly flawed in that more people have been released from death row because of DNA exoneration than have been actually executed in the last few decades. The state upheld the rights of prisoners, but many private citizens and justice officials were concerned by the prospect of abolishing capital punishment in the state altogether. In response, special interest groups, police and prosecutorial organizations, and many state legislators immediately sought ways to end the moratorium.

The criminal justice system is a part of society's formal social control apparatus. Three overall goals unite the three core agencies of the system:

1. Track down and punish those found guilty of committing crimes.
2. Maintain order.
3. Promote justice.

Table 8.1 lists the immediate goals and primary activities of the police, courts, and corrections. It is easy to see how one area relies on another. For example, a primary goal of the police is the detection and arrest of suspects. Unless that is accomplished, the courts have no one to process, and therefore cannot achieve their goals of determining guilt or innocence and promoting justice through fair punishment. Likewise, if no one is declared guilty by the courts, the goals of corrections cannot be achieved. Like any other system, the whole achieves its purpose only if the parts, or subsystems, accomplish theirs.

Table 8.1. The Goals and Primary Activities of the Criminal Justice System

Overall Goals of System
Track down and punish those guilty of committing crime
Maintain order
Promote justice

Three Functional Areas of the System

Police

Primary Goals
Enforce the Law
Maintain order
Prevent crime

Primary Activities in Support of the Goals
Detection and investigation of crimes
Identification and arrest of suspects
Routine patrol, surveillance, and intelligence gathering
Education and training of officers and citizens, including children (e.g., bicycle safety, DARE)
Community and problem-oriented policing

Courts

Primary Goals
Determine guilt or innocence of suspects
Set the appropriate penalty upon conviction
Uphold the cause of justice, including due process

Primary Activities in Support of the Goals
Prosecution and defense of suspects
Pretrial hearings
Impartial bench and jury trials
Plea negotiations
Sentencing
Appeals of conviction or sentence
Provide probation and parole services in conjunction with corrections

Corrections

Primary Goals
Apply court-ordered punishment
Maintain safety and security of correctional personnel and the community
Uphold due process and other constitutional rights of offenders

Primary Activities in Support of the Goals
Design, construct, and run prison and jail facilities with appropriate levels of security
Carry out the death penalty (in states where legal and prescribed)
Design and implement correctional programs
Provide probation and parole services in conjunction with courts

Decision Stages in the Criminal Justice System

The criminal justice system comes alive through the actions of the people who work in it and those who are processed by it. From the vantage point of criminal suspects, defendants, and victims, there are various key decision points that have markedly different outcomes depending on the actions taken. This section briefly describes where those points are in the system, the actions that may be taken, and their consequences. Figure 8.2 presents a flowchart summarizing the formal criminal justice process. The arrows show where the suspect or defendant goes after each decision is made. Some decisions involve considerable discretion, where criminal justice personnel act on the basis of their professional judgment; others are governed by strict rules allowing little leeway. Highly discretionary decisions are indicated by a +.

Key Police Decisions

The key decision points for police involve whether or not to:

- treat an event as a possible crime;
- investigate the crime;
- make an arrest; and
- turn the suspect over to the prosecution.

Most police decisions are highly discretionary. Even though the police rely heavily on complaints from the public, they must decide that an event is a possible crime and then investigate it in order to set the wheels of criminal justice in motion. It may take minutes or many months before a suspect is found, but only then can the police contemplate making an arrest. Many factors influence arrest decisions, but the essential legal criterion is **probable cause.** This means that a person

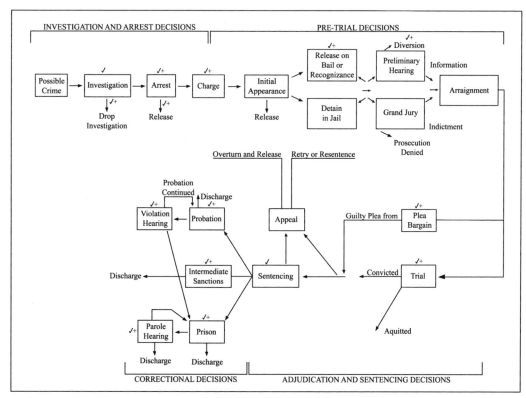

▲ **Figure 8.2.**
Criminal Justice System Flowchart

exercising reasonable judgment would believe that a crime is being or has been committed and that the suspect is responsible for it. Technically, suspects are arrested when they have been deprived of their freedom or believe that they have been placed in custody.

A suspect may be released quickly if the police realize they have made a mistake or believe they do not have sufficient probable cause. The same suspect can be rearrested if circumstances change, however. Suspects have the right to remain silent once they are arrested, but many end up talking to the police. Innocent or not, some suspects implicate others, and the police are trained to listen carefully to anything said by a suspect. Normally, the suspect must be formally charged with a crime or released within forty-eight hours of being arrested. Suspects who are charged are turned over to the prosecution, and thus enter the court phase of the criminal justice process.

Key Decisions of the Courts

Suspects that are turned over for prosecution become *defendants*. During the court phase of the criminal justice process the key decisions involve:

- Filing a formal complaint or charge
- Granting or denying of bail
- Issuing an *indictment* or *information*
- Entering a plea
- Plea negotiations
- Determination of guilt or innocence at trial
- Filing an appeal
- Determination of sentence

One of the first decisions made in the court phase is bail. The U.S. Constitution does not guarantee a defendant's right to be released on bail pending trial, but it does prohibit "excessive" bail. Bail can be denied if the court has grounds to believe that a defendant will not return for trial, would pose a threat to the community if released, or will interfere with the police or prosecution in the preparation of the case. Bail turns out to be one of the most significant decisions for defendants. For one thing, freedom helps in the preparation of a defendant's defense, while detention generally hinders it. It is much easier for attorneys to work on a case if their clients are readily accessible.

Other crucial decisions are made in the charging process. Many cases are screened out early in the process as prosecutors concentrate on pursuing cases they feel they can win or that they believe are important to the community, the criminal justice system, or themselves. When prosecutors take no further action, the case is called *nolle prosequi*; sometimes they may decide to pursue less serious charges than the crime itself might warrant. Prosecutors thus exercise considerable discretion in the charging phase.

Most felony cases go through one of two kinds of pretrial review designed to establish that there is sufficient evidence to proceed against the defendant. One is a **preliminary hearing**, held before a lower court judge, who summarizes the charge(s) listed by the prosecutor in a document called an *information*, and reviews the evidence. Prosecution and defense may each present testimony. Police procedures are sometimes challenged at this stage. If the judge or magistrate finds there is enough evidence to support the charges, the defendant is bound over for trial. The other review process, held in about half the states and the federal system, is conducted in secret before a panel of citizens, usually made up of twenty-three people, called a **grand jury**. The grand jury dates back to the reign of Henry II in the twelfth century, when it was composed of a group of royal knights assembled by the sheriff to decide who should be brought before the traveling court. Over the years, the grand jury gained in popularity because it was not afraid to challenge the crown by refusing to indict political opponents of the king. This reputation helped make the grand jury popular in the American colonies.

Today, only the prosecutor presents testimony before the grand jury, and there is no opportunity for cross-examination. For all intents and purposes the grand jury is an investigative arm of the prosecution. It sifts through the evidence presented and generates new evidence through the questioning of witnesses. If the grand jury accepts that there is probable cause to proceed with the case, it issues a *bill of indictment* listing the specific charges. Although the U.S. Constitution gives criminal defendants the right to a jury trial, approximately 90 percent of criminal convictions are the result of guilty pleas, and most of these are agreed upon by the prosecution and defense following some sort of negotiation. If the case goes to trial before a jury, the decision to convict must usually be a unanimous one. A guilty verdict sends the defendant on to sentencing; a not guilty verdict releases the defendant, who cannot normally be retried for the same offense. If the jury cannot make up its mind, it may be declared a *hung jury*, and the defendant may be retried at the discretion of the prosecution.

Some convicted defendants may decide to appeal the conviction, which can take months or years to complete. The appellate court will be asked to consider whether the defendant's legal rights were violated in some way. If the court finds that they were, a new trial may be ordered or the defendant may be freed altogether. Defendants are usually sentenced even when an appeal is pending. In misdemeanor cases, convicted defendants are usually sentenced the same day; in felony cases, it may be three or four weeks before sentencing is carried out. Judges used to have considerable discretion in the sentences they handed down; today, many states have **mandatory sentencing**, which requires the court to impose a specified penalty for each particular offense.

Key Decisions in Corrections

Even though the sentencing judge stipulates the penalties that will be imposed on convicted offenders, corrections officials have key decisions to make that impact offenders as well as the criminal justice system and the larger society. These decisions concern:

- classification of offenders;
- prison and jail management;
- type and extent of services provided; and
- inmate release and postrelease.

Some corrections decisions are more discretionary than others. For example, federal and state laws as well as court rulings may require that certain types of facilities be made available and that offenders receive certain services or be treated in a certain way. Increasing numbers of lawsuits filed by inmates and other offenders under correctional supervision continually test the constitutionality of practices and procedures. In 1980 a total of 42,781 suits were filed in U.S. District Courts; by 2005 the figure had grown to 104,466 (Maguire and Pastore, 2007). Although most suits are rejected, corrections officials know that their actions are subject to a level of public scrutiny that was unheard of twenty years ago.

Felony offenders headed to prison are generally classified according to the security risk they pose, and their likely response to the available educational and treatment programs. In these times of mandatory sentencing, prison overcrowding, reduced support for rehabilitation and other "liberal" programs, classification decisions focus on security rather than inmate needs. But overcrowding is also forcing the release of some inmates long before their time is served. This is seen by many people as a distinct threat to the community, and it fuels calls for more prison beds.

The new hope in correctional circles today lies with intermediate sanctions. The bulk of criminal offenders do not pose a serious safety risk to the community, even though a majority of known felons are repeat offenders and many commit new offenses while on probation or parole. Correctional officials around the country are challenging public fears and the skepticism of many politicians by advocating increased use of community-based corrections. The American Correctional Association lobbied Congress in 1996 to support legislation that provides alternatives to incarceration for the bulk of felony offenders.

An incarcerated offender's successful return into the community is never a foregone conclusion, and usually both offenders and correctional officials must work very hard at accomplishing it. More often than not the effort fails because offenders who leave prison have few marketable skills, few resources to fall back on, and few people willing and able to provide the emotional support and healthy companionship former inmates need to build a new life. Making matters worse is the stigma associated with street crime and prison time: Potential employers are reluctant to believe that former inmates are trustworthy, and the philosophy "once a criminal, always a criminal" sums up the view of many people. Notwithstanding the offense a person has committed—and former inmates have generally committed more serious ones—it is during the post-release phase of the criminal justice system that some of the most crucial decisions are made. These decisions are made by members of the public, not criminal justice personnel.

The Criminal Justice System Is a Leaky Funnel

Pour engine oil in a funnel with holes in it, and not much oil will reach the engine. Figure 8.3 illustrates this phenomenon using the criminal justice system as the funnel and criminal suspects as the oil. One can easily see that few of the people who start the journey through the system end up in prison.

Of course, it is unlikely that every one of the individuals arrested by the police for a felony crime actually committed it. But the picture is nonetheless sobering because it shows fairly convincingly that the system succeeds in weeding people out better than it does passing them through to the statutory punishment for a felony offense. This disturbs many people, both inside and outside criminal justice. However, other people are more disturbed by this fact: The people who are arrested in the first place are more likely to have committed conventional street crimes and are more likely to be from the lower classes and minority groups. These same people are the ones most likely to end up in prison. In this way, decisions made throughout the criminal justice system—including decisions about what constitutes serious crime in the first place—tend to have a cumulative negative impact on minority

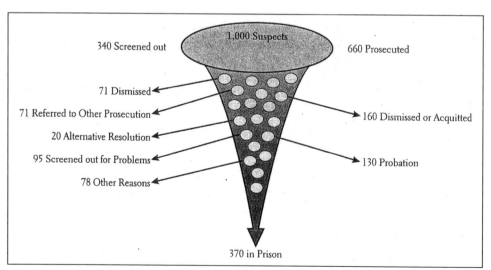

▲ Figure 8.3.
The Criminal Justice System Is a Leaky Funnel

individuals, especially African Americans. This is true for juveniles as well as for adults (Pope and Feyerherm, 1991). A combination of factors is responsible for this state of affairs: stereotypes of real crime and real criminals; bias and discrimination in the labeling practices of some criminal justice personnel; the nonrandom distribution of criminal opportunities and access to them; get-tough-on-crime policies that target street crimes, particularly drug sales; and the higher rates of violent crime among minorities and the poor who live in inner-city neighborhoods.

DISCRETION IN CRIMINAL JUSTICE

Discretion is exercised in situations where "criminal justice officials ... choose one action over another on the basis of their professional judgment" (Barlow, 2000: 681). Examples of these situations include decisions to interrogate a suspect, to make an arrest, to prosecute a defendant, to negotiate a plea, to follow the recommendations in a presentence report, and to release an inmate onto parole. There are both positive and negative aspects to the exercise of discretion. On the positive side, discretion allows criminal justice personnel to take into account individual characteristics and circumstances of people they are dealing with. The exercise of discretion inevitably results in some individuals and groups being treated differently than others, and this points up a major problem: Discretion undermines the constitutional right of all Americans to be treated equally under the law (Barlow and Barlow, 2000). Discretion means power, and if it is abused justice is compromised and respect for law—and for its enforcers—is diminished. This in itself may promote crime.

Police Discretion

In the daily routines of criminal justice, the police are typically the first officials to exercise discretion. Their decisions shape law

in action, and "through the exercise of discretion [patrol officers] define and redefine the meaning of justice" (Brown, 1988: 7). In similar circumstances one citizen may be arrested while another is let go, or perhaps one suspect's refusal to cooperate is handled in a different way than another's.

The scope of discretion—that is, the range of choices of action that can be made in a given situation—is enormous. Consider the case of traffic stops. There are at least 770 different combinations of actions that officers could appropriately take (Bayley and Bittner, 1989: 98–99). This number is calculated by multiplying ten different actions officers can choose when making initial contact by seven strategies used during the stop and by eleven options for exiting the encounter (10 x 7 x 11 = 770). Here are some of the exit options that officers can select when dealing with the driver:

- Release the car and driver.
- Release the driver with a warning.
- Release the driver with a traffic citation.
- Arrest the driver for a prior offense.
- Arrest the driver for being drunk.
- Arrest the driver for actions during the stop.
- Insist the driver proceed on foot.
- Transport the driver somewhere without making an arrest. (98)

Needless to say, dealing with traffic offenses is only one part of the police job; *all* routine police work involves choosing among alternative courses of action. Discretion is the core of policing.

Of necessity, the police engage in **selective enforcement** of the law. This means that "the police do not enforce all the laws all the time against every single violator" (Doerner 1998: 152; Petrocelli and Petrocelli, 2005). Some experts believe that the most important discretionary decisions are the *negative* ones, such as not to make an arrest, not to investigate a complaint, or not to make a deal. These decisions establish the line between people "getting into trouble," and "getting away with it." They define the limits of the law.

There is a strong incentive for police officers to avoid taking official action and it is this: Once they decide to take such action, whether it is responding to a complaint, writing a report, or making an arrest, that decision is subject to review by others. A review can mean a rewarding pat on the back or perhaps even a promotion; but it may also bring criticism, suspension, and even dismissal. Decisions to act unofficially or to do nothing, on the other hand, are rarely reviewed because they are usually of low visibility (Gottfredson and Gottfredson, 1988: 50). By their very nature, "do nothing" decisions will not be scrutinized by third parties except in extraordinary circumstances. Negative decisions contribute an element of mystery to the routine actions of police officers while lessening both internal (departmental) and external (public and legal) controls.

Discretion and the Field Interrogation

Police officers may choose to question individuals in the field, either while on routine patrol or as part of an investigative assignment. This is called a **field interrogation**. It may be a simple question or two, or it may be quite involved. The field interrogation is an integral part of the job, and another area in which discretion comes into play. Deciding whether to stop and question someone is important for police as well as for the general public. It not only determines whether a citizen will be detained, if only for a short time, but it could also determine the outcome of a case. How the interrogation is handled may also determine whether citizens later complain about the police officer's behavior.

Studies of police fieldwork show that officers are often very casual in their interviewing behavior, rarely taking detailed notes, sometimes none at all (Greenwood, Chaiken, and Petersilia, 1977; Sanders, 1977). Police carry

information in their heads, often for many hours, sifting and sorting it until a picture forms that guides their subsequent decisions. Throughout the process, they are trying to establish "what really happened" and "who really did it." Interrogations are designed primarily to develop information, but they often help officers decide what actually happened and what to call it.

Verbal information secured during field interrogation may point to inconsistencies or inaccuracies in the accounts of victims or witnesses, and it may also be used to "trip up" suspects in subsequent interrogations. Minor inconsistencies may be ignored, even in homicide cases, but a major inconsistency will be taken seriously and investigated further, perhaps during future questioning or through the collection of new evidence. Throughout the process, police categorize and sort the verbal information they receive, combining it with impressions—for example, if the suspect is acting "guilty"—and with evidence from the scene or from witnesses.

It is often heard that police unfairly target women and members of minority groups when conducting field interviews. One study of ethnic differences in field interrogations found that more blacks than whites reported (1) being stopped while in a vehicle or on foot; (2) being questioned about an offense, having their house searched, or being arrested; and (3) being asked for documents or to provide a statement (Bucke, 1997).

In response to charges of ethnic or racial bias, police often argue that they are responding to proven stereotypes of "suspicious" persons. Sometimes ethnic groups are believed responsible for periodic crime waves, and the police take these generalized racial stereotypes as a commonsense basis for targeting their field interrogations (see Weitzer and Tuch, 2006). According to one New York City police officer:

> One of the worst days in the police department is Good Friday. An awful lot of Gypsies

steal on Good Friday. . . . Christ on the cross is supposed to have said, "From now on and forevermore, Gypsies can steal and it's not a sin."

Good Friday is a big day for them. When I was working the Gypsies, we worked them for ten years, we would never take Good Friday off because it was a day we'd have to get up early and be on the run with them because they would be everywhere. (Fletcher, 1990: 222).

As for field interviews of women, a study in Miami uncovered evidence suggesting that some male police officers went out of their way to stop female drivers for traffic violations (Fyfe, 1988). Opportunities for sexual harassment are clearly present in the practice of field interrogation. Sex with female suspects has been called one of the "seductions of police work" for some male officers (Crank, 1998: 141–45). It is part of the excitement: the thrill that always lies around the corner. Although undercover cops who work the drugs and vice details may have more routine contact with women in settings that promote sexual opportunities, patrolling officers find such opportunities in a variety of situations: during traffic stops of lone women, when dealing with a female victim, when offering a runaway girl a ride or a meal, when making a field interrogation of a female suspect, and when responding to calls from lonely women. Not only do police have tremendous power by virtue of their job—including the power to overlook crimes in exchange for favors—they spend much of their time dealing with highly vulnerable and marginal populations. It is easy to be seduced by the opportunities for pleasure. Here is the story of one officer:

I really didn't have any offers or even really think about it until I was assigned to a 1-man car and one night I stopped a female subject for running a traffic light. She was really [the] first. The way she acted I just kind of hinted that maybe we could reach an understanding and she picked right up on it. Well, she had enough moving violations that another one could take her license and I guess she didn't

want that to happen. Anyway, I met her later that night and [we] had a wild session. I called again a few days later and she wouldn't even talk to me. Yeah, I've had a few similar experiences since but I'm real careful. (Sapp, 1994: 195)

Studies on the extent of police sexual activity on the job are few and far between, although one analysis of recent surveys of municipal and county police officers suggests that it may be widespread. For example, it has been estimated that as many as 1,520 incidents of sexual harassment, *witnessed by other officers*, occurred in Ohio and 3,175 in Illinois during a one-year period (Crank, 1998: 143). Presumably, far more incidents occurred that were not witnessed or not reported in the surveys.

Prosecutorial Discretion

Prosecutors do not proceed against all felony suspects brought to them by the police. Instead, they exercise considerable discretion, not only in deciding whether to proceed, but also in the selection of the particular charges that will be presented to the grand jury or at the preliminary hearing in open court.

One important factor affecting the decision to proceed with prosecution is the prosecutor's evaluation of the probability that the defendant will be convicted. Prosecutors avoid investing time and resources in prosecuting defendants who are likely to be acquitted. Prosecuting only those suspects who stand a good chance of being convicted helps serve the state's interest in convicting guilty people. It also confirms that the prosecutor's judgment is sound and that the taxpayers' money is not being wasted.

Important as these considerations are in making the decision to proceed with prosecution, this is by no means the whole story. The prosecutor's exercise of discretion is influenced by many considerations. Some are bound up with questions of justice; some with practical matters involving resources, evidence, and witnesses, some with politics and community interests; and yet others with the organization and culture of the criminal justice system itself. Let us review each of these in turn.

First, a prosecutor often worries about questions of justice. There may be times when a conviction is virtually guaranteed but the prosecutor has doubts about the suspect's actual guilt. Despite a prosecutor's obvious professional interest in obtaining guilty verdicts, conviction of an innocent person does not serve the interests of justice, which prosecutors are sworn to uphold. Concern that a defendant may actually be innocent would lead most prosecutors to delay prosecution pending further investigation. The defendant may have to be released, but this does not stop the prosecutor from coming back later with new charges.

Now consider the problem of resources: It is rarely feasible to prosecute all defendants that prosecutors believe can be convicted, and so a choice must be made among them. A prosecutor may therefore focus resources on the prosecution of people suspected of more serious crimes, or of people with extensive prior arrests, or of people suspected of specific types of crime, for instance, drug offenses or violent crimes.

The decision to prosecute is sometimes influenced by private individuals and groups who are able to put pressure on the district attorney. The fact that chief prosecutors are usually elected officials helps explain their responsiveness to public opinion. It would not be in their interest to spend time prosecuting crimes the public does not care about. In many cities, police and prosecutors have been under pressure to do something about gang violence and drug trafficking, so criminal justice officials respond with more arrests and prosecutions.

Prosecution decisions are also influenced by the need to maintain good working relations with police and other members of the courthouse work group, including those who work directly with the victims of crime. In some communities, for example, victim advocacy groups strongly favor the prosecution of certain types of offenders who previously may have been screened out—for example, those suspected of domestic violence or those arrested for spraying graffiti or other vandalism. Many police departments have special units to handle sex crimes. These units often work closely with victim advocacy groups to develop "prosecutable" cases.

Sometimes, evidence will come to light that the police made legal errors in their handling of a case, such as violations of search and seizure rules. This puts prosecutors in a difficult position and can cause strained relations with the police. When cases have been compromised in this way, prosecutors may still proceed with prosecution, but their chances of winning in court are significantly reduced.

As noted earlier, the boundaries of the criminalization process in any society are largely determined by negative decisions, that is, decisions to do nothing. In effect, negative decisions establish what people can get away with. Many criminal cases that come before prosecutors are screened out at an early stage or end up being dismissed later on. The decision not to prosecute is often made at an initial screening before the case is forwarded to the felony court. In most larger cities this initial decision is handled by assistant prosecutors who staff a warrant office. Besides determining whether initial charges will be filed or the case screened out, the warrant office is the major liaison between the district attorney and the public and also routinely advises the police on legal matters.

Discretion in Sentencing

Although the use of mandatory sentences and the spread of "three-strikes" laws have significantly curtailed the discretion allowed judges during sentencing, sentencing disparities still exist and reflect the exercise of discretion. When different sentences are imposed on offenders convicted of essentially the same offense, we have sentencing disparity. This could be the result of bias on the part of judges. For many years, criminologists have documented sentencing disparities by race (e.g., Mitchell, 2005; Sellin, 1935; Wolfgang and Cohen, 1970; Thornberry, 1973) and class (e.g., Hood, 1972), and the question of gender bias has been receiving increased attention in recent years (e.g., Steffensmeier and Stephen Demuth, 2006). This section reviews some of the evidence on the effects of discretion in sentencing.

Race and Sentencing

The so-called War on Drugs has had a greater impact on African Americans than any other group. The stiff penalties for crack cocaine offenses have resulted in a huge increase in the incarceration rate of blacks. This has been called a "hidden effect" of the criminal law, and "politicized sentencing" to reflect the political character of drug enforcement (Barnes and Kingsnorth, 1996; Mauer, 2000). Politicians and high-ranking government officials have been enthusiastic supporters of harsh measures against illicit drugs at least partly because it means votes at the ballot box and more resources for their home states or counties, or the agencies they head. When the War on Drugs is examined from the perspective of race, however, a startling picture emerges.

Data on illicit drug use compiled through nationwide household surveys shows slight differences in overall drug use patterns by race: Whites are somewhat more inclined than blacks to have ever used an illegal drug. But imprisonment rates bear little relationship to use rates. The rate at which African Americans are sentenced to prison for drug offenses is more than *six times higher* than that for white defendants. The trend over the past decade has been that black imprisonment rates for drug offenses increased, while those for whites have remained stable or decreased (Tonry, 1994). Though some of this difference is probably explained by legal factors such as

prior record and the severity of the current charge—for example, selling versus mere possession—much of it reflects the tough sentencing of crack cocaine offenders, who are mainly black.

When sentences for drug trafficking and drug possession are compared, African Americans still receive harsher sentences than whites. For example, the average sentences imposed by state courts in 1994 on white and black felony drug offenders were as follows:

Whites: possession—20 months; trafficking—33 months
Blacks: possession—31 months; trafficking—54 months. (Brown and Langan, 1998: 21)

More glaring, a recent study by Pettit and Western (2004), showed that of males born between 1965 and 1969, African American men were seven times more likely than white men to have served time in prison (22.1 percent for blacks versus only 3.2 percent for whites).

It is not possible to tell whether some of this disparity is due to blacks having worse criminal records than white drug offenders. However, even if that were true, the records themselves could reflect the cumulative impact of bias that occurred in earlier criminal justice decisions, for example, by legislators, the police, or prosecutors. During the charging and plea-bargaining processes, for example, prosecutors may take essentially the same events and reconstruct them into different crimes—carrying different penalties—on the basis of race (Crew, 1991; Mitchell, 2005). Studies have found that, all other things being equal, young black males are more likely than any other age-race-gender group to receive the harshest of criminal penalties (Mitchell, 2005; Steffensmeier, Ulmer, and Kramer, 1998).

Race, Social Class, and Sentencing

Race and social class are intertwined in American society, as are gender and class. African

Americans and women tend, on the whole, to have lower socioeconomic status and less power than whites and males. This makes distinguishing the individual relationship of these factors to sentencing more difficult.

It has been shown, for example, that the sentences given to juvenile offenders are affected by both race and class. In one study, the records of 9,601 juvenile court dispositions in Philadelphia were analyzed. Even when legal variables such as severity of offense and prior record were taken into account, blacks were more likely than whites to be prosecuted and institutionalized, and offenders of low socioeconomic status were more severely penalized than others (Thornberry, 1973). More recent studies of the sentencing have also shown class and race disparities (Leonard, Pope, and Feyerherm, 1995; Pettit and Western, 2004).

A study of early releases from prison in Ohio found race to be the most important factor in determining releases in certain situations (Leonard, Pope, and Feyerherm, 1995). For example, when the probation department recommended against early release, whites were twice as likely as blacks to be released, even after controlling for criminal record, current offense, and other variables. Some studies have shown that the effects of race and class on sentencing diminish when other factors, such as prior record and circumstances of the offense, are taken into account (Hagan, 1974: 379). However, Mitchell (2005) has found, after carefully reviewing previous studies, that this is not the case in general: Racial disparities still exist even when all other variables are held constant.

Research on sentencing in capital cases confirms that the killing of white victims results in harsher sentences than the killing of blacks (Eberhardt, Davies, Purdie-Vaughns, and Johnson, 2006). One study found that defendants convicted of killing whites were four times more likely than defendants who killed blacks to receive a death sentence (Baldus, Woodworth, and Pulaski, 1985). This finding could not be explained by conventional legal factors such as the circumstances of the crime or offenders' past records. A later study of death penalty sentences in eight states—Florida, Georgia, Illinois, Oklahoma, North Carolina, Mississippi, Virginia, and Arkansas—found a "clear pattern" of victim-based discrimination "unexplained on grounds other than race" (Gross and Mauro, 1989: 110).

In one study, disparities in sentencing based on the race of offenders and victims were most dramatic when the offenses were more serious. An analysis of 2,858 felony cases ranging from assaults to robberies and murders found that only in the case or murders and sexual assaults were marked racial disparities present in the sentences received (Spohn, 1994). Why this should be so is unclear. Two possibilities are that (1) judges see black-on-white sexual assaults and murders as a serious threat to the power structure of which they are a part, and (2) the violent intimacy of the crimes themselves gives rise to racial bias. Yet a Florida study of decisions to increase penalties using habitual offender laws shows that racial disparities were more common for *less* serious offenses (Crawford, Chiricos, and Kleck, 1998). The authors surmise that less serious offenses allow judges more room for flexibility in sentencing, including allowing nonlegal factors such as race to enter the picture. Only continued research will clarify the complex relationship between race and sentencing.

Gender and Sentencing

A review of research on juvenile court dispositions concludes that girls receive harsher treatment than boys for lesser crimes, but not for more serious offenses (Barlow and Ferdinand, 1992: 130–34). To some extent this reflects the impact of gender on referrals to juvenile court. A national study of juvenile court data found that girls were three times as likely as boys to be referred to juvenile court for status offenses—that is, acts (such as running away) that would not be crimes if committed by adults (Snyder and Finnegan, 1987). Once there, however, girls charged with status offenses were also more likely than boys to be incarcerated. This difference is a historical one (Chesney-Lind, 1987a; 1987b; 1988; 2006).

What explains this difference in the treatment of boys and girls? One study looked at gender bias in 36,680 juvenile court dispositions in Nebraska over a nine-year period (Johnson and Scheuble, 1991). Hypotheses were derived from two competing theories: sex role traditionalism and chivalry (or paternalism). The sex role traditionalism perspective predicts harsher punishment for females based on the argument that girls and women who commit crimes violate the traditional female role—being gentle, passive, and dependent. The chivalry model predicts an opposite gender bias: Female offenders will be given more lenient sentences because males—who dominate the criminal justice system—try to protect the "fairer sex."

The findings of this study support both models of gender bias. Overall, girls received more lenient dispositions than boys, suggesting a chivalry effect. Yet harsher penalties for girls were found in the case of repeat offenders who committed more serious offenses, suggesting a sex role effect. Over the nine years, however, the trend was toward greater leniency for females—"higher odds for girls being dismissed and higher odds for probation and lock-up for boys" (Johnson and Scheuble, 1991: 695).

One interesting study looked at sentencing practices as they take place in the courtroom (Daly, 1989). Courts in New York City and Seattle placed considerable weight on the family ties of defendants. Thus, black women with spouses, dependent parents, or children benefited most from sentencing leniency, and single and married men with children or dependent parents also did better than other men. Likewise, a study of 61,294 criminal cases in Pennsylvania in the late 1980s found that gender had only a small impact on prison

sentences; interviews with judges and courtroom observation showed that sentencing was influenced most by perceptions of a defendant's blameworthiness and by the practical consequences of incarceration (Steffensmeier, Kramer, and Streifel, 1993). When defendants had families to support and good jobs to lose, judges tended to be more lenient. A study of the sentencing of women in England reached the same conclusion (Hedderman and Gelsthorpe, 1997).

To conclude this discussion of discretion in criminal justice, suffice it to say that most crimes do not end up in an arrest and most arrests do not result in jail or prison for the offender. This is due in large part—though certainly not entirely—to the exercise of discretion. Unfortunately, discretion also results in some individuals and groups being more likely than others to be arrested and prosecuted, and to receive harsh punishments. These disparities tend to increase as the severity of the offense declines.

CRIMINAL JUSTICE AND CRIME PREVENTION

In this section we will consider whether and how the actions of the criminal justice system affect the amount of crime experienced in society. More particularly, can the criminal justice system prevent crime? This issue will come up again when we discuss opportunity-rationality theories of crime in chapter 10. Here, let us start with the police.

Crime Prevention and the Police

When police teach youngsters how to avoid being kidnapped or resist pressures to use drugs, when they help business owners burglarproof their premises or conduct neighborhood watch seminars, and when they place clearly visible surveillance cameras in subway stations, they are engaged in *crime prevention*. Even the mere visible presence of patrolling officers provides the police with a potential crime prevention aspect—people contemplating a crime may refrain from going through with it for fear of being caught and punished. When police enforce laws, they may also prevent crimes: Arresting a suspect may prevent a future crime—if not by that suspect, then by others who saw the arrest or know about it.

The law enforcement/crime prevention function of policing is the role that many police officers and many members of the public believe should be at the core of police operations. It certainly fits with the media image of policing, and the great success of crime-fighting fiction in film and books suggests that the public appetite for it is vast. Yet most of the time the police—or, more precisely, patrolling police officers—are neither actively enforcing the law nor actively preventing crime.

Proactive Policing and Crime Prevention

The traditional police response to crime is largely reactive: Crimes occur and the police respond. Reactive policing is unlikely to be a very effective crime prevention technique, although of course police reaction can prevent some crimes from being completed. Reactive policing is also not very effective for dealing with consensual crimes such as drug use and prostitution, nor for crimes occurring in neighborhoods where confidence in the police is low or where the police are regarded as enemies.

To address these problems, police departments across the United States have adopted a strategy of policing known as **proactive policing**: taking an active role in uncovering crime and trying to prevent it. Various methods have been employed:

- *Use of decoys.* Sometimes police pretend to be participants in crime, thereby inviting the real offenders to commit crimes in their presence. This strategy has been used for consensual crimes involving prostitution, homosexual activity in semipublic places such as highway rest areas and park restrooms, and money-laundering activities of drug traffickers and the transactions of fences and thieves. In some situations, as when a rash of assaults has been taking place in a certain neighborhood, undercover police act as inviting victims, hoping to lure potential rapists and muggers into committing a crime.

- *Directed patrols.* When crimes reach epidemic proportions, or when citizen complaints become politically embarrassing, police may turn to the "directed patrol." This involves concentrating patrol officers in particular locations or in surveillance of particular individuals or groups. This sort of saturation policing has been used successfully against youth gangs, as discussed below. Yet departments that adopt the strategy run the risk of merely moving crime to another neighborhood outside the area of saturation. Displacement effects such as this are an age-old problem in crime prevention, undermining proactive policing. The strategy of directed patrols has also been criticized for targeting black inner-city communities (Fishman, 1998: 116).

- *Crime-focused community relations programs.* One form of proactive policing is represented by the "gun buyback" programs that have sprung up around the country in recent years. Police departments ask citizens who own firearms, particularly handguns, to sell them to police with "no questions asked." The idea is to get guns off the street, thereby cutting down on the number of gun crimes. Thousands of guns have been turned in, often quickly exhausting the available buyback funds. But the success of buyback programs in actually reducing violent crimes committed with firearms is not proven (Rosenfeld, 1996).

Aggressive policing such as that advocated in some proactive strategies is believed to contribute to crime reduction through its

deterrent effect. The idea is that proactive policing raises the risks and costs of doing crime relative to its benefits, and this reduces the appeal of offending: "By stopping, questioning, and otherwise closely observing citizens, especially suspicious ones, the police are more likely to find fugitives, detect contraband (such as stolen property or concealed weapons), and apprehend persons fleeing from the scene of a crime" (Wilson and Boland, 1978: 373). Deterrence works if potential offenders see these outcomes as too costly and therefore refrain from committing crimes.

Aggressive policing may also lower crime rates by influencing the perceptions people hold of the likelihood of being arrested. As a rule, people have only a vague notion about the actual probability of arrest, which is low even for serious crimes. This means that potential offenders rarely witness an arrest going down, and if they do, they won't necessarily know what the person is being arrested for. But if the police engage in a rigorous proactive program of arrests—even for mostly relatively minor offenses such as drunkenness or traffic violations—"this is a very visible indicator of police activity . . . [and it may] send a signal to potential offenders that one's chances of getting caught are higher than they actually are" (Sampson and Cohen, 1988: 165). Thus, proactive policing may have a direct deterrent effect on crime by causing potential criminals to reconsider even when the actual risks of being arrested for a particular offense may not have changed.

In response to concerns about rising gun crimes among youth, the National Institute of Justice funded an experiment in directed police patrolling aimed at confiscating firearms that are illegal or illegally carried. When concentrated around gun crime hot spots, directed police patrols appear to reduce both the presence and use of guns at relatively modest cost. And it appears that the patrols do not result in a displacement of gun crime to other areas, where risks of police intervention are lower (Sherman and Rogan, 1995). However, repeated tests of the strategy are needed, and

there are still some possible hazards that need to be addressed. One of these is the possibility that intensified gun patrols provoke more violence "by making youths subjected to traffic stops more defiant of conventional society" (Sherman, Shaw, and Rogan, 1995: 9).

This problem does not seem to have occurred in New York City, where police claim that directed patrols have significantly reduced gun crimes (*New York Times*, July 30, 1995, p. 15). New York police first flooded a zone consisting of nine streets in northwest Harlem with plainclothes officers and detectives. Then the precinct moved many beat and uniformed narcotics officers from less violent streets to the "hot zone" to arrest low-level drug lookouts and dealers, often initially for minor violations. Meanwhile, patrolling officers in cars looked for legal excuses, such as lane changes without signaling, to stop and question drivers of cars with out-of-state licenses. When approaching suspects in the target zone, officers first looked for a bulge that may be a gun. If they thought the suspect was carrying a gun or responding to their questioning in a suspicious or nervous way, they frisked for a weapon. In June 1995, 30th Precinct officers frisked 450 people, a 150 percent increase from June 1994. The frisks produced only a handful of gun arrests, but shootings began to decline. The police believe potential offenders were leaving their guns at home in anticipation of encounters with police.

Aggressive police patrolling may be part of the answer to gang-related crimes as well as street violence associated with drug trafficking. However, there may be a cost in civil liberties that some Americans will find objectionable. The strategy also tends to target minority and poor neighborhoods, which raises the problem of overpolicing discussed earlier. In cities with large minority populations, there may be a political cost that elected authorities are reluctant to bear. This may explain why some police departments across the country have been reluctant to copy the New York City program.

Punishment and Crime Prevention

Punishment is any action designed to deprive someone of things of value because of something the person is believed to have done. Valued things include freedom, civil rights, money, health, identity, personal relationships, and life itself. Throughout the ages, rulers have devised all manner of punishments for people guilty of wrongdoing. The more serious an offense was considered to be, the harsher the penalties attached to it. Many people consider the harshest penalties to be those that cut offenders off from their families. Today, when a judge formally announces a sentence in a felony case, the penalty could be as light as twelve months on probation or as severe as life in prison; in thirty-eight states and the federal system, the penalty may be death.

An ideal punishment, according to eighteenth-century philosophers Jeremy Bentham (1948) and Cesare Beccaria (1963) is both proportionate to the offense *and* sufficient to outweigh the pleasure derived from it. The second factor is important, for it helps explain how punishment prevents crime: Crime is prevented when people refrain from offending so as to avoid the pain of punishment. This prediction is the central idea behind deterrence theory, discussed in more detail in the next section and in later chapters. But deterrence is only one way that punishment might prevent crime. In fact, as box 8.1 shows, there are at least *ten* different ways that punishment may prevent crime. Only the first four on the list have received much attention in criminal justice circles; these are deterrence, incapacitation, reformation, and rehabilitation. Let's look more closely at these four possibilities.

Reformation

The idea behind **reformation** is that punishment conveys a sense of shame and remorse to some offenders, building their consciences and thus promoting conformity to the law. The original penitentiary was an early ap-

plication of the idea that reformation occurs through punishment. Offenders were placed in solitary confinement so they could reflect on the evil of their ways and be reformed through penitence. Even an arrest may have a reformative impact with some criminal offenders. Some amateur shoplifters and many people charged with white-collar crimes experience a sort of moral jolt when arrested. The arrest demonstrates that they have slipped from law-abiding citizen to thief and prompts a return to lawful behavior—at least for a time. While true reformation implies a permanent change in behavior, even a temporary return to law-abiding behavior will have prevented some crime.

Incapacitation

Some forms of punishment render offenders no longer able to commit crimes. This consequence of punishment is called **incapacitation**. Potential offenders are incapacitated because punishment removes or diminishes their opportunities to commit crimes. Incapacitation is absolute when an offender is executed but it is relative for other forms of punishment. Consider imprisonment: Although putting someone behind bars reduces his opportunity to commit crimes, it does not rule out all offenses and may actually encourage some that the offender never before committed, for example, homosexual rape.

Capital punishment is the surest way to prevent future crime through incapacitation. But it is not foolproof, because offenders might still commit crimes while awaiting execution. Indeed, an infamous murderer awaiting execution in Illinois has found a way to delay his execution more than once: He has killed fellow prisoners, forcing new criminal investigations and trials, thereby postponing his own scheduled execution. It is surely preposterous to suggest execution as an incapacitation remedy for all types of offenses.

A study of persistent thieves found that imprisonment encourages "rationalization of

BOX 8.1. PUNISHMENT AND ITS POTENTIAL TO PREVENT CRIME

Punishment has the *potential* to prevent crime in the following ways:

1. *Deterrence.* People are scared away from criminal activity by fear of the consequences if they are caught.
2. *Incapacitation.* Offenders cannot commit crimes because the opportunity or ability to do so has been removed or reduced. Imprisonment is considered an incapacitating penalty, and so are some forms of mutilation.
3. *Reform.* Punishment conveys a sense of shame and remorse to some offenders, and this promotes subsequent conformity. In the original penitentiary, offenders were placed in solitary confinement so they could reflect on the evil of their ways and, through penitence, be reformed.
4. *Rehabilitation.* The alteration of behavior by nonpunitive means so that the individual no longer commits crimes. While not punishment in itself, rehabilitation is often attempted within the context of punishment. Work release and prison education programs are examples.
5. *Surveillance.* When people are watched closely or monitored by electronic means, their behavior is made visible to others. This may prevent some crimes from occurring. Obviously, deterrence may be involved here, too.
6. *Normative validation.* Punishment confirms and reinforces the view that an act is wrong. When a teacher or a judge says, "I'm going to make an example out of you," it reminds the offender and others how they ought to behave and what will happen if they do not.
7. *Retribution.* Punishing offenders in a just manner may prevent other crimes such as private vengeance or armed vigilantism. The "subway vigilante" Bernard Goetz is a real-life example. He shot three young men that he claimed were about to rob him, blaming his behavior on the inability of society to protect him from criminals.
8. *Stigmatization.* Punishment marks people as offenders, and the label "criminal" may stick long after the punishment is over. An individual may refrain from crime not because of the punishment itself, but because of the anticipated stigmatization that is associated with it. Laws requiring that neighbors be informed of convicted sex offenders in their midst are designed partly for their stigmatizing effect and partly to encourage surveillance.
9. *Normative insulation.* People tend to be influenced by the people they associate with. If people could somehow escape the influence of criminals there would be less crime. Parents who keep tight reins on their children may contribute to normative insulation—which children undoubtedly see as a punishment! Electronic monitoring of offenders on probation may contribute to normative insulation as well.
10. *Habituation.* Punishment can lead to the development of habitual behavior that conforms to the law. For example, driving tends to be slower in places where police routinely use speeding traps to catch violators. Habituation differs from deterrence because conforming behavior may persist long after enforcement has ended.

Source: Gibbs (1975).

crime" (Shover and Henderson, 1995: 236). Inmates learn from others how and why they were "busted," and this encourages a more calculating approach to their own criminal activity. In addition, many inmates leave prison reassured by the fact that they survived the ordeal, claiming in retrospect that prison was no big deal: "For too many of those who pass through it once, the prison experience will leave them less fearful and better prepared for a second trip if that should happen" (241).

Rehabilitation

It is traditional to think of the terms *reformation* and *rehabilitation* as interchangeable, but this is incorrect. Reform is a direct consequence of punishment, whereas **rehabilitation** is the alteration of an offender's behavior by nonpunitive means so that he or she no longer violates laws. While it is not in itself punishment, rehabilitation is usually attempted side by side with punishment. For almost a century the U.S. correctional system has included some efforts at rehabilitation while offenders are confined. Work release, prison educational and vocational programs, and halfway houses for offenders about to return to the community are examples. How much effort is put into rehabilitation generally depends on the security level of the prison: The higher the security level, the less the emphasis on rehabilitation.

Deterrence

The **deterrence doctrine** argues that people refrain from crime because they fear the punishment that might follow. This idea has probably received more attention from the scientific community than any other perspective on punishment, *and many important people believe in it.* For this reason we will spend a little more time discussing it here as well as in chapter 9.

It is conventional to distinguish between two classes of potential offenders who may refrain from crime because they fear punishment:

1. People who have directly experienced punishment for something they did in the past. If these people refrain from future criminal activity because they fear being punished again, this is **specific deterrence**.
2. People who have not experienced punishment themselves but are deterred from crime by the fear that they might get the same punishment experienced by others. This is **general deterrence**.

This distinction is important because the deterrent effect of experienced punishments may be quite different from that of threatened punishments. When a judge hands down a sentence and tells the offender, "This ought to make you think twice next time," the judge is thinking of the penalty as a specific deterrent; if the judge says, "I intend to make an example of you," the penalty's general deterrent value is being emphasized.

A second important distinction in deterrence research concerns three properties of punishment—severity, certainty, and speed. Beccaria and Bentham believed that the deterrent impact of punishment is greater when it is applied more swiftly, with greater certainty and greater severity. However, they considered severity to be less important as a deterrent than the others.

More than two hundred years have passed since Bentham and Beccaria laid the foundation of the deterrence theory of punishment. During that time a conventional wisdom emerged that punishment deters if it is swift, certain, and reasonably severe. But science has not confirmed that wisdom, and many experts would agree that the best answer to the question "Does punishment deter?" is "probably not" (Nagin and Paternoster, 1991).

The inability of the scientific community to substantiate—or reject—the conventional wisdom (and political belief) that punishment deters crime is difficult for many people to understand. Most of us can think of anecdotal illustrations of deterrence, from our own personal experience, perhaps, or from hearing about other people who refrained from committing crimes because they were fearful of the consequences. But serious researchers find that the complexities of the subject present formidable obstacles to developing conclusive answers. This is not to say that there has been *absolutely* no support in the literature of deterrence theory. Limited support of deterrence has been found in the realms of drunk driving (Freeman, Liossis, and David, 2006; Piquero and Paternoster, 1998; Walker, 1998), luggage and car theft in certain contexts (Di Tella and Schargrodsky, 2004; Trivizas and Smith, 1997), and crime trends more generally (D'Alessio and Stolzenberg, 1998).

Most surprising, perhaps, is the fact that few studies have uncovered a deterrent effect for capital punishment. Indeed, there is no good research that supports the oft-heard claim that there would be fewer murders if more killers were executed rather than sent to prison. Murders are often unplanned, spur-of-the-moment attacks, and alcohol is usually a factor in them. But even among hardened criminals, who may think about risks in planning their crimes (Horney and Marshall, 1992), fear of punishment does not seem to be a major factor in their decisions (Cromwell, 2006; Shover and Henderson, 1995; Wright and Decker, 1994; 1997).

On balance, the threat of formal punishments is much less worrisome to potential offenders than the threat of informal punishments imposed by relatives, friends, co-workers, or other close acquaintances (Cullen, 1994; Tittle, 1980; Paternoster, Saltzman, Waldo, and Chiricos, 1983; 1985; Braithwaite, 1989a). The average law-abiding citizen "is afraid of losing his job, of being ostracized by his business associates and friends, of the possible alienation of members of his family, of having to leave his neighborhood or even his town" (Shoham, 1970: 9).

One criminologist has argued that punishment may backfire under certain circumstances, and this may explain the lack of a deterrent relationship between crime rates and punishment (Sherman, 1993). Lawrence W. Sherman suggests that if punishment is seen as unfair or excessive, an attitude of defiance emerges. This defiance undermines any deterrent effect the threat of punishment might have had. It can also undermine any lingering respect for the law—a consideration in the sentencing of youthful and first-time offenders. Such a reaction has also been noted by James Gilligan (1996) in his research on incarcerated murderers, and to some extent by Charles R. Tittle (1995).

To summarize, deterrence clearly does not score high marks as the basis for a sentencing policy. Yet the lack of strong evidence does not mean that deterrence theory is disproved. The prospect of swift, certain, and reasonably severe punishment may deter some individuals from committing crimes under some circumstances. The difficulty is figuring out who those individuals are and which circumstances count. Still, rather than rejecting the deterrence doctrine, more research on these complex issues would seem the more prudent course. It would also seem appropriate for politicians, judges, and other court officials to refrain from claiming that harsher punishments will deter crime. The bulk of deterrence research simply does not support this claim.

CRIMES OF THE CRIMINAL JUSTICE SYSTEM

Some actions taken by some criminal justice personnel result in the victimization of suspects, offenders, witnesses, victims, and even the general public. Some of these actions are also illegal, either because they violate procedural laws—such as the constitutional protections against illegal search and seizure or cruel and unusual punishment—or because they violate the criminal law. In this section we will look at some of the ways in which citizens are victimized by the very people society employs to deal with crime and criminals.

Contexts and Varieties of Offenses

There are many ways that criminal justice officials may create victims in carrying out their work. Indeed, they run the gamut of occupational and organizational crimes discussed in chapter 6. Some of these crimes are for personal gain—as when police officers take drugs or money from criminal suspects—and some are committed on behalf of organizational goals—as when correctional officers use excessive force when handling resistant inmates or when prosecutors ignore or hide evidence that might hurt their case in court.

While all criminal justice operations provide opportunities for crime, the enforcement of public order crimes such as consensual drug and sex offenses is especially prone to lawbreaking. As noted earlier, police take a proactive approach in dealing with these offenses, and much of this work is undercover or involves informants. Armed with a strong public mandate but largely free from outside scrutiny, drug and vice officers have plenty of opportunities and incentives to break the law (Abadinsky, 1990; Luttwak, 1995). Sex and drugs are also big business, and money flows freely. By all accounts, it takes great self-control and immunity to the influence of corrupt peers for officers to resist the many opportunities and temptations in this line of policing (Jackson, 1969; Progrebin and Poole, 1993). Another context in which the opportunities and temptations for crime are strong is also largely hidden from public scrutiny: the prison. The public expects prisons to be harsh environments, so there is little interest in what goes on inside unless it seems extreme: deadly riots, on the one hand, or a country club atmosphere, on the other.

Indeed, for many years there existed a *hands-off doctrine* in correctional circles, allowing wardens to run their prisons pretty much as they liked. Although court rulings during the 1970s and 1980s severely curtailed authoritarian control strategies (Johnson, 1987), the history of prisons has been a brutal one. Consider torture and segregation. Torture has been outlawed in America and Europe for more than 150 years, yet cruel and vicious abuse of inmates has been documented. For example, in the late 1960s physical torture was commonplace in the Arkansas prison system (Murton and Hyams, 1969). In the Tucker prison farm, officers used the infamous "Tucker telephone" to punish inmates: Electrical wires from the "telephone" were attached to the feet and genitals of inmates, who were then "rung up" with an extremely painful electrical charge.

Segregation is also associated with brutality and abuse of inmates. Often referred to as "the hole," segregation units are used to discipline inmates or to keep them isolated from other inmates—sometimes at their own request. In some prisons, the hole is also used as a way of punishing inmates who are considered "difficult" or "subversive" by correctional staff (Scraton, Sim, and Skidmore, 1991: 85). Segregation units in older prisons were usually small, solid-walled cells, often without windows. Some sound terrifying: "When you step into the cell you see a box. That's the silent cell. Around this is all their strip-lights and big heaters. Also metal straps to keep the heat in. The inside is about three square yards. There are two spyholes, and two small air vents. It's a human furnace" (Scraton, Sim, and Skidmore, 1991: 84–85). In Pennsylvania during the 1960s, state courts ruled that inmates in segregation must have some light, so officials at one prison built a cell of Plexiglas known as the "glass cage"; bright lights were shone twenty-four hours a day (Hassine, 1996: 100).

Understanding Police Corruption

Most of the research on crimes of the criminal justice system has focused on the police, society's first official line of defense against crime. Every few years, it seems, a tale of police crime comes to light that receives national attention. This happened in New York City during the early 1970s, and the 1972 Knapp Commission found a widespread and "strikingly standardized" pattern of corruption involving patrol officers assigned to districts frequented by pimps, gamblers, and drug dealers. During the 1990s in both New York and Chicago, commissions were appointed to investigate charges of racketeering, extortion, stealing, and conspiracy among police officers. All three commissions reported the existence of a **blue code** (or "wall") **of silence**, a curtain of secrecy that unites police against outside scrutiny and protects them against informants from within (Crank, 2003). Police don't "rat" on their own kind, and anyone who does risks injury or death, as New York City narcotics officer Frank Serpico famously found out in 1970.

Explaining police corruption is a difficult task. Some evidence shows that serious police crime is mostly the product of so-called bad apples in a department. These people are portrayed as rogue cops who shouldn't have been placed in a police uniform in the first place. Other research has found that corruption is fairly widespread and that the very organizational structure and culture of policing itself contributes to corruption. For example, the police culture includes qualities and values such as solidarity, bravery, independence, the code of silence, and an "us versus them" mentality (Crank, 2003; Kappeler, Sluder, and Alpert, 1994). These features, along with significant opportunities to engage in crime, can be combined to help explain police crime. Police crime, as all crime, often has multiple causes.

A Typology of Police Corruption

An important step in understanding police crimes is to identify their similarities and differences. One of the few systematic studies of police corruption has identified eight types of police corruption:

1. *Corruption of authority* means receiving unauthorized, unearned material gains by virtue of police officer status. This includes free liquor, meals, discounts, and payments by merchants for more police protection. The corrupters are respectable citizens, there is considerable peer group support, there is little adverse departmental reaction, little organization is required, and the violation involved is primarily that of departmental regulations. This form of corruption is widespread, and most police officers know about it even if they have not participated themselves.

2. *Kickbacks* involve receipt of goods and services in return for referring business to a variety of patrons—doctors, lawyers, bondsmen, garages, taxicab companies, service stations, and so on. Corrupters are usually respectable persons who stand to gain from the scheme. Departments tend to ignore it or actually condone it, depending on the respectability of the corrupter; however, this practice usually violates formal departmental rules. Peer group support is often substantial, though its degree may depend on the reputation and trustworthiness of the patron. The organization involved is relatively simple, consisting basically of the ongoing relationship between the business and the police officer.

3. *Opportunist theft* consists of stealing goods or money from arrestees, victims, crime scenes, or unprotected property. It involves no corrupter and is clearly in violation of criminal laws as well as departmental rules. Reaction from departments is usually negative, and the reaction is likely to be more severe if the value of goods or cash taken is high, if the public knows about the theft, and if the victim is willing to prosecute. Peer group support depends on informal norms governing distinctions between "clean" and "dirty" money. Dirty money

is money that comes from crime, especially drug trafficking; some police officers treat this as fair game. Little organization is involved in opportunistic theft; as the term implies, it is a spontaneous act that occurs when an appropriate situation arises.

4. *Shakedowns* are also opportunistic behaviors. They occur when the police know about a crime but accept money or services from suspects in exchange for doing nothing. The corrupter may be either respectable or habitually involved in criminal activities. Shakedowns violate legal and departmental norms, and though peer group support is necessary for shakedowns to become routine, that support is often contingent on the suspect's criminal activity—bribes from drug dealers and armed robbers are frowned upon. Secrecy among participants is a key element of shakedowns.

5. *Protection of illegal activities* arises when corrupters want to continue illegal activities without risk of being arrested. Since they are doing something illegal, they purchase "protection" from police officers willing to be corrupted. This protection violates criminal and departmental rules and involves considerable collusion, peer group support, and organization. Though departmental reaction usually results in suspension, dismissal, or criminal charges, the severity and consistency of negative reactions may depend on the degree of community support of the illegal activities being protected.

6. *The fix* refers to quashing legal proceedings and "taking up" traffic tickets. Corrupters are suspects attempting to avoid arrest. Of course, the fix can occur anywhere in the criminal justice system—even in prison, where guards are paid not to "write up" an incident that could result in an inmate losing credit toward time served. Within policing, patrol officers, detectives, and even dispatchers may accept bribes to look the other way. The fix violates legal and departmental rules, and reaction is usually severe when cases are brought to light. In departments where the fix occurs frequently and with considerable regularity, it is a highly organized activity.

7. *Direct criminal activities* involve no corrupter, as the police alone are involved in the activity. Direct criminal activities include crimes of robbery, extortion, and other violence by police officers against suspects, victims, and citizens generally. Lack of peer group support and severe departmental reactions generally underscore the blatant criminal character of these practices. Even so, when officers engage in criminal activities in groups—whether stealing drugs or beating up suspects—the blue code of silence helps protect them from their law-abiding peers and effective control by their department or outside agencies.

8. *Internal payoffs* involve bribes within the police department for such things as assignments, hours, promotions, control of evidence, and credit for arrests. By virtue of their job assignments, some officers are in a particularly good position to take payoffs. An example is the dispatcher, who can give or deny patrolling officers all sorts of favors that ease the burdens of a shift. The internal payoff system is usually highly organized and there is extensive peer group support. Departmental reaction is tolerant if it means a more satisfied work force and does not involve breaking high-priority rules. (Roebuck and Barker, 1974)

Needless to say, these categories are not mutually exclusive in the life of any given police officer: He or she could be found engaging in more than one type at the same time. Furthermore, it is not uncommon to find a progression from corruption of authority to more serious violations. This is why some police departments have outlawed perks and have made taking them a suspendable offense—what begins as "just being friendly" may end up as bribery, kickbacks, payoffs, and direct criminal activities. Such was the case with former New York City police officer Michael Dowd. On July 12, 1994, Dowd was sentenced to fourteen years in prison on racketeering and drug charges. According to his own testimony, what began as petty perks taken on the job ended in ongoing criminal activities, shakedowns, and regular use of the fix.

Recognizing that improper police actions include various dysfunctional behaviors not clearly encompassed by the above typology—for example, sexual harassment, discrimination, violation of civil rights, and verbal mistreatment—there is an alternative way of looking at police deviance. It rests on the distinction between two types of police conduct: occupational deviance and abuse of authority. *Occupational deviance* concerns activities made possible by the nature and organization of normal work activity. Some are occupation specific:

> [M]any forms of deviance may be committed only by those who are in a given occupation. For example, only physicians can write fraudulent drug prescriptions and college professors may publish "research results" from false data in order to gain promotion, merit, and tenure. Similarly, only police officers can threaten to arrest in exchange for sexual favors or accept money in lieu of issuing a traffic ticket. The common elements in all of these acts is that they are committed by "normal" persons during the course of their occupational activity and the behavior is a product of the "powers" inherent in their occupation. (Barker and Carter, 1994: 7)

Occupational deviance thus includes many corrupt practices, as well as simple misconduct such as sleeping on the job. The key element is that occupational deviance has an internal locus: "It is concerned with how an officer performs as an organizational member, rather than the method by which the officer discharges his/her police duties" (9).

The second element in this model, *abuse of authority*, encompasses physical abuse such as brutality and misuse of force, psychological abuse, and legal abuse such as the violation of a person's constitutional rights. Unlike occupational deviance, abuse of authority has an external locus because it addresses the authority relation linking the police to the public—who make up the police "clientele"—and concerns the manner in which the police carry out their lawful function.

In addition to the distinction of locus, three other distinctions are noted. One concerns motivation, the second concerns police department liability, and the third involves peer tolerance. Abuse of authority is less likely to be motivated by personal gain or gratification, and, largely because of this, is more likely to be tolerated by police peers. But it is also more likely to result in lawsuits claiming civil rights violations. This occurs because the police have exceeded their lawful exercise of authority and may have violated constitutional protections.

CHAPTER SUMMARY

Criminal justice and criminology are highly related areas of study. The core components of the U.S. criminal justice system are the police, courts, and corrections, but the system also includes public interest groups, lawmakers, and assorted private industries. The criminal justice system can be thought of metaphorically as a leaky funnel. Very few people who are arrested end up in prison. The discretionary decisions by the police, prosecutors, and courts account for most of the leaks in the funnel. There is an abundance of evidence to show that gender, race, and class are related to the exercise of discretion. For example, the data on capital punishment clearly supports the notion that due process varies by social status.

Many popular, political, and scholarly views on crime hold that the nature and form of the U.S. criminal justice system has something to do with the causes of crime. The relationship between criminal justice and criminal behavior is complex. The police can deter some crime through proactive policing and patrol. The courts may be able to prevent some crime by incarcerating criminals and providing opportunities for reformation and rehabilitation. The most politically popular justification for punishment is deterrence, but the evidence on the effectiveness of the deterrence doctrine is mixed, and no study has clearly shown that the death penalty is a deterrent to crime.

Crimes by the criminal justice system, like crime generally, consists of many different activities. Some of these are blatant violations of the criminal law, while others are violations of administrative rules and regulations or constitutional protections. Nevertheless, they result in someone's victimization and may even target society as a whole by undermining respect for the law and encouraging lawbreaking generally. Although no criminal justice agency is immune from crimes among its members, the police have received most of the attention, perhaps because there are more of them and they have more opportunities for crime. Crimes of the police range from taking perks on the job—which can result in some people getting more police protection and others less—to theft, violence, and dealing drugs.

Key Terms

blue code of silence
criminal justice
deterrence doctrine
deterrent effect
discretion

field interrogation
general deterrence
grand jury
incapacitation
mandatory sentencing
preliminary hearing
proactive policing
probable cause
reformation
rehabilitation
selective enforcement
specific deterrence

Recommended Readings

Barlow, Hugh D. (2000). *Criminal Justice in America*. Upper Saddle River, NJ: Prentice-Hall.

Browne-Marshall, Gloria J. (2007). *Race, Law, and American Society: 1607 to Present*. New York: Routledge.

Currie, Elliott. (1998). *Crime and Punishment in America*. New York: Henry Holt.

Shelden, Randall G., and William B. Brown. (2002). *Criminal Justice in America: A Critical View*. New York: Allyn and Bacon.

Walker, Samuel, Cassia Spohn, and Miriam DeLone. (2003). *The Color of Justice: Race, Ethnicity, and Crime in America*. 3rd ed. New York: Wadsworth.

Recommended Web Sites

Sourcebook of Criminal Justice Statistics (http://www.albany.edu/sourcebook/). A voluminous collection of criminal justice data in easy-to-read tables.

National Criminal Justice Reference Service (http://www.ncjrs.org/database.htm). Thousands of abstracts and citations for those doing criminal justice research.

CRIMINOLOGICAL THEORY: ROOTS AND BRANCHES

Criminologists study how, why, when, where, and under what conditions crime and victimization occur. Criminologists look to social environments, the economy, institutions such as schools and families, group dynamics, and individual decision-making processes to help make sense of the nature, extent, distribution, and definition of crime. More formally, scholars of crime have created and tested dozens of theories in order to better understand, explain, and hopefully do something about crime in the real world. Such study and theorizing is not as straightforward and simple as it may sound. The truth is that there is "a lot going on" with crime, and criminological theories try to find out what exactly these things are.

Let's start with a classroom example. Occasionally we ask our students at the beginning of our criminology classes the difficult question "What causes crime?" In response, it is not uncommon for students to identify things such as poverty, dysfunctional families, racism, peer pressure, laziness, and the lack of good jobs. When probed to elaborate, some argue that if people can't find a good job, they can't pay the bills, and so they decide to commit crimes (for example, steal money or sell drugs) to get by. Other students say that when parents fail to provide rules and guidelines for their children's behavior, there can be no accountability, let alone discipline, and therefore kids will be more likely to get into trouble because they do not fear punishment. Criminologists have found that while both of these lines of reasoning may have some merit, they do not capture the real working dynamics or root causes of crime commission. Because crime is complicated, there are no easy answers. In the explanation of crime, as in real life, things are often easier said than done.

Attempts to explain why people violate rules is not new, and what we now call criminological theory dates back to the middle of the eighteenth century. The pioneers in the area of theoretical criminology were trained in a variety of disciplines. Cesare Beccaria (1738–1794) and Jeremy Bentham (1748–1833) were philosophers and students of law; Cesare Lombroso (1835–1909), regarded as the founder of criminology, was a physician and surgeon; Raffaele Garofalo (1852–1934) was a professor of law and a magistrate; Enrico Ferri (1856–1929) was a criminal lawyer and member of the Italian parliament. Although people from many disciplines continued to make important contributions to the field over the years, theoretical criminology found its primary academic home in departments of sociology, although it is ever more closely associated with criminal justice departments as well.

The basic goal of **theory** is *explanation*. Explanations are important because they help us figure out why things are the way they are and suggest what might be done to change things. In this sense, criminological theory's main job is to render crime more understandable. This simple way of conceptualizing theory reflects the diversity of applications that theories have in criminology. Every academic discipline has theory, for theory drives basic questions about the subject matter. Indeed, theory is inescapable in virtually all aspects of life and human activity. Without it "we would be lost in space and time" (Pfohl, 1985: 10). Sometimes theories are found in places not obvious to the causal observer. For example, when preparing to cross a busy street, one considers how best to do so by evaluating the flow of traffic versus the distance to be traveled. When parenting, decisions are made about the proper balance to strike between the discipline and support of a child. When you made the decision to enroll in college, your understanding of the value of education in the marketplace and in your vision of the future helped determine your course of conduct. In all of these cases, theories have instructed decision making by helping to make sense out of a situation, and by providing options and rationales for action. Theories exist in a wide range of popular culture contexts such as sports (there is plenty of theory behind baseball, football, golf, hockey, basketball, running, and almost every other sport), music (in which theories instruct how notes, rhythms, chords, and harmonies can be meaningfully organized), and card and casino games (which have plenty of mathematical theories that apply to player strategies, e.g., card counting in blackjack, probability play in poker). There are even theories about theories, known as metatheories.

As we discussed in chapter 1, criminology is the study of lawmaking, lawbreaking, and the reactions to crime. Criminology is a rich field of study with many ideological, intellectual, and methodological disagreements. This partially explains why there are several dozen theories in the field, all of which will be reviewed in this text. Many of the theories

attempt to explain why certain people commit crimes. Other theories attempt to explain why some places have higher crime rates than others or focus on the social conditions under which crime rates rise and fall. There is also a group of theories in criminology that try to explain lawmaking itself—the process by which certain behaviors or people are labeled criminal. Still other criminological theories attempt to shed light on the purpose of criminal justice itself, victimology, and the politics of crime and justice.

If the purpose of criminological theory is to explain crime, how do criminologists judge its success and value? Surely a theory should be logical, testable by research, and defensible in the face of criticism, but let's consider some less obvious criteria for evaluating the quality of a theory:

- *The theory should shed light on the topic under study.* Imagine yourself in a dark room. What do you see? Now flip on the light. Can you see things more clearly? Are things that were otherwise not in view now visible? A good theory should function like a light switch. Of course, the brighter the light it triggers, the better. As you will see in later chapters, some theories cast more light than others.
- *Theory should specifically point out the relationships between variables.* A variable is anything that changes or can have different values. Theories specify how relevant variables are logically linked to the problem in need of explanation. For example, a few theories of crime hold that economic status is linked to crime because of shifts and changes in the unemployment rate. A theorist adopting this approach must specify how changes in the independent variable (unemployment rates) impact the frequency and distribution of crime (the dependent variable). More generally, a good theory correctly predicts the outcomes produced by changing circumstances.

- *Theory should be helpful in guiding research and future theoretical developments.* To some, theory for its own sake is surely a stimulating intellectual exercise, but theory is especially meaningful when it can be articulated and applied in the real world. Although it is true that theories have an indirect influence on many aspects of criminal justice policy and practice, often the actors (lawmakers, police officers, judges, etc.) are not cognizant of the academic versions of theory and therefore not necessarily informed of the potential or substantiated drawbacks discovered in the academic community. Alternatively, some theorists we have talked to care little about the practical side of their work, choosing to instead leave those matters to others. Yet putting theory to work in the real world is, overall, a vitally important part of criminology (Barlow, 1995).

- *Theories should hold up under empirical scrutiny.* Flip through any major criminology journal and you'll likely find articles that in some way attempt to gauge the veracity and explanatory power of a theory. Such tests are important in any academic discipline, as theories that have been consistently shown to be weak should be reworked or eschewed in favor of better explanations. However, caution should be used when discussing whether or not a study or group of studies has actually "proved" or "disproved" a theory. In the social sciences such absolutism is difficult to achieve, and instead studies can either be said to have "supported" or "not supported" a theory.

- *Theories should be parsimonious.* Anything said in unnecessarily complicated ways is typically less useful than things said in a straightforward and direct manner. One of the reasons undergraduate students often dislike theory is because it seems unclear and abstract. At the same time, if a theory is not sufficiently broad to explain a given set of variables, it has little use in the academic community. This tension is better balanced by some theories than others, as we shall see in the chapters that follow.

In addition to considering how we can judge the quality and usefulness of theories, we also need to think about the goals of theory more generally. One of these is that a new theory should be able to shed a *different* sort of light on the topic under study than those previously applied. In this vein, several criminological theories are *oppositional*. Such theories develop from an explicit critique of existing modes of explanation. In the late eighteenth century, for example, classical theory (reviewed in this chapter and in chapter 10) introduced the notion of rational choice and in the process refuted supernatural explanations of crime. In like manner, Edwin Sutherland introduced his theory of differential association through a critique of earlier theories, which held that poverty was a major cause of crime. More recent theories reviewed in this book, such as postmodernism and feminism, are also oppositional, for they include fundamental critiques of other explanations of crime as a central step in advancing their own arguments.

Another function of theory is to guide social and criminal justice policy. If there is a need to convince anyone that crime is a highly significant social problem, consider that in the United States alone, billions of dollars are spent each year on governmental crime and criminal justice programs and institutions. Moreover, each year there are millions of victims of crime, and the fear of crime can be paralyzing for people whether they have been victimized or not. The large number of films and TV shows based on crime and criminal justice themes also suggests that there is a long-standing and significant interest in crime (see box 9.1). Perhaps the most compelling—and to some extent controversial—film on crime in recent years is Michael Moore's *Bowling for Columbine*, which is summarized in box 9.2.

BOX 9.1. CRIME IN FILM

For many years the American public has been fascinated with crime. Some of this interest may be because the fear of crime is so widespread. It may also be because people enjoy thinking about others taking chances that they themselves would never consider. Strong interest in crime is also reflected in popular culture, as there are literally thousands of television shows, films, and songs that in one way or another relate to crime or criminal justice.

Regarding crime films, Nicole Rafter writes in *Shots in the Mirror: Crime Films and Society* that the reason for their popularity is often tied to the nature of the heroes:

> Viewers delight in watching characters who can escape from tight spots and outsmart their enemies, all the while tossing down scotch and flipping jibes. Good-guy heroes please us by out-tricking the tricky, tracking down the psychos, solving impossible mysteries. Bad-guy heroes appeal by being bolder, nastier, crueler, and tougher than we dare to be by saying what they want, taking what they want, despising weaklings, and breaking the law with impunity. (2000: 141)

Our examination of the all time highest grossing films in the United States reveals that at least a quarter of them contain some kind of crime theme. The same is true with the American Film Institute's Top 100 Films of the American Century. Organized crime films seem especially popular, as movies such as *Goodfellas*, *Scarface*, and *The Godfather* series rank high in both popular and critics' lists.

Rafter (2000) proposes that crime films not only reflect society's interest in rule breaking, but that they also provide a way to frame the causes of crime as well. For example, if films depict someone committing a crime because of an addiction to hard drugs, viewers may come to believe that this is a cause of crime in the real world. As you read through the following chapters, keep a crime movie or two in mind and see if any of the academic explanations are similar to those provided in the films.

© Stephen J. Boitano / Alamy

Filmmaker Michael Moore speaks during a news conference at Capitol Hill in Washington, D.C., June 24, 2004.

Box 9.2. *Bowling for Columbine* as Pop Criminology

Michael Moore's Oscar-winning film *Bowling for Columbine* is regarded by many as one of the most powerful nonacademic treatments of real world crime to date. In the film, Moore raises fundamental questions about the relationship between social inequality, opportunity, and violence in the United States by exploring destructive individual, corporate, state, and special interest group practices and how they contribute to both interpersonal and social injury. Moore frames crime, especially gun violence, as the result of many factors, including youth alienation, racism, and poverty. He draws attention to the high level of gun violence in the United States by providing a series of powerful images, interviews, stories, and biographies. Among the more poignant of these are:

- An interview with musician Marilyn Manson about those who blame him for the Columbine shootings and similar forms of violence.
- Chilling video that until recently had only been viewed by the parents of children killed or injured at Columbine. The video shows dozens of students who panicked during the assault by Dylan Klebold and Eric Harris.
- Juxtaposing the U.S. government's bombing of an aspirin factory in Kosovo on the same morning that Harris and Klebold slaughtered thirteen people at Columbine High School. Predictably, Moore argues, then-president Bill Clinton only defined one of those actions as violent.
- Taking two young men—one in a wheelchair and the other with a bullet still embedded in his chest—who were shot by Klebold and Harris to Kmart's corporate headquarters to demand that the company stop selling handgun ammunition. After the predictable corporate neutralization of the situation, Moore and the two young men return a few days later—with the media in tow—to again demand some action. Several days later Kmart announces that it is phasing out the selling of such ammunition.
- The story of a woman who left her son to live with her brother because she was forced to work two jobs under Michigan's "welfare to work" program. Her son took a loaded handgun from his uncle's dwelling and then shot and killed one of his first-grade classmates. Moore implies that if Michigan's work policy were more lenient, the boy would have been with his mother and unable to access a firearm.
- Media obsession with the reporting of violent crime. In the case of the first-grade shooting, Moore shows how media agents frame stories without consideration of the effects of poverty on individual decision making and behavior. In another instance, Moore asks a field reporter what would be more attractive: covering a "guy with a gun" or a "baby that is drowning." The reporter picked the former.
- A friendly Moore randomly opening the doors of homes in urban areas in Canada and asking the residents why they really weren't scared when he appeared.
- Moore and sociologist Barry Glassner comfortably standing at the corner of Normandy and Florence in Los Angeles. They are unable to see the famous "Hollywood" sign because of massively thick air pollution. Moore asks a cop standing by if he could arrest the people responsible for poisoning his lungs. After a mumble or two, the cop walks away.

While Moore's film does not represent anything close to an academic breakthrough in the study of crime, it does present a number of compelling visual portraits of victims and offenders that encourages viewers to think about the causes and consequences of crime and violence. And while Moore has come under fire for the film's political slant, there are those in criminology who see this as unproblematic, as many theories of crime reflect ideological beliefs, as we will show later in this chapter.

CHARACTERISTICS OF THEORY

Before we examine particular theories of crime and criminality, it is helpful to consider how they differ. There are four main ways to classify theory: (1) by level of analysis, (2) by paradigmatic structure, (3) by range of explanation, and (4) by causal locus. We shall review each of these classifications in turn.

Levels of Analysis

Some theories deal mainly with large-scale social patterns such as social change or the social, economic, and political organization of society. Crime is viewed as a property of whole groups of people rather than as a property of individuals. Because they focus on how societies are organized, these theories usually relate crime to social structure. They are called **macro-level theories**, but this does not mean they lack relevance for the everyday lives of individuals. Rather, such theories attempt to make sense of the everyday behavior of people in relation to conditions and trends that transcend the individual, and even the individual's neighborhood and community. A macro-level analysis might also include the study of the social origins of criminal definitions, as well as how their enforcement affects group life, including crime itself. Some macro-level theorists are interested in why certain events and people are labeled criminal and others not; other scholars look into the process of constructing criminal definitions itself—among scientists, perhaps, or on the street or in the courtroom.

Some other theories focus on the ways individuals interact with others and with the groups to which they belong. These are called **micro-level theories**, and most share an inter-est in the way social interaction creates and transmits meanings. They emphasize the social processes by which people and events become criminal. For example, as people move from situation to situation, they are confronted with all sorts of messages, rules, and expectations, some of which are not obvious. Through a process of sending, receiving, and interpreting messages, individuals help construct the social reality of which they are a part.

Figure 9.1 provides one way to think about levels of analysis through concentric circles. Criminality is at the center, and around it are some of its influences, such as peer group associations and broader social forces such as the economy.

In reality, some theories do not neatly fit into these categories, while others seem to bridge the two levels. John H. Laub and Robert L. Sampson (1988), for example, predict that structural factors such as household crowding, economic dependence, residential mobility, and paren-

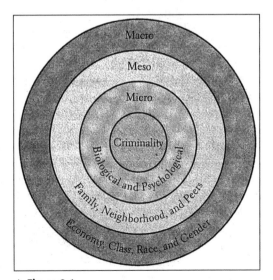

▲ Figure 9.1.
Levels of Analysis and Criminality

tal crime influence the delinquent behavior of children through their effects on the way parents relate to their children day by day. Sociological theories that attempt to explain "micro-macro" dynamics between individuals and society often take this approach. Indeed, it is a daunting but important task to explain how larger social forces shape institutions and groups, and ultimately find expression in the interactions of everyday life.

Paradigms and Criminological Theory

Paradigms are broad assumptions and presup-positions about the nature of social life (*ontology*) and how knowledge is to be gained about social life (*epistemology*). Paradigms are far more fundamental than theories or perspectives—they are indeed the foundation upon which theories are built. There are two basic paradigms in criminology: the **positivist paradigm** and the **social constructionist paradigm**. While some have argued that there are also Marxist, postmodernist, and feminist paradigms, we see these approaches as multidimensional: that is, they combine elements of both the positivist and constructionist paradigms.

The positivist paradigm holds that crime can be known and explained through the scientific method. Crime is considered an objective condition, or social fact, that can be analyzed and understood as an independent phenomenon, regardless of differing ideas about its development and constitution (Michalowski, 1985). A positivist theory of crime asks questions such as "What are the concrete causes of crime?" and "How can crime be controlled or reduced?"

In contrast, the social constructionist paradigm does not assume the objective existence of crime. It emphasizes instead how crime, law, and criminal justice are differently defined and conceptualized by social actors. To these theorists, crime is not an objective condition, nor is the law, the criminal, or the criminal justice system. Criminologists operating from the social construction-ist paradigm might build theories to explore questions such as "Who defines crime and for what purpose?" "How and why are labels attached to certain people and to certain acts at particular moments in time?" and "What are the consequences of the application of labels to people and groups over time?"

General and Restricted Theories

Another important way in which theories differ is in the range of phenomena they try to explain. **General theories** are meant to explain a broad range of facts. They are also not restricted to any one place or time. A general theory of crime, for example, is one that explains many (if not all) types of crime and can be applied to a variety of social and historical settings.

Although some theories in criminology purport to explain all or most crime, few really do meet a sufficiently generalizable level of analysis to satisfy crucial questions of causality or correlation. Sometimes this results in the production of **restricted theories**, explanations designed to apply to a narrower range of facts. A restricted theory of crime might apply to one type of crime or to various types under a limited set of circumstances. Most modern theories in criminology are regarded as restricted, but the development of general theory remains an important goal, and some recent efforts are promising.

Distant and Proximate Causes

Causation is not a simple concept, especially in the social and behavioral sciences. Think about your own behavior for a moment. Right now you are reading this book. How and why you are reading could probably be explained in many different ways; in other words, various causes might be at work. Some of the causes are closer or more immediate—called *proximate causes*—while others are more *distant causes*. A proximate cause might be that your professor assigned this chapter to be read before your next class, which is tomorrow. An even more proximate (and perhaps more powerful!) cause might be that your parents just told you that they would buy you a new car if you got an A in your criminology class. A more distant cause is the expectation that you will follow in your mother's footsteps and become a lawyer. An even more distant cause may lie in the fact that a university education is a requirement for many professional careers and increasingly for other jobs as well.

You look out the window and notice that a friend is not cracking the books, like you are. No surprise, since she's not a college student. But then you wonder why not. Because you know her, you comfortably reject personal explanations based on her intelligence, her drive, and her commitment to getting ahead, and start thinking about more distant factors, such as her background. You remember that neither of her parents has a university education; you recall that she has four brothers and sisters and that only her father works outside the home, as a house painter. You remember that one of her brothers is disabled and that a few years ago her father had an accident and was out of work for two years. You start thinking about other university students you know and about high school friends who never went to college or who dropped out.

Even though it is only a small sample of people, you begin to see patterns. You realize that a university education is explained by a combination of proximate and distant causes, some of which relate to the individual, some to the community and larger society, and some to the social situations people move in and out of in the course of their lives. You recognize, as well, that some causes seem to have a direct impact, while the effect of others is more indirect, working through their impact on something else. Some causes are both direct and indirect: for example, the impact of poverty on behavior may be indirect through its effects on family relationships, and direct through its impact on opportunities and access to them.

IDEOLOGY AND CRIMINOLOGICAL THEORY

The way criminologists visualize their field and its subject matter reflects their particular set of beliefs and values. These beliefs and values—called *ideology*—affect decisions about what to investigate, what questions to ask, and what to do with the knowledge gained. The intrusion of ideology is a normal aspect of the academic enterprise, and the study of crime is no exception. There are a number of competing ideological perspectives in criminology: conservative, liberal, and critical. The latter approach includes feminist, Marxist, postmodernist, and peacemaking theories, which we will review more fully in chapter 15.

Conservative Criminology

Conservative criminology is identified with the view that criminal law is a codification of moral precepts and that people who break the law are somehow psychologically or morally defective. Crimes are seen as threats to law-abiding members of society and to the social order on which their safety and security depend. The "right" questions to ask about crime include: "How are morally defective persons produced?" and "How can society protect itself against them?" The causes of crime are located in the characteristics of individuals, so the solution to the crime problem is couched in terms of a return to basic values wherein good wins over evil. For example, consider Gottfredson and Hirschi's (1990) self-control theory, a moderately conservative explanation of crime discussed later in this text. According to this theory, individuals with low self-control are most likely to commit crimes. The traits associated with low self-control include short-time perspective; low diligence, persistence, and tenacity; a tendency to be "adventuresome, active, and physical"; a tendency to be "self-centered, indifferent, or insensitive to the suffering and needs of others"; and a tendency to have "unstable marriages, friendships, and job profiles"

(91). The major cause of low self-control, according to the authors, is "ineffective parenting," a claim that has much more support in conservative than liberal circles. Until well into the twentieth century, most criminological thinking was conservative. In lay circles, the conservative view enjoyed a considerable boost during the Reagan and Bush years, and to some extent continued to enjoy popularity throughout the Clinton and George W. Bush administrations.

Liberal Criminology

Liberal criminology began to emerge as a force during the late 1930s and early 1940s, and it has remained dominant ever since. The most influential versions of liberal criminology explain criminal behavior either in terms of the way society is organized (social structure) or in terms of the way people acquire social attributes (social process). *Social structure* theories include strain theory, cultural transmission theory, and conflict theory. Strain theory argues that when people find they cannot achieve valued goals through socially approved means, they experience stress and frustration, which in turn may lead to crime. Cultural transmission theory draws attention to the impact on individuals of the values, norms, and lifestyles to which they are exposed day to day. Delinquency and crime are learned through exposure to a criminogenic culture—a culture that encourages crime. According to conflict theory, society is characterized by conflict, and criminality is a product of differences in power exercised when people compete for scarce resources or clash over conflicting interests.

Social process theories include associational theory, control theory, and labeling theory. Associational theories assert that people become criminal through close association with others (family members, friends, or coworkers) who are criminal. Control theory asserts that crime and delinquency result "when an individual's bond to society is weak or broken" (Hirschi,

1971: 16); more room is allowed for individual deviance when social controls are weak. Labeling theory suggests that some people become criminals because they are influenced by the way other people react to them. People who are repeatedly punished for "bad" behavior may eventually accept the idea that they are bad, and their subsequent behavior will be consistent with that identity.

Critical Criminology

Liberal criminologists locate criminogenic forces in the organization and routine social processes of society, yet they do not call for any change in its basic economic, cultural, or political structure. **Critical criminologists** (sometimes called *radical criminologists*) generally do. From a Marxist theoretical perspective, crime and criminal justice have reinforced and strengthened the power of the state and the wealthy over the poor, the working class, and the developing world. To some Marxists, crime and criminality are the products of the exploitative character of monopoly capitalism, and efforts to control crime are poorly disguised attempts to divert attention from the crimes committed by the state, corporations, and capitalists. While Marxism is but one school of thought within critical criminology, the overall approach has largely been shaped by Karl Marx's ideas, such as his call to work for social justice, encapsulated in his dictum: "[T]he philosophers have only interpreted the world in various ways; the point, however, is to change it" (quoted in Tucker, 1978: 143).

Feminist theories in criminology focus on how gender relations and patriarchy constitute and impact the nature, extent, and distribution of crime; responses to crime; and victimization. Theoretical criminology, like most academic areas, has historically been male centered, sexist, and either ignorant or dismissive of issues related to gender inequality and discrimination. Since the 1970s, however, there has been a substantial increase in the study of the gendered nature of the causes and consequences of crime, although the extent to which more radical forms of feminist criminology have impacted mainstream criminology is considerably less than that of liberal forms of feminism.

Another critical criminological approach is postmodernism, which employs notions of chaos and unpredictability in the understanding of crime and questions conventional ideas about the value of science in explaining crime (Ferrell, 2003; Henry and Milovanovic, 2003). Postmodernism is clearly an oppositional theory, and is really a loose collection of "themes and tendencies" that include the rejection of scientific methods, the notion of Truth, and the legitimacy of the state (Friedrichs, 1998: 83; Schwartz and Friedrichs, 1994). Criminological postmodernism also sensitizes us to the power of words, especially the so-called crime speak, which is how through language we think about and define the "reality" of crime and justice (Arrigo, 1998; Borkin, Henry, and Milovanovic, 2006; Henry and Milovanovic, 1996; 1999). For example, the phrase "war on crime" suggests a more militaristic than humanist strategy to reduce crime.

Critical criminology has also given rise to what is known as peacemaking criminology. Peacemaking criminologists theorize on how to bring victims, offenders, and communities together in the harmonious resolution of conflict. Borrowing heavily from the ideas of humanist thinkers such as Jane Addams and Mahatma Gandhi, this perspective holds substantial applicability to crime and criminal justice policy, most notably in the form of restorative justice.

All of these ideological positions—conservative, liberal, and radical/critical—can be found in the various theories reviewed in the next several chapters. As you can see, there is much variety within theories of crime, and in the real world of criminology, political ideology is partly responsible for this (see box 9.3). But there is much variety in lots of things.

BOX 9.3. POLITICAL IDEOLOGY AND CRIMINOLOGISTS' THEORETICAL PREFERENCES

A survey of criminologists lends considerable support to the notion that political ideology is related to theoretical preferences. In Anthony Walsh and Lee Ellis's (1999) survey of 138 scholars of crime, 70 identified themselves as liberal, 35 as moderate, 23 as conservative, and 10 as radical.

The study found that criminologists who regarded themselves as more politically conservative or moderate were more likely to favor theories that focus on low self-control and poor disciplinary practices as important causes of crime. Liberals were more likely to favor theories that focus on environmental factors that lead to crime, such as economic and educational inequality. Critical/radical criminologists were even stronger in their belief that these factors are important in the understanding of crime. Moreover, while radicals supported mostly Marxist and conflict theories, conservatives supported theories that do not implicate larger social factors in the causes of crime. Not surprisingly, those claiming to be liberal or moderate "fall in between" radicals and conservatives (14).

The authors indicate that it is unclear whether political ideology causes theoretical preference or whether theory influences a person's ideology. This is an interesting question, for if ideology alone informs theoretical preference, to what degree can criminology be "scientific"? If, however, certain theories are found to be supported in the research and this causes a change in ideology, does this mean that the discipline is more "objective" and committed only to the search for truth? Unfortunately, the answers to these questions are not easy, but what this study points out is that indeed criminology is—and perhaps has always been—"highly fragmented" by political ideology (14).

Consider, for example, tactics used in sports. Just as there are different ways to catch a fish, pitch a baseball, or hit a golf ball, there are different ways to approach the study of crime. Further, not all theories of crime are suitable at all times or in all places. What pitcher would only have one pitch in his repertoire? What angler would only have one lure? What golfer would use a putter on the tee? The same holds true with theories of crime, as criminologists have devised a number of different theories to explain what causes crime. But, as you will discover, the large number of theories in criminology is not necessarily negative, as crime itself is widely variable, changing over both time and space.

Another reason why there are so many criminological theories is that crime is an immensely variant phenomenon. From a strictly legalistic standpoint, crime includes a huge range of offenses, from property crimes like burglary and theft to violent crimes such as murder, rape, and assault. Criminologists also study white-collar crimes, which involve the violation of trust in the context of work. Examples of such crimes include embezzlement, environmental contamination, violations of worker safety laws, and genocide. With such a variety of behaviors that fall under the label "crime," it is clearly a daunting task to try to intelligently explain the causes and correlates of these various behaviors. But this is exactly what many criminologists attempt to do.

CHAPTER SUMMARY

The main purpose of theory is explanation. Criminologists create, test, and apply theories in order to understand the nature, extent, definition, and consequences of crime. Theories should be able to shed light on understudied or poorly understood problems, specify the relationship between variables, guide criminal justice policy, be economical, and hold up to empirical scrutiny. Theories are classified by their level of analysis, paradigmatic assump-tions, causal focus, and scope. Macro-level theories deal with large-scale social patterns; micro-level theories focus on the interaction of individuals and on the manner in which meanings are created and transmitted in social situations. General theories explain a broad range of facts; restricted theories apply to a narrower range of facts. A general theory thus subsumes more restricted theories. However, the development of general theory is extremely difficult, and most modern theories in criminology are regarded as restricted. Paradigms structure how theorists go about viewing the world in a fundamental way. The positivist paradigm assumes the objective existence of social phenomena, while the social constructionist perspective guides the investigation of subjective, interactive, and definitional processes.

Theories reflect the values, beliefs, and academic disciplines of those who propose them. Conservative criminological theories explain crime in terms of the moral or psychological defectiveness of individuals. Liberal theories explain crime in terms of normal social conditions and processes that characterize group life. Critical theories explain crime in terms of the exploitative character of capitalist society, patriarchy, or modernism. Crime is an immensely complex and variant phenomenon, requiring equally complex and variant attempts to explain it.

KEY TERMS

conservative criminology
critical criminologists
general theories
liberal criminology
macro-level theories
micro-level theories
paradigms
positivist paradigm
restricted theories
social constructionist paradigm
theory

CHAPTER

10

CLASSICAL AND RATIONAL CHOICE THEORIES

A5TC3N Alamy

Perry Ferrell, former lead vocalist of the band Jane's Addiction, sings of a simple rationale for shoplifting in the song "Been Caught Stealin'": Why pay for something if you can just take it? Indeed, why not do things that give you pleasure as long as you won't get in too much trouble for it? This kind of reasoning has intrigued criminologists, and whole theories of crime have been developed around the idea that people are rational because their behavior is a result of their quest to maximize pleasure and minimize pain. This is not a popular way of thinking about crime, as the phrase "It comes down to individual choice" is a comment we have heard many times from our criminology students. The logic behind this statement is that although

environmental conditions can affect a person's views and behavior, ultimately an individual makes a choice to act, including in ways that are criminal. Therefore, the individual should be at the center of attention when attempting to explain the causes of crime.

Modern criminological theory is no stranger to this line of reasoning, although it is not simply a matter of focusing on the person to the exclusion of all background factors. The **rational choice theory** of decision making predicts that individuals think about the expected rewards, costs, and risks of alternative actions and choose actions best suited to their goals. If such an explanation has merit, it should be revealed not only in the choice to commit crime, but also in the choice to commit one kind of crime rather than another and in the decision to direct crime against one victim rather than another. Before we discuss the foundations of rational choice theories, in box 10.1 we will consider the idea of rationality as it applies to attending a college class.

CLASSICAL THEORY

The end of the eighteenth century in Europe was a time of great transformation. As the Industrial Revolution motored on, populations swelled; people moved from the country to the city, working for wages rather than for themselves or rent; and a new political economy—capitalism—acted to fundamentally restructure the more simplified arrangements of barter exchange and feudal social organization. On the political level, the traditional authority of monarchies was under attack, as political radicals, some of whom were philosophers and scholars involved in the Enlightenment intellectual movement, championed the ideas of democracy, rationality, and free will. Intellectuals began to view people's behavior as motivated by their rational choice, not as a result of some supernatural or demonological force. This view of human nature was that people possessed free will and were guided

BOX 10.1. HOW RATIONAL IS COMING TO CLASS?

Think for a moment about your decision to attend a particular class meeting. Using rational choice theory, we would expect that this decision is based on your perception of the rewards and costs of doing so. What are some of the more immediate factors you might consider? Surely it would seem beneficial to come to class if the instructor rewards attendance, bases exams on lectures, or makes the class interesting. Some costs might be that you are tired and could use the sleep, you don't find the class interesting, or you think that the material to be covered in a particular class won't make much of a difference in your grade.

As college professors, we have noticed that attendance in our classes follows an interesting pattern. The first few weeks of class tend to have better attendance rates than those weeks in the middle of the semester. We also find that attendance peaks in a class right before an exam, while it decreases the class session immediately after the exam. Friday classes are almost always the most poorly attended, unless an exam is being given. From your experience, how do you think such patters can be explained through rational choice theory?

There may be larger, less immediate costs and benefits that enter into the equation as well. Perhaps you are so committed to the goal of graduating from college that you are willing to sacrifice being understimulated or poorly rewarded in a particular class. Even though you might have little to gain from attending the class, you might think that not doing so increases the risk of failure in some way. On the other hand, a person may not be all that committed to school, so the thought of missing an important class is not that big of a deal. Further consider that many college students work outside of class and have dependent family members, and that on some days work and family may have to take precedence over school. Another consideration is that every hour spent in the classroom is an hour not spent earning a wage. Students seem to be willing to justify that cost by thinking that in the long run, a college education will help them make more money. These are only a few things that could enter into the decision-making process involved in coming to class. Can you think of others?

Rare is the person who actually sits down with pencil and paper and meticulously calculates the overall costs and benefits of going to a class—or of engaging in criminal behavior, for that matter. Further, costs and benefits are bounded by space and time, and their relativity only underscores the fact that their salience can vary from individual to individual and context to context.

For further reading on the relativity of rationality in criminal decision making, consult Pogarsky (2002).

by a sort of cost/benefit analysis; thus, it was proposed that people choose their own destiny rather than being forced by circumstance or demons into action. Previously popular supernatural explanations of behavior lost their popularity rather quickly in the wake of the Enlightenment (Pfohl, 1985).

Cesare Beccaria and Jeremy Bentham, both products of this new intellectual movement, were among the first European scholars to write on issues pertaining to crime and criminal justice. Their writings were directed not only toward explaining crime, but also how a rational, fair, and democratic criminal justice system could be designed. The so-called **Classical School** had two main foci: (1) a program for changes in the administration of justice and (2) a limited theory of crime causation.

Regarding the relationship between the state and the control of its citizens, Beccaria wrote that: "every act of authority of one man over another, for which there is not an absolute necessity, is tyrannical. It is upon this then that the sovereign's right to punish crimes is founded" (1993: 9). Essentially, Beccaria and Bentham subscribed to the philosophy of **utilitarianism,** which holds that policies and deeds, particularly those associated with the government, should provide the greatest good for the greatest number of people. Applying this reasoning to law, Bentham wrote:

> The end of law is, to augment happiness. The general object which all laws have, or ought have, in common, is to augment the total happiness of the community; and therefore, in the first place, to exclude, as far as may be, every thing that tends to subtract from that happiness: in other words, to exclude mischief. (1973: 162)

The views of Becarria and Bentham are consistent with such modern notions as the presumption of innocence, judicial neutrality, and proportionality in sentencing. They were also opposed to the torture of prisoners and capital punishment. Further, Classical School scholars emphasized that punishment was a "necessary evil" and justifiable only if based on reasonable, humane, and rational processes. More specifically, Bentham believed that punishment should not be given when it is

a. *Groundless* (the act is not really mischievous)
b. *Inefficacious* (ineffective as a deterrent)
c. *Too expensive* (where the trouble it causes exceeds the benefits), and
d. *Needless* (where the crime may be prevented or dissolved in some other way). (1973: 162)

Bentham and Becarria also emphasized that punishment should be proportional to the harm caused to *society*, not tailored to the individual victim's preferences or the particular qualities of the individual offender. This approach is implied by the commonly used phrase "let the punishment fit the crime." In this way, classical theory's main focus is on the crime, not the offender. All persons were assumed to be operating under the same kind of rationality.

Classical scholars also provided a rough theory of crime causation. They believed that criminal behavior resulted from the rational calculation of costs and benefits associated with the criminal act. The idea that people are *hedonistic* (pleasure seeking) guided their work. A central prediction stemming from this idea is that people are more likely to commit a crime if the pleasure (perceived benefits) from the behavior outweighed the pain (perceived costs). Classical School thinkers thought that the most likely "cost" in the equation would be detection, apprehension, and punishment.

Not just any old punishment will do, they said. As discussed in chapter 8, the threatened punishment for criminal behavior was thought to work best as a deterrent if it was (a) certain, (b) proportionate to the harm caused by the crime, and (c) swiftly imposed. If these conditions were met, an individual would be less likely to recommit a crime (specific deterrence) and others would be deterred from crime because of the costs (general deterrence).

Beccaria and Bentham's ideas have also greatly influenced criminal justice policy both in the United State and abroad. Some of their views on the causes of crime and the criminal justice system have, in a sense, "stood the test of time," as deterrence and rational choice models of decision making are popular with the general public and many people working within the criminal justice system. But while seemingly related policies like "three strikes and you're out" and long mandatory minimums for minor offenses are often said to be guided by classical theory, they in actuality may be inconsistent with the original theory, especially if the punishment is too harsh for the crime. Ironically, the Classical School's emphasis on due process (such as fair trials and the right to appeal) is not as popularly supported in the United States.

THE ECONOMIC MODEL OF CRIME

More contemporary formulations of the classical view have been advanced by economists

BOX 10.2. MODERN-DAY RESEARCH ON DETERRENCE

To summarize, many amateur observers of crime often base their views on crime and punishment in a way first articulated by Classical School scholars, but deterrence theory has not been shown to be as valid as many believe.

Over two hundred years have passed since Bentham and Beccaria laid the foundation of the deterrence theory of punishment, and their ideas are still relevant to today. During that time a conventional wisdom emerged that punishment deters if it is certain, swift, and reasonably severe, but modern science has not confirmed that wisdom.

The inability of the scientific community to substantiate—or reject—the conventional wisdom (and political belief) that punishment deters crime must be difficult for many people to understand. Most of us can think of anecdotal illustrations of deterrence, from our own personal experience perhaps, or from hearing about other people who refrained from committing a crime because they were fearful of the consequences. But serious researchers find that the complexities of the subject present formidable obstacles to developing conclusive answers (Gibbs and Firebaugh, 1990; Stafford and Warr, 1993). This is not to say that there has been *absolutely* no support in the literature of deterrence theory. Limited support of deterrence has been found in the areas of auto theft (Di Tella and Schardrodsky, 2004), drunk driving (Piquero and Paternoster, 1998; Walker, 1998), luggage theft (Trivizas and Smith, 1997), and crime trends more generally (D'Alessio and Stolzenberg, 1998).

Most surprising, perhaps, is the fact that more than fifty years of research has yet to uncover a deterrent effect for capital punishment (Archer and Gartner, 1984; Bailey, 1998; Cochran, Chamblin, Mitchell and Smith, 1994; Peterson and Bailey, 1991). There is no good research that supports the oft-heard claim that there would be fewer murders if more killers were executed rather than sent to prison. Murders are often unplanned, spur-of-the-moment attacks, and alcohol is usually a factor in them. But even among hardened criminals who may think about risks in planning their crimes (Horney and Marshall, 1992), fear of punishment does not seem to be a major factor in their decisions (Cromwell, 1999; Shover, 1995; Wright and Decker, 1994; 1997).

On balance, the threat of formal punishments is much less worrisome to potential offenders than the threat of informal punishments imposed by relatives, friends, coworkers, or other close acquaintances (Cullen, 1994; Tittle, 1980; Paternoster, Saltzman, Waldo, and Chiricos, 1983 and 1985; Braithwaite, 1989). The average law-abiding citizen is probably more concerned about losing a good job, being ostracized by friends and coworkers, alienating family members (Shoham, 1970). Pogarsky (2002: 432) reminds us that some people are acute conformists, so that moral inhibition or worries over social isolation "may so effectively inhibit conduct that considerations of cost and benefit are not even brought into play."

One criminologist has argued that punishment may backfire under certain circumstances, and this may explain the lack of a deterrent relationship between crime rates and punishment (Sherman, 1993). Sherman suggests that if punishment is seen as unfair or excessive an attitude of "defiance" emerges. This defiance undermines any deterrent effect the threat of punishment might have had. It can also undermine any lingering respect for the law—a consideration in the sentencing of youthful and first-time offenders. Such a reaction has also been noted by Gilligan (1996) in his research on incarcerated murderers, and to some extent by Tittle (1995).

To summarize, deterrence clearly does not score high marks as the basis for a sentencing policy and crime control. Yet the lack of strong evidence does not mean that deterrence theory is disproved. The prospect of swift, certain, and relatively severe punishment may deter some individuals from committing crimes under some circumstances. The difficulty is figuring out who those individuals are, and which circumstances count. Still, rather than reject the deterrence doctrine, more research on these complex issues would seem the more prudent course. It would also seem appropriate for politicians, judges and other court officials to refrain from claiming that harsher punishments will deter crime. The bulk of deterrence research simply does not support this claim.

(Cherry and List, 2002; Cornwell and Trumbull, 1994), and chief among them is Gary Becker's (1968) work on crime, which was cited when he received the Nobel Prize for Economics in 1993. Many complicated models have been developed (Baltagi, 2006), but they all share certain key ideas. First, the approach assumes that individuals *choose* to commit crimes. Second, it is assumed that people will choose the same course of action when confronted by the same alternatives. This is *rationality*, as economists use the term. The choice itself is guided by maximization of satisfactions, or *utility*.

Individuals evaluate possible activities according to utility. The utility of a crime is the expected gain weighed against the probability of being caught and convicted, and the monetary costs, real and foregone, if convicted. When the expected utility of a criminal act is greater than the utility of a noncriminal alternative, the economic model predicts that the criminal act will be selected.

The classical model of criminal behavior assumes that crime follows a calculation in which the perceived rewards, costs, and risks of alternative actions are compared. In itself, this is a bold assumption because it implies not only that people are capable of making such calculations but also that they have the information necessary to do so.

Economists who develop models of criminal behavior often ignore noncriminal alternatives, concentrating instead on variations of estimated costs and benefits associated with crimes. The likelihood of a particular crime (robbery, for instance) is then calculated in terms of variations in the probabilities of arrest, conviction, and imprisonment, and in the economic gains to offenders for robbery, compared with other predatory property crimes. If the gains from robbery are small compared to the risks and costs, but the gains from burglary are greater, then a person acting rationally and voluntarily would choose to commit burglary.

The assumption that choice making is a fully rational exercise—a key assumption of the economic model and also implied in the writings of Beccaria and Bentham—is tempered by some authors who believe in a more limited rationality. It is argued, for example, that most people cannot know all the information necessary to evaluate all possible actions, but instead they reflexively react to opportunities that arise in ordinary situations (Trasler, 1986: 20).

The limited rationality view holds that behavioral choices arise in people's lives routinely and that some involve decisions to commit crime. These choices are structured by several factors, including the social distribution of opportunities and access to them; the knowledge, past experiences, and capabilities of individuals; the conditions that characterize and are created by the social situations in which individuals find themselves; and the measures taken by victims and authorities to prevent them. Individuals make behavioral decisions within the boundaries created by these factors. The chosen actions are rational to the extent that they are purposive (conscious and goal oriented) and reasonable (efficient and economical) in light of goals and alternatives. It is not necessary to assume that criminals carefully plan and execute their crimes or that they use the most sophisticated techniques (Ward, Stafford, and Gray, 2006). Rational choice theories need only assume that some minimal level of planning or foresight occurs (Clarke and Felson, 1993; Hirschi, 1983, Wright, Caspi, and Moffitt, 2004). Of course, whether or not an offender fears arrest or prosecution is crucial to the decision-making process. Box 10.3 reviews some research on this subject.

RATIONALITY AND CRIME: TWO EXAMPLES

Two examples of research on decisions by property offenders are Thomas Reppetto's (1974) study of residential burglary and robbery and Wright and Decker's (1994) study of burglars. Both studies show that offenders do have target preferences and that this was taken into account when they contemplated committing crimes. Burglars looked for unoccupied single-family homes (thus reducing the risk of being seen or heard), with easy access (thus reducing the amount of skill needed to gain entry), which appeared affluent (thus increasing the possible reward), and which were located in neighborhoods where offenders felt they "fit in" (another way to reduce the risk of being noticed) (Reppetto, 1974). At the very least, most burglars want to know *something* about the people who live in the house and the types of things the house contains (Mullins and Wright, 2003; Wright and Decker, 1994). This finding, as we shall see, is supported by more current research in the United States and abroad (Bernasco and Luykx, 2003).

The rationality model receives additional support from studies in England and Holland. Walsh's (1980) study of burglars in Exeter, England, found that although few burglars admitted doing much preplanning or "casing" of targets, most were very concerned about being seen and avoided entering houses likely to be occupied. A second study of English burglars is more detailed and lends further support to the rationality model, while pointing to the importance of situational cues in decision making. Using videotapes of thirty-six houses

seen from a passing van, Trevor Bennett and Richard Wright (1981, 1984) asked fifty-eight convicted burglars to evaluate the houses as potential burglary targets. Most of the burglars were very experienced, so there is no indication whether the findings would apply to occasional thieves or beginners. Although there was considerable variation in target choice, the burglars strongly agreed about certain blocks of houses or about one or two specific homes. When the authors grouped evaluations according to risk, reward, and skill factors, the authors found that the burglars most frequently mentioned the risk of being seen or heard as the decisive consideration. Reward factors became more important than those connected with skill only when given as reasons to disregard a target. Some houses were considered not worth burglarizing regardless of how easy they would be to enter.

These studies did not investigate actual criminal behavior, only what offenders said about it. For that reason they give only inferential support for the rationality model. However, a study of actual robberies of convenience stores and the crime prevention effectiveness of various security measures found that only six of eighteen measures were significantly related to the frequency of being robbed, and only two of these had the expected impact: Stores with space around them and those with only one employee on duty were robbed more often (Calder and Bauer, 1992). It is also true that criminals might not evaluate situational cues about ease of access and neighborhood surveillance all the time, especially when they are "desperate for money, feeling impulsive or bloody-minded, or simply too lazy" (Bennett and Wright, 1981: 16; Shover and Honaker, 1992; Wright, Caspi, and Moffitt, 2004).

It is important to remember that a full-fledged theory of criminal decision making needs to address not just the crime itself, but also the offender's initial involvement in crime. Such a theory must also account for decisions to continue and to terminate criminal activity (Cornish and Clarke, 1986a,

BOX 10.3. THE POSSIBILITY OF ARREST

Many who violate the law may actually spend little time contemplating the risks of crime. Several recent studies have found strong evidence of the insignificance of arrest and punishment in criminal decision making (Shover and Honaker, 1992; Tunnell, 1992; 2000; Wright and Decker, 1994; 1997). Interviews with forty-six persistent property offenders found that the majority gave little or no thought to the possibility of arrest and confinement. Here are some typical comments:

> Q. Did you think about getting caught?
> A. No.
> Q. How did you manage to put that out of your mind?
> A. [I]t never did come into it. . . . It didn't bother me.

Another subject said:

> A. I wasn't worried about getting caught or anything, you know. I didn't have no negative thoughts about it whatever.

And another said:

> A. When I went out to steal, I didn't think about negative things. 'Cause if you think negative, negative things are going to happen. . . . You just, you just put [the thought of arrest] out of your mind, you know. (Shover and Honaker, 1992: 5)

Another study found evidence of a similar line of reasoning:

> Q: As you did the burglaries, what came first—the crime or thinking about getting caught for the crime?
> A: The crime comes first because it's enough to worry about doing the actual crime itself without worrying about what's going to happen to you if you get caught. (Tunnell, 1990: 37)

Retrospective interviews are not without drawbacks, not least among which is the validity of reconstructions of events long past (Shover and Thompson, 1992). It remains to be seen whether more proximal memories confirm the lack of a negative relationship between perceptions of risk and criminal activity among able offenders.

Studying *active* offenders (those not imprisoned) has several obvious advantages over studying incarcerated persons. However, several recent studies of active burglars, robbers, and drug dealers have found that most crimes are not well planned out. However, there is a tendency for incarcerated offenders to make it sound as though they are (Wright and Decker, 1994).

Criminal justice policy is often misplaced in its assumption that active criminals seriously weigh the costs and benefits of committing a crime in a way envisioned by the average American. Just like any behavior, illegal behavior surfaces within a social context. This has been called the *socially bounded decision-making process*. As Shover and Honaker note:

> The lesson here for theories of criminal decision making is that while utilities and risk assessment may be properties of individuals, they are also shaped by the social and personal contexts in which decisions are made. Whether their pursuit of life as party is interpreted theoretically as the product of structural strain, choice, or even happenstance is of limited importance. . . . If nothing else, this means that some situations more than others make it possible to discount or ignore risk. (1999: 20)

1987). Traditionally, criminology has been more concerned with background influences such as social structure and prior experience and less with situational and transitory influences, which may influence certain types of criminal activity even more significantly.

CRIME DISPLACEMENT

Whenever criminally motivated persons decide not to commit a crime or avoid certain victims in favor of others, the substitution is commonly referred to as **crime displacement**. Five types of displacement have been identified:

- *Temporal displacement*: Here, an offender substitutes one time of day, week, or even season for another.
- *Spatial displacement*: An offender substitutes one street, neighborhood, area, or region for another.
- *Target displacement*: An offender substitutes an easier, less risky, or more rewarding target in the same location.
- *Tactical displacement*: An offender substitutes one modus operandi (method of operation) for another.
- *Type of crime displacement*: One type of crime is substituted for another, usually one that is less risky or more easily performed. (Hakim and Rengert, 1981)

Displacement is important for two reasons. First, its occurrence is predicted by the rationality model. The idea is that criminals generally take advantage of or seek the best criminal opportunities, those with the greatest rewards at the fewest risks and costs. Second, displacement is important because it is one of the potential costs of crime prevention efforts. For example, when criminal opportunities are reduced by police surveillance or other "target-hardening" measures, the net result may be an increase in crime in another place. Criminally motivated individuals simply move to the "safer" areas to commit crime. Therefore, one community may benefit from crime prevention efforts, while another may suffer because of them. It should be kept in mind, however, that offenders often take big risks for very small gains (Wright, 2000). This is partially explainable by the need to support a drug habit or a strong desire to continue "partying." It can also be understood as an irrational, sensual, or thrill-seeking activity not readily understandable to the outside viewer (Katz, 1988).

Research on crime displacement is sparse because it is extremely difficult to measure substitution behavior as it occurs. At the least, one would need to show that one criminal event occurred and some other did not because the offender changed his or her mind after evaluating the situation. Criminologists often infer displacement from studies of spatial or temporal changes in the volume of crime or by asking offenders if, when, and why they made substitutions. Most studies are further limited because they focus only on temporal or spatial displacement.

Spatial displacement is probably quite limited because "criminals prefer to operate in known territory" (McIver, 1981: 32; Bernasco and Luykx, 2003). This in itself is a sign of rationality, for familiarity reduces an offender's risk of being caught and may contribute to successful completion of the crime (Wright and Decker, 1994). Nevertheless, some studies show that police crime prevention efforts resulted in "spillover" effects: Crime rates increased in neighborhoods adjacent to areas with more concentrated police enforcement. However, displacement is more likely to occur with property crimes, not with crimes of violence. The latter may be relatively impervious to displacement pressures because they are more likely to be spur-of-the-moment and tend to occur at the criminals' homes, near local bars, and so forth.

English studies lend tentative support to the displacement argument, at least for some crimes. When steering locks were introduced in new British cars as a target-hardening measure, the rates of auto crime did not drop significantly. Apparently many thieves turned their attention to the abundant older cars that did not have steering locks. In addition, determined thieves quickly learned how to overcome the devices. This suggests that displacement brought about by changes in skill factors is probably limited to amateur and opportunistic thieves. However, a similar program in West Germany had the effect of lowering the overall rate of car theft because it required that *all* cars be equipped with the devices (Felson, 1998; Mayhew, Clarke, and Hough, 1992).

A third British study surveyed the impact of installing closed-circuit television in some London subway stations (Mayhew et al., 1979). Generally, stations with the greatest volume of traffic experienced more robberies and other property crimes. After authorities installed television cameras in high-traffic stations, the volume of robberies declined, but it increased dramatically in stations without surveillance. On the other hand, other thefts declined throughout the subway system during the three-year test period. This finding suggests that an offense-specific spatial displacement took place rather than any general displacement. Apparently robbers took the new surveillance into consideration, merely changing location. Other thieves—perhaps less committed or less experienced—were apparently more likely to view the TV cameras as evidence of a more concerted law enforcement effort. Reacting to this perception, offenders reduced their activity, at least for a time.

Displacement is thus not an inevitable result of crime prevention efforts such as target hardening (Clarke and Felson, 1993; Felson, 1998; Welsh and Farrington, 1999). Prostitution is another case in point: One study showed that increased police enforcement in a North London suburb did not cause prostitutes to move elsewhere (Matthews, 1986). Studies by Ronald V. Clarke and Patricia Mayhew (1988) of the effects of detoxification of the British gas supply on suicide rates showed marked decreases in suicides, but no evidence that suicide-prone individuals

were shifting to other means. Finally, the introduction of motorcycle helmets in various countries has apparently had the unintended consequence of reducing motorcycle thefts (presumably because thieves must carry a helmet with them), but there is no evidence that similar forms of crime—for example, auto theft—have increased as a result (Mayhew, Clarke, and Elliott, 1989).

It is unlikely that many offenders substitute new crimes for old when the calculus of risks, costs, and benefits changes. Income tax evaders, shoplifters, and employee thieves will not become burglars, con artists, and robbers. Some professional or habitual criminals may respond to such changes by increasing their skills and directing their energies only toward the most lucrative targets. They may become better criminals in the process, and they may also become more dangerous—willing to take greater risks, combining into more formidable groups, or increasing their willingness to use deadly force when confronted.

Those criminals most likely to shift from one crime to another, and least likely to continue a given line of crime in the face of increased risks and costs, are the less skilled but more experienced opportunistic offenders. They take advantage of easily accessible opportunities. They are unlikely to increase their efforts and risks in search of less hardened targets with which they may be unfamiliar or which may be too far from home. These are speculations although a study of decision making among property offenders lends them credence (Tunnell, 1992: 149). Considerably more work must be done in both theory and research to untangle the complexities of displacement.

OPPORTUNITY AND ROUTINE ACTIVITY THEORY

Let us now consider how the nature and distribution of opportunities for crime influence criminal activity and shape the contours of crime for specific groups of people.

It will help to think of crime as an event. Crime is not an event until it has occurred, for an event is an occurrence or happening. A criminal event occurs when a situation fortuitously brings together factors that facilitate it. Advocates of a situational approach look at crimes that have occurred and ask what things came together to make them happen.

Crimes differ in so many ways that any attempt to identify basic elements that all criminal events share would probably be doomed from the start. The **situational crime prevention** approach, sometimes referred to as *crime opportunity theory,* is based on ten principles:

1. Opportunities play a role in causing all crime.
2. Crime opportunities are highly specific.
3. Crime opportunities are concentrated in time and space.
4. Crime opportunities depend on everyday movements of activity.
5. One crime produces opportunities for another.
6. Some products offer more tempting crime opportunities.
7. Social and technological changes produce new crime opportunities.
8. Crime can be prevented by reducing opportunities.
9. Reducing opportunities does not usually displace crime.
10. Focused opportunity can produce wider declines in crime. (Clarke and Felson, 1993; Felson and Clarke, 1998: v–vi)

If there is a common element in all events, criminal or not, it is opportunity. An opportunity makes an event possible; a criminal opportunity makes a crime possible. One cannot rob a bank without the opportunity to do so—without the existence of banks. Notice, however, that banks provide not only criminal opportunities, but noncriminal ones as well. In fact, the purpose of most things is not crime, but their existence nonetheless creates criminal opportunities. A functionalist would say that

the above principle is a *latent dysfunction* of otherwise useful objects and institutions.

One version of opportunity theory is known as **routine activities theory**, which holds that there are three essential elements of a crime: (1) a motivated offender, (2) a suitable target, and (3) the absence of a capable guardian (Clarke and Felson, 1993; Felson, 1998). Therefore, the basic proposition of the theory is that "[t]he probability that a violation will occur at any specific time and place . . . is . . . a function of the convergence of likely offenders and suitable targets in the absence of capable guardians" (Cohen and Felson, 1979: 590). If any one of these elements is lacking, a criminal event will not occur. A routine activity is any recurring and prevalent goal-seeking activity. Work is a routine activity, but so are having sex, raising children, having lunch, going to the movies, and vacationing. Much crime can be viewed the same way.

Notice above that no mention is made of "capable" offenders, those able to "pull crimes off" (though they may later be caught). In fact, much crime is unsuccessful, making the distinction between completed and uncompleted crime an important one for theory and research. Indeed, the law has long recognized this distinction, treating attempted crimes less severely than completed ones. From the situational point of view, the distinction is interesting because it prompts one to compare attempted and completed crimes in order to establish the differences, and which elements account for the outcomes.

Technological change makes new activities possible, and some will be labeled criminal if those in authority accept that they should be (see Michalowski and Pfuhl, 1991). The United States government is obviously concerned: It has made changes to its legal currency in response to advanced computers and copying machines that have made counterfeiting easier, and all bills now contain a metal strip embedded within the paper.

Consider what many people now take for granted: electronic funds transfer. Not long ago this computer-based service was known and used only by banks and large corporations. Now the automated teller machine (ATM) is familiar to virtually everyone. Those with personal computers may also take advantage of home banking services. With the spread of electronic funds transfer has come growth in criminal abuse. Some types of crimes resulting from this newer technology include unauthorized use and fraud. Of course, growth in the use of personal computers has opened up many opportunities for crime as well. Such crimes include identity theft, fraud, embezzlement, and blackmail. It is also true that contacts between people have become easier via chat rooms, instant messaging, and e-mail. Thousands of arrests, for example, are made each year of adults soliciting sex from minors and running or viewing child pornography Web sites.

Marcus Felson (2002) offers a more detailed description of the impact of social change on crime in his book *Crime and Everyday Life*. He shows why it is that the United States maintains high crime rates by focusing on crime as an event rather than on the number and motivations of criminals. He concludes that crime has changed as a result of changes in where people live and work, where and when they interact, the type and storage of goods and services that are available, and the movement of goods and people. For example, as city populations dispersed, with more and more people living in single-family homes and in the suburbs and more and more property being spread over larger and larger space, it also became more difficult for people to control their environment and prevent crime. Cities that had previously been "convergent," bringing people and property together, became "divergent," spreading them apart. Work organizations and schools also became bigger, drawing thousands of people often from miles away. People can less readily monitor their own families, let alone the activities of strangers, under such circumstances. Both informal and formal social control, it can be argued, is therefore hampered.

Another way of looking at routine activities is to think of the locations where crimes are likely to occur. Where would you expect handgun crimes to occur most often? Your answer will depend on the routine activities of typical offenders and victims, and on the relationship between the two. Thus, handgun crimes involving relatives are most likely to occur in the home; those involving strangers are most likely to occur on the street. Urban structure has an impact on violent crime, and, within that context, the kinds of lifestyles (routines) people follow significantly affects their chances of being assaulted, robbed, or raped: People who go to bars, work, go to class, or go for a walk or drive at night are more likely to be victimized (Kennedy and Forde, 1990). Similar findings have been discovered in studies of elderly theft-homicide victimization (Nelsen and Huff-Corzine, 1998), homicide more generally (Caywood, 1998), sex worker victimization (Surratt et al., 2004), burglary victimization (Tseloni et al., 2004), and gender differences in all forms of criminal victimization (Felson, 2002; Mustaine, 1997).

CHAPTER SUMMARY

Classical theorists created a theory of justice and a simplified theory of the causes of criminal behavior. The theory of justice was based on utilitarian philosophy that prized a democratic and rationally designed system of punishment and deterrence. The primitive theory of crime causation held that individuals are fundamentally hedonistic, and that they will pursue a course of action if the outcome is perceived to offer more pleasure than pain. Many of Beccaria and Bentham's ideas remain quite popular today.

Modern-day rational choice theories of crime assume that criminals think about their crimes before doing them. Much research supports this basic contention, although the extent to which offenders actually weigh all or even most pertinent factors involved in a crime is probably small. The central message of opportunity-rationality theories is, first, that crime cannot be understood apart from the nature and distribution of opportunities for both criminal and noncriminal behavior, and second, that when criminals find themselves in situations in which they have opportunities to commit crime, the decision to do so or not to do so is a rational one.

The routine activity approach brings rationality and opportunities together to explain the distribution of crime in time and space. Advocates of the approach argue that the everyday activities of people influence the convergence of criminally motivated individuals and suitable, unguarded criminal targets. In this vein, social and technological changes can dramatically affect the nature, extent, and distribution of crime and victimization.

KEY TERMS

Classical School
crime displacement
rational choice theory
routine activities theory
situational crime prevention
utilitarianism

BIOLOGICAL, PSYCHOLOGICAL, AND EVOLUTIONARY THEORIES OF CRIME

23587481 Jupiter

tion within the field that has focused on the biological and psychological causes and correlates of crime. This chapter reviews several of these classical and contemporary theories.

The birth of criminology as science is usually traced to nineteenth-century Europe. By the latter half of that century, the scientific revolution was well under way. The armchair philosophizing of the classical theorists was grudgingly giving way to the logic and methodology of science. Observation, measurement, and experimentation are the basic tools of the scientific method, and their use in the study of human behavior heralded the development of disciplines now taken for granted—biology, anthropology, psychology, sociology, political science, and statistics. Thus was born the age of **positivism**, and crime was placed under the microscope of science. Theories now had to be spelled out, quantified, and falsifiable.

In this chapter we examine classic and contemporary theories of crime that have been influenced by the positivism of natural science. While most criminologists are not formally trained in the hard sciences, important contributions to theories of crime have come from physical anthropologists, biologists, behavioral psychologists, and evolutionary theorists.

It is not uncommon for popular television shows to suggest that crimes, especially violent ones, are committed by individuals with psychological, neurological, or biological abnormalities. However, media infatuation with strange and morbid crimes such as serial murder does not reflect the reality that relatively few crimes are gruesome, let alone violent. Criminal homicide, for example, makes up less than 1 percent of all reported crime, and serial murder but a fraction of all homicides. Yet, as one watches the latest example of serial murder in the news, it is tempting to say that the killer was someone "going mental." While most criminologists look to environmental factors to explain crime, there is a tradi-

Positivism and Early Criminology

The notion that crime could be studied through the methods of science was established early in the nineteenth century by two authors whose work earned them an honored place in the annals of criminology. Working independently, Adolphe Quetelet (1796–1874) and André Michel Guerry (1802–1866) compiled the first criminal statistics and used them to make predictions and comparisons about crime. Others soon followed suit, and these early ventures into social statistics became a model for the later work of Émile Durkheim (1858–1917). "For the first time in history," Leon Radzinowicz has observed, "crime became thought of as a social fact molded by the very environment of which it was an integral part" (1966: 35). This was an important break with the classical theorists, who viewed criminal behavior as stemming from the exercise of free will in the pursuit of pleasure.

A major impetus to the rise of positivism was the work of Charles Darwin (1809–1882) on animal evolution. Darwin's followers argued that human behavior is largely determined by *Homo sapiens'* position on the evolutionary scale and by the ongoing battle for survival. However, the specific impact of these forces on an individual was considered a matter for empirical investigation.

Positivism is not without its critics. The objections to positivism are varied, but primarily they consist of the argument that the so-called objective depiction of "concrete facts" in the world obscures a reality that is socially constructed by the participants in it. The facts are "constructed meanings produced within specific cultural, political, and economic contexts" (Michalowski, 1988: 18). Even the nature of crime itself cannot be taken for granted.

The debate about positivism versus social constructionism is unlikely to be resolved in the near future, and it is certainly possible for both to live side by side and for criminology to profit from their contributions to our knowledge and thinking about crime. Jack P. Gibbs (1988: 4) makes an important point, however: How else are scientific theories about crime to be assessed, if not by testing their predictions against a body of empirical data? This was the great insight of the early positivists, although there was actually very little research going on during this period (Garland, 1985: 128).

BIOLOGY AND THE SEARCH FOR THE CRIMINAL TYPE

Influenced by positivism, early criminologists were convinced that they could uncover the causes of criminal behavior if they could apply the methods of science to the study of human beings. Deviance, they believed, was caused rather than chosen (Pfohl, 1985; Rowe, 2001). The major figure was Italian physician Cesare Lombroso (1911). Like many of his contemporaries, Lombroso believed that criminals must be different from law-abiding people in some important way. The question, according to Lombroso, was *how* they differed, and the search for the criminal type consumed much of his career.

As a physician attached to the army and later to prisons and asylums, Lombroso examined thousands of individuals. Profoundly influenced by the evolutionary doctrine, he searched for physiological evidence of the link between deviant behavior and biological forces. In 1870 he claimed a triumphant discovery: In his view, many of the criminals he had studied were **atavistic**—biological throwbacks to a more primitive evolutionary state. Such "born criminals" could be identified by five or more physical stigmata, or anomalies: an asymmetrical cranium, a receding chin, a low forehead, large ears, too many fingers, a sparse beard, protruding lips, low sensitivity to pain, and deformities of the eye.

But the born criminal was not the only type Lombroso identified, nor did he argue that criminal behavior was solely the result of biological forces. He distinguished other categories of criminals, including insane criminals (idiots, imbeciles, alcoholics, degenerates), criminaloids (those with less pronounced physical stigmata and degeneracy, but pulled into crime by situation or environment), and criminals by passion (those who were neither atavistic nor degenerate, but drawn into crime by love, politics, offended honor, or other intense emotions).

Though the core of his theory was biological, Lombroso recognized the importance of precipitating situational and environmental factors. He mentioned poverty, emigration, high food prices, police corruption, and changes in the law as nonbiological determinants of criminal behavior (Wolfgang, 1961: 207). However, it remained for one of his followers, Enrico Ferri, to undertake serious investigation of the impact of environmental factors (see Sellin, 1937).

Lombroso and his followers had a tremendous impact on the emerging field of criminology. Especially important was the impetus their work gave to research on the individual criminal offender. For more than fifty years, scholars concentrated their efforts on describing and classifying criminals and on distinguishing them from noncriminals (for a critical analysis of this movement, see Garland, 1985).

Many felt that such research would identify traits and characteristics peculiar to criminals. One monumental study was done by anthropologist Earnest A. Hooton (1939). He studied 13,873 male criminals from ten different states, as well as 3,023 individuals regarded to be noncriminals. Hooton's study claimed to show that criminals are organically inferior to noncriminals, though he did not admit that environmental factors could be precipitating influences. Most controversial was his claim that certain types of crimes are committed by certain physical types of individuals: Tall, thin men tend to commit murder and robbery; short, heavyset men are prone to commit

assault and sexual crimes; and men of small frame commit theft and burglary. All this sounds ridiculous now (but see box 11.1), especially as one recognizes that the main differences between most assaults and most murders is the presence of a corpse, and a major difference between one type of stealing and another is the presence of an appropriate opportunity.

Another major study of the relationship between body type and criminality was conducted by William H. Sheldon in the early and mid-1940s. Sheldon (1949) studied a sample of two hundred young men, many of whom had previous involvement in juvenile delinquency. Sheldon examined each subject in great detail, noting each person's body type, temperament, recorded or reported delinquency, basic family history, and mental and physical health. In his book *Varieties of Delinquent Youth*, three pictures are presented of each of the men, from back, front, and side views, along with capsule summaries of their life histories. Sheldon categorized the young men's body forms into three basic types: endomorphic (soft and round), mesomorphic (muscular and athletic), and ectomorphic (slender and fragile). While many of his subjects' physiques were not entirely classifiable into one of the above categories, Sheldon

BOX 11.1. PHYSICAL APPEARANCE AND CRIMINALITY

Modern-day criminologists have little use for the idea that criminals share similar physical attributes. The exception to this is that it is well known that in many Western societies, people of color are more likely to be portrayed as criminal by the media. Numerous scholars, such as Barlow, Barlow, and Chiricos (1995a; 1995b); Greer and Jewkes (2005); and Weitzer and Kubrin (2004) have shown that media images often imply that criminals "look a certain way." As professors with many years of experience in college classrooms, we have heard similar suggestions from students. For example, we have heard that someone "looked like a child molester or serial murderer." We have even been told by a student that her former professor at a different university went to the FBI's "Ten Most Wanted" Web site so that students in his class could compare the suspects' physical similarities and differences. Modern-day criminologists have all but abandoned the search for physiological signs of criminality, but that doesn't seem to stop the media or popular belief that some people "look like criminals."

concluded that, overall, mesomorphs have a higher likelihood of being involved in crime because of their higher level of physical power and aggressiveness. Although Sheldon's research, like Hooton's, is now dismissed by most criminologists because of its questionable methodology and logical contradictions, Sheldon and Eleanor Glueck (1950) found some support for Sheldon's findings in their comparison study of five hundred delinquents and five hundred nondelinquents. Despite the shortcomings of the biological approach represented in the above studies, there are still serious scholars who argue that biological characteristics such as body type predispose individuals to commit crimes (see Wilson and Herrnstein, 1985).

The search for biological correlates of criminal behavior was largely discontinued in the United States during the 1950s and 1960s, partly because studies of human behavior in general were increasingly coming under the influence of the social and behavioral sciences, but also because the necessary research became too costly. There were also many people who simply believed that its focus on pathology was inaccurate (Pfohl, 1985). Although a few Scandivanian scholars (e.g., Christiansen, 1977) organized their studies around biology, U.S. criminologists essentially lost interest in it until the 1980s.

The biological perspective in criminology is by no means a unified approach. Its advocates draw on research from a variety of behavioral sciences, including genetics, physiological psychology, psychopharmocology, and endocrinology. Among the theoretical perspectives found within the biological camp are (1) evolutionary theories, which examine changing environmental conditions; (2) genetic theories, which focus on inherited traits, defects, or deficiencies; and (3) biochemical theories, which focus on hormonal or chemical imbalances.

One example of the third perspective is found in Lee Ellis's (1991) review of research on monoamine (MAO) and its relationship to criminal behavior. MAO is an enzyme that is believed to effect the transmission of impulses from one nerve to another. MAO is heavily concentrated in the brain stem, and its activity is believed to be influenced by both genes and hormones. The importance of MAO for brain functioning is well documented, and low MAO activity is thought to be associated with aggressiveness, feelings or anger and frustration, and various correlates of antisocial behavior such as defiance, poor academic performance, childhood hyperactivity, extroversion, and sensation seeking (Ellis and Walsh, 1997). These associations are modest, but Ellis believes that low MAO may be an important biological marker for criminality.

EVOLUTIONARY THEORIES

Some biologists believe that people are instinctively aggressive, basing their claim on studies of animal behavior. According to Konrad Lorenz (1971), nature gave animals an instinct for aggression for three reasons: (1) to ensure that the strongest males succeed in mating with the most desirable females, thus ensuring a kind of genetic quality control; (2) to protect the physical space, or territory, necessary for raising the young, securing food, and the like; and (3) to maintain hierarchies of dominance and through them a stable, well-policed society.

Following Lorenz and Desmond Morris—the author of *The Naked Ape*—Pierre van den Berghe believes that human behavior is not "radically discontinuous from that of other species," and he advocates a biosocial approach to understanding human violence (1974: 777). Essentially, the argument is that humans, like animals, have predispositions to violence that are innate—that is, biologically grounded. Though conclusive proof of this is still unavailable, one promising indication is that aggression is a universal behavior pattern for a species: In humans, aggression has been observed everywhere, despite widely differing habitats, cultures, and technologies. The viewpoint receives additional support from the documented relationship between aggression and the male hormone testosterone, and the discovery of "aggression centers" in the brain (van den Berghe, 1974; Bailey, 1976; Wilson and Herrnstein, 1985).

Robert L. Burgess (1979; Burgess and Draper, 1989) has drawn on evolutionary theory to explain variations in child abuse and family violence. Burgess argues that mature humans have two related problems: to pass on their genes through successive generations and to protect their offspring despite limited resources. The solution is for parents to invest most in those genetic offspring who show the best prospects for surviving and reproducing and least in nongenetic relatives and/or those genetic offspring who show the worst prospects of surviving and reproducing.

These problems and their solutions produce greater risk of abuse and neglect in families with stepchildren, in poorer families, in those with less education, in those with many children, in single-parent families, and in families whose children have mental or physical impairments. Burgess, along with Ellis and Walsh (1997), cites studies both in the United States and abroad that support these predictions (see also Daly and Wilson, 1988b). However, it should be emphasized that child abuse is not inevitable in families with these characteristics and it is found in many families without them (Ellis and Walsh, 1997).

Martin Daly and Margo Wilson make the following observation on step-relationships and violence:

In view of the costs of prolonged "parental" investment in nonrelatives, it may seem remarkable that step-relationships are ever peaceful, let alone genuinely affectionate. However, violent hostility is rarer than friendly relations even among nonrelatives; people thrive by the maintenance of networks of social reciprocity that will make them attractive exchange partners. . . . The fact remains, however, that step-relationships

lack the deep commonality of interest of the natural parent-offspring relationships, and feelings of affection and commitment are correspondingly shallower. Differential rates of violence are one result. (1988a: 520)

On a broader plane, Daly and Wilson's evolutionary psychological perspective (1988a; see also 1988b) explains the male propensity for violence as the result of the ubiquitous struggle over control and propagation. As Edward Green explains it:

Wife-murder and wife-abuse represent the striving for control over the reproductive capacities of women. Killings arising out of trivial altercations aim to deter rivals from threatening one's interests; they give tangible proof that any such attempt will be met with severe punishment. The predominance of males is due to the greater need of men for additional resources with which to check rivals and attract women. (1993: 32)

Ellis and Walsh (1997) have summarized the key points made by **evolutionary theorists** of crime that lead to the following claims about sexual assault:

- Males should be far more likely to engage in sexual assault. (Logic: males have more to gain because they do not become pregnant and in general have less commitment to their offspring.)
- Rape and sexual assault is found in both human and nonhuman species. (Logic: genes contributing to rape are suspected to be present in many animal types.)
- Victims of rape resist sexual attacks because it does not allow them the choice to select a mate who will help with child rearing. (Logic: some research supports the idea that females are far more choosier about their mates than males.)
- Victims of rape should be females in their child-bearing years. (Logic: while the goal of rape is not to exactly reproduce, it approximates such a drive.)

Theory is about explanation, and at issue here is *why* we see these patterns in sexual assault. Research does indeed support the age/rape, resistance, and gendered nature of sexual assault patterns noted in the points above, but the question is *how to explain* these facts. As we will see in the coming chapters, sociological theories have very different explanations.

Finally, we should note that genetic, evolutionary, and neurological explanations of crime continue to play some role in the modern-day search for the causes of crime (Janssen et al., 2005). Most theorists working in these areas agree that crime is best explained by studying how the social environment and internal physiological systems interact with one another to produce behavior (Ellis and Walsh, 1997; Jeffery, 1994). For example, it is quite true that the brain develops in concert with the environment. Any changes in the functioning of the brain, then, may be related to behavior—including criminal behavior. This means that the nutritional content of food, adverse chemical interactions caused by drug use, and brain trauma or disease may be involved in criminal decision making (Jeffery, 1994). Additionally, some recent genetic studies of twins and adoptees have found some evidence of a hereditary element of criminality, although the correlations are small and many of studies have major methodological limitations (Gottfredson and Hirschi, 1990; although see Ellis and Walsh, 1997). In sum, however, even biological and evolutionary theorists of crime understand that it is a serious mistake to ignore the role of the social environment in providing the context, opportunity, and motivation for much crime.

BIOSOCIAL THEORIES

Advocates of the biological perspective in criminology have been swimming against the tide for many years. However, James Q. Wilson and Richard Herrnstein (1985) helped spark renewed interest in the relationship between biology and criminal behavior. The tide hasn't turned, by any means, but a healthy interest in biological correlates of crime has emerged (Fishbein, 1990). Studies of chronic delinquents have found that, when compared with less delinquent youths, chronic offenders are more likely to suffer from minor birth defects, to have abnormal electrical activity in the brain, or to suffer from various other neurological defects (Buikhuisen, 1988). These correlates of chronic delinquency are believed to influence behavior through their impact on the socialization process. They impede a child's ability to learn and to develop attitudes consistent with self-control, deferred gratification, and restraint. The interaction between biology and social environment lies at the heart of the biosocial perspective.

Biology and Environment

Wilson and Herrnstein take a **biosocial approach** to explaining criminal behavior. They argue that certain constitutional factors, some of which are genetic, predispose people to commit crimes, but also that these predispositions are influenced by social forces as well as by the individual's own personality. In their view, neither biology nor environment alone is sufficient to explain why some people commit crimes and others do not, or why some people commit more crime than others. There is certainly no "crime gene," which means there is no "born criminal" (1985: 69; Ellis and Walsh, 1997). However, Wilson and Herrnstein emphasize that biological factors cannot be overlooked:

> The existence of biological predispositions mean that circumstances that activate criminal behavior in one person will not do so in another, that social forces cannot deter criminal behavior in 100 percent of the population, and that the distribution of crime within and across societies may, to some extent, reflect underlying distributions of constitutional factors . . . . [C]rime cannot be understood without

taking into account individual predispositions and their biological roots. (103)

These theorists infer the existence of biological influences from two observations. First, Wilson and Herrnstein's reading of the research shows that street crimes such as murder, robbery, and burglary are committed by young males who are disproportionately African American and possibly of lower intelligence. The most striking difference is observed for sex: Males are up to fifty times more likely to commit crimes than are females. Second, there is a large body of research suggesting something biologically distinctive about the "average offender." The typical male offender, in their view, is more muscular than other people and is likely to have biological parents who are (or were) themselves criminal.

Wilson and Herrnstein review a vast amount of research to help substantiate their claims, but how exactly are biological forces thought to influence criminal behavior? The authors are more cautious on this point—as well they might be, since many of the findings they review can be explained by other theories. However, their answer seems to rest in the impact biological factors have on (1) the things people consider rewarding, (2) the ability (or desire) of people to think about rewards and punishments that might come in the future, and (3) the ability of people to develop internal moral constraints—the "bite of conscience." Aggressive drives and needs are dominant in males; younger and less intelligent people are more inclined to be impulsive, to want rewards now rather later; and the cognitive skills involved in the development of conscience grow with age and are positively related to intelligence. People who are aggressive, impulsive, opportunistic, and less constrained by conscience are most likely to commit crimes.

Intelligence and Crime

One of the most enduring arguments found in scientific and popular literature is that an-

tisocial behavior is more likely among people with low intelligence. There is little disagreement that intellectual defects are heritable (Fishbein, 1990), and much of the research on intelligence and crime has concluded that boys with lower aptitude are more likely to become involved in delinquency and crime (Hirschi and Hindelang, 1977).

When a certain group of people is found to have disproportionate involvement in crime, the natural inclination is to look for things the people have in common and then attribute the criminal behavior to these things. This is the sort of reasoning that has linked intelligence to the disproportionately high rates of violent crime among African Americans compared with whites (Hindelang, 1978; Hindelang, Hirschi, and Weiss, 1979). To some, if African Americans consistently score lower than whites on intelligence tests, it is a short—but incorrect—step to conclude that African Americans are less intelligent because they are black (Fraser, 1995; Jensen, 1969). The rate of serious crime among African Americans is then explained as a result of biological differences in intelligence or aptitude.

The words *race, intelligence,* and *crime* are controversial in terms of meaning and measurement. Sociologists, for example, do not give any credence to the idea that race has any biological meaning. Rather, race is considered a pure social construction. Environmental differences such as neighborhood, upbringing, economic conditions, schools, nutrition, and discrimination could well account for most—if not all—of the difference in measured intelligence between African Americans and whites. Further, it is well known that the very methodology of intelligence tests is discriminatory, much like the ACT and SAT tests, which really measure exposure to the racially dominant (i.e., white) culture's language, tastes, hobbies, and artistic interests (Fraser, 1995).

Perhaps the most controversial statements on the relationship between intelligence and crime are rooted in Richard Herrnstein and

Charles Murray's (1994) book *The Bell Curve.* The authors argue that an "extensive research literature" shows that low IQ is a risk factor for criminal behavior. Claiming that differences in behavior result from differences in the characteristics of individuals (the classic psychological perspective), as well as differences in their circumstances (the sociological perspective), Herrnstein and Murray write that low intelligence may encourage crime in a variety of ways. First, they argue, low IQ may be associated with failure at school and work, which in turn causes frustration and perhaps resentment toward society and its laws. Second, it is claimed that a person with low IQ is more inclined to look for immediate gratification and tends to discount far-off risks such as arrest and incarceration. Third, the contention is made that a person with low IQ finds it harder to comprehend the moral and civil reasons for not hurting others and obeying rules.

While acknowledging that most people with low IQ are law abiding, Herrnstein and Murray maintain that the average intelligence of offenders is around ten points below that of non-offenders, and that offenders with lower IQs commit crimes more often, and those crimes are more serious. Citing research from abroad as well as self-report data from the United States, the authors conclude that individuals with the cognitive disadvantage implied by low IQ commit crimes at higher rates even when socioeconomic factors, family structure, and education are taken into account.

On the other hand, Herrnstein and Murray recognize that the changes in aggregate crime rates experienced over the past several decades cannot be explained by variations in intelligence. Large or sudden movements in crime rates are due to social forces rather than personal characteristics, yet these same forces nevertheless "may have put people of low cognitive ability at greater risk than before" (1994: 251). For example, while the downward shift in the age of the U.S. population due to the baby boomers, coupled with more permissive child-rearing practices, may largely account for the increased crime rate of the 1960s, Herrnstein and Murray would argue that the criminogenic impact of these forces was greatest among individuals with lower IQs.

Despite the convictions of the authors, the intelligence-criminality puzzle remains to be solved (Guay, Ouimet, and Proulx, 2005). For one thing, if cognitive disadvantage explains criminal behavior, how do we then explain the many varieties of white-collar crime, which are often committed by individuals with college degrees and require higher degrees of forethought, skill, and political capital? Also unclear is how constitutional and environmental factors come together to influence criminal behavior.

PERSONALITY AND AGGRESSIVE TEMPERAMENT

To say that people have an innate predisposition toward violence does not mean they will be violent, nor does it explain different levels and types of violence. Furthermore, as Green points out, "Most men proclaim their 'fitness' for progenitorship in non-violent ways" (1993: 32). The actual display of aggression is affected by triggers and inhibitors, controls that may be innate but also may be learned or situational.

Some psychiatrists believe that humans develop internal inhibitors during early childhood. According to Sigmund Freud, the individual psyche is composed of three parts: the ego, the id, and the superego. Behavior is motivated by those drives that are innate: the sex drive, the aggression drive, and even the death drive. These make up the id. As one develops and interacts with others, the superego emerges. This part of the psyche consists of social ideals and rules that are internalized through socialization. Finally, the ego strikes a balance between the demands of the id and the constraints of the superego.

The aggressive drive is expressed as violence, Freudians believe, when disturbances occur within the psyche. Mulvihill, Tumin, and Curtis put it this way:

> The id may overflow with violent drives: the individual hates too much, enjoys pain too much, or wants to destroy himself.
>
> Sometimes the id is just too much for the ego to control, and the individual breaks out into violent behavior. . . . Alternatively, the superego may be extremely overformed or underformed. If the superego tries to quash all expression of dislike or hatred, and to quell all fantasies about violence, the individual may build up a greater and greater reserve of unfulfilled desire, until he can no longer control himself. Then he becomes violent. If the superego is underdeveloped, the individual simply sees nothing wrong with violence; he will use it whenever the occasion seems to call for it. In the underdeveloped superego, we are not dealing with a "sick" man at variance with his environment; we are rather dealing with a sick environment which has encouraged violence as the "normal" mode of response. (1969: 460–61)

Some psychiatrists locate the seeds of emotional disturbance in parent-child relationships. It is suggested, for example, that the "love bonds" between parent and child are important to regulating the aggressive drive and that destructive behavior is prevented by the formation of stable human relationships in early childhood (Chodorkoff and Baxter, 1969). By the same token, excessive physical disciplining undermines these bonds and, further, teaches youngsters that there is a place for violence in relationships. Although psychiatrists may have much to tell about aggression and violence among those who are "disturbed" or "sick," their work is not helpful in understanding types of violence for entire populations and societies. Indeed, some people question the applicability of the psychiatric approach to even extreme forms of aggression. They point out that violent offenders do not suffer from mental disorders as a rule.

Summarizing the findings of investigations into mental disorders among murderers, psychiatrist Donald Lunde argues:

> I cannot emphasize too strongly the well-established fact that mental patients, in general, are no more murderous than the population at large. While it should not be surprising to find that psychotic killers have been previously hospitalized for treatment of psychosis, the incidence of psychosis among murderers is no greater than the incidence of psychosis in the total population. Furthermore, the percentage of murderers among former mental patients is actually slightly lower than that among persons who have never been in a mental hospital. Crimes committed by the mentally ill tend to receive disproportionate publicity, which reinforces a widespread myth about mental illness and violence. (1970: 93)

FRUSTRATION-AGGRESSION THEORIES

The **frustration-aggression hypothesis** was first advanced in the 1930s by psychologists at Yale University. Originally, the hypothesis asserted that "the occurrence of aggressive behavior always presupposes the existence of frustration, and . . . the existence of frustration always leads to some form of aggression" (Dollard et al., 1939: 1). Frustration arises whenever something interferes with an individual's attempt to reach a valued goal (see box 11.2).

It was soon recognized that this early statement of the frustration-aggression relationship required modification to accommodate the complexities of real life. Even though the impulse for aggression may be strong following some frustrating experience, the actual display of aggression may be inhibited by internal or external controls. Further, frustrations may be cumulative, one experience adding to another, and they may remain potent over a long period of time. It is now known that people evaluate frustrating experiences differently, according to whether they are arbitrary or unreasonable, for example. Finally, socialization teaches people how to respond

BOX 11.2. FALLING DOWN

> The film *Falling Down*, starring Michael Douglas, revolves around the main character's "mind snap" and subsequent aggressive criminal behavior. Douglas plays the role of Bill, an average man who starts to lose control of himself while sitting in a traffic jam on a hot day without air conditioning. Adding to his frustration, Bill has just lost his job and is late for his daughter's birthday party. After he is overcharged by a grocer for a soft drink, Bill stumbles upon a stash of high-powered weapons and begins an aggressive attack on various parties to exact his twisted sense of justice.
>
> Frustration-aggression theorists would examine the precipitating circumstances of such behavior and compare Bill's response to those who are similarly situated to look for differences. Although this theoretical perspective can be helpful in understanding sudden violent behavior, sociological theories reviewed in chapters 12 through 15 can also shed light on them. For example, an interesting study by Hipp, Bauer, Curran, and Bollen (2004) tests the temperature/frustration hypothesis (an idea first offered by Quetelet [1969] almost two centuries ago) against routine activities theory. The authors conclude that the latter theory better explains property crime but that both explanations offer some support for explaining violent crime.

to frustrations, and since the content of what is learned varies considerably from group to group and from society to society, the reactions to frustration can be expected to vary. In short, aggressive actions are not an automatic consequence of frustration, nor is the relationship between the two a simple one. As we will discuss in chapter 12, Robert Agnew has developed a more sophisticated way to explain the consequences of frustration and crime.

CHAPTER SUMMARY

The scientific foundations of criminology are traced to nineteenth-century Europe and the rise of positivism. The development of new techniques of data collection and analysis and Darwin's work on evolution spurred the application of science to problems of human behavior, including criminality. The work of Lombroso, Hooton, and Sheldon represent a kind of criminology inspired by the search for the biological and physiological causes of crime.

Among the theoretical perspectives found within modern biological approaches to crime are (1) evolutionary theories, which examine changing environmental conditions; (2) genetic theories, which focus on inherited traits, defects, or deficiencies; and (3) biochemical theories, which examine hormonal or chemical imbalances. Each of these perspectives has very modest empirical support and, for a variety of reasons, cannot be considered part of the core set of popular criminological theories today.

Biosocial theories maintain that there are important interactional effects between constitutional variables and the social environment that can lead to criminal behavior. The relationship between intelligence and crime has been a part of this theoretical tradition, but there is no clear evidence that IQ plays a substantial role in explaining either individual or structural variations in criminal involvement or crime rates in general.

KEY TERMS

atavistic
biosocial approach
evolutionary theory
frustration-aggression hypothesis
positivism

SOCIAL STRUCTURAL
THEORIES OF CRIME

A5TC3N Alamay

In the song "Breaking the Law," Rob Halford, lead singer of the heavy metal band Judas Priest, sings about familiar human and social problems: unemployment, instability, anger, disappointment, and boredom. The connection between a person's feelings, behavior, and social institutions has been a topic of intense scrutiny in academic quarters. In sociology, theories emphasize the social aspects of human behavior, including the organization, structure, and culture of group life as well as the interactions that occur among individuals and groups. As we discussed earlier, theories of crime that focus on social structure are generally macrosociological. They emphasize social conditions and patterns that transcend the immediate social situation. Theories of crime that focus on social interaction explain crime in terms of social process and are generally microsociological. They emphasize how the immediate social situation shapes the behavior of participants, and is in turn shaped by it. This chapter focuses on social structure, the next on social process, but it should be emphasized at the outset that some theories of crime defy easy classification because they bridge the conventional distinction between structure and process. This is true of the theories we review in this chapter, especially social disorganization and Chicago School theories, and it is true of conflict theory (discussed in chapter 14). In the end, all criminological theories are saying something about the behavior of individuals, for it is individuals who make and enforce rules or who behave in ways that violate them. The theories are grouped in different categories to emphasize their similarities and differences, and to show how they build upon each other and how they compete. Let us begin our study of structural theories with a look at the work of the eminent classical sociologist Émile Durkheim.

DURKHEIM ON CRIME, LAW, AND ORDER

Émile Durkheim is regarded by many as a founder of the sociological study of crime and law. The breadth of Durkheim's work is impressive, and it is easy to see from even a cursory examination of his scholarship that criminologists owe him a heavy intellectual debt. Indeed, two major social structural theories of crime—social disorganization theory and Robert Merton's anomie theory—have strong and direct ties to Durkheim's work.

Durkheim was a functionalist, and so it should not be surprising to find that he was concerned with how societies attempt to regulate behavior for the purposes of stability, control, and solidarity. Law, Durkheim believed, should ideally represent the collective will of the people. What should be considered criminal, then, are behaviors that compromise and jeopardize the social order. Durkheim (1893) used the term **collective conscience** to describe widely held social values and beliefs. He reasoned that something should be made or considered criminal if it offends the collective conscience, the basic normative standards of the society. Punishment, he argued, was necessary to reaffirm the collective conscience so that all members of society would understand the wrongfulness and immorality of criminal behavior. This, he explained, increases social solidarity.

Durkheim also pointed out that crime is not abnormal because it is found in every society. Further, he argued that crime and deviance are universal because every society must have norms and in every society someone will break those norms at one time or another:

> There is no society that is not confronted with the problem of criminality. Its form changes; the acts thus characterized are not the same everywhere; but everywhere and always, there have been men who have behaved in such a way as to draw upon themselves penal repression. . . . No doubt it is possible that crime will have abnormal forms, as, for example, when its rate is unusually high. . . . What is normal, simply, is the existence of criminality, provided that it attains and does not exceed, for each social type, a certain level, which it is perhaps not impossible to fix in conformity with the preceding rules. (1938: 64–66)

Crime and deviance are also functional or socially beneficial because they provide avenues for social change. Here Durkheim meant that norm or law violation can cause people to become aware of required changes in society. Using the example of Socrates, Durkheim noted that challenges to established rules may enlighten others so that laws and norms may adapt to ever-changing social conditions:

> Nothing is good indefinitely and to an unlimited extent. . . . To make progress, individual originality must be able to express itself. In order that the originality of the idealist whose dreams transcend his century may find expression, it is necessary that the originality of the criminal, who is below the level of his time, shall also be possible. One does not occur without the other. (1938: 71)

The defiant actions of people such as Martin Luther King Jr., Rosa Parks, and even Dr. Jack Kevorkian illustrate that lawbreaking or deviance can produce social change. Of course, how positive or negative the social change is thought to be is a matter of opinion rather than fact. Box 12.1 illustrates this point in the realm of popular music.

While Durkheim made numerous contributions to criminology, perhaps the most lasting was the introduction of the concept of **anomie**. In both *The Division of Labor* (1964a [1893]) and *Suicide* (1952 [1897]), anomie was explained as a social condition in which "normlessness" prevails. More specifically, anomie exists when systems of regulation and restraint in a society have diminished so much that individuals suffer a loss of external guidance and control in their goal-seeking endeavors. The structure regulating social relationships is disrupted and social cohesion and solidarity are undermined. Durkheim argued that anomie is more likely during periods of rapid social change, when traditional norms prove ineffective in regulating human conduct. This structural, macrosociological approach helped explain why some areas have higher suicide rates than others. This is important because suicide is often considered a very individual act and is perhaps more appropriately explained by psychological theories. However, Durkheim showed that suicide, as a social fact, is a phenomenon explainable by the careful study of large-scale social currents and forces. Sociologist Robert Merton was heavily influenced by the concept of anomie and used it to build a theory of crime, which we shall review later in this chapter. First, let's consider what is known as the first distinct sociological theory of crime in the United States: social disorganization theory.

BOX 12.1. DEPARTING FROM THE NORM CAN BE GOOD

Durkheim theorized that deviance can be beneficial to society. Let's apply this reasoning to changes over the years in popular music.

Every so often watershed moments in music are sparked by the unique charisma, style, and spirit of musical visionaries. Most popular musicians are able to trace back their influences to rebels who offered up something unusual and distinct. We have talked about such influences with many musicians and read about many more. Some of the names that pop up include the influence of Louis Armstrong and Count Basie on jazz; Robert Johnson and BB King on the blues; Elvis Presley on blues-rock; the Beatles and the Rolling Stones on rock; the Who, Jimmy Hendrix, and Motorhead on hard rock; Patty LaBelle and Aretha Franklin on soul music and rhythm and blues; Public Enemy, Easy E. and Run-DMC on hip hop; Michael Jackson and Madonna on pop; Ozzy Osbourne on all metal genres; the New York Dolls and Mötley Crüe on glam metal; Nirvana and Pearl Jam on grunge; Black Sabbath and Metallica on heavy metal; the Dead Kennedys and the Sex Pistols on punk; and Green Day and blink-182 on pop punk. What do all these folks have in common? First, they achieved some degree of success in the marketplace by offering something new and distinct. Such breakthroughs can forever change music. Second, these people challenged traditional rules and norms relating to music, whether by their style, substance, or presentation. Third, to a greater or lesser extent, they helped pave the way for new artists and act as symbolic reminders of the spirit of innovation.

Durkheim's ideas can also be applied to a variety of other popular culture subjects, such as film, television, and music videos. Regarding videos, in the early days of MTV, videos were simple and low budget, often depicting little more than images of the artists performing their song. Over time, as the popularity of cable television and visual media in general grew, landmark videos like Dire Straits' "Money for Nothin'" and Michael Jackson's "Billie Jean" set new standards for the visual presentation of music. Now, of course, some music videos are the equivalent of short films, containing complicated plots, hired actors or actresses, celebrity cameos, and lots of capital invested in their production. Times change, indeed—and often, according to a Durkheimian perspective, this change is triggered by those who go beyond the norm and push the envelope.

CRIME AND SOCIAL DISORGANIZATION

Crime and delinquency in cities have been given considerable attention in the academic community, and the general public's interest in urban problems is also high. One common understanding of the relationship between the city and social problems is that decaying urban environments generate high rates of crime and delinquency. Beginning in the early 1900s, sociologists at the University of Chicago published a series of studies of life in Chicago. Under the guidance of Robert Park and E. W. Burgess, these studies were designed to document the belief that problems such as crime and delinquency resulted from **social disorganization**. Simply put, social disorganization is the inability of a community to regulate itself (Bursik and Grasmick, 1995). Social organization is maintained by a group's commitment to social rules; when this commitment breaks down, social control breaks down. Members of the Chicago School and many contemporary criminologists believe that this breakdown in social control could occur through ecological changes, such as when communities experience rapid population change through social mobility and migration.

By examining voluminous data on the city of Chicago, Clifford Shaw and Henry McKay (1942) were able to confirm that certain areas of Chicago experienced relatively high rates of crime and delinquency and that these areas also showed the telltale signs of social disorganization. An area known as the *zone of transition* was found to have the highest crime rate. This zone was close to the central business district and, consequently, areas of population transition. Such areas of high crime were also characterized by overcrowding, physical deterioration, concentrations of minority and foreign-born residents, concentrated poverty, low rates of home ownership, lack of locally supported community organizations, and concentrations of unskilled and unemployed workers. Further analysis showed that these areas also had other problems: high rates of infant mortality, tuberculosis, mental disorder, and juvenile delinquency (Shaw and McKay, 1942; Morris, 1958). Shaw and McKay found that as the distance from the zone of transition increased, crime rates decreased.

Shaw summarized the links between ecological change, social disorganization, and the development of "delinquency areas" as follows:

> In the process of city growth, the neighborhood organizations, cultural institutions, and social standards in practically all areas adjacent to the central business district and the major industrial centers are subject to rapid change and disorganization. The gradual invasion of these areas by industry and commerce, the continuous movement of the older residents out of the area and the influx of newer groups, the confusion of many divergent cultural standards, the economic insecurity of the families, all combine to render difficult the development of a stable and efficient neighborhood for the education and control of the child and the suppression of lawlessness. (1931: 387)

One of Shaw and McKay's most important observations was that the relative levels of delinquency and crime in local communities tended to remain stable over many years, despite changing ethnic and racial composition (Bursik, 1988: 524; Bursik and Grasmick, 1993; 1995). Thus, a city area with high rates of delinquency compared to other areas would tend to remain that way, as would an area with low rates relative to another. They showed this to be true of Chicago over a period spanning several decades. Shaw and McKay argued that delinquent values and traditions were being passed from one generation of residents to another; in other words, a form of cultural transmission was taking place. In Shaw and McKay's view, the only way to combat the tendency for areas to become permanently crime prone was to develop neighborhood organizations that could help promote informal social controls and encourage residents to look out for each other's welfare (Sampson, 1986; 1987; Stark, 1987).

Shaw and McKay and their colleagues at Chicago had a major influence on the development of sociological criminology. They not only showed how social organization and culture unite to influence social behavior, but they drew attention to the processes by which youthful residents adopt the criminal lifestyles of an area and thus reinforce them. Even though their theory is essentially a macrolevel explanation of variations in group rates of crime, they clearly believed that interactions between parents and children, and between neighborhood youths themselves, helped mediate the influences of structure and culture (Bursik, 1988: 521). Indeed, Shaw spent many years helping youths find alternative solutions to their problems, and he persuaded former delinquents and crooks to help him reverse the spread of delinquent values and lifestyles. The resulting Chicago Area Project became a model for delinquency prevention efforts.

Social disorganization theory fell out of favor in the 1960s, as few criminologists identified themselves with the perspective. Various reasons can be advanced for this decline in popularity. For some it was sufficient to point out that many youngsters do not become delinquent despite living in high-crime areas. Others wondered whether crime and delinquency are not a part of social disorganization rather than a result of it. Furthermore, how could one explain the emergence of highly organized, cohesive youth gangs in neighborhoods that are supposedly so disorganized? Finally, there was concern that the social disorganization model diverts attention away from the delinquency and crime of middle-class neighborhoods and from non-street crimes such as price-fixing and the sale of unsafe products.

If Shaw and McKay's ideas were unpopular a few decades ago, what is happening in criminology now can only be seen as a resurrection of the theory (Kubrin and Weitzer, 2003; Pratt and Godsey, 2003). One example of this re-emergence of interest in the theory is found in Rodney Stark's theory of deviant places. Using human ecology theory and other classic Chicago School concepts, Stark's theory focuses on the following variables: density, poverty, mixed use, transience, and dilapidation. He argues that poor and densely populated neighborhoods are likely to be mixed use, and people tend to move in and out of these neighborhoods regularly. This can result in less community surveillance, more opportunities to engage in crime, and people who are disenchanted, cynical, or apathetic about their neighborhood. Neighborhoods that are dilapidated are also often stigmatized, Stark maintains, for they signify disorder and seem attractive to those seeking deviant opportunities. Furthermore, Stark proposes that

- more successful and conventional people will resist moving into a stigmatized neighborhood; and
- stigmatized neighborhoods will tend to be overpopulated by the most demoralized kinds of people and suffer from lenient law enforcement, which may increase the incidence of crime and deviance. (1987: 901–2)

Many of the basic propositions of social disorganization theory have been supported by scholarly research. For example, one study found that "busy places" in neighborhoods in Seattle have higher rates of violent crime (Rountree, Land, and Miethe, 1994). A study of Chicago neighborhoods found that the higher the level of informal community social control, cohesion, and trust, the lower the rate of violence in that area (Sampson, Raudenbush, and Earls, 1997: 922). This study also found that as there is more willingness on the part of people to help others in a community, the lower the level of violence in that area. However, there is also evidence to show that even nonintimates, or those removed from a person's daily or weekly routines, can also exercise considerable control over people's involvement in crime (Bursik, 2000). See box 12.2 to rate your neighborhood or community on these and other dimensions of social disorganization.

Another study using concepts from social disorganization theory has shown that there are significant community-level differences in the racial and ethnic distribution of crime and victimization, with the fundamental issue being the "embeddedness of black families in social environments with depleted resources" (McNulty and Bellair, 2003: 735). Similarly, a recent study of the distribution of black and white homicide rates in cities also supports this reasoning, but in a slightly different way. It may be that "the racial homicide differential is better explained by the greater resources that exist among whites than by the higher levels of disadvantage that exist among blacks" (Velez, Krivo, and Peterson, 2003: 645). In other words, whites may have more opportunities to affect neighborhood and institutional change, and therefore have increased regulatory power over their community.

Finally, we should consider how the dramatic increase in U.S. imprisonment rates over the last few decades could negatively impact neighborhood and community social organization. In this vein, Dina Rose and Todd Clear have proposed a very interesting theoretical argument:

> High incarceration rates may contribute to rates of criminal violence by the way they contribute to such social problems as inequality, family life deterioration, economic and political alienation, and social disorganization . . . [and] undermine social, political, and economic systems already weakened by the low levels of human and social capital produced under conditions such as high rates of poverty, unemployment, and crime. . . . The result is a reduction in social cohesion and a lessening of those communities' capacity for self-regulation. (1998: 441)

In sum, this argument proposes that imprisonment takes away fathers, mothers, neighbors, and workers from the very social relationships that are needed to keep community crime rates low. For example, children are less likely to be well supervised if one parent, or even an older brother or sister, is incarcerated; family members devastated by the imprisonment of one parent may move in and out of areas to be nearer to the prison; and the growth of collective political action movements that need young, energetic members is inhibited due to overincarceration.

It has been observed by many scholars that the imprisonment boom has taken its largest toll on poor African American communities (Mauer, 2000; Whitehead, 2000). Partial sup-

---

BOX 12.2. DO YOU LIVE IN A SOCIALLY DISORGANIZED COMMUNITY?

Consider the following questions:

- Do you know your neighbors?
- Do you say hello to them in passing?
- Do you ever hang out with them?
- Do they keep an eye on your children for you?
- When you are away, do they watch your house or apartment for suspicious activities?
- Do neighbors in your community occasionally congregate on the sidewalks or arrange for their to children play with one another?
- Do you know more than half of the people living in your immediate area?
- When problems arise, do you communicate and attempt to resolve them with your neighbors?

If you answered yes to all or most of these questions, you probably don't live in a highly disorganized area. Theoretically, then, your neighborhood would be expected to have a lower crime rate than one with less neighborhood cohesion, or what has been called *collective efficacy* (Sampson, Raudenbush, and Earls, 1998).

Other, more structural indicators of whether you live in a socially disorganized area are the ratio of rental properties to owner-occupied homes, how often people move in and out of your area (the transience rate), and the kinds of resources provided by the government, churches, community organizations, and recreational groups in the area.

Keep in mind that a socially organized community is not necessarily one that has to be so "tight" as to smother its residents in surveillance and social control. This might be dangerous: Charles Tittle's control balance theory, reviewed in chapter 15, maintains that people who feel overcontrolled have a tendency to seek out deviant ways of expressing themselves and their interests.

port of Rose and Clear's model suggests that this way of thinking about incarceration and its effects on social disorganization is promising (Clear, Rose, Waring, and Scully, 2003).

MERTON'S ANOMIE THEORY

Émile Durkheim's notion of anomie was extended and elaborated on by Robert K. Merton (1938; 1957), who made it a central feature of a strain theory of crime. According to Merton, a state of anomie exerts pressure on people to commit crime. While all societies establish institutionalized means, or rules, for the attainment of culturally supported goals, these means and goals are not always in a state of harmony or integration. The way the society or group is organized interferes with the attainment of valued goals by acceptable means for some of its members. A condition of anomie, or strain, therefore exists.

Looking at the United States in the 1930s, Merton saw an inordinate emphasis on material success, which was held up as achievable by all Americans. Not all segments of society, however, could realistically expect to have material success if they followed the rules of the game. African Americans and the lower classes were routinely excluded from access to legitimate means of achievement. The acceptable routes to success—a good education, a good job, the "right" background, promotions, and special skills—typically were not the routes

open to them. Unfortunately, things are only marginally better today (see Farley, 2005).

Strain is essentially the disjunction or lack of fit between socially desirable goals and the socially acceptable means to achieve those goals. Merton believes that various "modes of adaptation" are possible in response to the strain resulting from unrealized expectations: conformity, innovation, ritualism, retreatism, and rebellion. Refer to figure 12.1 as we proceed to discuss each of these adaptations to strain.

Many people will *conform*, simply accepting that they will never "make it big"—unless they win the lottery! Perhaps the "bite of conscience" (Wilson and Hernstein, 1985) holds them back from crime; perhaps they fear punishment; perhaps they have too much to lose, if not materially, then in terms of relationships with family and friends; perhaps they cannot recognize—or take advantage of—illegitimate opportunities. Merton prefers the idea that conformity reflects social acceptance of the rule of law.

Other people may engage in *ritualism*. They give up on the goals but continue to support the socially approved means. They cling "all the more closely to the safe routines and institutional norms" (Merton, 1957: 151). Imagine the platoon leader who gives up on the apparently impossible task of taking the enemy position but berates his soldiers for having dirty belt buckles, or the loyal corporate manager who gives up on being promoted himself but punishes his sub-

---

TABLE 11.1   Merton's Modes of Adaptation to Anomie

When confronted by a disjunction between legitimate means and socially approved goals—a condition of anomie, which produces strain—people may adapt in various ways. This table summarizes Merton's modes of adaptation.

ADAPTATION	SOCIALLY APPROVED GOALS	LEGITIMATE MEANS
Conformity	accept (+)	accept (+)
Innovation	accept (+)	reject (-)
Ritualism	reject (-)	accept (+)
Retreatism	reject (-)	reject (-)
Rebellion	reject and replace (±)	reject and replace (±)

▲ Figure 12.1.
Merton's Modes of Adaptation to Anomie

BOX 12.3. POSSIBLE MODES OF ADAPTATION TO STRAIN BY STUDENTS AND COLLEGE PROFESSORS

Merton's strain theory speaks not only to crime, but also other forms of deviance. Using the five adaptations to strain identified by Merton, let's consider how deviance might come about for both college students and college professors.

College Students

Let us suppose the overriding goal is to achieve very good to excellent grades in a class. What kinds of actions might be associated with the various adaptations to strain over this goal?

- Conformity: Diligent, careful, meticulous reading of course materials; not skipping class and coming to every class meeting prepared; asking the professor questions when clarification is needed; visiting the professor during office hours; properly using academic sources for papers; actively participating in any group work or discussion.
- Innovation: Cheating on exams; plagiarizing papers; having someone else take your exam or write your paper; relying on others' notes rather than taking them yourself.
- Ritualism: Achieving a passing grade, nothing more: this might be expressed by sporadic attendance and participation in the class; poor or uneven performance on exams and papers; cursory reading of course materials.
- Retreatism: Dropping out of class, or perhaps college altogether.
- Rebellion: Disengaging from the entire conventional higher education system; possibly embracing anti-intellectualism or intellectualism outside the confines of conventional education in the form of religious training, cults, or even home schooling.

College Professors

Now, let's think about college professors. Let us suppose the overriding goal is to be an effective teacher, productive scholar, and an active member of the community.

- Conformity: Putting in full work weeks; working on weekends; preparing and writing own lectures; giving all self-composed essay exams; carefully reading all student papers; publishing in peer-reviewed journals and with respectable presses; spending hours each week in committee meetings.
- Innovation: Copying lectures from textbooks; plagiarizing parts of papers; lying on their vitas (an academic resume); not reading papers but giving grades anyway; exaggerating the time and energy put into community work; stealing student work (as in the film *DOA*).
- Ritualism: Playing by the rules to achieve tenure, but content to stay within them even if it means missing out on other academic or educational opportunities.
- Retreatism: Being chronically late to class; communicating with students indifferently; using dated films and lectures; seldom changing exams from semester to semester; being unavailable to students; never writing or publishing; and doing little or no community service work.
- Rebellion: Subverting the dominant academic paradigm by using unconventional teaching methods (extreme participatory pedagogies, not giving grades, allowing

students control over the classroom experience) or overtly attempting to advance ideological, religious, or political agendas in class.

Although Merton never discussed these cases, it is interesting to note that his theory is sufficiently broad enough to be applied to specific roles and occupations. Such applications of Merton's theory are becoming more common among criminologists who study white-collar crime.

ordinates for not "playing the game."

Still others reject both means and goals. Such *retreatism* is an adaptation to anomic conditions in which people may even withdraw from society altogether. The inner-city heroin or crack addict is most often mentioned in this context. The drug-using antiestablishment "hippies" of the 1960s and the short-lived commune movement also come to mind. On the other hand, some people substitute new sets of norms and goals, and Merton calls this adaptation *rebellion*. Unfortunately, the logical separation between these two modes of adaptation is unclear. For example, are the antiestablishment hippies retreatists or rebels? Can rebellion occur without retreatism?

The adaptation Merton identifies most closely with crime is *innovation*. Innovators accept the goals, but they reject the institutional means and substitute illegal alternatives. Merton uses innovation to explain the relatively high rates of property crime among lower-class and minority segments of society. Their disadvantaged status, coupled with the high cultural priority given to material success as a goal for all, makes high rates of crime a "normal outcome" for those segments of society. Box 12.3 provides another way to understand the various modes of adaptation when applied to actors in higher education.

Merton's theory of anomic strain and crime had a profound influence on subsequent structural theories despite some serious criticisms. In many ways his "theory" is merely a catalog of potential reactions to anomie: It does not tell us when to expect one mode of adaptation rather than another, or whether different segments of the population are likely

to select different adaptations. Katz objects that Merton's theory is unconvincing as an explanation for "vandalism, the use of dope, intergroup fighting, and the character of initial experiences in property theft as sneaky thrills" (1988: 358, n9).

Another line of criticism repeats that directed at the social disorganization theory of Shaw and McKay: Too much is made of the high rates of crime officially observed among the lower classes. Even if the data are credible, the preoccupation with criminal behavior among the lower classes diverts theory and research from the behavior of other classes and from the power relations that exist between classes. More recent extensions of Mertonian strain theory, however, have been used to explain forms of white-collar crime. Kauzlarich and Kramer (1998), for example, have specifically studied how state strain brings about innovation by state and corporate organizations. They argue that state agencies use illegal means in order to achieve their operational goals, which may be financial health, legitimacy, national security, or political hegemony. For example, illegal human radiation experiments conducted by the U.S. government from 1940 to 1980 can be understood as the use of illegitimate means (violating international law and human rights) for the larger goal of winning the Cold War. In this way, white-collar crime can be understood in Mertonian terms, but this must be done by substituting the organization for the individual as the unit of analysis.

Another limitation of Merton's theory is that it provides no explanation of why the "success ethos" is so important in the United States. Indeed, Messner and Rosenfeld (2000) maintain in their **institutional anomie theory** that the larger U.S. *culture*, not simply its structure, prizes economic success over other forms of achievement. Good parenting and good grades in school are considered less valuable because they produce no capital—that is, no direct financial benefits. More broadly, according to the theory, institutions such as the family, school, and community become visualized in economic terms, and potential informal social control mechanisms within the culture become sterile. Crime, then, is not so much a product of those who are unable to achieve the American Dream, but those who are *locked in* to those values. Although institutional anomie theory has been subjected to only a few empirical tests, research has generally supported the theory's main contentions (Maume and Lee, 2003).

GENERAL STRAIN THEORY

Like Messner and Rosenfeld, Robert Agnew (1992; 2001) has redirected Merton's strain theory in the hopes of increasing the theory's explanatory power. Unlike institutional anomie theory, however, Agnew reframes strain theory on the social-psychological or micro level of analysis. In some ways this makes Agnew's theory more similar to the social process theories reviewed in the next chapter, but since Agnew's theory is rooted in Merton's work, we shall discuss it here.

Agnew's **general strain theory** (GST) starts with the assumption that negative relationships with others causes strain or stress in people's lives. Negative relationships are those "in which others are not treating the individual as he or she would like to be treated" (1992: 50). According to Agnew, Mertonian strain theory relies too heavily on the relationships that prevent the individual from reaching positively valued goals. GST, however, considers this and two other sources of strain that may lead to crime and delinquency: (1) when other individuals remove or threaten

to remove positively valued stimuli that one possesses, and (2) when others present or threaten to present a person with negatively valued stimuli (1992: 50; 2001). Some examples might help clarify these sources of strain.

The first type of strain—the failure to achieve positively valued goals—suggests that people have in some way not met their goals or expectations, or have received unfair or inequitable outcomes in social relationships. Examples include not meeting expectations to earn good grades in school, financial strength from working, and fair treatment by parents, teachers, and peers. Strain also stems from situations in which others remove or threaten to remove things that a person positively values. Think for a moment about the kinds of stressful life events we all probably encounter: the loss of partners (boyfriends, girlfriends, husbands, wives) and friends, for example, or a child's loss of a parent. All of these negative events can place considerable stress on individuals and may trigger involvement in crime. Finally, Agnew maintains that strain is also likely to develop when others present or threaten to present an individual with negative outcomes. Examples of this type of strain include a child who is abused, neglected, or otherwise criminally victimized (1992). The child may deal with these negative relationships by attempting to escape the environment all together (i.e., running or staying away from home) or exacting revenge upon the victimizers, who are usually family members. Further, these different types of strain can overlap:

> [F]or example, the insults of a teacher may be experienced as adverse because they (1) interfere with the adolescent's aspirations for academic success, (2) result in the violation of a distributive justice rule such as equity, and (3) are conditioned negative stimuli and so are experiences as noxious in and of themselves. (59)

Agnew (2001) has more recently theorized that those negative experiences that are perceived as highly unjust, undeserved, and threatening are most likely to trigger deviant activity.

Since most people probably experience these forms of strain at some point in their lives, the question remains: Who is more likely to commit crime or delinquent acts because of the strain? Agnew suggests that it is those who do not cope well with the stressful situations. Coping abilities, or adaptations, that moderate the effects of strain are things like the ability to "blow off," neutralize, or downplay the seriousness and/or significance of stressful life events. For example, lowering one's standards for the accumulation of wealth or grade point average helps neutralize strain. According to Agnew, personality traits, temperament, and social learning and bonding variables ultimately help determine whether a person's adaptation to strain is criminal or not. The theory therefore complements leading criminological theories such as social control theory and social learning theory, which we shall discuss in chapter 13. GST can also be partially integrated with social disorganization theory, as Agnew (1999) has attempted to do in order to explain community-level differences in crime rates.

Empirical tests of GST have generally confirmed that the theory has reasonably strong predictive power (Mazerolle, 1998; Paternoster and Mazerolle, 1994; Slocum, Simpson, and Smith, 2005). Of the several studies, two are particularly interesting because they examine the theory's ability to predict gender differences in offending (Broidy and Agnew, 1997; Mazerolle, 1998). Both found that GST did not predict the differences in overall offending very well, but that it did account for some differences in violent offending by gender. Specifically, one study found that losing a parent or family member and having negative relationships with adults are more likely to be criminogenic for males, but not for females (Mazerolle, 1997). This provides partial support to the notion that males tend to manifest anger and strain externally, while women more often manage these emotions inter-

nally. Another study of only African American youths, however, found that after controlling for prior offending and other factors, both boys and girls had similar delinquent responses to the anger and depression brought on by experiences with racial discrimination (Simons et al., 2003).

CULTURAL TRANSMISSION OF CRIME AND DELINQUENCY

As noted previously, ecological studies of crime and Merton's theory of anomie emphasized the high rates of crime officially observed among the poor. From 1940 to 1960, sociologists seemed preoccupied with explanations of criminal activity among the lower classes. Most of the theories produced in this period emphasized social structure, especially the ways in which the behavior of adolescents and young adults is shaped by the lifestyles and values to which they are exposed.

A number of theories focus on what is called the *delinquent subculture*. Any heterogeneous society is likely to have a parent, or dominant, culture and a variety of different subcultures. The dominant culture consists of the beliefs, attitudes, symbols, ways of behaving, meanings, ideas, values, and norms shared by those who regularly make up the membership of a society. Subcultures differ from the dominant culture and consist of the beliefs, values, and lifestyles shared by those members of society who belong to identifiable subgroups. For example, Goth kids, vegans, residents of a retirement community, homosexuals who have "come out," the hippies of the 1960s, and Polish Americans who belong to clubs and organizations that emphasize their common heritage are identifiable subgroups whose members share a common subculture.

Some subcultures are merely different from the dominant culture, while others are in active opposition to it. Delinquent subcultures fit neither characterization exactly. According to Richard Cloward and Lloyd Ohlin, a delinquent subculture "is one in which certain forms of delinquent activity are essential for the performance of the dominant roles supported by the subculture. It is the central position accorded to specifically delinquent activity that distinguishes the delinquent subculture from other deviant subcultures [such as homosexual activists]" (1960: 7). However, even in its support of delinquent activities, a delinquent subculture may nevertheless also share aspects of the dominant culture—for example, an emphasis on material possessions or an acceptance of gender differences in social roles.

In general, then, **subcultural theories** of crime and delinquency begin with the assumption that people are socialized into the norms and values of the immediate groups to which they belong. In a sense, all people are conformists, but the values and norms with which they conform may be different from, or at odds with, those of the dominant culture, and the behaviors that result are sometimes illegal. In other words, some kinds of conformity turn out to be delinquent or criminal. So it is with the activities central to delinquent subcultures.

Cohen's Theory

One of the first sociologists to propose a subcultural explanation of delinquency was Albert Cohen. In his book *Delinquent Boys*, Cohen (1955) suggests that high rates of lower-class delinquency reflect a basic conflict between lower-class youth subculture and the dominant middle-class culture. The delinquent subculture arises as a reaction to the dominant culture, which is seen as discriminating against lower-class people. Told in school and elsewhere to strive for middle-class goals and to behave according to middle-class values (be orderly, clean, responsible, ambitious, and so forth), lower-class youths find that their socialization has not prepared them for the challenge. They become "status frustrated" as a result of their inability to meet middle-class

standards and, in reaction, turn to delinquent activities and form delinquency-centered groups. Cohen describes the delinquency that results as nonutilitarian (for example, stealing "for the hell of it"), malicious (enjoying the discomfort of others), and negativistic (taking pride in doing things because they are wrong by middle-class standards).

Cloward and Ohlin's Differential Opportunity Theory

Expanding on Merton and Cohen, sociologists Cloward and Ohlin (1960) developed a theory of delinquency and youth crime that incorporates the concept of opportunity structures. The authors point out that society provides both legitimate and illegitimate opportunities for behavior, and that these opportunities (whether legitimate or not) meet different kinds of needs—some help a person achieve status (and with it, membership in the middle class); others help a person achieve economic success. Not all youths aspire to the same things, and Cloward and Ohlin believe that those youths who aspire to economic success but are denied legitimate opportunities to achieve it are at greatest risk of becoming embroiled in gang subcultures.

Cloward and Ohlin's theory is more than a rehash of strain theory because the introduction of opportunity variables enables them to explain why a particular form or type of deviance arises in response to structural strain (see Cullen, 1983: 41–45). While anomie theory predicts that strain is a motivating force behind deviance and crime, it does not explain why one form of deviance (say, retreatism) occurs rather than another (such as innovation). Cloward and Ohlin argue:

> The pressures that lead to deviant patterns do not necessarily determine the particular pattern of deviance that results. . . . Several delinquent adaptations are conceivably available in any given situation; what, then, are the determinants of the process of selection? Among delinquents who participate in sub-

cultures, for example, why do some become apprentice criminals rather than street fighters or drug addicts? These are distinctive subcultural adaptations; an explanation of one may not constitute an explanation of the other. (Quoted in Cullen, 1983: 44)

Applying opportunity theory to the world of business (conventionally thought to be a far cry from delinquency), John Braithwaite shows how a criminal subculture of price fixing might arise:

> Let us imagine, for example, that the government suddenly decides to double sales tax on beer in an effort to discourage consumption. The brewing companies might find as a consequence that legitimate opportunities are blocked for them to achieve their profit or growth targets. They might get together at trade association meetings to curse the government, to begin to suggest to each other that they have no choice but to conspire to fix prices, in other words to fashion a criminal subculture which rationalizes price fixing by blaming the government for it, appealing to the higher loyalty of saving the jobs of their workers, and which evolves new criminal conduct norms for the industry. (1989a: 33)

Cloward and Ohlin identify three delinquent subcultures to which lower-class youths may belong and that help structure a youngster's response to the absence of legitimate opportunities. These subcultures are *criminal*, *conflict*, or *retreatist*.

Criminal subcultures are characterized by illegal money-making activities and often provide a stepping-stone toward adult criminal careers. They tend to arise in slum areas where relatively well-organized age hierarchies of criminal involvement exist. This condition provides youths with adult criminal role models and encourages their recruitment into money-making crime. Also, the existence of adult roles such as "fixer" and "fence," which bridge the worlds of legitimate enterprise and crime, helps facilitate illegal money-making activities

as an alternate route to economic success.

Conflict subcultures are dominated by gang fighting and other violence. They arise in disorganized slum areas with weak social controls, an absence of institutionalized channels (legal or otherwise) to material goals, and a predominance of personal failure. Violence is a route to status as well as a release for pent-up frustrations.

Finally, retreatist subcultures are marked by the prevalence of drug use and addiction. This subculture arises as an adaptation for some lower-class youths who have failed in both the criminal and conflict subcultures, or have not successfully accessed either the legitimate or illegitimate opportunity structures. Like Merton's retreatists, they disengage from the competitive struggle for success goals.

Miller's Lower-Class "Focal Concerns"

The works of Cohen and of Cloward and Ohlin focus mainly on youthful gangs, and to that extent they ignore a tremendous amount of delinquency and crime that is not gang oriented. Their work also focuses on the organization and culture of the lower class, and to that extent it may not apply to lower-class behavior in other societies.

The same observations can be made of Walter Miller's (1958) well-known study of youth gangs, a study in which he delineates the special themes or issues prominent in lower-class youth culture. The material and social deprivations that are commonplace among the urban lower class contribute to the development of special themes, or **focal concerns**, as Miller calls them. Focal concerns command a high degree of emotional commitment. Among the focal concerns identified by Miller are *trouble* (a concern with avoiding entanglements with the law), *toughness* (an ability to handle physical and emotional challenges), *smartness* (being able to con, hustle, or outwit others), *autonomy* (remaining free from domination or control by others), and *excitement* (getting kicks; avoiding the routine and the monotonous).

Some of the activities shaped by these focal concerns are delinquent or criminal, for the law reflects and supports the dominant standards of middle-class society. But even when given a choice not to engage in delinquency or crime, youngsters will often find the "deviant" activity more attractive because the norms of groups with whom they identify, as well as peer group pressures, point to it as a means of acquiring prestige, status, and respect.

Finally, let's think about another subculture theory that bears similarities to Miller's perspective. Marvin Wolfgang and Franco Ferracuti (1967) advanced the idea that a **subculture of violence** can develop in poor urban areas. Such a subculture defines the use of physical force, aggression, and violence as appropriate and legitimate responses to a variety of social situations. Unlike Elijah Anderson's (1999) notion of the "code of the streets," Wolfgang and Ferracuti believed that the subculture of violence was widespread in some communities and revealed itself in both private and public ways.

In sum, the social structural theories reviewed thus far in this chapter purport to explain the relationship between the organization or structure of society and the behavior of its people. One problem with these theories as a whole is the almost exclusive focus on lower-class delinquency. This obviously limits the scope of the theories, and none of them was initially advanced as a general theory. Unfortunately, one of the undesirable (and probably unintended) consequences of the emphasis on the lower class has been the respectability it has given the stereotypical view of crime and criminals. This view associates being criminal with being a member of the lower class. Interestingly, the considerable media publicity given to crimes by members of the middle and upper classes sensationalizes their crimes, and by doing so seems only to confirm the idea that "real" crime is committed by the poor, the unemployed, and the disreputable. The misbehaviors of "real" criminals are, by definition, unsensational, because we expect crime from the "criminal classes." The objection to the criminological emphasis on lower-class crime is essentially that it lends the weight of "expert opinion" to this popular stereotype. If this (i.e., the lower class) is where criminologists look to find crime, then it must be where crime really is!

A common thread runs through social structural theories of crime, a thread that explains to a large extent why they have been almost exclusively theories of lower-class crime. These theories see crime as a consequence of inequality in the distribution of material resources. A lack of economic opportunities, the social disorganization of inner-city neighborhoods, the subculture of youth gangs, and unrealized expectations of affluence are the hallmarks of inequality. They are the products of a social organization that puts some people at a disadvantage in the competition for scarce resources. Crime is therefore an unexceptional consequence of economic, social, and political disadvantage.

This common thread reflects an assumption that is made about human nature: Human beings are basically good people. When they become "bad," it is because they are pushed or pulled into crime by adverse conditions. If the lot of the lower classes was improved, there would be less crime. Since food, clothing, and shelter are material resources, the bettering of conditions must begin with economic change that distributes material resources to segments of society where they are most needed. This is a major policy implication of social structural theories, but it is not as far-reaching as the implications of the critical theories reviewed in chapter 15.

CHAPTER SUMMARY

This chapter has reviewed theories of crime that emphasize the relationship between crime and social structure. Durkheim's work in sociology provides much of the intellectual foundation for both social disorganization theory and strain theory. As a sociologist, Durkheim was interested in the various roles that deviance and crime played in society, as well as how and why deviance persists but also changes over time. Durkheim also advanced the notion of anomie in order to explain how deviance results from weakened social solidarity and control.

Following Durkheim, social disorganization theories maintain that crime and delinquency result when there is a breakdown in social control. Members of the Chicago School believed that such a breakdown could result from ecological changes, as when communities experience rapid population change through social mobility and migration. Although this theory was almost forgotten, it has recently made a major comeback in criminology. Variations of the original theory have held up well to empirical scrutiny.

Merton's strain theory posits that when people find they cannot achieve valued goals such as wealth and status through socially approved means, they experience stress and frustration, which may lead to crime and deviance. In Merton's view, the poor are especially vulnerable to strain. Merton's theory is not without its faults, however. Two important revisions of Merton's theory—Messner and Rosenfeld's institutional anomie theory and Agnew's general strain theory—have expanded upon the theory's original position. The former seeks to extend Merton's argument to the macrocultural sphere, while Agnew's theory focuses on the more social-psychological dynamics of strain.

Subculture theories of crime revolve around the idea that crime and delinquency are connected to restricted opportunities and exposure to criminogenic cultures. Cloward and Ohlin's theory focuses on differential opportunities for delinquency. Cohen's subculture theory focuses on this as well, but is also concerned with how children from the lower class are treated in institutions such as the school. Miller's theory about lower-class gangs specifies how subcultural value systems develop to provide rationales for delinquency.

KEY TERMS

anomie
collective conscience
focal concerns
general strain theory
institutional anomie theory
social disorganization
strain
subcultural theories
subculture of violence

AK8W58 Alamy

Humans are social animals, and, for the most part, we like to have friends to share our time with and to help us navigate life. We need social support from our friends, parents, and teachers in order to develop emotionally and intellectually. For many years social scientists have been able to show that our relationships with intimate others substantially impact our values, beliefs, and behavior. Criminologists are especially interested in the manner in which friends, parents, and teachers "teach" us lessons about obeying or disobeying rules. Some criminological theories focus on parental behavior and practices, while others cast their gaze on peer groups. Still others examine how peer,

parental, and school experiences combine to push or pull an individual toward criminal values and behavior.

Social process theories, the type of explanations we shall review in this chapter, recognize that not all people exposed to the same social structure engage in the same behavior, nor do people who come from dissimilar social environments necessarily behave differently. Social process theories are more microsociological, as they are concerned with how individuals acquire social attributes through interaction with others. People's attributes are what identify them in the eyes of others, distinguishing one person from another. When thinking about attributes, it is important to keep in mind that their meaning is always contextual: How one person looks to another is always a matter of how other people in a similar situation look to that person.

Social attributes, such as being reliable or being nonconformist, convey messages about a person's behavior, status, and ideas. They are part of that person's social identity, and other people use those attributes to determine how they should behave toward that individual and to distinguish that person from others. A person is not born with these attributes, but acquires them through interaction with others. Criminality is a social attribute. People *become* criminals, and that status is confirmed when others treat them like criminals, and reinforced when people so identified actually engage in criminal behavior.

Social learning theorists owe a major intellectual debt to the ideas of the renowned social psychologist George Herbert Mead. Mead's **interactionist perspective** (sometimes called *symbolic interactionism*) sees human beings as *active agents* in the construction of the social world they experience. The idea is that during interaction, people construct meanings, expectations, and implications that shape everyone's behavior and thus create a certain social reality for participants. This experience influences what happens in later interactions, although each interaction creates its own social reality. Social order is therefore fluid and ever changing.

One of the most important elements of the interactionist perspective is the idea that actions arise out of situations (Blumer, 1969: 85). Whether people are at home with their families, in school, at work, or at play, each situation presents opportunities, demands, tasks, obstacles, pleasures—and sometimes dangers—that must be taken into account and evaluated by the actors. That assessment provides people with the basis for understanding the situation and forming their actions. Essentially, the meaning of a situation for each participant derives from the actions and reactions of the other participants.

For example, how do you decide that you are in control of a situation? By how others respond to you. Or consider how you know that a situation is safe or dangerous: You can "read" the situation through the actions of others, or you can put yourself in the shoes of another and imagine how he or she would act and what the likely results would be. Obviously, this becomes possible only when you have prior knowledge or experience with similar situations and people. Social order is constructed as people agree on the meanings and implications of the situations they are in, and act accordingly.

THE PROCESS OF ASSOCIATION

In criminology, social process theories attempt to describe and explain the ways in which individuals become criminal or adopt criminal values. These theories deal with the links between an individual's interaction with others and that person's motivations, perceptions, self-conceptions, attitudes, behavior, and identity. Although many interactionist theories seem to place greater emphasis on the behavior of others than on the behavior of "self," the goal is the same: to explain the emergence and consequences of behavior. An underlying assumption is that criminal

behavior can be explained within the same framework as any other behavior. A common theme in many social process theories is that criminal behavior is learned through interaction with others.

THE THEORY OF DIFFERENTIAL ASSOCIATION

In the 1939 edition of *Principles of Criminology*, Edwin H. Sutherland introduced **differential association theory**. According to this theory, criminal behavior patterns are acquired through processes of interaction and communication, just as other behavior patterns are. The principle of differential association accounts for the particular behavior pattern acquired through these processes: Individuals acquire criminal behavior patterns because they are exposed to situations in which the learning of crime outweighs the learning of alternative, noncriminal behaviors. Sutherland wanted it clearly understood that criminal behavior was not the result of biological or psychological pathology, but rather was one possible outcome of normal interactive processes. In their daily lives, people are participants in a variety of group situations, in which they are exposed to the behavior and influence of others. What they "pick up" in these situations helps shape their own behavior. When a person is more involved with delinquent or criminal groups, he or she is more likely to become delinquent or criminal as a result. The theory as a whole consists of the following nine propositions:

1. Criminal behavior is learned.
2. Criminal behavior is learned in interaction with other persons in a process of communication.
3. The principal part of the learning of criminal behavior occurs within intimate personal groups.
4. When criminal behavior is learned, the learning includes (a) techniques of committing the crime, which are sometimes

very complicated, sometimes very simple; (b) the specific direction of motives, drives, rationalizations, and attitudes.

5. The specific direction of motives and drives is learned from definitions of the legal codes as favorable or unfavorable.

6. A person becomes delinquent because of an excess of definitions favorable to violation of law [the principle of differential association].

7. Differential association may vary in frequency, duration, priority, and intensity.

8. The process of learning criminal behavior by association with criminal and anticriminal patterns involves all of the mechanisms that are involved in any other learning.

9. While criminal behavior is an expression of general needs and values, it is not explained by those general needs and values, since noncriminal behavior is an expression of the same needs and values. (Sutherland and Cressey, 1974: 75–77)

Figure 13.1 illustrates the process of differential association. Box 13.1 discusses how principles of differential association theory can be used to understand the idea that music affects behavior.

Three important observations should be made about this theory. First, the theory of differential association purports to explain noncriminal as well as criminal behavior. Noncriminal behavior emerges because of an excess of definitions unfavorable to law violation. Thus, if a child spends a great deal of time interacting intensely with people whose behavior and ideas stress conformity to the law, the child is likely to grow up a conformist (in terms of the law, at least).

Second, the theory can be used to explain variations in group rates of crime as well as individual criminality. Although the theory focuses on how individuals come to engage in criminal behavior, a compatible explanation of variations in rates of crime for whole populations is possible. Thus, relatively high crime rates are predicted for people and places having extensive exposure to definitions favorable to law violation, especially when there is a high probability that such definitions will be learned by a relatively large number of people. Shaw and McKay's delinquency areas, discussed in the preceding chapter, would meet these criteria.

Third, the theory can be applied to white-collar crime as well as traditional street crime. Sutherland invented the term *white-collar crime*, and he soundly criticized other theorists (like Shaw, McKay, and Merton) for failing to consider those crimes situated within the context of work. Sutherland believed that a general theory of crime cannot be based on a class-specific model of criminal behavior. Variables like poverty or neighborhood disorganization are insufficient explanatory variables, since people can—and do—learn criminal behavior and

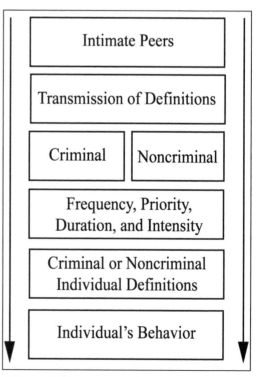

▲ **Figure 13.1.**
The Process of Differential Association

BOX 13.1. CONNECTIONS BETWEEN MUSIC AND DIFFERENTIAL ASSOCIATION THEORY

Every once in a while, a musician or band attracts the attention of those who would never be their fans. This is most often the case when the artist's style or lyrics receive widespread press coverage because they are seen by mainstream audiences as especially obscene, pornographic, offensive, or dangerous. It is the latter concern that is the most interesting to discuss from the perspective of differential association theory.

One early example that illustrates the fear in some quarters about corrupting the morals of youth stems from a performance that would surely now be considered conservative. By the time Elvis Presley made his third appearance on the *Ed Sullivan Show* (a very popular 1950s mainstream variety television program), Presley's gyrations and hip shaking were deemed so risqué that the cameras were aimed above the waist so the television audience wouldn't be exposed to his shaking lower body movements. Elvis's style was shocking to older generations but attractive to younger folks, and sometimes the former tried to "protect" the latter from the sensuous messages sent by Presley for fear that they would imitate him or adopt casual attitudes about sex.

Fast-forward fifty years and compare this to the infamous 2004 Super Bowl halftime fiasco involving Justin Timberlake and Janet Jackson. As they performed a highly sexualized dance, Timberlake tore some fabric from Jackson's chest and exposed her bare breast to millions of live viewers. It is unclear if the stunt was planned, but reactions to it ranged from laughter and ambivalence to shock and outrage. MTV, which produced the miniconcert, was told by the National Football League that they would never work together on a show like this again. Citing decency regulations, MTV and CBS, the television network that aired the halftime show, were threatened with fines and other penalties for the incident by the Federal Communications Commission.

Some social control agents (especially parents and teachers) have in other instances tried to prevent kids from getting the "wrong" message by attacking artists' music. Heavy metal artists such as Ozzy Osbourne and Judas Priest were early targets of such attacks in the 1980s; in fact, both were sued over the content of their lyrics. Marilyn Manson has been vilified by many as a modern-day devil who encourages young people to be disobedient, anarchist, hedonistic, and violent. He was singled out by some as encouraging the views that lead to the 1999 Columbine school shooting. Michael Moore's film *Bowling for Columbine* shows Manson's reaction to those who blamed him for that kind of violence. Several years ago Ice-T and his band, Body Count, were accused of encouraging youth violence against law enforcement officers for his song "Cop Killer." Led by police officers, a whole social movement sprung up against him and his music. More recently, Eminem has been accused of encouraging homophobia, sexual assault, and misogyny in his lyrics.

There appears to be a widely held popular belief that listening to music and watching musical performances can affect not only the attitudes of the young, but also their behavior. This is not dissimilar to the underlying logic of differential association theory. Let's think further about this. When you were younger teenagers, some of you might have been told by your parents to avoid contact with certain people. Parents often do this because there is something about another kid they don't like, and they are concerned that this person may negatively influence your values, attitudes, and behavior. Put more simply, the rationale is that parents don't want their kids "hanging out with the wrong crowd." Essentially this is Sutherland's argument, as it assumes that frequent and intense interactions with others might directly affect your attitudes and behavior. A similar line of reasoning applies to the possible effect of the media on beliefs. Clearly, many people believe that the media can indeed negatively influence children, as regulatory bodies that govern the content of television shows, films, and CDs all have some form of rating system designed to alert parents to adult content such as the use of profanity, violence, sex, or illegal drugs.

Of course, when Sutherland wrote differential association theory, the world was a very different place in terms of the mass media. Children—and, to some extent, adults—had less exposure to messages from outside of their immediate physical environment. Sutherland didn't give much credence to the idea that "picture shows" could influence the formulation of definitions favorable or unfavorable to law. This is one of the reasons he limited the theory to interactions with intimate others. In today's society, however, children and adults alike are surrounded by mass media, and the possible effects of media images on crime continues to draw scholarly interest.

attitudes in any economic or neighborhood context.

It is fair to say that the theory of differential association has been very influential in criminology. It is, after all, hard to argue with the idea that people learn criminal ways from others. Yet few theories have been subject to more criticism: The language is imprecise, the theory is untestable because major variables such as "definitions favorable or unfavorable to law violations" cannot be measured, it deals with the acquisition and performance of behavior and yet leaves out any mention of personality traits or other psychological variables, and it does not explain the fact that people often respond differently to the same situation. C. Ray Jeffery (1959) observes that since crime is learned, it must first exist. So what accounts for the first criminal act? How does one explain crimes that are committed "out of the blue," by people with no prior interaction with criminals?

BEHAVIORAL LEARNING THEORIES

According to *behavioral learning theories*, people tend to repeat activities for which they are rewarded and to avoid those for which they are punished. They also tend to copy others whom they see being rewarded. In this case the reward is experienced vicariously. The sanctioning effect of rewards and punishments may apply to any behavior.

One influential modification of Sutherland's original theory has been made by Robert Burgess and Ronald Akers (1966). They argue that Sutherland's formulation does not identify the mechanism by which individuals learn. Taking a social learning approach, the authors restate Sutherland's theory in terms of **operant conditioning**—a view that argues certain behaviors are learned because past examples have been rewarded. Thus, people engage in crime because it has been more highly rewarded in the past than has other behavior. That some people become criminals and others do not is explained by noting that not all people go through the same socialization process, nor are they exposed to the same nonsocial situations of reinforcement.

Another quasi-behavioral learning theory was proposed by Daniel Glaser, who argues that all forms of interaction between an individual and his or her social environment be incorporated in a modified theory of *differential identification*. "A person," writes Glaser, "pursues criminal behavior to the extent that he identifies himself with real or imaginary persons from whose perspective his criminal behavior seems acceptable" (1956: 440). These people serve as behavior models, and they need not come into direct personal contact with the individual. Hence Glaser acknowledges something that Sutherland did not: the possibility that portrayal of criminal roles in the mass media is linked with the adoption of criminal behavior patterns.

These modifications of Sutherland's theory have some parallels with a prominent theory that people learn violence by imitating or modeling the behavior of people they "look up to." Albert Bandura (1973) showed that the behavior of aggressive models is readily imitated by experimental subjects, whether observed in the flesh or via film. In one well-known experiment, Bandura played a film of a woman who beat, kicked, and hacked an inflatable doll. After witnessing the film, nursery school children placed in a room with a similar doll duplicated the woman's behavior and also engaged in other aggressive acts.

Experiments such as these have established the existence of immediate imitation, but how enduring are the behaviors learned, and does each new situation have to be virtually identical with the one originally observed in order for similar behavior to occur? While the jury is still out on these questions, there is evidence suggesting that imitated behaviors do survive over time and that people will generalize from the initial modeling situation to other, sometimes quite dissimilar, situations.

Violent behavior has its rewards, and many people learn what these are early in life. They learn that conflicts can be won through violence, that violence can be effective as a rule-enforcing technique, and that violence helps people get their way in the face of resistance. They also discover that respectable people often reward violence used in their interest, especially against "outsiders" and people regarded as a threat. From history, they learn that violence helped make America a better place to live. Closer to everyday life, they see that the successful use of violence often confers status, authority, and even riches.

This brief list by no means exhausts the rewards associated with violence. As people grow up, they have many opportunities to learn that violence is rewarded. But they also learn that violence has its costs. Violence is costly when used at the wrong time, in the

wrong place, or against the wrong person. But since there are differences of opinion as to when the use of violence is wrong, the costs and rewards of violence in any given situation are perceived differently by members of different groups (Stanko, 1990). One cannot assume that because one person or group refrains from violence in a certain situation, others will too.

PEER GROUPS AND SERIOUS DELINQUENCY

The observation that association with friends who are delinquent or criminal is associated with high rates of offending is not new, but it continues to be reconfirmed in study after study (Gorman and White, 1995; Hochstetler, Copes, and DeLisi, 2002).

Recall that the associational argument states that when youths are involved with delinquent friends, the association encourages further delinquency. How it does it is a matter of debate, but various mechanisms are possible: the group's power to sanction behavior of members, the social rituals that confirm membership and confer status, the role models provided by the group's leader(s), and the facilitation of activities that are not easily (or successfully) performed alone. The essential idea is that the delinquency of the group influences its members—and vice versa.

It all sounds simple enough, but the issue of peer influence remains controversial. In the first place, some studies have found that seriously delinquent youths are weakly attached to delinquent peers (e.g., Chapman, 1986; Gottfredson and Hirschi, 1990: 154–57). They are loners. Other studies have found quite the opposite, at least for youths involved in illicit drug use (Kandel and Davies, 1991). Youths in drug-using networks display extremely strong interactive ties with peers. Second, a study of incarcerated offenders found that group members who conformed to conventional standards were more popular than less conforming members (Osgood, Gold, and Miller, 1986). Third, at least two observational studies, one in the United States (Schwendinger and Schwendinger, 1985) and one in England (Parker, 1974), have shown that occasional and serious delinquents participate side by side in the same street-corner networks, and that the occasionals remain sporadic offenders.

Another issue further complicates what at first appeared to be a simple matter. Rather than influencing a youth's propensity to commit crimes, it has been suggested that delinquent peer groups merely facilitate crime among individuals whose tendencies are already compatible with it (Linden and Hackler, 1973; Gottfredson and Hirschi, 1988). A network of delinquency-prone individuals creates and responds to criminal opportunities in its milieu. The type and frequency of criminal acts will be determined largely by that milieu. A chronic delinquent is most often a lower-class street-corner male who keeps company with other lower-class street-corner males. This suggests that, quite apart from the intimate interaction among peers, the social structure of lower-class street-corner society is conducive to high rates of street crime (Barlow and Ferdinand, 1992: 60–79).

TESTING DIFFERENTIAL ASSOCIATION THEORY

Testing the original formulation of differential association is not easy, and both the methods used and the results have been inconsistent. Usually researchers infer support (or nonsupport) of the theory and do not test it directly. This is largely Sutherland's fault, because he did not specify how the theory might be tested and he left major concepts undefined. We shall now review a few studies that have attempted to test differential association.

One study involved interviewing 1,544 students in nine high schools in the southeastern United States (Paternoster and Ruth Triplett, 1988). The authors reported strong support for differential association. Friends' definitions of appropriate and inappropriate behavior and friends' actual behavior were significantly related to an individual's own use of marijuana, drinking behavior, petty theft, and vandalism. A study of more than 1,000 Dutch children found great support for the idea that the frequency of contact with deviant friends significantly influences definitions favorable to deviant behavior (Bruinsma, 1992). In another study, Mark Warr and Mark Stafford (1991) used National Youth Survey data to evaluate associational theory. They found that peers' behavior—what they actually do—was a more important predictor of self-reported delinquency than peers' attitudes about behavior.

Two tests of differential association have been conducted from data obtained from the Richmond Youth Project, a self-report survey of more than four thousand high school students. The first study found that definitions favorable to law violation predicted delinquency more strongly than any other variable (Matsueda, 1982; Matsueda and Heimer, 1987). However, in a recent reexamination of this data, it was found that the bonds to parents and friends more strongly explained delinquency (Costello and Vowell, 1999). More specifically, the authors found that definitions favorable to law violation were shaped or mediated by other factors, especially measures of the social bond (discussed in some detail later in this chapter). A similar finding was made by Ross Matsueda and Kathleen Anderson (1998).

Indeed, tests of differential association theory have supported the *mediation hypothesis*—the notion that larger social and structural factors shape the content and form of definitions favorable or unfavorable to crime (Heimer, 1997). This approach has been used to explain the gender differences in violent offending. A study by Karen Heimer and Stacy De Coster (1999) found that

- learning violent definitions is an important predictor of violent delinquency;
- aggressive peers and coercive discipline

each has a larger effect on boys' than girls' learning of violent definitions;

- emotional bonds to family influence girls' but not boys' learning of violent definitions;
- accepting traditional gender definitions significantly reduces violence among girls, but does not influence violence among boys; and
- boys engage in more violent delinquency than girls in part because they learn more violent definitions and more traditional gender definitions than girls and have more previous experience with violent offending than girls.

How and with whom we associate varies in a number of ways (e.g., by age, location, gender, and time). In the case of gender, role socialization reflects larger social norms and values, which help shape definitions of socially acceptable and unacceptable behavior in everyday interaction. When combined with a consideration of structural inequality in opportunities in schools, politics, and the workplace, one can see why there are differences in criminal offending by gender.

Differential association theory can also be helpful in explaining the causes of occupational and organizational crime. Indeed, partial support of the theory has been found in a number of studies of organizational crime (Kauzlarich and Kramer, 1998; Michalowski and Kramer, 2006). As Friedrichs notes:

> In some respects, white-collar crime may be better understood by reference to differential association than is true of conventional lower class crime and delinquency, both because of the broader range of learning options generally available to the white-collar crime offender and the complex nature of the offenses themselves. (2004: 205)

However, differential association theory is not equipped to explain the larger structural and organizational elements involved in the genesis and persistence of many organizational crimes. This limitation has prompted many scholars of white-collar crime to study how definitions of appropriate and inappropriate behavior are created and maintained in unique organizational climates.

For example, Vaughan's (1996) monumental study of the space shuttle *Challenger* explosion employs the notion of the **normalization of deviance**, a condition in which deviations from technical protocols gradually and routinely become defined as normative. Risky practices, which can be either an outcome of or a precursor to the normalization of deviance, are often caused by "environmental and organizational contingencies [which] create operational forces that shape world view, normalizing signals of potential danger, resulting in mistakes with harmful human consequences" (409).

SELF-CONCEPT

Most research and theorizing based in differential association theory addresses the ways in which youths, in particular, come to adopt patterns of delinquent or criminal offending. Learning, communication, and interaction are the fundamental processes by which individuals acquire their social identities. These processes are also crucial to the development of an individual's personality—motivations, ideas and beliefs, perceptions, feelings, preferences, attitudes, values, self-control, inhibitions, and awareness or sense of self. Some authors have argued that a person's sense of self, or self-concept, is a major element among the forces that control behavior.

Containment Theory

One of the first to propose a link between self-concept and criminal behavior was Walter Reckless. Reckless (1973) believes that the individual confronted by choices of action feels a variety of "pulls" and "pushes." The pulls are environmental factors—such as adverse living conditions, poverty, lack of legitimate opportunities, abundance of illegitimate opportunities, or family problems—that serve to pull the individual away from the norms and values of the dominant society. The pushes take the form of internal pressures—hostility, biopsychological impairments, aggressiveness, drives, or wishes—that may also divert the individual away from actions supported by dominant values and norms.

But not all people faced with the same pulls and pushes become delinquent or criminal. To explain why some do not, Reckless advances the **containment theory**. According to Reckless, there are two kinds of containment: inner and outer (1973: 55–56).

Inner containment consists mainly of "self" components, such as self-control, good self-concept, ego strength, well-developed superego, high frustration tolerance, high resistance to diversions, high sense of responsibility, goal orientation, ability to find substitute satisfactions, tension-reducing rationalizations, and so on. These are the inner regulators.

Outer containment represents the structural buffer in the person's immediate social world that is able to hold him or her within bounds. It consists of such items as a presentation of a consistent moral front to the person; institutional reinforcement of his norms, goals, and expectations; the existence of a reasonable set of social expectations; effective supervision and discipline (social controls); provisions for reasonable scope of activity (including limits and responsibilities) as well as for alternatives and safety valves; opportunity for acceptance; identity; and belongingness. Such structural ingredients help the family and other supportive groups contain the individual.

In Reckless's view, the inner control system, primarily self-concept, provides a person with the strongest defense against delinquency involvement. Commenting on the results of a follow-up study of white schoolboys in high-delinquency areas in Columbus, Ohio, Reckless and Simon Dinitz observe:

> In our quest to discover what insulates a boy against delinquency in a high delinquency area, we believe we have some tangible evidence that a good self-concept, undoubtedly a product of favorable socialization, veers slum boys away from delinquency, while a poor self-concept, a product of unfavorable socialization, gives the slum boy no resistance to deviancy, delinquent companions, or delinquent subculture. We feel that components of the self strength, such as a favorable concept of self, act as an inner buffer or inner containment against deviancy, distraction, lure, and pressures. (1967: 517)

The work of Reckless and his associates has not gone without criticism, but interest in self-concept and its connection with criminality has remained very much alive in some circles. One study seems to confirm the importance of favorable family experiences in protecting a child against criminogenic influences, even in slum neighborhoods. Joan McCord (1991) used case records of visits to the homes of 232 boys as well as records of their juvenile and adult criminal activity, covering a thirty-year period. She found that sons of mothers who were self-confident, offered leadership, and were affectionate and consistently nonpunitive in discipline tended to escape delinquency involvement. However, McCord also discovered that a different mechanism seemed to relate to whether a child subsequently became an adult criminal: a father's behavior toward his wife and children. Apparently, fathers who undermine their wives, who fight with the family, and who are aggressive "teach their sons how to behave when they become adults" (412). Thus, juvenile crime may be more susceptible to control mechanisms, including self-concept, whereas adult crime may be more susceptible to the influence of role expectations. More recent extensions of this approach have focused on how different identities, both between *and* within gender, influence the process of constructing one's self and the incidence of criminal offending and victimization (Giordano, Cernkovich, and Holland; 2003; Giordano et al., 1999). A central finding is that although involvement in crime by both men and women is strongly influenced by their peer and intimate relationships, women are less significantly affected than men by these relationships.

Techniques of Neutralization

One interesting theoretical contribution bearing on self-concept comes from David Matza and Gresham Sykes. Matza (1964) argues that individuals are rarely committed to or compelled to perform delinquent or criminal behavior. Rather, they drift into and out of it, retaining a commitment to neither convention nor crime. This so-called **drift theory** is also applicable to some instances of organizational crime (Braithwaite, 1989b).

In Matza's view, delinquents are never totally immune to the demands for conformity made by the dominant social order. At most they are merely flexible in their commitment to them. In a joint publication, Sykes and Matza (1957) argue that if delinquents do form subcultures in opposition to dominant society, they are surprisingly weak in their commitment to them. They show guilt and shame, though one would expect none; they frequently accord respect and admiration to the "really honest" and law-abiding people in their immediate social environment; and they often draw a sharp line between appropriate victims and those who are not fair game—all of which suggests that the virtue of delinquency is far from unquestioned. In terms of the dominant normative order, the delinquent appears to be both conforming and nonconforming.

Sykes and Matza believe that in order to practice nonconformity, delinquents must somehow handle the demands for conformity to which they accord at least some recognition. In their view, delinquents handle those

demands by learning to neutralize them in advance of violating them—that is, they redefine their contemplated action to make it "acceptable," if not "right." The authors identify five **techniques of neutralization** that facilitate the juvenile's drift into delinquency:

1. *Denial of Responsibility* ("Alcohol causes me to do it; I am helpless")
2. *Denial of Injury* ("My action won't hurt anyone")
3. *Denial of the Victim* ("He 'has it coming'")
4. *Condemnation of the Condemners* ("Those who condemn me are worse than I am")
5. *Appeal to Higher Loyalties* ("My friends, or family, come first, so I must do it")

Two other techniques of neutralization have been proposed and discussed in a classic study of occupational crime (see Hollinger, 1991; Klockars, 1974; Minor; 1981). They are *defense of necessity* and *metaphor of the ledger*. Defense of necessity relates to the fact that among business offenders, illegal acts are seen as standard business practice and necessary in a competitive marketplace. Metaphor of the ledger relates to the idea that a person can build up "good" credit so that he or she can later do something "bad" without feeling guilty—a form of cashing in the credits.

More recently, scholars of state crime and elite deviance have found strong evidence of how techniques of neutralization work (Jamieson and McEvoy, 2005; Kauzlarich, Matthews, and Miller, 2001; Rothe and Mullins, 2006; Simon, 2006). Obviously, one of the most important things separating victimizers from their victims is their power to exert their will. Most often, the perpetrators of state crime (e.g., human rights violations and illegal wars) do not acknowledge the degree to which their policies have caused harm. Instead, they concentrate on assessing the "effectiveness" of their policies, no matter how harmful they might be to others, to bring about desired changes or to maintain positions of dominance. Injury caused by criminal domestic and international policies can also be downplayed by employing bankrupt utilitarianism—that is, arguing that the ends justify the means—to neutralize reasonable imperatives (e.g., do no harm). Further, harms are neutralized by denying responsibility, dehumanizing the powerless for purposes of exploitation, and appealing to higher loyalties (i.e., the capitalist political economy and "national security") (Kauzlarich, Matthews, and Miller, 2001; Simon, 2006).

Political policy makers attempt to "neutralize" the destructive and harmful effects of their policies, as in the long history of U.S. abuses in Latin and Central America:

> U.S. policy makers have consciously decided (1) that the U.S. is entitled to control Central America and that the peoples of Central America are obligated to acquiesce in this power exercise; (2) that violence is permissible, and policy makers can live with themselves and conclude that they are ethical/moral persons and that these policies are ethical/moral even if they involve violence; (3) that the use of violence, intimidation, and threat of violence will produce the desired effect or minimize a more negative one; and (4) that the policy of violence and control will not unduly endanger the United States, and the country will neither sustain physical harm nor suffer legal, economic, or political consequences that will outweigh the benefits achieved through this violence. (Tifft and Markham, 1991: 125–26)

With respect to the historical treatment of Native Americans within the United States, "colonists quickly justified their violence by demonizing their enemies" (Takaki, 1993: 43). However, the transference of one's own negative tendencies to another group is not something new. While Native Americans were seen as unruly, "Godless" savages, Ronald Takaki (1993) notes that the atrocities committed by the civilized whites against the Native Americans were, in fact, savage. It is in this light, then, that Native

Americans became an enemy worthy of indiscriminate killing. In much the same manner, the indiscriminate killing of the "Godless" communists of Central America were also justified:

> [This] is a painful reality. Many of us face this reality with initial disbelief and denial, for it is difficult for us to see either the United States or ourselves as terrorists, as batterers. Terrorists and batters are someone else. To emotionally experience, to actually witness the destruction, the horror, the reality of destabilization, starvation, torture and death by design, by public planning, is beyond our comprehension. (Tifft and Markham. 1991: 131)

Empirical evaluations of the neutralization hypothesis are scarce, in part because of the difficulty of establishing what happens cognitively *before* a law violation occurs. Almost all research has looked at rationalizations after the fact, which provides at best only inferential evidence. The problem is one of establishing the causal order: neutralization before transgression.

In any case, with the exception of Robert Agnew's (1994) study and some indirect support from Lois Presser's (2003) interviews with violent men, the evidence is not very impressive in studies of most traditional street crimes. The absence of neutralizations, however, does not mean they might not have operated at some time in the mind of an offender. Neutralizations might arise after earlier transgressions and act as rationalizations for later ones, perhaps contributing to a "hardening" process that leads to a commitment to deviance (Hirschi, 1971: 208). John Hamlin goes even further and calls the prior sequencing argument "a fallacy" (1988: 432). He argues that the motives for doing things are created during the process of legitimizing actions that have been criticized or challenged.

Furthermore, neutralization may be necessary only for certain offenders. According to one scholar, "neutralization should only be necessary when a potential offender has both a strong desire to commit an offense and a strong belief that to do so would violate his personal morality. . . . If one's morality is not constraining, however, then neutralization or rationalization is simply unnecessary" (Minor, 1980: 103–20). Volkan Topalli (2005) has even found that some offenders neutralize being good rather than being bad. In other words, to survive on the streets and reach high status in their neighborhood, some offenders actively seek to enhance their "hard-core" reputations on the street and neutralize in the opposite direction than Sykes and Matza would predict.

There may be no adequate way to disentangle the causal order problem mentioned above, even with longitudinal data, since definitional learning ("This is right to do; this is wrong," and "I'm OK; I'm not OK," etc.) occurs concurrently with rule breaking. Even so, neutralization theory may have received a "bum rap" from critics, especially in light of his finding that neutralization may interact with age, younger people being less likely to neutralize than older ones (Hollinger, 1991).

SOCIAL CONTROL THEORY

Like Matza and others, control theorists emphasize the episodic character of much crime and delinquency, but, unlike their colleagues, they build in no assumptions about what motivates people to commit deviance. Indeed, "[t]hey assume that human beings are born free to break the law and will refrain from doing so only if special circumstances exist" (Box, 1981: 122).

The most prominent version of control theory is that of Travis Hirschi (1971). According to Hirschi, these special circumstances exist when the individual's bond to conventional, or moral, society is strong. As originally conceived, Hirschi's **social control theory** holds that this bond is based on four elements: *attachment, commitment, belief, and involvement*. *Attachment* refers to the individual's affective involvement with conventional others (e.g., parents, teachers, friends), including

sensitivity to their thoughts, feelings, and desires. When that attachment is weakened, the individual is free to deviate. *Commitment* is the "rational" component in conformity. It refers to the weighing of the costs and risks of deviance in light of that person's investment, or "stake," in conformity: "When or whenever he considers deviant behavior, he must consider the costs of this deviant behavior, the risks he runs of losing the investment he has made in conventional behavior" (20). The weaker the commitment to conformity, the lower the costs of deviance; hence the freer one is to deviate. Figure 13.2 illustrates the major thrust of the theory and box 13.2 provides further illustration.

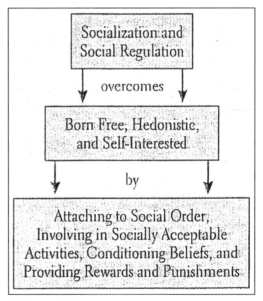

▲ **Figure 13.2.**
Hirschi's Social Control Theory

Hirschi defines *belief* as "a common value system within the society or group whose norms are being violated" (1969: 23). But individuals differ in the strength of their belief in the moral validity of these social rules. If for some reason these beliefs are weakened, the individual will be freer to deviate. By including *involvement*, Hirschi suggests that deviance is in part a matter of opportunities to deviate. He argues that the more one is involved in conventional things, the less one has the opportunity to do deviant things. This is one of the weakest parts of the theory, as Hirschi himself discovered in his research with more than four thousand California junior high and high school students, because opportunities for criminal or delinquent activities increase along with opportunities for noncriminal activities.

Both the clarity of its exposition and the many research findings supporting it have given Hirschi's control theory a prominent place in criminology. For example, one test of the theory conducted on the subject of misbehavior in school found that every measure of the social bond except involvement was shown to have significant effects in the predicted direction. As the study's author explains, the logic goes like this:

> Students who accept and believe in the dominant set of conventional school rules will be less likely to engage in delinquent behaviors and recognize the validity of those rules for maintaining a safe school environment. Those who care about and feel supported by their teachers and friends are more likely to develop affective ties to school and display socially acceptable behavior. Those with well-defined educational goals, who invest greater effort, and display higher aspirations for status attainment may be more committed to the educational process overall. As a result, they may recognize that involvement

in delinquent behavior may jeopardize their future goals. (Stewart, 2003: 493)

A study by Agnew (1985), however, questions social control theory's utility as an explanation of youth crime. He studied a national sample of 1,886 male youths interviewed first in the tenth grade and again at the end of the eleventh grade. He found delinquency involvement to be remarkably stable over the two-year period, with the delinquency measured in the tenth grade accounting for 65 to 68 percent of the delinquency measured later.

In contrast, Agnew (1985) found that the social bond variables of parental attachment, school grades, and commitment explained only 1 to 2 percent of the variance in delinquency. Agnew speculates that as children grow older, the importance of the bonds discussed by Hirschi may diminish, but he does not rule out their importance among younger children.

Hirschi's social control theory has also been heavily criticized for overstating the importance of the social bond. A recent reanalysis of the Richmond Youth Project data by David Greenberg found that while social control theory has its merits, the strength of theory has been overestimated by criminologists. For example, Greenberg (1999) found that (a) intimacy in communication between parent and child (a measure of attachment) is not highly correlated with delinquency, (b) a very modest

BOX 13.2. DIFFERENTIAL ASSOCIATION, SOCIAL CONTROL THEORY, AND *BOYZ IN THE HOOD*

The 1991 film *Boyz in the Hood* is still regarded as one of John Singleton's best movies. The story revolves around a father (played by Lawrence Fishburne) trying to shield his teenage son Tre (Cuba Gooding Jr.) from widespread crime and violence on the streets of their neighborhood in south central Los Angeles, where Singleton himself was raised. Criminologically, the film illustrates the difficulties parents have in connecting with their children, as there is competition from peer groups over what values and beliefs are most desirable. In real life, we know that as children enter the teenage years, they begin to model their friends' behavior more than their parents', and sometimes regard their parents as the enemy or cops, which can further add to the distances between them. If you haven't seen the movie, watch it and think about its connection to social process theories of crime. If it's been a while since you've seen it, give it another viewing.

negative relationship between involvement in school-related activities and delinquency, and (c) negative correlations between aspirations to attain higher levels of education (e.g., college) and delinquency are also quite small. However, another recent study also using the same data source found that measures of the social bond, especially belief, were the greatest predictors of delinquency (Costello and Vowell, 1999).

One final comment on this prominent theory is in order. Some criminologists contend that control theory ignores the criminal activity of career offenders, as well as the crimes of people in positions of economic and political power. The "upperworld" individual is actually freed by conventional society to engage in "indiscretions" because these are not viewed as especially disreputable, much less criminal (Hagan, 1985). Such a person may thus exhibit both strong social bonds to conventional society *and* considerable involvement in illegal activities. Indeed, if we are to take into consideration political and state crimes, many of the offenders would be discovered to be very bonded to the social order because of their high levels of education, employment status, familial relationships, and general belief sys-

tems. While there has been some support for social control theory in studies of occupational crime (Lasley, 1988; Makkai and Braithwaite, 1991), Hirschi's version is best suited to explain juvenile delinquency, not white-collar crime.

INTERACTIONAL THEORY

Terrence Thornberry (1987) developed an **interactional theory of delinquency** that highlights the relationship between delinquency and the family, school, and peers. While attention to these factors is certainly not new, Thornberry argues that criminologists have only explored their unidirectional (one-way) qualities. His theory unites insights from social control and differential association theories, among others.

Thornberry argues that instead of simply studying how a person's commitment to school affects his or her belief in conventional or unconventional values, we should also consider how beliefs shape the commitment to school, which in turn may further influence beliefs, which then may further effect commitment, and so on. He explains that "bonding variables appear to be reciprocally

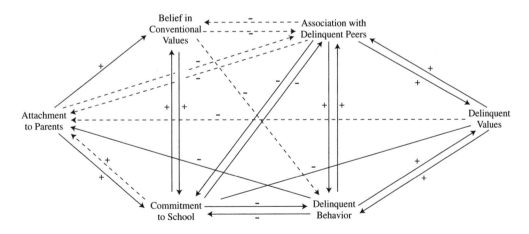

- - - - Broken line represents weaker effects.

———— Solid line represents stronger effects.

▲ **Figure 13.3.**
An Interactional Theory of Delinquency
Terrence Thornberry, "Toward an Interactional Theory of Delinquency," *Criminology* 25 (1987): 878. Reprinted with the permission of the American Society of Criminology.

linked to delinquency, exerting a causal impact on associations with delinquent peers and delinquent behavior; *they also are causally effected by these variables*" (Thornberry, 1987: 876; emphasis added). Interactional theory, then, suggests that many of the variables in social control theory and differential association theory can affect one another in all sorts of ways. Again, most people would think that strong attachment to parents reduces the extent to which youths associate with delinquent peers. But is it not true that associations with delinquent peers could affect a child's bond with his or her parents? Is it not also the case that delinquent peers could affect delinquency, just as delinquency affects association with delinquent peers? (Matsueda and Anderson, 1998). Figure 13.3 illustrates Thornberry's theory as applied to those in middle adolescence.

That the school, family, and peers have multiple and reciprocal effects is just part of the interactional theory. The second major part of the theory specifies how these variables affect people over the course of an individual's life. This developmental approach, which is similar to that of Sampson and Laub's (1992) theory, which we will review in chapter 15, suggests that the importance of these factors *varies by age*. For the very young, the family is the most important agent of socialization; when youths enter into middle adolescence, friends and the school become more important than before; and as the person enters adulthood, work and families of procreation (second families) become salient. All of this suggests that at different points in life, some associations more than others will be connected with our attitudes, beliefs, and behavior. It has been further argued that earlier delinquency has effects on later delinquency, and that low socioeconomic status can have compounding effects (Thornberry and Krohn, 2001).

There is no doubt that the journey from childhood to adulthood is marked with change. The likelihood of criminal offending is often affected by these developmental changes, and at least one empirical test of Thornberry's theory has been supportive (Jang, 1999).

THE LABELING PERSPECTIVE

Up to this point, the focus has been on crime and delinquency as behavior and on the distinctions between people who commit crimes and those who do not. The questions "What causes or influences criminal behavior?" and "What factors are associated with committing crime or becoming a criminal?" are underlying concerns in the work we have reviewed. However, the conception of crime and the criminal that underlies such questions is not the only one that has been recognized. Instead of simply viewing crime as illegal behavior and the criminal as one who engages in it, some criminologists draw attention to the behavior of other people with whom an individual interacts. Crime is a label attached to behavior, and the criminal is one whose behavior has been labeled crime. Crime is thus a question of social definitions and nothing intrinsic in behavior makes it a crime:

> Social groups create deviance by making the rules whose infraction constitutes deviance, and by applying those rules to particular people and labeling them as outsiders. From this point of view, deviance is not a quality of the act a person commits, but rather a consequence of the application by others of rules or sanctions to an "offender." *The deviant is one to whom that label has been successfully applied; deviant behavior is behavior that people so label.* (Becker, 1963: 9)

Labeling theory, or the societal reactions approach, gained immense popularity in the fields of crime and deviance during the 1960s. It was around this time that the social constructionist paradigm fully emerged in sociology. In its applications to the crime scene, labeling theory has been used to explain why

BOX 13.3. THE SAINTS AND THE ROUGHNECKS

William J. Chambliss (1973) followed the experiences of two small-town juvenile gangs whose members were students at "Hannibal High." The youths regularly broke the law. However, only the members of the Roughnecks were considered delinquent by officials and repeatedly arrested. The other gang, the Saints, largely escaped criminalization, and no members were ever arrested.

According to Chambliss, four factors played important roles in the differential response, and all related to the class position of the gang members. The Roughnecks came from the lower class, while the Saints came from more "respectable" upper-middle-class families.

First, the Roughnecks were more visible. Unlike the Saints, whose members had access to cars and could escape the local community, the Roughnecks had little choice but to hang out under the surveillance of neighbors and local authorities.

Second, the outward demeanor of the Saints deceived parents and officials. Around authority figures, they wore masks of courtesy and obedience, and when accused of deviant behavior they were apologetic and diplomatic. The Roughnecks, on the other hand, misbehaved openly and showed little regard for social customs or the feelings of others.

Third, when responding to the gangs' misbehavior, authorities displayed bias that favored the Saints. The Saints were characterized as typical adolescents who were merely sowing their wild oats, as normal boys do.

Finally, in defining the Roughnecks as boys who get in trouble, the community reinforced the "deviance" of gang members and helped produce a self-fulfilling prophecy: Deviant self-images promoted further deviance. The Saints, meanwhile, remained respectable in the eyes of the community, although in reality they continued to maintain a high level of delinquency.

Chambliss's study is one of the best examples of the importance of the labeling perspective to date. It clearly shows that "labeling, stigma and negative self-images have a powerful impact in determining who we are and what we become" (Chambliss, 1999: 120).

individuals continue to engage in activities that others define as criminal, why individuals become career criminals, why the official data on crime and criminals look the way they do, why crime waves occur, why law enforcement is patterned the way it is, why criminal stereotypes emerge and persist, and why some groups in society are more likely to be punished—and punished more severely—than others. Box 13.3 describes a well-known study by William J. Chambliss (1973) that vividly illustrates some of these points.

Though labeling theory gained popularity during the 1960s, it is based on the much earlier contributions of Frank Tannenbaum (1938) and Edwin Lemert (1951; 1972). Seventy years ago, Tannenbaum pointed out that

society's efforts at social control may actually help create precisely what those efforts are meant to suppress: crime. By labeling individuals as "delinquents" or "criminals" and by reacting to them in a punitive way, Tannenbaum argued, the community encourages those individuals to redefine themselves in accordance with the community's definition. A change in self-identification (or self-concept) may occur, so that individuals "become" what others say they are. Tannenbaum described the process:

From the community's point of view, the individual who used to do bad and mischievous things has now become a bad and unredeemable human being. From the individual's point of view there has taken place a similar change. He has gone slowly from a sense of grievance and injustice, of being unduly mistreated and punished, to recognition that the definition of him as a human being is different from that of other boys in his neighborhood, his school, street, community. This recognition on his part becomes a process of self-identification and integration with the group which shares his activities. It becomes, in part, a process of rationalization; in part, a simple response to a specialized type of stimulus. The young delinquent becomes bad because he is defined as bad and because he is not believed if he is good. There is a persistent demand for consistency in character. The community cannot deal with people whom it cannot define. Reputation is this sort of public definition. (17–18)

Even if people act in ways normally defined as good, their goodness will not be believed. Once stigmatized, they find it extremely difficult to be free of the label "delinquent" or "criminal." As Kai Erikson notes in *Wayward Puritans*, "The common feeling that deviant persons never really change . . . may derive from a faulty premise; but the feeling is expressed so frequently and with such conviction that it eventually creates the facts which later 'prove' it to be correct" (1966: 17).

A bad reputation doesn't just affect individuals. Peter Reuter, Jonathon Rubinstein, and Simon Winn (1983) describe the experience of corporations and even whole industries (for example, the vending machine business) whose bad reputations have led to an increase in crime. The reason, they argue, is that when labeled crooked, respectable people do not apply for jobs or work with such businesses—leaving them open and attractive to risk takers and criminals—a kind of self-selection is going on, "bad" places attracting "bad" people.

Societal reaction to crime and delinquency helps turn offending individuals away from seeing themselves as basically "straight" and "respectable" and toward an image of themselves as criminal. Thus, some people who are reacted to as criminals come to think of themselves as criminals, or at least they participate in what becomes a self-fulfilling prophecy. In a study of used-car fraud, one of John Braithwaite's informants said, "They think because you're a used car dealer you're a liar. So they treat you like one and lie to you. Can you blame the dealer for lying back?" (1978).

The term **secondary deviation** refers to the criminal acts associated with the individual's acquired status as a criminal and his or her ultimate acceptance of it (Lemert, 1951; 1972). Secondary deviation emerges from a process of reaction and adjustment to the punishing and stigmatizing actions of significant others, such as schoolteachers, parents, and law enforcement officials. Although initially individuals engage for a short time in deviant acts they regard as incompatible with their true selves (suggesting the need for the techniques of neutralization discussed earlier), they eventually come to accept their new identities as deviants and are well advanced toward careers in deviance:

> The sequence of interaction leading to secondary deviation is roughly as follows: (1) primary deviation [initial acts of deviance prompted by any number of reasons]; (2) social penalties; (3) further primary deviation; (4) stronger penalties and rejections; (5) further deviation, perhaps with hostilities and resentments beginning to focus upon those doing the penalizing; (6) crisis reached in the tolerance quotient, expressed in formal action by the community stigmatizing of the deviant; (7) strengthening of the deviant conduct as a reaction to the stigmatizing and penalties; (8) ultimate acceptance of deviant social status and efforts at adjustment on the basis of the associated role. (Lemert, 1951: 77)

Whether an individual moves from primary to secondary deviation depends greatly on the degree to which the disapproval of others finds expression in concrete acts of punishment and stigmatization. In a later paper, Lemert notes: "While communication of invidious definitions of persons or groups and the public expression of disapproval were included [in earlier discussions] as part of the societal reaction, the important point was made that these had to be validated in order to be sociologically meaningful. Validation was conceived as isolation, segregation, penalties, supervision, or some kind of organized treatment" (1974: 457). Support for the criminogenic impact of validation comes from Lyle Shannon's (1991) famous cohort study in Racine, Wisconsin, which found that boys who experienced repeated contact with the police were at much greater risk of chronic delinquency.

A more recent version of the theory that has been empirically supported in the literature posits that official intervention during adolescence can negatively impact educational attainment and employment opportunities in direct ways. In regard to education, children labeled as troublemakers are more likely to be harshly disciplined. They may even be suspended or expelled. This may not only create animosity in the child toward the school system and administrators, but also preclude the child from eventually landing a good job. It is theorized that this leads to reduced opportunities for legitimate ways to achieve income and status, and thus raises the probability of secondary deviation, as the individual does not see him- or herself fitting into mainstream society (Bernburg and Krohn, 2003).

Some critics have attacked labeling theory, arguing that many of its key assumptions are not supported by the bulk of available evidence. Indeed, Charles Wellford asserts that the supposed connection between punitive reactions, changes in self-concept, and secondary deviation is "a simplistic view of behavior causation, one that stresses the explanation of intellectual as opposed to behavioral characteristics of the subject" (1975: 342). More contemporary critics argue that the claim that changes in self-concept produce changes in behavior has yet to be demonstrated. Some prefer to view behavior as situationally determined, and thus crime may well occur quite independently of the actor's self-concept.

To be sure, labeling theory has come in for its share of criticism—perhaps even a disproportionate share—but it is far from dishonored as a theoretical perspective on crime, nor is it about to be abandoned by the field. Braithwaite's (1989) theory of reintegrative shaming (discussed in detail in chapter 15) and Sampson and Laub's (2003; 1997) continuing work in developmental criminology both take labeling theory seriously, giving it a prominent place in their theories of crime.

While differential association theory, social control theory, and varieties of strain/ anomie theory are more frequently tested than labeling theory, several studies in addition to the ones mentioned above have found that labeling theory is helpful in explaining some of the dynamics involved in crime and deviance. For example, because of the stigma surrounding being "mentally ill," people who may in fact be mentally ill might avoid treatment, keep their problems secret, or withdraw from the very audiences (friends, family) that might be able to help them improve the quality of their lives (Link and Cullen, 1983; Triplett, 2000). Criminal justice policies are also instructively viewed through labeling theory, as Ruth Triplett (2000) notes in the context of social reactions to juvenile delinquency in the 1990s. Furthermore, two studies found that while the effects of labeling theory are not as direct as the initial authors of the theory suggest, the effects of labeling are mediated through differential association (Adams, 1996; Downs, Robertson, and Harrison, 1997). Another study found that the effects of labeling were far stronger—a child's perception of teacher disapproval was highly associated with delinquency, independent of prior delinquency. However, the effects of labeling were less direct when considering a child's delinquent peer associations (Adams and Evans, 1996). Other research has found that the effects of labeling were highly significant in explaining adolescent drug use (Edwards, 1993).

CHAPTER SUMMARY

This chapter has considered the social processes by which people acquire the criminal attributes. A common theme running through many social process theories is that criminal behavior is learned through association with others who have criminal attributes. Sutherland's differential association theory is among the most well-known social process theories, and it has received considerable empirical support. Sutherland's theory, like several other social process theories, also draws attention to the ways in which relationships with others provide opportunities and incentives to learn criminal behavior patterns.

Self-concept theories of criminality suggest that a person's sense of self, which is grounded in the reactions of others, is an important element in the internal control of behavior. A strong self-concept is a defense against criminal influence. Neutralization theories suggest that self-respecting individuals will occasionally drift into crime or delinquency, as long as they can rationalize their misdeeds so as to protect their self-image as essentially good and honest people.

Control theory, on the other hand, asserts that by nature people will tend to do whatever they want, including crime, so the important theoretical question is: What stops them? Hirschi believes that people are less likely to become criminals the more attached they are to the people, values, and activities of conventional (i.e., noncriminal) society.

Labeling theory revolves around the idea that crime is a label attached to behavior and to people; there is nothing intrinsic in behavior that makes it a crime. Labeling theory emphasizes how the stigmatizing reactions of others may turn an individual's infrequent or spontaneous criminal behavior into persistent involvement that matches a criminal identity.

KEY TERMS

containment theory
differential association theory
drift theory
interactional theory of delinquency
interactionist perspective
normalization of deviance
operant conditioning
secondary deviation
social control theory
social process theories
techniques of neutralization
normalization of deviance
operant conditioning
secondary deviation
social control theory
social process theories
technique of neutralization

14 CRITICAL THEORIES OF CRIME

23107280 Jupiter

The lack of good jobs and homelessness are enduring social problems in the United States and in many other countries of the world. Hope that "things will get better" often hinges on the idea that financial security will bring about greater happiness. For the most unfortunate, hope might simply be for a meal or a home. Many more dream of a life free from abuse, assault, and neglect. As critical theorists point out, however, forces external to the individual—such as gender, economic class, and race—have a lot to do with who "makes it" in any given society. Critical criminological theorists are openly critical of social forces that limit opportunities for some groups while expanding them for others.

What distinguishes critical criminologists from other theorists is their *opposition* to—not just interest in—unequal political, economic, and social structures and relationships. The major forms of critical theories reviewed in this chapter include Marxist, left realist, feminist, postmodernist, and peacemaking perspectives. Respectively, their critiques are centered on capitalism, stratification and inequality, patriarchy, modernity, and war making. Critical theories of crime have roots in conflict theory.

While the social structural theories reviewed in chapter 13 consider the impact of social and economic inequities on crime, they do so only up to a point. **Conflict theory** goes a step further by seeing society as shaped by conflicts among people who have competing self- and group interests. Even though at a given time a society may seem to agree on basic values and goals, the existence of scarce resources and the tendency for them to be allocated unequally means that someone (or some group) is benefiting at the expense of someone else. In American society, groups at an overall disadvantage are women, minorities, and the poor. People on the "losing end" may not recognize or admit that their interests are in conflict with the interests of others, when in fact they are. Even though the struggle over scarce resources may be unrecognized or acknowledged, conflict theorists believe it is historic and ubiquitous. It usually consists of a struggle over three related things: money, power, and influence. Those who have more of them try to keep things the way they are; those who have less of them favor change so that they can obtain a bigger share. The groups with wealth, power, and influence are favored in the conflict precisely because those resources put them in a dominant position. It is the "haves"—rather than the "have-nots"—who make the rules, control the content and flow of ideas and information, and design (and impose) the penalties for nonconformity. Dominance means people are in a position to promote their own self-interest, even at the expense of others.

Sometimes the struggle over scarce resources is blatant and bloody, but more often it is subtle and restrained. Conflict theorists point to various factors that form the complex reasons for the restraint. For example, by controlling ideas and information, the dominant group is able to promote beliefs and values that support the existing order. In this way, the disadvantaged classes in society may develop what Karl Marx and Friedrich Engels (1947) called "false consciousness": a belief that prevailing social conditions are in their interest, when in fact they are not. Marx and Engels illustrate how this happens in the case of law. Law is presented to the masses as "the will of the people," and this "juridical illusion" undermines the development of opposition and resistance among the disadvantaged. People are likely to feel uncomfortable challenging a law that they believe reflects public consensus. In reality, law reflects the interests of the ruling class, according to Marx and Engels (39). In like manner, contemporary feminists theorize that law is biased not only against the poor, but also against women.

A second means of keeping the struggle over scarce resources in check is through the institutionalization of conflict. Special mechanisms such as courts, tribunals, and (in modern times) arbitration and civil rights hearings are set up to settle disputes. Disputes between individuals and groups are often conflicts over the distribution of scarce resources. When institutionalized avenues of settling disputes exist, the underlying struggle tends to be moderated and obscured. Aggrieved parties in the immediate dispute are pacified—if not by talk of "justice," then by the emphasis on procedures. Nowhere is this more evident than in the realm of crime, where victims often experience a complete loss of purpose as they face interminable delays and the intricacies of judicial procedure.

The *consensus*, or functionalist, view sees law and other political arrangements as useful for society as a whole, which justifies their existence. Conflict theorists, on the other hand, see them as useful for the dominant groups (i.e., the wealthy, men, and, in Western societies, whites) and perhaps even harmful to other groups or to the larger society. Law and politics protect the interests of the powerful, who in turn resist efforts to change them. Before we examine various critical and feminist theories in detail, let's first look at an influential t conflict theory that is one source of contemporary critical criminology.

TURK'S CONFLICT THEORY

Austin Turk's (1966; 1969) conflict theory of criminality illustrates many of the points made above. What makes Turk's work distinctive is his emphasis on authority and power relations, rather than on economic inequality.

Turk begins by rejecting the conception of crime as behavior, arguing instead that crime is a status acquired when those with authority to create and enforce legal rules (lawmakers, police, prosecuting attorneys, judges) apply those rules to others (the "subjects" in authority relations). He then constructs a theory to explain this process of criminalization. Turk believes that criminology needs a theory "stating the conditions under which cultural and social differences between authorities and subjects will probably result in conflict, the conditions under which criminalization will probably occur in the course of conflict, and the conditions under which the degree of deprivation associated with becoming a criminal will probably be greater or lesser" (1969: 53).

Turk hypothesizes that conflict between groups is most likely when authorities and subjects disagree about a particular activity, but the actions of each group (social norms) correspond with what they think ought to happen (cultural norms). For example, if the authorities hold that marijuana use is wrong and refrain from using it themselves, but a group of subjects holds that marijuana use is OK and use it, then conflict is likely because there is no room for compromise. In such a case, Turk argues, the authorities are likely to resort to coercion in order for their view to prevail. Conflict is least likely when neither the authorities nor the subjects act in accordance with their beliefs: Neither group is sufficiently committed to a value or belief to make an issue out of it. Other factors can affect the probability of conflict, including the degree to which subjects who resist are organized and the level of their sophistication. Conflict is more likely when norm resisters are poorly organized and unsophisticated.

Given the existence of conflict, the probability of criminalization depends on power differentials between authorities and subjects and on the realism of the moves (i.e., tactical skills) employed by opposing parties. Criminalization is more likely when the power difference favors authorities and the moves adopted by resisters are unrealistic. Examples of unrealistic moves are those that (1) increase the visibility of an attribute or behavior perceived by authorities as offensive; (2) draw attention to additional offensive attributes or violate even more significant norms upheld by authorities; (3) increase the level of consensus among authorities, for example, by turning opposition to a particular rule into an attack on the whole system; or (4) increase the power differences in favor of the enforcers (Turk, 1969: 72).

Turk's theory has not been tested as much as other theories reviewed in this chapter, but one of the very few empirical studies found considerable support for the notion that poor organization and a lack of sophistication among norm resisters tend to produce conflict. However, Turk's more specific claims regarding the relative importance of organization and sophistication were not well supported (Greenleaf and Lanza-Kaduce, 1995).

It should be noted that, for a number of reasons, Turk's theory represents one of the finest examples of theory construction in criminology. Foremost among these is the nature of the relationship between those who create, interpret, and enforce legal rules and those who are subject to them. Crime has no objective reality apart from the meanings attached to it, and criminality is an expression of those meanings. As Turk makes clear, the structure of authority relations must be included in a comprehensive theory of criminalization. Turk's theory focuses on authority relations and explains how it is that some people are labeled as criminals. Marxist theorists go further, casting conflicts of authority and criminal labeling within a general theory of political economy having roots in the work of Karl Marx.

MARXIST CRIMINOLOGICAL THEORY

While Karl Marx said little about crime, some criminologists, especially critical criminolo-

While Karl Marx wrote little about crime, his critique of capitalism inspired many social scientists, including criminologists, to study how economic inequality impacts behavior, processes, and institutions.

5265123 photos.com

gists, recognize a substantial debt to this nineteenth-century scholar. Marx believed that a society's mode of economic production—the manner in which relations of production are organized—determines in large part the organization of social relations, or the structure of individual and group interaction (1859; 1970: 20–21). Marx put it this way:

> In the social production in which men carry on they enter into definite relations that are indispensable and independent of their will; these relations of production correspond to a definite stage of development of their material powers of production. The totality of these relations of production constitutes the economic structure of a society—the real foundation, on which legal and political superstructures arise and to which definite forms of social consciousness correspond. The mode of production of material life determines the general character of the social, political, and spiritual process of life. It is not the consciousness of men that determines their being, but, on the contrary, their social being determines their consciousness.

Under a capitalist mode of production, there are those who own the means of production and those who do not. The former group is known as the *bourgeoisie* and the latter as the *proletariat.* The bourgeoisie, or ruling class, controls the formulation and implementation of moral and legal norms, and even ideas. Both classes are bound in relationship to one another, but this relationship is asymmetrical and exploitive.

This relationship affects law and, by extension, crime. Laws are created by the bourgeoisie, to protect their interests, at the expense of the proletariat. However, the image of law promoted to the masses is one that implies democracy and consensus. For example, nearly everyone would agree that killing another without legitimate reason should be criminal. However, what is a legitimate reasons? War? Corporate violations of safety laws that result in worker deaths? Marxists might point out that even presumably simple and well-supported laws may not work in the interests of the have-nots, though they may be perceived to be a representation of the collective will of a society. In this spirit, Marxist scholars have noted:

> The fact is that the label "crime" is not used in America to name all or the worst of the actions that cause misery and suffering to Americans. It is primarily reserved for the dangerous action of the poor. (Reiman, 1999: 25)
>
> [I]t is not the social harms punishable by law which cause the greatest misery in the world. It is the lawful harms, those unpunishable crimes justified and protected by law, the state, the ruling elites that fill the earth with misery, want, strife, conflict, slaughter, and destruction. (Tifft and Sullivan, 1980: 9)

Marxist criminology hit its high point in the 1970s, after many of Marx's early writings were translated to English and made available in the United States. The perspective is still a force in criminology, but not in its original formulation, as its applicability to the study of crime and law has been realized more fully by contemporary critical criminological scholarship. However, before we examine these newer versions, let's take a look at the classic work of the Dutch criminologist Willem Bonger.

Bonger on Crime and Economic Conditions

As previously discussed, Marx himself wrote little about crime. However, Willem Bonger, an intellectual follower of Marx, applied some of Marx's arguments to crime in capitalistic societies. In *Criminality and Economic Conditions* (1969; first published in English in 1916), Bonger observed that capitalistic societies appear to have considerably more crime than others. Furthermore, as capitalism developed, crime rates increased steadily.

Under capitalism, Bonger argued, the characteristic trait of humans is self-interest (egoism). Given the emphasis on profit maximization and competition and the fact that social relations are class structured and geared to economic exchange, capitalistic societies spawn intraclass and interclass conflicts as individuals seek to survive and prosper. Interclass conflict is one sided, however, since those who own and control the means of production are in a position to coerce and exploit their less fortunate neighbors. As one instrument of coercion, criminal law is used by the ruling class to protect its position and interests. Criminal law "is principally constituted according to the will of" the dominant class, and "hardly any act is punished if it does not injure the interests of the dominant class" (1969: 379, 380). Behavior that threatens the interests of the ruling class is designated as criminal.

Since social relations are geared toward competition, profit seeking, and the exercise of power, altruism is subordinated to egoistic tendencies. These tendencies lead, in Bonger's view, to a weakening of internal restraint. Both the bourgeoisie and the proletariat become prone to crime. The working class is subject to further demoralization, however, because of its inferior exchange position and its exploitation at the hands of the ruling class: "Long working hours and monotonous labor brutalize those who are forced into them; bad housing conditions contribute also to debase the moral sense, as do the uncertainty of existence, and, finally, absolute poverty, the frequent consequence of sickness and unemployment" (1969: 195).

In Bonger's view, economic conditions that induce egoism, coupled with a system of law creation and enforcement controlled by the capitalist class, account for (1) higher crime rates in capitalistic societies than in other societies, (2) the increase in crime rates with industrialization, and (3) the working-class character of official crime.

A Sampling of Marxist Criminology: 1970s to the Present

In the 1970s the first systematic Marxist statements on crime began to appear in the United States. Many works by Marx (such as the *Economic and Philosophic Manuscripts* of 1844) became widely available to U.S. scholars at this time. Also adding to the appeal of Marx's scholarship were the sweeping social movements of the 1960s and the accompanying cultural and political changes that occurred at this time. Students, professors, and social activists looked to alternative literature to help them answer big questions about social problems such as crime, racism, sexism, and war. Marxist theory is still a valuable tool for analyzing the nuances of the political economy's impact on crime and victimization, but much of the contemporary relevance of Marxian criminology is attributable to the work of David Gordon, Richard Quinney, Stephen Spitzer, and William Chambliss, whose work we will now review.

According to David Gordon (1971; 1973), most crime is a rational response to the structure of institutions found in capitalistic societies. Crime is "a means of survival in a society within which survival is never assured" (1971: 59). Gordon identifies three types of crime in the United States as the best examples of this rationality: ghetto crime, organized crime, and corporate (or white-collar) crime. These types of crime offer a chance at survival, status, and respect in a society geared toward competitive forms of social interaction and characterized by substantial inequalities in the distribution of social, economic, and political resources.

Involvement in different types of crime is explained by class position. Those in the upper socioeconomic classes have access to jobs in which paper transactions, large amounts of money, and unobtrusive communication are important features. Illegal opportunities are manifest in the many forms of white-collar crime. Those in the lower classes, especially those who are "raised in poverty," do not have easy access to money and nonviolent means to manipulate it. Accordingly, illegal activities tend to involve taking things by force or physical stealth. Gordon sees duality in American justice in that the state tends to ignore certain kinds of crime, most notably corporate and white-collar crime, and concerns itself "incessantly" with crimes among the poor. According to Gordon, this duality is understandable only if one views the state through the radical perspective. First of all, government in a capitalistic society exists primarily to serve the interests of the capitalist class, and preservation of the system itself is the priority. So long as power and profits are not undermined, the offenses that tend in general to harm members of other classes receive little interest. Second, even though offenses of the poor tend to harm others who are poor, they are collectively viewed as a threat to the stability of the system and the interests of the ruling class. Furthermore, an aggressive lower class is a dangerous class, and the spread of ghetto crime (conveniently identified with African Americans) to other parts of the nation's cities heightens the fears of the affluent classes, who are in a position to influence policy. Gordon's critical approach provides a framework for explaining both the status of criminality and the behavior of the criminal (see also Spitzer, 1975).

Richard Quinney, one of the most prolific criminologists in the world, has written on crime from a number of theoretical perspectives, but here we will consider his Marxist theory of crime, first published as *Class, State, and Crime* in 1977 and elaborated in *Criminology* (1979). This work is really not a theory of crime causation per se, but a call, through critique, for the use of Marxist theory in the scholarly understanding of law, justice, and crime.

Quinney starts with a number of presuppositions. First, to understand the meaning of crime in capitalist society, one must take into account how capitalist economics develop. By this, Quinney means that to understand crime in U.S. society, we should have a sense of the historical evolution of political economy and how it instructs our everyday lives and ideas. Second, says Quinney, it is important to get a grasp on how systems of class domination and repression operate for the benefit of the

capitalist class through the vehicle of the state. Here Quinney suggests that law is one weapon in the arsenal of the bourgeoisie to exploit the proletariat and to deflect scrutiny from its own harmful actions. Additionally, Quinney writes that ideas about crime and justice are created through human experiences within a capitalist society, and therefore the dominant ideology of crime reflects that bias. Justice, too, is ideological in this sense, as it is constituted through the prism of capitalist logic and interests. Crime itself, according to Quinney, is a manifestation of class struggle as well:

> Much criminal behavior is of a parasitical nature, including burglary, robbery, drug dealing, and hustling of various sorts. . . . [T]he behavior, although pursued out of the need to survive, is a reproduction of the capitalist system (1979: 61).

Crimes such as murder, assault, and rape, he continues, often stem from those who are already "brutalized by the conditions of capitalism" (61). The solution to crime, according to Quinney and others working from this perspective, involves a fundamental restructuring of society on socialist principles.

Quinney called criminologists to the carpet for their role in all of this as well: He viewed uncritical criminologists as tacit agents of the capitalist state, for the discipline of criminology "seeks to control anything that threatens the capitalist system of production and its social relations" (1979: 176). What Quinney meant is that by divorcing the study of crime from the study of class domination, criminologists are involved in reproducing the inequalities caused by capitalism. Many mainstream criminologists have taken issue with the claim that they are capitalist patsies because they study crime in traditional ways, but Quinney's claim is defensible from a Marxist point of view: As the old saying goes "if you are not part of the solution, you are part of the problem." Indeed, from this perspective, the problem of crime is rooted in capitalism, and thus the study of anything else is uncritical and indirectly supportive of the system. It is therefore part of the problem because it detracts attention from the real issues.

At about the same time Richard Quinney was making his important stance in criminology, another Marxist-inspired conceptualization of crime was offered by William Chambliss (1975). Chambliss, also a highly productive criminologist, argued that the state was a tool used by the elite to control the poor and to protect their own wealth, status, and privilege. If this wasn't the case, he asked, how is it that many wrongs committed by the rich represent an even greater threat than traditional street crimes in terms of injury, yet are either not defined as criminal or are not prosecuted and punished? While in today's world it may seem there that there is more attention paid to elite crime by both the public and the state (e.g., publicity surrounding the Enron fiasco), there is hardly equity in enforcement and punishment. This is not to say that traditional street crimes such as murder and robbery should not be taken seriously, but rather that if an important rationale for criminalization and punishment is the seriousness of injury, white-collar crimes (including state crimes like genocide, illegal war, and repression) must also be taken seriously. Chambliss maintained that crimes in the suites are often off the radar screen because of the elite's grip on power and their influence on those who control the creation and enforcement of law. Unless the proletariat achieves class-consciousness—a Marxian term for the collective realization of the proletariat that capitalism must end—the crimes of the elite will escape proper scrutiny. In sum, Chambliss argued that:

- Acts are criminal because it is in the interests of the ruling class to so define them.
- The lower classes are labeled criminal and the bourgeoisie is not because the bourgeoisie's control of the means of production gives them control of the state and law enforcement as well.

- Socialist and capitalist societies should have significantly different crimes rates since class conflict will be less in socialist societies.

In a similar vein, Steven Spitzer has maintained that people become candidates for formal social control in a capitalist society when they "disturb, hinder, or call into question" any of the following:

- Capitalist modes of appropriating the product of human labor (theft)
- The social conditions under which capitalist production takes place (those unable or unwilling to perform labor)
- Patterns of distribution and consumption in capitalist society (drug use)
- The process of socialization for productive and nonproductive roles (youths who refuse schooling or traditional family life)
- The ideology which supports the functioning of capitalist society (revolutionaries and other political deviants) (1975: 352)

Because there has never been a genuine socialist society that would meet Marx's definition, it is difficult to gauge the validity of Chambliss's and Quinney's assertions that crime would be lower in communist societies. However, elements of Chambliss's first two points identified above can be tested, and studies have found that some lawmaking and law enforcement is as classist as he suggests. In support of Spitzer's theory, some deviance is clearly defined as such by authorities because it threatens the principles of the economic system (e.g., almost all forms of theft), but the extent to which the laws are passed with this specific intent on the part of the bourgeoisie is less clear.

This points to one of the problems with early efforts in Marxist criminology: their overly instrumentalist theme. **Instrumental Marxism,** which has fallen out of favor in critical criminology circles, grants too much importance to the direct relationship between the economy and crime. The theorized supremacy of economics results in overgeneralization, as it is now commonly understood that, rather than conscious capitalist interests dictating the whole content of law and the working of the criminal justice system, other interests and actors shape institutions and social structures such as criminal justice and law. Another major problem with the instrumentalist treatment of the structural sources of crime is its vision of the ruling class itself. Sometimes the image conjured up is of a small band of powerful individuals in collusion with one another to determine the destinies of all. Some early Marxists also portrayed those whose criminal actions were political as victimized prisoners of circumstance, whose crimes were not their responsibility. A final tension in instrumental Marxist theory can be identified: Some adherents to the perspective are against short-term reforms of the criminal justice system because such actions would undermine the militant opposition necessary for a socialist revolution. This matter has been a source of tension between critical criminologists, as less radical scholars have argued that even small change is better than nothing. Left realists (discussed later) have grounded their integrative theory with specific attention to this issue.

As the years passed, Marxist criminology began to develop into more sophisticated sets of ideas about crime and law. David Greenberg (1977), for example, developed an explanation of juvenile delinquency that focused on teenagers' exclusion from the labor market. Greenberg noted that since children and teenagers do not normally engage in "serious work," they have little ability to achieve status through money. Everyone knows that it is difficult, if not impossible, for teens to work at a place like McDonald's while in high school and make the rent. Some parents, of course, have neither the means nor the desire to buy their children all the clothes, toys, concert tickets, and cars they might want. Youths, then, because they are not capable of buying these items themselves, might turn to delinquency (such as theft) to upgrade their lifestyle or status. By showing how the lack of participation in a capitalist labor market might be connected to crime, Greenberg's theory adds some explanatory power to Marxist criminological theory, as many of the explanations for crime causation by earlier Marxist criminologists were somewhat crude.

Another influential Marxist theory of juvenile delinquency was developed by Mark Colvin and John Pauly (1983). Juvenile delinquency, they argued, begins with parenting. While this perspective does not seem particularly Marxist, the authors argued that parenting styles are influenced by relationships and experiences at work. First, many delinquents come from working-class families, where the breadwinners are employed in "dead-end" jobs (so-called Fraction I jobs) and are subject to coercion, threats, and the possibility of dismissal at any time. Such jobs include nonunionized industrial, textile, and agricultural work. Workers in this category tend to be highly alienated from their jobs, and this tends to carry over at home. Such parents are more likely to be punitive (sometimes physically), inconsistent with discipline, and generally more abusive than parents employed in better jobs. As a result of this type of parenting, children are more likely to become alienated from their parents, leading to a greater likelihood of alienation at school and association with other alienated peers. Along with the disadvantages of their class position, the table then becomes set for the formulation of delinquent attitudes and behavior. Colvin and Pauly's theory was a major contribution to critical criminology at the time, as it showed, like Greenberg's, that both cultural forces and insights from other theories of crime can be integrated into Marxist theory to form a potentially more valuable explanation of crime.

Marxist criminology matured immensely in the 1990s. Perhaps the best illustrations of this change are recent socialist feminist theories (discussed later in this chapter) and Chambliss's **structural contradictions theory** (Chambliss and Zatz, 1993). Let's examine the latter now.

Rejecting theories (and, to some extent, his earlier work) that maintained that the capitalist mode of production exclusively determines law—and, by implication, crime—the new theory posits that every society attempts to resolve conflicts and dilemmas caused by fundamental contradictions. The creation of law, then, is more complicated than simply the ruling class plotting against the interests of the working class (see figure 14.1). The basic contradiction within capitalism is between labor and capital, and it

produces conflicts between workers and capitalists, and for the state it creates a set of dilemmas. Should the state represent only the

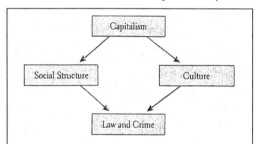

Instrumental Marxist Approach: Capitalism and capitalist interests determine the particular form of institutions, organizations, ideology, and social processes. Law is used to control the proletariat and to shield the crimes of the bourgeoisie.

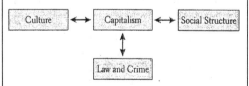

Structural Marxist Approach: Capitalism and capitalist interests shape institutions, organizations, ideology, and social processes, which then further shape the political economy of capitalism. Law and crime are strongly influenced by the interests of the economy, not simply elites conspiring to control the proletariat.

For in depth discussions of these perspectives, see Raymond J. Michalowski (1985) and William Chambliss and Marjorie Zatz (1993).

▲ **Figure 14.1.**
Instrumental and Structural Marxist Theories

interests of capitalists, the conflicts will increase in intensity, with workers pitted against the state. . . . Were the state to side with the workers . . . the system would likewise collapse and a new social order would have to be constructed. Faced with this dilemma, officials of the state attempt to resolve the conflict by passing laws, some which represent the interests of capitalists and some the interests of workers. (Chambliss and Zatz, 1993: 10)

This refinement of Marxist theory allows for the idea that the state has *relative autonomy* from the capitalist class. While elite interests surely shape law, they do not exclusively instruct it. Consider the example of white-collar crime. A major goal of the capitalist state has been to promote capital accumulation (corporate money making). However, there is quite a bit of regulation of business as well. Harold Barnett has argued that while this is true, the state's regulatory function "must not be so severe as to diminish substantially the contribution of large corporations to growth in output and employment" (1981: 7). So from this structural—rather than instrumental—Marxist view, while state regulatory agencies have been created to help protect workers (the Occupational Safety and Health Administration), the environment (the Environmental Protection Agency), and consumers (the Consumer Product Safety Commission), they cannot do anything to seriously compromise an industry's basic contributions to the functional requirements of the economy (Matthews and Kauzlarich, 2000). While regulatory agencies can help protect the environment and make workplaces and commodities safer, the laws and regulations will never be so strong as to disable business from the ability to reap profits. This is seen as problematic by Marxists, as the main motivation of corporate crime can be linked to the desire to maximize profits (Friedrichs, 2004). Ultimately, laws governing business will not be created or enforced if they seriously compromise principles designed to facilitate capitalist accumulation. In fact, to some Marxists, their very existence increases false consciousness, as the illusion of protection is enhanced when the "front" put up by the state seems legitimate on the surface (Pearce and Tombs, 2002).

Research by Raymond Michalowski and Susan Carlson (1999) illustrates the enduring value of the Marxist criminology. The authors have shown that unemployment rates and new court admissions to prison can be linked to swings and qualitative changes in the U.S. economy. These changes include shifts in the productive dimension of the overall economy, the workforce, and various state interventions. Thus, periods characterized by high unemployment, deteriorating job quality, low social welfare benefits, and a growing surplus population of young, disaffected, unemployed men will generate a greater reliance on punitive strategies than other periods in time (227). In sum, the study illustrates how discrete changes in capitalist economies effect aggregate levels of crime.

LEFT REALISM

Several years ago British criminologists led by Jock Young started to systematically critique some radical Marxist criminological theories. Young proposed that the "left idealism" of the radical perspective be replaced by **left realism**. According to Young (1986; 1997), left idealism has tended to downplay the severity of crime and the fact that it is most often intraclass and intraracial. Rick Matthews explains:

> While not ignoring crimes of the powerful, new left realists have taken the position that the effects of street crime are both serious and real, that the criminal class is not revolutionary, and that critical (i.e., Marxian, conflict, feminist, and radical) criminologists must pay attention to it. What ties new left realism to Marxian criminology, however, is its emphasis on understanding crime within the larger political economy. (2004: 9)

In addition, Young charges that left idealism failed to build on past theories of criminal etiology and consequently failed in its theoretical mission to explain crime. For example, Young writes:

> [T]here is no evidence that absolute deprivation (e.g. unemployment, lack of schooling, poor housing, and so forth) leads automatically to crime. Realist criminology points to relative deprivation in certain conditions as being the major causes of crime; i.e., when people experience a level of unfairness in their allocation of resources and utilize individualistic means to attempt to right this condition. . . . To say that poverty in the present period breeds crime is not to say that all poor people are criminals. Far from it: most poor people are perfectly honest and many wealthy people commit crimes. Rather, it is to say that the rate of crime is higher in certain parts of society under certain conditions. (1997: 30–31)

Young believes that the central tasks of radical or critical criminology still remain "to create an adequate explanation of crime, victimization, and the reaction of the state" (1986: 25). The alternative realist criminology deals with that agenda while uncovering the reality of crime, "its origins, its nature, and its impact" (21). Official data and research are not to be rejected out of hand, nor will current definitions of crimes and their severity constrain the realist's search for this reality (Matthews, 1986: 8). Left realism emphasizes going behind appearances that pass as reality. A "central tension" in left realism is working both "in" and "against" the state. The question is this: How can the victimization and suffering of crime, especially among the lower classes, be reduced without extending the coercive and bureaucratic apparatus of the state? (DeKeseredy et al., 2003; Matthews, 1986: 14).

Like other social structural perspectives, one of the central ideas of realist criminology leads to the lower classes. But rather than looking there only for offenders the realists see the lower class as a victim of crime "from all sides"

(Young, 1986: 23). The lower class generally, and racial minorities in particular, are doubly vulnerable to crime because they are victims of predatory street crimes as well as white-collar crimes: They are victims of both the poor and the powerful (Young, 1997; 2000).

In the tradition of both left realism and strain theory, Elliott Currie (1997) has theorized about crime in so-called *market societies*. These types of societies (e.g., the United States and Great Britain) have significant economic inequality as well as a scarcity of stable and rewarding jobs. Market societies are characterized by the pursuit of personal economic gain in all facets of life. This one-dimensional motivation, Currie argues, comes at the expense of peoples' interest and ability to invest in powerful social, cultural, and human forces (so-called social capital), which are known to be negatively related to violence in any given society. In such societies, people have little or marginal interest in furthering their relationships with others outside their immediate group, such as the larger community or neighborhoods.

According to Currie (1997), market societies are criminogenic—they provide fertile grounds for crime to flourish—in a number of ways. First, while market economies like the U.S. can produce lots of jobs, many of them are low paying and without benefits. So even though the unemployment rate in the United States is currently low, many people are working very hard to earn very little. This continues to produce economic and social inequalities that positively correlate with the overall crime rate. Second, market societies tend to have limited formal and informal social supports. For example, the strains between family and work are profound for many working people. There is little formal support by employers or the government to provide paid parental leave and quality universal health care, or to do something about the disintegration of neighborhoods and communities. Third, market societies often place "competition and consumption over the values of community, contribution, and work" (Currie, 1997: 161).

We should therefore expect that in a "dog-eat-dog" world, people will care less about others' well-being—and not caring about other people makes it easier to victimize them. Fourth, Currie believes that it is possible that the amount of firearm violence in the United States could be reduced with more sensible gun regulation. The United States leads the advanced industrialized world in the rate of gun crime and violence—and it also has the weakest national regulations on the sale and possession of guns. Finally, Curries notes that, at least in the United States, the lack of alternative political discussion leads people to believe there is nothing that can be done about social problems such as crime. Crime is thus easily divorced from its larger structural roots, which in turn lessens peoples' ability to envision a safer and less violent society.

Left realism is surely here to stay, for it provides a richer approach than traditional Marxist theories to understanding the links between crime and the economy. In fact, the approach may soon be as recognizable as any other criminological theory discussed in this text, especially given its clear practical implications (see box 14.1).

FEMINIST THEORIES OF CRIME

Feminist theory has challenged many of the biases of traditional academic disciplines, including criminology. For years, criminology was very androcentric, as criminologists were mostly males studying males and either ignoring women altogether, stereotyping them, or otherwise downplaying their importance. While there are many different forms of **feminist criminology** (e.g., liberal socialist, and radical), at the most basic level feminism in criminology is about centering gender and its relationship to lawmaking, lawbreaking, and reactions to crime (Iadicola and Shupe, 1998: 78; Miller, 2003). Several years ago Kathleen Daly and Meda Chesney-Lind published a landmark paper on feminism and criminology in which they identified five elements of feminist thought that distinguish it from other forms of social and political perspectives. These are:

1. Gender is not a natural fact but a complex social, historical, and cultural product . . . .
2. Gender and gender relations order social life and social institutions in fundamental ways.
3. Gender relations and constructs of masculinity and femininity are not symmetrical but are based on an organizing principle of men's superiority and social and political economic dominance over women.
4. Systems of knowledge reflect men's views of the natural and social world.
5. Women should be at the center of intellectual inquiry, not peripheral, invisible or appendages to men. (1988: 108)

Taken together, these points suggest that a small physiological difference at birth between males and females (that is, our sex) becomes the basis for drastically different expectations, opportunities, and socialization throughout the course of our lives. Open almost any introductory sociology textbook and read the chapter on gender. There you will find overwhelming evidence of the significance of (a) gender role socialization (the teaching of girls to be feminine and boys to be masculine) and (b) gender inequality (the differences in political, social, and economic power, authority, and status among men and women). There is simply little doubt that in the aggregate, men and women have very different social statuses.

Criminologists who take gender seriously use these larger sociological realities to help understand issues such as (a) different offending rates; (b) differential involvement in types of crime; (c) police, prosecutorial, and judicial discretion in criminal justice; (d) institutional discrimination against women in criminal justice; and (e) differential victimization (Flavin, 1998; Miller, 2003; Stanko, 1995). This last area has played a key role in the development of criminological research and theory on domestic assault, sexual assault, child maltreatment, pornography, and prostitution. While there is considerable debate among criminologists about the impact of feminism on criminology

BOX 14.1. POLICY PROPOSALS OF LEFT REALISM

Left realist criminological theory has a number of clear policy implications, some of which are similar to those of Merton's strain theory. Which of the following left realist proposals do you think have a good chance to reduce crime?

- Job creation and training programs
- A higher minimum wage
- Government-sponsored day care
- Housing assistance
- Teaching of entrepreneurial skills in high school
- Linking school, business, and state services
- Creating universal health care

As Walter DeKeseredy, one of the preeminent left realists of our time, notes, the perspective emphasizes the importance of making changes in the area of *social policy* more than criminal justice policy (DeKeseredy, 2004: 37). Do you agree?

Source: DeKeseredy (2004)

more generally (Rafter and Heidensohn, 1997), there is little question that feminist criminology is a growing area of scholarship, and, in our view, makes considerable contributions to the understanding of crime.

There are two issues that lie at the heart of the feminist challenge to theoretical criminology: (1) whether traditional theories of crime apply to girls and women, and (2) why women offend significantly less than men (Miller, 2004). Regarding the first issue, it is important to examine the question of whether interactions and relationships with friends and family are qualitatively different for boys and girls. For example, research has shown that parents tend to be more controlling in some aspects of their daughters' lives, but not their sons' lives. Instead of "control" being a gender-neutral variable, it could be that girls are subject to different forms of control—say, in the monitoring of physical appearances and sex. If parents exercise control and tolerance in gendered ways, a seemingly objective measure of the social bond such as the quality or time of "parental interaction" may be measuring different things for boys than girls. Further, how do we know there are not significant variations in the causes of offending within gender categories? To explore this question, feminist criminologists are working on new ways to understand the intersections of race and class with gender (Miller, 2004).

The second issue relates to what is know as the gender ratio problem. The concern here is rooted in the fact that official statistics and other measures of crime indicate that men and boys are much more involved than girls and women in criminal activity. From a feminist perspective, any legitimate theory of crime must be able to address this relationship, as it is among the more universal facts about crime. We turn to one such theory now.

Gender Class Theory

As we have seen, theories of crime that focus on class relations and economic inequality owe a heavy debt to Marx and Engels. However, some criminologists believe that an adequate theory of crime requires the incorporation of a second aspect of social structure, what James Messerschmidt calls *relations of reproduction*. "[I]n all societies," Messerschmidt writes, "people need to reproduce, socialize, and maintain the species. Consequently, people organize into relations of reproduction to satisfy these needs" (1986: ix).

From a socialist feminist perspective, in capitalist societies such as the United States, "relations of reproduction take the form of patriarchal gender relations, in which the male gender appropriates the labor power and controls the sexuality of the female gender" (Messerschmidt, 1986: ix–x). However, the domination of women as a group by men as a group is intertwined with class domination: "Women labor in both the market and the home, and suffer masculine dominance in each. But in addition, their experience in both realms is determined by their class" (xi). In production and in reproduction, behavior is shaped by power relations that cut across both spheres. In the United States, "we do not simply live in a 'capitalist' society, but rather a 'patriarchal capitalist' society" (35). One can therefore distinguish two basic groups: "a powerless group, comprising women and the working class, and a powerful group, made up of men and the capitalist class" (41).

Messerschmidt endeavored to show how interlocking class and gender relations affect both criminal behavior and its control. For example, the well-documented gap between female rates of serious crime (which are low) and male rates (which are high)—the so-called gender ratio problem discussed above (Daly and Chesney-Lind, 1988: 119; see also Chesney-Lind and Shelden, 1992: 7–28; Miller, 2003)—is explained in terms of the lack of female opportunities for legitimate and illegitimate activities that results from the fact that women are subordinate "and therefore less powerful in economic, religious, political, and military institutions" (Messerschmidt, 1986: 43). On the other hand, males have power, which provides them with far more opportunities to commit crime. When class is brought into the picture, the argument is this: Lower-class males have less power, hence commit less crime, than capitalist and middle-class males, but in all social classes, males are more powerful than females. "Their powerful position allows some men to engage in crimes specifically as men to maintain their dominant position" (45), for example, rape and wife beating.

While socialist feminist theories of crime can be criticized for their lack of attention to race (Rice, 1990), the theory offers a more sophisticated way to think about the relationship between gender and class and how both operate to structure the nature and extent of crime and victimization.

Power-Control Theory

John Hagan and his colleagues have developed what has become known as the *power-control theory* of crime, which attempts to explain gender differences in offending. The theory focuses on the relations of girls and boys to their parents, and argues that in patriarchal (male-dominated) families, male delinquency will be greater because parents encourage, support, and socialize boys into masculine roles and behaviors. Girls in patriarchal families, however, commit less crime because they are more subject to regulation by their parents and are encouraged to adopt more feminine roles and behaviors. On the other hand, girls in more egalitarian families, where each parent has equal power and status, are more likely to engage in delinquency because fewer controls are exercised over their behavior. In sum, the theory holds that as women enter the paid labor force and assume more powerful positions in the workplace, mothers—and, by extension, their daughters—might become freer and less controlled. Thus, daughters could become more like sons in their willingness to take risks and their involvement in de-

linquency (McCarthy, Hagan, and Woodward, 1999: 762).

What makes the work of Messerschmidt and Hagan important is its improvement over other critical theories that focus only on economic inequality, and particularly its specification of how class and gender together affect crime. Even so, the approaches, specifically Hagen's, are not without critics. Meda Chesney-Lind (1987a), for example, objects that Hagen's work represents a "not-so-subtle variation" of the now-discredited view that "liberated" females commit more crime. The *liberal feminist theory* of crime to which Chesney-Lind is referring maintains that women's involvement in crime is linked to their increased opportunities in society, especially in the workplace. The argument goes like this: The women's liberation movement has pushed for equality between the sexes. The result, Freda Adler (1975) and Rita Simon (1975) have suggested, has been a convergence of gender roles as many of the experiences and opportunities previously reserved for males (and a few "lucky" females) open to more and more females. In Adler's terms, a "virilization" of women has taken place, and the masculine female becomes less distinguishable from her male counterpart in all areas of life, including crime. These changes, because they affect home life and the socialization process, presumably will filter down to young girls. This **liberation/opportunity theory** predicts that the crime rates of women and girls will increase and broaden. Under empirical scrutiny, this theory has been shown to be weak. This is partly due to the fact that females are still more likely to hold low-paying jobs that are often auxiliary to the "more important" and better-paying jobs of men. Some have suggested that many women are actually *less free* today than they were forty years ago. They are expected to contribute to family income, yet childcare facilities are woefully inadequate. This is particularly burdensome on young single mothers, many of whom are teenagers (Morris, 1987: 72).

Hagan and his colleagues have recognized the merit of such criticism by Chesney-Lind, and have pointed out in a test of a revised power-control theory that there is a "further possibility that changes in women's work and family experiences might affect their relationships with their sons and their sons' fathers, thus altering, and perhaps diminishing delinquency among males" (McCarthy, Hagan, and Woodward, 1999: 761). This richer, more dynamic power-control theory has been to some extent empirically supported, and the revised power-control theory now awaits further test.

A Sampling of Feminist Works

There are hundreds—perhaps thousands—of feminist studies and tests of theories in criminology. As with our review of Marxist criminological theories, however, we can provide only a snapshot of these works. Let's review a few that illustrate the continuing value of contemporary feminist scholarship in criminology.

Jody Miller (1998b) has studied the similarities and differences between male and female robbers. Based on interview data from St. Louis, Miller found that while the *motivations* for engaging in robbery for men and women were similar, the *accomplishment* of robbery was very different. She found that (a) female robbers targeted female victims more than male victims, however, (b) some of the female robbers used men's perceptions of women as weak and sexually available to facilitate the robbing of male victims. These differences suggest that women who commit violent crimes may do so quite differently than men because of the gendered nature of their environment, wherein "the differences that emerge reflect practical choices made in the context of a gender-stratified environment, one in which, on the whole, men are perceived as strong and women are perceived as weak" (Miller, 1998b: 60–61). Other research by Miller on girls and gangs also suggests similar social processes and structures at work (Miller, 1998b). In a different vein, Lisa Maher (1997) has found evidence that women who engage in violent crime often do so to protect or defend themselves. While Miller (1998b) found that the motivations for men and women to commit robbery were similar, Maher found that women often "vicced" (robbed) male clients in part because of their increased economic marginalization and vulnerability to abuse and assault on the street. Women, then, according to Maher, clearly have different motivations than men for engaging in violent crime.

A study of the impact of gender on residential burglars by Mullins and Wright (2003) has found further evidence of this. Regardless of gender, the majority of burglars indicated that they stole money and other items to enhance a "party" lifestyle (i.e., buying drugs, alcohol, fancy clothes, and jewelry). However, women were far more likely to report that the money gained from the burglaries would be in some way used to take care of their children. Consider the following statement:

> I needed money, cause I needed a roof over my head, food to eat, things for my baby . . . cause I needed diapers and I was broke and, you know, my hours had been cut and I didn't have the money to pay rent plus to get the baby what it needed. You know, it's gonna be cold soon, I need winter clothes for my kid. (821–22)

Men rarely mentioned such problems.

Another interesting type of feminist criminological theory has developed around the relationship between masculinities and crime. Promoted by James Messerschmidt, **structured action theory** "emphasizes the construction of gender as a situated social and interactional accomplishment. . . . [G]ender grows out of social practices in specific social structural settings and serves to inform such practices in reciprocal relation" (1994; 2000: 6). Essentially, the theory suggests that when men "do" crime or violence, they are often acting out a role within a specific social context that can be related to the presentation of masculinity.

But this performance of masculinity is relative and intermittent. Obvious affronts to a boy's or man's masculinity are called *masculinity challenges*, and it is these challenges, such as insults and threats, that can give rise to the motivation to violent behavior or masculine social action (Messerschmidt, 2000). However, many threats to masculinity may not result in violent behavior.

Using structured action theory to help understand the identities of nine boys, Messerschmidt notes that each of the boys, and all males presumably, construct or "do" gender differently. The difficult part is identifying who is most at risk and how to promote a "democratic manhood" in which men and boys separate violence, authority, and domination from being masculine (2000: 139). Closing this section with the words of Messerschmidt seems appropriate. His take on the future directions of feminist criminology is consistent with ours:

> [R]ather than conceptualizing gendered crime simplistically in terms of, for example, males commit violence and females commit theft, new directions in feminist theory enable us to explore which males and which females commit which crimes, and in which social situations. (1997: 185)

Indeed, it is quite fair to say that criminology can only benefit from this type of analysis.

POSTMODERN CRIMINOLOGY

Like other critical criminologies, postmodern theories of crime are oppositional—but for this perspective the opposition is to modernity, or, more specifically, privileged discourses (i.e., writing and speaking by the more powerful members of society) that drown out and marginalize the less powerful in society. Grounded in a critique of the notion that rationality, reason, science, and technology lead to progress (as implied by Enlightenment-era thought) **postmodern criminology** has its intellectual roots in the writings of French scholars such as Jacques Lacan, Michel Foucault, Jean Baudrilland, and Jean-François Lyotard. Postmodernism openly questions conventional ideas about the value of science in explaining crime and posits that the world is chaotic and unpredictable (Ferrell and Hamm, 1998; Henry and Milovanovic, 2003; Milovanovic, 1997). According to Bruce Arrigo (2004), there are three themes of the postmodernist perspective: (1) the importance of language, (2) the notion of partial knowledge and provisional truth, and (3) deconstruction, difference, and possibility. Let us consider each of these in turn.

Criminological postmodernism sensitizes us to the power of words, especially the so-called crime speak, and how the use of language is linked to how we think about and define the supposed "being" of crime and justice (Arrigo, 1998; Henry and Milovanovic, 1996; 1999). For example, a postmodern *constitutive theory* of crime offered by Arrigo maintains that:

- Language is never neutral. It is encoded with multiple desires and multiple ways of knowing.
- Certain conversations about crime are valued and esteemed over others. Crime talk provides one accented or anchored representation of reality.
- There is an inherent problem when crime talk signs are reduced to perpetuate conventional criminological meanings . . . this semiotic cleansing of being . . . denies. . the possibility for emerging alternative or replacement narratives on crime, on criminal behavior, and on the criminal law.
- Theories of crime [are the] product of coterminous forces, the subject in process and economic conditions that give rise to notions of crime. (1998: 56)

While postmodern criminology has yet to make a significant impact on the discipline of criminology as a whole, it clearly raises important questions, such as: How do we know what we think we know? This is the second important theme of the perspective, and perhaps the most powerful. Philosophically speaking, truth is not absolute, nor is it something that can ever really exist on its own. A simple way to think about it is by picturing all the different situations that people find themselves in as they make decisions about their lives. While there surely may be shared statuses (e.g., race, educational level, and gender), human beings are infinitely different, and, from the postmodern perspective, there is no compelling reason to assume their behavior has the same universal cause. Lyotard even goes so far as to "wage war on totality," the so-called metanarrative of grand social theories (1984: 82).

Postmodernist opposition to general or macro-level theories of crime also stems from the idea that some "texts" or "discourses" (e.g., discussions, images) of crime are given more credence than others for no other reason than that they come from people in a position of power. Such texts should be deconstructed to reveal the interests that guide them—which may, for example, be racist, sexist, or economic. This dismantling of dominant understandings of crime leaves room for the creation of *replacement discourses*, stories that have been neglected or dismissed not because they are necessarily inaccurate, but because they do not fit into the dominant paradigm. As Henry and Milovanovic note, replacement discourse "is designed to displace harmful moments in the exercise of power with discourses that tell different stories about the world" (2004: 67). An example would be busting myths about crime being primarily committed by the underclass and minorities (which would be one logical conclusion if official government statistics are the primary source of data) by placing narratives from workers and consumers victimized by wealthy corporations into the story of crime.

PEACEMAKING CRIMINOLOGY

Critical criminology has given rise to what is known as **peacemaking criminology**, a perspective that sees crime and suffering as part of the larger problem of domination caused by the unequal distribution of power in society. The perspective shares much in common with the nonviolent philosophies articulated by thinkers as Jane Addams, Dr. Martin Luther King Jr., and Gandhi. Some peacemaking criminologists credit Zen Buddhism and Quakerism as inspirations as well. First developed in 1991 by Richard Quinney and Hal Pepinsky, the perspective sees human existence as being characterized by suffering; crime is a most vivid example of this. Through compassion and genuine care for ourselves and others, this view maintains, the suffering can end as personal and collective awareness grows. Peacemaking criminology is therefore a criminology of "compassion and service" that seeks to eliminate suffering and therefore all crime (Quinney and Pepinsky, 1991). This is done by working for peace at all levels of social and personal life.

Peacemaking criminologists see that much of criminal justice is geared toward "war making." Of course, this is not a particularly novel observation, as the phrase "War on Crime" is well integrated into the common vernacular in the United States. The use of the term *war* assumes that there is an enemy. The word also implies that violence is an acceptable way to resolve problems. Peacemaking criminologists, however, subscribe to the view that violence begets violence and that war making is the least effective way to bring about justice and healing for the individual, self, and society. More specifically, violent responses to suffering undermine the ability of victims, offenders, and communities to communicate and cooperate. As Pepinsky explains:

> People cannot talk, listen together, and fight one another at the same time. Peacemaking is a matter of injecting doses of conversation into our social space—conversation that

embraces the greatest victims and the most powerful oppressors of the moment at the same time. The sooner dialogue begins, the less likely explosive and violent relations will develop. The sooner the dialogue commences, the sooner power imbalances will be mediated, and the sooner peace will be made. (1999: 69)

While peacemaking criminology is regarded by some as too philosophical or even metaphysical, John Fuller (2004) has identified some basic principles of the perspective that are more amenable to practice in the day-to-day criminal justice context, and perhaps life more generally:

1. *Nonviolence* (force, especially the physical variety, is counterproductive)
2. *Social justice* (fairness and equality in all aspects of social policy and social structure)
3. *Inclusion* (all stakeholders should participate in the process)
4. *Correct means* (no coercion or discrimination)
5. *Comparable knowledge* (everyone should know what's going on)
6. *Categorical imperative* (act as though it was universal law; do no harm)

As you can see, peacemaking criminology is not just theoretical, but can be applied to a number of real-life situations, both inside and outside of the criminal justice system. One such way that peacemaking criminology is practiced in criminal justice is through victim-offender reconciliation programs, where a trained mediator oversees face-to-face meetings between the offender and victim. Now a fairly common practice in the United States and Australia, the idea here is that the offender is placed in the situation of actually thinking about how his or her actions have affected others. Studies have shown that victims often feel some sense of catharsis in the process, and offenders, often for the first time, are confronted with the victim's reaction to

the crime. Unlike the traditional model of criminal justice, where there is little to no interaction between the main participants in a crime, the hope is that victims and offenders can collaboratively discuss issues and develop solutions to their problems (Fuller, 2004). Another way that peacemaking criminology can be put into practice is through family group conferencing in the juvenile justice system, where family members of the offender and the victim discuss how the crime has impacted their lives. As with all forms of restorative justice, the hope is that the wounds from crime can be healed through genuine dialogue designed to promote forgiveness, introspection, and change.

CHAPTER SUMMARY

Critical theories of crime include Marxist, left realist, feminist, postmodernist, and peacemaking perspectives. Respectively, their critiques are centered on capitalism, stratification and inequality, patriarchy, modernity, and war making. Critical theories of crime have roots in general sociological conflict theory, which sees society shaped by conflicts among people who have competing self- and group interests.

Stemming from Marx's critique of capitalism, early Marxist criminological theory saw law as a tool of the bourgeoisie used to control the proletariat and to shield the harms committed by the elite from scrutiny. Crime was seen as a reaction of the proletariat to its oppression. This instrumentalist approach gave way to more sophisticated Marxist theories of crime, some of which maintained that economic class influences everyday activities, making crime more attractive to the economically marginalized. Other structural Marxist theories see the state as relatively autonomous from elite interests, but still a reflection of the logic of capitalism. Left realism developed out of a critique of the tendency of Marxist theory to downplay the importance of street crime and victimization. The perspective emphasizes the relationship between the nested contexts of racial, gender, and class stratification.

Feminist criminological theory developed through the critique of the andocentric nature of criminology and theories of crime. There are several different varieties of the perspective (e.g., liberal socialist and radical), but at the most basic level of analysis, feminism in criminology is about centering gender and its relationship to lawmaking, lawbreaking, and reactions to crime. Two of the most important questions raised by feminist criminologists are: (1) Do extant theories of crime apply to girls and women? and (2) How are the tremendous gender differences in criminal offending to be explained? Studies of burglars and robbers show that while offenders may share some similarities across gender, there are notable differences as well.

Postmodern criminology has attacked the notion that an absolute truth exists about crime. The deconstruction of dominant crime stories is considered necessary to allow room for replacement discourses, which are marginalized perspectives on crime that don't fit into the dominant or publicized understanding of crime. Peacemaking criminology holds that crime is a part of human suffering, and that violence by both individuals and social institutions like the criminal justice system are equally unacceptable. From this perspective, the ultimate solution to crime is to be found in sweeping cultural changes that emphasize nonviolence and social justice in all aspects of life.

KEY TERMS

conflict theory
feminist criminology
instrumental marxism
left realism
liberation/opportunity theory
peacemaking criminology
postmodern criminology
structural contradictions theory
structured action theory

RECOMMENDED READINGS

Meda Chesney-Lind and Katherine Irwin. (2007). *Beyond Bad Girls: Gender, Violence and Hype.* London: Routledge.

Shaun L. Gabbidon and Helen Taylor Greene. (2005). *Race and Crime.* Thousand Oaks, CA: Sage.

Martin D. Schwartz and Suzanne Hatty. (2004). *Controversial Issues in Criminology: Critical Criminology.* Cincinnati: Anderson.

Dennis Sullivan. (2006). *Handbook of Restorative Justice: A Global Perspective.* London: Routledge.

15

GENERAL AND INTEGRATED THEORIES OF CRIME

AOBJEY Alamy

Students and professors alike experience a certain degree of frustration when trying to answer the seemingly straightforward question: "What causes crime?" Without a doubt, the question is deceiving in its simplicity, but in reality crime is an immensely complex and ubiquitous problem. When asked what does crime boil down to, professors often tell students to raise more questions before attempting to pursue an answer: "What type of crime?" "Crime rates, or individual criminal activity?" "Juvenile or adult crime?" Even after whittling down the question, the truth of the matter is that there is still a large degree of controversy and disagreement about the nature, extent, and distribution of particular types of crime. Inevitably some students get the impression that criminological theory is incapable of generalizing about crime, but this opinion is not shared by general and integrative criminological theorists. Let us first discuss general criminological theory.

The period of time from the late 1980s to the mid-1990s may very well go down in history as the time criminology finally took stock of its achievements and rediscovered general and integrated theory. **General theories** explain a broad range of facts and are not restricted to any one time or place. This does not mean that a particular general theory has to explain all crime, but if exceptions keep turning up, its generality becomes suspect. By the same token, successful tests of a general theory with a particular crime—say, armed robbery—cannot be the basis for inferring that the theory applies equally well to embezzlement or even to other forms of robbery. Only repeated tests of a theory, with different people, places, or events, will establish its degree of generality.

Crime varies in many ways. There are variations between populations, places, times and individuals; there are variations in the frequency with which people commit crimes (called the *incidence* of crime) and variations in the proportion of people who commit those crimes (the *prevalence* of crime); there are variations in the way crimes are committed and in the consequences that follow for offenders as well as for victims; and there are variations in criminalization, from the declaration that certain activities are crimes to the imposition of penalties.

A general theory that could explain all these variations would be impressive indeed. In the first place, it would need to explain variations at the individual level as well as variations at the societal level. The things that account for differences among individuals may not account for differences among societies, and vice versa. As Braithwaite asserts: "There is some evidence, for example, that while unemployment is a strong predictor of individual criminality, societies with high unemployment rates do not necessarily have high crime rates" (1989a: 104). In the second place, a theory that accommodates all these variations would have to explain not only the behavior that constitutes crime, but also the propensity of people to engage in those behaviors and the propensity of others to apply criminal labels to those people and acts.

A third reason such an all-encompassing theory would be impressive relates to the conceptualization of crime as an event. One way to think of crime as an event is illustrated by the routine activities approach, discussed in chapter 10. In this conceptualization, crime occurs when opportunities and motivated offenders fortuitously come together in the absence of capable guardians. From this vantage point, a general theory of crime would have to explain variations in the situational matrix that gives rise to criminal events.

The central concepts of a theory usually reflect the training of its author(s). It comes as no surprise when a sociologist includes social variables in a theory of crime, a psychologist includes personality variables, a biologist includes constitutional variables, or a geographer includes spatial variables. Yet some scholars see discipline boundaries as a hindrance to the development of a general theory of crime. Gottfredson and Hirschi make this point, arguing that "much of the research generated by these disciplines is beyond the reach of their own explanations of crime" (1990: 274). They "find no adequate positivistic theory that accounts for a range of well-documented facts about crime (e.g., the age curve [crime rates peak at age twenty to twenty-four and fall off rapidly thereafter], the gender gap, the disproportionate involvement of minorities, the high correlation between crime rates and rates of other 'deviancy'), and the characteristics of crime itself" (Barlow, 1991: 231). And so Gottfredson and Hirschi claim to base their theory on a conception of human nature and of crime that escapes the fetters of disciplines.

If the disciplinary baggage theorists carry around restricts their ability to construct a general theory of crime, the competition among different theoretical perspectives within a discipline is surely more restrictive. This has led some criminologists to seek **integrated theories** that borrow from otherwise competing paradigms. In sociological criminology, for example, attempts have been made to unite control theory with rationality-opportunity theory, associational theory with strain theory, and cultural deviancy theory with control theory. These efforts expose some of the commonalities among ostensibly competing theories (Barlow and Ferdinand, 1992: 201–22), though tests of integrated theories (usually with juveniles) have had mixed success. To the extent that an integrated theory explains a wider range of phenomena, it is more general than the individual theories of which it is constructed, and that makes theoretical integration a worthwhile challenge. We examine integrated theories at the end of this chapter.

SIX GENERAL THEORIES OF CRIME

Our observations above might well evoke pessimism regarding the possibility of constructing a general theory of crime. Yet the challenge has now been taken up, although it should be said that Katz (1988) makes no claim that his work constitutes a general theory. In truth, his is as much method as theory, but the two are so intertwined as to be indistinguishable, as we shall see. Here, then, are the six theories. There is space here to do only a superficial job, and readers are strongly advised to read the original sources in their entirety.

We begin with two theories that share a common grounding in sociobiology, although one is an evolutionary theory and the other is a behaviorist learning theory.

Wilson and Herrnstein's General Theory

Wilson and Herrnstein offer an integrative theory of criminal behavior that combines sociobiological, psychological (behaviorist), and rationality-opportunity perspectives on crime. Their theory is about "the forces that control individual behavior," and it incorporates behavioral, biological, and environmental factors to explain why some people commit "serious" street crimes and others do not (1985: 42).

An underlying assumption of the theory is that when individuals are facing a choice among possible actions, they will choose the action with the highest anticipated ratio of rewards to costs. When individuals behave this way, their behavior is considered rational. Therefore, both stealing and bestiality can be rational. Even if people feel restrained by the "bite of conscience," this is a cost that can be overcome by a sufficient level of anticipated reward. Therefore, Wilson and Herrnstein believe, individuals can still choose to commit or not commit a crime, and they will select crime over noncrime whenever the reward-cost ratio is greater for the crime than for the noncrime.

What any given individual considers rewarding (or costly) is part human nature (i.e., it satisfies such primary drives as hunger and sex) and part learned behavior. These rewards may be material or nonmaterial, certain or uncertain, and immediate or delayed. The evaluation of any particular action will be influenced by how well a person handles uncertainty and delay, which Wilson and Herrnstein believe is influenced by nature, temperament, and social environment. Aggressive individuals, for example, are inclined to be more impulsive and less able to delay gratification, a trait characteristic also of youth. The rewards of noncrime are often delayed, whereas the rewards of crime generally precede their costs and will therefore be preferred by less mature and more impulsive individuals. Finally, there is the important question of equity: Crime may be preferred to noncrime if it is perceived to correct an imbalance in distributive justice. Such an imbalance occurs when people feel that, in comparison to themselves, others get more than they deserve on the basis of their contribution.

Wilson and Herrnstein's theory is controversial partly because of their claim that the theory is general enough to encompass most sociological theories of criminal behavior (1985: 63–66), partly because it is used to justify conservative crime control policies (528–29), and, perhaps most of all, because it links criminal behavior to constitutional factors. On the other hand, Wilson and Herrnstein have explored new avenues—and some old ones—in a way that merits serious study.

A major criticism of their approach is its focus on "serious" street crime—murder, theft, and rape—to the exclusion of other forms of criminality. A general theory of crime that explains only a small range of behaviors is not so general, and in any case it is certainly not established that embezzlers, con artists, organized criminals, fences, and pilferers are constitutionally different from noncriminals—or, for that matter, from other criminals. It is also curious that despite their declared focus on serious street crime, the voluminous research Wilson and Herrnstein bring to bear on their theory often does not make that distinction. Finally, Wilson and Herrnstein's approach manifests the ideology of conservative criminology in its thinly veiled search for the criminal type (for additional criticisms, see Gibbs, 1985).

Inferential support for Wilson and Herrnstein's theory (and also that of Gottfredson and Hirschi, discussed later in this chapter) comes from a survey of college undergraduates by Daniel Nagin and Raymond Paternoster (1993), who asked students to describe their involvement in three distinctive offenses—drunk driving, sexual assault, and theft. Students were presented with various scenarios that were experimentally varied across the sample. They were asked to estimate the chances that they would commit the act specified in the scenario, as well as the chances that they would be arrested. They were also questioned about their perceptions of the costs and benefits of committing the offense and were also given questions designed to measure their level of self-control.

Nagin and Paternoster found evidence of individual differences in the propensity to commit crime (individuals lacking self-control were more likely to say they would commit an offense), as well as evidence that students took the vulnerability of the target and perceived benefits and costs of doing the crime into account. The authors thus concluded that individual differences and situational factors both influence the decision to commit crime—although, in this case, the crimes were hypothetical. The authors advocate more research along these lines.

Cohen and Machalek's Evolutionary Theory

The evolutionary ecological theory proposed by Lawrence Cohen and Richard Machalek (1988) is also integrative, and what is remarkable is the simplicity of the result. The theory is heavily influenced by biological developments and is described as a general theory even though the authors apply it to a restricted range of crimes (although see Vila, 1994, for an attempt to extend the theory to all forms of criminal behavior). Even though the theory remains to be fully developed, it unites the perspectives of routine activity, structure, social psychology, and biology.

Cohen and Machalek argue that variation in individual behavior is explained by the "alternative behavioral strategies" that are used as people try to meet their needs (1988: 467). Some of these strategies are *expropriative*, because they involve depriving others of valuable things. Many crimes are expropriative, and it is these crimes to which the theory is applied.

Behavioral strategies develop over time as people (like other organisms) strive to meet their needs. The successful strategies tend to become "major" ones. However, the more prevalent a strategy becomes within society, the more vulnerable the population is to "invasion" by alternative strategists, or to "non-

conformists" who are willing to be creative. This is one way in which new strategies evolve and behavior diversifies.

In addition, individuals differ in their physical and behavioral traits and resources. These differences may result in the selection (intentional or not) of different strategies, just as they may help or hinder a person's successful adoption of a preferred strategy. In this way, "conditional" strategies arise alongside major strategies, and behavioral diversity grows.

Human beings possess intelligence, meaning they can think; however, people do not always act with conscious purpose: "It is thus unnecessary to assume that criminal acts are perpetrated by rational, calculating individuals who understand fully the strategic implications of their chosen actions" (Cohen and Machalek, 1988: 479). Indeed, people may have resource advantages they do not realize or intentionally create, and yet these advantages explain why they have adopted a particular strategy. If a strategy works well it will probably be tried again, although the individual may never question or realize why it worked.

Cohen and Machalek argue that property crimes, as expropriative strategies, are promoted by various factors—some pertaining to individuals; others to the type and mix of noncriminal strategies that exist in a time and place. Deficiencies in social, cultural, and physical resources may promote criminal strategies (such as burglary) that are employed as alternatives to inaccessible noncriminal strategies. However, criminal alternatives may also be promoted by resource advantages: "[An] individual who is rich in [resources] may be even more predisposed to commit a criminal act precisely because he or she commands the resources required to implement an expropriative strategy successfully" (Cohen and Machalek, 1988: 483).

If both resource deficiencies and advantages promote crime, it is difficult to see how resource differences can explain individual or group differences in the selection of ex-propriative crime. Cohen and Machalek get around this problem by taking a conventional and conservative approach: People who are socially and economically disadvantaged are more likely to be exposed to values and experiences that encourage criminal behavior—but they do not tell us why this should be so. On the other hand, resource variability can explain the type of crime selected, for, as we saw repeatedly in chapter 11, access to criminal opportunities often requires the right combination of resources.

Because expropriative strategies arise as alternatives to legitimate production activities, they are promoted by the expansion and proliferation of noncriminal activities. For example, Cohen and Machalek observe that "large-scale concentrations of producers offer rich and inviting opportunities" to both advantaged and conditional strategists (1988: 480). Once discovered, a particular theft strategy is likely to proliferate through conventional social-psychological processes such as imitation and social learning, and through independent discovery.

This brief sketch does not do justice to Cohen and Machalek's theory, which contains other elements and emphasizes the evolutionary dynamics that underlie the development and acquisition of behavioral strategies (see also Machalek and Cohen, 1991; Vila and Cohen, 1993; Vila, 1994). Nevertheless, it is important to note again that none of the elements described above is new. One can find them in the theories reviewed in the last several chapters. A new idea that does emerge is the notion that crime is shaped by "strategy evolution" in general, and that the characteristics, frequency, and mix of behavioral strategies explain the amount and types of crime that exist in any particular place, time, or group. An evaluation of their theory using real-world data has not yet been accomplished; however, computer simulations have not disproved the theory (Vila and Cohen, 1993: 907).

Gottfredson and Hirschi's General Theory of Crime[1]

Crime can be thought of as a form of cheating, where one person or group extracts resources from another without compensating the victim (Machalek and Cohen, 1991: 223). What crimes have in common is the fact that they victimize. When crime is conceptualized this way, questions about the ubiquity and evolution of crime follow naturally enough, for how can societies survive in the face of such parasitic conduct? Gottfredson and Hirschi (1990) take a different approach in conceptualizing crime, although they acknowledge that suffering occurs. Much of the account that follows is taken from a critical review of their theory (Barlow, 1991).

Taking classical (rational choice) theory as a starting point, Gottfredson and Hirschi (1990) argue that crime, as any other behavior, turns on the likelihood that it will bring pleasure. Its characteristics must generally be consistent with that result, irrespective of the specific motives, interests, or talents of the people doing it. Gottfredson and Hirschi observe that most crimes are in fact attempts, and this implies something about the nature of crimes: They are unlikely to be carefully thought-out, skillful acts involving special expertise, technology, or organization. Criminal acts are relatively easy to commit, involve little skill or planning, and tend to be exciting, risky, or thrilling.

What makes crimes distinct from analogous acts is that they entail the use of force and fraud, and this helps make gratification immediate. On the other hand, force and fraud also threaten the self-interests of victims and are therefore universally resisted. Like Machalek and Cohen (1991) and Durkheim (1964a) before them, Gottfredson and Hirschi (1990) see potential retaliation as the inseparable other side of crime. And so we have three other characteristics of crimes: they provide immediate gratification, but they also produce pain and suffering for victims and

---

[1] Parts of this section are from Barlow (1991). Reprinted with permission.

the risk of long-term costs for offenders.

Beyond the commonalities already noted, a crime will not occur unless an appropriate opportunity exists. Opportunity is defined by the logical structure of the crime itself, and therefore varies from one specific offense (say, embezzlement) to another (say, rape). Gottfredson and Hirschi (1990) describe the "typical" or "standard" characteristics and the logical structures (necessary elements or conditions) of burglary, robbery, homicide, auto theft, rape, embezzlement, and drug use. The characteristics and elements of the offenses are strikingly similar. However, it is also apparent that the likelihood of any particular crime being committed is influenced by the availability of opportunities and a person's access to them, issues the authors do not explore. Presumably, the characteristics of situations and the personal properties of individuals jointly affect the use of force or fraud in pursuit of self-interest.

Gottfredson and Hirschi (1990) maintain that crimes are interchangeable not only among themselves but also with analogous acts that do not involve force or fraud. They call this the **versatility construct.** And so they end up rejecting traditional distinctions among crimes (e.g., petty and serious, personal and property, attempted and completed, street and suite) as "without import" and "a waste of time." They look for what crimes have in common as a basis for inferring what criminals have in common.

Criminality: Low Self-Control

If crimes differ in the opportunity for their commission, individuals differ in the extent to which they are vulnerable to the temptations provided by those opportunities. Gottfredson and Hirschi (1990) use the notion of self-control to represent that vulnerability, and criminality is synonymous with low self-control. **Criminality** refers to the propensity to use force and fraud in the pursuit of self-interest. Its characteristics are inferred from the char-

acteristics of crime. In this way, Gottfredson and Hirschi ensure that the conception of criminality is consistent with their conception of crime.

The traits associated with **low self-control** include short-time perspective; low diligence, persistence, and tenacity; a tendency to be "adventuresome, active, and physical"; a tendency to be "self-centered, indifferent, or insensitive to the suffering and needs of others"; and a tendency to have "unstable marriages, friendships, and job profiles" (1990: 89–90). Since these traits are also implicated in many noncriminal acts (e.g., alcohol use, accidents, smoking, running away, truancy) "crime is not an automatic or necessary consequence of low self-control" (Gottfredson and Hirschi, 1990:91). In other words, there is no theoretical basis for predicting which of many possible crimes and analogous acts will be committed by individuals with low self-control.

Gottfredson and Hirschi (1990) identify the major cause of low self-control as "ineffective parenting." However, individual differences among children (and parents) may affect the prospects for good parenting. Thus, low intelligence tends to compromise the recognition of low self-control and the willingness or ability to do anything about it. Other factors affecting parental control and the prospects for effective socialization include parental criminality and anything that interferes with the monitoring and supervision of children. Gottfredson and Hirschi acknowledge that schools and other socializing institutions (marriage, work, Boy or Girl Scouts) may have a positive effect on self-control, but the further from early childhood one moves, the harder it is to make up for early deficiencies. Besides, the traits characteristic of low self-control are inconsistent with success in school, work, and interpersonal relationships. In their view, this explains why delinquent youths end up in the company of each other ("birds of a feather") and why failure in school, marriage, and work correlates strongly with delinquency and crime (they all require diligence, hard work, and willingness to defer gratification).

The Stability Postulate

Central to the theory is the proposition that levels of self-control are relatively stable throughout the life course. Put another way, "differences between people in the likelihood that they will commit criminal acts persist over time" (Gottfredson and Hirschi, 1990: 107). This *stability postulate* is predicated on the belief that the early failure of control and socialization cannot readily be overcome later in life, any more than effective control and socialization of a child can later be undone. Together with the notion that there are many noncriminal acts that are analogous to crimes, the stability postulate explains why the so-called age curve of crime is invariant across space and across crimes, as well as why "[m]en are always and everywhere more likely than women to commit criminal acts" (145).

To summarize, the central proposition of Gottfredson and Hirschi's general theory of crime is as follows: Crime rate differences among individuals are explained by the independent effects of variations in the characteristics of crime itself (i.e., the opportunity to pursue self-interest through the use of force or fraud) and variations in self-control (criminality, or the propensity to use force or fraud in the pursuit of self-interest). When criminal opportunities are held constant, low self-control predicts relatively high rates of offending, low self-control earlier in life predicts criminality later in life, and criminality earlier in life predicts low self-control later in life.

Scope of the Theory

Despite continued reference to "ordinary" or "common" crimes, Gottfredson and Hirschi call their theory general, going so far as to claim that the theory "is meant to explain all crime, at all times, and, for that matter, many forms of behavior that are not sanctioned by the state"

(1990: 117). In short, the independent effects of crime opportunities and criminality explain bait-and-switch scams in appliance stores, police brutality, bid rigging, employee theft, fraudulent advertising, insider trading, tax evasion, smuggling, gang crimes, labor racketeering, prison rape, armed robbery, arson, burglary, murder, rape, and shoplifting; they also explain drug use, accidents, smoking, and eating between meals. No specialized theories are needed, because all crimes and analogous acts "provide relatively quick and relatively certain benefit with minimal effort" (190).

Unfortunately, Gottfredson and Hirschi do not develop the opportunity (crime) side of their theory sufficiently well to predict which of these varied acts individuals are likely to commit (at a high or low rate) at any given time, or when they might switch from one crime to another or from a crime to a noncriminal but analogous act. Nor do they provide a basis for deducing what kind of social or cultural setting would experience a high (or low) rate of any particular crime or analogous act. Their treatment of these issues as theoretically irrelevant or inconsequential hardly lessens the theory's vulnerability to attack. In fact, it is quite clear that Gottfredson and Hirschi have a very unique—and, in our view, myopic—understanding of crime, especially those committed in the context of an organization or institution.

The theory is most vulnerable in its application to white-collar crime, both organizational and occupational. Gottfredson and Hirschi (1990) present FBI arrest data on embezzlement and fraud to show that correlates of white-collar crime are similar to those of murder (and therefore other common crimes), and they also refer to "good research" that shows just how mundane, simple, and easy occupational crimes are and that the people who commit them also tend to commit analogous acts (using drugs and alcohol, for example).

The evidence is at the very least inconclusive about these issues, and at most contrary to the claims of Gottfredson and Hirschi

(1990). Indeed, much research into organizational and occupational crime clearly challenges another assertion of their theory—that crime is more prevalent among those outside the occupational structure than among those in it (see Barlow, 1991). The lack of consistent evidence of a relationship between unemployment and crime is one challenge, but another comes from abundant evidence that employee fraud and theft, though often mundane, are widespread in all sectors of the U.S. economy as well as in other countries. Furthermore, evidence of widespread crime in the fields of health, real estate, banking, insurance, defense contracting, and politics hardly supports the contention that high-end occupations are incompatible with criminality (Reed and Yeager, 1996; Yeager and Reed, 1998).

Gottfredson and Hirschi (1990) do not assert that criminality is absent among corporate executives or other high-level employees, merely that it is less prevalent the higher one climbs the occupational ladder. Even if this is true, many of the crimes committed at the high end of the ladder display characteristics opposite to those indicative of low self-control. Compared to low-end crime, high-end crime is much more likely to involve planning, special expertise, organization, delayed gratification, and persistence—as well as considerably larger potential gains with arguably less potential long-term cost. Such distinctions are also apparent when comparing the activities of fences with thieves, "good" burglars with "kick-it-in men," pickpockets with purse snatchers. Gottfredson and Hirschi's theory can accommodate these observations in only one of two ways: Either temptations to commit force and fraud in the pursuit of self-interest overwhelm the resistance associated with self-control, or many individuals with low self-control manage somehow to become managers, professionals, and entrepreneurs.

If the stability postulate is wrong, however, it is possible for people with low self-control early in life to develop it later and for individuals with self-control early in life

to lose it later. Braithwaite's (1989a) theory of reintegrative shaming (discussed below) presumes this to be true, while Gottfredson and Hirschi's (1990) theory requires that it not be. Recall that low self-control is inconsistent with effective control and socialization, and that includes socialization into as well as out of crime. Hence the groups and organizations to which offenders belong are regarded as facilitating crime among people who already lack self-control. Gottfredson and Hirschi thus dismiss as misguided (or poor) research suggesting that the social and cultural milieu of an organization generates criminality among its members. Besides, they argue, there is little social support of white-collar offenders, because their offenses usually victimize the organizations in which they work and are detrimental to fellow employees.

Our reading of wide-ranging research is very different. Whether the subject is police corruption, employee pilfering, the ethics of corporate managers, antitrust violations, city politics, or state crime, one finds social support of criminality through subcultures of criminality—accommodating norms, goals, means, and values and networks of cooperation. Gottfredson and Hirschi's (1990) view that such support relates to the nature and context of crime itself rather than to the propensity of individuals to commit it would perhaps constitute a fatal counterattack if they could also show that self-control cannot be undermined by external (group) influence. This has not been established, however, and, contrary to the general theory, rational choices are "far from being self evident and stable"; rather, they are "socially constructed in group interaction" (Yeager and Reed, 1998: 894).

Minority Crime

Among the facts about crime in America are these: African Americans constitute roughly 14 percent of the population; yet nearly 50 percent of those arrested for violent crime are black, as are 33 percent of those arrested for property crimes, 40 percent of those serving jail time, and 47 percent of those in state prisons (Maguire and Pastore, 2007). How would the general theory of Gottfredson and Hirschi explain these facts?

Gottfredson and Hirschi (1990) reject traditional explanations of minority involvement in crime (e.g., inequality and subcultural theories) and resort to an emphasis on the self-control component of their theory. In their view, parental management of children is the key to understanding racial variations in crime, and, within the realm of parenting, discipline is considered more important than supervision, which affects access to criminal opportunities. However, Gottfredson and Hirschi cite no evidence, saying only that "[p]artitioning race or ethnic differences into their crime and self-control components is not possible with currently available data" (153).

On Gottfredson and Hirschi's side, the relationship between parenting and delinquency is one of the strongest in the literature, and evidence is piling up that the impact of structural factors (e.g., family composition or socioeconomic status) on delinquency is mediated by parental management. Nevertheless, if poverty, community disorganization, large family size, and family instability impact negatively on parental management, rates of crime and delinquency will be affected. Such structural conditions are prevalent in inner-city African American communities (Anderson, 1999; Wilson, 1987), where rates of victimization by force and fraud are also high (Stewart and Simons, 2006). Gottfredson and Hirschi do not explore the implications of this for their theory.

In rejecting inequality theories of race differences in crime, Gottfredson and Hirschi point out that "[offenders] tend to victimize people who share their unfortunate circumstances" (1990: 152). True, but then this question arises: Are there race differences in the tendency for offenders to victimize people who are like themselves? According to their theory, crime is a matter of "proximity, ease, and convenience of rewards"; hence, there is no a priori basis for predicting such differences. Nevertheless, studies of the urban distribution of crime indicate that African American offenders have a more restricted image of the city than white offenders, who can move around more freely and need not concentrate their criminal activities in areas close to home, thereby forgoing "easy marks" (Carter and Hill, 1979; Boggs, 1964). This suggests that while most crime tends to be intraracial, crimes committed by whites are likely to be more dispersed and hence potentially more rewarding—but also more costly and risky—than crimes committed by blacks. If access to profitable criminal opportunities is skewed in favor of whites, Gottfredson and Hirschi are silent on the issue and its implications for their theory.

Gottfredson and Hirschi's general theory of crime has come under considerable empirical scrutiny since its publication. An example of the most common approach to testing the theory is a study of drunk driving and self-control. Here, a composite measure of low self-control was found to relate to DUI offenses for both men and women, and the authors found a strong risk-taking component to drunk driving—for example, not wearing seat belts. However, they also found that teenagers did not have higher blood alcohol levels than others, and speculate that a minimum drinking age of nineteen might have been a factor. Furthermore, "it may be that teenagers express more of their criminality in other and more demanding [i.e., physical] ways" (Keane, Maxim, and Teevan, 1993: 40). As seems fairly typical of tests of this general theory to date, self-control is found to relate to crime or analogous acts and therefore the theory cannot be rejected (Gibbs, Giever, and Higgins, 2003; Piquero et al., 2005; Winfree et al., 2006).

Braithwaite's Theory of Reintegrative Shaming

Like Gottfredson and Hirschi, Braithwaite believes that "there is sufficient in common between different types of crime to render a general explanation possible" (1989a: 1). However, Braithwaite explicitly rejects the idea that crimes are inherently similar, arguing instead that they are qualitatively similar by virtue of the stigma attached to them and by the fact that the offender makes a "defiant choice" in taking the opportunity to perpetrate a crime:

> The homogeneity presumed between disparate behaviors such as rape and embezzlement in this theory is that they are choices made by the criminal actor in the knowledge that he is defying a criminal proscription which is mutually intelligible to actors in the society as criminal. (3)

Braithwaite excludes acts that are formally crimes but whose criminalization is without support in the society at large, for example, "laws against marijuana use in liberal democracies or laws that create political crimes against the state in communist societies" (1989a: 3). Braithwaite's theory applies to predatory crimes—acts that involve victimization of one person or group by another.

We encountered some of the ideas of Braithwaite's theory in previous chapters. But the theory is much more than this. Braithwaite offers yet another integrative theory, one that incorporates elements of major sociological theories of crime and delinquency: control theory, labeling theory, subcultural theory, associational theory, strain theory, and social learning theory.

Braithwaite's diagram of his theory is reproduced in figure 15.1. The arrows indicate the direction or flow of influence between linked variables, and the signs indicate whether the relationship between them is positive (i.e., a plus sign indicates the more of one, the more

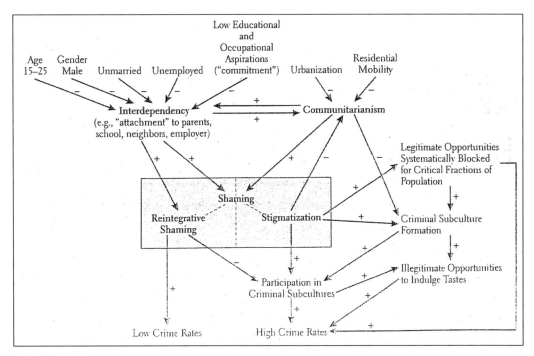

▲ **Figure 15.1.**
Summary of Braithwaite's Theory of Reintegrative Shaming.
Reprinted with permission.

of the other) or negative (i.e., a minus sign indicates the more of one, the less of the other). On the integrative and original aspects of his theory, Braithwaite has this to say:

> The top left of [the figure] incorporates the key variables of control theory; the far right—opportunity [strain] theory; the middle and bottom right—subcultural theory; the right side of the middle box—labeling theory. With one crucial exception (reintegrative shaming), there is therefore no originality in the elements of this theory, simply originality of synthesis. (1989a: 107)

The central proposition of the theory is this: Crime rates of individuals and groups are influenced directly by processes of shaming. High crime rates result from shaming that stigmatizes, because rule breakers who are shamed but not forgiven are more likely to become "outlaws" and to participate in subcultures of crime. This is referred to as **disintegrative shaming**, a stigmatizing approach that involves

- disrespectful disapproval and humiliation;
- ceremonies to certify deviance but no ceremonies to decertify deviance;
- labeling the person, not just the deed, as evil; and
- allowing deviance to become a master status trait. (Braithwaite, 1995: 194)

On the other hand, when rule breakers are shamed but then forgiven and welcomed back to the fold, the unpleasant, punitive experience of being shamed is offset by the pleasant relief of discovering that one is still accepted (loved, wanted, cared about) despite the transgression. This what Braithwaite refers to as **reintegrative shaming**. The process of reintegrative shaming confirms the validity of the rules and reestablishes the transgressor's place as a member in good standing. This process involves

- disapproval while sustaining a relationship of respect;

- ceremonies to certify deviance terminated by ceremonies to decertify deviance;
- disapproval of the evil of the deed without labeling the persons as evil; and
- not allowing deviance to become a master status trait. (Braithwaite, 1995: 194)

While Braithwaite hypothesizes that either kind of shaming is likely to be more successful at combating predatory crime than "punishment without associated moralizing and denunciation" (86), systems of punishment that encourage reintegration should experience the lowest crime rates.

As a mechanism of social control, shaming works best among closely connected people whose fortunes, reputations, and futures are interdependent—as in families, for example, or among workmates, colleagues, and friends. Justice officials in Western industrialized societies are at a decided disadvantage: "Most of us will care less about what a judge (whom we meet only once in our lifetime) thinks of us than we will care about the esteem in which we are held by a neighbor we see regularly" (Braithwaite, 1989a: 87). Interdependence among individuals has a societal correlate—**communitarianism**—which has three elements:

> (1) densely enmeshed interdependency, where interdependencies are characterized by (2) mutual obligation and trust, and (3) are interpreted as a matter of group loyalty rather than individual convenience. Communitarianism is therefore the antithesis of individualism. (Braithwaite, 1989a: 86)

Western industrialized societies, with their high rates of urbanization and residential mobility, are more individualistic than less developed agrarian societies. The model in figure 15.1 shows that communitarianism has a positive effect on shaming, but is itself undermined by shaming that is merely stigmatizing. This is because shaming without reintegration makes criminal subcultures more attractive and encourages their formation "by creating populations of outcasts with no stake in conformity" (Braithwaite, 1989a: 102). Criminal subcultures are also fostered by blocked legitimate opportunities, and once formed, they encourage crime directly by providing illegitimate opportunities and incentives to deviate from the norms of conventional society.

At the individual level, **interdependency** is associated with age, marital status, gender, employment status, and aspirations within society-wide approved opportunity systems. More so than other people, older teenagers and young adults—especially if they are male—are freed from the constraints and obligations of interdependency, as are single people, those without work, and those with low commitment to legitimate ways of "getting ahead." Absent the close ties of interdependency, such people are less likely to be exposed to or affected by shaming. They are more susceptible to crime because controls are weak.

Evaluation of the Theory

Braithwaite's work is an important contribution to criminological theory. Not only does he show how "old" competing theories can be integrated into one model, but his addition of the social-psychological variable *shaming* is a major innovation. Along with associational theories, his theory is one of the few that can be applied to occupational and organizational crimes. Other notable accomplishments are that the theory of reintegrative shaming can be applied at both individual and societal levels of analysis, and that it incorporates background and foreground variables, although discussion of the lived experience of shaming is largely limited to the mechanics of gossip (see Braithwaite, 1989a: 75–77). The latter is certainly an area for future research and elaboration, and will be considered when we discuss Katz below.

Braithwaite suggests ways in which his theory could be tested and even mentions modifications that could be made to accommodate additional variables. Few specific tests of the theory have been conducted to date, but at least a dozen or so studies have found some empirical support of some of Braithwaite's theses (Botchkovar and Tittle, 2005; Chamlin and Cochran, 1997; Makkai and Braithwaite, 1994; Vagg, 1998). Despite the absence of focused tests, Braithwaite confidently asserts the merits of his theory by claiming that it accounts for the thirteen best-established findings in criminology, which no other existing theory can do. Among these findings are the high rates of crime among males, people living in large cities, certain categories of young people (e.g., those with low aspirations, poor school performance, and weak attachments to school or parents, or strong attachments to delinquent peers), and disadvantaged people. The theory also accounts for the low rate of crime in Japan—an industrialized nation—when compared with other industrialized nations such as the United States (see Braithwaite, 1989a, especially pages 61–66).

One of the most interesting aspects of the theory is its implications for criminal justice policy in highly individualized societies such as our own. Given that reintegrative shaming works best in the informal contexts of family, friends, and neighborhood, a justice policy aimed at preventing or reducing crime should be a community-based, largely informal system that uses traditional process and punishment as a last resort. Such an approach has come to be known in recent years as **restorative justice.** Box 15.1 provides some information on restorative justice practices that are consistent with Braithwaite's theory.

Expanding on the policy implications of the theory, Braithwaite and Pettit (1990) advocate a "republican" approach to criminal justice in which formal interventions are minimized and subjective assurances of liberty, equality, fraternity, and dialogue are guaranteed all citizens (also see Braithwaite, 1991; 1995). In such a setting, the reintegrative prospects of community shaming are enhanced and the likelihood is greater that offenders will rec-

BOX 15.1. RESTORATIVE JUSTICE

Restorative justice involves a holistic approach to criminal justice and crime prevention that promotes the healing of the victim, the offender, and the community. It is inspired by a genuine desire to right a wrong (crime), but in fair and humane way. Restorative justice differs from traditional criminal justice in several ways. First, its focus is on the future. Healing requires an understanding of the past harm, but recovering from the injury, rebuilding the community, and forging interdependencies should be paramount. Second, the process by which justice is to be achieved is through dialogue, mediation, and negotiation, not through adversarial "warlike" techniques. Healing, not sending people to prison, is the goal. Third, the offender takes responsibility for the crime and repentance is encouraged. This is crucial for reintegration, as traditional punishment and revenge philosophies generally do not facilitate healing. Fourth, restorative justice carries not only a concern for the victims of crime, but also a sincere concern for the well-being of the offender. Historically, offenders have been considered violators of the abstracted "society" and unfit for membership in the community.

There are many types of restorative justice practices in Australia, New Zealand, and the United States. Here are some that are consistent with Braithwaite's shaming theory:

- Victim-offender, community accountability, and family group conferences where offenders, victims, and communities come together to reintegratively shame and restore community and victim health
- Community and neighborhood advisory boards, which offer input and advice for the handling of deviance and deviants in the community
- Peer mediation and conferencing, where the offender is shamed by peers and intimates and then reintegrated into the group
- Victim services and victim impact statements, where victims can be heard by both state officials, special victims agents, and the offender
- Offender community service, in which the offender gives back to the community harmed
- Offender competency development, such as the teaching of life, civic, and parenting skills

Many county courts, prosecutor's offices, and probation departments in the United States have embraced the philosophy of restorative justice. To the many practitioners who have seen the failures of traditional justice, restorative justice is seen as an attractive approach, but it is still unclear whether restorative justice movement will become the dominant form of doing justice in the years to come.

Sources: Coates, Umbreit, and Vos (2006); Minnesota Department of Corrections (1998)

ognize their offense and shame themselves. In this manner, shaming becomes conscience building, the essence of crime prevention in Braithwaite's view.

Despite its originality, broad scope, and impressive integration of existing theories, the theory of reintegrative shaming leaves at least one important issue unresolved. For example, Braithwaite claims his theory accommodates the existence of "multiple moralities" in modern societies whereas some others do not. He argues that "[a] severe limitation of theories that deny this, like Hirschi's control theory, is that they give no account of why some uncontrolled individuals become heroin users, some become hit men, and others price fixing conspirators" (1989a: 13). This is fair enough, but aside from identifying criminal subcultures as the milieu in which crime is learned and via which tastes may be indulged in illegitimate ways, it is by no means clear how one would derive predictions about variations in the prevalence and incidence of particular types of crime, or about crime selection by predisposed individuals.

Tittle's Control Balance Theory

Recall from chapter 13 that Hirschi's (1971) social control theory holds that people who are not strongly bonded to conventional society are those most likely to commit crime. Hirschi's argument, then, is that this *lack of control* produces criminal outcomes. But what about people who have a lot of control or those who are overcontrolled? Are they likely to commit crimes as well? Would they commit different types of crime than those who are undercontrolled?

Charles Tittle has produced an integrative *control balance theory* of deviance that addresses these and other questions. First, Tittle intends for his theory to explain deviance, not just crime. Deviance, according to Tittle, is "any behavior that the majority of a given group regards as unacceptable or that typically evokes a collective response of a negative type" (1995: 124).

The central thesis of control balance theory is that the "amount of control to which people are subject relative to the amount of control they can exercise" affects the probability of deviance more generally, as well as the *type* of deviance (Tittle, 1995: 142). Being controlled or *experiencing* control means that a person is subject to the will of others, through, for example, rewards and punishments. If a teenager is not free to stay out all night, drink beer, choose his or her friends, or go to con-

certs, one might say he or she is experiencing control. When people *exercise* control, they have the ability to limit the options, choices, and behaviors of others. The parent who sets the limits in the above example is exercising control.

The relationship of control to deviance is found in the **control ratio**, which is the overall level of control people have in their lives. The ratio is calculated by weighing the total level of control a person exercises against the total level of control the person is subject to. People who control others more than they are controlled have a **control surplus**, while those who are controlled more than they control others have a **control deficit**. Tittle provides the following example:

> [A] man may have a control surplus in the domestic realm but a control deficit in the work environment, a youth may have a control deficit in the society as a whole, but a control surplus in the recreational domain, and a woman may have a control surplus in the realm of interpersonal relations, but a control deficit with respect to the physical environment. (1995: 266)

Another example is in order. Think of the class for which you are reading this book. How much control do you have over the course? How much control are you subject to in the course? You have probably been subject to control in the following ways: You must meet the class requirements, such as earning passing grades on papers and examinations, and even the number, nature, and length of the papers and examinations is generally out of your control. You may also be required to attend lectures and participate in classroom discussions. You must also earn a certain amount of points or a certain overall grade to have this class "count" for credit. You probably have little, if any, control over decisions such as the selection of the textbook, whether class is canceled, or if it dismissed early. Clearly you are subject to great amounts of control and regulation in a typical college classroom. Now, what kinds of things *can* you control in the course? Unless the professor is extremely unfair, most students have some control over their performance on exams and the relative content of their papers. You may also have some control in group discussions and by making observations or raising questions to the professor. Of course, you also have the ability to drop the course, be more or less interested in the course, and express your views about the course and the instructor on teaching evaluations. All told, however, you can see how most students have a control deficit when it comes to the typical college course. Can you think of how this control deficit might lead to deviance on the part of students? How might the professor act deviantly as a result of his or her control surplus?

According to Tittle (2004; 1995), those who have a **control balance** are least likely to engage in deviance, but the probability and seriousness of deviance rises in correlation with control deficit and surplus (see figure 15.2). This is straightforward enough, but Tittle goes one step further by theorizing that the *type* of resulting deviance differs depending on whether one has a surplus or deficit: Those with a control deficit seek to escape or rectify their problem through deviance, while those with a surplus seek to extend their control.

Critical Variables

Surely a control imbalance is not by itself sufficient to cause a deviant act to take place.

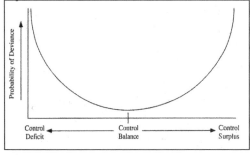

▲ **Figure 15.2.**
Control Balance.
Source: Piquero and Hickman (1999). Reprinted with permission.

Tittle rightly acknowledges that other independent variables play a role in the genesis and persistence of deviant behavior:

1. the *predisposition* toward deviant motivation;
2. the situational stimulation of deviance (*provocation*);
3. the likelihood of *constraint* in the face of deviance; and
4. the *opportunity* to commit deviance. (1995: 142)

Let us briefly review each of these variables.

Tittle argues that the predisposition to deviance is rooted in a fundamental aspect of human nature: the desire for autonomy. This means that people generally want to escape the control of others as well extend their control over others. This universal drive for freedom and power is likely to result in deviance when control is imbalanced. Thus, while the theory is called control balance, a major motivation for deviance is the elimination of the control imbalance. Tittle also suggests that autonomy and control are embedded not only in the personal, individual context, but also in organizational contexts, such as family and work.

While motivation is a necessary component of the deviant act, certain events and circumstances trigger the behavior. This is what Tittle calls *provocation*, which includes "contextual features that cause people to become keenly cognizant of their control ratios and the possibilities of alter them through deviant behavior" (1995: 163). Examples of provocation include being insulted or dismissed from employment, and any number of threats or challenges that might trigger an attempt to balance the control ratio.

Constraint refers to the "probability or the perceived probability that control will actually be exercised" (Tittle, 1995: 167). Constraint, then, could be manifested in the form of the probability that the deviant act would result in, for example, arrest or discovery by a significant other. It also can be generally understood to be a calculation of the *risk* associated with deviance.

The last major variable in control balance theory is opportunity. Like the rational-opportunity theories reviewed in chapter 10, Tittle agrees that a situation or circumstance must be available for the performance of deviance. This means that there must be, for example, available victims, people to rob and assault, drugs to sell and use, and things to steal and destroy. Finally, in a refinement of the theory, Tittle (2004) has proposed integrating insights from Gottfredson and Hirschi's (1990) self-control theory.

Evaluation of the Theory

There are many strengths of control balance theory. First, the theory is truly *general*. It provides us with sound ways of understanding both white-collar and traditional street crime and deviance. Unlike Gottfredson and Hirschi's theory, Tittle does a splendid job of dealing with the conceptually difficult issues that distinguish occupational from organizational crime. Indeed, Tittle understands that there is more to white-collar crime than simple embezzlement.

Second, Tittle's theory is intended to explain deviance, not just those things which legislators happen to define as crime. While Hirschi and Gottfredson claim they transcend a narrow definition of crime, they do it poorly. Tittle's sociological approach to crime and deviance provides a measure of breadth and depth not found in many other theories of crime.

Third, control balance theory weaves many of the most well-supported findings in criminological theory into the novel idea of control ratio. Tittle's specificity and attention to detail to these matters in many ways breaks the mold. While Braithwaite (1989a) also explains the relationship of his novel concept (shame) to other well-tested variables in criminology, Tittle does it more meaningfully, with keen attention to how the theory may be empirically tested in the future.

It usually takes several years for a theory in criminology to undergo rigorous testing. Tittle's theory has been tested in several studies, including one by Piquero and Hickman (1999). While overall support was found for the notion that control imbalance leads to deviance, the types of deviance predicted by Tittle were not supported. More specifically, it was found that predation and defiance were significantly related to those with a control surplus, not just those with a control deficit. This finding confirms the suspicion voiced by Braithwaite (1997) that it would be better to collapse the types of deviance categories into simpler, broader constructs (e.g., reducing the types of autonomous deviance into a larger "predation" category). Tittle (1997) has agreed with a few of Braithwaite's suggestions along these lines. Indeed, Tittle (2004) has revised the theory to take into account some of the mixed empirical findings on the theory and some conceptual flaws. One of the main changes Tittle to the earlier version of the theory was admitting that the qualitative categories of deviance expected as results of a control imbalance are not especially valid. Instead, Tittle now proposes that a person's control balance desirability—that is, the long-term usefulness and resolutive capacity of a deviant act—is a central predictor of the type of deviant outcome.

Katz's Seductions of Crime

A fascinating book hit the shelves in the late 1980s: Jack Katz's (1988) *Seductions of Crime: Moral and Sensual Attractions in Doing Evil*. In this book, Katz explores the relationship between doing crime and the emotional states of the offender. His focus is the foreground of crime, as opposed to the background variables traditionally emphasized in positivistic criminology. It is an analysis of the seductions and compulsions that are felt by people as they engage in criminal activity and that draw them into and through criminal "projects." To understand and explain crime as action, it is first necessary to reconstruct criminal events as they are experienced by participants. Criminology, Katz argues, should move from the inside of crime outward, rather than the other way around.

For Katz, the commonality among such diverse crimes as pilfering, robbery, gang violence, and apparently senseless robbery-murders is the "family of moral emotions" that are subjectively experienced by offenders: "humiliation, righteousness, arrogance, ridicule, cynicism, defilement, and vengeance. In each [crime] the attraction that proves to be most fundamentally compelling is that of overcoming a personal challenge to moral—not material—existence" (1988: 9). The following passage illustrates Katz's central argument:

> The closer one looks at crime, at least at the varieties examined here, the more vividly relevant become the moral emotions. Follow vandals and amateur shoplifters as they duck into alleys and dressing rooms and you will be moved by their delight in deviance; observe them under arrest and you may be stunned by their shame. Watch their strutting street display and you will be struck by the awesome fascination that symbols of evil hold for the young men who are linked in the groups we often call gangs. If we specify the opening moves in muggings and stickups, we describe an array of "games" or tricks that turn victims into fools before their pockets are turned out. The careers of persistent robbers show us, not the increasingly precise calculations and hedged risks of "professionals," but men for whom gambling and other vices are a way of life, who are "wise" in the cynical sense of the term, and who take pride in a defiant reputation as "bad." And if we examine the lived sensuality behind events of cold-blooded "senseless" murder, we are compelled to acknowledge the power that may still be created in the modern world through the sensualities of defilement, spiritual chaos, and the apprehension of vengeance.
>
> Running across these experiences of criminality is a process juxtaposed in one manner or another against humiliation. In committing a righteous slaughter, the impassioned assailant takes humiliation and turns it into rage; through laying claim to a moral status of transcendent significance, he tries to burn humiliation up. The badass, with searing purposiveness, tries to scare humiliation off; as one ex-punk explained to me, after years of adolescent anxiety about the ugliness of his complexion and the stupidity of his every word, he found a wonderful calm in making "them" anxious about his perceptions and understandings.
>
> Young vandals and shoplifters innovate games with the risks of humiliation, running along the edge of shame for its exciting reverberations. . . . Against the historical background of a collective insistence on the moral nonexistence of their people, "bad niggers" exploit ethically unique possibilities for celebrating assertive conduct as "bad." (Katz, 1988: 312–13)

Katz's "empirical" theory is, then, a theory of moral self-transcendence constructed through examination of the doing of crime as experienced and understood by its participants. Crime becomes a "project" through which offenders transcend the self that is caught up in the mundane routines of modern life. Crime embodies a creative exploration of emotional worlds beyond the realm of rational controls—it is spiritual, nonrational, self-fulfilling, and self-proclaiming. The lure of crime is, inter alia, its promise of providing "expanded possibilities of the self . . . ways of behaving that previously seemed inaccessible" (Katz, 1988: 73).

Katz argues that there are three necessary and sufficient steps through which the construction of crime takes place: "(1) a path of action—distinctive practical requirements for successfully committing the crime; (2) a line of interpretation—unique ways of understanding how one is and will be seen by others; and (3) an emotional process—seductions and compulsions that have special dynamics" (1988: 9).

If there is a link between the foreground and background in Katz's theory, the path of action is one obvious place to look:

As a consequence of the inequality of re-sources in society, some of the ways of transcending mundane life are more open to some groups of people than to others. Sky diving, for example, may offer a transcendent experience, but it is unlikely to be available to many young black members of the urban under-class. Crack, on the other hand, may provide a similarly transcending experience . . . but unlike sky diving is available to all, rich and poor. Moreover, the poor, perhaps more than any others in modernity, are faced with lives in which meaninglessness and the destruction of the self are ever present possibilities. (O'Malley and Mugford, 1991: 16)

Pat O'Malley and Stephen Mugford make this observation in the face of criticism that Katz cannot explain the shape of crime—that is, its distribution among social classes, between cities, or among racial or ethnic groups—because he rejects structural perspectives, particularly strain theory. Yet one strength of Katz's work likes precisely in the fact that it begins with no assumptions about how predispositions to crime might be distributed and concludes that only through examination of the experience of elite (or white-collar) crime can we construct the necessary comparative picture (Katz, 1988: 313–24). However, Katz is not confident of criminology's ability to study the foreground of white-collar crime:

Now, where would we get the data? With white-collar crime, we have a special problem in locating facts to demonstrate the lived experience of deviance. Despite their presumably superior capacity to write books and the healthy markets that await their publication efforts, we have virtually no "how-I-did-it-and-how-it-felt-doing-it" autobiographies by corrupted politicians, convicted tax frauds, and chief executive officers who have been deposed by scandals over inside trading. (319)

Katz goes on to suggest that what will turn out to be distinctive about elite crime is not its motivations or consequences but its emo-tional quality: Feelings of shame often attend its discovery. In contrast, "[s]tickup men, safecrackers, fences, and drug dealers often wear the criminal label with pride, apparently relishing the opportunity to tell their criminal histories in colorful, intimate detail" (1988: 319).

Bringing up the issue of shame returns us to the central element in Braithwaite's (1989a) theory of crime. We noted that Braithwaite is largely silent on the emotional process involved in shaming except to say that people find shaming a humiliating experience that provokes fear and anxiety and, consequently, avoidance behavior on the part of the person shamed. The avoidance may come in the form of conformity (most likely if the shamed also experience pangs of conscience), or it may come in the form of withdrawal from the group and participation in deviant subcultures—behavior that provoked shaming now becomes behavior that is rewarded. If the shaming is followed by forgiveness and other reintegrative processes, it becomes a particularly powerful mechanism for reinforcing cultural (group) values and identity.

Katz complements Braithwaite in his documentation of the emotions moving around the edge of shame. His analysis of the process of transcendence may help criminologists understand more completely the dynamics of shaming, especially when it fails. The humiliating subordination that is shaming (when there is no self-participation or reintegration) represents a moral affront that must be "put right" through a transcendent process of self-reaffirmation—of reconstruction that salvages honor, identity, and worth. The formation and persistence of criminal subcultures, crucial to understanding the forms that deviance takes, and an important criminogenic source in Braithwaite's model, can be explored within the framework of foreground analysis of the kind Katz has demonstrated.

Importantly, Katz's (1988: 52–79) analysis of *sneaky thrills*—shoplifting, pilfering, vandalism, joyriding (some of which were discussed in chapter 5)—also shows how shaming, a generally unpleasant consequence of getting caught, can also be a stimulus for crime. It is precisely the people who have some emotional investment in the conventional order (especially their standing in it) who are likely to be responsive to shaming—otherwise, who cares if a parent, teacher, police officer, or judge bawls you out? Yet the euphoria or thrill of sneaky theft—the seduction of the crime itself—lies precisely in the risk that one will be shamed if caught:

> Thus, the other side of the euphoria felt from being successful is the humiliation from being caught. What the sneak thieves are avoiding, or getting away with by not being caught, is the shame they would feel if they were caught. . . . The thrills of sneaky thefts are metaphysically complex matters. On the one hand, shoplifters and vandals know what they are doing is illegal; the deviant character of the practice is part of the appeal. On the other hand, they typically register a kind of metaphysical shock when an arrest induces a sense that what they are doing might be treated as real crime. . . . Once an arrest occurs, the shoplifting career typically ends in response to an awareness that persistence would now clearly signal a commitment to a deviant identity. (64–66)

INTEGRATED THEORY

As we explained in chapter 12, social process theories deal with the dynamic aspects of the relationship between individuals and their immediate social environments. They explain how it is that certain people learn criminal behavior patterns and how they acquire criminal status. Where social structural theories (discussed in chapter 13) focus on the relationship of organization and culture to values, norms, resources, and opportunities, social process theories consider how the actions of individuals and groups influence what people do and become.

Even though process has been separated from structure in this review of prominent theories, the two are, in reality, intimately connected. One way to think of that connection is to visualize structure as setting the stage for process, which, in turn, brings structure to life. When thinking about crime, structure promotes and restrains criminal activity among different segments of the population, while process determines which individuals within those segments will become criminally active (or be singled out for criminal labeling) and which will not.

Two questions are therefore relevant when considering why crime varies from place to place or from group to group: (1) How do social structures compare? and (2) How do the activities and experiences of individuals compare? Often it is not possible to answer both questions at the same time because the kinds of information or methodologies needed are not available or not used. Sometimes the criminologist who engages in research is simply not interested in process questions, for example, but wants to evaluate the relationship between structure and crime, perhaps at a class or societal level.

It is nevertheless helpful to illustrate how structure and process can be linked in research. While there are many integrated theories, one fairly recent study (Laub and Sampson, 1988) assesses the criminal behavior of individuals who live in different family and neighborhood environments (structure) and are exposed to different interactional experiences (process). It is based on a reanalysis of data compiled by Sheldon and Eleanor Glueck some sixty years ago.

The Gluecks (1950) collected data on five hundred officially defined delinquents and five hundred nondelinquents. All subjects were white males growing up in poor, deteriorated neighborhoods close to the industrial and commercial zones of Boston. Their average age was just under fifteen. Data on all sorts of social, psychological, and biological variables were collected in a multifactor design. Despite a variety of criticisms leveled at the Gluecks' research design, the study remains a classic in the field (Laub and Sampson, 1988: 357–61).

The reanalysis of the Gluecks' data by Laub and Sampson focused primarily on the relationship between family factors and delinquency. The family factors were divided into two categories that reflect the distinction between structure and process. Structural factors included household crowding, economic dependence, residential mobility, and parental criminality. Process factors included parental discipline and supervision of a child, and emotional rejection.

Laub and Sampson hypothesized that parental child-rearing practices and other family management skills would be most directly related to the delinquent behavior of a child, since they constitute the emotional atmosphere and control environment to which the child is exposed while growing up. Basing their argument on work by Hirschi (1983) and others, Laub and Sampson predicted that good parenting skills and a supportive emotional climate would help prevent the emergence of delinquency in a child because they enhance family social control.

The authors also predicted, however, that parental discipline and family emotional climate would be directly influenced by background factors such as economic dependency, irregular employment, and parental criminality. Thus, the structural variables influence delinquency through their impact on family process: "For instance, it is likely that residential mobility and irregular employment by mothers are related to difficulties in supervising and monitoring children. Similarly, family disruption not only affects supervisory capacity, but also attachment and disciplinary practices" (Laub and Sampson, 1988: 367–68).

In this manner, Laub and Sampson showed how structure and process can be linked in the explanation of delinquency. When they reanalyzed the Gluecks' data to test this model, they found that the quality of family social control was indeed directly and strongly related to serious and persistent delinquency among boys.

Equally important, however, was the finding that the social structural variables helped set the stage by directly influencing the ways in which parents supervise and discipline their children and the quality of the emotional relationship between parent and child.

The relationship between family life and delinquency, it must be said, is one of the most researched issues in criminology. Yet a review of nearly three hundred studies came up with few clear-cut conclusions, except to reiterate that a relationship *does* exist—deviance begins at home (Wright and Wright, 1994). The lack of definitive conclusions about the specifics of the link between family life and crime reflects in part the many inconsistencies plaguing the methods and findings of so much of the research. It also reflects problems in resolving the issue of causality:

> For example, when researchers observe an association between family conflict and delinquency, any one of three explanations may describe the actual relationship between the variables. Family conflict may, in fact, actually cause delinquency. Alternatively, having a delinquent child may create considerable conflict within the family. Or, perhaps family conflict and delinquency are unrelated, but increase or decrease in relation to one another because of their mutual relationship to yet a third variable, for instance, aggression proneness among family members. Researchers never prove causality but endeavor to eliminate alternative explanations by using more complex models and methods that allow them to rule out other possibilities. (2)

On the whole, one can safely say that family structure and family interaction *together with* external factors such as the economic condition, opportunity structure, quality of schools, and institutional stability of the neighborhood and surrounding community go a long way toward explaining the antisocial behavior of youths. How relevant these same factors are for explaining adult crime, especially occupational and public order crimes, is another matter. The fact that most youths "mature" out of crime by their late teens and early twenties indicates that something is operating to halt or perhaps even reverse the impact of these factors for a majority of children once they reach adulthood.

Some criminologists believe that key adult roles such as spouse, full-time worker, and parent make continued criminality too costly. Perhaps people become concerned about losing their family's respect (e.g., Rowe, Lindquist, and White, 1989), or perhaps participation in family life bonds a person more closely to conventional society, including values and attitudes about marital, parental, and work responsibility (e.g., Thornberry, 1987; Sampson and Laub, 1990). On the other hand, Gottfredson and Hirschi (1990) argue that criminality reflects impulsivity, short-time perspective, and other characteristics of low self-control. Such individuals are unlikely to make successful marriage partners, parents, or workers as adults—just as they are unlikely to do well in school as children. Any relationship between marriage and family life and crime is therefore spurious, meaning that the three are related only through their association with low self-control.

Kevin Wright and Karen Wright (1994) conclude that the research on this issue is inconclusive. But here is another thought: Some forms of crime—small business crime and perhaps some occupational and professional crimes—may actually thrive on strong family and work relationships. Since the emphasis in most criminological research is on street crime, it is easy to forget that robbery, burglary, drug pushing, rape, assault, and murder actually represent just the tip of the crime iceberg. An adequate description and explanation of the relationship between family life and crime must surely move beyond these crimes into the world of business crime, money laundering, fraud, and bribery—offenses not usually committed by children or by people whose backgrounds automatically suggest a delinquent childhood.

The Life Course Perspective

Sampson and Laub (1992; 1993; 2003) have proposed a very promising integrated theory of crime. Their theory centers on the notion of the life course, through which all individuals travel from birth to death. The **life course** consists of *trajectories*, which are long-term sequences and patterns of behavior (for example, schooling, work life, marriage, parenthood, or criminal career), and *transitions*, which are specific life events within a trajectory, such as getting a job, getting married, going to college, or joining a gang (Piquero and Mazerolle, 2001).

Sampson and Laub's review of research shows that individuals have fairly stable attributes that are established early in life and that provide continuity and consistency as individuals age; aggression might be one, with adult manifestations in the form of spousal abuse and harsh punishment of children. But they also find evidence that a childhood trajectory may be modified or even halted by key life course events, such as getting married, getting a job, or moving from one town to another. Sampson and Laub believe that in the transition to adulthood, it is not so much the timing of discrete life events such as marriage, but rather "the [resulting] quality or strength of social ties" that influences behavior (1992: 73).

Sampson and Laub call for a deeper examination of how continuity and change work together in an individual's life course to inhibit or promote antisocial behavior. In proposing a dual focus on continuity and change within the individual life course, they nevertheless recognize that structural conditions, including social opportunities and the actions of social control agencies, impact on the life experiences of individuals and therefore the chances that an individual's criminal behavior will begin, end, continue, or undergo modification over time.

Perhaps the most interesting conclusion of Sampson and Laub's (2003) prodigious series of studies is that crime involvement for all persons—including serious, persistent offenders—declines significantly with age. This finding, although somewhat contested (e.g., Blokland, Nagin, and Nieuwbeerta, 2005) is that desistance from crime as one ages is a universal fact, regardless of the differences in individuals' early childhood experiences.

CHAPTER SUMMARY

Consistent with the goal of general theory, the theories reviewed in this chapter seek to identify the things diverse crimes have in common and to build explanations around them. Most of the theories are heavily indebted to existing ideas about crime, and what is new is more in the packaging than in the substance. On the other hand, Katz shows us a way of thinking about crime that departs significantly from the other approaches even as it complements Braithwaite's.

It is safe to say that criminologists will be examining these theories closely in the years ahead. Do not expect that one will emerge as *the* explanation of crime. For one thing, criminologists disagree on the definition of their subject matter. For another, the data and methodology for adequate tests of all theories do not yet exist. What is likely to happen is continued refinement and reshaping, so that the dominant theories a decade from now will show their indebtedness but will not be the same.

Remember, too, that the criminological enterprise is affected not only by the ideas and values of its participants, but also by the ideology underlying public policy. That ideology affects the funding of research. Theories that challenge established paradigms tend, in any case, to be embraced with great caution—all the more so if they conflict with the funding priorities of governments and universities.

If the measure of criminology is its success at explaining crime, where do you think we stand? We certainly know a lot about the crime scene, and well we should after more than one hundred years of research. We can also point to theories that have remained prominent for many, many years—differential association is perhaps the best example. Some of the general theories we have reviewed in this chapter address crime at both the micro and macro levels of analysis, and some integrate theories that once appeared incompatible. Some also bring together behaviors that were once thought to be so different as to require different explanations—rape and shoplifting, for example. It is noteworthy, too, that an argument made long ago by French sociologist Émile Durkheim now seems more relevant than ever: that crime and punishment are two parts of an inseparable whole and that one cannot be explained without also explaining the other.

KEY TERMS

communtarianism
control balance
control deficit
control ratio
control surplus
criminality
disintegrative shaming
general theories
interdependency
intergrated theories
life course
low self-control
reintegrative shaming
restorative justice
versatility construct

CRIMINOLOGICAL THEORY

At the very least, a course in criminology should enable students to offer the casual observer some insight into the character and causes of crime. However, as is true with many apparently simple questions, thoughtful answers rarely come easily. For one thing, there are dozens of theories of crime and the sheer variety of competing explanations can be overwhelming. For another, *crime* and *criminality* cover many different things, so an explanation of one may hardly touch another. And, as we saw in chapter 15, attempts to construct general theories of crime that apply to many forms are fraught with difficulties and pitfalls. Small wonder students who have completed criminology courses often feel more confused about crime than when they started.

We believe that some of the confusion can be lessened if students keep the following seven points in mind when thinking about criminological theory.

1. There are many different types of crime. A cursory glance at annual crime statistics shows that while petty theft, vandalism, and simple assault make up the bulk of crimes known to the police, many other offenses are committed in a given year, among them sexual assaults, forgery, liquor law violations, weapons

violations, drug crimes, gambling offenses, disorderly conduct, robbery, auto theft, vagrancy, embezzlement, prostitution, fraud, and murder. There are also many types of crime that are not listed at all, from so-called white-collar offenses and state and governmental crimes to domestic violence. But the implication is this: A theory of crime that does well for one type of crime may not do as well—or even be relevant—for another (a simple example: a theory that explains barroom violence is hardly relevant for corporate price-fixing or safe cracking by professional thieves).

2. Criminality varies among individuals as well as among groups. This is an important distinction because the clues to variations among individuals may be different from those relevant for groups. Explaining individual differences draws us toward psychological and social-psychological theories, while variations among groups are better addressed with social-structural theories.

3. Variations in criminality are not the same as variations in crime. This important distinction has been addressed by Ron Clarke and Travis Hirschi, among others. *Criminality* can be thought of

as the propensity to commit crime, and is a property of individuals or groups. *Crime* refers to offenses as events that occur with greater or lesser frequency, duration, intensity, and so on. Crime is all about opportunities, while criminality is all about motivations. Theories designed to explain variations in criminality are unlikely to shed enough light to also explain variations in crime as an event—and vice versa.

4. Among the ways crimes differ is in the resources and ability needed to commit them. This means that even though an opportunity for crime exists, it must still be accessed (taken advantage of), and the ability to do this varies among individuals and groups. Almost anyone can punch someone else (a simple assault) or shoplift (a petty theft); safe cracking is another story, as are price-fixing and bomb making. To the degree that opportunities for crime and access to them vary independently, a promising theory will address both these aspects of crime.

5. Just as crimes differ objectively in opportunity and accessibility, they also differ subjectively. Simply put, while an opportunity for crime must exist objectively for the offense to occur, subjective perceptions will influence whether the opportunity is seized. Just as objective opportunities for crime (and access to them) vary among places and times as well as among individuals and groups, so do perceptions of those opportunities (and access to them). A promising theory will also address these variations.

6. Crime is a social construction. From a legalistic point of view, an act is not criminal until lawmakers say it is—and assign a penalty for violations. Generally speaking, the seriousness of offenses is gauged by the penalties assigned to them: the lighter the penalty, the less serious the crime. So crimes vary by seriousness, where seriousness is a judg-

ment made by people with the legal authority to do so. Although by no means exact, there is a connection between the legal seriousness of an offense and its perceived wrongness among the public at large. The two tend to vary together—that is, if one is high, so is the other. Thus, a person who plants a bomb that kills twenty people faces execution or life in prison without parole; this same act receives the highest severity scores in national surveys of the general public. On the other hand, vagrancy and trespassing are relatively minor crimes in terms of penalties; not surprisingly, they receive among the lowest severity scores from the general public.

This has some bearing on the likelihood that crimes will be committed, if only because the more serious a contemplated act is perceived to be, the less likely it will occur. There are two reasons for this: (1) More serious crimes carry higher penalties (or costs and risks)—this is the core of the deterrence argument—and (2) more serious crimes incur greater moral objection—this is the "normative" or wrongness argument found in neutralization theory. A promising theory of crime will address both the legal and moral aspects of seriousness.

7. Finally, external counter-control may reduce both crime and criminality. By this we mean that criminal events and the propensity to participate in them are each susceptible to efforts by others (police, courts, parents, teachers, friends, neighbors, witnesses, etc.) to prevent them from occurring in the first place, or to lessen their impact if they do arise. At the level of events, effective counter-control works on the opportunities for crime and/or access to them—it makes a given *situation* less prone to crime; at the level of motivations, effective counter-control reduces the likelihood that an individual or group finds crime appeal-

ing—it makes *people* less prone to committing crime. A promising theory of crime will address the impact of counter-control on both events and people.

The primary goal of any theory is to predict differences—that is, when there will be more or less of something. In our case, theory should result in predictions about crime and criminality. Policy makers can then use these predictions to make strategic decisions in the effort to reduce crime and criminality.

Some scholars (e.g., Gibbs, 1972, 1994) believe that predictive power is the only appropriate criterion when assessing theories. But there is a hitch: To achieve such assessments, it is necessary that theories be stated formally, so that their logical structures are exposed in a parsimonious way and their arguments are made explicit. Unfortunately, this is rarely the case in social science theory, and criminology is no exception. If convincing is necessary, simply look back through the chapters you have read and try to derive testable predictions from the mostly discursive theories presented. In many cases it will be a difficult, if not impossible, task. Worse, just when you think you've nailed down a testable prediction derived from one of the theories, the author of the theory could very easily say, "That's not what I meant."

So when friends or acquaintances bemoan the "crime problem" and ask you to suggest solutions, you should first ask them to be more specific. What kind of crime are they talking about? Are they talking about criminal events or criminal people? If it is the latter, are they talking about individuals or groups of people? If the former, are they interested in the objective features of a situation or the subjective ones? An even more fundamental question you should ask is this: What do they mean by the words *crime* and *criminal*? A legalistic answer will focus your attention on acts and situations defined as crime by legislatures and on the people who commit those acts. An answer that emphasizes social harm or moral prohibitions will focus your attention on a much broader range of acts—and potentially a broader range of people. The definitions of *crime* and *criminal* thus have important implications for theory. Indeed, some criminologists (e.g., Black, 1976) believe that variations in crime and criminality are directly linked to the behavior of law itself.

This book is an *introduction* to criminology and criminological theory. We have only scratched the surface. If our effort helps students respond coherently and helpfully to questions about crime, then we will have achieved our purpose. The links to popular culture are our way of making criminology more understandable and relevant to every day life. We hope these examples show that while crime is a major theme in modern day popular culture, it is important to critically analyze these images and texts—because more often than not, they are incomplete, if not totally distorted, representations of crime.

Academic criminologists can spend their entire careers studying very specific problems and topics. We hope you find that this text allows you to consider some of this work and be better prepared to think more academically about a popular subject that won't go away any time soon.

REFERENCES

Abadinsky, Howard. (1990). *Organized Crime*. 3rd ed. Chicago: Nelson-Hall.

Abdelrahman, A. I., Gloria Rodriguez, John A. Ryan, John F. French, and Donald Weinbaum. (1998). "The Epidemiology of Substance Use Among Middle School Students: The Impact of School, Familial, Community and Individual Risk Factors." *Journal of Child & Adolescent Substance Abuse* 8, no. 1: 55–75.

Adams, Mike S. (1996). "Labeling and Differential Association: Towards a General Social Learning Theory of Crime and Deviance." *American Journal of Criminal Justice* 20, no. 2: 147–64.

Adams, Mike S., and David T. Evans. (1996). "Teacher Disapproval, Delinquent Peers, and Self-Reported Delinquency: A Longitudinal Test of Labeling Theory." *Urban Review* 28, no. 3: 199–211.

Adler, Freda. (1975). *Sisters in Crime: The Rise of the New Female Criminal*. New York: McGraw-Hill.

Adler, Patricia A. (1993). *Wheeling and Dealing: An Ethnography of an Upper-Level Drug Dealing and Smuggling Community*. 2nd ed. New York: Columbia University Press.

Agnew, Robert (1985). "Social Control Theory and Delinquency." *Criminology* 23: 47–60.

———. (1992). "Foundation for a General Strain Theory of Crime and Delinquency." *Criminology* 30: 47–87.

———. (1994). "The Techniques of Neutralization and Violence." *Criminology* 32: 555–80.

———. (1999). "A General Strain Theory of Community Differences in Crime Rates." *Journal of Research in Crime and Delinquency* 36, no. 2: 123–55.

———. (2001). "Building on the Foundation of General Strain Theory: Specifying the Types of Strain Most Likely to Lead to Crime and Delinquency." *Journal of Research in Crime and Delinquency* 38, no. 4: 319–63.

Agnew, R., and Helene Raskin White. (1992). "An Empirical Test of General Strain Theory." *Criminology* 30, 4: 475–500.

Alexander, Reginald. (1994). "Confessions of a Drug Kingpin." *Prison Life*, January: 31–35.

Allen, Chris. (2005). "The Links between Heroin, Crack Cocaine and Crime: Where Does Street Crime Fit In?" *British Journal of Criminology* 45: 355–72.

Allen, Francis A. (1974). *The Crimes of Politics*. Cambridge, MA: Harvard University Press.

Allen, John. (1977). *Assault with a Deadly Weapon: The Autobiography of a Street Criminal*. New York: Pantheon.

Allison, Julie A., and Lawrence S. Wrightsman. (1993). *Rape: The Misunderstood Crime*. Newbury Park, CA: Sage.

Alvarez, A., and R. D. Bachman. (2005). "American Indians and Sentencing Disparity." In Shaun L. Gabbidon and Helen Taylor Greene, eds., *Race, Crime, and Justice: A Reader*. New York: Routledge.

American Association for World Health. (1997). *Denial of Food and Medicine: The Impact of the U.S. Embargo on the Health and Nutrition in*

Cuba. Washington, DC: American Association for World Health.

American Society of Criminology. (1999) *Draft Code of Ethics.* Unpublished manuscript.

Amir, Menachim. (1971). *Patterns in Forcible Rape.* Chicago: University of Chicago Press.

Anastasia, George. (1993). *Blood and Honor: Inside the Scarfo Mob.* New York: Morrow.

Anderson, Elijah. (1990). *Streetwise: Race, Class, and Change in an Urban Community.* Chicago: University of Chicago Press.

———. (1994). "The Code of the Streets." *Atlantic Monthly* 273: 81–94.

———. (1999). *Code of the Street.* New York: Norton.

Anglin, Douglas M., and George Speckart. (1988). "Narcotics Use and Crime: A Multisample, Multimethod Analysis." *Criminology* 26: 197–233.

Archer, Dane, and Rosemary Gartner. (1984). *Violence and Crime in Cross-National Perspective.* New Haven, CT: Yale University Press.

Aronowitz, Alexis A. (1994). "Germany's Xenophobic Violence: Criminal Justice and Social Responses." In Mark S. Hamm, ed., *Hate Crime: International Perspectives on Causes and Control.* Cincinnati, OH: Anderson.

Arrigo, Bruce. (1998). "Marxist Criminology and Lacanian Psychoanalysis: Outline for a General Constitutive Theory of Crime." In Jeffrey I. Ross, ed., *Cutting the Edge: Current Perspectives in Radical/Critical Criminology and Criminal Justice.* Westport, CT: Praeger.

———. (2003). "Postmodern Justice and Critical Criminology: Positional, Relational, and Provisional Science." In Martin D. Schwartz and Suzanne E. Hatty, eds., *Controversies in Critical Criminology.* Cincinnati, OH: Anderson.

———. (2004). "Postmodern Criminology." In Martin D. Schwartz and Suzanne Hatty, eds., *Controversial Issues in Criminology: Critical Criminology.* Cincinnati: Anderson.

Ashley, Barbara Renchkovsky, and David Ashley. (1984). "Sex as Violence: The Body against Intimacy." *International Journal of Women's Studies* 7: 352–71.

Association of Certified Fraud Examiners. (2006). *Report to the Nation on Occupational Fraud and Abuse.* http://www.acfe.com/resources/publications.asp?copy=rttn.

Attenborough, F. L. (1963). *The Laws of the Earliest English Kings.* New York: Russell and Russell.

Aulette, Judy R., and Raymond J. Michalowski. (1993). "Fire in Hamlet: A Case Study of State-Corporate Crime." In Kenneth Tunnell, ed., *Political Crime in Contemporary America.* New York: Garland.

Ayres, Ian, and John Braithwaite. (1992). *Responsive Regulation: Transcending the Deregulation Debate.* New York: Oxford University Press.

Bachman, Ronet. (1994). *Violence against Women.* Washington, DC: U.S. Department of Justice.

Bailey, Ronald H. (1976). *Violence and Aggression.* New York: Time Life Books.

Bailey, William C. (1998). "Deterrence, Brutalization, and the Death Penalty: Another Examination of Oklahoma's Return to Capital Punishment." *Criminology* 36: 711–33.

Baker, Michael A., and Alan F. Westin. (1987). *Employer Perceptions of Workplace Crime.* Washington, DC: U.S. Department of Justice.

Baldus, David, George Woodworth, and C. A. Pulaski. (1985). "Monitoring and Evaluating Contemporary Death Sentencing Systems: Lessons from Georgia." *University of California Davis Law Review* 18, no. 4: 1375–1407.

Baltagi, Badi. (2006). "Estimating an Economic Model of Crime Using Panel Data from North Carolina," *Journal of Applied Econometrics* 21, no. 4: 543–47.

Bandura, Albert. (1973). *Aggression: A Social Learning Analysis.* Englewood Cliffs, NJ: Prentice-Hall.

Barak, Gregg (1991). *Crimes by the Capitalist State.* Albany: State University of New York Press.

———. (1994). *Media, Process, and the Social Construction of Crime: Studies in Newsmaking Criminology.* New York: Garland.

———. (2000). *Crime and Crime Control: A Global View.* Westport, CT: Greenwood.

Barak, Gregg, Jean Flavin, and Paul Leighton. (2001). *Class, Race, Gender and Crime: Social Realities of Justice in America.* Los Angeles: Roxbury.

Barker, Thomas, and David L. Carter. (1994). *Police Deviance.* 3rd ed. Cincinnati, OH: Anderson.

Barlow, David E., and Melissa Hickman Barlow. (2000). *Police in a Multicultural Society: An American Story.* Prospect Heights, IL: Waveland.

Barlow, Hugh D. (1983). "Factors Affecting the Lethality of Criminal Assaults." Presented at the annual meeting of the American Society of Criminology, Denver.

———. (1985). "The Medical Factor in Homicide Victimization." Presented at the Fifth International Symposium on Victimology, Zagreb, Yugoslavia.

———. (1991). "Explaining Crimes and Analogous Acts, or the Unrestrained Will Grab at Pleasure Whenever They Can." *Journal of Criminal Law and Criminology* 82: 229–42.

———. (1995). *Crime and Public Policy: Putting Theory to Work.* Boulder, CO: Westview.

———. (2000). *Criminal Justice in America.* Upper Saddle River, NJ: Prentice-Hall.

Barlow, Hugh D., and Lynne Schmidt Barlow. (1988). "More on the Role of Weapons in Homicidal Violence." *Medicine and Law* 7: 347–58.

Barlow, Hugh D., and Theodore N. Ferdinand. (1992). *Understanding Delinquency.* New York: Harper-Collins.

Barlow, Melissa Hickman, David E. Barlow, and Theodore G. Chiricos. (1995a). "Economic Conditions and Ideologies of Crime in the Media: A Content Analysis of Crime News." *Crime and Delinquency* 41: 3–19.

———. (1995b). "Mobilizing Support for Social Control in a Declining Economy: Exploring Ideologies of Crime within Crime News." *Crime and Delinquency* 41, no. 2: 191–202.

Barnes, Carole Wolf, and Rodney Kingsnorth. (1996). "Race, Drugs, and Criminal Sentencing: Hidden Effects of the Criminal Law." *Journal of Criminal Justice* 24: 39–55.

Barnett, Harold. (1981). "Corporate Capitalism, Corporate Crime." *Crime and Delinquency* 27: 4–23.

Baron, Larry, and Murray A. Straus. (1990). *Four Theories of Rape in American Society.* New Haven, CT: Yale University Press.

Barr, Kellie E. M., Michael P. Farrell, Grace M. Barnes, and John W. Welte. (1993). "Race, Class, and Gender Differences in Substance Abuse: Evidence of Middle-Class/Underclass Polarization among Black Males." *Social Problems* 40: 314–27.

Bartol, Curt. (1995). *Criminal Behavior: A Psychosocial Approach.* Englewood Cliffs, NJ: Prentice-Hall.

Baumer, Terry L., and Dennis P. Rosenbaum. (1984). *Combatting Retail Theft: Programs and Strategies.* Boston: Butterworths.

Bayley, David H., and Egon Bittner. (1989). "Learning the Skills of Policing." *Law and Contemporary Problems* 47: 35–59.

Beare, Margaret E. (1998). "Corruption and Organized Crime: Lessons from History." *Crime, Law, and Social Change* 28, no. 2: 155–72.

Beccaria, Cesare. (1963). *Essay on Crimes and Punishments.* Translated by Henry Paolucci. Indianapolis: Bobbs-Merrill.

Becker, Gary S. (1968). "Crime and Punishment: An Economic Approach." *Journal of Political Economy* 76: 493–517.

Becker, Howard S. (1963). *Outsiders: Studies in the Sociology of Deviance.* New York: Free Press.

Beckett, Katherine, Kris Nyrop, and Lori Pfingst. (2006). "Race, Drugs, and Policing: Understanding Disparities in Drug Delivery Arrests." *Criminology* 44, no. 1: 105–37.

Beirne, Piers. (1983). "Generalization and Its Discontents: The Comparative Study of Crime." In Israel L. Barak-Glantz and Elmer H. Johnson, eds., *Comparative Criminology.* Beverly Hills, CA: Sage.

Beirne, Piers, and James Messerchmidt. (2000). *Criminology.* 3rd ed. Boulder, CO: Westview.

Bell, Daniel. (1965). "Crime as an American Way of Life: A Queer Ladder of Social Mobility." In *The End of Ideology.* Rev. ed. New York: Free Press.

Bennett, Trevor, and Richard Wright. (1981). "Burglars' Choice of Targets: The Use of Situational Cues in Offender Decision Making." Presented at the annual meeting of the American Society of Criminology, Washington, DC.

———. (1984). *Burglars on Burglary.* Aldershot, UK: Gower.

Benson, Michael L., and Francis T. Cullen. (1998). *Combating Corporate Crime: Local Prosecutors at Work.* Boston: Northeastern University Press.

Bentham, Jeremy. (1948). *The Principles of Morals and Legislation.* New York: Hofner.

———. (1973). *The Principles of Morals and Legislation.* New York: Hofner.

Bergen, Raquel Kennedy. (1996). *Wife Rape.* Thousand Oaks, CA: Sage.

———. (1998). *Issues in Intimate Violence.* Thousand Oaks, CA: Sage.

———. (2006). Marital Rape: New Research and Directions. National Online Resource Center on Violence against Women. http://new.vawnet.org/Assoc_Files_VAWnet/AR_MaritalRapeRevised.pdf.

Berlin, Peter. (1996). *National Report on Shoplifting.* Jericho, NJ: Shoplifters Anonymous.

Bernasco, Wim, and Floor Luykx. (2003). "Effects of Attractiveness, Opportunity, and Accessibility to Burglars on Residential Burglary Rates of Urban Neighborhoods." *Criminology* 41: 981–1001.

Bernburg, Jon Gunnar, and Marvin D. Krohn. (2003). "Labeling, Life Chances, and Adult Crime: The Direct and Indirect Effects of Official Intervention in Adolescence on Crime in Early Adulthood." *Criminology* 41, no. 4, 1287–1319.

Berton, Margaret, and Sally D. Stabb. (1996). "Exposure to Violence and Post-Traumatic Stress Disorder in Urban Adolescents." *Adolescence* 31: 489–98.

Best, Joel. (1999). *Random Violence: How We Talk about New Crimes and New Victims.* Berkeley and Los Angeles: University of California Press.

Bichler, Gisela, and Stefanie Balchak. (2007). "Address Matching Bias: Ignorance Is Not Bliss." *Policing* 30, no. 1: 32–50.

Birzer, Michael L., and Gwynne Harris Birzer. (2006). "Race Matters: A Critical Look at Racial Profiling, It's a Matter for the Courts." *Journal of Criminal Justice* 34, no. 6: 643–51.

Black, Donald J. (1976). *The Behavior of Law.* New York: Academic Press.

Blankenship, Michael B., ed. (1993). *Understanding Corporate Criminality.* New York: Garland.

Bleecker, E. Timothy, and Sarah K. Murnen. (2005). "Fraternity Membership, the Display of Degrading Sexual Images of Women, and Rape Myth Acceptance." *Sex Roles* 53: 487–93.

Block, Alan A. (1991). *The Business of Crime: A Documentary Study of Organized Crime in the American Economy.* Boulder, CO: Westview Press.

Block, Carolyn Rebecca. (1991). "Trends in Homicide Syndromes and Economic Cycles in Chicago over 25 Years." Presented at the annual meeting of the American Society of Criminology, San Francisco, November 18–23.

———. (1993). "Lethal Violence in the Chicago Latino Community." In Anna Victoria Wilson, ed., *Homicide: The Victim/Offender Connection.* Cincinnati, OH: Anderson.

———. (1995). *Major Trends in Chicago Homicide: 1965–1994.* Chicago: Criminal Justice Information Authority.

Block, Carolyn Rebbecca, and Richard Block. (1993). "Street Gang Crime in Chicago." *NIJ Research in Brief*, December: 1–11.

Block, Richard, and Carolyn Rebecca Block. (1991). "Beginning with Wolfgang: An Agenda for Homicide Research." Presented at the annual meeting of the American Society of Criminology, San Francisco, November 18–23.

Blokland, Arjan, Daniel Nagin, and Paul Nieuwbeerta. (2005). "Life Span Offending Trajectories of a Dutch Conviction Cohort." *Criminology* 43, no. 4: 919–48.

Blumer, Herbert. (1969) *Interactionism: Perspective and Method.* Englewood Cliffs, NJ: Prentice-Hall.

Boggs, Sarah Lee. (1964). "The Ecology of Crime Occurrence in St. Louis: A Reconceptualization." PhD diss., Washington University, St. Louis.

Bohm, Carol. (1974). "Judicial Attitudes toward Rape Victims." *Judicature*, Spring 303–307.

Bohm, Robert M. (1998). "Understanding Crime and Social Control in Market Economies: Looking Back and Moving Forward." In Jeffrey Ian Ross, ed., *Cutting the Edge: Current Perspectives in Radical/Critical Criminology.* Westport, CT: Praeger.

Bonger, Willem, (1969). *Criminality and Economic Conditions.* Abridged ed. Bloomington: Indiana University Press.

Borkin, Joseph. (1978). *The Crime and Punishment of I. G. Farben.* New York: Pocket Books.

Borkin, Julie, Stuart Henry, and Dragan Milovanovic. (2006). "Constitutive Rhetoric and Constitutive Criminology: The Significance of the Virtual Corpse." In Walter S. DeKeseredy, Shahid Alvi, and Martin D. Schwartz, eds., *Advancing Critical Criminology: Theory and Application.* New York: Rowman and Littlefield.

Botchkovar, Ekaterina, and Charles R. Tittle. (2005). "Crime, Shame and Reintegration in Russia." *Theoretical Criminology* 9, no. 4: 401–42.

Bourgois, P. (2004) *In Search of Respect: Selling Crack in El Barrio.* 2nd ed. Cambridge: Cambridge University Press.

Box, Steven. (1981). *Deviance, Reality, and Society.* 2nd ed. London: Holt, Rinehart, and Winston.

Box-Grainger, Jill. (1986). "Sentencing Rapists." In Roger Matthews and Jock Young, eds., *Confronting Crime.* Beverly Hills, CA: Sage.

Boyle, Kathleen, and M. Douglas Anglin. (1994). "To the Curb: Sex Bartering and Drug Use among Homeless Crack Users in Los Angeles." In Mitchell S. Ratner, ed., *Crack Pipe as Pimp: An Ethnographic Investigation of Sex-for-Crack Exchanges.* New York: Lexington Books.

Bradshaw, Tausha L., and Alan E. Marks. (1990). "Beyond a Reasonable Doubt: Factors That Influence the Legal Disposition of Child Sexual Abuse Cases." *Crime and Delinquency* 36: 276–85.

Braithwaite, John. (1978). "An Exploratory Study of Used Car Fraud." In P. R. Wilson and J. B. Braithwaite, eds., *Two Kinds of Deviance: Crimes of the Powerless and Powerful.* Brisbane: University of Queensland Press.

———. (1985). *To Punish or Persuade: Enforcement of Coal Mine Safety.* Albany: State University of New York Press.

———. (1988). "White-Collar Crime, Competition, and Capitalism." *American Journal of Sociology* 94: 627–32.

———. (1989a). *Crime, Shame and Reintegration.* Cambridge: Cambridge University Press.

———. (1989b). "Organizational Theory and Organizational Shame." *Justice Quarterly* 6: 401–26.

———. (1991). "Inequality and Republican Criminology." Presented at the annual meeting of the American Society of Criminology, San Francisco, November 18–23.

———. (1995). "Reintegrative Shaming, Republicanism, and Policy." In Hugh D. Barlow, ed., *Crime and Public Policy: Putting Theory to Work.* Boulder, CO: Westview.

———. (1997). "Charles Tittle's Control Balance and Criminological Theory." *Theoretical Criminology* 1, no. 1: 77–97.

Braithwaite, John, and Philip Pettit. (1990). *Not Just Desserts: A Republican Theory of Criminal Justice.* Oxford: Oxford University Press.

Bresler, Fenton (1992). *Interpol.* London: Penguin.

Brezina, Timothy. (1998). "Adolescent Maltreatment and Delinquency: The Question of Intervening Processes." *Journal of Research in Crime and Delinquency* 35, no. 1: 71–89.

Broidy, Lisa, and Robert Agnew. (1997). "Gender and Crime: A General Strain Theory Perspective." *Journal of Research in Crime and Delinquency* 34: 275–306.

Brown, Brenda A. (1974). "Crime against Women Alone." Mimeograph. Memphis, TN: Memphis Police Department.

Brown, Jodi M., and Patrick A. Langan. (1998). *State Court Sentencing of Convicted Felons, 1994.* Washington, DC: U.S. Department of Justice.

Brown, Michael. (1988). *Working the Streets: Police Discretion and Dilemmas of Reform.* New York: Russell Sage.

Brown, Richard Maxwell. (1969). "Violence in America." In Donald J. Mulvihill, Melvin Tumin, and Lynn Curtis, eds., *Crimes of Violence.* Washington, DC: U.S. Government Printing Office.

Browne, Angela. (1987). *When Battered Women Kill.* New York: Macmillan.

Browne, Angela, Kirk R. Williams, and Donald G. Dutton. (1999). "Homicide between Intimate Partners: A 20-Year Review." In M. D. Smith and M. Zahn, eds., *Homicide: A Sourcebook of Social Research.* Thousands Oaks, CA: Sage.

Browne-Marshall, Gloria J. (2007). *Race, Law, and American Society: 1607 to Present.* London: Routledge.

Brownmiller, Susan. (1975). *Against Our Will.* New York: Simon and Schuster.

Bruinsma, Gerben. (1992). "Differential Association Theory Reconsidered: An Extension and Its Empirical Test." *Journal of Quantitative Criminology* 8, no. 1: 29–49.

Bryan, James H. (1965). "Apprenticeships in Prostitution." *Social Problems* 12: 287–97.

Buchmueller, Thomas C., Mireille Jacobson, and Cheryl Wold. (2005). "How Far to the Hospital? The Effect of Hospital Closures on Access to Care." *Journal of Health Economics* 25, no. 4: 740–61.

Bucke, Tom. (1997). "Ethnicity and Contracts with the Police: Latest Findings from the British Crime Survey," *Research Findings,* UK Home Office 59: 1–4.

Buckle, Abigail, and David P. Farrington. (1984). "An Observational Study of Shoplifting." *British Journal of Criminology* 24: 63–72.

Buikhuisen, Wouter. (1988). "Chronic Juvenile Delinquency: A Theory," in Wouter Buikhuisen and Sarnoff A. Mednick, eds., *Explaining Criminal Behavior.* Linden, Netherlands: E. J. Brill.

Bureau of Justice Statistics. (1988). *BJS Data Report, 1987.* Washington, DC: U.S. Department of Justice.

———. (1993). *National Update,* vol. 3. Washington, DC: U.S. Department of Justice.

———. (1994). *Criminal Victimization, 1993.* Washington, DC: U.S. Department of Justice.

———. (1998). www.ojp.usdoj.gov/bjs.

———. (2006). *Criminal Victimization, 2005.* Washington, DC: U.S. Department of Justice.

———. (2007). *Criminal Victimization, 2006*. Washington, DC: U.S. Department of Justice.

Burgess, Robert L. (1979). "Family Violence: Some Implications from Evolutionary Biology." Presented at the annual meeting of the American Society of Criminology, San Francisco.

Burgess, Robert L., and Ronald L. Akers. (1966). "A Differential Association-Reinforcement Theory of Criminal Behavior." *Social Problems* 14: 128–47.

Burgess, Robert L., and Patricia Draper. (1989). "The Explanation of Family Violence: The Role of Biological, Behavioral, and Cultural Selection." In Lloyd Ohlin and Michael Tonry, eds, *Family Violence*. Chicago: University of Chicago Press.

Burns, Ronald G., and Michael J. Lynch. (2004). *Environmental Crime: A Sourcebook · Environmental Crime: A Sourcebook*. New York: LFB Scholarly Publishing.

Bursik, Robert J., Jr. (1988). "Social Disorganization and Theories of Crime and Delinquency: Problems and Prospects." *Criminology* 26: 519–51.

———. (2000). "The Systematic Theory of Neighborhood Crime Rates." In Sally S. Simpson, ed., *Of Crime and Criminality: The Use of Theory in Everyday Life*. Thousand Oaks, CA: Pine Forge Press.

Bursik, Robert J., and Harold G. Grasmick. (1993). *Neighborhoods and Crime: The Dimensions of Effective Community Control*. Lexington, MA: Lexington Books.

———. (1995). "Neighborhood-Based Networks and the Control of Crime and Delinquency." In Hugh D. Barlow, ed., *Crime and Public Policy: Putting Theory to Work*. Boulder, CO: Westview.

Bush, Tracey, and John Hood-Williams. (1995). "Domestic Violence on a London Housing Estate." *Home Office Research Bulletin* 37: 11–18.

Calavita, Kitty, and Henry N. Pontell. (1990). "Heads I Win, Tails You Lose: Deregulation, Crime, and Crisis in the Savings and Loan Industry." *Crime and Delinquency* 36: 309–41.

———. (1991). "Other People's Money Revisited: Collective Embezzlement in the Savings and Loan and Insurance Industries." *Social Problems* 38: 94–112.

Calder, James D., and John F. Bauer. (1992). "Convenience Store Robberies: Security Measures and Store Robbery Incidents." *Journal of Criminal Justice* 20: 553–66.

Calhoun, George. (1927). *The Growth of Criminal Law in Ancient Greece*. New York: Law Book Exchange.

Callahan, Charles M., and Frederick P. Rivara. (1992). "Urban High School Youth and Handguns." *JAMA* 267: 3038–42.

Cameron, Mary Owen. (1964). *The Booster and the Snitch*. New York: Free Press.

Campbell, Jacquelyn, Nancy Glass, Phyllis W. Sharps, Kathryn Laughon, and Tina Bloom. (2007). "Intimate Partner Homicide." *Trauma, Violence, and Abuse* 8, no. 3: 246–69.

Carey, James T. (1968). *The College Drug Scene*. Englewood Cliffs, NJ: Prentice-Hall.

Carter, Ronald L., and Kim Q. Hill. (1979). *The Criminal's Image of the City*. New York: Pergamon.

Caulfield, Susan L. (1991). "The Perpetuation of Violence through Criminolgoical Theory: The Ideological Role of Subculture Theory." In H. Pepinsky and R. Quinney, eds., *Criminology as Peacemaking*. Bloomington: Indiana University Press.

Caulfield, Susan L., and Nancy A. Wonders. (1993). "Personal *and* Political: Violence against Women and the Role of the State." In Kenneth D. Tunnell, ed., *Political Crime in Contemporary America: A Critical Approach*. New York: Garland.

Caywood, Tom. (1998). "Routine Activities and Urban Homicides: A Tale of Two Cities." *Homicide Studies* 2, no. 1.: 64–82.

Centers for Disease Control and Prevention. (2007). *Youth Violence at a Glance*. http://www.cdc.gov/injury.

Cernkovich, Stephen A., Peggy C. Giordano, and Meredith D. Pugh. (1985). "Chronic Offenders: The Missing Cases in Self-Report Delinquency Research." *Journal of Criminal Law and Criminology* 76: 705–32.

Chaiken, Marcia R. (1993). "The Rise of Crack and Ice: Experiences in Three Locales," *NIJ Research in Brief*, March: 1–8.

Chambliss, William J., ed. (1972). *Box Man: A Professional Thief's Journey*. New York: Harper and Row.

Chambliss, William J. (1973). "The Saints and the Roughnecks." *Society* 11: 24–31.

———. (1975a). *Criminal Law in Action*. Santa Barbara, CA: Hamilton.

———. (1975b). "The political economy of crime: A comparative study of Nigeria and the U.S.A.," in Ian Taylor, Paul Walton, and Jock Young, eds., *Critical Criminology*. London: Routledge and Kegan Paul.

———. (1988). *On the Take: From Petty Crooks to Presidents*. 2nd ed. Bloomington: Indiana University Press.

———. (1999). *Power, Politics, and Crime*. Boulder, CO: Westview.

Chambliss, William J., and Marjorie Zatz. (1993). *Making Law: The State, the Law, and Structural Contradictions*. Bloomington: Indiana University Press.

Chamlin, Mitchell B., and John K. Cochran. (1997). "Social Altruism and Crime." *Criminology* 35, no. 2: 203–27.

Champion, Dean. (2000). *Research Methods for Criminal Justice and Criminology*. Upper Saddle River, NJ: Prentice-Hall.

Champion, Jane Dermot. (1999). "Life Histories of Rural Mexican American Adolescents Experiencing Abuse." *Western Journal of Nursing Research* 21, no. 5: 699–717.

Chancer, Lynn S. (1987). "New Bedford, Massachusetts, March 6, 1983–March 22, 1984: The 'Before and After' of a Group Rape." *Gender and Society* 1: 239–60.

Chapman, William R. (1986). "The Role of Peers in Strain Models of Delinquency." Presented at the annual meeting of the American Society of Criminology, Atlanta, GA.

Cherry, T., and J. List. (2002). "Aggregation Bias in the Economic Model of Crime." *Economic Letters* 75, no. 1: 81–86.

Chesney-Lind, Meda. (1987a). *Girls' Crime and Women's Place: Toward a Feminist Model of Female Delinquency*. Honolulu: University of Hawaii Youth Development and Research Center.

———. (1987b). "Female Status Offenders and the Double Standard of Juvenile Justice: An International Problem." Presented at the annual meeting of the American Society of Criminology, Montreal, November 11–14.

———. (1988). "Girls in Jail." *Crime and Delinquency* 34: 150–68.

———. (2006). "Patriarchy, Crime, and Justice: Feminist Criminology in an Era of Backlash." *Feminist Criminology* 1, no. 1: 6–26.

Chesney-Lind, Meda, and Katherine Irwin. (2007). *Beyond Bad Girls: Gender, Violence and Hype*. London: Routledge.

Chesney-Lind, Meda, and Randall G. Shelden. (1992). *Girls, Delinquency, and Juvenile Justice*. Pacific Grove, CA: Brooks/Cole.

Chiricos, Ted, Kathy Padgett, and Marc Gertz. (2000). "Fear, TV News, and the Reality of Crime." *Criminology* 38, no. 3: 755–86.

Chodorkoff, Bernard, and Seymour Baxter. (1969). "Psychiatric and Psychoanalytic Theories of Violence and Its Origins." In Donald J. Mulvihill, Melvin Tumin, and Lynn Curtis, eds., *Crimes of Violence*. Washington, DC: U.S. Government Printing Office.

Christiansen, K. O. (1977). "A Preliminary Study of Criminality among Twins." In Sarnoff A. Mednick and K. O. Christiansen, eds., *Biosocial Basis of Criminal Behavior*. New York: Wiley.

Churchill, Ward, and Jim Vander Wall. (1990). *Cointelpro Papers: Documents from the Fbi's Secret Wars against Domestic Dissent*. Cambridge, MA: South End Press.

Clarke, R. V., and M. Felson, eds. (1993). *Routine Activity and Rational Choice: Advances in Criminological Theory*. Vol. 5. New Brunswick, NJ: Transaction, 1993.

Clarke, Ronald V., and Patricia Mayhew. (1988). "The British Gas Suicide Story and Its Criminological Implications." in Michael N. Tonry and Norval K. Morris, eds., *Crime and Justice: A Review of Research*, vol. 10. Chicago: University of Chicago Press.

Claster, Daniel. (1992). *Bad Guys and Good Guys: Moral Polarization and Crime*. New York: Greenwood.

Clear, T. R., D. R. Rose, E. Waring, and K. Scully. (2003). "Coercive Mobility and Crime: A Preliminary Examination of Concentrated Incarceration and Social Disorganization." *Justice Quarterly* 20: 33–64.

Clifford, Nancy. (1998). *Environmental Crime: Enforcement, Policy, and Social Responsibility*. Gaithersburg, MD: Aspen.

Clinard, Marshall B. (1989). "Reflections of a Typologic, Corporate, Comparative Criminologist." *Criminologist* 14: 1, 6, 11, 14–15.

Clinard, M., and R. Quinney. (1973). *Criminal behavior systems: A typology*. New York: Holt, Rinehart, and Winston.

Cloward, Richard A., and Lloyd E. Ohlin. (1960). *Delinquency and Opportunity: A Theory of Delinquent Gangs*. New York: Free Press.

CNN. (2000). "Q&A with Emmanuel Goldstein of *2600: The Hacker's Quarterly*." http://www.cnn.com/TECH/specials/hackers/qandas/goldstein.html.

Coates, R., S. Umbreit, and B. Vos/ (2006). "Responding to Hate Crimes through Restorative Justice Dialog." *Contemporary Justice Review* 9, no. 1: 7–21.

Cochran, John K., Mitchell B. Chamlin, and Mark Seth. (1994). "Deterrence or Brutalization: An Impact Assessment of Oklahoma's Return to Capital Punishment." *Criminology* 32: 107–34.

Cohen, Albert K. (1955). *Delinquent Boys: The Culture of the Gang*. New York: Free Press.

Cohen, Lawrence E., and Marcus Felson. (1979). "Social Change and Crime Rate Trends: A Routine Activity Approach." *American Sociological Review* 44: 588–608.

Cohen, Lawrence E., and Richard Machalek. (1988). "A General Theory of Expropriative Crime: An Evolutionary Ecological Approach." *American Journal of Sociology* 94: 465–501.

Cohen, Mark A. (1998). "Sentencing the Environmental Criminal." In Nancy Clifford, ed., *Environmental Crime: Enforcement, Policy, and Social Responsibility*. Gaithersburg, MD: Aspen.

Collins, James T., Robert L. Hubbard, and J. Valley Rachel. (1985). "Expensive Drug Use and Illegal Income: A Test of Explanatory Hypotheses." *Criminology* 23: 743–63.

Colvin, Mark, and John Pauly. (1983). "An Integrated Structural-Marxist Theory of Delinquency." *American Journal of Sociology* 89, no. 3: 513–51.

Conklin, John E. (1972). *Robbery and the Criminal Justice System*. Philadelphia: Lippincott.

———, ed. (1973). *The Crime Establishment: Organized Crime and American Society*. Englewood Cliffs, NJ: Prentice-Hall.

Conklin, John E., and Egon Bittner. (1973). "Burglary in a Suburb." *Criminology* 11: 206–32.

Cook, Philip J. (1987). "Robbery Violence." *Journal of Criminal Law and Criminology* 78: 357–76.

Cornish, Derek B., and Ronald V. Clarke. (1986a). "Situational Prevention, Displacement of Crime and Rational Choice Theory." In Kevin Heal and Gloria Laycock, eds., *Situational Crime Prevention*. London: HMSO.

———. (1986b). *The Reasoning Criminal: Rational Choice Perspectives on Offending*. New York: Springer-Verlag.

———. (1987). "Understanding Crime Displacement: An Application of Rational Choice Theory." *Criminology* 25: 933–47.

Cornwell, C., and W. Trumbull. (1994). "Estimating the Economic Model of Crime with Panel Data." *Review of Economics and Statistics*: 360–67.

Costello, Barbara J., and Paul R. Vowell. (1999). "Testing Control Theory and Differential Association: A Reanalysis of the Richmond Youth Project Data." *Criminology* 37, no. 4: 815–42.

Crank, John P. (1998). *Understanding Police Culture*. Cincinnati, OH: Anderson.

———. (2003). "Institutional Theory of Police: A Review of the State of the Art." *Policing: An International Journal of Police Strategies & Management* 26, no. 2: 186–207.

Crawford, Charles, Theodore Chiricos, and Gary Kleck. (1998). "Race, Racial Threat, and Sentencing Habitual Offenders." *Criminology* 36: 481–511.

Cressey, Donald R. (1953). *Other People's Money: A Study in the Social Psychology of Embezzlement*. New York: Free Press.

———. (1965). "The Respectable Criminal." *Transaction* 3: 12–15.

———. (1969). *Theft of the Nation: The Structure and Operations of Organized Crime in America*. New York: Harper and Row.

Crew, B. Keith. (1991). "Race Differences in Felony Charging and Sentencing: Toward an Integration of Decision-Making and Negotiation Models." *Journal of Crime and Justice* 14, no. 1: 99–122.

Criminal Justice Collective of Northern Arizona University. (2000). *Investigating Difference: Human and Cultural Relations in Criminal Justice*. Boston: Allyn and Bacon.

Croall, Hazel. (1989). "Who Is the White Collar Criminal?" *British Journal of Criminology* 29: 157–74.

Cromwell, Paul F., ed. (1999). *In Their Own Words: Criminals on Crime*. 2nd ed. Los Angeles: Roxbury.

———. (2006). *In Their Own Words: Criminals on Crime*. 4th ed. Los Angeles: Roxbury.

Cromwell, P., J. Olson, and D. Avary. (1991). *Breaking and Entering: An Ethnographic Analysis of Burglary*. Newbury Park, CA: Sage.

Cromwell, Paul F., Lee Parker, and Shawna Mobley. (1999). "The Five-Finger Discount: An Analysis of Motivations for Shoplifting." In Paul F.

Cromwell, ed., *In Their Own Words: Criminals on Crime.* 2nd ed. Los Angeles: Roxbury.

Crowell, Nancy, and Ann W. Burgess. (1996). *Understanding Violence against Women.* Washington, DC: National Academy Press.

Cullen, Francis T. (1983). "Paradox in Policing: A Note on Perceptions of Danger." *Journal of Police Science and Administration* 11: 457–62.

———. (1994). "Social Support as an Organizing Concept for Criminology: Presidential Address to the Academy of Criminal Justice Sciences." *Justice Quarterly* 11: 527–59.

Cullen, Francis T., William J. Maakestad, and Gary Cavender. (1987). *Corporate Crime Under Attack: The Ford Pinto Case.* Cincinnati, OH: Anderson.

Cupples, Thomas, and David Kauzlarich. (1997). "La Cosa Nostra in Philadelphia: A Functionalist Perspective." *Criminal Organizations* 11, no. 1–2: 17–24.

Currie, Elliott. (1997). "Market, Crime, and Community: Toward a Mid-range Theory of Postindustrial Violence." *Theoretical Criminology* 1, no. 2: 147–72.

———. (1998). *Crime and Punishment in America.* New York: Henry Holt.

D'Alessio, Stewart J., and Lisa Stolzenberg. (1998). "Crime, Arrests, and Pretrial Jail Detention: An Examination of the Deterrence Thesis." *Criminology* 36, no. 4: 735–61.

Daly, Kathleen. (1988). "The Social Control of Sexuality: A Case Study of the Criminalization of Prostitution in the Progressive Era." *Research in Law, Deviance and Social Control* 9: 171–206.

———. (1989). "Neither Conflict nor Labeling nor Paternalism Will Suffice: Intersections of Race, Ethnicity, Gender and Family in Criminal Court Decisions." *Crime and Delinquency* 35: 136–68.

Daly, Kathleen, and Meda Chesney-Lind. (1988). "Feminism and Criminology." *Justice Quarterly* 5: 101–43.

Daly, Martin, and Margo Wilson. (1988a). "Evolutionary Social Psychology and Family Homicide." *Science* 242: 519–24.

———. (1988b). *Homicide.* New York: Aldine De Gruyter.

Davis, F. James. (1962). *Law as a Type of Social Control.* New York: Free Press.

Davis, J. K. (1992). *Spying on America.* Westport, CT: Praeger.

DeKeseredy, Walter S. (2004). "Left Realism on Inner-City Violence," In Martin D. Schwartz and Suzanne E. Hatty, eds., *Controversies in Critical Criminology.* Cincinnati, OH: Anderson.

DeKeseredy, W., S. Alvi, M. Schwartz, and A. Tomasceski. (2003). *Under Siege: Poverty and Crime in a Public Housing Community.* New York: Lexington Books.

DeKeseredy, Walter S., and Martin D. Schwartz. (1998). *Woman Abuse on Campus: Results From the Canadian National Survey.* Thousand Oaks, CA: Sage.

Dible, Debra A., and Raymond H. C. Teske Jr. (1993). "An Analysis of the Proesecutory Effects of a Child Sexual Abuse Victim-Witness Program." *Journal of Criminal Justice* 21: 79–85.

Di Tella, R., and E. Schardrodsky. (2004). "Do Police Reduce Crime? Estimates Using the Allocation of Police Forces after a Terrorist Attack." *American Economic Review* 94, no. 1: 115–33.

Doerner, William G. (1998). *Introduction to Law Enforcement: An Insider's View.* Boston: Butterworth-Heinemann.

Dollard, John, N. Miller, L. Doob, O. H. Mowrer, and R. R. Sears. (1939). *Frustration and Aggression.* New Haven, CT: Yale University Press.

Donziger, Steven (1996). The Real War on Crime. New York: HarperPerennial.

Dorman, Michael. (1972). *Payoff: The Role of Organized Crime.* New York: David McKay.

Dowler, Kenneth (2004) "Comparing American and Canadian Local Television Crime Stories: A Content Analysis." *Canadian Journal of Criminology and Criminal Justice* 46, no. 5: 573–96.

Downs, William R., Joan F. Robertson, and Larry R. Harrison. (1997). "Control Theory, Labeling Theory, and the Delivery of Service for Drug Abuse to Adolescents." *Adolescence* 32: 1–24.

Dowty, Alan. (1994). "Sanctioning Iraq: The Limits of the New World Order." *Washington Quarterly* 17, no. 3: 180.

Drug Enforcement Administration. (2007). www.usdoj.gov/dea.

Dunford, Franklyn W., and Delbert S. Elliott. (1984). "Identifying Career Offenders Using Self-Reported Data." *Journal of Research in Crime and Delinquency* 21: 57–86.

Dunlap, Eloise, Bruce D. Johnson, Ali Manwar. (1997). "A Successful Female Crack Dealer: Case Study of a Deviant Career." In Larry K. Gaines and Peter B. Kraska, eds., *Drugs, Crime, and*

Justice: Contemporary Perspectives. Prospect Heights, IL: Waveland.

Durkheim, Émile. (1893). *De la Division du Travail Social.* Paris: Alcan.

———. (1952 [1897]). *Suicide.* London: Routledge and Kegan Paul.

———. (1964a [1893]). *The Division of Labor in Society.* New York: Free Press.

———. (1964b). *The Rules of Sociological Method.* New York: Free Press.

Eberhardt, Jennifer L., Paul G. Davies, Valerie J. Purdie-Vaughns, and Sheri Lynn Johnson. (2006). "Looking Deathworthy: Perceived Stereotypicality of Black Defendants Predicts Capital-Sentencing Outcomes." *Psychological Science* 17, no. 5: 383–86.

Edwards, Loren E. (1958). *Shoplifting and Shrinkage Protection for Stores.* Springfield, IL: Charles C. Thomas.

Edwards, S. S. M. (1986). *The Police Response to Domestic Violence in London.* London: Central London Polytechnic.

Edwards, Willie J. (1993). "Constructing and Testing a Multiple-Theory Integrated Model of Juvenile Delinquency." *Mid American Review of Sociology* 17, no. 1: 31–43.

Egger, Steven A. (1998). *The Killers among Us: An Examination of Serial Murder and Its Investigation.* Upper Saddle River, NJ: Prentice-Hall.

———. (2002). *The Killers among Us: An Examination of Serial Murder and Its Investigation.* 2nd ed. New York: Prentice Hall.

Einstadter, Werner J. (1969). "The Social Organization of Armed Robbery." *Social Problems* 17: 64–83.

Elias, Robert. (1993). *Victims Still.* Newbury Park, CA: Sage.

Elliott, Delbert S., Beatrix A. Hamburg, and Kirk R. Williams. (1998). *Violence in American Schools.* Cambridge: Cambridge University Press.

Ellis, Lee. (1991). "Monoamine Oxidase and Criminality: Identifying an Apparent Biological Marker for Antisocial Behavior." *Journal of Research in Crime and Delinquency* 28: 227–51.

Ellis, Lee, and Anthony Walsh. (1997). "Gene-Based Evolutionary Theories in Criminology." *Criminology* 35, no. 2: 229–76.

Empey, LaMar T., and Maynard L. Erickson. (1972). *The Provo Experiment: Evaluating Community Control of Delinquency.* Lexington, MA: Lexington Books.

Erikson, Kai T. (1966). *Wayward Puritans: A Study in the Sociology of Deviance.* New York: Wiley.

———. (1976). *Everything in Its Path: Destruction of Community in the Buffalo Creek Flood.* New York: Simon and Schuster.

Ermann, David M., and Richard J. Lundman. (1982). *Corporate Deviance.* New York: Holt, Rinehart and Winston.

Eschholz, Sarah, Matthew Mallard, and Stacey Flynn. (2004). "Images of Prime Time Justice: A Content Analysis of *NYPD Blue* and *Law & Order.*" *Journal of Criminal Justice and Popular Culture* 10, no. 3: 161–80.

Evans-Pritchard, E. E. (1940). *The Nuer.* Oxford: Clarendon Press.

Exxon Valdez Oil Spill Trustee Council. (2000). www.oilspill.state.ak.us.

Fagan, Jeffrey. (1990). "Intoxification and Aggression." In Michael Tonry and James Q. Wilson, eds., *Drugs and Crime,* vol. 13: *Crime and Justice: A Review of Research.* Chicago: University of Chicago Press.

———. (1996). *The Criminalization of Domestic Violence: Promises and Limits.* Washington, DC: U.S. Department of Justice.

Farley, John E. (2005). *Majority-Minority Relations,* 5/E. Upper Saddle River, NJ: Pearson.

Farley, Melissa, Isin Baral, Merab Kiremire, and Ufuk Sezgin. (1997). "Prostitution in Five Countries: Violence and Post-Traumatic Stress Disorder." *Feminism and Psychology* 8, no. 4: 405–26.

Farrington, Jan. (2000). "Resisting Cocaine's Tragic Lure." In Hugh T. Wilson, ed., *Annual Editions: Drugs, Society, and Behavior.* Guilford, CT: Dushkin/McGraw-Hill.

Faupel, Charles E. (1991). *Shooting Dope: Career Patterns of Hard-Core Heroin Users.* Gainesville: University of Florida Press.

———. (1999). "The Drugs-Crime Connection among Stable Addicts." In Paul F. Cromwell, ed., *In Their Own Words: Criminals on Crime.* 2nd ed. Los Angeles: Roxbury.

Federal Bureau of Investigation. (1991). *Crime in the United States, 1990.* Washington, DC: U.S. Department of Justice.

———. (1998). *Crime in the United States, 1997.* Washington, DC: U.S. Department of Justice.

———. (2005). *Crime in the United States, 2004.* Washington, DC: U.S. Department of Justice.

———. (2006a). *Crime in the United States, 2005.* Washington, DC: U.S. Department of Justice.

———. (2006b). *Uniform Crime Reports, 2005.* Washington, DC: U.S. Department of Justice.

———. (2007). *Crime in the United States, 2006.* Washington, DC: U.S. Department of Justice.

———. (2008). *Crime in the United States, 2007.* Washington DC: U.S. Department of Justice.

Feeney, Floyd. (1999). "Robbers as Decision Makers." In Paul Cromwell, ed., *In Their Own Words: Criminals on Crime.* 2nd ed. Los Angeles: Roxbury.

Felson, Marcus. (1998). *Crime and Everyday Life.* 2nd ed. Thousand Oaks, CA: Pine Forge.

———. (2002) *Crime and Everyday Life.* 3rd ed. Thousand Oaks, CA: Sage.

Felson, Marcus, and Ronald V. Clarke. (1998). "Opportunity Makes the Thief: Practical Theory for Crime Prevention." Policing on Reducing Crime Unit. http://www.homeoffice.gov.uk/rds/prgp-dfs/fprs98.pdf.

Felson, Richard B., and Alison C. Cares. (2005). "Gender and the Seriousness of Assaults on Intimate Partners and Other Victims." *Journal of Marriage and Family* 67, no. 5: 1182–95.

Feltey, Kathryn (1991). "Sexual Coercion Attitudes among High School Students: The Influence of Gender and Rape Education." *Youth And Society* 23: 229–50.

Ferrell, Jeff. (1993). *Crimes of Style: Urban Graffiti and the Politics of Criminality.* New York: Garland.

———. (2003). "Cultural Criminology." In Martin D. Schwartz and Suzanne E. Hatty, eds., *Controversies in Critical Criminology.* Cincinnati, OH: Anderson.

Ferrell, Jeff, and Mark S. Hamm. (1998). *Ethnography at the Edge.* Boston: Northeastern University Press.

Feucht, Thomas E. (1997). "Prostitutes on Crack Cocaine: Addiction, Utility, and Marketplace Economics." In Larry K. Gaines and Peter B. Kraska, eds., *Drugs, Crime, and Justice: Contemporary Perspectives.* Prospect Heights, IL: Waveland.

Finkelhor, David, and Kersti Yllo. (1985). *License to Rape: Sexual Abuse of Wives.* New York: Free Press.

Finley, Laura L. (2002). "The Lyrics of Rage Against the Machine: A Study in Radical Criminology?" *Journal of Criminal Justice and Popular Culture* 9, no. 3: 150–66.

Fishbein, Diana H. (1990). "Biological Perspectives in Criminology." *Criminology* 28: 27–72.

Fisher, Dawn, Anthony Beech, and Kevin Browne. (1999). "Comparisons of Sex Offenders to Non-offenders on Selected Psychological Measures," *International Journal of Offender Therapy and Comparative Criminology* 43, no. 4: 473–91.

Fishman, Laura (1998). "The Black Bogeyman and White Self-Righteousness." In Coramae Richey Mann and Marjorie S. Zatz, eds., *Images of Color, Images of Crime.* Los Angeles: Roxbury.

Flavin, Jeanne. (1998). "Razing the Wall: A Feminist Critique of Sentencing Theory, Research, and Policy." In Jeffrey I. Ross, ed., *Cutting the Edge: Current Perspectives in Radical/Critical Criminology and Criminal Justice.* Wesport, CT: Praeger.

Fleming, Zachary. (1999). "The Thrill of It All: Youthful Offenders and Auto Theft." In Paul Cromwell, ed., *In Their Own Words: Criminal on Crime.* Los Angeles: Roxbury.

Fletcher, Connie. (1990). *What Cops Know.* New York: Pocket Books

Fleury, R. E., C. M. Sullivan, D. I. Bybee, and W. S. Davidson. (1998). "Why Don't They Just Call the Cops? Reasons for Differential Police Contact among Women with Abusive Partners." *Violence and Victims* 13, no. 4: 333–46.

Fogarty, Kate. (2006). *School and Youth Violence.* http://fycs.ifas.ufl.edu/newsletters/rnycu06/2006/10/school-and-youth-violence.html.

Food Safety and Inspection Service (2000). "Grand Rapids firm guilty of selling adulterated meat and poultry." Press release. Washington, DC: USDA.

Fox, James Alan and Jack Levin. (1999). "Serial Murder: Popular Myths and Empirical Realities." In M. Dwayne Smith and Margaret A. Zahn, eds., *Homicide: A Sourcebook of Social Research.* Thousand Oaks, CA: Sage.

———. (2000). *The Will to Kill: Making Sense of Senseless Murder.* Boston: Allyn and Bacon.

———. (2005). *Extreme Killing: Understanding Serial and Mass Murder.* Thousand Oaks, CA: Sage.

Fox, James G., and Elizabeth Szockyj. (1996). *Corporate Victimization of Women.* Boston: Northeastern University Press.

Fox, James, and Marianne Zawitz. (1999). *Homicide Trends in the United States.* Washington, DC: Bureau of Justice Statistics.

Fraad, Harriet. (1997). "At Home with Incest." *Rethinking Marxism* 9, no. 4: 16–39.

Fraser, S. (1995). *The Bell Curve Wars*. New York: Basic Books.

Freeman, James, Poppy Liossis, and Nikki David. (2006). "Deterrence, Defiance and Deviance: An Investigation Into a Group of Recidivist Drink Drivers' Self-Reported Offending Behaviours." *Australian and New Zealand Journal of Criminology* 39, no. 1: 1–19.

Freeman, Kenneth R., and Terry Estrada-Mullaney. (1988). "Using Dolls to Interview Child Victims: Legal Concerns and Interview Procedures." *NIJ Reports* 207: 2–6.

French, John F. (1994). "Pipe Dreams: Crack and the Life in Philadlephia and Newark." In Mitchell S. Ratner, ed., *Crack Pipe as Pimp: An Ethnographic Investigation of Sex-For-Crack Exchanges*. New York: Lexington Books.

Friedman, Monroe. (1992). "Confidence Swindles of Older Consumers." *Journal of Consumer Affairs* 26: 20–46.

Friedman, Robert I. (2000). *Red Mafia: How the Russian Mob Has Invaded America*. Boston: Little, Brown.

Friedrichs, David O. (1996). *Trusted Criminals: White Collar Crime in Contemporary Society*. New York: Wadsworth.

———. (1998). State Crime. Aldershot, UK: Dartmouth.

———. (2004). *Trusted Criminals: White Collar Crime in Contemporary Society*. 2nd ed. Belmont, CA: Thomson/Wadsworth.

———. (2006). *Trusted Criminals: White Collar Crime in Contemporary Society*. 3rd ed. New York: Wadsworth.

Frisby, Tana. (1998). "The Rise of Organised Crime in Russia: Its Roots and Social Significance." *Europe-Asia Studies* 50, no. 1: 27–49.

Fuller, John Randolph. (2004) "Peacemaking Criminology." In Martin D. Schwartz and Suzanne E. Hatty, eds., *Controversies in Critical Criminology*. Cincinnati, OH: Anderson.

Fyfe, James J. (1988). *The Metro-Dade Police/Citizen Violence Reduction Project: Final Report*. Washington, DC: Police Foundation.

Fyfe, James J., David A. Klinger, and Jeanne M. Flavin. (1997). "Differential Police Treatment of Male-on-Female Spousal Violence." *Criminology* 35: 455–73.

Gabbidon, Shaun L., and Helen Taylor Greene. (2005). *Race and Crime*. Thousand Oaks, CA: Sage.

Gabor, Thomas, Micheline Baril, Maurice Cusson, Daniel Elie, Marc LeBlanc, and Andre Normandeau. (1988). *Armed Robbery: Cops, Robbers, and Victims*. Springfield, IL: Thomas.

Gallagher, J. (1999, October 8). "State Farm Stops the Use of Aftermarket Parts; Action Comes as a Result of Suit; Judgment Is Being Appealed." *St. Louis Post-Dispatch*.

Garland, David. (1985b). "The Criminal and His Science." *British Journal of Criminology* 28: 109–37.

Gasser, Robert Louis. (1963). "The Confidence Game." *Federal Probation* 27: 47–54.

Gegax, T. Trent, and Sarah Van Boven. (2000). "Heroin High." In Hugh T. Wilson, ed., *Annual Editions: Drugs, Society and Behavior*. Guilford, CT: Dushkin/McGraw-Hill.

Geis, Gilbert (1978a). "Deterring Corporate Crime." In M. David Ermann and Richard J. Lundman, eds., *Corporate and Governmental Deviance*. New York: Oxford University Press.

———. (1978b). "Lord Hale, Witches, and Rape." *British Journal of Law and Society* 5: 26–44.

———. (1988). "From Deuteronomy to Deniability: A Historical Perlustration on White-Collar Crime." *Justice Quarterly* 5: 7–32.

———. (1997–98). "Crime and the Czech Republic: Summary Observations." *Crime, Law, and Social Change* 28, no. 3–4: 311–23.

Giacopassi, David J., Jerry R. Sparger, and Preston M. Stein. (1992). "The Effects of Emergency Medical Care on the Homicide Rate: Some Additional Evidence." *Journal of Criminal Justice* 20: 249–59.

Gibbs, Jack P. (1972). *Sociological Theory Construction*. Hinsdale, IL: Dryden.

———. (1975). *Crime, Punishment and Deterrence*. New York: Elsevier.

———. (1985). "Review Essay." *Criminology* 23: 381–88.

———. (1988). "Reply to Michalowski." *Criminologist* 13, no. 4: 4–5.

———. (1994). *A Theory about Control*. Boulder, CO: Westview.

Gibbs, Jack P., and Glenn Firebaugh. (1990). "The Artifact Issue in Deterrence Research." *Criminology* 28: 347–67.

Gibbs, John J., Dennis Giever, and George E. Higgins. (2003). "A Test of Gottfredson and Hirschi's General Theory Using Structural Equation Modeling." *Criminal Justice and Behavior* 30: 441–58.

Gibbs, Nancy. (1991). "When Is It Rape?" *Time,* June 3.

Gilchrist, Gail, Jacqui Cameron, and Jane Scoular. (2000). "Crack and Cocaine Use among Female Prostitutes in Glasgow: Risky Business." *Drugs: Education, Prevention, Policy* 12, no. 5, 381–91.

Gilligan, James. (1996). *Violence: Our Deadly Epidemic and its Causes.* New York: Grosset/Putnam.

Giordano, P. C., S. A. Cernkovich, and D. D. Holland. (2003). "Changes in Friendship Relations over the Life Course: Implications for Desistance from Crime." *Criminology* 41: 293–327.

Giordano, Peggy C., Toni J. Millhollin, Stephen A. Cernkovich, M. D. Pugh, and Jennifer L. Rudolph. (1999). "Delinquency, Identity, and Women's Involvement in Relationship Violence." *Criminology* 37, no. 1: 17–40.

Glaser, Daniel. (1956). "Criminality Theories and Behavioral Images." *American Journal of Sociology* 61: 433–44.

Glazer, Sarah. (1992). "Violence in Schools: Can Anything Be Done to Curb the Growing Violence?" *CQ Researcher* 2, no. 34.

Glueck, Sheldon, and Eleanor Glueck. (1950). *Unraveling Juvenile Delinquency.* New York: Commonwealth Fund.

Goffman, Erving. (1952). "On Cooling the Mark Out: Some Aspects of Adaptation to Failure." *Psychiatry* 15: 451–63.

Goldstein, Herman. (1990). *Problem-Oriented Policing.* New York: McGraw-Hill.

Goldstein, Paul J. (1993). "Drugs and Violence." In Carolyn Rebecca Block and Richard L. Block, eds., *Questions and Answers in Lethal and Non-Lethal Violence.* Washington, DC: U.S. Department of Justice.

Gordon, Cyrus H. (1957). *The Code of Hammurabi: Quaint or Forward Looking?* New York: Holt, Rinehart and Winston.

Gordon, David M. (1971). "Class and the Economics of Crime." *Review of Radical Economics* 3: 51–75.

———. (1973). "Capitalism, Class and Crime in America." *Crime and Delinquency* 19: 163–86.

Gorman, D. M., and Helene Raskin White. (1995). "You Can Choose Your Friends, but Do They Choose Crime? Implication of Differential Association Theories for Crime Prevention Policy." In Hugh D. Barlow, ed., *Crime and Public Policy: Putting Theory to Work.* Boulder, CO: Westview.

Gottfredson, Michael R., and Don M. Gottfredson. (1988). *Decision-Making in Criminal Justice.* 2nd ed. New York: Plenum.

Gottfredson, Michael R., and Travis Hirschi. (1988). "Science, Public Policy, and the Career Paradigm." *Criminology* 26: 37–55.

———. (1990). *A General Theory of Crime.* Stanford, CA: Stanford University Press.

Grabowski, John. (1984). *Cocaine: Pharmacology, Effects and Treatment of Abuse.* Washington, DC: National Institute of Drug Abuse.

Grace, Sharon. (1993). "Resisting Sexual Assault: A Review of the Literature." *Home Office Research Bulletin* 34: 18–25.

———. (1995). *Policing Domestic Violence in the 1990s.* London: HMSO.

Gracia, Enrique. (2004). "Unreported Cases of Domestic Violence against Women: Towards an Epidemiology of Social Silence, Tolerance, and Inhibition." *Journal of Epidemiology and Community Health* 58: 536–37.

Green, Edward. (1993). *The Intent to Kill.* Baltimore: Clevedon.

Greenberg, David F. (1977). "Crime and Deterrence Research and Social Policy." In Stuart S. Nagel, ed., *Modeling the Criminal Justice System.* Beverly Hills, CA: Sage.

———. (1999). "The Weak Strength of Social Control Theory." *Crime and Delinquency* 45, no. 1: 66–81.

Greenleaf, Richard G., and Lonn Lanza-Kaduce. (1995). "Sophistication, Organization, and Authority-Subject Conflict: Rediscovering and Unraveling Turk's Theory of Norm Resistance." *Criminology* 33, no. 4: 565–73.

Greenwood, Peter W. (1992). "Substance Abuse Problems among High-Risk Youth and Potential Interventions." *Crime and Delinquency* 38: 444–58.

Greenwood, Peter, Jan Chaiken, and Joan Petersilia. (1977). *The Criminal Investigation.* Lexington, MA: D. C. Heath.

Greer, C., and Y. Jewkes. (2005). "Extremes of Otherness: Media Images and Social Exclusion." *Social Justice* 32, no. 1: 20–38.

Greider, William. (2002). "Enron Democrats." *Nation,* April 8. http://www.thenation.com/doc/20020408/greider.

Gross, Samuel R., and Robert Mauro. (1989). *Death and Discrimination: Racial Disparities in Capital Sentencing.* Boston: Northeastern University Press.

Guay, J., M. Ouimet, and J. Proulx. (2005). "On Intelligence and Crime: A Comparison of Incarcerated Sex Offenders and Serious Non-Sexual Violent Criminals." *International Journal of Law and Psychiatry* 28, no. 4: 405–17.

Hagan, Frank (1982). *Research Methods in Criminal Justice and Criminology.* New York: Macmillan.

Hagan, John. (1974). "Extra-legal Attributes and Criminal Sentencing: An Assessment of a Sociological Viewpoint." *Law and Society Review* 8: 357–83.

———. (1985). *Modern Criminology: Crime, Criminal Behavior and Its Control.* New York: McGraw-Hill.

Hagan, John, A. R. Gillis, and J. Chan. (1978). "Explaining Official Delinquency: A Spatial Study of Class, Conflict and Control." *Sociological Quarterly* 19: 386–98.

Hagedorn, John. (1991). "Gang Neighborhoods and Public Policy." *Social Problems* 38: 529–40.

Hakim, Simon, and George F. Rengert, eds. (1981). *Crime Spillover.* Beverly Hills, CA: Sage.

Hale, Robert. (1997). "Motives of Reward among Men Who Rape." *American Journal of Criminal Justice* 22: 101–20.

Hall, Jerome (1952). *Theft, Law, and Society.* Rev. ed. Indianapolis: Bobbs-Merrill.

Hall, Richard. (1987). "Organizational Behavior: A Sociological Perspective." In J. W. Lorsch, ed., *Handbook of Organizational Behavior.* Englewood Cliffs, NJ: Prentice-Hall.

Haller, Mark H. (1990). "Illegal Enterprise: A Theoretical and Historical Interpretation." *Criminology* 28: 207–35.

———. (1991). *Life under Bruno: The Economics of an Organized Crime Family.* Philadelphia: Pennsylvania Crime Commission.

Hamlin, John E. (1988). "The Misplaced Role of Rational Choice in Neutralization Theory." *Criminology* 23: 223–40.

Hamm, Mark S. (1993). *American Skinheads: The Criminology and Control of Hate Crime.* Westport, CT: Praeger.

———. (1994). *Hate Crime: International Perspectives on Causes and Control.* Cincinnati, OH: Anderson.

Hanson, R. Karl, Otto Cadsky, Andrew Harris, and Coralie Lalonde. (1997). "Correlates of Battering among 997 Men: Family History, Adjustment, and Attitudinal Differences." *Violence and Victims* 12, no. 3: 191–208.

Harlow, Caroline Wolf. (1991). *Female Victims of Violent Crime.* Washington, DC: U.S. Department of Justice.

Harries, Keith D. (1989). "Homicide and Assault: A Comparative Analysis of Attributes in Dallas Neighborhoods, 1981–1985." *Professional Geographer* 41: 29–38.

Harrison, Lana D. (1992). "The Drug-Crime Nexus in the USA." *Contemporary Drug Problems* 19, no. 2: 203–45.

Hart, Timothy C., and Callie Rennison. (2003). *Reporting Crime to the Police, 1992–2000.* Washington, DC: U.S. Bureau of Justice Statistics.

Hartjen, Clayton. (1974). *Crime and Criminalization.* New York: Praeger.

Hass, R. N. (1998). *Economic Sanctions and American Diplomacy.* Washington, DC: Brookings University Press

Hassine, Victor (1996). *Life without Parole.* Los Angeles: Roxbury.

Hawkins, Darnell F. (1999). "What Can We Learn from Data Dissaggregation? The Case of Homicide and African Americans." In M. Dwayne Smith and Margaret A. Zahn, eds., *Homicide: A Sourcebook of Social Research.* Thousand Oaks, CA: Sage.

Hedderman, Carol, and Loraine Gelsthorpe. (1997). *Understanding the Sentencing of Women.* London: HMSO.

Heidensohn, Frances (1997). *International Feminist Perspectives in Criminology: Engendering a Discipline.* Buckingham: Open University Press, 176–188.

Heimer, Karen. (1997). "Socioeconomic Status, Subcultural Definitions, and Violent Delinquency." *Social Forces* 75: 799–833.

Heimer, Karen, and Stacy De Coster. (1999). "The Gendering of Violent Delinquency." *Criminology* 37, no. 2: 277–318.

Heiner, Robert. (1996). *Criminology: A Cross-Cultural Perspective.* New York: West.

Heis, Lori L. (1998). "Violence against Women: An Integrated, Ecological Framework." *Violence against Women* 3, no. 3: 262–90.

Henry, Stuart. (1978). *The Hidden Economy.* Oxford: Martin Robinson.

Henry, Stuart, and Dragan Milovanovic. (1996). *Constitutive Criminology: Beyond Postmodernism.* Thousands Oaks, CA: Sage.

———. (1999). *Constitutive Criminology at Work: Applications to Crime and Justice*. Albany: State University of New York Press.

———. (2003). "Constitutive Criminology." In Martin D. Schwartz and Suzanne E. Hatty, eds., *Controversies in Critical Criminology*. Cincinnati, OH: Anderson.

Hentig, H. von. (1948) *The Criminal & His Victim: Studies in the Sociobiology of Crime*. New Haven, CT: Yale Univeristy Press.

Hepburn L., M. Miller, D. Azrael, and D. Hemenway. (2007). "The US Gun Stock: Results from the 2004 National Firearms Survey." *Injury Prevention* 13: 15–19.

Herrnstein, Richard, and Charles Murray. (1994). *The Bell Curve: Intelligence and Class Structure in American Life*. New York: Free Press.

Hickey, Eric W. (1991). *Serial Murderers and Their Victims*. Pacific Grove, CA: Brooks/Cole.

———. (1997). *Serial Murderers and Their Victims*. 2nd ed. Pacific Grove, CA: Brooks/Cole.

Hills, Stuart L. (1971). *Crime, Power, and Morality*. Scranton, PA: Chandler.

Hindelang, Michael J. (1974). "Decisions of Shoplifting Victims to Invoke the Criminal Justice Process." *Social Problems* 21: 580–93.

———. (1978). "Race and Involvement in Common Law Personal Crimes." *American Sociological Review* 43: 93–109.

Hindelang, Michael J., Travis Hirschi, and Joseph G. Weiss. (1979). "Correlates of Delinquency: The Illusion of Discrepancy between Self-Report and Official Measures." *American Sociological Review* 44: 995–1014.

Hinkle, William G., and Stuart Henry. (2000). "Preface." *Annals of the American Academy of Political and Social Science* 567: 8.

Hipp, J., D. Bauer, P. Curran, and K. Bollen. (2004). "Crimes of Opportunity: Testing Two Explanations of Seasonal Change in Crime." *Social Forces* 82, no. 4: 1333–72.

Hirschi, Travis. (1971). *Causes of Delinquency*. Berkeley and Los Angeles: University of California Press.

———. (1983). "Crime and the Family," In James Q. Wilson, ed., *Crime and Public Policy*. San Francisco: Institute for Contemporary Studies.

Hirschi, Travis, and Michael R. Gottfredson. (1987). "Causes of White-Collar Crime." *Criminology* 25: 949–74.

Hirschi, Travis, and Michael J. Hindelang. (1977). "Intelligence and Delinquency: A Revisionist View." *American Sociological Review* 42: 572–87.

Hochstetler A., H. Copes, and M. DeLisi. (2002). "Differential Association in Group and Solo Offending." *Journal of Criminal Justice* 30, no. 6: 559–66.

Hoebel, E. Adamson. (1941). *The Cheyenne Way*. Norman: University of Oklahoma

Hollinger, Richard C. (1991). "Neutralization in the Workplace: An Empirical Analysis of Property Theft and Production Deviance." *Deviant Behavior* 12: 169–202.

———. (2004). National Retail Security Survey Final Report http://web.crim.ufl.edu/research/srp/srp.html.

———. (2005). National Retail Security Survey Final Report. http://web.crim.ufl.edu/research/srp/srp.html.

Holmes, Ronald M., and Stephen T. Holmes. (1994). *Murder in America*. Thousand Oaks, CA: Sage.

Hood, Roger. (1972). *Sentencing the Motoring Offender*. London: Heinemann.

Hooton, Earnest A. (1939). *Crime and the Man*. Cambridge, MA: Harvard University Press.

Horney, Julie, and Ineke Haen Marshall. (1992). "Risk Perceptions Among Serious Offenders: The Role of Crime and Punishment." *Criminology* 30: 575–92.

Horowitz, Ruth. (1987). "Community Tolerance of Group Violence." *Social Problems* 34: 437–49.

Hotchkiss, Susan. (1978). "Realities of Rape." *Human Behavior*, December: 18–23.

Hufbauer, G., J. Schott, and A. Elliot. (1990). *Economic Sanctions Reconsidered*. 2nd ed. Washington, DC: Institute for International Economics.

Hunt, Dana F. (1990). "Drugs and Consensual Crime." In Michael Tonry and James Q. Wilson, eds., *Drugs and Crime*. Vol. 13: *Crime and Justice: A Review of Research*. Chicago: University of Chicago Press.

Hutchinson, John. (1969). "The Anatomy of Corruption in the Trade Unions." *Industrial Relations* 8: 135–37.

Iadicola, Peter, and Anson Shupe. (1998). *Violence, Inequality, and Human Freedom*. Dix Hills, NY: General Hall.

Ianni, Francis A. J. (1974). "New Mafia: Black, Hispanic and Italian styles," *Society* 11:30-36.

———. (1975). *Black Mafia: Ethnic Succession in Organized Crime.* New York: Pocket Books.

———. (1998). "New Mafia: Black, Hispanic, and Italian Styles." *Society* 35, no. 2: 115–29.

Ianni, Francis A. J., and Elizabeth Reuss-Ianni. (1973). *A Family Business: Kinship and Control in Organized Crime.* New York: Russell Sage.

Illinois Motor Vehicle Theft Prevention Council. (1993). *1999 Annual Report.* http://www.icjia.org/public/pdf/mvtpc/annreport99.pdf.

International Court of Justice. (1996). *Legality of the Use by a State of Nuclear Weapons in Armed Conflict.* http://www.un.org/law/icjsum/9622.htm.

Jackall, Robert. (1988). *Moral Mazes: The World of Corporate Managers.* New York: Oxford University Press.

Jackson, Bruce. (1969). *A Thief's Primer.* New York: Macmillan.

Jacobs, Bruce A. (1999a). "Crack to Heroin? Drug Markets and Transition." *British Journal of Criminology* 39, no. 4: 555–74.

———. (1999b). *Selling Crack: The Social World of Streetcorner Selling.* Boston: Northeastern University Press.

Jacobs, Bruce A., Volkan Topalli, and Richard Wright. (2000). "Managing Retaliation: Drug Robbery and Informal Sanction Threats." *Criminology* 38: 171–98.

Jamieson, Ruth, and Kieran McEvoy. (2005). "State Crime by Proxy and Juridical Othering." *British Journal of Criminology* 45, no. 4: 504–33.

Jang, Sung Joon. (1999). "Age-Varying Effects of Family, School, and Peers on Delinquency: A Multilevel Modeling Test of Interactional Theory." *Criminology* 37, no. 3: 643–86.

Jankowski, Martin Sanchez. (1991). *Islands in the Street: Gangs and American Urban Society.* Berkeley and Los Angeles: University of California Press.

Janssen, P., T. Nicholls, R. Kumar, H. Stefankis, A. Spidel, and E. Simpson (2005) "Of Mice and Men: Will the Intersection of Social Science and Genetics Create New Approaches for Intimate Partner Violence?" *Journal of Interpersonal Violence* 20, no. 1: 61–71.

Jaspan, Norman, and Hillel Black. (1960). *The Thief in the White Collar.* New York: Lippincott.

Jeffery, C. Ray. (1959). "An Integrated Theory of Crime and Criminal Behavior." *Journal of Criminal Law, Criminology, and Police Science* 49: 533–52.

———. (1994). "Biological and Neuropsychiatric Approaches to Criminal Behavior." In Gregg Barak, ed., *Varieties of Criminology.* Westport, CT: Praeger.

Jenkins, Phillip. (1993). "African Americans and Serial Homicide." *American Journal of Criminal Justice* 17, no. 2: 47–60.

———. (1994). *Using Murder: The Social Construction of Serial Homicide.* New York: Aldine De Gruyter.

Jensen, A. R. (1969). "How Much Can We Boost IQ and Scholastic Achievement?" *Harvard Educational Review* 39: 1–123.

Jerin, Robert A., and Charles B. Fields. (1994). "Murder and Mayhem in *USA Today*: A Quantitative Analysis of the National Reporting of States' News." In G. Barak, ed., *Media, Process, and the Social Construction of Crime: Studies in Newsmaking Criminology.* New York: Garland.

Jesilow, Paul, Henry N. Pontell, and Gilbert Geis. (1993). *Prescription for Profit.* Berkeley and Los Angeles: University of California Press.

Jewkes, Yvonne. (2004). *Media and Crime.* Thousand Oaks, CA: Sage.

Johnson, Barbara E., Douglas L. Kuck, and Patricia R. Schander. (1997). "Rape Myth Acceptance and Sociodemographic Characteristics: A Multidimentional Analysis." *Sex Roles* 36: 693–707.

Johnson, David R., and Laurie K. Scheuble. (1991). "Gender Bias in the Disposition of Juvenile Court Referrals: The Effects of Time and Location." *Criminology* 29: 677–99.

Johnson, Robert. (1987). *Hard Time: Understanding and Reforming Prison.* Monterey, CA.: Brooks/Cole.

Jones, David P. H., and J. Melbourne McGraw. (1987). "Reliable and Fictitious Accounts of Sexual Abuse to Children." *Journal of Interpersonal Violence* 2: 1–6.

Kandel, Denise, and Mark Davies. (1991). "Friendship Networks, Intimacy, and Illicit Drug Use in Young Adulthood: A Comparison of Two Competing Theories." *Criminology* 29: 441–69.

Kantor, Glenda Kaufman, and Murray A. Straus. (1987). "The 'Drunken Bum' Theory of Wife Beating." *Social Problems* 34: 214–30.

Kappeler, Victor E., Mark Blumberg, and Gary W. Potter. (2000). *The Mythology of Crime and Justice.* 3rd ed. Prospect Heights, IL: Waveland Press.

Kappeler, Victor E., Richard D. Sluder, and Geoffrey P. Alpert. (1994). *Forces of Deviance: Understanding the Dark Side of Policing*. Prospect Heights, IL: Waveland.

Katz, Jack. (1988). *Seductions of Crime: Moral and Sensual Attractions of Doing Evil*. New York: Basic Books.

Kauzlarich, David. (1997). "Nuclear Weapons on Trial: The Battle at the International Court of Justice." *Social Pathology* 3, no. 3: 157–64.

———. (2007). "Seeing War as Criminal: Peace Activist Views and Critical Criminology." *Contemporary Justice Review* 10, no. 1: 67–85.

Kauzlarich, David, and Ronald C. Kramer. (1993). "State-Corporate Crime in the U.S. Nuclear Weapons Production Complex." *Journal of Human Justice* 5, no. 1: 4–28.

———. (1998). *Crimes of the American Nuclear State: At Home and Abroad*. Boston: Northeastern University Press.

Kauzlarich, David, Rick A. Matthews, and William J. Miller. (2001). "Toward A Victimology of State Crime." *Critical Criminology: An International Journal* 10, no. 3: 173–94.

Keane, Carl, Paul S. Maxim, and James J. Teevan. (1993). "Drinking and Driving, Self-Control, and Gender: Testing a General Theory of Crime." *Journal of Research in Crime and Delinquency* 30: 30–46.

Kennedy, Leslie W., and David R. Forde. (1990). "Routine Activities and Crime: An Analysis of Victimization in Canada." *Criminology* 28: 137–52.

King, Harry. (1972). *Boxman: A Professional Thief's Journey*. Edited by William Chambliss. New York: Harper and Row.

Kinsey, Richard, John Lea, and Jack Young. (1986). *Losing the Fight against Crime*. Oxford: Basil Blackwell.

Kleck, Gary, and Susan Sayles. (1990). "Rape and Resistance." *Social Problems* 37: 149–62.

Klemke, Lloyd. (1992). *The Sociology of Shoplifting: Boosters and Snitches Today*. New York: Praeger.

Klockars, Carl B. (1974). *The Professional Fence*. New York: Free Press.

Klofas, John M. (1993). "Drugs and Justice: The Impact of Drugs on Criminal Justice in a Metropolitan Community." *Crime and Delinquency* 39: 204–24.

Knowles, G. (1996). "Dealing Crack Cocaine: A View from the Streets of Honolulu." *FBI Law Enforcement Bulletin* 65, no. 7: 1–8.

Kovandzic, Tomislav V., Lynne M. Vieraitis, and Mark R. Yeisley. (1998). "The Structural Covariates of Urban Homicide: Reassessing the Impact of Income Inequality and Poverty in the Post-Reagan Era." *Criminology* 36: 569–99.

Kramer, Ronald C. (1992). "The Space-Shuttle *Challenger* Explosion: A Case Study of State-Corporate Crime." In Kip Schlegel and David O. Weisburd, eds., *White Collar Crime Reconsidered*. Boston: Northeastern University Press.

———. (2000). "Poverty, Inequality, and Youth Violence." *Annals of the American Academy of Political and Social Science* 567: 123–39.

Kramer, Ronald C., and David Kauzlarich. (1999). "The Opinion of the International Court of Justice on the Use of Nuclear Weapons: Implications for Criminology." *Contemporary Justice Review* 2, no. 4: 395–413.

Kramer, Ronald C., and Raymond J. Michalowski. (1987). "The Space between the Laws: The Problem of Crime in a Transnational Context." *Social Problems* 34: 34–53.

———. (1990). "State-Corporate Crime." Presented at the annual meeting of the American Society of Criminology, Baltimore.

———. (1991). "State-Corporate Crime." Paper based on the 1990 presentation at the annual meeting of the American Society of Criminology, Baltimore.

———. (1995). "The Iron Fist and the Velvet Tongue: Crime Control Policies in the Clinton Administration." *Social Justice* 22, no. 2: 87–97.

———. (1999). "The Changing Nature of State Crime in an Era of Globalization." Presented at a meeting of the American Society of Criminology, Toronto.

———. (2005). "War, Aggression, and State Crime: A Criminological Analysis of the Invasion and Cccupation of Iraq." *British Journal of Criminology* 45, no. 4: 446–69.

Kramer, R. C., R. J. Michalowski, and D. Rothe. (2005). "The Supreme International Crime: How the U.S. War in Iraq Threatens the Rule of Law." *Social Justice* 32, no. 2: 52–81.

Kraska, Peter B. and Louis J. Cubellis. (1997). "Militarizing Mayberry and Beyond: Making Sense of American Paramilitary Policing." *Justice Quarterly* 14: 607–29.

Krinsky, M., and D. Golove. (1993). *U.S. Economic Measures against Cuba: Proceedings in the United Nations and International Law Issues*. Northampton, MA: Aletheia Press.

Krippendorff, D. (2004). *Content Analysis: An Introduction to Its Methodology*. Thousand Oaks, CA: Sage.

Kubrin, C., and R. Weitzer. (2003). "New Directions in Social Disorganization Theory." *Journal of Research in Crime and Delinquency* 40, no. 4: 374–402.

Kurz, D. (1993). "Physical Assaults by Husbands— A Major Social Problem." In R. Gelles and D. Loseke, eds., *Current Controversies on Family Violence*. London: Sage.

LaFree, Gary D. (1989). *Rape and Criminal Justice: The Social Construction of Sexual Assault*. Belmont, CA: Wadsworth.

LaFree, Gary D., Barbara F. Reskin, and Christy Visher. (1991). "Jurors' Responses to Victims' Behavior and Legal Issues in Sexual Assault Trials." *Social Problems* 32: 389–407.

LaGrange, Randy L., Kenneth F. Ferraro, and Michael Supancic. (1992). "Perceived Risk and Fear of Crime: Role of Social and Physical Incivilities." *Journal of Research in Crime and Delinquency* 29: 311–32.

Lamberth John. (1998). "Driving While Black: A Statistician Proves That Prejudice Still Rules the Road." *Washington Post*, August 16.

Lasley, Jim. (1988). "Toward a Control Theory of White-Collar Offending." *Journal of Quantitative Criminology* 4: 347–62.

Laub, John H., and Robert J. Sampson. (1988). "Unraveling Families and Delinquency: A Reanalysis of the Gluecks' Data." *Criminology* 26: 355–80.

Lawrence, Richard A. (1997). *School Crime and Juvenile Justice*. New York: Oxford University Press.

Lee, Matthew R. (2000). "Concentrated Poverty, Race, and Homicide." *Sociological Quarterly* 41, no. 2: 189–206.

Lee, Matthew R., and Erica DeHart. (2007). "The Influence of a Serial Killer on Changes in Fear of Crime and the Use of Protective Measure: A Survey-Based Case Study of Baton Rouge." *Deviant Behavior* 28, no. 1: 1–28.

Lee, Matthew R., and Graham C. Ousey. (2005). "Institutional Access, Residential Segregation, and Urban Black Homicide." *Sociological Inquiry* 75, no. 1: 31–54.

Lein, Laura, Robert Richard, and Tony Fabelo. (1992). "The Attitudes of Criminal Justice Practitioners toward Sentencing Issues." *Crime and Delinquency* 38: 189–203.

Leiser, Burton M. (1973). *Liberty, Justice and Morals*. New York: Macmillan.

Lemert, Edwin M. (1951). *Social Pathology*. New York: McGraw-Hill.

———. (1972). *Human Deviance, Social Problems and Social Control*. 2nd ed. Englewood Cliffs, NJ: Prentice-Hall.

———. (1974). "Beyond Mead: The Societal Reaction to Deviance." *Social Problems* 21: 457–68.

Leonard, Kimberly Kempf, Carl E. Pope, and William H. Feyerherm. (1995). *Minorities in Juvenile Justice*. Thousand Oaks, CA: Sage.

Letkemann, Peter. (1973). *Crime as Work*. Englewood Cliffs, NJ: Prentice-Hall.

Levin, Jack, and Jack McDevitt. (1993). *Hate Crimes: The Rising Tide of Bigotry and Bloodshed*. New York: Plenum.

Liddick, Donald R. (2004). *The Global Underworld: Transnational Crime and the United States*. Westport, CT: Praeger.

Light, Roy, Claire Nee, and Helen Ingham. (1993). *Car Theft: The Offender's Perspective*. London: HMSO.

Linden, E., and J. C. Hackler. (1973). "Affective Ties and Delinquency." *Pacific Sociological Review* 16: 27–47.

Link, Bruce, and Francis T. Cullen. (1983). "Reconsidering the Social Rejection of Ex-Mental Patients: Levels of Attitudinal Response." *American Journal of Community Psychology* 11: 261–73.

Lippmann, Walter. (1931). "The Underworld as Servant." In Gus Tyler, ed., *Organized Crime in America*. Ann Arbor: University of Michigan Press.

Lizotte, Alan J. (1985). "The Uniqueness of Rape: Reporting Assaultive Violence to the Police." *Crime and Delinquency* 31: 169–90.

Lombroso, Cesare. (1911). *Crime, Its Causes and Remedies*. Boston: Little, Brown.

Long-Onnen, Jami, and Derral Cheatwood. (1992). "Hospitals and Homicide: An Expansion of Current Theoretical Paradigms." *American Journal of Criminal Justice* 16, no. 2: 57–74.

Lorenz, Konrad. (1971). *On Aggression*. New York: Bantam.

Luckenbill, David F. (1977). "Criminal Homicide as a Situated Transaction." *Social Problems* 25: 176–86.

Lunde, Donald T. (1970). *Murder and Madness.* San Francisco: San Francisco Book Company.

Luttwak, Edward N. (1995). "Going Dutch: The Unending Cost of the Drugs War." *Times Literary Supplement* 1 September: 4–5.

Lyotard, J. (1984). *The Postmodern Condition: A Report on Knowledge.* Minneapolis: University of Minnesota Press.

Maas, Peter. (1968). *The Valachi Papers.* New York: Putnam.

Machalek, Richard, and Lawrence E. Cohen. (1991). "The Nature of Crime: Is Cheating Necessary for Cooperation?" *Human Nature* 2: 215–33.

MacKinnon, C. (1989). *Toward a Feminist Theory of the State.* Cambridge, MA: Harvard University Press.

Maguire, Kathleen, and Ann L. Pastore, eds. (1996) *Sourcebook of Criminal Justice Statistics, 1995.* Washington, DC: U.S. Department of Justice.

———. (1998). *Sourcebook of Criminal Justice Statistics, 1997.* Washington, DC: U.S. Department of Justice.

———. (2000). *Sourcebook of Criminal Justice Statistics, 1999.* Washington, DC: U.S. Department of Justice.

———. (2007). *Sourcebook of Criminal Justice Statistics, 2006.* Washington, DC: U.S. Department of Justice.

———. (2008). *Sourcebook of Criminal Justice Statistics, 2007.* Washington, DC: U.S. Department of Justice.

Maher, Lisa (1997). *Sexed Work: Gender, Race, and Resistance in a Brooklyn Drug Market.* Oxford: Clarendon Press.

Maine, Sir Henry Sumner. (1905). *Ancient Law,* 10th ed. London: John Murray.

Makkai, Toni, and John Braithwaite. (1991). "Criminological Theories and Regulatory Compliance." *Criminology* 29: 191–217.

———. (1994). "Reintegrative Shaming and Compliance with Regulatory Standards." *Criminology* 32: 361–83.

Malinowski, Bronislaw. (1926). *Crime and Custom in Savage Society.* New York: Harcourt Brace Jovanovich.

Mann, Coramae Richey. (1996). *When Women Kill.* Albany: State University of New York Press.

Mannheim, Hermann. (1946). *Criminal Justice and Social Reconstruction.* London: Routledge and Kegan Paul.

Manning, Peter K. (1994). "The Police, Symbolic Capital, Class, and Control." In George Bridges and Martha A. Myers, eds., *Inequality, Crime, and Social Control.* Boulder, CO: Westview Press.

Marino, R., J. Browne, and M. Jamieson. (1999). "A Profile of the Clients of Male Sex Workers in Three Australian Cities." *Australian and New Zealand Journal of Public Health* 23, no. 5:511–18

Mars, Gerald (1982). *Cheats at Work: An Anthropology of Workplace Crime.* London: George Allen and Unwin.

———. (1983). *Cheats at Work: An Anthropology of Workplace Crime.* London: Unwin Paperbacks.

Martin, Elaine, Casey T. Tafta, and Patricia A. Resick. (2007). "A Review of Marital Rape." *Aggression and Violent Behavior.* 12, no. 3: 329–47.

Martin, J. B. (1952). *My Life in Crime.* New York: Harper and Row.

Martin, Susan E. (1994) "Outsider within" the Station House: The Impact of Race and Gender on Black Women Police," Social Problems, 41,3: 383–400.

Marx, Karl. (1859; 1970). *A Contribution to the Critique of Political Economy.* Moscow: Progross Publishers.

Marx, Karl, and Friedrich Engels. (1947). *The German Ideology.* New York: International Publishers.

Matoesian, Gregory. (1993). *Reproducing Rape: Domination through Talk in the Courtroom.* London: Polity Press.

Matsueda, Ross L. (1982). "Testing Control Theory and Differential Association: A Causal Modeling Approach." *American Sociological Review* 47: 489–504.

Matsueda, Ross L., and Karen Heimer. (1987). "Race, Family Structure, and Delinquency: A Test of Differential Association and Social Control Theories." *American Sociological Review* 52: 826–40.

Matsueda, Ross L., and Kathleen Anderson. (1998). "The Dynamics of Delinquent Peers and Delinquent Behavior." *Criminology* 36, no. 2: 269–308.

Matthews, Rick A. (2004). "Marxist Criminology." In *Controversies in Critical Criminology,* edited by Martin D. Schwartz and Suzanne E. Hatty. Cincinnati, OH: Anderson.

Matthews, Rick A., and David Kauzlarich. (2000). "The Crash of ValuJet Flight 592: A Case Study in State-Corporate Crime." *Sociological Focus* 3: 281–98.

Matthews, Roger. (1986). "Policing Prostitution." In Roger Matthews and Jock Young, eds., *Confronting Crime*. Beverly Hills, CA: Sage.

Matza, David. (1964). *Delinquency and Drift*. New York: Wiley.

Mauer, Marc. (2000). "The Racial Synamics of Imprisonment." In John P. May, ed., *Building Violence: How America's Rush to Incarcerate Creates More Violence*. Thousand Oaks, CA: Sage.

Maume M.O., and M. Lee. (2003). "Social Institutions and Violence: A Sub-national Test of Institutional Anomie Theory." *Criminology* 41, no. 4: 1137–72.

Mayhew, P., R. V. G. Clarke, J. N. Burrows, J. M. Hough, and S. W. Winchester. (1979). "Crime in Public Places." *Home Office Research Study No. 49*. London: HMSO.

Mayhew, Patricia, Ronald V. Clarke, and David Elliott. (1989). "Motorcycle Theft, Helmet Legislation and Displacement." *Howard Journal* 28: 1–8.

Mayhew, Patricia, Ronald V. Clarke, and J. M. Hough. (1992). "Steering Column Locks and Car Theft." In R. V. Clarke, ed., *Situational Crime Prevention: Successful Case Studies*. New York: Harrow and Heston.

Mayhew, Pat, Natalie Aye Maung, and Catriona Mirrlees-Black. (1993). *The 1992 British Crime Survey*. London: HMSO.

Mazerolle, Paul. (1997). "Delinquent Definitions and Participation Age: Assessing the Invariance Hypothesis." *Studies on Crime and Crime Prevention* 6: 151–67.

———. (1998). "Gender, General Strain, and Delinquency: Empirical Examination." *Justice Quarterly* 15: 65–91.

McCaghy, Charles H. (1967). "Child Molesters: A Study of Their Careers as Deviants." In Marshall B. Clinard and Richard Quinney, eds., *Criminal Behavior Systems: A Typology*. New York: Holt, Rinehart and Winston.

McCaghy, Charles H., and Timothy A. Capron. (1994). *Deviant Behavior: Crime, Conflict, and Interest Groups*. 3rd ed. New York: Macmillan

McCarthy, Bill, John Hagan, and Todd S. Woodward. (1999). "In the Company of Women: Structure and Agency in a Revised Power-Control Theory of Gender and Delinquency." *Criminology* 37, no. 4: 761–88.

McClennen, Joan C. (2005). "Domestic Violence between Same-Gender Partners." *Journal of Interpersonal Violence* 20, no. 2: 149–54.

McCord, Joan. (1991). "Family Relationships, Juvenile Delinquency, and Adult Criminality." *Criminology* 29: 397–417.

McDermott, M. Joan. (1979). *Rape Victimization in 26 American Cities*. Washington, DC: U.S. Department of Justice.

McFarlane, J., and A. Malecha. (2005). *Sexual Assault among Intimates: Frequency, Consequences, and Treatments* (NCJ 211678). Washington, DC: U.S. Department of Justice.

McGarrell, Edmund F., and Timothy J. Flanagan, eds. (1985). *Sourcebook of Criminal Justice Statistics*. Washington, DC: U.S. Government Printing Office.

McIver, John P. (1981). "Criminal Mobility: A Review of Empirical Studies." In Simon Hakim and George F. Rengert, eds., *Crime Spillover*. Beverly Hills, CA: Sage.

McMillan, Edward J. (2006). *Policies and Procedures to Prevent Fraud and Embezzlement: Guidance, Internal Controls, and Investigation*. New York: Willan.

McNeely, R. L., and Carl E. Pope. (1981). *Race, Crime, and Criminal Justice*. Beverly Hills, CA: Sage.

McNulty, T. L., and P. E. Bellair. (2003). "Explaining Racial and Ethnic Differences in Adolescent Violence: Structural Disadvantage, Family Well-Being, and Social Capital." *Justice Quarterly* 20: 1–31.

Merrill, Gregory S. (1998). "Understanding Domestic Violence among Gay and Bisexual Men." In Raquel Kennedy Bergen, ed., *Issues in Intimate Violence*. Thousand Oaks, CA: Sage.

Merry, Sally Engle. (1981). *Urban Danger: Life in a Neighborhood of Strangers*. Philadelphia: Temple University Press.

Merton, Robert K. (1938). "Social Structure and Anomie." *American Sociological Review* 3: 672–82.

———. (1957). *Social Theory and Social Structure*. New York: Free Press.

Messerschmidt, James W. (1986). *Capitalism, Patriarchy, and Crime*. Totowa, NJ: Rowman and Littlefield.

———. (1994). *Masculinities and Crime*. Totowa, NJ: Rowman and Littlefield.

———. (1997). "From Patriarchy to Gender: Feminist Theory, Criminology, and the Challenge of Diversity." In Nicole Hahn Rafter and Frances Heidensohn, eds., *International Feminist Perspectives in Criminology: Engendering a Discipline*. Buckingham, UK: Open University Press.

———. (2000). *Nine Lives: Adolescent Masculinities, the Body, and Violence*. Boulder, CO: Westview.

Messner, Steven F., and Richard Rosenfeld. (1994). *Crime and the American Dream*. Belmont, CA: Wadsworth.

———. (2000). *Crime and the American Dream*. 3rd ed. Belmont, CA: Wadsworth.

Metz, Tim. (1971). "Hot Stocks." In Michael Gartner, ed., *Crime as Business*. New York: Dow Jones Books.

Michalowski, Raymond J. (1985). *Order, Law, and Crime*. New York: Random House.

———. (1988). "Response to Nettler." *Criminologist* 13, no. 4: 4.

Michalowski, Raymond J., and Susan Carlson. (1999). "Unemployment, Imprisonment and Social Structures of Accumulation: Historical Contingency in the Ruschh-Kircheimer Hypothesis." *Criminology* 37, no. 2: 217–50.

Michalowski, Raymond J., and Ronald C. Kramer. (2006). *State-Corporate Crime: Wrongdoing at the Intersection of Government and Business*. New Brunswick, NJ: Rutgers University Press.

Michalowski, Raymond, and Erdwin H. Pfuhl. (1991). "Technology, Property, and Law." *Crime, Law and Social Change* 15: 255–75.

Miethe, Terance D., and Richard McCorkle. (1998). *Crime Profiles: The Anatomy of Dangerous Persons, Places, and Situations*. Los Angeles: Roxbury.

Mihalic, S. W., and D. Elliott. (1997). "If Violence Is Domestic, Does It Really Count?" *Journal of Family Violence* 12, no. 3: 293–311.

Miller, Eleanor M. (1986). *Street Women*. Philadelphia: Temple University Press.

Miller, Jody. (1998a). "Gender and Victimization Risk among Young Women in Gangs." *Journal of Research in Crime and Delinquency* 35, no. 4: 429–53.

———. (1998b). "Up It Up: Gender and the Accomplishment of Street Robbery." *Criminology* 36, no. 1: 37–65.

———. (2004). "Feminist Criminology." In Marty Schwartz and Suzanne Hatty, eds., *Controversies in Critical Criminology*. Cincinnati, OH: Anderson.

Miller, Walter B. (1958). "Lower Class Culture as a Generating Milieu of Gang Delinquency." *Journal of Social Issues* 14: 5–19.

———. (1973). "Ideological and Criminal Justice Policy: Some Current Issues." *Journal of Criminal Law and Criminology* 64: 141–62.

Milovanovic, Dragan. (1997). *Postmodern Criminology*. New York: Garland.

Milovanovic, Dragan, and Stuart Henry. (2004). "Constitutive Criminology." In Martin D. Schwartz and Suzanne Hatty, eds., *Controversial Issues in Criminology: Critical Criminology*. Cincinnati: Anderson.

Minnesota Department of Corrections (1998). "Restorative Justice." http://www.doc.state.mn.us/rj/Default.htm.

Minor, William. (1980). "The Neutralization of Criminal Offense." *Criminology* 18: 103–20.

———. (1981). "Techniques of Neutralization: "Reconceptualization and Empirical Examination." *Journal of Research in Crime and Delinquency* 18: 295–318.

Mintz, Morton. (1970). *The Therapeutic Nightmare*. Boston: Houghton Mifflin.

Mirrlees-Black, Catriona, Pat Mayhew, and Andrew Percy. (1996). "The 1996 British Crime Survey." *Home Office Statistical Bulletin*, September: 1–78.

Mitchell, Ojmarrh. (2005). "A Meta-Analysis of Race and Sentencing Research: Explaining the Inconsistencies." *Journal of Quantitative Criminology* 21, no 4: 439–66.

Mokhiber, Russell. (1988). *Corporate Crime and Corporate Violence*. San Francisco: Sierra Club.

———. (1999). *The Decade's Worst Corporate Criminals*. http://www.corporatepredators.org/top100.html.

Monitoring the Future (2007). http://www.monitoringthefuture.org/

Moore, Joan. (1998). "Understanding Youth Street Gangs: Economic Restructuring and the Urban Underclass." In Meredith W. Watts, ed., *Crosscultural Perspectives on Youth and Violence*. Stamford, CT: JAI.

Moore, Mark H. (1986). "Organized Crime as a Business Enterprise." Presented at the annual meeting of the American Society of Criminology, Atlanta, November.

Morris, Allison. (1987). *Women, Crime and Criminal Justice*. Oxford: Basil Blackwell.

Morris, Terrence. (1958). *The Criminal Area*. New York: Humanities Press.

Mullins, Christopher W. (2006). *Holding Your Square: Masculinities, Streetlife And Violence*. Portland, OR: Willan.

Mullins, C. W., and Dawn L Rothe. (2007). "The Forgotten Ones." *Critical Criminology* 15: 2.

———. (2008). *Blood, Power, and Bedlam: Violations of International Criminal Law in Post-Colonial Africa*. New York: Peter Lang.

Mullins, C. W., and R. Wright. (2003). "Gender, Social Networks, and Residential Burglary." *Criminology* 41, no. 3: 813–40.

Mullins, C. W., R. Wright, and B. Jacobs. (2004). "Gender, Streetlife and Criminal Retaliation." *Criminology* 42, no. 4: 911–40.

Mulvihill, D., Melvin Tumin, and Lynn Curtis, eds. (1969). *Crimes of Violence*. Washington, DC: U.S. Government Printing Office.

Murphy, J. E. (1984). "Date Abuse and Forced Intercourse among College Students." Presented at the National Conference for Family Violence Researchers, University of New Hampshire.

Murton, Tom, and Joe Hyams. (1969). *Accomplices to the Crime: The Arkansas Prison Scandal*. New York: Grove.

Mustaine, Elizabeth E. (1997). "Victimization Risks and Routine Activities: A Theoretical Examination Using a Gender-Specific and Domain-Specific Model." *American Journal of Criminal Justice* 22, no. 1: 41–70.

Muzzatti, Stephen L. (2000). *Crotch Rocket Heroes: Reflections on Speed, Youth Identity and Delinquency through Consumerism*. Presented at the annual meeting of the Midwest Sociological Society, Chicago.

Nagin, Daniel S., and Raymond Paternoster. (1991). "The Preventive Effects of the Perceived Risk of Arrest: Testing an Expanded Conception of Deterrence." *Criminology* 29: 561–87.

———. (1993). "Enduring Individual Differences and Rational Choice Theories of Crime." *Law and Society Review* 27: 467–96.

Natarajan, Mangai, and Belanger, Mathieu. (1998). "Varieties of Drug Trafficking Organizations: A Typology of Cases Prosecuted in New York City." *Journal of Drug Issues* 28, no. 4: 1005–25.

National Center for Education Statistics (2006). http://nces.ed.gov/

National Center for Victims of Crime. (2007). Constitutional Rights for Crime Victims. http://www.ncvc.org/ncvc/main.aspx?dbName=DocumentViewer&DocumentID=32463.

National Committee on Violence [Australia]. (1989). "Racist Violence." *Violence Today* 8: 1–7.

National Crime Victimization Survey. (2000). http://www.ojp.usdoj.gov/bjs/pub/pdf/ncvs104.pdf.

———. (2006). http://www.ojp.usdoj.gov/bjs/pub/pdf/ncvs104.pdf.

National Institute of Drug Abuse. (2006). http://www.nida.nih.gov/researchreports/researchindex.html.

National Institute of Justice. (1997). http://www.ncjrs.gov/.

National Research Council. (1996). http://sites.nationalacademies.org/nrc/index.htm

National Retail Security Survey. (2005). http://www.lpinformation.com/Default.aspx?tabid=142.

———. (2006). http://www.lpinformation.com/Default.aspx?tabid=142.

National Youth Survey. (2007). http://www.icpsr.umich.edu/cocoon/ICPSR/STUDY/08506.xml.

Nelsen, C., and Lin Huff-Corzine. (1998). "Strangers in the Night: An Application of the Lifestyle-Routine Activities Approach to Elderly Homicide Victimization." *Homicide Studies* 2, no. 2: 130–59.

Nettler, Gwynne. (1974). "Embezzlement without Problems." *British Journal of Criminology* 14: 70–77.

Newsweek, July 22, 1991.

Nielsen, Marianne O. (2000). "Stolen Lands, Stolen Lives: Native Americans and Criminal Justice." In Criminal Justice Collective of Northern Arizona University, ed., *Investigating Difference: Human and Cultural Difference in Criminal Justice*. Boston: Allyn and Bacon.

Nielsen, Marianne O., and Robert A. Silverman. (1996). *Native Americans, Crime, and Justice*. Boulder, CO: Westview.

O'Brien, Robert M. (1996). "Police Productivity and Crime Rates: 1973–1992." *Criminology* 34: 183–207.

O'Conner and Bush (2006a). "Ryan convicted in corruption trial: Co-defendant Warner also guilty," *Chicago Tribune*, April 17.

O'Conner and Bush (2006b). "Ryan gets 6 ½ years: Ex-governor regrets conviction, but doesn't admit to wrongdoing," *Chicago Tribune*, September 7, 2006.

Odem, Mary E., and Jody Clay-Warner. (1998). *Confronting Rape and Sexual Assault.* Wilmington, DE: SR Books.

Office of Justice Programs. (1996). http://www.ojp.usdoj.gov/.

———. (2003). http://www.ojp.usdoj.gov/BJA/

———. (2006). http://www.ojp.usdoj.gov/BJA/

Office of National Drug Control Policy. (2007). www.whitehousedrugpolicy.gov/

O'Malley, Pat, and Stephen Mugford. (1991). "Crime, Excitement and Modernity." Presented at the Annual Meeting of the American Society of Criminology, San Francisco, November 18–23.

Orchowsky, S. (1998). *Unique Nature of Domestic Violence in Rural Areas. Justice Research and Statistics Association.* Washington, DC: U.S. Department of Justice, Bureau of Justice Statistics.

Osgood, D. Wayne, Martin Gold, and Carolyn Miller. (1986). "For Better or Worse?" Peer Attachment and Peer Influence among Incarcerated Adults." Presented at the annual meeting of the American Society of Criminology, Atlanta, GA.

OSHA. (2006). OSHA Briefs. http://www.osha.gov/

———. (2007). "OSHA Identifies 14,000 Workplaces with High Injury and Illness Rates." Press release. Washington, DC: U.S. Department of Labor.

Packer, Herbert L. (1964). "The Crime Tariff." *American Scholar* 33: 551–57.

———. (1968). *The Limits of the Criminal Sanction.* Stanford, CA: Stanford University Press.

Parker, Howard J. (1974). *View from the Boys.* London: David and Charles.

Passas, Nikos. (1999). *Transnational Crime.* Aldershot, UK: Ashgate.

Paternoster, Raymond, and Paul Mazerolle. (1994). "General Strain Theory and Delinquency: A Replication and Extension." *Journal of Research in Crime and Delinquency* 31: 235–63.

Paternoster, Raymond, Linda E. Saltzman, Gordon P. Waldo, and Theodore G. Chiricos. (1983). "Perceived Risk of Social Control: Do Sanctions Really Deter?" *Law and Society Review* 17: 457–79.

———. (1985). "Assessments of Risk and Behavioral Experience: An Exploratory Study of Change." *Criminology* 23: 417–33.

Paternoster, Raymond, and Ruth Triplett. (1988). "Disaggregating Self-Reported Delinquency and Its Implications for Theory." *Criminology* 26: 591–620.

Pearce, Frank, and Steve Tombs. (2002). *Toxic Capitalism: Corporate Crime and the Chemical Industry.* Aldershot, UK: Dartmouth.

Pennsylvania Crime Commission. (1989). Untitled memo. Conshohocken, PA.

Pepinsky, Hal. (1999). "Peacemaking Criminology and Social Justice." In Bruce A. Arrigo, ed., *Social Justice/Criminal Justice: The Maturation of Critical Theory in Law, Crime, and Deviance.* Belmont, CA: West/Wadsworth.

Perry, S. W. (2004). *American Indians and Crime.* Washington, DC: U.S. Department of Justice.

Peterson, Ruth D., and William C. Bailey. (1991). "Felony Murder and Capital Punishment: An Examination of the Deterrence Question." *Criminology* 29: 367–95.

Petrocelli, Matthew, and Joseph Petrocelli. (2005). *Anatomy of a Motor Vehicle Stop: Essentials of Safe Traffic Enforcement.* Flushing, NY: Looseleaf.

Pettit, B., and B. Western. (2004) "Mass Imprisonment and the Life Course: Race and Class Inequality in US Incarceration." *American Sociological Review* 69: 151–69.

Pfohl, Stephen J. (1985). *Images of Deviance and Social Control.* New York: McGraw-Hill.

Pileggi, Nicholas. (1968). "1968 Has Been the Year of the Burglar." *New York Times Magazine,* November 17.

Piquero, A., and M. Hickman. (1999). "An Empirical Test of Tittle's Control Balance Theory." *Criminology* 27, no. 2: 319–34.

Piquero, A., J. MacDonald, A. Dobrin, L. Daigle, and F. Cullen. (2005). "Self-Control, Violent Offending, and Homicide Victimization: Assessing the General Theory of Crime." *Journal of Quantitative Criminology* 21, no. 1: 55–81.

Piquero, Alex, and Paul Mazerolle. (2001). *Life-Course Criminology.* Belmont, CA: Wadsworth.

Piquero, Alex, and Raymond Paternoster. (1998). "An Application of Stafford and Warr's Reconceptualization of Deterrence to Drunk Driving." *Journal of Research in Crime and Delinquency* 35, no. 1: 3–39.

Pogarsky, Greg. (2002) "Identifying "Deterrable" Offenders: Implications for Research on Deterrence." *Justice Quarterly* 19, no. 3: 431–532.

Polk, Kenneth. (1991). "Male-to-Male Homicides: Scenarios of Masculine Violence." Presented at the annual meeting of the American Society of Criminology, San Francisco, November 18–23.

Pollack, J. M. (2004). *Ethics in Crime and Justice*. Belmont, CA: Thomson Wadsworth.

Polsky, Ned. (1967). *Hustlers, Beats, and Others*. Chicago: Aldine.

Pontell, Henry N., and Kitty Calavita (1993). "The Savings and Loan Industry," in Michael Tonry and Albert J. Reiss, Jr., eds., *Beyond the Law: Crime in Complex Organizations*. Chicago: University of Chicago Press.

Poortinga, Ernest, Craig Lemmen, and Michael Jibson. (2006). "A Case Control Study: Whie-Collar Defendants Compared with Defendants Charged with Other Nonviolent Theft." *Journal of the American Academy of Psychiatry and Law* 34: 82–89.

Pope, Carl C., and William Feyerherm. (1991). "Minority Status and Juvenile Justice Processing." *Criminal Justice Abstracts* 22: 327–36 (part 1); 22: 527–42 (part 2).

Post, James E., and Edwin Baer. (1978). "Demarketing Infant Formula: Consumer Products for the Developing World." *Journal of Contemporary Business* 7: 17–37.

Pound, Roscoe. (1943). "A Survey of Social Interests." *Harvard Law Review* 57: 1–39.

Pratt, T. C., and T. W. Godsey. (2003). "Social Support, Inequality, and Homicide: A Crossnational Test of an Integrated Theoretical Model." *Criminology* 41: 611–43.

Preble, Edward A., and John J. Casey. (1969). "Taking Care of Business—The Heroin User's Life on the Street." *International Journal of the Addictions* 4: 8–12.

Preble, John M., A. Nicholas Groth, and Suzanne M Sgroi. (2002). *Male Victims of Same-Sex Abuse: Addressing Their Sexual Response*. Lutherville, MD: Sidron Press.

Presser, Lois. (2003). "Remorse and Neutralization among Violent Male Offenders." *Justice Quarterly* 20, no. 4: 801–25.

Progrebin, Mark R., and Eric D. Poole, (1993). "Vice Isn't Nice: A Look at Working Undercover." *Journal of Criminal Justice* 21: 383–94.

Putnam, F. W. (2003). "Ten-Year Research Update Review: Child Sexual Abuse." *Journal of the American Academy of Child and Adolescent Psychiatry* 42: 269–78.

Quetelet, A. (1969). *Sur l'Homme et le Development de Ses Facultes*. Paris: Wiley and Sons.

Quinney, Richard. (1970). *The Problem of Crime*. New York: Dodd, Mead.

———. (1977). *Class, State, and Crime*. New York: Longman.

———. (1979). *Criminology*. 2nd ed. Boston: Little, Brown.

Quinney, Richard, and Hal Pepinsky. (1991). *Criminology as Peacemaking*. Bloomington: Indiana University Press.

Radcliffe-Brown, A. R. (1948). *The Andaman Islanders*. New York: Free Press.

Radzinowicz, Leon. (1966). *Ideology and Crime*. New York: Columbia University Press.

Rafter, Nicole. (2000). *Shots in the Mirror: Crime Films and Society*. New York: Oxford University Press.

Rafter, Nicole Hahn, and Frances Heidensohn. (1997). *International Feminist Perspectives in Criminology: Engendering a Discipline*. Buckingham, UK: Open University Press.

Rand, Michael. (1990). *Handgun Crime Victims*. Washington, DC: U.S. Department of Justice.

Raphael, Jody, and Deborah L. Shapiro. (2004). "Violence in Indoor and Outdoor Prostitution." *Violence against Women* 10, no. 2: 126–39.

Ratner, Mitchell S. (1994). *Crack Pipe as Pimp: An Ethnographic Investigation of Sex-for-Crack Exchanges*. New York: Lexington Books.

Reckless, Walter. (1973). *The Crime Problem*. 5th ed. Englewood Cliffs, NJ: Prentice-Hall.

Reckless, Walter C., and Simon Dinitz. (1967). "Pioneering with Self-Concept as a Vulnerability Factor in Delinquency." *Journal of Criminal Law, Criminology, and Police Science* 58: 515–23.

Reed, Gary, and Peter Yeager. (1996). "Organizational Offending and Neoclassical Criminology: Challenging the Reach of a General Theory of Crime," *Criminology* 34, no. 3: 357–82.

Reid, Sue Titus. (1989). *Criminal Law*. New York: Macmillan.

Reiman, Jeffrey. (1999). *The Rich Get Richer and the Poor Get Prison*. 6th ed. Boston: Allyn and Bacon.

———. (2007). *The Rich Get Richer and the Poor Get Prison*. 8th ed. Boston: Allyn and Bacon.

Renzetti, Claire M. (1998). "Violence and Abuse in Lesbian Relationships: Theoretical and Empirical Issues." In Raquel Kennedy Bergen, ed., *Issues in Intimate Violence*. Thousand Oaks, CA: Sage.

———. (1992). *Violent Betrayal: Partner Abuse in Lesbian Relationships*. Thousand Oaks, CA: Sage.

Renzetti, Claire M., Jeffrey L. Edleson, and Raquel Kennedy Bergen. (2001). *The Sourcebook on*

Violence Against Women. Thousand Oaks, CA: Sage.

Renzetti, Claire M., and Lynne Goodstein (2001). *Women, Crime, and Criminal Justice: Original Feminist Readings*. Los Angeles: Roxbury.

Reppetto, Thomas A. (1974). *Residential Crime*. Cambridge, MA: Ballinger.

Reuter, Peter. (1983). *Disorganized Crime: Illegal Markets and the Mafia*. Cambridge, MA: MIT Press.

Reuter, Peter, Jonathon Rubinstein, and Simon Winn. (1983). *Racketeering in Legitimate Industries: Two Case Studies*. Washington, DC: U.S. Department of Justice.

Rice, Marcia. (1990). "Challenging Orthodoxies in Feminist Theory: A Black Feminist Critique." In Loraine Gelsthorpe and Allison Morris, eds., *Feminist Perspectives in Criminology*. Milton Keynes, UK: Open University Press.

Riedel, Marc. (1993). *Stranger Violence*. New York: Garland.

Robinson, Matthew B., and Barbara H. Zaitow. (1999). "Criminologists: Are We What We Study?" *Criminologist* 24, no. 2: 1,4,17–19.

Roebuck, Julian B., and Thomas Barker. (1974). "A Typology of Police Corruption." In Ronald L. Akers and Edward Sagarin, eds., *Crime Prevention and Social Control*. New York: Praeger.

Roebuck, Julian B., and Ronald C. Johnson. (1964). "The 'Short Con' Man." *Crime and Delinquency* 10: 235–48.

Romenesko, Kim, and Eleanor M. Miller. (1989). "The Second Step in Double Jeopardy: Appropriating the Labor of Female Street Hustlers." *Crime and Delinquency* 35: 109–35.

Rose, Dina R., and Todd R. Clear. (1998). "Incarceration, Social Capital, and Crime: Implications for Social Disorganization Theory." *Criminology* 36, no. 3: 441–f80.

Rosenfeld, Richard (1996). "Gun Buy-Backs: Crime Control or Community Mobilization?" In M. Plotkin, ed., *Under Fire: Gun Buy-Backs, Exchanges, and Amnesty Programs*. Washington, DC: Police Executive Research Forum.

Rosoff, Stephen M. Henry N. Pontell, and Robert Tillman. (2007). *Profit without Honor: White-Collar Crime and the Looting of America*. 4th ed. Upper Saddle River, NJ: Prentice-Hall.

Roth, Jeffrey A. (1994). "Psychoactive Substances and Violence." *NIJ Research in Brief*, February: 1–8.

Rothe, Dawn, and Christopher W. Mullins. (2006). *Symbolic Gestures and the Generation of International Social Controls: The International Criminal Court*. Lexington, MA: Lexington Books.

Rountree, Pamela Wilcox, Kenneth C. Land, and Terrence C. Miethe. (1994). "Macro-Micro in the Study of Victimization: A Hierarchal Logistic Model Analysis across Seattle Neighborhoods." *Criminology* 32, no. 3: 387–409.

Rowe, Alan, John H. Lindquist, and O. Z. White. (1989). "A Note on the Family and Crime in the United States." *Psychological Reports* 65: 1001–1002.

Rowe, David C. (2001). *Biology and Crime*. Los Angeles: Roxbury.

Runkle, Gerald. (1976). "Is Violence Always Wrong?" *Journal of Politics* 38: 367–89.

Russell, Diana E. H. (1983). *Rape in Marriage*. New York: Collier.

Rynbrandt, Linda J., and Ronald C. Kramer. (1995). "Hybrid Nonwomen and Corporate Violence: The Silicone Breast Implant Case." *Violence against Women* 1, no. 3: 206–27.

Salerno, Ralph, and John S. Tompkins. (1969). *The Crime Confederation*. Garden City, NY: Doubleday.

Sampson, Robert J. (1986). "Crime in Cities: The Effects of Formal and Informal Social Control." In Albert J. Reiss and Michael Tonry, eds., *Communities and Crime*. Chicago: University of Chicago Press.

———. (1987). "Communities and Crime," In M. R. Gottfredson and T. Hirschi, eds., *Positive Criminology*. Beverly Hills, CA: Sage.

Sampson, Robert J., and Jacqueline Cohen. (1988). "Deterrent Effects of the Police on Crime: A Replication and Theoretical Extension." *Law and Society Review* 22: 163–89.

Sampson, Robert J., and John Laub. (1990). "Crime and Deviance Over the Life Course: The Salience of Adult Social Bonds." *American Sociological Review* 55: 609–27.

———. (1992). "Crime and Deviance in the Life Course." *Annual Review of Sociology* 18: 63–84.

———. (1993). *Crime in the Making*. Cambridge, MA: Harvard University Press.

———. (1997). "Life-Course Desisters? Trajectories of Crime among Delinquent Boys Followed to Age 70." *Criminology* 41, no. 3: 555–93.

———. (2003). *Shared Beginnings, Divergent Lives: Delinquent Boys to Age 70*. Cambridge, MA: Harvard University Press.

Sampson, R. J., S. W. Raudenbush, and F. Earls. (1997). "Neighborhoods and Violent Crime: A Multilevel Study of Collective Efficacy." *Science* 277: 918–24.

Sanchez–Jankowski, Martin. (1991). *Islands in the Street: Gangs and American Urban Society*. Berkeley and Los Angeles: University of California Press.

Sanday, Peggy Reeves. (1996). *A Woman Scorned: Acquaintance Rape on Trial*. New York: Doubleday.

Sanders, William B. (1977). *Detective Work: A Study of Criminal Investigators*. New York: Free Press.

———. (1983). *Criminology*. Reading, MA: Addison-Wesley.

———. (1994). *Gangbangs and Drive-bys*. New York: Aldine De Gruyter.

San Francisco Task Force on Prostitution. (2000). *Final Report*. http://www.bayswan.org/1TF.html.

Sapp, A. D. (1994). "Sexual Misconduct by Police Officers." In T. Barker and D. L. Carter, eds., *Police Deviance* (187–89). Cincinnati, OH: Anderson.

Sartin, Robert M., David J. Hansen, and Matthew T. Huss. (2006). "Domestic Violence Treatment Response and Recidivism: A Review and Implications for the Study of Family Violence." *Aggression and Violent Behavior* 11: 425–40.

Schafer, Stephen. (1969). *Theories in Criminology*. New York: Random House.

Schneider, Anne L. (1977). *The Portland Forward Check of Crime Victims: Final Report*. Eugene: Oregon Research Institute.

Schneider, Hans Joachim. (1997). "Sexual Abuse of Children: Strengths and Weaknesses of Current Criminology." *International Journal of Offender Therapy and Comparative Criminology* 41: 310–24.

Schneider, Sandra L., and Robert C. Wright. (2004). "Understanding Denial in Sexual Offenders." *Trauma, Violence, and Abuse* 5, no. 1: 3–20.

Schrager, Laura S., and James F. Short. (1978). "Toward a Sociology of Organizational Crime." *Social Problems* 25: 407–19.

Schultz, Pamela D. (2005). *Not Monsters: Analyzing the Stories of Child Molesters*. New York: Rowman & Littlefield.

Schwab-Stone, Mary, Chuansheng Chen, Ellen Greenberger, David Silver, and Judith Lichtman. (1999). "No Safe Haven II: The Effects of Violence Exposure on Urban Youth." *Journal of the American Academy of Child & Adolescent Psychiatry* 38, no. 4: 359–67.

Schwartz, Martin D., and Walter S. DeKesseredy. (1997). *Sexual Assault on the College Campus: The Role of Male Peer Support*. Thousand Oaks, CA: Sage.

Schwartz, Martin D., and David O. Friedrichs. (1994). "Postmodern Thought and Criminological Discontent: New Metaphors for Understanding Violence." *Criminology* 32: 221–46.

Schwartz, Martin D., and Suzanne Hatty. (2004). *Controversial Issues in Criminology: Critical Criminology*. Cincinnati: Anderson.

Schwendinger, Herman, and Julia Siegel Schwendinger. (1970). "Defenders of Order or Guardians of Human Rights?" *Issues in Criminology* 5, no. 2: 123–57.

———. (1985). *Adolescent Subcultures and Delinquency*. New York: Praeger.

Scraton, Phil, Joe Sim, and Paula Skidmore. (1991). *Prisons under Protest*. Milton Keynes, UK: Open University Press.

Scully, Diana, and Joseph Marolla. (1985). "Riding the Bull at Gilley's: Convicted Rapists Describe the Rewards of Rape." *Social Problems* 32: 251–63.

Searles, Patricia and Ronald J. Berger (1995). *Rape and Society: Readings in the Problem of Sexual Assault*. Boulder, Co.: Westview.

Sellin, Thorsten. (1935). "Race Prejudice in the Administration of Justice." *American Journal of Sociology* 41: 212–17.

———. (1937). "The Lombrosian Myth in Criminology." *American Journal of Sociology* 42: 898–99.

———. (1938). *Culture Conflict and Crime*. New York: Social Science Research Council.

Shannon, Lyle W. (1991). *Changing Patterns of Delinquency and Crime*. Boulder, CO: Westview.

Shaw, Clifford R. (1930). *The Jack-Roller: A Delinquent Boy's Own Story*. Chicago: University of Chicago Press.

———. (1931). *Delinquency Areas*. Chicago: University of Chicago Press.

Shaw, Clifford R., and Henry D. McKay. (1942). *Juvenile Delinquency and Urban Areas*. Chicago: University of Chicago Press.

Shearing, Clifford D. (1979). "Subterranean Processes, the Maintenance of Power: An Examination of the Mechanisms Coordinating Police Action." Presented at the annual meeting of the American Sociological Association, August 17–21.

Sheehy, Gail (1973). *Hustling: Prostitution in Our Wide-Open Society*. New York: Delacorte.

Shelden, Randall G., and William B. Brown (2002) *Criminal Justice in America: A Critical View*. Boston: Allyn and Bacon.

Sheldon, William. (1949). *Varieties of Delinquent Youth*. New York: Harper.

Shelley, Louise I. (1981). *Crime and Modernization: The Impact of Industrialization and Urbanization on Crime*. Carbondale: Southern Illinois University Press.

Sherman, Lawrence W. (1992). "Attacking Crime: Police and Crime Control." In Michael Tonry and Norval Morris, eds., *Modern Policing*. Chicago: University of Chicago Press.

———. (1993). "Defiance, Deterrence, and Irrelevance: A Theory of the Criminal Sanction." *Journal of Research in Crime and Delinquency* 30: 445–71.

Sherman, Lawrence W., and Richard Berk. (1984). "Specific Deterrent Effects of Arrest for Domestic Assault." *American Sociological Review* 49: 261–72.

Sherman, Lawrence W., and Dennis P. Rogan. (1995). "Effects of Guin Seizures on Gun Violence: Hot Spot Patrol in Kansas City." *Justice Quarterly* 12: 673–93.

Sherman, Lawrence W., James Shaw, and Dennis P. Rogan. (1995). "The Kansas City Gun Experiment." *NIJ Research Brief*, January: 1–11.

Shihadeh, Edward S., and Graham C. Ousey. (1998). "Industrial Restructuring and Violence: The Link between Entry-Level Jobs, Economic Deprivation and Black and White Homicide." *Social Forces* 77: 185–206.

Shihadeh, Edward S., and Wesley Shrum. (2004). "Serious Crime in Urban Neighborhoods: Is There a Race Effect?" *Sociological Spectrum* 24, no. 4: 507–33.

Shoham, Shlomo. (1970). *The Mark of Cain*. Dobbs Ferry, NY: Citadel.

Shover, Neal. (1973). "The Social Organization of Burglary." *Social Problems* 20: 499–514.

———. (1991). "Burglary." In Michael Tonry and James Q. Wilson, eds., *Crime and Justice: A Review of Research*, vol. 14. Chicago: University of Chicago Press.

———. (1996). *Great Pretenders: Pursuits and Careers of Persistent Thieves*. Boulder, CO: Westview.

Shover, Neal, and Belinda Henderson. (1995). "Repressive Crime Control and Male Persistent Thieves." In Hugh D. Barlow, ed., *Crime and Public Policy: Putting Theory to Work*. New York: Westview.

Shover, Neal, and David Honaker. (1992). "The Socially Bounded Decision Making of Persistent Property Offenders." *Howard Journal of Criminal Justice* 31: 276–93.

———. (1999). "The Socially Bounded Decision Making of Persistent Property Offenders." In Paul Cromwell, ed., *In Their Own Words: Criminals on Crime*. Los Angeles: Roxbury.

Shover, Neal, and Carol Y. Thompson. (1992). "Age, Differential Expectations, and Crime Desistance." *Criminology* 30: 601–16.

Shover, Neal, and John Paul Wright. (2001). *Crimes of Privilege: Readings in White-Collar Crime*. New York: Oxford University Press.

Sieh, Edward W. (1987). "Garment Workers: Perceptions of Inequity and Employee Theft." *British Journal of Criminology* 27: 174–90.

Simon, David R. (2006). *Elite Deviance*. 6th ed. Boston: Allyn and Bacon.

Simon, David R., and Frank E. Hagan. (1999). *White-Collar Deviance*. Boston: Allyn and Bacon.

Simon, Rita J. (1975). *Women and Crime*. Lexington, MA: Lexington Books.

Simons, R. L., Y.-F. Chen, E. A. Stewart, and G. H. Brody. (2003). "Incidents of Discrimination and Risk for Delinquency: A Longitudinal Test of Strain Theory with an African American Sample." *Justice Quarterly* 20: 827–54.

Skogan, Wesley G. (1986). "Fear of Crime and Neighborhood Change." In Albert J. Reiss Jr. and Michael Tonry, eds., *Communities and Crime; Crime and Justice: A Review of Research*, vol. 8. Chicago: University of Chicago Press.

Slocum, L., S. Simpson, and D. Smith. (2005). "Strained Lives and Crime: Examining Intra-individual Variation in Strain and Offending in a Sample of Incarcerated Women." *Criminology* 43, no. 4: 1067–1111.

Smith, Douglas A. (1986). "The Neighborhood Context of Police Behavior." In Albert J. Reiss Jr. and Michael Tonry, eds, *Communities and Crime*. Chicago: University of Chicago Press.

Smith, Lorna J. F. (1989). *Concerns about Rape*. London: HMSO.

Snyder, Howard N., and Terrence A. Finnegan. (1987). *Delinquency in the United States, 1983*. Washington, DC: U.S. Department of Justice.

352

References

Southern Poverty Law Center. (2007). *Intelligence Report: Hate Group Numbers Up by 48% Since 2000.* http://www.splcenter.org/news/item.jsp?aid=300.

Spergel, Irving. (1964). *Racketville, Slumtown, Haulberg: An Exploratory Study of Delinquent Subcultures.* Chicago: University of Chicago Press.

Spitzer, Steven. (1975). "Toward a Marxian Theory of Deviance." *Social Problems* 22: 638–51.

Spohn, Cassia. (1994) "Crime and the Social Control of Blacks: Offender/Victim Race and the Sentencing of Violent Offenders." In George S. Bridges and Martha Myers, eds., *Inequality, Crime, and Social Control.* Boulder, CO: Westview.

Stafford, Mark C., and Mark Warr. (1993). "A Reconceptualization of General and Specific Deterrence." *Journal of Research in Crime and Delinquency* 30: 123–35.

Stanko, Elizabeth. (1990). *Everyday Violence.* London: Pandora.

———. (1995). "Gendered Criminological Policies: Femininity, Masculinity, and Violence." In Hugh D. Barlow, ed., *Crime and Public Policy: Putting Theory to Work.* Boulder, CO: Westview.

Stark, Rodney. (1987). "Deviant Places: A Theory of the Ecology of Crime." *Criminology* 25: 893–909.

State of Texas. (1998). Indictment of the Accused Murderers of James Byrd.

State of Wyoming. (1998). Indictment of the Accused Murderers of Matthew Shepard.

Steffensmeier, Darrell J. (1986). *The Fence: In the Shadow of Two Worlds.* Totowa, NJ: Rowman and Littlefield.

———. (1995). "A Public Policy Agenda for Combating Organized Crime." In Hugh D. Barlow, ed., *Crime and Public Policy: Putting Theory to Work.* Boulder, CO: Westview.

Steffensmeier, Darrell J., and Stephen Demuth. (2006). "Does Gender Modify the Effects of Race-Ethnicity on Criminal Sanctioning? Sentences for Male and Female White, Black, and Hispanic Defendants." *Journal of Quantitative Criminology* 22, no. 3: 241–61.

Steffensmeier, Darrell J., John Kramer, and Cathy Streifel. (1993). "Gender and Imprisonment Decisions." *Criminology* 31: 411–46.

Steffensmeier, Darrell J., and Robert M. Terry. (1986). "Institutional Sexism in the Underworld: A View from the Inside." *Sociological Inquiry* 56: 305–23.

Steffensmeier, Darrell J., Jeffrey Ulmer, and John Kramer. (1998). "The Interaction of Race, Gender, and Age in Criminal Sentencing: The Punishment Cost of Being Young, Black, and Male." *Criminology* 36: 763–97.

Stein, Bradley D., Lisa H. Jaycox, Sheryl Kataoka, Hillary J. Rhodes, and Katherine D. Vestal. (2003). "Prevalence of Child and Adolescent Exposure to Community Violence." *Clinical Child and Family Psychology Review* 6, no. 4: 247–64.

Stewart, Eric. (2003). "School Social Bonds, School Climate, and School Misbehavior: A Multilevel Analysis." *Justice Quarterly* 20, no. 3: 575–604.

Stewart, E., and R. Simons. (2006). "Structure and Culture in African American Adolescent Violence: A Partial Test of the Code of the Street Thesis." *Justice Quarterly* 23, no. 1: 1–34.

St. Louis Post-Dispatch, October 6, 1988.

St. Louis Post-Dispatch, October 16, 1988.

St. Louis Post-Dispatch, November 27, 1991: B1.

Sullivan, Dennis. (2006). *Handbook of Restorative Justice: A Global Perspective.* London: Routledge.

Surette, Ray. (2006). Media, *Crime, and Criminal Justice: Images, Realities and Policies.* Belmont, CA: Wadsworth.

Surratt, Hilary L., James A. Inciardi, Steven P. Kurtz, and Marion C. Kiley. (2004). "Sex Work and Drug Use in a Subculture of Violence." *Crime and Delinquency* 50, no. 1: 43–71.

Sutherland, Edwin H. (1937a). *Principles of Criminology.* New York: Lippincott.

———. (1937b). *The Professional Thief.* Chicago: University of Chicago Press.

———. (1939). *Criminology.* 2nd ed. New York: Lippincott.

———. (1945). "Is 'White-Collar Crime' Crime?" *American Sociological Review* 10: 132–39.

———. (1949). *White Collar Crime.* New York: Dryden.

Sutherland, Edwin H., and Donald R. Cressey. (1974). *Criminology.* 9th ed. Philadelphia: Lippincott.

Sutton, Mike. (1993). "From Receiving to Thieving: The Market for Stolen goods and the Incidence of Theft." *Home Office Research Bulletin* 34: 3–8.

Sykes, Gresham M., and David Matza. (1957). "Techniques of Neutralization: A Theory of

Delinquency." *American Sociological Review* 22: 664–70.

Takaki, Ronald T. (1993). *A Different Mirror: A History of Multicultural America*. Boston: Little, Brown.

Tannenbaum, Frank. (1938). *Crime and the Community*. New York: Columbia University Press.

Tappan, Paul W. (1947). "Who Is the Criminal?" *American Sociological Review* 12: 96–102.

Thomas, Anthony R., Stephen H. Thomas, Gene A. Fisher, and David J. Hirsch. (2002). "Murder and Medicine: The Lethality of Criminal Assault, 1960–1999." *Homicide Studies* 6, no. 2: 128–66.

Thomas, D. A. (1967). "Sentencing: The Basic Principles." *Criminal Law Review*: 514–20.

Thornberry, Terence P. (1973). "Race, Socioeconomic Status, and Sentencing in the Juvenile Justice System." *Journal of Criminal Law and Criminology* 64: 90–98.

———. (1987). "Toward an Interactional Theory of Delinquency." *Criminology* 25: 863–91.

Thornberry, Terence P., and Marvin D. Krohn. (2001). "The Development of Delinquency: An Interactional Perspective." In Susan O. White, ed., *Handbook of Youth and Justice*. New York: Plenum.

Tifft, Larry, and Lynn Markham. (1991). "Battering Women and Battering Central Americans: A Peacemaking Synthesis." In Richard Quinney and Hal Pepinsky, eds., *Criminology as Peacemaking*. Bloomington: Indiana University Press.

Tifft, L., and D. Sullivan. (1980). *The Struggle to be Human: Crime, Criminology, and Anarchism*. Sanday, Orkney, UK: Cienfuegos Press.

Time, July 22, 1991.

Time, July 29, 1991.

Tittle, Charles R. (1980). *Sanctions and Deterrence*. New York: Praeger.

———. (1995). *Control Balance: Toward a General Theory of Deviance*. Boulder, CO: Westview.

———. (1997). "Thoughts Stimulated by Braithwaite's Analysis of Control Balance Theory." *Theoretical Criminology* 1, no. 1å: 99–110.

———. (2004). "Refining Control Balance Rheory." *Theoretical Criminology* 8, no. 4: 395–428.

Tonry, Michael. (1994). "Racial Disproportion in US Prisons." *British Journal of Criminology* 34: 97–115.

Topalli, Volkan. (2005). "When Being Good Is Bad: An Expansion of Neutralization Theory." *Criminology* 43, no. 3: 797–836.

Trasler, Gordon. (1986). "Situational Crime Control and Rational Choice." In Kevin Heal and Gloria Laycock, eds., *Situational Crime Prevention: From Theory into Practice*. London: HMSO.

Triplett, Ruth. (2000). "The Dramatization of Evil: Reacting to Juvenile Delinquency during the 1990s." In Sally S. Simpson, ed., *Of Crime and Criminality: The Use of Theory in Everyday Life*. Thousand Oaks, CA: Pine Forge Press.

Trivizas, Eugene, and Philip T. Smith. (1997). "The Deterrent Effect of Terrorist Incidents on the Rates of Luggage Theft in Railway and Underground Stations." *British Journal of Criminology* 37, no. 1: 63–75.

Tseloni, Andromachi, Karin Wittebrood, Graham Farrell, and Ken Pease. (2004) "Burglary Victimization in England and Wales, the United States and the Netherlands; A Cross-National Comparative Test of Routine Activities and Lifestyle Theories." *British Journal of Criminology* 44, no. 1: 66–92.

Tucker, James. (1989). "Employee Theft as Social Control." *Deviant Behavior* 10: 319–34.

Tucker, Robert C. (1978). *The Marx-Engels Reader*. 2nd ed. New York: W.W. Norton.

Tunnell, Kenneth D. (1990). "Choosing Crime: Close Your Eyes and Take Your Chances." *Justice Quarterly* 7: 4.

———. (1992). *Choosing Crime: The Criminal Calculus of Property Offenders*. Chicago: Nelson-Hall.

———. (1993). Political Crime in Contemporary America. New York: Garland.

———. (2000). *Living Off Crime*. Chicago: Burnham.

Turk, Austin T. (1966). "Conflict and Criminality." *American Sociological Review* 31: 338–52.

———. (1969). *Criminality and Legal Order*. Chicago: Rand McNally.

Turner, J. W. Cecil, ed. (1966). *Kenney's Outlines of Criminal Law*. 19th ed. Cambridge: Cambridge University Press.

Tyler, Gus, ed. (1962). *Organized Crime in America*. Ann Arbor: University of Michigan Press.

United Nations. (2006). *Charter of the United Nations*. http://www.un.org/aboutun/charter/.

U.S. Department of Education. (1999). http://www.ed.gov.

———. (2000). http://www.ed.gov/about/pubs/intro/index.html?src=gu.

U.S. Department of Health and Human Services. (2007). http://www.hhs.gov/news/press/2007. html.

U.S. Department of Justice. (1976). *The LEAA: A Partnership for Crime Control.* Washington, DC: U.S. Government Printing Office.

———. (1999). *American Indians and Crime.* Washington, DC: USDOJ.

———. (2006). http://www.usdoj.gov/

U.S. Department of Labor. (2000). Injuries, Illnesses, and Fatalities. http://www.bls.gov/iif/home.htm.

U.S. Drug Enforcement Agency. (2007). Drugs of Abuse. http://www.usdoj.gov/dea/index.htm.

Vagg, Jon. 1998. "Delinquency and Shame: Data from Hong Kong." *British Journal of Criminology* 38: 247–64.

Van den Berghe, Pierre L. (1974). "Bringing Beasts Back In: Toward a Biosocial Theory of Aggression." *American Sociological Review* 39: 777–78.

Vander-May, Brenda J., and Donald L. Neff. (1984). "Adult-Child Incest: A Sample of Substantiated Cases." *Family Relations* 33: 549–57.

Vaughan, Diane. (1996). *The Challenger Launch Decision: Risky Technology, Culture, and Deviance at NASA.* Chicago: University of Chicago Press.

Vega, William A., and Andres G. Gil. (1999). "A Model for Explaining Drug Use Behavior among Hispanic Adolescents." *Drugs and Society* 14, no. 1–2: 57–74.

Velez, Maria B., Lauren J. Krivo, and Ruth D. Peterson. (2003). "Structural Inequality and Homicide: An Assessment of the Black-White Gap in Killings." *Criminology* 41, no. 3: 645–73.

Venkatesh, Sudhir-Alladi. (1998). "African American Organized Crime: A Social History." *American Journal of Sociology* 103, no. 6: 1747–49.

Vila, Bryan J. (1994). "A General Paradigm for Understanding Criminal Behavior: Extending Evolutionary Ecological Theory." *Criminology* 32: 311–59.

Vila, Bryan J., and Lawrence E. Cohen. (1993). "Crime as Strategy: Testing an Evolutionary Ecological Theory of Expropriative Crime." *American Journal of Sociology* 98: 873–912.

Waldrop, A. E., and P. A. Resick. (2004). "Coping among Adult Female Victims of Domestic Violence." *Journal of Family Violence* 19, no. 5: 291–302.

Walker, Samuel. (1998). *Sense and Nonsense about Crime and Drugs: A Policy Guide.* 4th ed. New York: West/Wadsworth.

———. (2005). *Sense and Nonsense about Crime and Drugs: A Policy Guide.* 6th ed. New York: Thomson Learning.

Walker, Samuel, Cassia Spohn, and Miriam DeLone. (2003). *The Color of Justice: Race, Ethnicity, and Crime in America.* 3rd ed. New York: Wadsworth.

Wall Street Journal, June 14, 1991

Walsh, Anthony, and Lee Ellis. (1999). "Political Ideology and American Criminologists' Explanations of Criminal Behavior." *Criminologist* 24: 1–27.

Walsh, Dermot. (1980). *Break-ins: Burglary from Private Houses.* London: Constable.

Walsh, Marilyn. (1977). *The Fence.* Westport, CT: Greenwood Press.

Waltz, Jon R. (1953). "Shoplifting and the Law of Arrest." *Yale Law Journal* 62: 788–805.

Ward, D., M. Stafford, and L. Gray. (2006). "Rational Choice, Deterrence, and Theoretical Integration." *Journal of Applied Social Psychology* 36, no. 3: 571–598.

Warr, Mark, and Mark Stafford. (1991). "The Influences of Delinquent Peers: What They Think or What They Do?" *Criminology* 29: 851–66.

Warshaw, R. (1989). *I Never Called It Rape.* New York: Harper and Row.

Watkins, B., and A. Bentovim. (1992). "The Sexual Abuse of Male Children and Adolescents: A Review of Current Research." *Journal of Child Psychology and Psychiatry* 33: 197–248.

Webster, Barbara, and Michael S. McCampbell. (1992). "International Money Laundering: Research and Investigation Join Forces." *NIJ Research in Brief,* September: 1–8.

Weinbaum, Donald. (1998). "The Epidemiology of Substance Abuse among Middle School Students: The Impact of School, Familial, Community, and Individual Risk Factors." *Journal of Child and Adolescent Substance Abuse* 8, no. 1: 55–75.

Weinberg, Martin S., Frances Shaver, and Colin J. Williams. (1999) "Gendered Sex Work in the San Francisco Tenderloin." *Archives of Sexual Behavior* 28, no. 6: 503–21.

Weis, Kurt, and Sandra S. Borges. (1973). "Victimology and Rape: The Case of the Legitimate Victim." *Issues in Criminology* 8: 85–89.

Weisburd, David, Elin Waring, and Ellen Chavet. (1991). *White-Collar Crime and Criminal Careers.* Cambridge: Cambridge University Press.

Weiss, T. G. (1997). *Political Gain and Civilian Pain: Humanitarian Impacts of Economic Sanctions.* Lanham, MD: Rowman and Littlefield.

Weitzer, Ronald. (2005). "New Directions in Research on Prostitution." *Crime, Law, and Social Change* 43: 211–35.

———. (2006). "Moral Crusade against Prostitution." *Society* 43: 33–38.

Weitzer, R., and C. E. Kubrin. (2004). "Breaking News: How Local TV News and Real-World Conditions Affect Fear of Crime." *Justice Quarterly* 21, no. 3: 497–523.

Weitzer, R. J., and S. A. Tuch. (2006). *Race and Policing in America: Conflict and Reform.* New York: Cambridge University Press.

Wellford, Charles. (1975). "Labeling Theory and Criminology: An Assessment." *Social Problems* 22: 332–45.

Welsh, B., and D. Farrington. (1999). "Value for Money? A Review of the Cost and Benefits of Situational Crime Prevention." *British Journal of Criminology* 39, no. 3: 345–69.

Whitcomb, Debra. (1985). "Prevention of Child Sexual Abuse: Innovations in Practice." *NIJ Research in Brief,* November: l–7.

Whitcomb, Debra, Gail S. Goodman, Desmond K. Runyan, and Shirley Hook. (1994). "The Emotional Effects of Testifying on Sexually Abused Children." *NIJ Research in Brief,* April: 1–7.

White, Leslie T. (1972). "The Definitions and Prohibitions of Incest." In John N. Edwards, ed., *Sex and Society.* Chicago: Markham.

Whitehead, Tony L. (2000). "The "Epidemic" and "Cultural Legends" of Black Male Incarceration: The Socialization of African American Children to a Life of Incarceration." In John P. May, ed., *Building Violence: How America's Rush to Incarcerate Creates More Violence.* Thousands Oaks, CA: Sage.

Widom, Cathy Spatz. (1992). "The Cycle of Violence." *NIJ Research in Brief,* October: 1–6.

Wilbanks, William. (1985). "Is Violent Crime Intraracial?" *Crime and Delinquency* 31: 117–28.

Wilson, James Q., and Barbara Boland. (1978). "The Effect of the Police on Crime." *Law and Society Review* 12: 367–90.

Wilson, James Q., and Richard J. Herrnstein. (1985). *Crime and Human Nature.* New York: Simon and Schuster.

Wilson, William Julius. (1987). *The Truly Disadvantaged: The Inner City, the Underclass, and Public Policy.* Chicago: University of Chicago Press.

Wiltz, Christine. (1999). *The Last Madam: A Life in the New Orleans Underworld.* New York: Faber and Faber.

Winfree, L., T. Taylor, N. He, and F. Esbensen. (2006). "Self-Control and Variability over Time: Multivariate Results Using a 5-Year, Multisite Panel of Youths." *Crime and Delinquency* 52, no. 2: 253–79.

Wired Strategies, 2006, available at http://www.wiredstrategies.com/shepardx.html

Wolfgang, Marvin E. (1958). *Patterns in Criminal Homicide.* Philadelphia: University of Pennsylvania Press.

———. (1961). "Pioneers in Criminology: Cesare Lombroso (1835–1909)." *Journal of Criminal Law, Criminology, and Police Science* 52: 361–91.

Wolfgang, Marvin E., and Bernard Cohen. (1970). *Crime and Race.* New York: Institute of Human Relations Press.

Wolfgang, Marvin E., and Franco Ferracuti. (1967). *The Subculture of Violence.* London: Tavistock.

Wright, B., A. Caspi, and T. Moffitt. (2004). "Does the Perceived Risk of Punishment Deter Criminally Prone Individuals? Rational Choice, Self-Control, and Crime." *Journal of Research in Crime and Delinquency* 41, no. 2: 180–213.

Wright, James D., and Peter H. Rossi. (1981). *Weapons, Crime, and Violence in America.* Washington, DC: National Institute of Justice.

Wright, James D., Joseph F. Sheley, and M. Dwayne Smith. (1992). "Kids, Guns, and Killing Fields." *Society* 30: 84–89.

Wright, Kevin N., and Karen E. Wright. (1994). *Family Life, Delinquency, and Crime: A Policymaker's Guide.* Washington, DC: Office of Juvenile Justice and Delinquency Prevention.

Wright, Richard T. (2000). Comments made at a presentation at Southern Illinois University Edwardsville, March.

Wright, Richard T., and Scott H. Decker. (1994). *Burglars on the Job: Streetlife and Residential Break-ins.* Boston: Northeastern University Press.

————. (1997). *Armed Robbers in Action*. Boston: Northeastern University Press.

Yeager, P., and G. Reed. (1998). "Of Corporate Persons and Straw Men: A Reply to Herbert, Green, and Larragoite." *Criminology* 36, no. 4: 885–97.

Yin, Robert. (2002). Case *Study Research: Design and Methods*. 3rd ed. Thousand Oaks, CA.: Sage.

Yogan, Lissa J. (2000). "School Tracking and Student Violence" *Annals of the American Academy of Political and Social Science* 567: 108–22.

Young, Jock. (1986). "The Failure of Criminology: The Need of Radical Realism." In Roger Matthews and Jock Young, eds., *Confronting Crime*. Beverly Hills, CA: Sage.

————. (1997). "Left Realism: The Basics." In Brian MacLean and Dragan Milovanovic, eds., *Thinking Critically about Crime*. Vancouver, BC: Collective Press.

————. (2000). *The Exclusive Society*. London: Sage.

————. (2007). *The Vertigo of Late Modernity*. Los Angeles: Sage.

Zeitz, Dorothy. (1981). *Women Who Embezzle or Defraud: A Study of Convicted Felons*. New York: Praeger.

Zimring, Franklin E. (1972). "The Medium Is the Message: Firearm Caliber as a Determinant of Death from Assault." *Journal of Legal Studies* 15: 97–123.

Zinn, Howard. (1999). *A People's History of the United States, 1492–present*. New York: HarperCollins.

INDEX

f indicates figure or illustration; *t* indicates table

ABOUT THE AUTHORS

Hugh Barlow is Professor Emeritus at Southern Illinois University Edwardsville. He now resides in Albuquerque, New Mexico, where he teaches an occasional course at the University of New Mexico. Most of his spare time is spent playing poker and exploring the Land of Enchantment. During his career he has been a visiting professor at the University of Wisconsin, Milwaukee and at the University of North Carolina, Chapel Hill, and was a visiting scholar at the Institute of Criminology of Cambridge University in England, and a member of Clare Hall. In 1993 he received the Herbert Bloch Award from the American Society of Criminology for services to the society and the profession of criminology. His most recent book, *Dead for Good: Martyrdom and the Rise of the Suicide Bomber* was released in 2007.

David Kauzlarich is Professor and Chair in the Department of Sociology and Criminal Justice Studies at Southern Illinois University Edwardsville (SIUE). He earned his master's and doctoral degrees in sociology at Western Michigan University in the early 1990s. He has been the recipient of several honors for his teaching and research including the William and Margaret Going Endowed Professor Award, SIUE College of Arts and Sciences (2008), the SIUE Great Teacher Award (2005), and the Critical Criminologist of the Year Award from the American Society of Criminology's Critical Criminology Division (2005). He has published over thirty articles and essays as well as two other books on criminological and sociological topics. He specializes in the study of state crime, human rights, and victimology.